Abraham Lincoln

Beyond the American Icon

FRED REED

www.whitman.com

Atlanta, Georgia

Beyond the American Icon

www.whitman.com

© 2013 Whitman Publishing, LLC
3101 Clairmont Road • Suite G • Atlanta, GA 30329

Correspondence concerning this book may be directed to the publisher, Attn: Abraham Lincoln, at the address above.

ISBN: 0794837417
Printed in China

This book was prepared to document the biography of Abraham Lincoln and the public's perception of his image. It includes a wide variety of promotional materials used in historical political campaigns along with cartoons, advertisements, magazine covers, and other popular-media materials that provided commentary and publicized Lincoln's popular image. The reader will find commentary and analyses of the included materials, which allow the historian and collector to perform their own analysis and form their own opinions. We hope this book is helpful in your study of Abraham Lincoln and his public image over the past 160-plus years.

About the cover: "Lincoln" is artist Cat Clausen's most well-known portrait. The piece has been displayed at the Triennale Bovisa Museum in Milan, Italy, and became imprinted on Chicago, where it was used in a city-wide advertising campaign. Clausen selected Abraham Lincoln as her subject due in part to her admiration of the 16th president and her desire to "spend a day with the man." Cat lives and paints in Dwight, Illinois. To view the artist's entire collection, visit CatClausen.com.

About the frontispiece: "The idea behind most of my work, including my portraits of Abraham Lincoln, is to take a familiar cultural image and to give it new meaning through the interpretations of viewers. . . . I chose Lincoln originally as a subject, because the photograph I based my work on is of such high quality, and is widely regarded as one of the finest examples of early photographic portraiture. This fact, coupled with Lincoln's powerful and instantly recognizable features, made him a perfect subject. The life of Abraham Lincoln and his achievements make any manipulation of his image much more powerful and I have been amazed at the variety of interpretations I have heard from viewers of these pieces." —Lola Dupré, 2010. Visit the artist at loladupre.com.

If you enjoy *Abraham Lincoln: Beyond the American Icon,* you will also enjoy *Abraham Lincoln: The Image of His Greatness* (Reed), *America's Money, America's Story* (Doty), *The Great American West: Pursuing the American Dream* (Rendell), and other books by Whitman Publishing. For a complete catalog, visit Whitman Publishing online at Whitman.com.

⊰ **Contents** ⊱

Dedication

This book is dedicated to my grandkids, Grace, Nathan, and Jacob, the finest of sequels. May you always draw upon good inspirations from our past, and have the freedom to do so. May you all find something in your lives that gives you as much lasting enjoyment and satisfaction as your granddad has. May you always remember how much your parents and grandparents love each of you.

—Grandpa

Acknowledgments

I owe much to a great many persons who have enabled me to write this second Lincoln book. First I'd like to thank my editors in the various numismatic periodicals for publishing a good many of my Lincoln articles in the last few years. These include Beth Deisher, David Harper, Robert Van Ryzin, and Barbara Gregory. Additionally, Bob and Beth provided me images of newsworthy Lincoln items. My interest in Abraham Lincoln remains unbounded and these editors and their wonderful periodicals are my primary outlet. In these days of shrinking periodicals markets, it is wonderful to have developed good working relationships with such fine professionals as these editors.

Next I would like to thank Cathee A. "Cat" Clausen for the use of her vibrant and emotional Lincoln portrait as the cover illustration for this book. Ms. Clausen hails from "The Land of Lincoln," and her adaptation of the familiar, intimate "Gettysburg Lincoln" image bespeaks the best of the "beyond the icon" imagery of recent times. Likewise, my thanks go out to Lola Dupré, who allowed me to use one of her unique Lincoln collages as this book's frontispiece. The internationally known Ms Dupré (she was based in Scotland when I became acquainted with her work several years ago, and is now in Portugal) also employed Alexander Gardner's November 8, 1863, photograph as the basis for her artwork. Each work makes a statement. Their vitality conveys something of the spark Old Abe still holds for creative souls.

Once again this book was much improved by Jim Halperin and Steve Ivy's permission to borrow freely from the incomparable treasure trove that is the Heritage Galleries Internet archive. Additionally Jim permitted photography of his unique James Earle Fraser Lincoln cent plaster model. My association with Steve and Jim dates back to the early 1980s, including the opportunity to catalog the G.F.C. Smillie family archives, which added a great deal to my knowledge and appreciation of Smillie's Lincoln and other engravings. My thanks, too, go out to friends Len Glazer, Allen Mincho, Frank Clark, Tom Slater, Paul Minshull, and Mark Van Winkle at Heritage.

Dealer and longtime colleague Q. David Bowers is to be especially thanked for contributing the fine foreword to this volume. I value Dave's kindnesses over many years greatly. Dave's firm, Stack's Bowers Galleries, provided a real diversity of choice Lincolniana for this book. In addition to many Lincoln tokens from his personal collection, Dave permitted me to use images of the Eliasberg gold Lincoln medals, five unique U.S. currency essays, and various other items from Stack's varied sales. Additionally, Dave supplied me the photo of Victor David Brenner sculpting a model for a standing statue of Lincoln. I would also like to thank Doug Plasencia, Bruce Hagen, and Chris Karstedt of Stack's Bowers Galleries.

Dealer Scott Winslow furnished me rare Lincoln items from his inventory, specifically for this book, as did scripophily dealer Bob Kerstein. Champion Stamp Co. supplied some noteworthy check specimens. William Langs permitted use of the circa 1960 Herb Lubalin photographic stamp essays.

John Herzog, former principle of the late, lamented R.M. Smythe & Co., "downsized" two very wonderful Lincoln items my way after publication of my first Lincoln book. The first was a framed pristine example of the William Edgar Marshall 1866 Lincoln portrait that influenced a host of commercial imitations among the banknote companies and product brands. The second was a framed, signed broadside of Edwin Markham's *Lincoln, the Man of the People,* which the poet recited during the dedication of the Lincoln Memorial in 1922. Both items had hung on Herzog's office walls for many years, and now are special features of the undersigned's "Lincoln Room." John also kindly permitted reproduction of his wonderful World War I Liberty bond, with the familiar Lincoln money-image vignette that is illustrated in chapter 3.

Other individuals and their auction houses who also supplied items include Scott Treppel and John Zuckerman, Siegel Auction Galleries; Dr. Robert Schwartz, H.R. Harmer and Archives International Auctions; Donald Ackerman, The Railsplitter; Dana Linett, Early American History Auctions, who additionally provided a history on the Leidersdorf revenue-tax-paid labels; Spink USA; and Doreen Mileto at Timothy J. Hughes.

I relied heavily once again on Dick Johnson's *Abraham Lincoln on Coins, Medals and Tokens: A Complete List of Lincoln Items by Known Artists,* a then-unpublished catalog that Dick unselfishly shared with me for the first Lincoln book, *Abraham Lincoln: The Image of His Greatness.* Additionally, Dick and his business partner Mark Schlepphorst furnished to me excellent images of their SAMCO Lincoln plaques, and Mark provided me access to their artists, including U.S. Mint sculptor/engraver Don Everhart and illustrator, coin, medal, and stamp designer Joel Iskowitz. Both Don and Joel were very accommodating, as readers of this volume will readily observe.

Peter Huntoon furnished me a great number of unique Bureau of Engraving and Printing proofs from the National Numismatic Collection (Smithsonian Institution), including proofs and mockups of notes, bonds, and war savings stamps having Lincoln vignettes. Peter also supplied the illustrations of the previously unknown $20 Lincoln food coupon essays with the "Gettysburg Lincoln" portrait, and provided me his listing of Lincoln National Banks.

A special "thank you" to Glenn King, the granddaughter of artist Vincente Aderente, who supplied me images and new information on the artist, and registered my Lincoln portrait by Aderente (which appeared on the cover of *The Image of His Greatness*) with the SIRIS (Smithsonian Institution Research Information System) Art Database.

Once again, collector Alan Weinberg furnished interesting Lincolniana for the excellent photography of Tom Mulvaney for this book. Although I've never met Alan personally, his selfless contributions to both my Lincoln books are not only very much appreciated, they also helped make both books much better.

Cigar-art dealer David Beach supplied many of the great Lincoln tobacco labels shown herein, and also the important incorporation papers for Lincoln Motor Co.

Thanks to Vera Feltz, executive director of the American Topical Association, for her assistance. Vera assisted me in chronicling the foreign Lincoln Bicentennial stamps.

I am very grateful to Dr. Richard Doty and Dr. Harry R. Rubenstein, curators of numismatics and of political history, respectively, at the Smithsonian Institution, for information supplied.

Tim Grant of the U.S. Mint supplied the photo of engraver Don Everhart and his model for the Lincoln Presidential dollar. I am also thankful for the assistance of Travis Alford of the Bureau of Engraving and Printing Office of External Relations, who availed me the images and text of the BEP's three Lincoln Bicentennial exhibits, and Dr. Franklin Noll and Barbara Bither of the BEP Historical Resource Center. Once again I made considerable use of the extensive spreadsheet BEP HRC's Margaret Richardson prepared for me on the Lincoln portrait dies in the Bureau's die vault for my first Lincoln book.

Hal Smith, director of "Looking for Lincoln," answered my questions and supplied me additional information, as did Jeff Harris, director of local history services for the Indiana Historical Society, who additionally supplied images of the Society's grand Lincoln bicentennial exhibits.

Donn Pearlman provided me images and information on the unique 1943-D $1.7 million Lincoln bronze cent.

Longtime friend and SPMC president Mark Anderson gifted me the wonderful Ainsworth catalog, and succumbed to my entreaties to sell me his very rare Lincoln scrip note from his precious hometown of Brooklyn, New York.

Thanks to Ray Lockwood for hosting my Lincoln lecture at the Central States Numismatic Society Educational Symposium at Fort Wayne, Indiana, in April 2011.

A special thanks to Cindy Van Horn, Allen County Public Library Lincoln Room reference librarian, for the personal tour of their collection and assistance with my research.

Dr. Thomas R. Turner, editor of the *Lincoln Herald,* and Michelle Ganz, archivist, Abraham Lincoln Library and Museum (Lincoln Memorial University Archives, Harrogate, Tennessee) provided information.

American Numismatic Association library director RyAnne Scott, Ellen S. Peachey at the American Philatelic Research Library, and American Numismatic Society librarian Elizabeth Hahn provided reference material.

I would like to thank Dan Weinberg and Bjorn Gustafson for the opportunity to present *Abraham Lincoln: The Image of His Greatness* at one of the Abraham Lincoln Book Shop virtual book signings in April 2009.

I thank Kathy Lawrence for being my excellent moderator for my lecture at the spring 2010 Fort Worth American Numismatic Association convention. David Lisot made an excellent videotaping of that talk despite mechanical malfunctions that beset me, and my own lack of experience as a public speaker. Bureau of Engraving and Printing photographer Gino Wang kindly photographed my book signing at the summer 2010 ANA Boston convention.

I would also like to thank the White House Historical Association for information on the former Lincoln suite of offices and present Lincoln Bedroom.

As you read this text you will note a great many mentions of eminent Lincoln image historian Harold Holzer, who happened to be cochairman of the United States Abraham Lincoln Bicentennial Commission, a very busy job over the past several years. Incidentally, Harold's "day job" is as vice president of the Metropolitan Museum of Art in New York City, and over many years has been a patient tutor on my quest to understand Abraham Lincoln and his image.

Once again Mark Reinhart, the world's great authority on Abraham Lincoln films, answered my questions and made various helpful suggestions.

Lincoln statue authority Dave Wiegers answered my many questions and was specifically very helpful in my understanding the differences between the Pelzer statue and the Segesman copies. Dave also provided me several illustrations from his personal project to photograph every Lincoln statue for some future publication. That's quite a chunk Dave has bitten off. He's been to more than 250 sites already.

Matt Hansen provided information and census data on the Lincoln, Nebraska, municipal scrip. Joseph Boling provided information on MFC (Military Fest Currency) depicting Lincoln shrines. Paul Cunningham shared information on Lincoln exonumia from his vast experience as a collector, dealer, and lead cataloger/editor for the Token and Medal Society King revision committee. Longtime colleagues Tom DeLorey and David T. Alexander provided me excellent insights into the Lincoln medals of coin dealer Tom Elder, and the importance of Victor David Brenner's round, medallic Lincoln profile portraits in the development of the one-cent coin effigy, respectively. Researcher-author Roger Burdette was also very helpful on the latter topic, too.

Many of the persons acknowledged in *The Image of His Greatness* were specifically helpful once again, or generally helpful to my overall understanding of Lincoln or my collecting pursuits. Included especially are Hugh Shull, Tom Denly, Dennis Forgue, and Lyn Knight, four outstanding paper-money dealers who have enabled me to acquire many of the interesting Lincoln items in my collection. Other dealers, too, should be mentioned with appreciation, including Ken Barr, Rex Stark, Dennis Forgue, Bruce Hagen, Austin Sheheen, Joe Levine, Eric Jackson, Larry Phillips, J.W. "Doc" Carberry, Intergovernmental Postal Consultants, Bill Smith, Nuno Felipe, Doug Hammerman, Roger West at Avion Stamps, Rob Kravitz, Jay Parino, and Wendell Wolka.

David DeLisle supplied the image of his wonderful 19th-century folk-art plaque. Jennifer Cooper supplied an image of her Exemplar cigar tin sign. Brad Burton supplied images of some interesting Lincoln pinbacks, and Dave Schenkman supplied a great many Lincoln tokens and storecards from his fine collections, most particularly the Merrimack made-from medal. Thanks go to Jim Castetter for permission to use his image of his rare 1915 Lincoln Stars Negro League pennant. C. Baker gave me permission to reproduce his image of his rare Baby Lincoln slot machine. Antonio Reid graciously permitted reproduction of his Portuguese Lincoln medal. Great Storm Galleries provided access to their finely crafted replicas of vintage Lincoln plaques.

Rob Stoddard permitted examination and reproduction of his rare, largely unknown Lincoln carte de visite reproducing a Lincoln portrait by artist John Wood Dodge, which led me to my discovery of a jumbo cabinet card of the same image. Jeremy B. Katz, JK Coin Photography, provided images of Lincoln medals. Peter Schwartz permitted use of many of his rare Lincoln stamp essays. Seth Bienstock provided the illustration of his rare large bronze plaque attributed to Ralph J. Menconi. William Tinsley furnished the illustration of the Towle Log Cabin Syrup centennial tin. Nici, the 99-cent goddess, permitted use of her World War II–era Lincoln-FDR pamphlet. Ron Sherman furnished an illustration of a rare Lincoln ribbon. Cheryl Duck provided me a rare illustrated Lincoln funeral newspaper account. Historical photo collector Chris Nelson shared his original Lincoln images with this writer. David W. Lange provided the example of the early Lincoln penny board shown here. Delbert Wallace shared a rare Washington-Lincoln memorial ribbon. Dr. Tony Hyman provided a very early Lincoln tobacco label. Lev Linkner shared information on a 1909 lead Lincoln cent obverse die trial without the motto "In God We Trust" (Pollock 3527).

Britisher Angus Lincoln, a collecting friend for 30 years, provided me information on recent worldwide Lincoln philatelic items. Doug Murray helped me understand early Lincoln greenback varieties. Additional collectors and dealers who assisted me by providing me specific data and/or illustrations useful to this book include Karl Kabelac, Bob Julian, Terry Bryan, Larry Adams, Neil Shafer, Larry Schuffman, Ed Dauer, Jamie Yakes, Ron Horstman, Art Paradis, David Tretter, Saul Teichman, Wayne Homren, Michael Sanders, Cheryl Duck, Paul Elman, Gary Young, Roger D. Best, Graham Pilecki, Ira Goldberg, Daniel Carr, George LaBarre, Colin Bruce, George Cuhaj, William Hallam Weber, Rich Jewell, and Benny Bolin. Carlson Chambliss supplied printage figures for various Lincoln federal notes. His coauthor of the *Comprehensive Catalog,* the great U.S. federal currency and bond authority Gene Hessler has been a constant source of ready information on note and bond engravers, vignettes and related topics however obscure. Longtime colleague David Ganz answered a thorny question that came up right on my deadline.

Fred Bart contributed the Series of 1928C $5 Lincoln note salvaged at Pearl Harbor from aboard the sunk USS *Arizona.* Bill McBride of www.archivesofadvertising.com identified the 1930 Lincoln touring car. Movie producer Chris Lukeman supplied illustrations from his camp vampire film *The Transient.* Publisher Rob Sequin permitted reproduction of a *Havana Journal* photograph of an Augustus Saint-Gaudens *Standing Lincoln* statue located in Cuba. Lorraine and Phil Shapiro provided me insights into Havana's Parque de la Fraternidad, the location of another famous Lincoln bust. Dave Greene shared his rare Lincoln Club badge.

As a journalist for more than 40 years, I spent a good deal of time since *Abraham Lincoln: The Image of His Greatness* tracking down contemporary artists who are creating vibrant, modern Lincoln imagery. U.S. Mint sculptor/engraver Don Everhart shared his unpublished "other" design for the Lincoln Presidential dollar, and provided me with real insights on the design process. Stamp, coin, and medal designer Joel Iskowitz provided unpublished designs and insights into his design process, too. BEP engraver Tom Hipschen shared with me his personal vision of Abe on the new $5 bill. Prolific Lincoln artist Wendy Allen permitted use of several of her most revealing Lincoln portraits. Renowned Lincoln actor Fritz Klein provided me with images of his work. Sculptor Jim Nance provided me images of his fine Lincoln busts, statue, and medallion designs. William Leigh Hunt supplied his Lincoln portrait from 544 tiled family photographs. Inventive steel portraitist Alan Derrick explained his artistic process to me, and granted me permission to reproduce his wonderful *The People, The Union, Forever.* Graphic artist Maury McCoy explained the genesis and furnished photos of the Penny Portrait plaque that he and his educator wife Elizabeth developed. Sculptor Rhin Choi, fabulist artist Brian Gubicza, and pop artists Marty Defranco and "Dillon" (James Dillon Wright) shared their contemporary Lincoln works with me.

I would also like to thank the artists and photographers who answered my inquiries, provided images, or otherwise assisted this study, including Galen R. Frysinger, Eric Amend, William S. Nawrocki, Richard McCoy, Jen Yates, and Fred L. Reed IV for his Lincoln art. Fred IV also called my attention to the then breaking news that Steven Spielberg had signed Oscar-winner Daniel Day-Lewis to play Lincoln in his stalled project to bring Doris Kearns Goodwin's *Team of Rivals,* about Lincoln and his Cabinet, to the big screen. Then late in the process my brother Michael Reed found me the first release of the trailer for the Spielberg movie that was still in post-production as this is finalized.

Among those whom I would be remiss not to mention are my Civil War mentor Dr. LeRoy H. Fischer whose encouragement and great breadth of knowledge were equally freely given and beneficial to me during a large portion of my formative years. Since that time many individuals have assisted in a variety of ways. I count the great Lincoln authority Lloyd Ostendorf a special friend for his many kindnesses through the years. Curator and author Mark Neely has been exceptionally kind with his valuable time and resources. Others include Matt Rothert, photographer Paul Agnew, Martin Gengerke, Michael Aldrich, Ben Coming, John and Nancy Wilson, Curtis Radford, Ken Prag, Neil Sowards, Jack Donahue, Gerry McClafferty, Lee Crumbaugh, Mary Nowesnick (then editor of *Savings Institutions*), Sam Daniel (then Reference Librarian at the Library of Congress), Jeanne Howard (then in the Public Affairs Section of the BEP), Paul R. Prey (then executive assistant to the BEP director), Vem Potter and Alex Perakis. Also, Jenny B. Lee and Nancy Versaci (then curators of Printed Books at the Brown University Library, Jane Reed (then librarian at the Union League Club of New York City), curators at the Frick Art Reference Library of New York and National Portrait Gallery in Washington, D.C., Dr. L.C. Rudolph (then curator of Books at the Lily Library, Indiana University, Bloomington), various staff members at the Library of Congress and especially of the WC Photo Duplication Service, photographer David Repp, William R. Venters, Gary Hendershott, George LaBarre, George Rinsland, Charles T. Rodgers, Theodore Kemm, J. and D. Paschke, Yancy Green, Harold Goldstein, and Ray Hanser. I would like to express a special thank-you to David and Rachel Benning for permitting the use of their daughter Olivia Benning's photo in this book, and Olivia's uncle Jon Benning for the use of his cute photo of Olivia in the Babe Lincoln onesie that he designed and created.

Last, but not least, I would like to thank my grandchildren Grace, Nathan, and Jacob, for sharing their Lincoln bicentennial penny finds with their grandpa when he could not seem to find any of these new cents in circulation to save his life. Kids, this book is dedicated to you and your love of Abraham Lincoln.

Finally, I would also like to express my appreciation to the staff of Whitman Publishing, whose vision for my two Lincoln books and whose hard work have brought my life's ambitions to fruition once again.

Fred Reed
Dallas, Texas

Foreword

In a field as popular and as crowded as Abraham Lincoln scholarship, to create a reference book that contains significant information not available elsewhere is indeed a daunting task.

Of all the presidents after George Washington, Lincoln has been the most studied. Every aspect of his life has been examined—his childhood in Kentucky, his law practice in Illinois, his debates with Stephen Douglas, his entry as a dark horse Republican candidate in 1860, his election later that year, his inauguration, and, of course, his leadership during the Civil War, followed by his unfortunate assassination. Past studies by others have included volumes reprinting every known letter by Lincoln, a day-by-day account of his life during the Civil War, and more. Indeed, a comprehensive Lincoln library would fill a huge room of bookshelves.

If anyone is qualified to break new ground in Lincoln scholarship, it is Fred Reed. I have been a friend of Fred's for many years, since the 1960s in fact, and have followed his award-winning career. A consummate researcher and a gifted writer, he has created standard reference articles and books on several historical subjects, his *Abraham Lincoln: The Image of His Greatness* being a recent example. Both broad and deep in its scope, that book was recognized with literary awards from national organizations representing several branches of numismatics. Beyond that, it has been embraced by the mainstream of the Lincoln research community, as well as by more casual armchair historians and Lincoln fans.

Now, in his latest work, *Abraham Lincoln: Beyond the American Icon*, Reed has created a perspective of Lincoln from a new angle: Lincoln seen not from the viewpoint of military history or presidential accomplishments, but as he was regarded by the American public in his time, followed by his legacy since 1865.

Before immersing myself in Reed's new book, I was quite familiar with Lincoln cents, had read of the development of the Lincoln Highway, and as a kid had played with Lincoln Logs. In *Beyond the American Icon* I learned that Abraham Lincoln is, in countless additional ways, a part of American life. Banks, insurance companies, and other businesses have added Lincoln to their names, hoping that in their own way they will become great as well. Consumer products from fruit-crate labels to automobiles to utilitarian coins and postage stamps have borne his name and image.

In many ways Fred Reed's new book adds to the appreciation of Lincoln as a human being. In the years after the president's passing, satire was rare, and appreciation, indeed adulation, was common. For an artist or sculptor to be commissioned to create a statue, plaque, coin, or other item depicting Lincoln was a high tribute. Reed traces the shift in public opinion, showing how the once universally revered president has become touched by controversy and parody, and yet endures as one of the most fascinating figures in our collective history. Lincoln's image has become so familiar to Americans that the beloved president has been increasingly called upon to serve any number of agendas, from the "Honest Abe" persona that advertisers and business owners appropriate in order to gain credibility and the public's trust, to the rawboned pioneer scrapper, who is called upon to bodyslam evildoers in graphic novels and films.

The present book is indeed comprehensive; it would be a rare find indeed to locate a significant image of Lincoln as a product advertisement, medal, civic monument, or other manifestation not known to the author. This unique volume covers every aspect of Lincoln's life in the public eye, from the late 1850s, continuing through the Civil War and into the more complicated and changeable territory of the American view of Lincoln from 1865 onward. Its lavish illustrations encompass hundreds of examples of fascinating Lincoln imagery, from the most elevated (such as the Mount Rushmore likeness) to the most commercial (Garbage Pail Kids) and even to the fantastical *(Abraham Lincoln: Vampire Hunter)*. Reed illustrates curiosities unknown to all but the most zealous collector of Lincolniana and shares fascinating, little-known behind-the-scenes information about the creation of different likenesses of the great man.

I anticipate that any reader of this book—ranging from a dedicated scholar to a longtime collector to anyone interested in American history and tradition—will find it to be not only a fact-filled and interesting reference but also a good read.

My congratulations to Fred Reed on a job well done!

Q. David Bowers
Wolfeboro, New Hampshire

Introduction

For a gentleman seven score and seven-plus years deceased, Abraham Lincoln just won't stay dead and buried. Private and popular views of Lincoln have changed repeatedly before, as each age grappled toward understanding the man's character and accomplishments. His legacy is so transcendent that his image is still in transition as I put pen to paper.

In philosophy, anthropology, law enforcement, and many sciences the observer attempts to divorce himself and his act of observation from influencing, by the very process of his observing, the substance and the meaning of what he sees. Phenomenologists, especially, attempt to separate the percipient from the perception, leaving only the objective reality. For most of us mere mortals in the real world of men and human affairs, however, what we see is subjective, often highly so.

Thus for the last two centuries our individual and collective perceptions and judgments regarding Nancy Hanks Lincoln's son tell as much about *us* frequently as they illuminate him. They don't illuminate where he stands but where we are standing. Views of Lincoln are a moving stream: one cannot step into the same water twice. This is especially so with Lincoln's image and legacy. The practical Lincoln of acerbic law partner William Herndon became the elevated Lincoln of presidential secretaries John Nicolay and John Hay, which became alternately the folksy Lincoln of Ida Tarbell, the prairie warrior of Carl Sandburg, the venal opportunist of Gore Vidal, and most recently the racist, despondent, sexually ambiguous Lincoln of modern revisionists.

This changing perception is demonstrated most dramatically in Lincoln statuary. Lincoln was a Romanesque solon to Sarah Fisher Ames in a bust from life, but following his death was perched atop a very tall column as a demigod stationed in the heavens to be admired by mere humans in Lot Flannery's and Larkin Meade's visions. For Augustus Saint-Gaudens, this elevated demigod was brought down a notch as a father figure gazing benevolently on his children, but to George Grey Barnard Lincoln was a tall, Bunyanesque rustic treading the ages at ground level. From Gutzon Borglum to the present, Lincoln has become more the village elder on a park bench visitors cuddle up to and commune with for photo ops. Searching for new imagery, contemporary sculptors have increasingly portrayed Lincoln not as a man at all, but as a child or youth frequently with a dog, or a book, or a discarded axe; or, if a man, in a domestic ensemble with his wife and/or kids.

On canvas, too, Abraham Lincoln has melded from the imperial presence of G.P.A. Healey, to the inscrutable fellow of Freeman Thorp, to the socialist icon of Boardman Robinson, to the common man of Douglas Volk, to the splendid laborer of Norman Rockwell. Increasingly today we have come to see Old Abe as a fiery, emotional character, as in colorist Cat Clausen's portrait (see the cover of this book), or the somewhat simian-looking Lincoln of collagist Lola Dupré (on the title page), or the ghoulish Lincoln of Mark Ryden or Van Arno (both inside). On stage and screen the kind-hearted president of *Lincoln's Clemency,* and the congressional dupe of *Birth of a Nation,* became the love-worn Lincoln of *Young Mr. Lincoln* and its many derivatives, and the time-traveling hale fellow well met of Bill & Ted's comic history, and the sitting duck of the various conspiracist film fictions.

While Lincoln was transiting through these formal arts, the pop-culture view of him was changing too. The Indian Hunter Lincoln of the 1950s comics became the What Me Worry? Abraham E. Neuman everyman of *Mad* magazine in the 1960s. Today Lincoln and Buffy Summers slay myriad Cullen-like vampires, and Lincoln and the Village People dance merrily across the stage in new liberation follies.

In *Abraham Lincoln: The Image of His Greatness* I attempted to demonstrate this changing Lincoln consciousness through what I labeled as its transitional stages covering the 200 years from Lincoln's birth to his bicentennial. In that book we traced the evolving image through epochs I called Abraham Lincoln: 1809–1865; Lincoln the Ideal: 1865–1909; Lincoln the Idol: 1909–1959; and Lincoln the Icon: 1959–2009. Although these epochs are not rigid, they do provide a useful framework for understanding the evolution of Lincoln consciousness over time. Abraham Lincoln successively morphed from the preserver of the Union and emancipator of a race into an American icon and ultimately into a world figure in the universal struggle for liberty and humane and progressive values. I am very gratified at the reception that the book received. It won "Book of the Year" honors from three national organizations: the Society of Paper Money Collectors, the Professional Currency Dealers Association, and the Numismatic Literary Guild. It also received favorable commentary outside the collecting community, among Lincoln enthusiasts.

On the eve of Lincoln's bicentennial in that book, I also posed the question: Is Lincoln irrelevant going forward? The progress of the bicentennial celebration and the pandering self-identification of political opportunists partially answered that question. In one sense, Lincoln was seemingly everywhere during his bicentennial year. But the most significant commemoration, a national distribution of the U.S. Mint's four celebratory cents coined for the event, was dead on arrival, bungled by the administration, and never got off the ground. Most of the public never noticed even *one* of these cents in circulation in 2009. By persistence and pluck I managed to find exactly five—and four of them were gifts from my grandkids, who obviously circulate in a better marketplace than do I! I have yet to find a Professional Aspect "Lincoln in Illinois" cent in circulation, and I spent weeks in Illinois during the bicentennial celebration where they were supposedly "launched" prior to my arrival.

Most Americans in 2009 didn't even know these commemorative cents were being minted.

Even more maddening for a Lincolnphile, Lincoln's actual presence in his omnipresence became increasingly irrelevant in many of the commemorations. Let me explain. To too many today, in this man's view, Lincoln has become as relevant as, say, Paul Bunyan or Frosty the Snowman. We don't need to know them or much of anything about them to imagine into existence tales of Bunyan or Frosty in alternate universes of existence and experience. It has become commonplace and quite acceptable in today's "anything goes" climate to posit Abe (or Frosty, or Paul) in fanciful, imaginary scenarios. Any bearded, tall-hatted, plainly dressed character named Abe Lincoln can play seemingly any role, however turgid, immoral, or contrary to the better nature of Abe's being it is. It just doesn't seem to matter anymore. People who know little, and couldn't care less, about the real Abe, feel free to use Abe for their own purposes.

So what else is new? People have been misappropriating Lincoln's image and legacy since his own time. There's probably little harm in sticking Lincoln's face on a tobacco product and christening it Honesty Cigars. It's quite another thing, however, to ascribe to Lincoln a contrary character trait—say, dishonesty—and create a streetwise thug named Abe Lincoln who brutally cheats his way to the top of the mob. Everything is entertainment, theater of the absurd. "I'm sorry, Mrs. Lincoln; other than that, how did you enjoy the play?"

But in contemporary times, this transmogrification doesn't end with flight-of-fancy fictive exercises. Today Lincoln is just an empty suit to some opportunists who pour their own neuroses and aberrant character qualities into the Lincoln mold. The picture that emerges from some of these fictions is truly aberrant. These concoctions christen the creators' own psychological quirks as the lost, but now refound, one true Lincoln. These five-foot-tall troll Lincolns have become all too commonplace today, whether appearing on the stage, or in television commercials, or in graphic novels, or in footnoted hatchet tomes. Alas, such contemporary foggy visions become part and parcel of the story of Lincoln image transition, just as much as the simian caricatures that proliferated in Lincoln's own time. As will be seen, I have not shirked from showing some of them, too.

Abraham Lincoln: The Image of His Greatness was a success, and in some ways the culmination and realization of my closely held half-century dream. So: why another Lincoln book now, especially so close on the heels of the first endeavor? Simply put, it is because I still have Abe-eagerness in my sinews, and my publisher thinks our public still has Abe-receptivity, too. As readers will note, this new work has entirely new text, and all new illustrations, and the emphasis has shifted. Its predecessor book was more heavily slanted toward Lincoln the man and Lincoln the ideal—the mythmaking phase of the story. This book is more heavily slanted toward Lincoln the idol and Lincoln the icon—the branding phase.

Abraham Lincoln: Beyond the American Icon gives me an opportunity to amplify and extend on previous commentary; in short, to draw a finer point to the first book's arguments. It also provides an opportunity to drill down on certain aspects treated cursorily in the first text, and present interesting additional data or details (such as the Henry Clay medal presented by Daniel Ullman to Lincoln, or the City of Lincoln, Nebraska, municipal scrip with Lincoln portraits), and to show interesting different varieties/types of previously illustrated Lincolniana. Furthermore, this book presents the opportunity to put down on the record a broad canvas of celebrations surrounding the Lincoln bicentennial. We might wish that someone had done as much a century ago, shortly after the Lincoln centennial!

It also presents the perfect opportunity to correct unfortunate errata that crept into the first volume despite our combined best efforts. I alone am responsible for these muffs. Three stand out to my mind. Although I got many things right, I misidentified Thomas Lincoln's Goosenest Prairie cabin (figure 1.18), south of Charleston, Illinois (in the former settlement of Farmington), as a Lincoln boyhood home in Farmington, Kentucky, due to an unfortunate handwritten caption on the back of the photo. I consistently misspelled Lincoln photographer Alexander Hesler's surname as *Hessler,* probably because that's the way one of my mentors, paper-money expert Gene Hessler, spells his own surname. And in figure 1.164 I identified Lincoln's youngest son as Thaddeus, not Thomas or "Tad"—a frequent contemporary mistake also seen on the period carte de visite shown. I instantly knew all three of those things were wrong when I got my first copy of the printed book. Mea culpa. After all that work, I regret my errors more than you can imagine.

This new work also provides me the abundant and very much relished opportunity to share additional treasures from my own half century of collecting Lincolniana. When I reported that I had upward of 4,000 Lincoln items, some may have scoffed—but they may be less likely to do so now. Especially important in the present volume are images from my collection of the great many statues and monuments erected in Lincoln's honor. These were only sampled in the previous volume. This book also permits me the distinct privilege to share the fruits of others' collections, too. Once again, I have checked my personal ego at the door, and given others the opportunity to take bows. These gentlemen and ladies, companies, and institutions are thanked in the acknowledgments and listed in the photo credits.

Finally, this book gives me the opportunity to reiterate my basic conception. I feel as if some readers may have misinterpreted *Abraham Lincoln: The Image of His Greatness* by taking the word "image" too literally and being overly impressed by its 900-plus illustrations. I attempted to make my intention clear in the book's introduction. I wrote, regarding Lincoln consciousness, that this included Lincoln imagery in poetry, film, and the plastic arts as much as in pictures, whether on card photographs, medals, or money. My purview was the entire gamut of Lincoln celebration and criticism, not just Lincoln *this*es and Lincoln *that*s. Although other authors had written illustrated works on Lincoln photos, Lincoln movies, Lincoln statuary, Lincoln stamps, Lincoln postcards, and the like, nobody, to my thinking, had ever attempted to take a catholic (i.e., universal) look at Lincoln mythmaking as a whole except literarily. My earlier book was— and this book continues—a survey attempting to take the temperature of Lincoln consciousness in its evolving chronological manner across the ages, spectra of human endeavor and geographical loci.

History records about 130 photographs of Lincoln, and assorted paintings, busts, and sketches, from life. All failed to record the essential Lincoln, according to his secretary, John Nicolay. Writing in 1891, a quarter century after Lincoln's death, Nicolay bemoaned the inability of the camera or graphic arts to capture the essential Lincoln's spirit and soul, much less the transitory emotions of his face. Nicolay wrote, "There are many pictures of Lincoln. But there is no portrait of him." Be that as it may, Lincoln was an astute politician and he understood the power of Brady's Cooper Union photograph (O-17) in making him knowable and electable in 1860. In truth, that image and the Hesler near-profile public-relations photo (O-26) that the Illinois Republicans commissioned after his nomination were important vehicles in the 1860 campaign. But these were only of fleeting importance in creating the historic Lincoln image. A half dozen other photos—the bearded C.S. German photos (O-41/42) taken in January 1861; Gardner's Gettysburg Lincoln facing portrait (O-77) taken in November 1863; five photos taken by Anthony Berger the same day, February 9, 1864 (O88/89, O-91, O-92, and O-93); and a drawing by Francis B. Carpenter based on a virtual snapshot by Berger for Carpenter in April 1864 (O-97)—were the real workhorses in creating the evolving Lincoln image for the past century and a half. Throw into consideration the Volk life mask, and Lincoln statuary by Augustus

Saint-Gaudens, Daniel Chester French, and Gutzon Borglum, and the portraits/engravings by William Edgar Marshall and John H. Littlefield/Henry Gugler, and that pretty much covers the bases for Lincoln's changing image in the mind's eye of the public during that time. And even among this select group, as I have demonstrated in my pioneering articles in *Paper Money, Coin World, The Numismatist,* and the *Lincoln Herald* and my two Lincoln books, those images that were reproduced on the nation's money set the agenda for Lincoln consciousness. Even today traditionalist artists model their paintings, engravings, and sculptures on one or the other of these enduring models for the most part.

To be sure, in 2009 there were a great many commemorations carried out to observe the bicentennial of Lincoln's birth, including an outpouring of new sculptures. But no further evidence need be shown that the age of the heroic is long gone than to examine the monuments dedicated to Lincoln in 2009 and in the years leading up to the celebration. Taken as whole these might correctly be aggregated under the rubric "Lincoln at Street Level." Abraham Lincoln is no longer the austere godlike figure our grandparents saw surmounting a 10- to 12-foot-tall hunk of granite above the sea of his fellow citizens. He has been brought down off his pedestal to mingle with the hoi polloi. In essence these memorials do not commemorate Lincoln so much as they salute us ourselves—our brushes with his greatness in times gone past. There is an almost "George Washington slept here" mentality to many of these modern memorials. Lincoln spoke here to us! Lincoln lawyered here among us! Lincoln surveyed this ground for us! Lincoln passed this way in our view! Increasingly, it seems, we commemorate Lincoln no longer for his extraordinariness, but for his sameness to ourselves.

According to the new Lincoln consciousness of our day, Lincoln is not only a mere mortal, but a mundane one at that! We no longer *revere* Lincoln as we *relate* to him. Today, any tall dude with a black hat and a high-pitched voice will do as well as the Great Emancipator. Please understand I am not begrudging Lincoln his humanity by this criticism. Lincoln's associates—some of them, at least—told stories of a worldly man who engaged in profanity and drink. Who among us has not? But it is a pretty perverse turn of affairs that some find it necessary to drag into the muck the man who saved the crumbling Union at its darkest hour—saved it by moral courage, sheer will, and political adroitness—to make us feel good about our own shortcomings.

Lincoln's legacy was never the possession of the Lincoln Cult only. Robert Todd Lincoln and the professional apple-polishers from among his personal friends and political allies are long since buried, but that doesn't justify a "free-for-all" approach. Just because the kid gloves are off, Lincoln needn't be treated with rough hands. He has gone from ideal to idol to icon but not to irrelevancy. Today Lincoln is *very* relevant, but in popular culture mostly in irreverent, speculative, or fanciful ways. Today's "creative" artists pour the Lincoln identity into roles and suits of clothes as foreign to the flesh-and-blood Lincoln as can be imagined. Lincoln's persona has become an empty suit to be filled with all kinds of perversions.

Putting Lincoln in a red beanie may bring a chuckle because it pokes good-natured humor at his austere image. But would we feel the same about depicting him in a red dress, as some do? Putting Lincoln in shades strumming a rock guitar is a lesser metaphor than contemporary political illustrations of Lincoln and a banjo, whistling "Dixie" while the nation perished. However, treating him like one of the Village People in gross displays says nothing about Lincoln the human being, but a lot about the perpetrators of such a scene. Today it has become de rigueur to put a Lincolnesque character into absurdist plots, such as vampire tales. These campy efforts exploit the Lincoln identity and mystique. Their current popularity owes much to our exploitative culture that flocks to the reprehensible and cheap like a moth to a candle flame.

But whether these fictions do harm is another line of inquiry. More than one influential member of the Lincoln establishment has validated such chestnuts as "Anything that attracts people to Lincoln is a positive." That might be self-evident, but do such curiosities really attract people to Lincoln, or do they put up a cheap shellac on a rich rosewood? I don't mean to be the "Lincoln police," sanctioning or censuring the use or abuse of Lincoln's image. There once was a very real Lincoln mafia that sought to control public dissemination of Lincoln to the masses. It was centered in the person of the president's surviving heir, attorney and statesman Robert Todd Lincoln, and his allies, "friends" of Lincoln such as secretaries John Nicolay and John Hay. During the period of Lincoln idealizing and Lincoln idolizing, contrarians felt the censure of this mythmaking mob. Even close Lincoln associates could get hammered if they misspoke. We only have to look at what happened to Lincoln's close colleagues, law partner William Herndon and secretary W.O. Stoddard, or the vendetta Robert Todd Lincoln waged against entrepreneur Osborn H. Oldroyd. Both Lincoln's widow and his surviving son chilled Herndon. Robert especially vituperated against Stoddard's Lincoln, and threw Oldroyd out of the Lincoln homestead in Springfield as a heretic. One only has to examine the lists of those who lined up for and against the proliferation to Europe of the George Grey Barnard "upset stomach" statue to note more of these self-appointed caretakers of Lincoln's legacy.

Throughout history, as discussed both in *The Image of His Greatness* and herein, the Lincoln persona and our understanding of his legacy have undergone an evolution. Whether you accept my epochs or not, and however you choose to view this transition, it is clear today that Lincoln has emerged beyond the American icon. Today Abraham Lincoln has become *idiom*—that is, an expression whose meanings cannot be inferred from the meanings of the words that make it up. Novelists, artists, and other creators speak the Lincoln idiom, but it's impossible for anybody who knows Lincoln's past to understand much of Lincoln's present in many contemporary portrayals.

Lincoln is no longer an icon. An icon brands a product or message with known content. Thus, when a manufacturer stuck the president's face on his coffee can, he was appealing to the buying public's sense of Lincoln's sterling qualities of worth and value. Same when Henry Leland named his luxury automobile the Lincoln, or when the Waterman Company brought out its Lincoln pen. This was the avowed intent of the founders of Lincoln National Life Insurance . . . to run a company that lived out the Lincoln ideal. Often, today, when Lincoln's face is stuck on a product, it is gratuitous or (worse yet) attempts to attribute to the Lincoln persona uncharacteristic qualities or attributes. Through history it has been common to illegitimately appropriate the Lincoln persona; promoters with motives as disparate as alcohol purveyors and temperance pledgers, and politicians of opposing stripes, have all manipulated Lincoln consciousness to their selfish purposes.

Putting Lincoln on a can of coffee might imply good value, but the proof of the connection is in the taste and worthiness of the coffee itself. If there is a disconnect in the mouth or wallet of a coffee buyer, he'll likely not be fooled a second time. Branding only works if the product lives up to the iconic promise. Today, what we see increasingly is something new. If Lincoln stood for integrity, stick a Lincoln face on lawlessness; if Lincoln was courageous, paint a coward with a Lincoln brush; if Lincoln was a nationalist, put the Lincoln mask on a one-worlder.

Part of the value of studies like *Abraham Lincoln: The Image of His Greatness* and the present work is their breadth. I've examined how Lincoln was portrayed in many media from poetry to bronze statuary to motion pictures to money. Some of these portrayals were commemorative (passive, i.e., a mirror directed toward the object of commemoration). Some were projective (active, a beacon propelling the object onto something outside itself). We should not be surprised that today's commemorations continue to be both passive and active.

Passive commemorations are easily understood: Lincoln freed a race, so put Lincoln and a freedman on a monument, a stamp, or a medal. Lincoln activism is not so easily understood. It may be helpful to take a metaphor from our pop-culture experience, in the mythos of *Batman*. Think of Commissioner Gordon's Bat-Signal projected on the clouds. This was a call for help from the Gotham City police. Generally in the past, creators projected the Abe-Signal narrowly—a rifle approach on likely targets. But today's creators project the Abe-Signal broadly and indiscriminately. This scattergun broadcast approach brings the Lincoln identity into precincts foreign to Abe himself. By virtue of such misappropriation, Lincoln's character and legacy are diluted to meaninglessness. Today Lincoln has not become irrelevant, but his use is often illegible. It's impossible to see the real Lincoln in many of these modern depictions. This is not successful branding, because the product does not live up to the Lincoln qualifications. It is ephemeral and it too will pass.

Abraham Lincoln has emerged beyond the nation's icon in other ways also. In the last 150-plus years, Lincoln has burst onto the international stage. In this volume I document the outpouring from the worldwide community at Lincoln's death, the memorials erected to his honor in England, Denmark, Mexico, Cuba, Norway, the Philippines, Argentina, and other foreign climes. From an early date Lincoln was not just an American hero; he has been a popular or inspirational figure since the 1860s in many lands beyond our borders. That foreign interest has increased in recent decades, as American aid and military might has flowed around the globe. Lincoln has become an international patron saint in struggles for human rights and moral treatment for all. The sheer volume of foreign stamps shown in this volume is one measure of this international interest. Another is that of the 937 new Lincoln titles recorded at worldcat.org (a global catalog of library collections) in 2008–2010 for the Lincoln bicentennial, 21 are in Spanish, 12 are in German, 8 in Japanese, 7 in Chinese, 4 in French, and others in Dutch, Albanian, Armenian, Hindi, and Gujarati.

I have accepted my publisher's challenge to write a sequel to the very successful *Abraham Lincoln: The Image of His Greatness.* I am fully aware that most sequels flop. For every *Godfather Part II* there are a dozen *Blues Brothers 2000*s. But then, *Superman II* and *Rocky II* were fine films, and very worth the doing. I am taking my personal inspiration from Augustus Saint-Gaudens. Even after sculpting the widely acclaimed greatest Lincoln statue, his *Standing Lincoln,* for Chicago's Lincoln Park in the mid- to late 1880s, he accepted a commission from the same source to do another Lincoln memorial for the Windy City. Saint-Gaudens labored 12 years on a second masterpiece. He completed the statue in 1906, but died before it was cast. When it was cast posthumously, President Theodore Roosevelt was so impressed by Saint-Gaudens's sensitive treatment of an introspective Lincoln that he secured the sculptor's widow's permission to have that bust engraved for the official Lincoln centennial U.S. two-cent commemorative postage stamp in 1909. Eventually, after his bronze *Seated Lincoln* was exhibited in New York City and San Francisco to great acclaim, it was installed in 1926 in Chicago's Grant Park—a fitting memorial to both its subject and its sculptor. In short, another masterpiece.

Abraham Lincoln: Beyond the American Icon is slanted toward interest in the Civil War sesquicentennial. Lincoln is a natural subject; a century and a half ago, for four long years he did something significant virtually every single day. Here is my interpretation. May it prove of some value to your enjoyment and edification.

The most important image of Abraham Lincoln during and after his presidency was this engraving, by Charles Burt, which appeared on millions of $10 notes issued from 1861 to 1869. A similar vignette also appeared on federal government bonds, $20 Interest Bearing Treasury Notes, bank notes, and other "official" documents. This image embodied Lincoln the man. A similar image also graced the first U.S. stamps to depict Lincoln, issued in 1866 and 1869.

Chapter 1

Abraham Lincoln

1869 – 1865

History has given us about 130 legitimate photographs of Abraham Lincoln, innumerable pretender images, several portraits from life, two life masks, and assorted contemporary sketches, so we are not unaware of how Lincoln actually looked. Over the years various adaptive images produced by sculptors and other artists have been added to the canon, so today there is no shortage of Lincoln likenesses.

Today nobody is confused about how Lincoln actually appeared. In Abe's own day, however, this was not the case. He was largely unknown outside his intimate circle. The first recorded legitimate image of Lincoln is the congressional daguerreotype showing a well-kempt 37-year-old Abe as a congressman-elect in 1846. Thereafter Lincoln was apparently photographed sporadically for the next decade. All these images were private affairs, and it was only much later that any of them came to be known to the public. Even 30 years after his death fewer than two dozen different Lincoln photographs were known to Lincoln historians.

The first real notice of Lincoln following his series of joint speaking appearances with Democrat Stephen Douglas was in late winter 1860, when his New York City young Republican hosts trotted the Westerner before Mathew Brady's camera lens in New York City. The so-called Cooper Union photograph caught a raw-boned, tousle-haired lawyer ill at ease in his skin. But the photographer retouched the image sufficiently that following Lincoln's nomination that May it rose to popular notice.

The Cooper Union photograph became the first widely dispersed image of the beardless candidate Lincoln. He reportedly said something along the lines of the Cooper Union speech and that photograph having made him president. The quote may be apocryphal, but is generally accepted by Lincoln historians. If he actually said anything of the kind, it shows how genuinely astute he was about the power of the mass media in shaping his image. This photograph alone is said to have been distributed on upward of 100,000 small cartes de visite during the campaign. It was also widely reproduced as woodcut and other engraved images in periodicals like *Harper's Weekly*, *Leslie's Illustrated*, the *New York Illustrated News*, and even the *London Illustrated News*. These were likewise copied by additional CDVs both here in the United States and abroad in London, Paris, and the German states.

Other partisans, too, grasped the camera's special effect of making their candidate known to the masses. Shortly after Lincoln's nomination, his Republican handlers in Illinois engaged Chicago photographer Alexander Hesler to take a series of photographs for campaign purposes. These images were recorded in Lincoln's hometown of Springfield, and were widely duplicated through effigies on small medals and ribbons during the campaign.

Fig. 1.1. This axe handle inscribed "A. Lincoln / New Salem 1834" attests to Lincoln's frontier upbringing. It was dug up near the old location of the Lincoln-Berry store and traces to the 1952 Oliver Barrett Collection Sale, lot 31.

Lincoln spent the entire election season at home in Illinois, as was the practice of that time. His backers took the stump throughout the Northern states, and his campaign literature spread his image and his message in profusion. This included illustrated sheet music, illustrated campaign envelopes and stationery, biographies and songsters with illustrated covers, banners, and similar printed and woven material. During the election and immediately following, additional photographers, artists, and sculptors visited the Lincolns in Springfield to catch his likeness for a curious media and for posterity.

When Lincoln commenced his beard following his election (and the excellent suggestion of young Grace Bedell), all these previous images were outdated. So local photographer C.S. German recorded Lincoln's new chin whiskers and his evolving image makeover as presidential timbre.

On Sunday, February 25, the very day after president-elect Lincoln entered the nation's capital, he was escorted to Mathew Brady's Washington, D.C., gallery for another series of photographs to feed the needs of the illustrated tabloids of the day. Throughout the four-plus years of his presidency, Lincoln frequently visited or was visited by additional lensmen and other artists on private or public commissions.

Early in the war, when Congress met Lincoln's call for troops with a bond and paper-money issue, Lincoln's secretary of the Treasury, Salmon P. Chase, insisted that the president have a "correct picture" taken that could be duplicated on the nation's bonds and currency, to serve the needs of the nation's finances and its preservation in those trying times. Chase suggested Lincoln use the official government photographer for this purpose, but the image ultimately selected was one of the excellent likenesses captured by C.S. German in Springfield in January 1861.

We know this image best today as the $10 greenback portrait, cataloged as Ostendorf-41/42. It was the model for a bond portrait engraved by a National Bank Note Co. engraver of uncertain identity. Historically this engraving was credited to Henry Gugler, but research for *Abraham Lincoln: The Image of His Greatness* (2009) shows it much more likely to have been engraved by George Baldwin for NBNCo. Bonds utilizing this engraving hit the ground almost immediately in July 1861, and were issued to investors periodically throughout the war as needs warranted and as appropriations made possible.

Fig. 1.2. A youthful teenaged Abe is here depicted by the Abraham Lincoln Presidential Library and Museum.

Fig. 1.3. Lincoln's law partner, William Herndon; biographer Ida Tarbell; poet Edgar Lee Masters, and others were responsible for embroidering the problematic legend of Lincoln's star-crossed love affair with New Salem girl Ann Rutledge, played here by the beautiful, winsome Ruth Clifford in *The Dramatic Life of Abraham Lincoln* (1924). Hollywood embellished the ill-fated love story by employing only the most striking young actresses in the Ann role. Actresses reprising Clifford's Ann included Una Merkel, Pauline Moore, Mary Howard, Grace Kelly, and Joanne Woodward

Fig. 1.4. Over a long, distinguished career, and for the rest of his life, Raymond Massey was Identified with his role in *Abe Lincoln in Illinois,* created first on the stage in 1938 and two years later on the silver screen. Here twenty-something Abe attends to a customer at the Lincoln-Berry New Salem store. The business partnership lasted only three months but is a highlight of all Lincoln film biographies.

Fig. 1.5.
The alleged
"smoking gun" proving the validity
of the Lincoln-Rutledge love affair was this
betrothal stone, purportedly dug up in New Salem, scratched
"A. Lincoln / Ann Rutledge / were betrothed / here July 4 / 1833."
This fraud roped in collector Oliver Barrett and Lincoln biographer
Carl Sandburg. It appeared as lot 29 in the Barrett sale, with the
scratched inscription highlighted as shown.

Fig. 1.6. It was a real tear-jerker in 1930 when the great dramatic actor
Walter Huston grieved at Ann Rutledge's grave in director-producer
D.W. Griffith's film *Abraham Lincoln.* The script was written by novelist
Stephen Vincent Benet.

Fig. 1.7. Abraham Lincoln
found favor with his New
Salem neighbors, who sent
him to successive terms in the
Illinois State House as their
representative. This facsimile
reproduction of his March 1,
1841, pay warrant as an Illinois
legislator promised six-percent
interest until redeemed by the
state. Such replicas are
available to modern-day
visitors to the old Capitol
building in Springfield.

Fig. 1.9. Abraham Lincoln is the only U.S. president to
hold a patent. In 1849 he improvised a method of
floating a riverboat off a sandbar. This model of his
invention illustrates his "improved method of lifting
vessels over shoals," patented May 22, 1849.

Fig. 1.8. Hoaxes have been part and parcel of the unfurling of the
Lincoln legend over time. This photograph was put forward purporting
to show Congressman Abraham Lincoln and wife Mary (second and
third from left) at George Washington's grave at Mount Vernon in the
1840s. Although both Abraham and Mary visited Washington's grave,
their visits were at different times, 13 years apart. Lincoln visited the
site in February 1848.

Fig. 1.10. Lincoln was the most experienced trial lawyer to be elected president up to that time. He spent a quarter century in the profession. Here Henry Fonda lawyers as Lincoln in director John Ford's motion picture *Young Mr. Lincoln* (1939).

A companion likeness, also based on the C.S. German photographic images, was engraved in the first month of Lincoln's presidency for the competing American Bank Note Co. This engraving was long credited to Frederick Girsch, and the Bureau of Engraving and Printing Historical Resource Center persists in this erroneous attribution to this day. However, we have known this engraver's true identity precisely because the die he engraved and all its attendant paperwork were preserved in the archives of ABNCo until 2005, when the die and provenance material were sold at public auction. The following year the actual roller die that transferred the original engraved portrait to the currency plates likewise came up for public sale.

We now know correctly that the engraver of this image was none other than Charles K. Burt, and his masterpiece was approved on March 31, 1861. Both the cataloger of the auction and the winner of the steel-plate intaglio die, steel roller die, and documentary material (who happens to be the present author) widely publicized their contents in a series of important articles in three of the most influential publications devoted to numismatics (*Paper Money*, *Bank Note Reporter*, and *The Numismatist*), and later in the prestigious *Lincoln Herald*. The original die and roller die were also illustrated in *Abraham Lincoln: The Image of His Greatness*. This information was also reported to the BEP Office of External Relations and to BEP HRC contract personnel directly, but the BEP never registered the message, and misattributed the engraver of this *most* important contemporary Lincoln engraving (of the man's own lifetime) in its Lincoln bicentennial exhibition in 2009.

Beginning in August 1861, through April 1869, this Lincoln money image by Charles Burt was duplicated on nearly 14 million $10 Demand Notes and Legal Tender Notes. This was the portrait of himself that Lincoln carried in his own pockets. It was also the official government portrait of Lincoln that his contemporaries saw daily. These notes circulated and re-circulated through the marketplace throughout Lincoln's lifetime and in the years following his death.

The Lincoln on the money was the Lincoln that people knew, loved, or hated during his lifetime, and subsequently revered following his martyrdom. The money image sparked a host of copycat likenesses in the media and elsewhere. This was both the most impor-tant and the dominant Lincoln likeness of his lifetime. No other competing image came close in creating the contemporary Lincoln persona.

Fig. 1.11. This gaunt and noble portrait envisions how Lincoln would have looked in the 1850s as a prosperous and successful lawyer in Illinois.

Fig. 1.12. Francis (sometimes given as Frank) B. Carpenter spent six months in the White House working on a grand canvas of Abraham Lincoln's first reading of the Emancipation Proclamation to his Cabinet. This portrait of a pre-presidential Lincoln, also by Carpenter, shows the more ordinary day-to-day Lincoln that the artist had come to know through close association.

Fig. 1.13. For those familiar only with the stern images of a war-bedraggled, aging Lincoln, artist Jasper Conant's circa-1860 "smiling Lincoln" with rounded, soft facial features provides a differing perspective.

Fig. 1.14. Easterners were curious about Westerner Lincoln. Boston photographer John Adams Whipple traveled to Springfield, Illinois, to take photos of the Republican candidate in summer 1860. He recorded this image (O-38) of Lincoln and sons Willie and Thomas ("Tad" is barely seen peeking out from behind the corner fence post) outside the family's residence at Eighth and Jackson. The identities of the man and boy in the foreground are unknown.

1835 FEBRUARY 5. In the Illinois legislature, Abraham Lincoln votes to withdraw state school funds from the Bank of the United States at St. Louis and tender them to the state treasurer.

1854 AUGUST 11. Lincoln loans Rita Angelica da Silva $125 at 10 percent interest, payable annually, with principal to be paid in four years. The loan was secured by a mortgage on a Springfield lot. The account was satisfied in full on November 24, 1858. Lincoln would make the woman another loan for $125 in 1855, which would also be repaid, on June 9, 1860.

1856 FEBRUARY 21. Abraham Lincoln writes to George P. Floyd, of Quincy, Illinois, regarding a payment Floyd had sent for legal work. Lincoln determined that Floyd has overpaid him, and he wrote his client, "I have just received yours of 16th, with check on Flagg & Savage for twenty-five dollars. You must think I am a high-priced man. You are too liberal with your money. Fifteen dollars is enough for the job. I send you a receipt for fifteen dollars, and return to you a ten-dollar bill."

1858. Lincoln sits for an ambrotype (O-14), which Lloyd Ostendorf credits as "probably by Roderick M. Cole, Peoria, Illinois, probably 1858." A print in the Alfred Whital Stern Collection of Lincolniana at the Library of Congress has, written in pencil on the back, "This is the photograph from the original ambertype [sic] owned by the Latham family of Lincoln, Illinois. It was posed for by Mr. Lincoln at the time the city of Lincoln was named for him. The photographer is unknown and is called the lost ambrotype. [Signed] Gillespie, 7/5/35." The LOC cataloging of the image is "c. 1853."

1859 APRIL 16. Lincoln writes Peoria editor Thomas J. Pickett: "I must, in candor, say I do not think myself fit for the Presidency. I certainly am flattered and gratified that some partial friends think of me in that connection; but I really think it best for our cause that no concerted effort, such as you suggest, should be made. Let this be considered confidential."

1860 MAY 12. *Harper's Weekly* publishes a two-page centerfold captioned "Prominent Candidates For The Republican Presidential

Nomination At Chicago." Shown were 11 contenders, with the most prominent being William Seward from New York. Shunted off near the lower-left corner was a woodcut of "Lincoln" based on the Mathew Brady Cooper Union photograph.

1860 MAY 20. According to sculptor Leonard Volk, "By previous appointment I was to cast Mr. Lincoln's hands on the Sunday following the Nomination, at nine a.m. I found him ready at his house. I wished him to hold something in his right hand and looked for a piece of paste-board but could find none. I told him a round stick would do as well as anything, thereupon he went to the woodshed and I heard the saw go, and he soon returned to the dining room (where I did the casting) whittling on the end of a piece of broom handle. I remarked to him that he need not whittle off the edges. 'Oh, well' he said 'I thought I would like it nice.' The right hand appeared swollen as compared to the left on account of the excessive hand-shaking the evening before. The difference is distinctly shown in the casts."

1860 SPRING. Sometime after Lincoln wins his party's presidential nomination on May 18, the New York lithographic firm of H.H. Lloyd & Co. publishes a large (approximately 36 by 28 inches)

broadside titled "National Republican Chart—Presidential Campaign 1860." The principal feature was a large, color lithographic portrait of Abe, based on the Cooper Union photo taken in New York City in February, and another of his running mate, Hannibal Hamlin of Maine. A map of the free and slave states, biographies of the candidates, portraits of the first 15 U.S. presidents, and statistical charts were also given. This wasn't a partisan venture for the lithographic company, which also produced one for the Democratic candidates and one listing the candidates of all four national parties in the canvas.

1860 JUNE 3. Two weeks after his nomination, Chicago photographer Alexander Hesler takes a near-profile photograph of Abraham Lincoln in the State Capitol in Springfield. It would become a popular model for political-campaign tokens.

1860 JULY 13. Lincoln pens a note to a well-wisher: "Dear Sir, You requested an autograph; and here it is. Yours truly A. Lincoln."

1860 SEPTEMBER 1. Abraham Lincoln appears on the front page of *Broughton's Monthly Planet Reader and Astrological Journal*. The editor described candidate Lincoln very favorably, writing in part:

Fig. 1.15. Today we know this famous image, generally credited to Peoria, Illinois, photographer Roderick M. Cole, as O-14. Reproductions of the image were very popular on campaign buttons (ferrotypes) and ribbons during the election of 1860. This print at the Library of Congress supplies this spurious information written in pencil on back: "This is the photograph from the original ambertype [sic] owned by the Latham family of Lincoln, Illinois. It was posed for by Mr. Lincoln at the time the city of Lincoln was named for him. The photographer is unknown and is called the lost ambrotype. [Signed] Gillespie, 7/5/35." Lincoln, Illinois, was incorporated in 1853. Lincoln photograph historians now believe this likeness was taken circa 1858.

Fig. 1.16. For decades wire services circulated photographs of this "We Honor the Honest Abraham Lincoln" as a Lincoln poster from the senatorial canvass of 1858. It was actually only a series of notices printed in a newspaper, but "poster" is more impressive-sounding.

After careful examination of his Nativity, we are of the opinion that he was born near two o'clock in the morning. Should we have ascertained the correct time of Abraham Lincoln's birth, he was born under the planets Jupiter and Saturn, as the sign Sagittary was ascending at the above-named time; and the planet Saturn was in the ascendant. Saturn in Sagittary describes a large person, not stout, but raw-boned; dark-brown hair, good make, and rather dark in complexion; careful, choleric, and will not bear an affront, yet willing to do to all; a lover of his friends and merciful to his enemies.

Later in its review of Lincoln's prospects, *Broughton's* unabashedly predicted "Mr. Lincoln has a rather fortunate Nativity for becoming popular, and for rising in the world with care and industry. But we are sorry to say that he has some rather unfortunate aspects coming on . . . all of which aspects make us inclined to judge that he will be defeated this next coming Presidential election, and we think it will be caused by some intrigue or political manoeuvres." The Lincoln cover and planetary and astrological reading was one of four *Broughton's* published for the contenders in the 1860 presidential election. Stephen A. Douglas appeared on the August 1 cover, and John Breckinridge and John Bell on the October 1 and November 1 issues, respectively.

Broughton's incorrectly predicted the election of Judge Douglas.

1860 SEPTEMBER. New York Young Men's Republican Club secretary Erasmus Sterling issues a circular on behalf of the organization, which had invited Western lawyer Abraham Lincoln to address the public in New York (this speech became his noted Cooper Union Address): "We will furnish for $1 sixteen copies of Mr. Lincoln's Address, similar to the copy enclosed, or forty copies of a cheaper edition, for the same type, but on ordinary paper,

Fig. 1.17. *Broughton's Monthly Planetary Reader and Astrological Journal* was published in Philadelphia by L.D. (Luke Dennis) Broughton. From the looks of this September 1, 1860, issue, the periodical commenced on April 1 of that year. Broughton star-gazed all four presidential candidates' electoral chances. Stephen A. Douglas appeared in August, and Abraham Lincoln was followed by John Breckinridge and John Bell in October and November, respectively. Mr. Broughton erred in his prognostication; he picked Douglas. After Lincoln's election, Broughton (who styled himself as a "prognostic astronomer") chalked up his lapse to something akin to beginner's luck.

Fig. 1.18. This representation of one of the 1858 Lincoln-Douglas debates is located at the Lincoln Boyhood Memorial in Indiana.

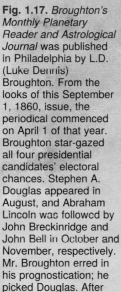

Fig. 1.19. This isn't another "lost ambertype" of Abraham Lincoln, but this Lincoln-esque gentleman's hand-tinted ambrotype (wet collodion positive image on glass) was offered up as a newly discovered Lincoln photograph in the last decade. It dates from circa the 1850s; perhaps Abe grew out his chin whiskers to look more like this resolute brother of the brush?

Fig. 1.20. On August 8, 1860, Chicago photographer William A. Shaw recorded this image (O-34) of Abraham Lincoln and dozens of his fellow townsmen after a Lincoln rally in Springfield. The photograph was taken in front of the candidate's home.

without a cover; or, if preferred, eight of the former and twenty of the latter. We will also furnish associations with the cheap edition at $15 per thousand."

1860 OCTOBER 20. *Frank Leslie's Illustrated Newspaper* publishes a full-page woodcut based on Mathew Brady's three-quarter-length Cooper Union photograph of Lincoln. "The Republican candidate for the Presidency is one of a class which belongs especially to our Republic," editor Frank Leslie wrote.

No other nation on the face of the globe can boast of men who, by the mere force of individual hardihood and merit, rise through all the gradations of toil to the highest offices in the State. Common labor, which brutalizes and degrades man in other lands, in our own country strengthens him mentally as well as physically, and the cabinet maker and the rail-splitter, after having earned a compe-

tency by the honest labor of their hands, finally meet face to face as contestants for the highest office in the gift of the people.[1]

1860 NOVEMBER 9. Lincoln's election is not popular in the South. Three days after he was elected, the *New Orleans Delta* reported: "A consignment of Lincoln medals from New York have been returned. An exhibition for sale of Portraits of Lincoln exasperated the people so that the exhibitor barely escaped with his life."

1860 NOVEMBER 17. Winning candidate Abraham Lincoln and his running mate appear on the front page of the *New York Illustrated News*.

1860 DECEMBER 15. A woodcut of Mary Todd Lincoln and sons Tad and Willie appears on the full front page of *Frank Leslie's Illustrated Newspaper*.

Fig. 1.21. This campaign-used cover was postmarked in Lansing, Michigan, on October 23 (1860). It features a woodcut illustration based on the famous Mathew Brady Cooper Union photograph (O-17) taken in New York City on the afternoon of February 27, 1860. A previous owner tore off the stamp, presumably for his collection.

Fig. 1.22. The Wide Awakes were young Republican boosters of candidate Lincoln. The Cooper Union image engraved by "CRAP" adorns this fine 1860 campaign ribbon for "Honest Old Abe. / The People's Choice." It is unlisted in Sullivan, but clearly tied to AL-30.

Fig. 1.23. Interest in Lincoln was intense in Europe. A. Ken, located at 10 Montmartre Boulevard in Paris, France, was one of the finest Parisian photographers of his day, and important in the history of photography. His works reside in famous museum collections, and this carte de visite in the collection of the author. The image reproduces a print based on the Cooper Union photograph. "B.S.G.D.G." on the back of the mount stands for "breveté sans garantie du gouvernement" (French meaning "patented without government guarantee")—in other words, Monsieur Ken was claiming copyright to his artistic product.

Fig. 1.24. Chicago photographer Alexander Hesler came to Springfield to photograph Abraham Lincoln at the behest of his Republican backers in late spring 1860. This image (O-26) was one of at least five he took on June 3. Said Lincoln: "That looks better and expresses me better than any I have ever seen. If it pleases the people I am satisfied." It was especially popular as a model for die-struck 1860 presidential-campaign tokens.

Fig. 1.25. Parisian photographer André Adolphe Eugène Disdéri was most famous for his cartes de visite, such as this fine example. He perfected a method of mass-producing these small photographs, which became the rage on the Continent and in the United States. Like his competitor A. Ken, Disdéri reproduced a printed image based on the Cooper Union photograph.

Fig. 1.26. This is one of the several types of 1860 campaign ferros reproducing a Currier & Ives print based on the Roderick Cole image of Lincoln. It is of the type of DeWitt/Sullivan AL 1860-89/90.

Fig. 1.27. The Lincoln likeness on this wonderful Lincoln-Hamlin jugate pin is a print based on the Cole ambrotype. It is not listed in DeWitt/Sullivan because it is a paper, not tintype, composite image.

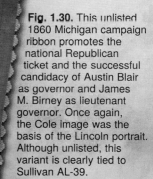

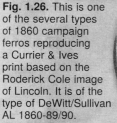

Fig. 1.28. Philadelphia diesinker Robert Lovett, who is also credited with the fantasy "Confederate" cent, created this marvelous campaign token (King-48) for Abraham Lincoln in 1860, proclaiming "Protection to American Industry / Free / Homes / For / Free Men," both Republican planks. The portrait is the Hesler photograph, O-26. It is a 27-millimeter masterpiece. However, its concentric reverse design has only 32 stars, when there were 33 states at the time.

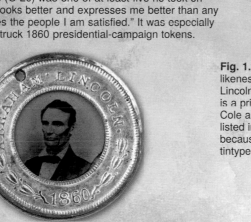

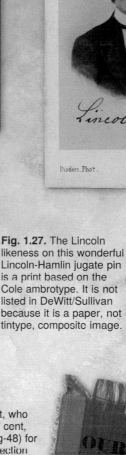

Fig. 1.29. Charles Lang of Knox & Lang, Worcester, Massachusetts, cut the portrait on this "Freedom / National / Slavery / Sectional" campaign token (King-52) based on the same Hesler photographic model as did Lovett. Although a creditable likeness, this stern visage is much inferior to the Philadelphia medalist's work.

Fig. 1.30. This unlisted 1860 Michigan campaign ribbon promotes the national Republican ticket and the successful candidacy of Austin Blair as governor and James M. Birney as lieutenant governor. Once again, the Cole image was the basis of the Lincoln portrait. Although unlisted, this variant is clearly tied to Sullivan AL-39.

1861 JANUARY 25. New York attorney Daniel Ullman writes Lincoln:

Some years ago a number of citizens of New York caused dies to be sunk, in which to strike a medal commemorative of the life and public services of the great Clay & — in order that they might thereby transmit to remote posterity, in the most enduring and classic form, a correct resemblance of his lineaments. A medal was accordingly struck in gold, and presented to him. One hundred and fifty were also struck in bronze. After which the dies were broken. Many of the medals were presented to various States of the Union, and to leading public Institutions, at home and abroad. I reserved, at the time one of them, with the intention, if ever such a result should occur in my day, of presenting it to the citizen of the school of Henry Clay, who should first be elected to the Presidency of the United States. I rejoice that that event has, at last, occurred, and, recognizing in you, a true disciple of our illustrious friend, I take great pleasure in carrying out my purpose, by hereby transmitting the medal to you, and begging your kind acceptance of it.[2]

1861 JANUARY 31. Five days after posing for C.S. German in Springfield (for the photograph that later that year would be engraved for the $10 bill), the president-elect visits his stepmother to bid adieu for the last time. Sarah Lincoln was staying with her daughter Matilda Johnston Hall Moore in Farmington while repairs were being made to her cabin at Goosenest Prairie. Lincoln visited his father's grave in Shiloh Cemetery and returned to the Moore home for a big banquet. After dinner, Lincoln, looking just like his photo, told his stepmother farewell. She embraced him and said, "My dear boy, I always thought there was something great in you." Lincoln returned to Charleston that night to catch the train to Springfield the following day. In 1861, he would write about Sarah Lincoln: "She has been my best friend in this world and no son could love a mother more than I love her."

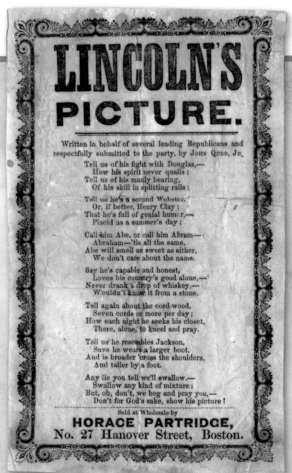

Fig. 1.31. This colorful red-white-and-blue paper ribbon was marketed by the Satin & Paper Badge Depot of Philadelphia. The printed Lincoln portrait is also based on the Fassett image. It has the erroneous but prevalent conceit from early in the 1860 campaign that frequently misidentified the candidate's Christian name as "Abram." Its textile counterpart is listed as Sullivan AL-52. That author points out a similar design was issued for George B. McClellan, giving rise to the somewhat remote possibility that this undated beardless ribbon was an 1864 and not an 1860 production.

Fig. 1.32. This jocular poem, "Lincoln's Picture," was allegedly written by John Quod Jr. It circulated during the campaign of 1860. The author gently criticizes Abraham Lincoln's humble face. We'll swallow any lie \you tell us about him, but please, its author begs, "Don't for God's sake, show [us] his picture!"

Fig. 1.33. Chicago lithographer Ed Mendel created this Lincoln portrait after fellow Chicagoan Samuel Fassett's photograph. The enterprising Mendel used it on campaign ribbons such as this one (Sullivan AL-26, not illustrated), on campaign covers and companion stationery, and even on merchant scrip he printed for a Kentucky merchant (see figure 1.103a in *Abraham Lincoln: The Image of His Greatness*).

1861 FEBRUARY 1. Abraham Lincoln writes to Daniel Ullman to thank him for "the bronze medal of Mr. Clay," which had arrived by express that morning. Lincoln wrote to convey "the extreme gratification I feel in possessing so beautiful a memento." According to the *Chicago Tribune*, New York attorney Daniel Ullman, who had been the Know-Nothing candidate for governor in 1854, had been saving one of the 150 examples of the limited-edition bronze medals struck in honor of Henry Clay "some years before" for presentation to the first president elected from the "school of Henry Clay."[3] On April 15, 1861, Lincoln appointed nearly a dozen New Yorkers to political patronage jobs, including Daniel Ullman to the U.S. Mint in some capacity.[4] Ullman accepted a commission in the Army instead, as a colonel of the 78th New York. He would be promoted to brigadier general in 1863. Ullman recruited black soldiers in Louisiana for the Corps d'Afrique. Near war's end, he would be promoted to brevet major general.[5]

Ullman leaked Lincoln's response to the press. Southerners, particularly the *Richmond Dispatch*, as Harold Holzer points out, mocked Lincoln's reference to Clay as "his teacher." "What lesson of Henry Clay has he learned?" the paper asked. "Where does he follow his leader's (the Great Compromiser's) footsteps?"[6]

1861 APRIL 22. Mathew Brady pens a note to photographer Alexander Gardner: "Mr. Gardner, President Elect Lincoln will visit the Gallery on the 24th. Please ready equipment."

1861 MARCH 9. After Abraham Lincoln's inauguration on March 4, the first image many Americans get of their new president is of Lincoln bravely raising the American flag over Independence Hall two weeks earlier on February 22, during his trip east from Illinois to take up the reins of the government. Lincoln approached the task of celebrating George Washington's birthday courageously, disregarding death threats upon his person, and appeared in public to reassure Americans that all was well. He addressed the crowd from a flag-draped dais. "I would rather be assassinated on this spot, than surrender it," he thundered defiantly. The new 34-star flag that Lincoln raised recognized the admission of the new state of Kansas on January 29, 1861. The unattributed full-page illustration on the cover of *Harper's Weekly* of this date was based on "photographs" taken by F. DeBourf Richards, of Philadelphia. Ostendorf lists three extant images of this scene (O-46 to O-48), none of which actually show Lincoln in the process of raising the flag over the cradle of the nation's independence.

Fig. 1.34. Contemporary campaign banners (or flags, as they are sometimes called) like this red-white-and-blue patriotic takeoff on Old Glory for Lincoln and Hannibal Hamlin are among the most cherished and pricey of campaign collectibles. A similar design in a Heritage Auctions sale brought more than $80,000, but this particular design is being sold on the Internet today based on an unknown referent. The Lincoln portrait appears to be a print after the October 4, 1859, photograph (O-16) by Samuel M. Fassett of Chicago.

Fig. 1.35. On the morning of the 12th day of his 1861 rail trip east to be inaugurated, in an event marking George Washington's birthday on February 22, Abraham Lincoln bravely spurned caution of having been under death threats and publicly raised the new 34-star flag in honor of Kansas over Independence Hall in Philadelphia. Lincoln is the hatless gent above the single star at left on the draped flag; his young son Tad is the lad leaning on the rail above the cluster of stars at right. The patriotic significance of Lincoln's bravery ignited a firestorm of contemporary prints memorializing the occasion, and a half century later of a series of memorable commemorative paintings by J.G.L. Ferris.

1861 MARCH 9. Folks get another view of the president-elect's progress to the nation's capital on the back cover of *Harper's Weekly*; a four-panel illustration covers most of the page. In panel one, Lincoln in bedclothes is advised of "the fact that an organized body of men had determined that Mr. Lincoln should never leave the City of Baltimore alive." In panel two, Lincoln is counseled over his wishes to play it safe. In the third box a furtive Lincoln rushes madly to a special train. "He wore a Scotch plaid Cap and a very long Military Cloak, so that he was entirely unrecognizable," the text advises. Finally, safe at Washington, Lincoln and New York senator William Seward pay their respects to outgoing president James Buchanan.

1861 MARCH 20. Medalist Salathiel Ellis submits a proposal to newly installed Commissioner of Indian Affairs William P. Dole to supply Indian Peace medals with portraits of recently inaugurated president Abraham Lincoln for presentation to Native American allies. Ellis promised to supply 100 each of small (62 mm) and large (76 mm) silver medals, with $1,250 in silver for $3,250 delivered. Work on the medal was delayed. Congress finally appropriated $5,000 on July 5, 1862, for production/distribution of "medallions of the President of the United States for distribution to Indian Tribes," as part of an "Act making Appropriations for the current and contingent Expense of the Indian Department, and for fulfilling Treaty Stipulations with various Indian Tribes, for the Year ending June thirtieth, eighteen hundred and sixty-three."[7]

Fig. 1.36. This particular example of Salathiel Ellis and Joseph Willson's 1862 Lincoln Indian Peace medal design (Julian IP-38) is struck in fine gold. Silver examples, both large and small size, were presented to Native American allies of the United States. Julian lists this medal in gold, but a check of his appendix fails to disclose a 19th-century striking of this medal in gold at the U.S. Mint. It is believed this example was probably struck to order for a 20th-century collector.

Fig. 1.37. Lincoln's inauguration was noted in England by this woodcut in the *Illustrated London News*, March 30, 1861. The text of his inaugural address had appeared in the newspaper the previous week, but it took additional time to complete the massive engraving for the illustration.

Fig. 1.38. A National Bank Note Co. engraver created this excellent portrait of Abraham Lincoln based on Christopher S. German's January 13, 1861, photo (O-42) for use on government-contract printing work such as this $100 six-percent registered bond proof (Hessler X128B). Two hundred and fifty million dollars were authorized by the acts of July and August 1861. This fine engraving would grace this and successive emissions which financed the suppression of the insurrection. The Lincoln vignette is sometimes attributed to Henry Gugler, but research for *Abraham Lincoln: The Image of His Greatness* revealed it was probably done by George D. Baldwin instead.

Fig. 1.39. Almost simultaneously, a second but very similar Lincoln security portrait was engraved by American Bank Note Co. contract engraver Charles Burt based on the companion, similar C.S. German photograph (O-41). It appeared also on $10 Demand Notes printed by that company by contract for the Treasury that summer. When the Legal Tender greenbacks were authorized the following February, Burt's image was transferred to the $10 notes of that class of currency. Circulated on these federal currencies by the millions of impressions, Burt's Lincoln became the most prevalent view of Abraham Lincoln that his fellow citizens had of him during the Railsplitter's presidency and aftermath. Money was the mass media of the day, and other media were quick to copy the "official" government money portrait that people knew and carried in their pockets.

1861 JULY 13. In a *Harper's Weekly* editorial cartoon Abe Lincoln apprehends a scraggly Jefferson Davis stealing a U.S. Treasury portfolio. Officer Lincoln, with billy club in hand, says: "I guess I've got you now, Jeff." Davis replies: "Guess you have—well now, let us Compromise."

1861 SEPTEMBER. One of the perimeter-defense forts built to defend Washington, D.C., in the far northeast quadrant of the city along the Baltimore & Ohio Railroad line, is named Fort Lincoln in the president's honor by General Order #10.

1862. Alfred H. Satterlee privately publishes in New York the first list of Lincoln medals in his *An Arrangement of Medals and Tokens Struck in Honor of the Presidents of the United States, and of presidential candidates, from the administration of John Adams to that of Abraham Lincoln.* Included were 26 medals, exclusive of metal varieties (58 total counting varieties), including several store cards.

Fig. 1.40. During the 2009 Lincoln Bicentennial, curators at the Smithsonian Institution discovered and revealed a hidden message scratched into the plate inside Abraham Lincoln's pocket watch, which had been repaired in New York in 1861. The craftsman doing the repair inscribed this benediction: "Jonathon Dillon April 13, 1861. Fort Sumpter [sic] was attacked by the rebels on the above date . . . thank God we have a government."

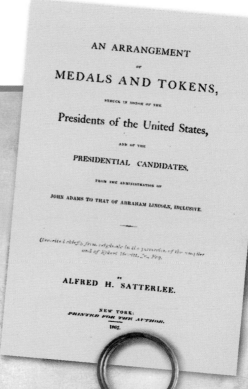

Fig. 1.41. Alfred Satterlee's privately printed pamphlet *An Arrangement of Medals and Tokens, Struck in Honor of the Presidents of the United States* was the first publication to quantify and catalog the proliferation of numismatic tributes to Honest Abe.

Fig. 1.42. Orthodox Christians, Deists, and atheists alike claim a spiritual kinship with Old Abe. This undated document, brought forth in 1942, claims that Lincoln donated $150 and became a "Life Director" of the Missionary Society of the Methodist Episcopal Church. Both Lincoln and his wife were, in fact, honorary "Life Directors" (patrons) of the organization, but how that reflects on his personal spirituality is an unsettled question.

Fig. 1.43. This contemporary tintype souvenir copied—but flopped—the C.S. German photographic image that was popular with the folks because it was the Lincoln on the $10 bill.

1862. Sarah Fisher Clampitt Ames sculpts a white marble bust of Abraham Lincoln dressed in robes, like a Roman senator, in Classical style. She would use that bust, in 1868, as a model for a larger version of the bust which was acquired by the U.S. Senate and is displayed in the Capitol. The original smaller bust is in the collection of the Union Pacific Railroad Museum, Council Bluffs, Iowa, one of the oldest corporate art collections in the country. In 1859 Lincoln had traveled to Council Bluffs to meet with Grenville Dodge, an engineer who recommended the location as the eastern terminus of a transcontinental railroad. As president, Lincoln approved land-grant incentives to provide for construction of such a railroad across the American West. In 1869 a line comprising the Union Pacific and the Central Pacific would be completed from Council Bluffs to Sacramento, California; combined with railroads in the East, it effectively spanned the continent from sea to shining sea.

1862 June 23. President Abraham Lincoln vetoes a bill that would have allowed the federally chartered banks in the federal District of Columbia to issue "small notes," i.e., bank notes of value less than $5. In his veto message to the U.S. Senate, Lincoln tells legislators that

> during the existing war it is peculiarly the duty of the National Government to secure to the people a sound circulating medium. . . . The object of the bill submitted to me . . . can be fully accomplished by authorizing the issue, as part of any new emission of United States notes made necessary by the circumstances of the country, of notes of a similar character but of less denomination than $5. Such an issue would answer all the beneficial purposes of the bill, would save a considerable amount to the Treasury in interest, would greatly facilitate payments to soldiers and other creditors of small sums, and would furnish to the people a currency as safe as their own Government.

Fig. 1.45. New York City lithographer Charles Magnus's output was prodigious. Early on he fixed upon a likeness similar to the federal $10 portrait and festooned all kinds of paper ephemera with the image in a variety of contexts, borders, and colors. This elegant "Souvenir of Victory" all-over cover pairs Abe with General George B. McClellan. It was circulated after General William Tecumseh Sherman's victory at Savannah, Georgia.

Fig. 1.44. These similar-appearing merchants' scrip were printed by Boston lithographer Louis Prang. One (presumably the first issue) *(a)* was redeemable in bank bills, and the other (presumably subsequent) *(b)* was redeemable in federal currency. The present author is unaware that any numismatist has reported this important changeover in these merchant due bills following the introduction of federal Legal Tender Notes in 1862.

Fig. 1.46. This enigmatic small plaque bears a profile nude bust of Lincoln and the inscription "President / Abraham Lincoln / 1st / Co / Guard Patrol / 1862." It might not date from the Civil War era.

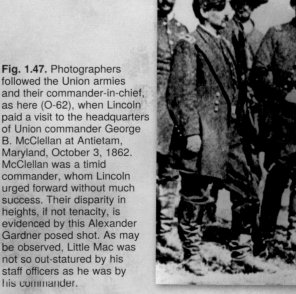

Fig. 1.47. Photographers followed the Union armies and their commander-in-chief, as here (O-62), when Lincoln paid a visit to the headquarters of Union commander George B. McClellan at Antietam, Maryland, October 3, 1862. McClellan was a timid commander, whom Lincoln urged forward without much success. Their disparity in heights, if not tenacity, is evidenced by this Alexander Gardner posed shot. As may be observed, Little Mac was not so out-statured by his staff officers as he was by his commander.

Accordingly, the Act of July 11, 1862, authorizing an additional $150 million in fiat paper notes, would include provisions for these "change notes." $1, $2, and $3 notes were anticipated, but only the first two were eventually issued, the $1 denomination bearing the portrait of Lincoln's secretary of the Treasury (and political rival), Salmon P. Chase.

1862 July 14. President Lincoln signs legislation authorizing the Medal of Honor to members of the Army for valorous service. A similar medal for members of the Navy had been authorized earlier.

1862 November 14. H.H. Van Dyck, superintendent of the New York State Bank Department, reports the organization of the Lincoln Bank, Clinton, New York, during the third quarter of 1862. William C. Churchill was president and C.E. Marston cashier. Its capital was $100,000. The bank would issue sheets of $1—$1—$2—$3 notes, engraved and printed by the National Bank Note Co., with the same engraved Lincoln portrait that was currently appearing on the bonds that company printed for the U.S. Treasury (and the $20 interest-bearing Treasury Notes the Treasury would circulate later). The bank's notes were issue-dated April 8, 1862, possibly pre-dating the bank's organization.

1863 May 2. *Harper's Weekly* publishes two-page and full-page illustrations of Lincoln on horseback, reviewing the Army of the Potomac on April 9, from drawings by illustrator A.R. Waud.

1863 August 11. President Lincoln writes out check number 52 on his personal account at Riggs & Co.: $5.00 payable to "Colored Man, with one leg." It was one of 222 small checks totaling $37,403.31 that Lincoln drew on his Riggs account. Due to its content, it is considered the most famous presidential check of all time. Flowery stories have grown up surrounding it, although nothing is known of its payee or the circumstances of its issue. The check has been known since at least 1893, traced from son Robert Lincoln through a presidential secretary to a Denver collector; its location thereafter became a mystery. For many years, the bank's successor, Riggs National Bank, had a facsimile of it from an 1899 magazine article gracing its president's desk. The facsimile also appeared in a 1948 advertising campaign for the bank. In 1953 the check's content was published in *The Collected Works of Abraham Lincoln*. During the Lincoln Sesquicentennial in 1959, the bank unsuccessfully offered a $500 reward for it, resulting in a flurry of press accounts, where various "experts" speculated on how much it

Fig. 1.48. This is widely celebrated, because of its content, as the most famous presidential check of all time. On August 11, 1863, Abraham Lincoln drew it out on his personal account at Riggs & Co. to "Colored man, with one leg." A great deal of baloney narrative has been embroidered around the circumstances of its issue, which are completely unknown. Although known and cataloged in *The Collected Works of Abraham Lincoln* in 1953, the check's whereabouts were unknown and subject to a national search spearheaded by Riggs National Bank, which offered a substantial reward for it. It finally reemerged in a Sotheby's auction sale in 1984, from the estate of the heirs of a Denver lawyer who had received it as collateral for unpaid services.

Fig. 1.49. Capitalizing on Lincoln's image and character began in his own lifetime. One of the first instances was the Abraham Lincoln Tobacco Co., purveyors of Honest Old Abe Havana cigars. The image on the cigar-box label is a print after the familiar Brady Cooper Union photograph.

Fig. 1.50. Artist Alonzo Chappel was among the first to pair Abraham Lincoln with the "Father of His Country," George Washington. Chappel's painting was widely reproduced in Civil War–era books, as in this hand-tinted illustration.

Fig. 1.51. Administration critic and Philadelphia illustrator L.H. Stephens blistered the president's conduct of the war in a series of 1864 anti-Lincoln campaign cartoons that circulated as cartes de visite and cabinet cards. In this drawing, titled *This Little Joker for President*, an Ape Lincoln Crow dances merrily, cracks jokes, and sucks on molasses candy. In 1930 R.E. Townsend and a partner reissued Stephens's illustrations, lithographed by A. Hoen & Co.

THIS LITTLE JOKER FOR PRESIDENT

might be worth if found. The actual check finally emerged from hiding a quarter century later, on October 31, 1984, at a Sotheby's "fine printed and manuscript Americana" auction, consigned by the granddaughters of a Denver businessman. According to family tradition, he had received it as security for a loan that was never repaid.

1863 August 18. Abraham Lincoln writes to photographer Alexander Gardner to thank him for sending cards of the recent photos Gardner had taken of him. "I think they are generally very successful," Lincoln wrote. "The imperial photograph in which the head leans upon the hand [Ostendorf-74] I regard as the best that I have yet seen."

1863 October. In a speech at Indianapolis, Indiana, Treasury Secretary Salmon P. Chase remarks,

> The next question was, "Will you borrow the paper of the banks and give six per cent. interest for it, and then pay that to the soldiers in place of gold?" Don't you think that after awhile something would have happened if I had done this? Have you not heard somewhat of revulsions and panics and crashes? Well, what would you have had me do? Would you not have said to me: "Here am I, Smith, a farmer; here am I, Jones, a mechanic; here am I, Robinson, a merchant. Take our property and our credit and us, and make a currency for the country based on the country itself. In other words, go to work and make 'greenbacks.'" I know that is what you would have advised me to do; and therefore, as my business was to interpret your will—to know what you would have me do, and then do it—I went to work and made "greenbacks," and a good many of them. I had some handsome pictures put on them; and as I like to be among the people, and was kept too close to visit them in any other way, and as the engravers thought me rather good looking, I told them they might put me on the end of the one-dollar bills. [Cheers and laughter.][8]

1864 February 23. President Lincoln interviews Comptroller of Currency Hugh McCulloch on money matters.

1864. Abraham Lincoln Grammar School on Fifth Street, San Francisco, is established. Ex–state superintendent of public instruction, Ira G. Hoitt, became the first principal of this exclusively boys' school. Medals were awarded annually to top students. It was outside the school's building that Pietro Mezzara's Lincoln statue would find a home as the first such memorial raised in tribute following his assassination. In 1892 *The Californian Illustrated Magazine* reported on "The Lincoln medal fund of three thousand dollars, the interest of which exceeds the annual cost of the medals." Twenty medals were then being awarded annually, to graduates, for scholarship and meritorious conduct. A later, but perhaps similar, medal is listed as King-1046.[9]

1864 April 15. John Williams offers to sell $5,000 (50 shares) of his own paid-in stock in the First National Bank of Springfield, Illinois (charter no. 205, of which he is president), to Abraham Lincoln as an investment. "The stock holders would feel proud of your association with them as one of the share holders," Williams wrote. He added that he didn't wish Lincoln to do anything improper, and concluded with, "of course you will understand that the offer is made in all good faith & without any wish that you should do any thing that would compromise your high position."[10]

1864 April 25. Lincoln replies to John Williams, president of the First National Bank of Springfield, Illinois, that he'll think about the offer to purchase stock in the paid-up bank. "Thanks for your kind remembrance," Lincoln replied. "I would accept your offer at once, were it not that I fear there might be some impropriety in it, though I do not see that there would. I will think of it a while."[11]

1864 June, circa. Shortly after Lincoln's nomination for a second term as president, engraver John Chester Buttre publishes a cam-

Fig. 1.52. New York commercial steel-plate engraver John Chester Buttre was one of the principal hands in popularizing an image of Lincoln based on the February 9, 1864, photograph by Anthony Berger that we know as O-92. He created this exciting portrait, which was popular as a print and very popular as a book illustration.

Fig. 1.53. J.F. Feeks published *The Lincoln Catechism*, a scathing, albeit anonymous, indictment of Abraham Lincoln and his reelection attempt. Its author referred to Lincoln as "Abraham Africanus." He accuses the president of trampling the Constitution, and dividing and bankrupting the country. This pamphlet was issued in both English and German.

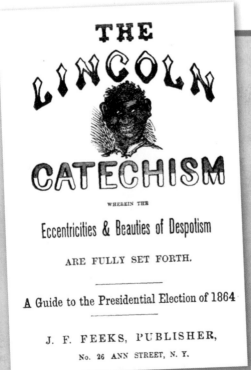

paign engraving of him based on the February 9, 1864, photograph (O-92) by Anthony Berger, which we know chiefly from its further reproduction on the small-size $5 notes of the 20th century.

1864. J.F. Feeks, 26 Ann Street, New York, publishes *The Lincoln Catechism,* a pamphlet "wherein the Eccentricities & Beauties of Despotism are Fully Set Forth" as a "guide to the Presidential Election of 1864." The lessons teach that the Constitution has been made obsolete by "Abraham Africanus the First," that Congress is a body organized to make laws to protect the president from being punished for his crimes and "for the purpose of taxing the people to buy negroes," and that the meaning of "coining money" is printing green paper. The business of the secretary of the Treasury, the publication said, is "to destroy State Banks and fill the pockets of the people full of worthless, irredeemable U.S. shinplasters."

1864 AUGUST 26. The *British Journal of Photography* publishes notice of a "New and Unusual Photo of Lincoln in New York City."

> A New York photographer has published a portrait of President Lincoln, which is likely to prove acceptable to all parties. At first glance it appears to be a photograph of 'Old Abe,' taken when he had the smallpox a few months ago; but on a closer examination the seeming pustules are found to be minute photographic likenesses of the distinguished generals, statesmen, politicians, literary and scientific men, actors.... The likenesses, which are scattered all over the physiognomy of the President, number upwards of 400 . . . and are so exceedingly well executed as to be at once recognized . . . yet, taken together, they constitute as ugly a picture of 'Old Abe' as any of the others that have been published.

1864. During Lincoln's presidential reelection campaign and attendant congressional races, L. Towers prints Isaac N. Arnold's *Reconstruction: Liberty the Cornerstone, and Lincoln the Architect for the Union (Republican) Congressional Committee.*

1864 SEPTEMBER 17. A *Harper's Weekly* anonymous editorial cartoonist's drawing titled "This Reminds Me of A Little Joke," showing Lincoln holding General George McClellan in his palm, noticeably reproduces Lincoln's portrait based on the Anthony Berger photograph (O-92) of February 9, 1864, in which Lincoln's hair is erroneously parted on the right side.

1864 OCTOBER 1. *Harper's Weekly* publishes a two-page editorial cartoon, "Rally Around the Flag," depicting Lincoln holding Old Glory aloft, surrounded by admiring soldiers and sailors "who have maintained the honor and integrity of the nation."

1864 OCTOBER. *Broughton's Monthly Planet Reader and Astrological Journal* features an anachronistic beardless woodcut engraving of Lincoln, after the Cooper Union photograph pose, on its front page, with this bold prediction: "[S]hortly after the election is over, Mr. Lincoln will have a number of evil aspects afflicting his Nativity (I do not think any of them will begin to be felt until the election is past) they will be in operation in Nov. and Dec. of this year. During these months, let him be especially on his guard against attempts to take his life; by such as firearms, and infernal machines." (See figure 1.59.)

Fig. 1.54. This detail from a rare vocational carte de visite shows a sign painter in the midst of painting a pro-Lincoln message on a wall.

Fig. 1.55. The radical comic magazine, *The Funniest of Phun,* commenced in June 1864 to assist Chase and Fremont's attempts to topple the presidency of dark monarch Abraham the Last. The journal's invective was pointed and bitter. On the front page of its August 1864 issue, a cartoonist (probably Frank Ballew) depicted Lincoln as an evil beast trampling civil liberties and the press, dangling his emancipation joke just outside the grasp of the slave, while his henchman Seward arrested administration opposition. Such anti-Lincoln propaganda helped galvanize his negative image in contemporary media and among his political opposition.

Fig. 1.56. In 1863 Schoharie, New York, artist Amos Hamilton painted this portrait of Abraham Lincoln based on the familiar pose he saw on the nation's $10 bills.

1864 FALL. Poet Walt Whitman goes out for a Saturday night on the town during the Lincoln-McClellan political campaign. At a beer dive on New York's Lower East Side, he noticed his waitress was wearing a McClellan pin. "The air is full of the scent of thievery, druggies, foul play, and prostitution gangrened," Whitman wrote. He called to her and pointed to the McClellan medal attached to her bosom. "Are the other girls here for McClellan too?" he inquired. "Yes, every one of them, and they won't tolerate a girl in the place who is not," she replied. Whitman counted 20 such bar girls. "I should think nine-tenths, of all classes, are Copperheads here," he recalled.[12]

1864 OCTOBER 29. Abraham Lincoln shows Sojourner Truth at the Executive Mansion the Bible presented to him by the Colored People of Baltimore. It would later become famous by way of a celebrated illustrated cabinet card of a painting.

1864 NOVEMBER 8. Lincoln becomes only the sixth U.S. president to be reelected to a second term, and the first since Andrew Jackson in 1832.

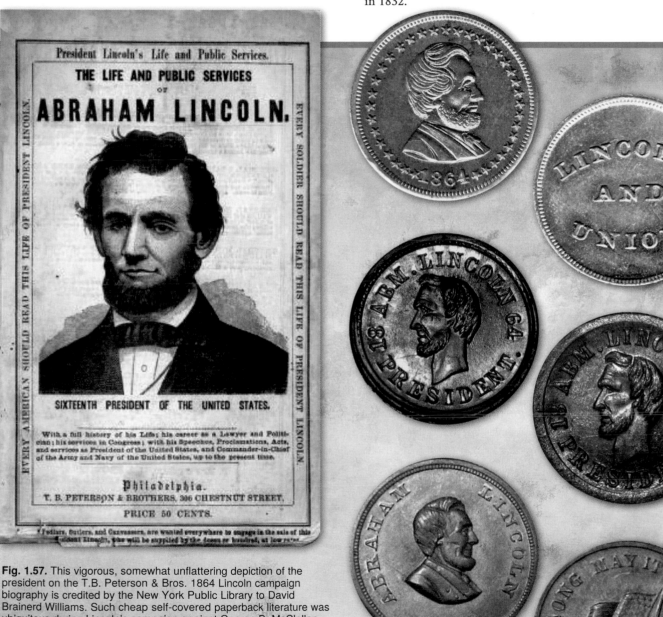

Fig. 1.57. This vigorous, somewhat unflattering depiction of the president on the T.B. Peterson & Bros. 1864 Lincoln campaign biography is credited by the New York Public Library to David Brainerd Williams. Such cheap self-covered paperback literature was ubiquitous during Lincoln's campaign against George B. McClellan.

Fig. 1.58. Whereas most campaign tokens for 1860 were quarter-sized (24.3 mm) or larger, 19-millimeter cent-sized medalets such as these (a, b) dominated the 1864 campaign. The reason, of course, was economic. Northern diesinkers had spent the past two years cranking out cent-sized tokens (c) to replace government cents, which were hoarded by the public. In the early 1980s, the present author was given the problematical assignment by the Civil War Token Society of divining which of these were probably issued as medalets and which were struck as small-change substitutes, for the revised fourth edition of the Fulds' *Patriotic Civil War Tokens*.

BROUGHTON'S
MONTHLY PLANET READER,
AND
ASTROLOGICAL JOURNAL.

Entered according to the Act of Congress in the year 1864, by DR. L. D. BROUGHTON, in the Clerk's Office of the District Court for the Southern District of New York,

Vol. 5.   NEW YORK, OCT. NOV. & DEC., 1864.   **No.1**

THE NATIVITY OF
ABRAHAM LINCOLN,
President of the United States.

In Vol. 1, No. 6, of the "*Planet Reader*", I published the Nativity of Abrm. Lincoln, and to that No., I refer the reader for the chart of the Heavens at the time of his birth. In the above named No. there may also be found the following short description of his personal appearance, mental abilities, and general fortune, &c.; which I prefer to copy, rather than re-write the same :—

Hon. Abrm. Lincoln was born February 12th 1809; After careful examination of his Nativity, we are of the opinion that he was born near two o'clock in the morning. Should we have ascertained the correct time of Abraham Lincoln's birth, he was born under the planets Jupiter and Saturn, as the sign Sagittary was ascending at the above-named time ; and the planet Saturn was in the ascendant. Saturn in Sagittary describes a large person, not stout, but raw-boned ; dark-brown hair, good make, and rather dark in complexion ; careful choleric, and will not bear an affront, yet willing to do good to all : a lover of his friends and merciful to his enemies.

The Moon in good aspect to Jupiter, will cause him to be of a good natured and benevolent disposition, and very sociable, and one that will be very popular and very much esteemed among the poorer classes of people. It will likewise cause him to be of sound judgment, and of a practical turn of mind. Saturn in the ascendant will cause him to be of a plodding, thoughtfull, careful character, and one that will try to provide something against a rainy day.

The planet Mercury having no aspect to the Moon, will show that his mental abilities are not of the highest order, and we may venture to predict that he will never become noted for his learning or scholarship. But at the same time Mercury being in good aspect to the planet Herschel, will cause him to be of an original turn of mind, and one that will think and act for himself, and not care about following fashions or the rules of etiquette ; and it would cause him to appear rather blunt or abrupt in his deportment and language, and to have a rather comical way of expressing himself.

As the Moon first makes an aspect to the planet Mars, his wife is denoted by that planet; which describes a person rather short, well built. but not stout made, rather light in complexion, light brown hair, and oval face ; disposition cheerful, but rather fond of dress and fine outside, of a quick temper but soon over, fond of company, and would be very much respected both by male and female acquaintences and friends, but on account of the Moon making an evil aspect of Mars, they would not live in the most happy manner in a married life. And it would indicate that he would outlive his wife.

This Nativity would not indicate a very large family of children, we should say that they would have some five or six altogether, but there would be much danger of burying some of them when quiet young.

Mr. Lincoln has a rather fortunate Nativity for becoming popular, and for rising in the world with care and industry. But we are sorry to say, that he has some rather unfortunate aspects coming on, and that is the planet Saturn coming in square to his own place and in opposition to Mercury; and the planet Jupiter in opposition to the sun's place ; all of which aspects make us inclined to judge that he will be defeated this coming Presidential election, and we think it will be caused by some intrigue or political manœuvres.

At the time Mr. Lincoln was elected Pres-

1864 CIRCA. One of the first Lincoln portraits—if not the first—based on the Anthony Berger February 9, 1864, photograph (O-92) is painted by self-taught Philadelphia African American artist David Bustill Bowser (1820–1900). From a prominent and early free-Black Philadelphia family, Bowser was an ardent abolitionist and a friend and supporter of John Brown's. He was a sign painter who also created flag designs for black Union regiments, and painted landscapes and portraits (including famously of Brown). The 1864 attribution date is accepted by the Smithsonian American Art Museum's "Inventories of American Painting and Sculpture" database. Critics have labeled the painting amateurish and exaggerated, and pointed out liberties taken with the photographic model. Nevertheless art historian Van Deren Coke says that the painting does convey "something of the sensitivity and determination of the subject [even if] in a rudimentary fashion." At any rate, both the artist and Lincoln must have been happy with this portrait. Bowser sold the canvas to the president as soon as the paint was dry. He painted additional likenesses of Lincoln. One source states Bowser painted "Twenty-one portraits of Abraham Lincoln, one of which Lincoln himself posed for."[13] There is no evidence that Lincoln ever sat for this artist, but he did paint a number of Lincoln portraits. One, then belonging to a South Carolina antique shop, was featured in the May 1960 issue of *Antiques* magazine. A(nother) Lincoln portrait, an oil painting, by Bowser (perhaps the same painting), belonging since 1971 to the Fort Wayne Lincoln Library and Museum, was illustrated in the February 1975 issue of *Antiques*.

Fig. 1.60. Philadelphia African American artist David Bustill Bowser painted several likenesses of Lincoln, including (in 1864) this portrait, based on the same photographic model as, or a print like, Buttre's. Bowser was primarily a painter of emblems and seals, but he made portraits of eminent persons to supplement his income.

Fig. 1.61. The famous British illustrated magazine *Punch, or the London Charivari,* was highly critical of Lincoln's administration and conduct of the Civil War. Here its artist, John Tenniel, depicts Lincoln hogtied by indebtedness.

Fig. 1.62. A week before his 56th (and what would prove to be his last) birthday, Abraham Lincoln and his constant companion, son Tad, visited Washington, D.C., photographer Alexander Gardner's studio for a series of pictures. These are recorded in Lloyd Ostendorf's book as O-114 to O-118. Gardner published the carte de visite of O-116 in 1864. At a somewhat later point, to create an additional photo, L.C. Handy made the similar print also illustrated here, which is not listed in Ostendorf's chronological corpus although it fits nicely between O-115 and O-116. The darkroom operator has married the slightly more turned head of O-116 with the bottom of O-115, in which Lincoln holds a pencil and his spectacles. You can note that the pencil moved when O-115 was taken. The fixing of that defect, and a retouched, more defined image of the specs, makes the combined image "new" and saleable. Such photo-manipulations are what Ostendorf would label a "variant." He called this one "Variant of O-116D."

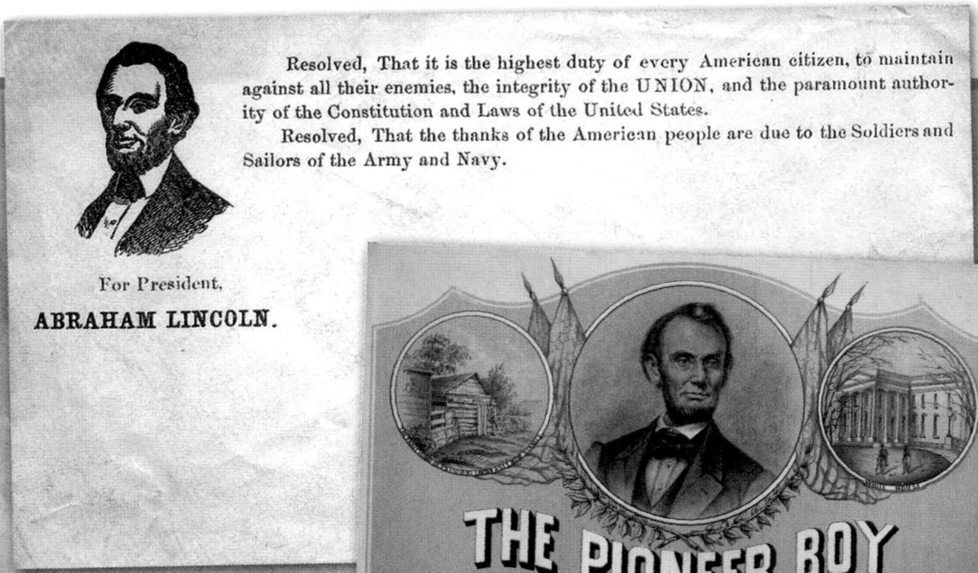

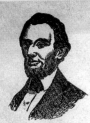

Resolved, That it is the highest duty of every American citizen, to maintain against all their enemies, the integrity of the UNION, and the paramount authority of the Constitution and Laws of the United States.
Resolved, That the thanks of the American people are due to the Soldiers and Sailors of the Army and Navy.
For President,
ABRAHAM LINCOLN.

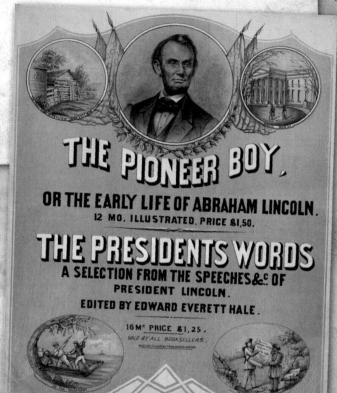

Fig. 1.63. This 1864 political cover, on laid paper, championing Lincoln's reelection, has the $10 Lincoln money image and two planks from the National Union Baltimore Convention (Republican) platform of June 7, 1864.

THE PIONEER BOY,
OR THE EARLY LIFE OF ABRAHAM LINCOLN.
12 MO. ILLUSTRATED. PRICE $1,50.
THE PRESIDENTS WORDS
A SELECTION FROM THE SPEECHES &c. OF
PRESIDENT LINCOLN.
EDITED BY EDWARD EVERETT HALE.
16 M° PRICE $1,25.
SOLD BY ALL BOOKSELLERS.

Fig. 1.64. Boston publishers Walker, Fuller & Co. advertised two works in 1865. The first work listed was actually published by Walker and Fuller beginning in 1865 as the 28th thousand copies of *The Pioneer Boy and How He Became President,* by William Makepeace Thayer. Thayer's work had been first published by Walker, Wise & Co. in 1863, becoming a bestseller. After Lincoln's death the work continued to be popular. The 34th thousand copies appeared in 1871, revised and enlarged.

ABRAHAM LINCOLN FOR PRESIDENT
1864
US

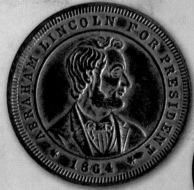

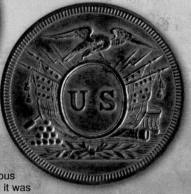

Fig. 1.65. Not all 1864 Lincoln campaign tokens were small size. This 31-millimeter militaristic, silvered-brass issue (O-80) had a low-relief anonymous and amateur Lincoln profile, but it was nearly the size of a half dollar.

Executive Mansion.
Washington, Oct 6th 1864.

Dear Gumpert

I send Thomas Cross to see you about the Carriage Bill. It was sent to me and I ant got any money to pay the man with.

And Oblidge
Thomas Lincoln
Your Friend
Tad

[NUMBER 528]

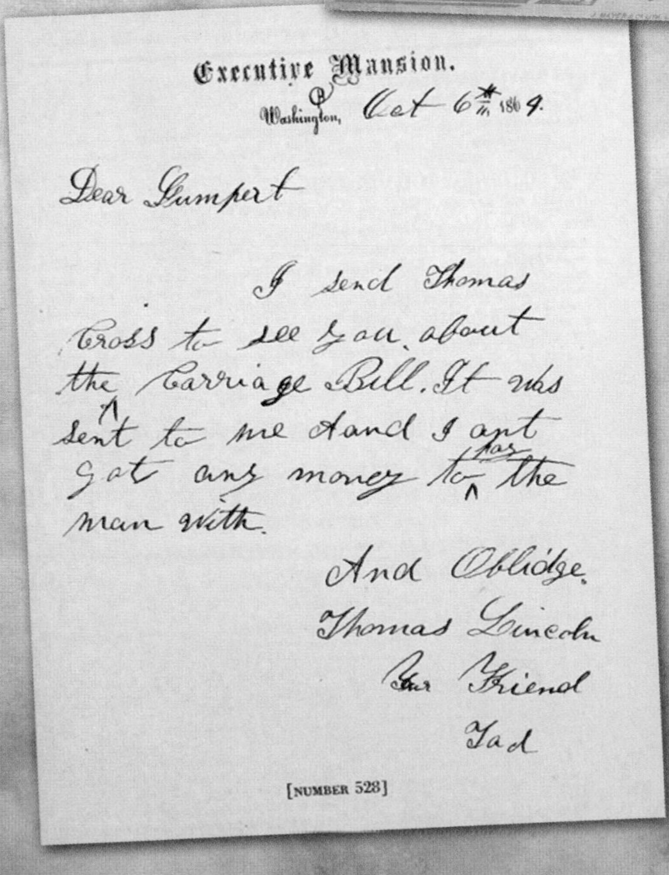

Fig. 1.66. This autographed note, signed by Lincoln's 11-year-old son, which appeared as Lot 528 in the great Oliver Barrett Collection sale, refers a carriage bill to his friend, Philadelphia cigar dealer Gustav E. "Gus" Gumpert, who had befriended the young boy. "I ant (sic) got any money to pay the man with," Tad pleaded.

Fig. 1.67. Thomas Stevens Co., Coventry, England, produced this elegant woven ribbon (Sullivan AL-13) to mark Lincoln's second inaugural. When the president was assassinated shortly thereafter, Stevens altered it to a memorial ribbon.

Fig. 1.68. Collector Oliver Barrett owned Lincoln's presidential seal, which was used to impress a wax seal to documents.

Fig. 1.69. This silvered brass shell (King-764) was likely issued as a pin in 1865, following Lincoln's death, and worn with a memorial ribbon of some kind. It is not listed as silvered by King. That omission will be corrected in the revision of King's classic catalogs, being undertaken by a quartet of Token and Medal Society members, including the present author.

Fig. 1.70. Lincoln's former political foe Salmon P. Chase had matriculated from ex–secretary of the Treasury to chief justice of the United States when Lincoln appointed him to uphold post-war challenges to administration and congressional actions such as enacting legal-tender legislation. Here Chase administers the oath of office at Lincoln's second inaugural, March 4, 1865, in the *Harper's Weekly* front-page illustration of March 18. The caption says "Photographed by Gardner, Washington"—however, the reference image for this unsigned woodcut illustration is unknown today.

PRESIDENT LINCOLN.

Photographed on the Balcony at the White House,
March 6, 1865, by

H. F. WARREN,   WALTHAM, MASS.

Fig. 1.71. In recent years the fame of obscure Waltham, Massachusetts, lensman Henry F. Warren has risen, as he has been christened "the first of the paparazzi." Warren was a portrait painter who had accompanied Lincoln to Alexander Gardner's studio on February 5, 1865, to obtain a model for a portrait he desired to paint. A month later, after the second inaugural, he importuned Lincoln at the White House for additional snapshots, three of which were taken outside on the balcony of the South Portico in the late afternoon. The wind mussed Lincoln's hair and his expression is one of irritation. These candid snapshots are the last taken of Lincoln prior to his assassination. At first Warren marketed the image as the "latest" photo of the president, but after the assassination he changed the label on the photo mount to "last" photo.

Fig. 1.72. This 1861 quarter dollar is said to have been one of the coins placed over the eyelids of the deceased Abraham Lincoln to seal the corpse's eyes. The provenance of this item was said to trace through Maunsell B. Field, assistant Treasury secretary in the Lincoln administration. Regardless of the "evidence" tendered for this piece, skeptics point out that an 1861 quarter dollar could not have achieved the extensive wear evidenced by the time of Lincoln's death, especially because silver change was hoarded by the public by mid-1862 and did not circulate during the rest of the war.

Fig. 1.73. Boston medalist Joseph Merriam created some of the finest 1860 Lincoln campaign medals. Although his obverse portrait die was used to strike this post-war store card (King-597), it probably wasn't made by Merriam. The issuer of this soft white-metal piece, presumptively J.A. Bolen, used Merriam's 27-millimeter die after it had cracked across its entire surface. This shows how eagerly such pieces were pursued by contemporary collectors, and what avarice promoters would succumb to in order to fill this demand.

1864 December 31. Artist Thomas Nast's two-page illustration in *Harper's Weekly*, "The Union Christmas Dinner," features Lincoln hosting a gala feast for representatives of the various states—with chairs for the states remaining in rebellion being vacant.

1865 February 6. The Illinois General Assembly grants a charter to Cumberland Presbyterian Church to establish Lincoln University, Lincoln, Illinois. Groundbreaking would be held six days later, on the president's birthday.

1865 February 12. Ground is broken for Lincoln University, on property donated by the town's proprietors, Robert B. Latham, John D. Gillett, and Virgil Hickon. The school was named in the honor of their friend, Abraham Lincoln. He was aware that the school would be named in his honor—the only such one established during his lifetime. The school would open to both men and women in November 1866. The first graduates would be awarded degrees in 1868. Today the Lincoln, Illinois, school is styled as Lincoln College, with an undergraduate enrollment of approximately 1,100.

1865. Capitalizing on the return of Lincoln to office and the war's end, Boston publisher Walker, Fuller & Co. packages William Makepeace Thayer's *The Pioneer Boy, and How He Became President* and Edward Everett Hale's *The President's Words, a Selection from the Speeches &c. of President Lincoln*, priced at $1.50 and $1.25 respectively.

1865. Before his 22nd birthday, Philadelphia artist William Sartain creates an exceptionally fine, large mezzotint portrait of Abraham Lincoln, justly praised for its "delicacy of tone," based on the Anthony Berger February 9, 1864, photograph (O-92). Sartain posed his Lincoln in the somber and austere glimmer of soft clerestory lighting. The universal image casts a weighty shadow behind it. Its somber tones echo the turmoil of its subject as he weighs the country's fate in its darkest hours. Many consider this the finest Lincoln portrait engraving of the period. The subtle tonal ranges of the lifelike portrait and luxurious woolen garments the president wears in the mezzotint original are not done justice by today's traditional offset-printing methods. This is especially true in the deep gray tones of Lincoln's coat, vest, and tie. Sartain's shading is subtle. This print was meant to be as splendid as it appears. Mezzotint

Fig. 1.74. In its April 29 issue, *Frank Leslie's Illustrated Newspaper* ran this Albert Berghaus woodcut based on a sketch by the publication's artist "Gus," showing the relative positions in the presidential box of the assassin John Wilkes Booth, Abraham Lincoln, his wife, and their guests. *Harper's Weekly* published a similar illustration on the same date, but inside its issue.

gives a rich, velvety print, more so than any other engraving method. Every shade of tone can be obtained, from the deepest blacks to the whitest whites. Sartain's Lincoln has them all. Its fine line and exquisite detail have been widely praised. This was the high art of engraving in the golden age of the craft. Sartain's Lincoln is splendid in both its technical and its artistic aspects. The print was published by Bradley & Co., Philadelphia. The plate was reprinted and a number of these reprints have come down to the collecting community through the hands of deceased Philadelphia antiquities-and-coins dealer Stephen Nagy and the late Confederate and obsolete-currency dealer Grover Criswell. Nagy acquired the original Sartain plate together with a half dozen other Sartain plates (of P.G.T. Beauregard, Robert E. Lee, Mrs. Lincoln, Philip Sheridan, William Sherman, and George Thomas) in the course of his business. Around the 1930s he caused approximately 50 prints of each mezzotint to be pulled from the original plates, including the Lincoln. Nagy was the uncle of a modern hobby dealer, who with his wife was still very active in several historical collectibles fields until recent years. According to my source, who was also a protégé of Nagy's, the Philadelphia dealer sold the Lincoln plate and thereafter donated the rest of the historic mezzotint plates to the Smithsonian Institution. Remaining prints were marketed during the Civil War Centennial along with similar items by A.B. Walter and Hall and Perrine as "Rare and

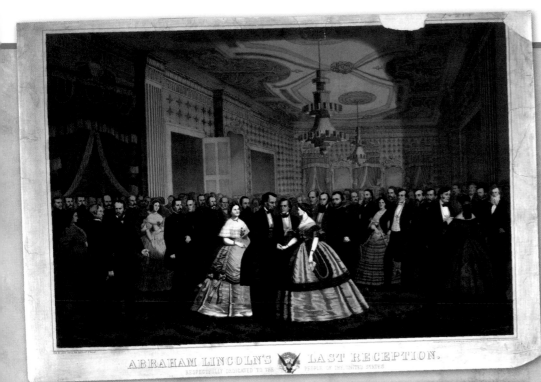

Fig. 1.75. Philadelphia publisher John Smith dedicated this lush hand-colored print, *Abraham Lincoln's Last Reception,* to "the People of the United States." Andrew Johnson, William Seward, U.S. Grant, Salmon P. Chase, and other celebrities of the day are easily recognizable among the crowd gathered in the East Room of the White House. For years a framed example of this print hung in the Lincoln Bedroom of the White House.

Head Quarters Armies of the United States,
City-Point, April, 2. 8.45 P.M. 1865.

Lieut. General Grant.

Allow me to tender to you, and all with you, the nations grateful thanks for this additional, and magnificent success. At your kind suggestion, I think I will visit you to-morrow.

A. Lincoln

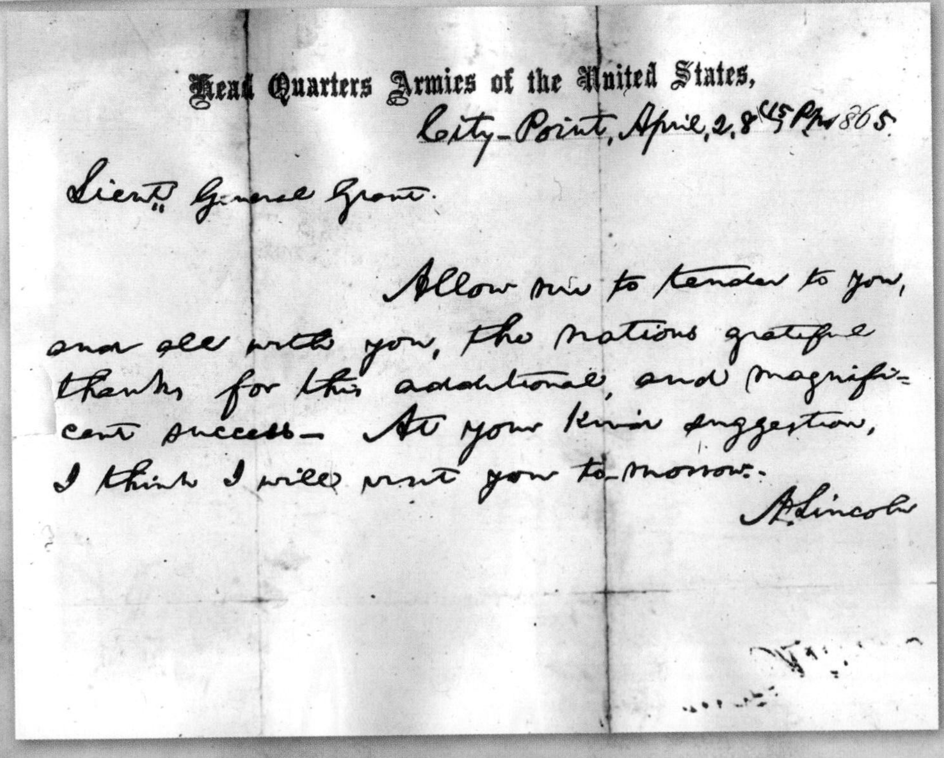

Fig. 1.76. On the evening of April 2, 1865, Abraham Lincoln dashed off this telegram to his commanding general at City Point, congratulating him on the fall of Richmond, Virginia, and advising him he would be visiting the following day. Lincoln had just returned to the White House from a visit with his commanders, where they met on board the steamship *River Queen* on March 28. This historic meeting is commemorated by G.P.A. Healy's painting *Council of War,* depicting Lincoln meeting with generals Grant and Sherman and Commodore Porter. On the day after this additional confab, Lincoln and Tad were escorted up the James River to Richmond, where the president toured the fallen Confederate capital—the "additional and magnificent success" that is the subject of this missive.

Superb Civil War Engravings by famous 19th century artists. Made from original plates by master engravers on high grade heavy format suitable for coloring." Copies of the colored Walter print have circulated widely down to the present day.

1865 April 4. On his tour of Richmond, Virginia, the surrendered Confederate capital which had fallen a day earlier, President Lincoln acquires a Confederate Treasury note. The 1864 Confederate $5 bill was later found in the box containing the contents of Lincoln's pockets on the night he was assassinated. The president had picked it up 10 days earlier, when he and his son Tad toured the fallen Confederate capital. This is according to John Sellers, Library of Congress curator of the Lincoln Bicentennial exhibit "With Malice Toward None." He told it to C-Span cameras during a tour through the exhibition on March 20, 2009.

1865 April 13. Abraham Lincoln writes check No. 2 on his new account at the First National Bank of Washington to "Self" for $800, and the check is cashed the same day. The following evening he would be assassinated.

Fig. 1.78. *Leslie's Illustrated* of April 22, 1865, showed the triumphant Lincoln riding through the fallen Confederate capital on April 4, 1865. Although he was greeted by a crowd of freedmen and curious white citizens alike, the former slaves had abundant reason to be gleeful, as depicted by artist Joseph Becker and engraved for publication by Albert Berghaus. The appearance of this jubilant illustration a week after Lincoln's death was no doubt a melancholy event.

Fig. 1.77. Attending Ford's Theatre on April 14 was a celebratory occasion, as depicted sedately in this diorama at the Abraham Lincoln Presidential Museum.

Fig. 1.79. When Lincoln arrived in Washington, D.C., he took out a personal checking account at Riggs and Co., from which he wrote some 222 mostly small checks. During his second administration, for some unaccounted reason, he took out a second personal account at the First National Bank of Washington (charter #26). On April 13, the day before his assassination, Lincoln wrote this check, no. 2, to himself, for $800. He probably took out the second account to show his support for the poorly received system of national banks that he had advocated, but at the time he wrote this check, Lincoln had four uncashed pay warrants in his desk drawer.

Abraham Lincoln.

Bureau, Engraving & Printing.

Chapter 2

Lincoln the Ideal

1865 – 1969

Engraver Charles Burt created four Abraham Lincoln money portraits for American Bank Note Co. and the U.S. Treasury Department that were used on federal paper money. His 1861 portrait, based on the C.S. German photos (O-41/42), which was used on the $10 greenbacks through 1869, defined how Lincoln's contemporaries viewed the president and then martyr. His two excellent 1869 portraits achieved two very different results. The engraving based on the Anthony Berger O-97 snapshot portrait was used on 50-cent Fractional Notes, which suffered the ignominy of almost immediate vitiation by counterfeiters and were withdrawn within months of their first issue.

Burt's other engraving, however, of the more formal O-92 Berger photo, became the mainstay for a generation on the new Legal Tender Notes. It also appeared briefly on Series of 1870 and Series of 1875 $500 Gold Certificates. But the portrait's legacy was to become much more enduring than that. The O-92 money portrait so conditioned Lincoln image consciousness that among its sequels were a succession of postage stamps with similar likenesses, and additional money uses that branded this portrait as a national icon in the 20th century, as detailed in chapter 4.

In 1881, circumstances converged and the U.S. Treasury Department called upon Charles Burt a fourth time to once again create a new Lincoln portrait engraving for currency use. This was an important commission: Burt's first new Lincoln currency portrait in a dozen years. Lincoln's son, corporate lawyer Robert Todd Lincoln, had recently arrived in the nation's capital as Civil War–vet president James A. Garfield's new secretary of war. Robert believed he was to become Garfield's Edwin Stanton. However, several months into their

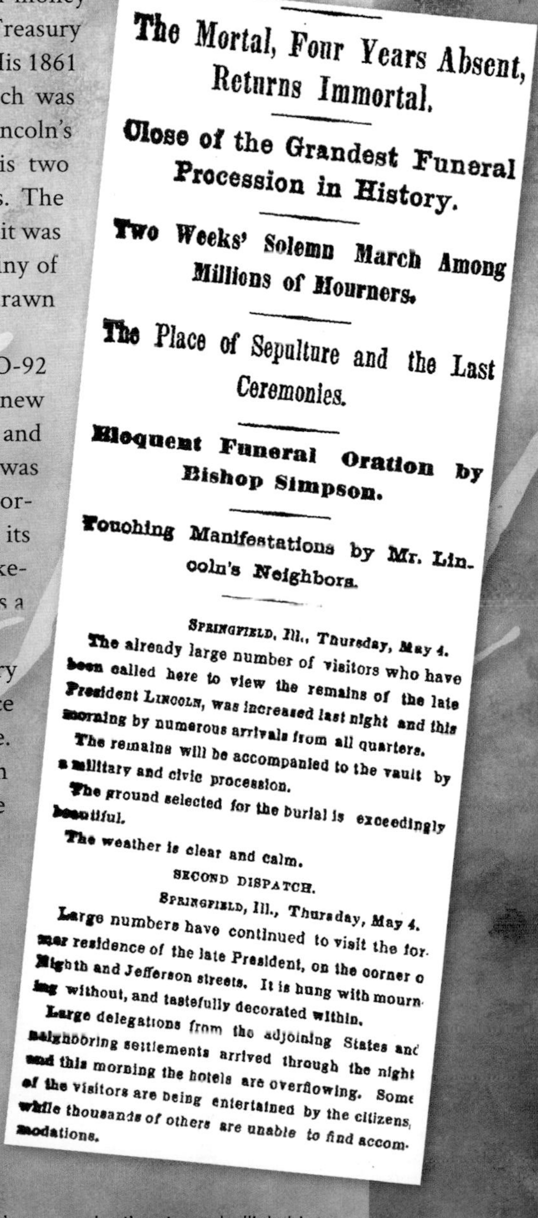

The Mortal, Four Years Absent, Returns Immortal.

Close of the Grandest Funeral Procession in History.

Two Weeks' Solemn March Among Millions of Mourners.

The Place of Sepulture and the Last Ceremonies.

Eloquent Funeral Oration by Bishop Simpson.

Touching Manifestations by Mr. Lincoln's Neighbors.

SPRINGFIELD, Ill., Thursday, May 4.

The already large number of visitors who have been called here to view the remains of the late President LINCOLN, was increased last night and this morning by numerous arrivals from all quarters.

The remains will be accompanied to the vault by a military and civic procession.

The ground selected for the burial is exceedingly beautiful.

The weather is clear and calm.

SECOND DISPATCH.

SPRINGFIELD, Ill., Thursday, May 4.

Large numbers have continued to visit the former residence of the late President, on the corner of Eighth and Jefferson streets. It is hung with mourning without, and tastefully decorated within.

Large delegations from the adjoining States and neighboring settlements arrived through the night and this morning the hotels are overflowing. Some of the visitors are being entertained by the citizens, while thousands of others are unable to find accommodations.

Fig. 2.1. According to the *New York Times*, May 5, 1865, when Abraham Lincoln left Springfield in 1861 he was merely human, but when he returned he truly belonged to the ages, for he was "immortal."

Every private and official attempt was made after Abraham Lincoln's assassination to embellish his image and legacy. This included the U.S. Treasury commissioning Charles Burt, who had engraved Lincoln's likeness for the U.S. currency in 1861 and 1869, to produce another security engraving for federal paper money. Burt created this magnificent engraving in 1882, and it was immediately placed on the new $500 Gold Certificates. The pleasing image represented Lincoln the Ideal for the succeeding half century.

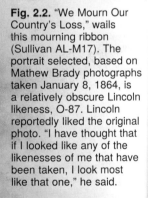

Fig. 2.2. "We Mourn Our Country's Loss," wails this mourning ribbon (Sullivan AL-M17). The portrait selected, based on Mathew Brady photographs taken January 8, 1864, is a relatively obscure Lincoln likeness, O-87. Lincoln reportedly liked the original photo. "I have thought that if I looked like any of the likenesses of me that have been taken, I look most like that one," he said.

Fig. 2.3. "In Victory We Mourn," stresses this mourning card in the collection of the Library of Congress. Its $10 bill image emphasizes the bittersweet emotions felt by Abraham Lincoln's countrymen in the aftermath of the week between Robert E. Lee's surrender on April 9 and the president's death on April 15, 1865.

relationship, while Lincoln was accompanying Garfield to New England to speak at Williams College, the president was assassinated in his presence at the Washington, D.C., train station. "How many hours of sorrow have I passed in this town," Robert was heard to say on the spot.

The slaying of a second U.S. president chilled the nation. But Garfield's assassination instantly linked him to the Lincoln legacy, and a new outpouring of sympathy and reverence was visited upon the Union's savior and martyr. The young Lincoln remained in Washington to serve in Chester Arthur's Cabinet. Robert had also become the practical arbiter of Lincoln's legacy, and anything other than love and fond regard toward his late father was anathema. So meeting Robert Lincoln's expectations and those of the Republican administration was paramount for Burt.

The Garfield assassination refocused attention on Abraham Lincoln, and revived interest in the Lincoln legacy. Although Lincoln's image was already circulating on the $100 Legal Tender Note and the $500 Gold Certificate (both in the form of Burt's 1869 engraving based on the O-92 photographic model), a new and even more regal Lincoln portrait was called for. An imperial image was necessary to reestablish Lincoln's legacy on a high footing following a decade of trivializing anecdotes spun forth by myriad Lincoln associates capitalizing on the public want of Lincoln reminiscence. The new engraving would be more fitting. It would idealize the nation's savior and the emancipator of a race.

Once again Charles Burt was equal to the challenge. The model selected for his fourth Lincoln currency portrait was Anthony Berger's February 9, 1864, O-91 seated photograph of Lincoln at Brady's Washington, D.C., gallery. Lincoln is erect, facing right, glancing slightly back to his left, a classically conditioned and regal pose. Burt's engraving captures the high principles and steely resolve of the sitter. The result was to be the masterpiece of Burt's long engraving career. The engraving was utilized immediately on a new Series of 1882 $500 Gold Certificate. Specie payments, i.e., payments of gold and silver coins for federal paper currency, had only recently been resumed by the U.S. Treasury in 1879. This momentous event in the country's history occurred nearly 17 years after Civil War fiat paper-money inflation had caused bankers and the Lincoln Treasury to suspend specie ayments to greenback note holders.

Burt's full large engraving (shown on page 28) depicts a great deal of the original photographic model, much more than could be utilized on the face of the $500 gold note. Although the note renders Burt's original in a cropped fashion, it nevertheless reveals the intensity of the Lincoln idealization. This image is the finest security portrait engraving to appear on U.S. currency to that time—or since, in the opinion of many specialists, including this author.

The notes it graced were heavyweights in banking and commercial circles. These circulating notes were golden promises that the U.S. Treasury made investors and capitalists when they deposited their gold coins and bullion. They specifically state on their face: "There have been deposited in the Treasury of the

United States Five Hundred Dollars in Gold Coin Repayable to the Bearer on Demand." To demonstrate this pledge the note back was printed in a bright golden-orange ink, and a yellow overprint was applied to the note face. Honest Abe's image sealed this promise that the restored Union Treasury would honor its commitment and never suspend specie payments again. The note was as good as the government's word—good as gold.

The idealized Lincoln portrait proved a durable one on this nation's Gold Certificates. Successive issues of this golden-inked note during the next 40 years totaled more than 350,000 such certificates that were issued as needed. These paper issues spanned new wartime periods with Spain and with the German kaiser. Through it all, the U.S. Treasury kept its promise to depositors and honored the memory of Honest Abe. It did not suspend specie payments again, but met each payment on request, in gold.

As readers of this volume know, Berger's O-92 photograph would be called upon late in the 20th century to make an appearance on the nation's money once again. But it would be a new O-92 for the new times and new purposes . . . a "Twinkle Eye" portrait, vouchsafing the public's identification with the iconic Lincoln on the $5 bill.

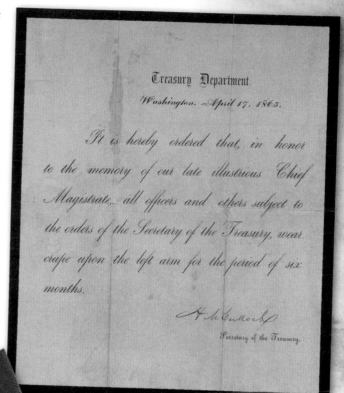

Fig. 2.4. Lincoln's third and last Treasury secretary, Hugh Mulloch, issued this order "in memory of our late illustrious Chief Magistrate." All Treasury employees were to wear mourning crepe for a period of six months, in Lincoln's memory.

Fig. 2.5. New York medalist George H. Lovett created a fine likeness for this memorial medal (King-257) to commemorate "The Martyr President."

Fig. 2.6. This Lincoln campaign ferrotype pin (AL 1864-95) was repurposed as a mourning ribbon in the days following news of the president's death.

Fig. 2.7. This small 1864 Lincoln campaign medal is another that was repurposed as a memorial item in 1865.

1865 APRIL 17. Secretary of the Treasury Hugh McCulloch issues an order instructing all persons subject to his authority to wear a (black) crepe on their left sleeve for a period of six months in "honor to the memory of our late illustrious Chief Magistrate."

1865 APRIL 19. An ad in the *National Intelligencer* reads: "THE LATE PRESIDENT – CARTES DE VISITES OF ABRAHAM LINCOLN, Photographed from Life by Gardner – Mr. Lincoln's last sitting. Price, 55 cents, mailed free. PHILP & SOLOMONS, Metropolitan Bookstore."

1865 APRIL 22. Irony of ironies: a large cover illustration by J. Becker on the front page of the popular weekly, *Frank Leslie's Illustrated Newspaper,* shows Abraham Lincoln jubilantly and warmly welcomed on April 4 in Richmond, Virginia, by the freed former slaves. What should have been seen as a triumphant culmination of Lincoln's steadfast service to his country during four hard years of internecine warfare was by then only a bittersweet, symbolic week-old commentary on his martyrdom.

1865 APRIL 24. New York lensman Jeremiah Gurney surreptitiously photographs Abraham Lincoln's open casket with the president lying in state under a military guard in New York City Hall. When this comes to the attention of Secretary of War Edwin Stanton, he orders the images confiscated—but one is later found,

in 1952, among the papers of Lincoln's secretaries archived at the Illinois State Historical Library. The discoverer was a perspicacious 14-year-old, Ronald Rietveld, who would go on to become a university professor in the California state university system. He retired in 2009 from Cal State–Fullerton.

1865 APRIL 24. The Committee of Arrangements in Springfield, Illinois, adopts resolutions relating to the canvassing for funds during the second week in May for the Lincoln National Monument Association to erect a suitable monument there in Lincoln's memory. The following day, Illinois governor Richard Oglesby took the reins of the association as its president, and state treasurer James H. Beveridge became the association's treasurer.

1865 APRIL 26. A young Teddy Roosevelt witnesses the Lincoln funeral procession proceeding up Broadway from the second-story window of his grandfather Cornelius Roosevelt's mansion.

Fig. 2.8. E. & H.T. Anthony published this image as part of a stereoview card showing the Lincoln funeral procession down Broadway in New York City.

IN VICTORY

We Mourn a Martyred PATRIOT.

Fig. 2.9. Another of the melancholy mourning ribbons (Sullivan AL-M19) with a portrait based on the O-87 Brady photograph is this "martyred patriot" ribbon.

Fig. 2.10. After Lincoln's death, Sangamo Insurance Co., Springfield, Illinois, headed up by Lincoln's friend and fellow Illinois legislator Jesse K. DuBois, wasted no time in trading on the president's name, reputation, and legacy. Their 1865 advertising poster features the familiar, ubiquitous Lincoln $10 money image. The poster was lithographed by Ehrgott, Forbriger & Co., Cincinnati.

1865. Philadelphia coin dealer John W. Kline publishes a broadside indicating "The undersigned has published a beautiful medal, two inches in diameter, of Abraham Lincoln, late president of the United States." This was likely the 51-millimeter Broken Column medal (King-247), with dies by Philadelphia engraver William H. Key. Its dies later fell into the hands of Charles K. Warner, who caused restrikes to be made on thinner planchets.

1865 MAY 6. Readers, after flipping past the front-page illustration of *Harper's Weekly*, with its large woodcut illustration of Abraham Lincoln and Tad perusing the carte-de-visite sample book at Brady's Gallery, immortalized by photographer Anthony Berger on February 9, 1864 (O-93), are given details of the president's funerary events in New York City. Illustrations included exteriors of Ford's Theatre, the house where Lincoln died, Lincoln's deathbed scene, the assault on Secretary Seward, Lincoln's catafalque, Lincoln lying in state at the White House, the funeral processions in Washington, D.C., and in New York City, and Lincoln lying in state at New York's City Hall.

1865 MAY 13. The *Harper's Weekly* two-page double-truck illustration shows Abraham Lincoln's funeral parade in New York City, and a half-page illustration depicts the transfer of Lincoln's remains from City Hall to the funeral car. Additional illustrations depicted the hunt for John Wilkes Booth, and Booth's post-mortem examination on board the Monitor *Montauk*.

1865 MAY 15. P.T. Barnum telegraphs Secretary of War Edwin Stanton: "I will give five hundred dollars to Sanitary Commission or Freedman's Association for the petticoats in which Jeff. Davis was caught, P.T. Barnum."

1865 MAY 20. The *London Illustrated News* publishes a full-page illustration, *Arrival of the Body of President Lincoln at the City Hall, New York.*

1865. Shortly after the president's assassination, Lincoln campaign biographer Abott A. Abott updates his 1864 work to include the war's end and the sad events of Lincoln's death. In the haste to rush the work into print (to capitalize on the morbid Lincoln fascination following the slaying), Abott and publisher T.R. Dawley, "Publisher for the Million," put the small book out onto the street with an anachronistic 1864 copyright date, according to copyright deposit copies sent to the Copyright Office attached to the Library of Congress.

1865. New York City lithographers Currier & Ives (152 Nassau Street)—"printmakers to the millions"—in their rush to supply myriad memorials to the martyred Lincoln, reissue their 1860 beardless lithograph (which they had updated in 1861 by adding a beard), and title it "Abraham Lincoln. The Martyr President. Assassinated April 14th. 1865." Their prints still bore the anachronistic 1860 copyright date in small lettering under the bust.

1865. At about the same time, Currier & Ives commemorate the Emancipation Proclamation by adapting the famous Berger O-92 head to a standing Lincoln body for use on a lithograph titled *Free-*

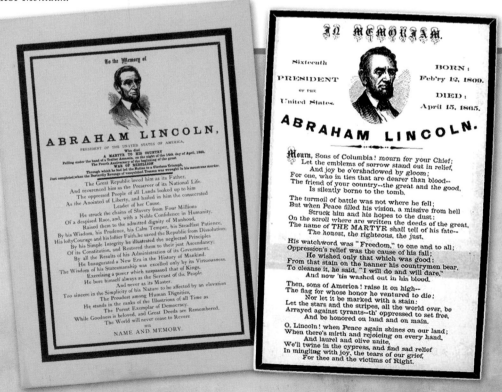

Fig. 2.11. These two mourning cards feature very similar likenesses patterned after the Lincoln money image, and they express similar sentiments. Abraham Lincoln, "the purest exemplar of democracy," will be remembered for all time as "honest . . . righteous . . . [and] just."

Fig. 2.12. This finely made, but rare and unlisted, "best son" mourning ribbon, with its $10 currency portrait design, is believed to have been the official U.S. Treasury mourning ribbon that department employees wore in the week after Abraham Lincoln's demise, during obsequies in Washington, D.C.

dom to the Slaves, showing the Lincoln figure facing left, raising his right hand toward Providence, and his left hand extended to a supplicating ex-slave. Although the face in this portrayal is a mirror image of the normal Lincoln depiction that would become a universal icon in the 20th century, and the artist has lowered the presidential eyes to gaze upon the black man at his feet, this mid-19th-century depiction's reliance on the Berger image is unmistakable.

1865 SPRING. According to researchers at the National Parks Service and Harvard University's W.E.B. DuBois Institute for Afro-American Research, French historian and abolitionist Edouard-René Lefebvre de Laboulaye suggested, at a dinner party, a liberty monument as a gift to America. The monument would celebrate French-American amity and the abolition of slavery, and serve as a tribute to the life of Abraham Lincoln. The liberal history professor's just-completed three-volume history of the United States had proposed America as "the dawn of a new work" in which "liberty arose . . . to enlighten the universe." Sculptor Frédéric Auguste Bartholdi was at the dinner. As executed by Bartholdi, Liberty is shown with a broken shackle on her foot. By the time it was completed and installed in New York Harbor, however, the statue was heralded not as a celebration of freedom of the slaves, but of freedom of the dispossessed fleeing the Old World for the promises of the New World.

1865. A make-believe illustration of the Lincoln family by Gustave E. Gumpert correctly shows Lincoln and son Tad perusing a photograph sample album—at Brady's Washington, D.C., gallery—and not a book (or, particularly, the Bible), as it was then in vogue to describe the scene.

1865 MAY. An anonymous English poet, "R," publishes "Abraham Lincoln" in *Macmillan's* magazine, which is reprinted in June in Littrell's *The Living Age* magazine. According to "R," Lincoln "wrought the great work of his age" and "fought and fought the noblest fight / and marshalled it from stage to stage. . . . Lincoln, the man who freed the slave; / Lincoln, whom never self enticed; / Slain Lincoln, worthy found to die / A soldier of his captain Christ."

1865 JUNE 1. Ribbons for the National Day of Mourning bear the verse, "Like Him long since crucified, / For Humanity he died / Mourns his Country not alone / Mourns the world for him, her own."

1865 JUNE 1. Abolitionist William Lloyd Garrison speaks at the Union League "Remember Lincoln" rally at City Hall, Providence, Rhode Island.

Fig. 2.13. President Andrew Johnson declared a National Day of Mourning for June 1, 1865. This rare memorial ribbon (Sullivan-unlisted) in the collection of the Library of Congress utilizes a likeness based on the Anthony Berger January 9, 1864, O-91 photo. It also contains an anonymous verse analogizing Lincoln's death to that of Christ.

Fig. 2.14. Memorial services were held throughout the nation on the National Day of Mourning. Ceremonies held by the Union League of Providence, Rhode Island, featured a speech by abolitionist William Lloyd Garrison at City Hall. "Those joining in the Procession and wearing badges will be first admitted to the body of the Hall, which will be closed until the Procession arrives," this poster advised.

1865 JUNE 2. The U.S. consul in Paris, John Bigelow, writes Secretary of State William Seward to report progress of the popular subscription being undertaken in France to strike a memorial medal to Lincoln. The movement started in and around Nantes, France. "Up to the 30th of last month, 11,129 subscribers had been enrolled and their names published from time to time in the *Phare de la Loire*."[1] Note that contributions were deliberately limited to about 2¢ (variously described as 2 sous or 10 centimes) per person, so a large number of individuals could participate. Eventually 40,000 French citizens donated a total of about $800 toward execution of the dies and striking of the gold medal.

1865. New York lithographers Kimmel and Forster produce a lovely pastel hand-colored lithographic portrait of Abraham Lincoln based on the Berger O-92 image of February 9, 1864. Kimmel and Forster's Lincoln print exhibits the president's good humor. Their depiction is anything but austere. It's not somber, as is the Sartain mezzotint produced at nearly the same time. Lincoln's countenance is warmer. He is human; the print is humane. Lincoln is portrayed as a more accessible, less aloof man. As can be seen by comparing both prints to the source photograph, each artist was extremely faithful to the original, yet each imbued his likeness with its own individualities of detail. Compare the Kimmel flesh tones to the higher art of the Sartain. The Sartain was created for the drawing room of the finest mansions. The Kimmel was executed for the hearths of the frame dwellings of the masses; its workmanship is of the finest execution and detail for a mass-produced lithograph. The print was produced shortly after the president's untimely demise, probably priced at 25 cents. It was made to be displayed on the wall, and its possessor could be justifiably proud to hang such a portrait in his or her home.

1865 JULY 4. Adolph Leconte, of New York City, receives design patent no. 2,108 for a medallion of Abraham Lincoln.

1865 JUNE 22. The Abraham Lincoln 50-cent spade-shaped Internal Revenue stamp design (Scott-RN V1-4) is approved by the U.S. Treasury.

1865. W.H. & O.H. Morrison, of Washington, D.C., publish B.F. Morris's compilation *Memorial Record of the Nation's Tribute to Abraham Lincoln.* Although this work carries an 1865 copyright date, it also describes events of 1866.

Fig. 2.15. Only six weeks following Lincoln's death the die proof to the Lincoln five-cent Internal Revenue stamp imprint (Scott RN P2-P6) was approved by J.J.L. (probably a U.S. Treasury employee).

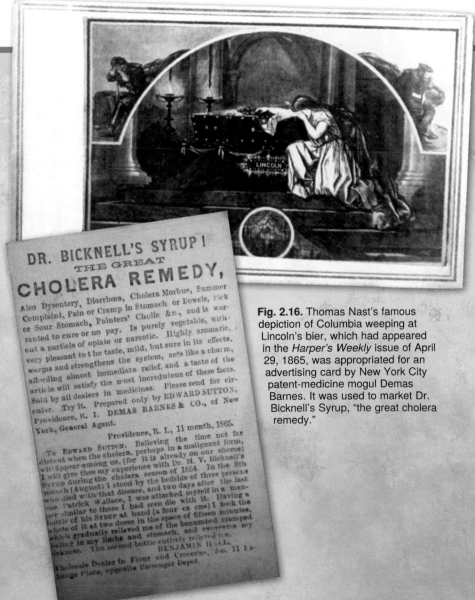

Fig. 2.16. Thomas Nast's famous depiction of Columbia weeping at Lincoln's bier, which had appeared in the *Harper's Weekly* issue of April 29, 1865, was appropriated for an advertising card by New York City patent-medicine mogul Demas Barnes. It was used to market Dr. Bicknell's Syrup, "the great cholera remedy."

1865 DECEMBER 18. Congress passes a joint resolution expressing a desire to "testify their sensibility upon the occasion of the public bereavement of the tragic death of President Lincoln, and a purpose to meet on February 12th, in the hall of the House, and listen to an address upon the life and character of the deceased."

1866 FEBRUARY. The Executive Committee of Ashmun Institute, Chester County, Pennsylvania, the "first institution found anywhere in the world to provide a higher education in the arts and sciences for male youth of African descent" (founded in April 1854), resolves to make application to the Pennsylvania Legislature to change the school's name to Lincoln University after President Abraham Lincoln. The Legislature approved the name change in April 1866, and it was promptly signed into law by Republican governor Andrew Curtin.[2] The university admitted female students in 1952. Its distinguished alumni include poet Langston Hughes (1929), jurist Thurgood Marshall (1930), president of Nigeria Benjamin Azikiwe (1931), president of Ghana Kwame Nkrumah (1939), and actor/author Roscoe Lee Browne (1946). In addition to producing doctors, lawyers, educators, and scientists, Lincoln University has a distinguished tradition in athletics. Monte Irvin attended Lincoln before going on to the New York Giants. In track and field Lincoln's teams have won 15 NCAA Division III championships. Recognized today as the first "historically Black" institution of higher education in the United States, it currently enrolls about 2,000 students.

1866 FEBRUARY 12. At 10 minutes past noon members of the U.S. Senate solemnly file into the chamber of the House of Representatives and occupy seats reserved for them on the sides of the main aisle. Shortly afterward they were joined by President Andrew Johnson and his Cabinet, followed immediately afterward by the chief and associate justices of the Supreme Court. Also on hand were a host of other dignitaries, military officials, many governors, mayors, additional federal judges, and historian George Bancroft, the latter selected to present the memorial eulogy on the life and character of Abraham Lincoln that day. At 12:20 the Marine Corps band played. At 12:30 the two houses of Congress were called to order. Chaplain of the House Reverend Dr. Charles Brandon

Fig. 2.17. Philadelphia publisher A. Bancroft's memorial "To the memory of Abraham Lincoln" included a poem by Bancroft, and an albumen-copy photograph of an etching of Lincoln's portrait, based on the Anthony Berger O-92 photograph, in an oval format.

Fig. 2.18. Hatch Lithographic Co., New York City, issued a trade card "in Everlasting Memory" with the firm's version of the Lincoln $10 money photo within a black memorial border.

Boynton offered a prayer, and then Bancroft was introduced. His remarks were printed and bound together with a frontispiece employing the National Bank Note Co. Lincoln bond portrait in a memorial cartouche.

1866 MARCH 8. The American Numismatic and Archaeological Society listens to an undated report by its Special Committee on the Lincoln Medal, regarding delays and difficulties in the production of the medal for subscribers to the project by New York die sinker Emil Sigel. It then resolved to forward an example in "block tin" (white metal) to the Society's agents in London, Messrs. Stevens Bros., No. 17 Henrietta Street, Covent Garden. This example would subsequently be reproduced by the English minters Wyon Bros. (see entry for November 8, 1866).

1866 APRIL 7. Congress appropriates $30,000 "for defraying the expenses incident to the death and burial of Abraham Lincoln, late President of the United States."

1866 APRIL. A fire consumes a steel-plate engraving in progress by Alexander Hay Ritchie of the *Death of President Lincoln.* In the same fire, a reduced-size copy of Carpenter's *First Reading of the Emancipation Proclamation Before the Cabinet,* from which example Ritchie was in the process of engraving, was also consumed, but Ritchie's partially finished plate was saved.[3]

1866 APRIL 14. The only known first-day-of-issue cover for the Lincoln memorial 15-cent black U.S. postage stamp (Scott 77), nominally officially released the following day to observe the first anniversary of Lincoln's death, is mailed via the steamer *Bavaria* to Hamburg, addressed to Heinrich Runk in Eichelsachsen, Germany. The cover is today in the collection of noted Chicago philatelist Eliot A. Landau.

Engraved & Printed at the Treasury Department.

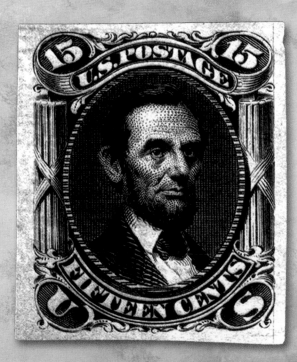

Fig. 2.19. The National Currency Bureau turned the former National Bank Note Co. Lincoln portrait bond die to good use, placing it within a memorial cartouche, for the frontispiece of publication of historian George A. Bancroft's "Memorial Address on the Life and Character of Abraham Lincoln." The address was to a joint session of Congress on the occasion of the 57th anniversary of Lincoln's birth, February 12, 1866. This design was reprised by the BEP on a 2012 souvenir card.

Fig. 2.20. The issuing of a memorial stamp to Abraham Lincoln followed closely on the heels of the joint session of Congress (in February 1866) in Lincoln's honor. A U.S. postage stamp was issued on April 15, 1866, to mark the first anniversary of Lincoln's death. Engraver Joseph Ourdan created a miniature version of the official governmental money portrait for the stamp. This is a trial color essay in blue ink (Scott 77tc3). The issued 15-cent stamp was in mourning black.

Fig. 2.21. Burnham's American Business College was founded in 1864 in Springfield, Massachusetts. Students filled out these notes and used them in model transactions while learning business principles. Each bears Hatch & Co.'s lithographed version of the Lincoln money image, chosen to lend credibility to the school scrip. Both of these varieties (type of Schingoethe MA-400-2.A/2.B), circa 1865–1866, are unlisted in the Schingoethe college-currency catalog.

Fig. 2.22. George F. Nesbitt Co., New York City, had a contract with the U.S. Post Office Department to produce pre-stamped envelopes since 1852, a contract held until 1870. Circa 1866 Nesbitt created these two stamp indicia with embossed Abraham Lincoln profile portraits. The 3-cent (Undersander E25Bd) *(a)* rate was the standard domestic postage rate, and the 15 cent (Undersander E25Ac) *(b)* rate was the standard international rate to Europe at the time. Neither was adopted, although a 15-cent U.S. postage stamp (Scott 77) in black was issued as a memorial tribute to the slain president. This official government portrait, like Lincoln's money image, was based on the C.S. German 1861 photographic model.

Fig. 2.23. This elegant silk ribbon with its O-92–style portrait was made in 1866 by Jordan Tchapp, Basel, Switzerland. For some reason the paraphrased clauses from Lincoln's Second Inaugural Address are inverted.

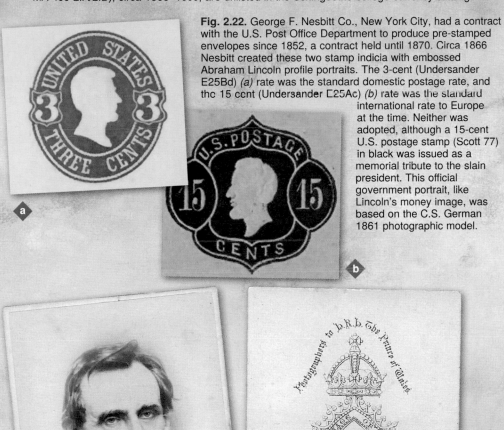

Fig. 2.24. The London Stereoscopic & Photographic Co., 54 Cheapside, London, grafted whiskers to the well-known pre-presidential Brady Cooper Union beardless pose for this post-assassination memorial carte de visite. The card back is Type IIc, employed by the studio circa 1864–1868.

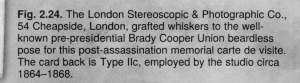

1866 APRIL 14. Sculptor Pietro Mezarra's standing figure of Lincoln as Emancipator is installed at Lincoln Grammar School, San Francisco, California. When it was displayed at the Mechanics Institute Fair the previous summer, it was the first large-size memorial sculpture of Lincoln.

1866 APRIL 21. A large front-page illustration of the Abraham Lincoln School for Freedmen in New Orleans dominates the front page of *Harper's Weekly.* According to the publication, the school opened October 3, 1865, in a building belonging to the University of Louisiana. Soon after opening it had 800 students and 14 teachers, the largest school of its kind in the United States. Tuition was $1.50 per month.

1866 MAY. In the first "Bulletin of the American Numismatic and Archaeological Society" (*American Journal of Numismatics*), the editor reports the history of the society's salute to Abraham Lincoln in "The Lincoln Medal." The society contracted with New York City die sinker Emil Sigel, and medal production was repeatedly delayed. "Imperfect copies" were presented to President Andrew Johnson and historian George Bancroft on the occasion of Congress's com-

memoration of Lincoln on February 12, 1866. Perfectly stuck copies were not available until the middle of that March. However, after a few white-metal trial strikes were taken and only 16 bronze medals produced, "by some accident not yet fully understood, the dies were broken so badly as to necessitate the abandonment of all idea of striking from them medals in hard metal." Consequently the committee in charge of the medal investigated, exonerated Sigel of blame, and accepted his proposal to make a new set of dies "and complete the medal as originally proposed," by August 1. "The few impressions of the medal that were successfully struck, leave nothing to be desired, either in sharpness and force of outline or in the life-like appearance of the portrait," the report noted. "The medal will be a credit to the artist and to the country," it added.[4]

1866 JUNE 28. The American Numismatic and Archaeological Society receives "a small medal of Mr. Lincoln" from die sinker J.A. Bolen of Springfield, Massachusetts. Bolen also presented the Boston Numismatic Society a white-metal Lincoln medal "having on the reverse his famous words, 'With malice toward none, with charity for all.'"

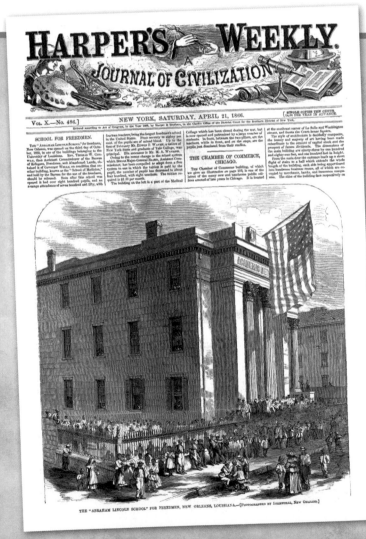

Fig. 2.25. The Abraham Lincoln School for Freedmen in New Orleans was opened October 3, 1865, and enrollment peaked at 800, making it the largest institution of its kind. Enrollment dropped after a tuition rate of $1.50 per month was enacted. By the time it was featured on the front page of *Harper's Weekly* (April 21, 1866), the school had 400 students and occupied this former University of Louisiana Medical College building.

Fig. 2.26. The movement to commemorate the fallen Abraham Lincoln on a U.S. postage stamp in 1865–1866 was strong. This stamp essay (Turner 52a-3) created during that period is modeled after one of the Anthony Berger photos of February 9, 1864—probably O-91.

Fig. 2.27. This excellent post-war ivory cameo has a wonderful sculpted version of Mathew Brady's January 8, 1864, photo (O-87).

1866. Essayist and poet Dr. J(osiah). G(ilbert). Holland publishes a one-sheet broadside, *Proposals for Publishing a Popular Life of Abraham Lincoln, Late President of the United States,* to be published by Gurdon Bill & Co., Springfield, Massachusetts. When Holland's *Life of Abraham Lincoln* is published later that year, it becomes the first of the great seminal works on its subject. It is also published in the same year in German by Gurdon Bill as *Das Lebens Abraham Lincoln's.*

1866 JULY 7. To celebrate America's 90th anniversary of independence, *Harper's Weekly* publishes Thomas Nast's chilling full-page illustration *Why He Cannot Sleep.* It depicted Lincoln's skeleton haunting an insomniac Jefferson Davis with Death itself clawing at Davis's prison bars. Columbia is the stage manager of an ethereal tableau of slave and battlefield deaths. Immediately behind the distraught Davis, Lincoln's skeleton points to the bullet hole in his own skull.

After the assassination, Confederate president Jefferson Davis had been arrested and incarcerated in Fortress Monroe, Virginia. During this period, he repeatedly wrote his wife Varina about his acute insomnia. In a letter dated September 26, 1865, he told her: "It is true that my strength has greatly failed me, and the loss of sleep has created a morbid excitability." On October 10, 1865, Varina wrote to Dr. John J. Craven begging that he intercede with "the authorities to let him sleep without a light. He is too feeble to escape, and could not bear a light in his room when in strong health." Davis also complained about interruptions by passing guards, "which caused him broken sleep." And again, "For say, three months after I was imprisoned here, two hours consecutive sleep were never allowed me." Another time, he said he "did not sleep an hour in the night."

Nast's portrayal provided a reason for Davis's lack of sleep, an indictment for causing the deaths of so many—including Lincoln himself. In one moving letter, Davis told his wife that "sleep has many stages, and that only is perfect sleep which we call Death." The former president of the Confederate States of America was released from Fortress Monroe in May 1867. He died December 6, 1889.

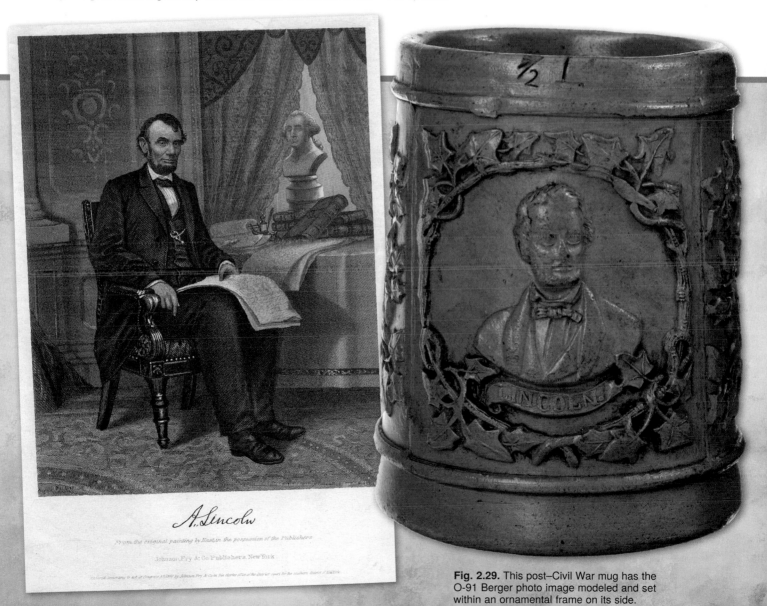

Fig. 2.28. In 1866, New York City publishers Johnson & Fry issued this engraving of a Thomas Nast painting. It embroidered on the imagery of the Anthony Berger February 9, 1864, photograph (O-92) with the addition of a formal backdrop that linked Abraham Lincoln with George Washington.

Fig. 2.29. This post–Civil War mug has the O-91 Berger photo image modeled and set within an ornamental frame on its side.

1866 July 24. The U.S. House of Representatives passes a bill to accept a gift from Antonio Salviati of an enamel mosaic portrait of Lincoln, modeled on the "Speed photograph," measuring approximately 22.75 by 20.25 inches. The U.S. Senate immediately concurred. Salviati was an Italian artist and businessman. In making the gift, he called the martyred Lincoln "one of the world's greatest heroes." The mosaic was made by Salviati, Burke & Co., of Venice and London.

During the second half of the 19th century Salviati became internationally renowned for his fine mosaics. Following the assassination of James A. Garfield, in 1883 he proposed a gift of a companion mosaic portrait of Garfield, formally accepted by Congress by a concurrent resolution in May 1884. Both mosaics hung for many years on the third floor of the Senate wing of the U.S. Capitol.

1866 August 9. U.S. Treasurer F.E. Spinner signs Treasury Warrant 6398 for $1,653.84 to Sergeant Boston Corbett for his share of the reward for the capture of Lincoln assassin John Wilkes Booth.

1866 August 23. The U.S. Treasury pays Treasury Warrant 6398 for $1,653.84 to Sergeant Boston Corbett for his share of the reward for the capture of John Wilkes Booth.

1866. Artist Francis Bicknell Carpenter publishes his reminiscences of his time spent with Abraham Lincoln developing his great historical narrative painting, *First Reading of the Emancipation Proclamation*, in *Six Months at the White House with Abraham Lincoln: The Story of a Picture*, published by Hurd and Houghton in New York. In it, Carpenter also describes Lincoln's daily life as he observed it in 1864. In addition to his painting, and the engravings which emanated from it, many of the most famous and important Lincoln photographic portraits were taken at the behest of Carpenter's progress on the project, including Anthony Berger's February 9, 1864, portrait series, among which notable images of Lincoln seated in the "Brady posing chair" have been adapted for United States coins (O-88/89, for Victor David Brenner's cent), and paper money (O-92, for $1 Silver Certificates, $100 U.S. Notes, $500 Gold Certificates, and all classes of large- and small-size paper money in the denomination of $5 since 1914, exclusive of large-size National Bank Notes; and O-91 for $500 Gold Certificates and current $5 Federal Reserve Notes).

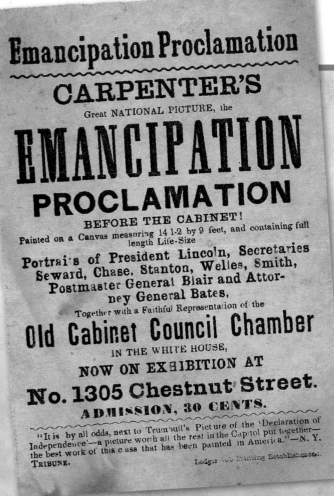

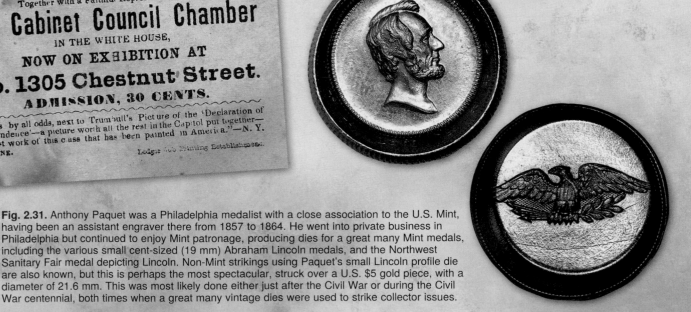

Fig. 2.30. Francis B. Carpenter spent six months at the White House painting his great historical canvas *First Reading of the Emancipation Proclamation to the Cabinet*. Upon its completion, it was exhibited to the public in the East Room of the White House and then in the U.S. Capitol. It was engraved by Ritchie, and popularized by a book Carpenter wrote on his experiences in the nation's household with the Lincoln family. When Congress did not immediately buy the painting, Carpenter exhibited it commercially. This poster advertises one such appearance in Philadelphia. Eventually, after Carpenter had reworked the painting (including the Lincoln portrait overly much), it was purchased and donated to the United States by Elizabeth Thompson of New York City, in 1877. The work was formally dedicated at the Capitol on February 12, 1878.

Fig. 2.31. Anthony Paquet was a Philadelphia medalist with a close association to the U.S. Mint, having been an assistant engraver there from 1857 to 1864. He went into private business in Philadelphia but continued to enjoy Mint patronage, producing dies for a great many Mint medals, including the various small cent-sized (19 mm) Abraham Lincoln medals, and the Northwest Sanitary Fair medal depicting Lincoln. Non-Mint strikings using Paquet's small Lincoln profile die are also known, but this is perhaps the most spectacular, struck over a U.S. $5 gold piece, with a diameter of 21.6 mm. This was most likely done either just after the Civil War or during the Civil War centennial, both times when a great many vintage dies were used to strike collector issues.

Fig. 2.32. Italian artist and businessman Antonio Salviati was moved by Abraham Lincoln's death. In honor of "one of the world's heroes" (his words) he created this wonderful mosaic *(a),* about two feet long on each side, as a gift to the United States. Salviati's portrait, modeled on the "Speed photograph" (O-55), was accepted by Congress in 1866. The artisan went on to international acclaim. Following President James Garfield's assassination, he created a similar mosaic gift for Congress. Both tributes hung in the U.S. Capitol *(b).*

1866. Clarke & Co., Chicago, publishes Isaac Newton Arnold's *The History of Abraham Lincoln, and the Overthrow of Slavery.*

1866 OCTOBER 13. The French gold medal in honor of Abraham Lincoln, struck in Switzerland, is brought back to Paris for presentation.[5] "A committee of French Liberals brought the medal to the American minister, to be sent to Mrs. Lincoln. 'Tell her,' said Eugène Pelletan, 'the heart of France is in that little box,'" Nicolay and Hay wrote in their Lincoln biography.[6]

1866 NOVEMBER 8. At a regular meeting of the American Numismatic and Archaeological Society, the corresponding secretary reads a letter from Stevens Brothers of London "offering to have the Lincoln medal duplicated by the new process of the Messrs.

Wyon," which elicited a lengthy discussion. The members finally resolved that the secretary inform the Messrs. Stevens that the medal in their possession may be used for that purpose, "but that the number of copies must be limited to six only." The "process" mentioned was the use of the Janvier reducing machine, which permitted perfect mechanical copies of three-dimensional bas-relief surfaces. Negotiations must have gone swimmingly, because Wyon & Co. eventually produced reductions of the three-inch (83 mm) medal (King-244) in three sizes: 35 mm (King-252), 16 mm (King-288), and 7 mm (King-290). According to King, these smaller-sized medals were not issued by the Society, and examples of them are, in fact, rarer than the originals.

Fig. 2.33. "Columbia's Noblest Sons" were the Father of Our Country, George Washington, and the Preserver of the Nation, Abraham Lincoln, according to a widely circulated print showing the goddess crowning joint portraits of the two men. The lithograph was published in 1865 by Kimmel & Forster, and the image pirated later (detail shown) by the maker of this carte de visite. The portrait is the O-92 Berger image that became increasingly popular following Lincoln's death.

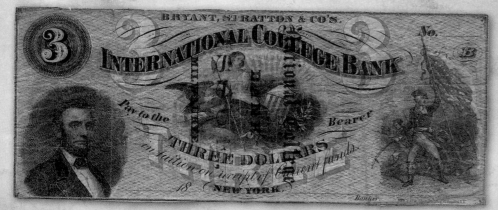

Fig. 2.34. Dr. J.C. Bryant and his partner H.D. Stratton founded a commercial college in 1854. It grew into a chain of similar institutions in many of the principal cities of the United States. Their institution continues down to the present day at Buffalo, New York, and additional locations. In its heyday following the Civil War, the school operated at Milwaukee and two additional locations in Wisconsin. This rare note lithographed by Hatch & Co., New York, was originally issued for the New York City branch of the school, but was overprinted "National College / Bank / Issue, / Milwaukee" circa 1863–1869 for use at the school branch in that location. This is the Schingoethe plate specimen (WI-300-3).

Fig. 2.35. This rare promissory note was printed for B.M. DuRell & Co., which had a mine and milling operation in Idaho City, Idaho Territory. The note was drawn against the company's account at the First National Bank of Idaho, Boise City, Idaho Territory. It is the more common of the two varieties known. The unique (only one example known) variety was shown as figure 2.53 in *Abraham Lincoln: The Image of His Greatness.* It lists the location as Silver City (Owyhee). This variety, although not unique, is still scarce, with about six known. The example shown was once stolen from a dealer's inventory, but subsequently surfaced in a currency auction.

1866 December 7. John Bigelow, U.S. ambassador to France, writes Mary Todd Lincoln from Paris:

> Legation of the United States.
>
> Madam,
>
> In compliance with the request of a Committee composed of many of the most illustrious among the Republicans of France, I send you herewith a medal in gold designed to commemorate the glory and martyrdom of the great citizen whose name you bear. It is the product of the spontaneous offerings of Forty Thousand Frenchmen eager to testify in this manner their sympathy with your immeasurable sorrows, and their deep respect for those exalted virtues which in President Lincoln, transcending the sphere of usefulness in which he lived and labored, have become the property and pride of the human race. Deeply sensible, Madam, of the honour that is done me in making me the medium of transmission of an offering so precious, I beg the privilege of adding the expression of my profound respect and heartfelt sympathy.
>
> — *John Bigelow*

1866 December 26. Theodore Dimon, charged by Secretary of State William Seward with conveying the French citizens' gold medal to Mary Todd Lincoln, sends a note to the widow requesting an appropriate audience for that purpose. Mrs. Lincoln replies the following morning, requesting the envoy come at 2 p.m. that day. Mrs. Lincoln receives the medal and letter of transmittal from the French citizens on December 27. Dimon tells her:

> The wisdom and purity of character for which our beloved President was pre-eminent among us has touched the hearts of the people throughout the whole civilized world. In this beautiful record we may see an affecting and enduring emblem of the profound emotion of regard which inspired the republicans of France to communicate to you the heartfelt sentiments of their condolence.

Dimon reports the circumstances of the presentation to Seward on January 7, 1867.[7]

a

[3271]

Legation of the United States
Paris. December 7. 1866.

Madam

In compliance with the request of a Committee composed of many of the most illustrious among the Republicans of France, I send you herewith a medal in gold designed to commemorate the glory and martyrdom of the great citizen whose name you bear.

It is the product of the spontaneous offerings of Forty Thousand Frenchmen eager to testify in this manner their sympathy with your immeasurable sorrows and their deep respect for those exalted

Mrs. Abraham Lincoln

42640

b

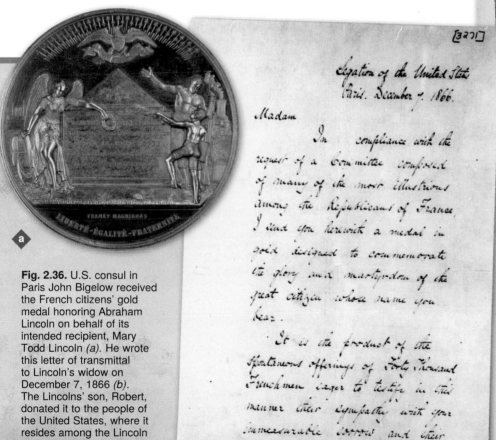

Fig. 2.36. U.S. consul in Paris John Bigelow received the French citizens' gold medal honoring Abraham Lincoln on behalf of its intended recipient, Mary Todd Lincoln *(a)*. He wrote this letter of transmittal to Lincoln's widow on December 7, 1866 *(b)*. The Lincolns' son, Robert, donated it to the people of the United States, where it resides among the Lincoln Papers at the Library of Congress. The numbers at top and bottom are docketing numbers. Also shown is the reverse of the actual gold medal presented to Lincoln's widow, with the signature of medalist Franky Magniadas. The obverse bears a Lincoln portrait. Bronze duplicates were given to officials, including Bigelow and William Seward, and sold to the public.

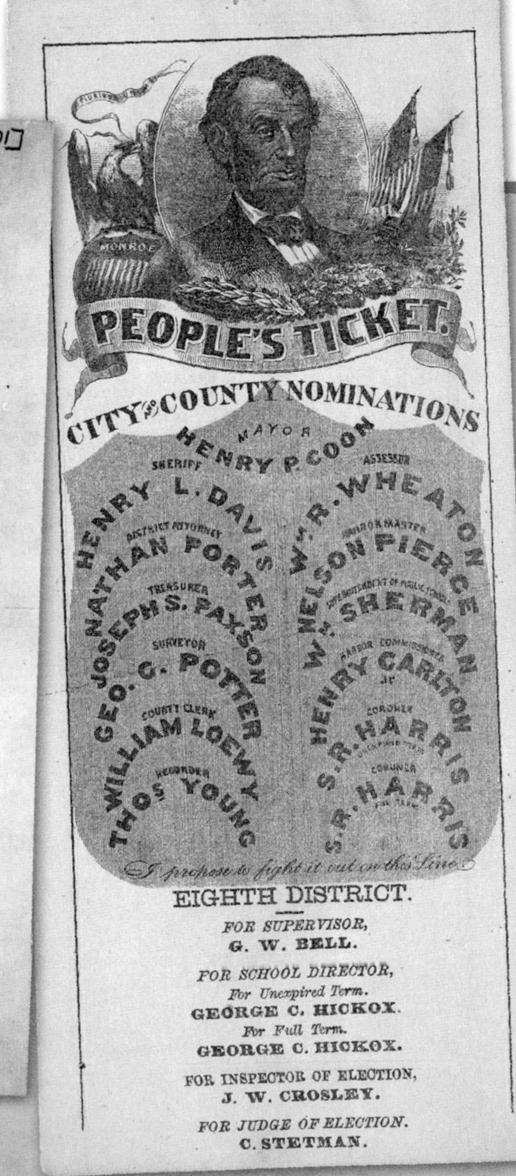

Fig. 2.37. This circa-1865 San Francisco election "People's Ticket" headed by Henry Perrin Coon of the Vigilance People's Party was attributed to 1862 by a cataloger at the Library of Congress. However, the picture (O-92) on which the Lincoln likeness at top was based was not taken by Anthony Berger until February 9, 1864. Since Coon served as San Francisco's mayor from 1863 to 1867, it would have been helpful to the Library of Congress cataloger to be more familiar with Lincoln imagery.

1867 JANUARY 3. Mary Todd Lincoln writes to thank the French committee for the gold medal presented her by subscription.[8]

Gentlemen:

I have received the medal you have sent me. I cannot express the emotion with which this proof of the sentiments of so many thousands of your countrymen fills me. So marked a testimony to the memory of my husband, given in honor of his services in the cause of liberty, by those who in another land work for the same great

end, touches me profoundly, and I beg you to accept, for your selves and those whom you represent, my most grateful thanks. I am, with the profoundest respect, your most obedient servant.

Mary Lincoln.

1867 JANUARY 11. William H. Seward transmits a copy of the "proceedings consequent upon the delivery to Mrs. Mary Lincoln of the gold medal presented by citizens of France."[9]

1867. The Currier & Ives lithograph *The Lincoln Family* depicts Mary and Robert seated at a table at left and Tad (Thomas, misidentified

ABRAHAM LINCOLN AND THE DRUMMER-BOY.—(SEE PAGE 257.)

Fig. 2.38. This maudlin full-page illustration in the April 27, 1867, issue of *Harper's Weekly*, called *Abraham Lincoln and the Drummer-Boy*, by Thomas Nast, was clearly intended to gin up emotion. Artist Nast also clearly based the seated portrait of Lincoln on the Anthony Berger O-92 photograph.

Fig. 2.39. The U.S. Treasury attempted to coerce the contracting banknote companies, on which it had relied, to surrender dies used in printing Treasury notes and bonds to finance the Civil War. The government wanted to start up its own in-house engraving-and-printing bureau. The National Bank Note Co. capitulated. Its surrendered Lincoln bond portrait die was used by the Treasury to print $20 interest-bearing notes and more bonds (among other things, such as land warrants). The American Bank Note Co. did not give in. Its original steel plate die and roller die came down to the present, where they were purchased from the ABNCo archives sales by the present author.

After NBNCo relinquished its Lincoln portrait die to the government, around 1867 an unknown engraver at the company created this similar die for use on commercial work. As can be readily observed, it is also based on the same model as the (by then ubiquitous) Lincoln money portrait.

Fig. 2.40. Published in 1866 by Bradley & Co., Philadelphia, this rich mezzotint engraving by William Sartain, based on a painting by Samuel B. Waugh, was considered the best parlor-print portrait of the Lincoln family at the time. Artist's proofs fetched $20 and even the regular print sold for $7.25. The artist has placed the family group in the White House with the U.S. Capitol in view out the window. The Lincoln portrait is not strictly modeled on any known photographic model, but bears a striking resemblance, with artistic license, to the O-91 Berger photo. Tad reclines by the president, and Willie's portrait peers over the standing figure of Robert at center. Once again, a bust of George Washington clearly associates Lincoln with the Founding Father.

as Thaddeus) standing by the seated president, based on the famous Anthony Berger February 9, 1864, photograph (O-93) of Lincoln and his son examining a photograph album. Detailed inspection of the litho, however, reveals Lincoln is supposedly reading a passage from Isaiah in the Bible.

1867 MARCH 29. The American Numismatic and Archaeological Society receives a bronze copy of the French gold medal honoring Lincoln presented to his widow, Mary Todd Lincoln. The agent for the sales of these bronze duplicates in the United States was Mr. Caylus of E. Caylus, De Ruyter & Co., 57 Beaver Street, New York. The price for one medal in a case was $5.

1867 JULY 3. William Leggett Bramhall explains the circumstances surrounding his striking of political and Lincoln medals during the period of 1859–1860, in a letter to the editor of the *American Journal of Numismatics*. Bramhall said he obtained a photo of Abraham Lincoln immediately following his nomination in May 1860, through the "kind assistance of my friend, George B. Lincoln, of Brooklyn, a profile photograph of his honest face, which was taken at Springfield for my special purpose. [Note: This is an Alexander Hesler photo taken June 3, 1860; probably O-26.] I engaged the services of Mr. George H. Lovett, of New York, who immediately commenced

engraving the dies for a small Medalet, which soon after appeared, and it was the first and bore the best likeness of Mr. L. among the very many issued during that long and exciting political contest." The medalet Bramhall described is the cent-sized ABRA-HAM LIN-COLN "Honest Abe of the West" and "The Hannibal of America" piece (Sullivan AL 1860-73, King 70) struck in silver, copper, brass, copper-nickel, and white metal. According to Bramhall, the comparison to the Carthaginian general "was intended to illustrate his [Lincoln's] reputed boldness, and his success in political warfare." Further, Lincoln's name was punctuated erratically "to exhibit the singular fact that the last syllable of the Christian name and the first of the surname of Mr. Lincoln comprised the surname of his 'political Lieutenant,' Mr. Hamlin." The quantity of minting brought about by additional demand for the medalet caused the reverse die to break and the "Wide Awakes" design (Sullivan AL 1860-74, King-71) was substituted, struck in silver, copper, brass, nickel, and white metal.

1867 OCTOBER 10. The American Numismatic and Archaeological Society's Lincoln medal committee reports that new dies "were now completed, and that the medals would be issued forthwith." However, after considering and rejecting the purchase of its own press on which to strike the Lincoln memorial medal, a contract was not

Fig. 2.41. After much political wrangling, Thomas Ball's *Emancipation Group* was finally installed and dedicated in Washington, D.C., on the 11th anniversary of Lincoln's assassination, April 14, 1876, just prior to the United States Centennial. Once again Lincoln's proclamation emancipating the Southern slaves is seen to rest firmly upon authority, in this case a plinth (small column) bearing the fasces, a federal shield, and a portrait of George Washington, among other patriotic symbols. A plaque was headed "Freedom's Memorial in Grateful Memory of Abraham Lincoln."

Fig. 2.42. Following the war, 1866-dated and 1868-dated (shown, Pollock-5105) privately made patterns for $3 gold coins were struck with a profile portrait of Abraham Lincoln, conjectured (without much substantiation) to have been done by Boston medalist Joseph Merriam. The U.S. Mint also experimented with Lincoln and Washington portrait nickel patterns, but it would be another four decades before a U.S. president would appear on a regular-issue coin, in 1909—the Lincoln cent.

Fig. 2.43. This small (25.5 mm) commemorative medal (King-275) links George Washington and his "most worthy successor" Abraham Lincoln in a very direct manner. Lincoln's profile portrait sports Washington's colonial peruke. Several varieties of this small medal are known, including some with the obverse die cancelled before striking with a wedge-shaped occlusion behind Lincoln's head that reads "Treas. / Dept. / 1869."

presented to Emil Sigel of New York City to do so until February 13, 1868. The committee reported back a signed agreement at its meeting of February 27. At contest were the funds already given Sigel for manufacturing the medal, and his bill for the new dies. According to the terms of the agreement, Sigel would pay the Society a sum of money less medals already received by them from the first set of dies, and additional medals from old or new dies at $5 in bronzed copper or $1 in tin "until the demand of said Society therefor shall be fully satisfied." Until the agreed-upon sum in favor of the Society ($720) was fully satisfied, the Society would have first lien on both old and new dies, including their collar and hub, and Sigel would agree not to strike copies for any third party, after which the dies would belong to the die sinker and not to the Society. At its May 14, 1868, meeting the committee reported that 70 impressions of the medal were ready and would be delivered at the next meeting. However, on May 28, only 36 were presented. Distribution was reported at 54 a month later (June 25), at which time the members voted that the Lincoln medal "now provisionally in the possession of the Mint, be presented definitely to the Cabinet there." At the same time a committee was appointed to present a specimen to the Union League Club. In August 1868, the Society reported delivery of impressions from the first dies "which were found to be perfectly able, with judicious han-

dling, to bear the requisite pressure" to nearly all advanced subscribers. The committee thus pronounced the medal "published."

Although it praised Sigel's work, the committee acknowledged that the delays had caused the Society to be "annoyed and embarrassed . . . beyond measure and for a long time. Undertaken in a moment of patriotic enthusiasm and wild excitement, it has proved too much for our resources. . . . This medal ought to be a warning to all our sister Societies not to attempt anything of the kind themselves." Nevertheless, collectors were urged to purchase the variety from the second dies also. The design differs materially from that of the old ones. In the bust on the obverse there are those appreciable differences of detail which present themselves even where a facsimile is attempted. But such differences were not the case here, for it was Mr. Sigel's ambition to improve upon his former work. The new reverse varies still more widely from the original, the word ACTS being suppressed, so that the inscription reads "IN MEMORY OF THE LIFE AND DEATH OF ABRAHAM LINCOLN, &c." According to King, no medals were struck from this second pair of dies, which then resided in the collection of the Society.[10]

1868 FEBRUARY 12. The first annual meeting of the Lincoln Association of Jersey City is held at Taylors' Hotel with David W. Weiss in the chair as president. The organization had been founded a year

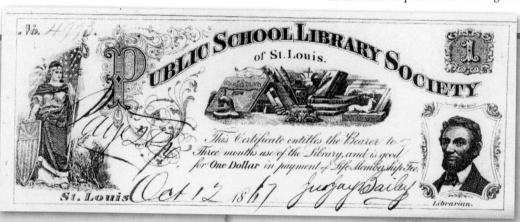

Fig. 2.44. The St. Louis Public School Library Society was a fee-paid membership organization. Its receipt, likely printed by R.P. Studley of St. Louis, had a lithographed Lincoln portrait based on the $10 money image.

Fig. 2.45. The Lincoln Association of Jersey City, New Jersey, was organized in 1865 and formally founded in 1867 to commemorate and perpetuate Abraham Lincoln's legacy. It was the first of many such organizations in the country. Annually at an observance on Lincoln's birth date, February 12, the organization holds a dinner, hears a lecture, or conducts similar activity. This 1889 banquet menu reproduces the French citizens' medal obverse by Franky Magniadas.

Fig. 2.46. Lincoln was reputed to be a teetotaler who abstained from hard drink, although he had a liquor license and doubtless sold alcohol as a shopkeeper. The Lincoln Temperance Association was formed in 1867. It adopted the new NBNCo Lincoln image, with its then-current facsimile of the $10 money portrait, for its attractive pledge cards.

earlier to preserve the memory and the legacy of the slain president. The hotel continued to be identified with the organization. Its banquets were held there from 1880 to 1892 and 1895 to 1899, after which the group moved its annual Lincoln tributes to the Jersey City Club. The elaborately engraved menu for the 24th annual function (held February 12, 1889, with Major Z.K. Pangborn in the chair as president) bears the image of the obverse of the French medal presented by the citizens of France to Abraham Lincoln's widow, Mary Todd Lincoln, engraved by Franky Magniadas and struck in Switzerland when the French government refused to permit it to be struck in France. The original medal for Mary Todd Lincoln was struck in gold and its letter of transmittal was penned by novelist Victor Hugo. Examples for presentation to other dignitaries and for sale were struck in bronze and in silvered bronze.

1868. Sculptor Sarah Fisher Clampitt Ames models a classical white-marble 35-inch-high bust of Abraham Lincoln based on her smaller 1862 bust from life; it is acquired by the United States for $2,000, and is displayed in the Senate wing. According to a U.S. Capitol historian, little is known about the early life of Mrs. Ames

(wife of artist Joseph Alexander Ames). She produced at least six busts of Lincoln, "but the circumstances of their production are not well documented. While Ames was able to patent a bust of the 16th president in 1866, the drawings were later destroyed in a U.S. patent and Trademark building fire," the historian wrote.[11]

Ames's bust in the Capitol has been widely praised for nearly a century and a half. One art historian wrote in 1873: "But any one who ever saw . . . his living humanity must thank Mrs. Ames for having reflected and transfixed it in the brows and eyes of this marble." The bust has been the model for many U.S. postage-stamp engravings, including the 1870 six-cent stamp (Scott 137), the 1870/1871 Reay six-cent embossed covers (Scott U85), and the 1873 six-cent U.S. official department stamps (various), as well as the 1938 Presidential Series 16-cent stamp (Scott 821). In addition to the bust purchased by the Joint Committee on the Library in 1868, other Lincoln busts by Ames reside in collections of the Massachusetts Statehouse, the Williams College Museum of Art, the Lynn (Massachusetts) Historical Society, the Woodmere Art Museum in Philadelphia, and the Union Pacific Railroad Museum in Council Bluffs, Iowa.

Fig. 2.47. The National Lincoln Monument Association collected moneys to finance a memorial to Lincoln in Washington, D.C. Its treasurer was U.S. Treasurer Francis E. Spinner, and its receipts were engraved and printed at the U.S. Treasury Department with the Lincoln money and bond image originally created by a National Bank Note Co. contract engraver.

Fig. 2.48. Henry Bryan Hall became famous in the mid-19th century as an engraver and publisher of portraits of prominent individuals. His firm was H.B. Hall & Sons. This engraving was done by H.B. Hall Jr. He based the fine likeness on the Berger profile photographs (O-88/89) taken February 9, 1864. It was published by Jno. B. Bachelder, New York.

Fig. 2.49. Sarah Fisher Clampitt Ames produced this fine white marble bust of Lincoln, purchased by Congress in 1868 and placed in the U.S. Senate wing of the Capitol. It was highly praised. The bust overall is 35 inches tall.

1868 APRIL 11. Sculptor Henry Jackson Ellicott's life-size plaster statue of Abraham Lincoln is displayed in the Rotunda of the U.S. Capitol. Dr. Louis A. Warren once made the claim that Ellicott's was the first life-size study of Lincoln, but this assertion was subsequently disproved and credit still belongs to Pietro Mezzara, who first displayed his plaster figure of Lincoln at the San Francisco Mechanics Fair in August 1865.[12]

1868 APRIL 16. Lot Flannery's statue of Lincoln atop a tall monolith is unveiled in Washington, D.C.

1868 JUNE 18. Sylvester Sage Crosby exhibits three sizes of the Wyon copy of the American Numismatic and Archaeological Society Lincoln memorial medal at a meeting of the New England Numismatic and Archaeological Society.

Fig. 2.50. In 1869 the U.S. Treasury engaged Charles Burt, who had engraved the Lincoln portrait for the $10 bill, to engrave a new portrait for the nation's money. Burt produced two images, the more formal of which appeared on the C-note, $100 U.S. Legal Tender Notes. Based on the Berger O-92 full-length seated photograph cropped as a portrait, the engraving appeared first on the Series of 1869 "Rainbow Notes," so called because of their vibrant colored inks. It would remain emblazoned on successive issues of these $100 notes through World War I.

Fig. 2.51. In 1869 Burt's second new Lincoln money portrait, based on another of Anthony Berger's photos (O-97) taken April 20, 1864, appeared on the highest value of U.S. Fractional Currency, 50-cent notes of the Fourth Issue, necessitated by the withdrawal of silver coinage from circulation during the Civil War due to hoarding. A sheet of 12 is shown.

Fig. 2.52. Lot Flannery's white marble Abraham Lincoln towers over common humanity atop a 35-foot Tuscan pillar of white marble—the first memorial to Lincoln in the nation's capital. A similar statue atop a tall pillar was the first design suggested by Larkin Mead for the Lincoln monument in Springfield, Illinois. The monument in D.C. was dedicated on the third anniversary of Lincoln's death. In Flannery's vision, Lincoln's left hand rests on a fasces, the symbol of authority. With its extremely tall pediment, the monument's symbolism of the elevated Lincoln could not be lost on any observer.

1869. J.B. Bachelder, New York City, publishes Isaac N. Arnold's *Sketch of the Life of Abraham Lincoln,* an abridgement of his 1866 work on Lincoln and the overthrow of slavery.

1869 MARCH 20. The U.S. Senate refers to its committee on Military Affairs Joint Resolution SR 35, "Donating the Lincoln Hospital to the Columbia Hospital for Women and Laying-in-Asylum." The resolution was reported with amendments on April 9, and on April 20 further consideration was "postponed indefinitely."

1869 MARCH 20. The U.S. Senate receives a memorial from the trustees, faculty, and friends of Lincoln University of Oxford, Pennsylvania, "praying a donation of a portion of public lands," which was referred to the Committee on Public Lands.

1869 SEPTEMBER 16. The New England Numismatic and Archaeological Society receives a gift from J.F. Pratt of a Lincoln medal struck from a piece of copper taken from the rebel ram *Merrimac* in 1862 by Pratt, then an Army surgeon. Ten pieces were struck by

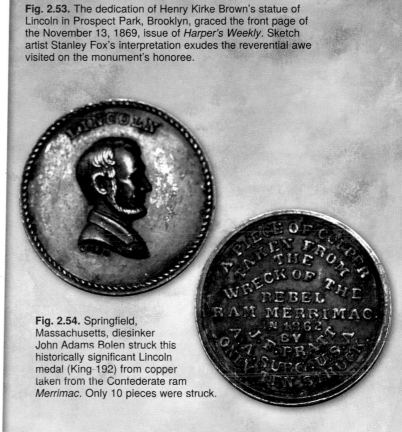

Fig. 2.53. The dedication of Henry Kirke Brown's statue of Lincoln in Prospect Park, Brooklyn, graced the front page of the November 13, 1869, issue of *Harper's Weekly.* Sketch artist Stanley Fox's interpretation exudes the reverential awe visited on the monument's honoree.

Fig. 2.54. Springfield, Massachusetts, diesinker John Adams Bolen struck this historically significant Lincoln medal (King-192) from copper taken from the Confederate ram *Merrimac.* Only 10 pieces were struck.

Fig. 2.55. In 1869 the federal government put Abraham Lincoln's image on a new series of bicolor postage stamps. The portrait on the 90-cent stamp (Scott 77) by Joseph Ourdan was carried over from the 15-cent stamp (issued three years earlier) that had been patterned after the Lincoln money image. It perpetuated the official government imprimatur for a single Lincoln image.

Fig. 2.56. Fisk Mills was the son of Clark Mills, who had made the second life cast of Lincoln's face on February 11, 1865. The younger Mills invented and patented this "United States Postal Currency" to facilitate transfer of small amounts by mail. It bears a Lincoln portrait modeled on the Berger profile photos, O-88/89. Note that "Patent Applied For" appears at lower right. Mills's patent was granted June 15, 1869, but the government did not adopt his early version of a money order.

John A. Bolen in Springfield, Massachusetts. "It possesses a valuable historic worth as commemorating the destruction of one of the most formidable war vessels by our 'Little Monitor,' which latter class of vessels have since become so famous," it was said.

1869 OCTOBER 21. The Lincoln statue in Prospect Park, Brooklyn, was "unveiled . . . and dedicated with imposing ceremonies," according to *Harper's Weekly,* November 13, 1869, which features a front-page illustrated article on the fete. Cost of the statue, executed by Henry K. Brown, was underwritten by "dollar subscriptions." Abraham Lincoln, clad in a cloak, is pointing to the U.S. Constitution, held in his left hand. The woodcut illustration was based on a sketch by Stanley Fox. (See figure 2.53.)

1870 JANUARY 19. The Lincoln-Vicksburg Memorial is dedicated at the statehouse in Columbus, Ohio. The memorial has a marble

bust of Lincoln by Charles M. Niehaus, and a bas relief of the surrender of the Confederates at Vicksburg.

1870 JANUARY 29. The *Brooklyn Daily Eagle's* Washington correspondent laments "[I]t will hardly be believed that there is no provision to prevent contractors for engraving and printing Government paper retaining possession of the plates after the contract is completed. Yet such is the fact, and the plates often are retained. The opportunities for their criminal use are obvious."

1870 CIRCA. Boston sculptor Martin Milmore, an apprentice to Thomas Ball and a close friend of Daniel Chester French's, creates a parian-ware bust of Abraham Lincoln for sale as an appointment for rich Victorian parlors.

Fig. 2.57. This circa-1870s fine Lincoln textile bandana has a Lincoln image (modeled on O-91), federal eagles, flags, and clasping hands.

Fig. 2.58. Martin Milmore was an American sculptor who studied with Thomas Ball. Milmore was active after the Civil War. In addition to public monuments, he specialized in commercial busts and statues of parianware (bisque porcelain) sold to individuals and institutions. His Abraham Lincoln bust was produced in 1870. Milmore died in 1883 at age 38.

Fig. 2.59. This circa-1870s Delft porcelain charger from the Netherlands has an excellent painted likeness based on either the Berger O-91 photograph or, more likely, an engraving based on the photo. It is signed "Van Durn."

Fig. 2.60. Following the Civil War, in 1868 and 1869, Abraham Lincoln appeared on several small U.S. Mint medals. They bore a profile portrait copied by assistant Mint engraver William Barber from an earlier small medalet by former Mint engraver Anthony C. Paquet (by then in private business in Philadelphia). The three gold strikes shown feature Lincoln and George Washington (Julian PR-31) *(a)*; Lincoln and a broken column symbolizing the abridgement of his life (Julian PR-38) *(b)*; and Lincoln and U.S. Grant (Julian PR-39) *(c)*.

Fig. 2.61. In 1866 the U.S. Congress commissioned teenage artist Vinnie Ream to create a statue of Abraham Lincoln for the Capitol. Her marble standing figure is shown in this stereoview card.

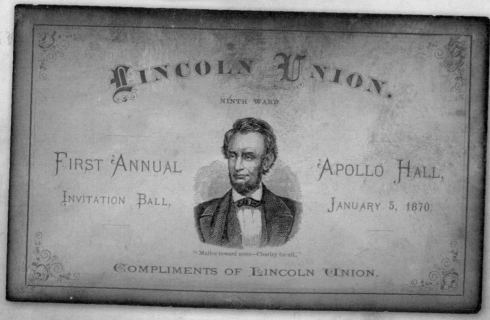

Fig. 2.62. The Lincoln Union sent out this invitation to its first annual ball of January 5, 1870. The portrait chosen for the invitation is a copy of the Lincoln 50-cent Fractional Currency image in circulation at the time, from a pose modeled on O-97. It is believed this event was held in Brooklyn.

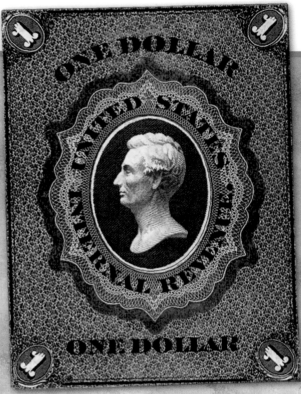

Fig. 2.63. This wonderful $1 Internal Revenue stamp essay (Turner 21a), with its nude profile bust of Lincoln and fugitive colorful inks to avoid tampering, was unfortunately never adopted.

Fig. 2.64. John Rogers's commercial sculptures for the home, such as his realistic *The Council of War*, showing U.S. Grant, Edwin Stanton, and Abraham Lincoln, were very popular in the decades following the war.

Fig. 2.65. In 1871 U.S. Mint engraver William Barber created this medal for the "Medal Series of the U.S. Mint," a project of Mint Director James Pollock to keep his staff occupied and to raise funds for the Mint numismatic collection. This gold specimen, possibly struck many years later, was formerly owned by legendary coin collector Louis Eliasberg.

1870 SEPTEMBER 16. Sculptor Henry Kirke Brown's bronze statue of Lincoln, *The Orator*, commemorating his second inaugural address, is dedicated in Union Square, New York City.

1871 JANUARY 25. Vinnie Ream's white marble statue of Abraham Lincoln is dedicated inside the U.S. Capitol Rotunda. The statue was unveiled by Lincoln's friend, U.S. Supreme Court Associate Justice David Davis, in the presence of President Ulysses S. Grant and other dignitaries. Miss Ream was the first woman to receive a congressional commission to create artwork for the Capitol Rotunda.

1871 AUGUST 10. The *New York Times* reports several counterfeit $10 Lincoln Legal Tender Notes in circulation.

1871 SEPTEMBER 22. Sculptor Randolph Rogers's bronze statue of *Lincoln, the Emancipator* is dedicated at Philadelphia's Fairmount Park before a crowd numbering 50,000.

1871 OCTOBER. New York City collector Andrew C. Zabriskie writes on "Lincoln Medals" in the *American Journal of Numismatics,* page 42. He would do so again in the October 1872 issue of the publication, page 43. In the latter article, Zabriskie bemoaned the fact that no one had adequately cataloged and described the numerous Lincoln political and memorial medals. "I hope at no very distant day," Zabriskie wrote, "to issue a catalogue of the pieces, and wish to make it as full and valuable as possible. To this end I am collecting scarce medals and medalets, and would request all collectors who have any in their possession, to send me either a rubbing or a minute description" of same.[13] Zabriskie would follow through on his promise: his *Descriptive Catalogue of the Political and Memorial Medals Struck in Honor of Abraham Lincoln, Sixteenth President of the United States* would be published in early 1873.

1871 OCTOBER 11. Chicago's Lincoln Park proves a sanctuary for thousands of unfortunates fleeing the rushing inferno known as the Great Chicago Fire. The *Chicago Tribune* reported on the scene: "Striking Lincoln Park, the trace of the bosom of destruction is visible even there. The fences have all gone, and some of the railings around the graves in the Old Cemetery are scorched and burned. The fire did not penetrate far into the park, as it did not reach it until about 11 o'clock on Monday night, when the welcome rain was falling in torrents."

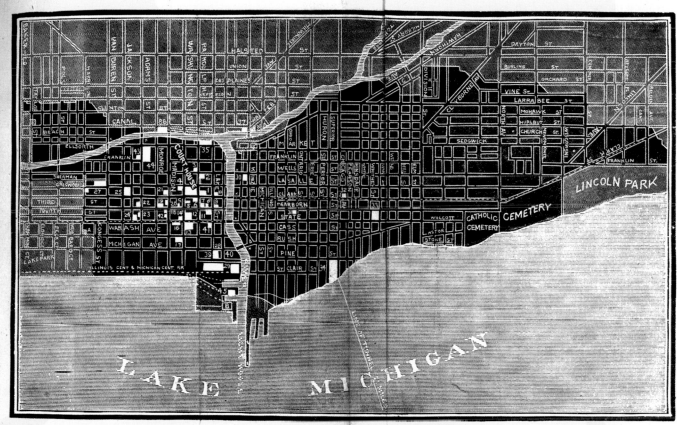

Fig. 2.66. Lincoln Park, in the far-north precincts of Chicago, was created by city fathers to honor the deceased Illinoisan. When the Great Chicago Fire burned through the city's center (the area shown in black) in October 1871 the park was a refuge for thousands of victims fleeing the wrath of the flames.

1871 OCTOBER 14. In the wake of the Great Chicago Fire, three days later *Chicago Tribune* newspaper editor Horace White writes his colleague, *Cincinnati Commercial* editor Murat Halstead, about the "thousands of men, women, and tender babes huddled together in Lincoln Park, seven miles to the north of us, with no prospect of food, exposed to rain, if it should come, with no canopy but the driving smoke of their homes."

1872. Artist and author Francis Bicknell Carpenter amplifies his earlier work on Lincoln, and Hurd and Houghton publish his *The Inner Life of Abraham Lincoln: Six Months at the White House.* Carpenter's detailed observations were praised as providing "an intimate character study such as few men of the time, even among those brought into close official relations with Mr. Lincoln, were qualified to make." Both of Carpenter's Lincoln volumes "were wisely read and many men and women of to-day can refer their first attempts to idealize the man Lincoln to the word-pictures so skillfully drawn by Mr. Carpenter," literary critic and Lincoln image historian Albert Shaw wrote at the time of the 1909 Lincoln centennial.[14]

1872. Boston publisher J.R. Osgood brings out Ward Hill Lamon's *The Life of Abraham Lincoln, From His Birth to His Inauguration as President.* Since Lamon's Lincoln biography covered his pre-presidential years, it stressed Lincoln's views at the time in favor of gradual and compensated emancipation "by the voluntary action of the people of the Slave States, and the transportation of the whole negro population to Africa as rapidly as they should be freed from service to their masters."

"It was," Lamon continued, "a favorite scheme with Mr. Lincoln then, as it was long after he became President of the United States. 'Compensated' and 'voluntary emancipation,' on the one hand, and 'colonization' of the freedmen on the other, were essential parts of every 'plan' which sprung out of his own individual mind."[15] Lamon also refuted Holland's assertion that Lincoln made a pilgrimage to Henry Clay's Ashland estate to visit with him at his home in Lexington, Kentucky.

1872 APRIL 15. Lincoln, Nebraska, officials receive a quote from the Continental Bank Note Co. for printing $1 and $2 municipal scrip depicting deceased president Abraham Lincoln. The notes evidently were delayed for two years when local officials were advised that their issue would be illegal.

1872 MAY 20. Lincoln, Nebraska, mayor E.E. Brown and councilmen J.J. Gosper (McGosper), S.G. Owen (chairman of the city council finance committee), and L.A. Scoggin are authorized to negotiate with bank-note companies to manufacture a municipal scrip to pay

Fig. 2.67. Lincoln, Nebraska, was named in Abe's honor. When the city council sought to fund improvements in the early 1870s, they contracted the Continental Bank Note Co. to print notes with Lincoln portraits on them. This is the plate from which CBNCo printed the faces of the notes. A Lincoln profile appears at bottom right on the $2 face. CBNCo's portrait, patterned after the Lincoln federal currency image, appears on the back of the $1 note.

off outstanding debts. On August 20, 1872, the city council authorized $10,000 worth of the scrip to be printed by Continental Bank Note Co. Fifteen hundred sheets of $1 and $2 notes with images of Abraham Lincoln were printed, but the legality of their issue came into question. On October 16, 1874, the *Nebraska State Journal* reported "that the U.S. Secret Service had come to the city to confiscate the notes for possible destruction," according to numismatic historian James L. McKee. Nothing more was heard of the notes until the State National Bank remodeling in 1894 "found the entire supply." Some notes would be overprinted as advertising notes. Others would be signed falsely and dirtied up in an attempt to circulate them. Examples known to collectors today include both those falsely handled to appear "well circulated," and remainders of high grade.

1873 June. *Potter's American Monthly* praises the new pamphlet by Andrew Christian Zabriskie, *A Descriptive Catalogue of the Political and Memorial Medals Struck in Honor of Abraham Lincoln, Sixteenth President of the United States,* calling it "beautifully printed. It is the work of a careful, intelligent and enthusiastic young numismatologist and antiquary . . . [and] a most interesting and useful monograph, for which the author is entitled to the thanks of numismatologists and numismatic students."

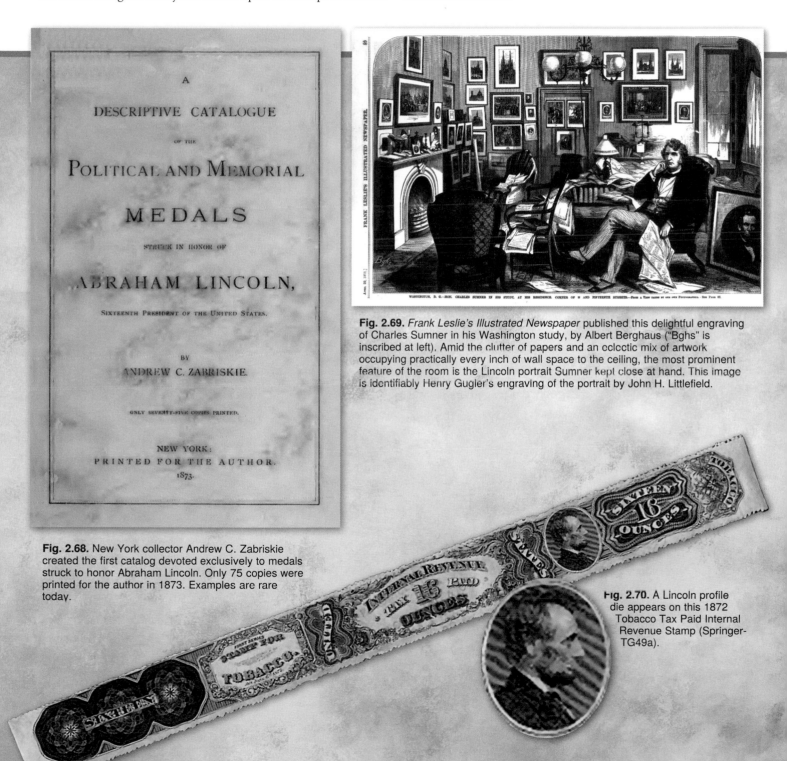

Fig. 2.69. *Frank Leslie's Illustrated Newspaper* published this delightful engraving of Charles Sumner in his Washington study, by Albert Berghaus ("Bghs" is inscribed at left). Amid the clutter of papers and an eclectic mix of artwork occupying practically every inch of wall space to the ceiling, the most prominent feature of the room is the Lincoln portrait Sumner kept close at hand. This image is identifiably Henry Gugler's engraving of the portrait by John H. Littlefield.

Fig. 2.68. New York collector Andrew C. Zabriskie created the first catalog devoted exclusively to medals struck to honor Abraham Lincoln. Only 75 copies were printed for the author in 1873. Examples are rare today.

Fig. 2.70. A Lincoln profile die appears on this 1872 Tobacco Tax Paid Internal Revenue Stamp (Springer-TG49a).

1872 December. The *American Historical Record,* volume 1, no. 12, edited by historian Benson J. Lossing, publishes a page-and-a-half illustrated article on the French gold medal presented to Lincoln's widow. According to Lossing, funds for the medal were contributed by "forty thousand Democrats of France," which he takes from the obverse legend "Dedicated by the French Democracy. Twice Elected President of the United States." All other writers characterized the contributors as French *republicans,* i.e., those favoring restoration of a republic.

1873 December 12–14. At the New York auction of George A. Leavitt & Co., an A. Lincoln "10 dollars" spielmark token in Proof brings the high sales price of $5.00, an exceptional price for exonumia at the time. These counters were made in Nuremberg, Bavaria, in the workshops of the Lauers. The founder of the firm was Ludwig Sigmund Lauer (1762–1833). In charge of the family business at the time the Lincoln gaming money was coined was his grandson Ludwig Christian Lauer (1817–1873).

1874 June 14. The City of Lincoln, Nebraska, belatedly attempts to circulate municipal notes with portraits of Abraham Lincoln, which it had ordered in 1872 from the Continental Bank Note Co. Most of the notes, however, remained in storage for two decades until they were brought out surreptitiously, and then stained and otherwise distressed to make them resemble well-circulated bills. (See entry for 1872, May 20.)

1874 July 9. The foundation stone is laid for the Lincoln Memorial Tower in London, by the U.S. ambassador to the Court of St. James's, General Robert C. Schenk.

1874 October 29. The Lincoln Tomb in Springfield, Illinois, is opened to public viewing.

1875 January. The *American Journal of Numismatics* publishes the article "Lincoln Medals" (pages 59 and 60), an open letter from numismatist Henry W. Holland pointing out errors in Andrew C. Zabriskie's 1873 *Descriptive Catalog of the Political and Memorial Medals Stuck in Honor of Abraham Lincoln,* to which Holland had initially appended a listing of additional pieces. Holland's addenda included 110 medals not listed in Zabriskie's work or his prior listing. He also issued this appeal: "I hope that some of the owners of Lincoln medals not in Zabriskie's list, or this appendix to it, will describe them, and thus assist in the compilation of a complete list, which is much desired." The next issue of the *Journal,* published in April, presented (pages 83–85) Zabriskie's defense of his listing. He challenged Holland's inclusion of pieces made from green clay, terra cotta, rubber, etc., since "these medals have no right to the title of medals." Further, Zabriskie intoned sarcastically, "I have a Lincoln piece made from soap, which has as much right in the list as the articles just mentioned." The issue also published Holland's rejoinder, saying that although he regretted Mr. Zabriskie's ire, the pieces he listed were struck from medal dies and deserved listing.

1875. Springfield, Illinois, publisher Edwin A. Wilson & Co. publishes the "Monumental Edition" of John Carroll Power's Lincoln biography, *Abraham Lincoln, His Life, Public Services, Death and Great Funeral Cortege,* together "With a Report and Description of the National Lincoln Monument."

1875 October 5. U.S. Secret Service operative Patrick D. Tyrrell of St. Louis arrests Ben Boyd, "who manufactured the fifty cent Lincoln vignette counterfeit plate, and he is considered the best letterer on steel in the country or the world."

Fig. 2.71. Counterfeiting was rife in the years following the Civil War, and the U.S. Treasury and Justice departments were inept in controlling this scourge, although the U.S. Secret Service had been created specifically for the purpose. The relatively high-denomination 50-cent Lincoln fractionals were an especially prime target, and the Lincoln notes were withdrawn and replaced after only several months by a new issue with a portrait of Edwin M. Stanton. This very-high-grade counterfeit was one of the felonious productions that doomed the Lincoln bill to a short life.

The source of these bills was a subject of diligent inquiry by Government officials, and a kind of dissolving view was obtained of the same, in Canada, St. Louis, and elsewhere, now here and now there. After a time, the talents and activity of Boyd, as well as the ability and wealth of his partners, became known to the Treasury Department and the Secret Service Division came to recognize the imperative necessity of breaking up the combination of which the skill of Ben Boyd was the heart and soul.[16]

1875 OCTOBER 15. The National Lincoln Monument is dedicated at Springfield, Illinois. Local dry-goods dealer Hall & Herrick issued a cabinet card for the occasion, with an engraving of the monument and details of its size and cost ($212,000). Larkin Mead's bronze statue of Lincoln the Emancipator on the front of the monument was unveiled at the dedication.

Fig. 2.72. Springfield, Illinois, merchants Hall & Herrick issued this trade card in 1874 with a fine likeness of the National Lincoln Monument (100 feet high, cost $212,000).

Fig. 2.73. The Funding Act of March 3, 1875, enumerated various items on which taxes were to be collected. Distilled Spirits revenue stamps were issued by volume, 10 to 130 gallons, and were printed by the American Bank Note Co. This stamp proof for 20 to 29 gallons has a unique Lincoln engraved portrait (BEP die MISC 3040) modeled on a Mathew Brady photo (O-57) "probably taken in 1862," according to Lincoln photo historian Lloyd Ostendorf. The BEP Historical Resource Center credits this original portrait to Henry Gugler for the National Bank Note Co., for a "Draft on Interior Warrant."

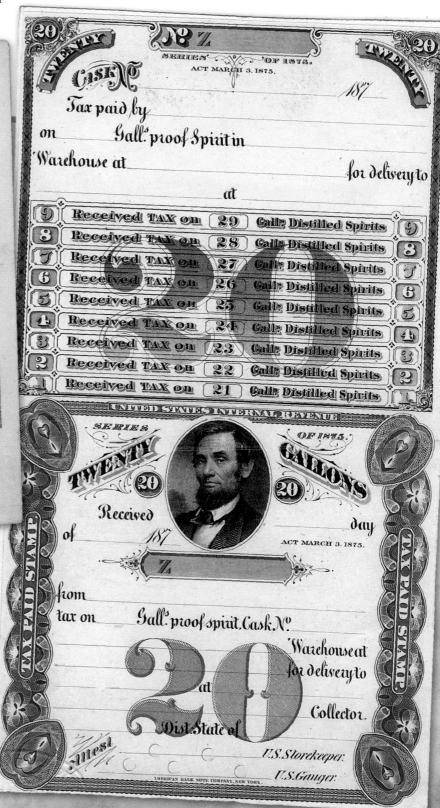

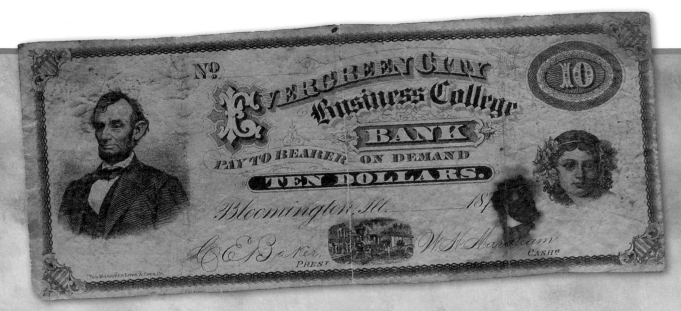

Fig. 2.74. Circa 1873, Evergreen City Business College, Bloomington, Illinois, engaged the Milwaukee Lithographic and Engraving Co. to print bills for use in its curriculum. This unlisted $10 note (type of Schingoethe IL-200) is unique. Interestingly, the Lincoln portrait note patterned after O-92 is similar to the federal money portrait then coming into vogue on the $100 greenbacks.

Fig. 2.75. On October 1, 1872, the assistant U.S. treasurer at Philadelphia returned this counterfeit Lincoln 50-cent note to a depositor, writing "Counterfeit" in ink twice on its face and pinning it to the Fractional Currency deposit.

Fig. 2.76. Series of 1869 Lincoln $100 notes were preyed upon by counterfeiters, causing the notes to be vitiated, i.e., compromised. The Treasury instituted a new Series of 1874/1875 to replace the sullied notes. Laban Heath was allowed by the Treasury to publish this canceled plate image, of the business end of the note face, in his ubiquitous counterfeit detectors.

Fig. 2.77. Alexander Hay Ritchie engraved this Lincoln deathbed scene circa 1868. His tableau crowded two dozen mourners into the small room in which Lincoln actually died. Ritchie's engraving was based on his own original painting. Artists bowed to personal conceits, as everybody wanted to be associated with such epochal, historic events.

Fig. 2.78. This silk jacquard portrait was characterized as "spectacular" by the auction cataloger who wrote the lot description—a judgment with which we certainly agree. Unfortunately the cataloger misread the piece itself when he wrote "It is marked 'Carquillen Tex . . . Allardet del.'" This excellent interpretation of the O-92 money portrait is a Carquillat textile. The famous manufacturer's detailed, woven-textile portraits of historical figures such as Alexander II, George Washington, and Napoleon III dated back as far as the 1840s. Michel-Marie Carquillat perfected the process, and François Carquillat founded Carquillat & Porton, Rambaud & Co., in Lyon, France. This silk was designed by Allardet. According to the Smithsonian Institution volume *Threads in History*, this piece was made for exhibition at the U.S. Centennial in Philadelphia.

Fig. 2.79. The portrait on this patriotic dish is modeled on Alexander Gardner's November 8, 1863, image (O-78) that was taken at the same time as the famous "Gettysburg Lincoln" portrait, O-77. The seller of this item figured that it dated from the time of the U.S. Centennial Exposition in 1876.

1875 December 6–9. At a Thomas Birch & Son Philadelphia auction, cataloged by John W. Haseltine, a silver Abraham Lincoln Wide Awakes badge, size 40, brought the high price of $16.50, and a smaller, size 22, silver Wide Awakes badge brought $5.87. An 1860 brass Lincoln campaign token fetched $2.50, and an 1864 brass Lincoln political token, $2.87.

1876 January 18. At an American Numismatic and Archaeological Society regular meeting, Andrew C. Zabriskie exhibits "one hundred and thirty-five Lincoln's, different metals, among which was the broken column in silver by Key, size 32; the large Mint medal, size 48, in silver; the Emancipation Proclamation medal, size 28, of the Mint series in silver; also, a white metal Lincoln, size 24, three-quarters bust to right encircled by stars; reverse, a recumbent female figure with the word 'Amerika.'" Also at the meeting, Benjamin Betts displayed 63 different Grant pieces; Daniel Parish Jr., 45 Grants; and Isaac F. Wood, 82 Grant items and the rare misspelled variety of the Swiss Lincoln medal by Bovy (King-229).

1876 April 14. Frederick Douglass speaks at the dedication of Thomas Ball's Freedmen's Memorial in Washington, D.C. Three years later, a replica would be installed in Boston near the Boston Common.

1876. Sculptor Leonard Volk, who posed Lincoln in 1860 for his famous life mask, hand casts, and marble bust, completes a full-size plaster standing statue of a bearded Lincoln as president. The statue was never cast in bronze; instead, Volk's plaster would be coated with a bronze-looking compound. The work is presently displayed in the second-floor rotunda of the Illinois State Capitol, opposite a statue of Lincoln's political opponent, Stephen A. Douglas.

1876 July 4. The Lincoln Memorial Tower, a Gothic Revival tower in London, opens on the centenary of American independence.

1879 November 27. "A friend of her martyred Son" erects an appropriate grave marker for Lincoln's mother, Nancy Hanks Lincoln, who died "Oct. 5 A.D. 1818 / Aged 35 years," according to the tombstone, on a half acre (donated by Henry Lewis) surrounding her grave. A public subscription placed a low fence around the plot. The friend of Mrs. Lincoln's son was Peter E. Studebaker, who chose to remain anonymous.

Fig. 2.80. Peter E. Studebaker anonymously contributed a fitting stone for Lincoln's mother's grave in 1879, on a half acre donated by Henry Lewis. Today this site lies within Indiana's Nancy Hanks Lincoln–Lincoln Boyhood Memorial, administered by the National Park Service.

Fig. 2.81. Harriet Hosmer's original design for the Lincoln Monument in the nation's capital was this extravagant, multi-tiered affair, which failed to be funded. Instead the organizing committee accepted Thomas Ball's more straightforward design of a standing Lincoln and a kneeling freedman breaking the chains of slavery.

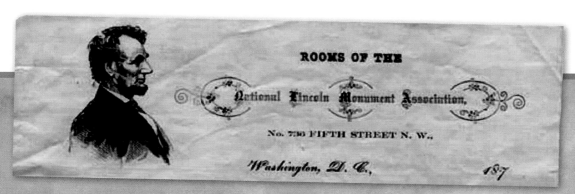

Fig. 2.82. A letterhead of the National Lincoln Monument Association, 736 Fifth Street NW, bore a profile Lincoln portrait based on the familiar Anthony Berger model (O-88/89).

Fig. 2.83. Card games date back far in history. This "Commander in Chief" card is believed to hail from an 1880s game.

Fig. 2.84. By 1882 Charles Burt's Lincoln portrait, based on the O-92 Berger photograph, not only appeared on the $100 United States Legal Tender Note, but for a dozen years had also appeared on Series of 1870 and Series of 1875 $500 Gold Certificates. In 1882 the Treasury Department engaged Burt for a fourth Lincoln money image. He created this magnificent portrait based on the Berger O-91 photograph, which displaced his O-92–style portrait on the high-value $500 Gold Certificates, but not on the $100 greenbacks that continued to be issued for the next three decades.

Fig. 2.85. Artist Freeman Thorp produced several Lincoln portraits, this one circa 1879. It was acquired in 1920 by the Congressional Joint Committee on the Library. Beauty being in the eye of the beholder, some complained that it was "too dark," while others complimented its "richness of tone."

Fig. 2.86. In 1870 W.L. Troxell issued this rare 25-cent scrip note as a receipt for his First National Photographic Bank, 319 Fulton Avenue, in Brooklyn, New York. The printer used a near likeness to the Lincoln $10 bill image. Troxell was a highly successful photographer in St. Louis and then Brooklyn, specializing in cartes de visite. He also marketed a proprietary "erasive soap" guaranteed to diminish skin blemishes.

1879 DECEMBER 9. New England poet John Greenleaf Whittier's poem for the unveiling ceremony at Boston's Park Square of expatriate Boston sculptor Thomas Ball's *Emancipation Group,* a copy of the monument installed in Washington, D.C., in 1876, reads in part: "Let man be free! The mighty word / He spake was not his own; / An impulse from the Highest stirred / These chiselled lips alone."

Ball's 12-foot-high sculpture shows Lincoln symbolically liberating a slave in chains. It rests on a tall pediment inscribed "A Race Set Free and the Country at Peace Lincoln Rests from His Labors." The bronze replica for Boston was cast in 1877 at von Müller's Royal Foundry in Munich, Bavaria, at a cost of $17,000.[17] The statue was donated to the city by resident Moses Kimball.

1880 FEBRUARY 12. The Lincoln Guard of Honor is organized at the Memorial Hall of the National Lincoln Monument, Springfield, Illinois, for the purpose of "raising a fund with which to purchase and keep in repair the former home of President Lincoln; to open the house, under proper regulations, to visitors, and to hold the premises in trust for the public." The group also pledged to hold memorial services on suitable occasions and to collect and preserve mementoes of his life and death. The most important of its relics was the body of Lincoln, which had barely escaped being stolen in 1876. The group pledged "to guard the precious dust of Abraham Lincoln from vandal hands." Its first formal function would be to observe the 15th anniversary of Lincoln's death on April 15, 1880, in a memorial service commencing at 7:22 a.m., the precise time of Lincoln's demise.

Fig. 2.87. The U.S. Mint added a 19-millimeter Lincoln-Garfield medalet (Julian PR-41) to its sales list in fall 1881. The obverse employed William Barber's Lincoln profile after Paquet, while the reverse was entirely Barber's design. He also created 25-millimeter medals of similar style (Julian PR-40). The example shown is gold.

Fig. 2.88. Union veterans, organized as the Grand Army of the Republic and supporting the Republican Party, managed to "wave the bloody shirt" with great success in the second half of the 19th century. Reunions, such as the one in 1880 in Massachusetts represented by this invitation, kept up camaraderie and extended the political pull of the vets in local, state, and national affairs. This circa-1880 invite bears the American Bank Note Co. money image, the Lincoln portrait that would have been familiar to all the ex-Union soldiers.

Fig. 2.89. The assassination of President James Garfield in 1881 linked him indelibly to the beloved Lincoln, who had been felled sixteen years earlier. Various items depicted the two fallen Civil War heroes—such as this glass cup, which has embossed likenesses of both men.

Fig. 2.90. In 1881 New York music publisher P.A. Wunderman published this Lincoln-Garfield National Funeral March, lithographed by R. Teller, New York City.

1880 MAY 11. J.J. Cooke Co., New York, receives its first patent for its foil packaging with a "tax paid" imprint, used by Western Steam Tobacco Works, Milwaukee, and first used by B. Leidersdorf & Co., Milwaukee, on June 1, 1880, for its Old Abe brand.

1880 JULY 6. J.J. Cooke Co., New York, receives a second patent for its foil Old Abe Fine Cut tobacco tin-foil label with a revenue-stamp imprint, employed on tobacco pouches of Western Steam Tobacco Works, Milwaukee, sold by Leidersdorf & Mendel, Milwaukee. In 1881 Leidersdorf & Mendel sold the loose tobacco in one- and two-ounce packages, with stamps dated July 1, 1881, and May 1, 1881, respectively. The tax rate was 16¢ per pound. By 1883

the firm was styled B. Leidersdorf & Co. The Act of March 3, 1883, cut the tax rate to 8¢ per pound. The stamp date on the wrapper was May 1, 1883.

1881. When George B. Ayres bought Alexander Hesler's Chicago photographic studio, he acquired the four original campaign photographic plates that Hesler had shot of Lincoln in Springfield on June 3, 1860. In 1881 Ayres made "some fine prints direct from the plates, which he copyrighted and sold." They bear the imprint on verso: "Copyright / Geo. B. Ayres / Phila." Ayres also made a duplicate set of glass negatives, which were eventually acquired by the Chicago Historical Society, now the Chicago History Museum.

Fig. 2.91. In 1882 the Bureau of Engraving and Printing created these two essays for the new $500 Gold Certificate, with the idealized portrait of Abraham Lincoln at left. One had the printed facsimile signatures of the register and treasurer stacked at right *(a)*, while the other had the signatures in-line *(b)*. The latter display won out, and the issued notes have in-line signatures.

Fig. 2.92. This circa-1880s carved wood Lincoln Emancipation plaque sold on the Internet, in very competitive bidding, for thousands of dollars. It is illustrated here courtesy of the seller.

Fig. 2.93. George B. Ayres acquired several of Chicago photographer Alexander Hesler's original glass-plate negatives of Lincoln portraits. In 1881 he copyrighted and issued prints from O-26 in several sizes.

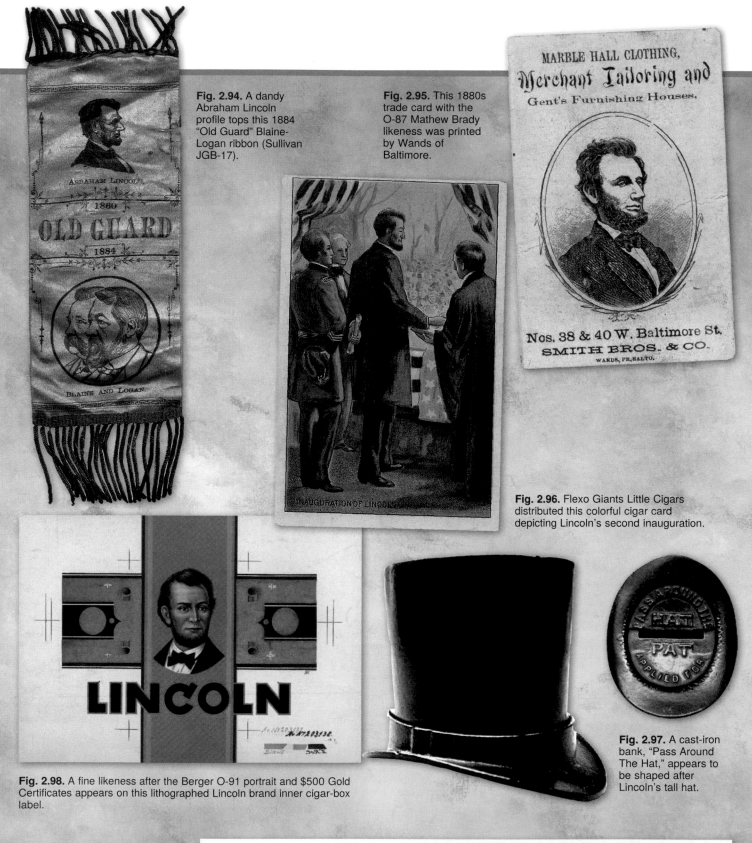

Fig. 2.94. A dandy Abraham Lincoln profile tops this 1884 "Old Guard" Blaine-Logan ribbon (Sullivan JGB-17).

Fig. 2.95. This 1880s trade card with the O-87 Mathew Brady likeness was printed by Wands of Baltimore.

Fig. 2.96. Flexo Giants Little Cigars distributed this colorful cigar card depicting Lincoln's second inauguration.

Fig. 2.97. A cast-iron bank, "Pass Around The Hat," appears to be shaped after Lincoln's tall hat.

Fig. 2.98. A fine likeness after the Berger O-91 portrait and $500 Gold Certificates appears on this lithographed Lincoln brand inner cigar-box label.

Fig. 2.99. Lincoln pens have been marketed since shortly after the president's death. In 1887 the Lincoln Fountain Pen Co. sold this straightforward hard-rubber (probably gutta percha) pen, with a gold pen point, for a buck—guaranteed, "your money back if you want it."

$1 LINCOLN FOUNTAIN PEN $1

LINCOLN FOUNTAIN PEN

Solid Gold Pen—Hard Rubber Engraved Holder—Simple Construction—Always Ready—Never blots— No better working pen made—A regular $2.50 pen.
To introduce, mailed complete, boxed, with filler, for $1.00. Your money back—*if you want it.* Agents Wanted.
LINCOLN FOUNTAIN PEN CO., ROOM 5, 108 FULTON ST., NEW YORK

Fig. 2.100. Honest Old Abe cigars traded blatantly on Lincoln's reputation for integrity. The company's memorabilia is plentiful, but this circa-1880s poster was affixed to the side of a store. The likeness mirrors the proliferation of Charles Burt's money image on the $500 Gold Certificates from the 1880s forward.

Fig. 2.101. Collectors of Victorian redware would be pleased to own this decorated vase with Abraham Lincoln surrounded by a wreath of oak leaves and topped by a federal eagle.

Fig. 2.102. When longtime friend, dealer Joe Levine, found this bois-durci Lincoln medal I knew I had to have it. Long ago some contemporary numismatists railed against such productions, cast or struck in nonmetals, calling them "nae numismatic" (not numismatic). Bois-durci (French, meaning *hardened wood*) products are pressed from fine sawdust, from a wood such as rosewood, mixed with blood. Such medallions were popular in the 19th century. Who could deny the appeal of this medallion (which appears to be signed with an omega in the field beneath the truncation)?

Fig. 2.103. The gold medal *(a)* is Julian PR-12, U.S. Mint engraver George Morgan's highly praised excellent likeness of Abraham Lincoln, considered one of the finest U.S. Mint medals of the 19th century. The obverse does not have Morgan's name on the truncation, which Julian indicates was the first die state in 1886. Examples in the present author's collection indicate that Morgan's design was so admired that it was used on a host of commercial issues. It is unclear whether these were sanctioned or pirated. The second, similar, example *(b)* is a white-metal splasher of the principal devices, of uncertain origin.

Fig. 2.104. Every president or political figure to come down the pike following Abraham Lincoln sought to link himself with the Washington-Lincoln "founder-savior" tradition. Democratic candidate Grover Cleveland's claim to the savior mantle was "will save from Corruption," according to this circa-1884 campaign print featuring a copy of the Lincoln $100 bill image.

Fig. 2.105. Colorful lithographed calling cards were the rage in polite society during the late-19th century. This patriotic design employs the Lincoln $100 bill image and urges the recipient to "Forget Me Not."

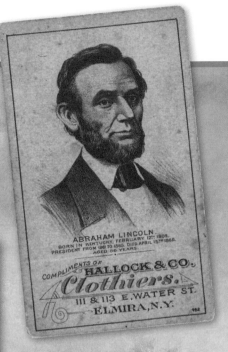

Fig. 2.106. The Lincoln $100 pose appears on this upstate New York Lincoln Club political ribbon. Republican Congressman Charles S. Baker was the incumbent, and he won reelection.

Fig. 2.107. In the 1880s this Lincoln portrait stock trade card, numbered 492 in the lower right corner, was extremely popular with advertisers. The present author has observed dozens of merchants' names imprinted beneath the portrait, which mirrored the Lincoln image on the Civil War–era $10 and $20 notes.

Fig. 2.108. Multilingualism has a long history in this largely immigrant nation. Abraham Lincoln's ancestors came from England. A great many German soldiers fought under Lincoln as commander-in-chief during the war. This "auf Deutsch" 1885 memorial-service program printed by Henry Rauth of St. Louis was issued to mark the 20th anniversary of Lincoln's death. Organizing groups from St. Louis and Springfield participated. The Lincoln tomb illustration is copyrighted, but the fine profile is not.

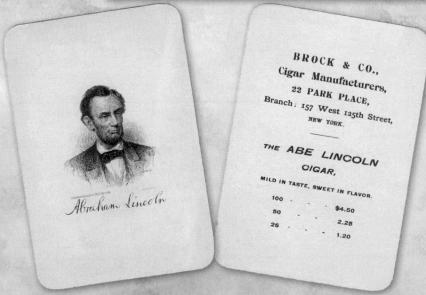

Fig. 2.109. Brock & Co. in New York City manufactured the Abe Lincoln nickel cigar. Quantity discounts were available. This wonderful trade card has the Baldwin & Gleason engraving of the Anthony Berger O-97/98 Lincoln portrait that Charles Burt had also engraved in 1869 for abbreviated use on U.S. Fractional Currency. Baldwin & Gleason patented its engraving (245-E1) in 1886.

A great many proofs of this B&G portrait die, likely engraved by Marcus Baldwin, exist. In fact, most of the proofs observed (especially at Memphis International Paper Money Show exhibits) offered up as the Lincoln fractional portrait are actually proofs from the B&G die and not the BEP die.

Fig. 2.110. This unobtrusive item is one of my favorite Lincoln pieces. It was sold to me as a "rare BEP Fractional Currency die proof," which of course it is not. Instead it is a Baldwin & Gleason progressive die proof. Above the Lincoln Fractional Currency–type portrait the engraver has added a shield with the motto "Liberty and Prosperity."

1881 JUNE 16. In a paper read before the Royal Historical Society in London, Isaac N. Arnold tells those present that when Thomas Lincoln was but six years old his father Abraham was "shot and instantly killed by an Indian" while working in his field with young Thomas. The Indian had then grabbed the young boy, whereupon his older brother Mordecai, having witnessed the attack, ran to the family cabin, grabbed "his ready loaded rifle . . . and aiming at a silver (Indian Peace) medal, conspicuous on the breast of the Indian, he instantly fired. The Indian fell, and the lad, springing to his feet, ran to the open arms of his mother, at the cabin door."[18] Thomas Lincoln was born in 1778, and his father Abraham died in 1786, so Abe Lincoln's pa actually would have been about eight years old when this happened.

1882 JANUARY 1. Chicago sculptor Leonard Volk sends his manuscript contribution for *The Lincoln Memorial: Album-Immortelles* to the book's editor, Lincolniana collector O.H. (Osborn Hamiline) Oldroyd. The book was published after July 1882, by American Union Publishing Co. Its subtitle describes the contents of this compilation: *Original life pictures, with autographs, from the hands and hearts of eminent Americans and Europeans, contemporaries of the great martyr to liberty, Abraham Lincoln. Together with extracts from his speeches, letters, and sayings.*

According to Volk, Lincoln was a toiler, who carried the "cares of state . . . Atlas-like, the destinies of the Western Continent upon his brawny and herculean shoulders."

Other contributors included Benson Lossing, Joshua Speed, and Jesse W. Fell. The book's introduction was penned by the Reverend Matthew Simpson, and a biographical sketch was provided by Isaac Arnold. Oldroyd had begun collecting Lincolniana during the 1860 election campaign. By 1882 he owned more than 2,000 items. "The fact is, I have collected everything I could find sacred to Lincoln's memory, from a newspaper scrap to his large cook-stove and other household articles," he wrote in the book's preface. "I shall always be thankful for any Lincoln relic sent me, no matter how trifling it may seem to the owner," he added.

In November 1883, Oldroyd would lease and turn the Lincoln home in Springfield into his personal museum to display his holdings. He charged visitors a fee to view what he styled the Oldroyd Lincoln Memorial Collection. In 1893, after the Lincoln home had been donated to the State of Illinois, Oldroyd (with the government's permission) would move his family into the Petersen House in which Lincoln had died in Washington, D.C., live rent free, and charge tourists a quarter to view his memorabilia there.

1882 APRIL 15. Illinois abolitionist attorney and congressman Isaac N. Arnold, who had lectured on Abraham Lincoln before the Royal Historical Society in London in 1881, delivers a lecture titled "Reminiscences of Lincoln and of Congress During the Rebellion," in an anniversary address marking the death of Lincoln before the New York Genealogical and Biographical Society. The paper is then published by the *New York Genealogical and Biographical Record.*

1883 CIRCA. According to local legend relayed by Illinois State Museum curator of anthropology Jonathan Reyman, a Tlingit chief of the Proud Raven clan named Yalgeewee (Yahl-jeeyi), commissioned a Tshimian carver named Tkleedah (Thleda) to carve a commemorative totem pole to honor his ancestors' first sighting of a white man.

Never having seen a white man, the carver was given pictures of Abraham Lincoln found at a nearby post office and at an Army post. "Lincoln was at that time still the best-known white man in North America," Reyman remarked. "So . . . he carved it into this image which sat on top of the pole." Said to have originally been 51 feet tall (although legend had it at 150 feet tall approximately), the pole was carved at Tongass Village on Tongass Island in southeast Alaska. In the 1930s replicas of the pole were carved by the Civilian Conservation Corps. A five-story fiberglass copy was made in the 1960s. The original deteriorated. A CCC copy ended up in a museum in Ketchikan, Alaska. Another CCC copy found its way to the Illinois State Museum in Springfield, where the fiberglass copy also resides.[19]

1883. Springfield, Illinois, photographer F. McNulty copyrights the C.S. German photograph of Lincoln (O-41) taken January 13, 1861, which was rendered as security engravings in 1861 for use on U.S. currency and bonds by, respectively, engraver Charles Burt for the American Bank Note Co. and a National Bank Note Co. engraver believed to have been George D. Baldwin. Imprinted on the back of McNulty's prints, erroneously, is: "Abraham Lincoln. From an original negative taken in 1861, just before leaving his home for Washington City, and believed to be the only one in existence taken previous to his inauguration as President of the United States. This is the last negative taken of him in Illinois."

1884 FEBRUARY 12. An entirely hand-engraved silver medal recording the award of $1,000 to Captain G. Cottingham by Brigadier General Lafayette C. Baker from the reward pool established by federal authorities for the capture of the Lincoln conspirators, with its engraved likeness of the Lincoln $10 bill image, surpasses its reserve price of $25 and sells for $42 to T. Harrison Garrett in an H.G. Sampson auction sale of the J.C. Hills Collection. That piece has sold only once since. In the 1981 Garrett/Johns Hopkins University auction, it brought $26,000. It was figure 2.15b in *Abraham Lincoln: The Image of His Greatness.*

1884 APRIL 29. The *Buffalo Evening Courier & Republic* reports that the Oldroyd Collection in Springfield, Illinois, has more than 100 Lincoln campaign medals of 1860 and 1864 as well as Old Abe smoking tobacco and a can of Lincoln brand tomatoes.

1884. Notman Photo Co., Boston, produces a composite cabinet-card photograph of Abraham Lincoln and his Union commanders. The seated image of Lincoln is based on the Berger photograph (O-92) taken February 9, 1864, which was then appearing on the nation's $100 bills. A companion cabinet-card photo depicts the Confederate commanders. After cabinet cards of both images were sold to the public, large prints of the Union image were offered to clients by the Travelers Insurance Co. This hearkens to the photographic composites made famous by studio operators during Lincoln's time.

The print's chief appeal is its exceptional fidelity in copying the Berger original. It employs the entire seated portrait and places it in the context of the Union military commanders. Its other distinction is its method of reproduction, which was one of the first successful, commercial uses of the dot-halftone process. The print is truly an artistic success, resplendent in its visual imagery.

1884 NOVEMBER 11. Augustus Saint-Gaudens signs a contract to provide a statue of Abraham Lincoln, not less than 11 feet in height, for the Chicago Parks System. According to John H. Dryfhout, an authority on the work of Saint-Gaudens, the contract was for $10,000.

1885. Sculptor Augustus Saint-Gaudens comes to Cornish, New Hampshire, "to find a place to model his latest commission, a statue of Abraham Lincoln. He chose the area," according to research by a U.S. National Park Service historian, "because he had been told by a friend that it was an area with 'plenty of Lincoln-shaped men.'"[20] Saint-Gaudens would spend summers there through 1897. He used Langdon Morse, "a tall Yankee model," from nearby Windsor, Vermont, as his model. Morse was six feet, four inches in height, and the same build as Lincoln. The sculptor modeled the head and hands after the life casts made by Leonard W. Volk in 1860.[21]

1885. Abolitionist U.S. congressman and Lincoln intimate, Illinoisan Isaac N. Arnold, authors his highly regarded biography *The Life of Abraham Lincoln*, published by Jansen, McClurg & Co., Chicago. In 1866 Arnold had written one of the first of the Lincoln post-assassination biographies, *The History of Abraham Lincoln and the Overthrow of Slavery*, published in Chicago by Clarke & Co.

Arnold, who was a devout evangelical, contended Lincoln too was a "reverent Christian," which other contemporary writers had denied. "He was by nature religious; full of religious sentiment. It is not claimed that he was orthodox. For creeds and dogmas he cared little. But in the great fundamental principles of the Christian religion he was a firm believer. Belief in the existence of God; in the immortality of the soul; in the Bible as the revelation of God to man; in the efficacy and duty of prayer; in reverence toward the Almighty and in love and charity to man, was the basis of his religion."[22]

1885 MARCH 25. Former Lincoln presidential secretary William O. Stoddard, who had published his account of the Lincoln White House entitled *Abraham Lincoln: The True Story of a Great Life* (1884, Fords, Howard & Hulbert, New York City), writes his former colleague John Hay (who with John Nicolay had been working on a monumental insiders' account of their own regarding the professional jealousy exhibited): "I want to say a word or so. I did not suppose I was copying your track or 'taking away your market' and so said in my preface. I have left that unchanged in the edition now going out. Long ago I wrote you and Nicolay that I had a book in my mind and it was my idea, year after year, that yours would come out first. Is it too much to say that the idea died of old age?"[23]

1885. The public could purchase Lincoln medals at the U.S. Mint in Philadelphia at the following prices:[24]

> 3-inch Lincoln Presidential medal (Julian PR-12), copper-bronzed, for $2
>
> 5/8-inch medalets:
>
> > Lincoln-Garfield (Julian PR-41) in fine gold, $4.50
> >
> > Lincoln-Garfield in fine silver (Julian PR-41), 25 cents
> >
> > Lincoln-Washington in silver (Julian PR-31), 25 cents
> >
> > Lincoln-Grant in silver (Julian PR-39), 25 cents
> >
> > Lincoln–broken column in silver (Julian PR-38), 25 cents.

1885 APRIL 17. John Hay circulates part of the draft of the handwritten manuscript of his and John Nicolay's Lincoln biography to Robert Todd Lincoln, "who approved of the effort." The president's son wrote in part: "I read [the manuscript] carefully and was delighted with the way you had done your work." The younger Lincoln had provided access to his father's papers to the authors.

1885. Sculptor Augustus Saint-Gaudens completes a bust of Abraham Lincoln as a study for his monumental standing bronze Lincoln figure to be placed in Chicago two years later. A bronze casting of this model is in the collection of the Saint-Gaudens National Historic Site, a unit of the National Park Service, in Cornish, New Hampshire.

1885/1886 WINTER. The Volk life casts used by August Saint-Gaudens for modeling his standing Lincoln figure for the Chicago Park System are re-discovered in the possession of the sculptor's artist-friend Wyatt Eaton.

1886 FEBRUARY 1. *Century Illustrated Magazine* owner/editor Richard Watson Gilder, sculptor August Saint-Gaudens, and prominent New Yorkers Erwin Davis and Thomas Clark circulate a letter to philanthropists, companies, institutions, and others, soliciting funds to purchase Leonard Volk's original 1860 life mask of Lincoln, and the 1870 mold of the mask Volk had made in Italy. These were to be purchased from the sculptor for presentation to the Smithsonian Institution. Each subscriber to the syndicate was to pay $50 for plaster copies of the mask and also copies of the hands Volk had cast of Lincoln in Springfield following his nomination for president. Subscribing $85 would net the donor bronze copies. Thirty-three individuals and institutions responded to the plea, including Lincoln's former secretary John Hay, novelist Bram Stoker, and Saint-Gaudens himself. Saint-Gaudens supervised the castings. It is unknown how many bronzes were cast. After casting the subscribers' copies, the original mask and the Italian mold, as well as a bronze casting by Saint-Gaudens, were indeed presented to the Smithsonian by 1888.

1886 NOVEMBER. Serialization of John Nicolay and John Hay's Lincoln biography, *Abraham Lincoln: A History,* commences in *The Century Magazine,* continuing without interruption until February 1890. The authors were paid the unprecedented sum of $50,000 for the serialization rights. They had been at work on the project on and off for two decades. "One benefit of serialization was that it allowed the authors to collect additional information from other participants in the events that they described, as knowledgeable readers would write in to make additions and corrections to their work," according to Brown University curator Holly Snyder's exhibition "John Hay's Lincoln & Lincoln's John Hay." The series was a great success for the magazine as it brought it many thousands of new subscribers.

1887 MARCH 9. Poet Walt Whitman complies with John Hay's request to supply him with a handwritten copy of his poem "O Captain! My Captain!" about his emotional reaction to Lincoln's assassination. Hay acknowledges receipt of the poem on March 12.

1887. Robert Todd Lincoln donates Abraham and Mary Todd Lincoln's home in Springfield, Illinois, at Eighth and Jackson streets, to the State of Illinois. His conditions included that it should always be open free to the public, and be well maintained. It was immediately opened to the public, becoming one of the earliest publicly held historical sites in the country.

1887 October 22. Lincoln's only grandson and namesake, 14-year-old Abraham "Jack" Lincoln II, the middle child of Robert Todd Lincoln and Mary Eunice Harlan, unveils Augustus Saint-Gaudens's 12-foot-tall (not including pedestal) standing bronze figure of Lincoln. The president is depicted as if he's just risen from the chair behind him to speak "a few appropriate remarks" in Lincoln Park, on Chicago's north side.[25] The statue, located on the east lawn of the former Chicago Historical Society (presently the Chicago History Museum), is widely acclaimed as the finest Lincoln statue.

Saint-Gaudens had personal memories of Lincoln. As a youth he had observed the president-elect riding in a carriage in New York City.[26] "Lincoln stood tall in the carriage, his dark, uncovered head bent in contemplative acknowledgement of waiting people," Saint-Gaudens later recalled. Further, as a teenager, he recalled his parents crying over news of Lincoln's assassination. He had been one of the mourners to observe the fallen hero's remains lying in state at New York's City Hall, and had even gone through the long queue a second time to fix his mental image of the presidential face.

The sculptor portrayed the heroic figure erect, but deep in thought. The president holds his lapel with his left hand, his right arm behind his back and his legs spread slightly in an easy stance. His head is slightly lowered, so viewers can gaze directly into his eyes. Saint-Gaudens's plaster model was cast in bronze by Henry-Bonnard

Bronze Co., New York. The memorial was such a success that eight years later the city commissioned Saint-Gaudens to provide a suitable second memorial to Lincoln in Chicago. Saint-Gaudens labored for many (12) years on the new work. In 1904, it was lost in a great fire which destroyed much of his work, sketches, and notes. The ailing sculptor finished the work two years later, in 1906, with help from his assistants Henry Hering and Elsie Ward. Saint-Gaudens succumbed from a long bout with cancer on August 3, 1907. His widow finally had the plaster masterpiece cast in bronze in 1908. After an odyssey that took the statue to both coasts for display (to great acclaim) at the Metropolitan Museum of Art in New York City and the 1915 San Francisco World's Fair, the bronze casting spent years in storage awaiting construction of a suitable venue. Saint-Gaudens's seated bronze figure of the Great Emancipator was finally installed to rave reviews in 1926 in Chicago's Grant Park, on the city's south side. It was nearly two decades after the master artist had last laid down his sculptor's tools.

Fig. 2.111. By 1887, when the magnificent standing Lincoln statue by Augustus Saint-Gaudens was dedicated in Lincoln Park, Chicago, other sculptors' works had been erected in Washington, D.C., New York City, San Francisco, Brooklyn, Boston, and Philadelphia. Critics and the public alike marveled at the sensitivity and strength of the new Lincoln monument, declaring it a masterpiece. That acclaim has not faded in the succeeding six score years.

Fig. 2.112. Monuments great and small marked the diffusion of Lincoln consciousness in the decades following his death, as men and women unborn during Lincoln's lifetime learned of his character and legacy. Shortly after the Saint-Gaudens standing Lincoln was dedicated, one observer created this simple yet elegant silhouette shadow portrait of the statue. It was discovered in a Victorian scrapbook.

Fig. 2.113. The Funding Act of March 3, 1883, set revised rates for internal revenue duties, occasioning a new series of Manufactured Tobacco revenue stamps engraved and printed at the Bureau of Engraving and Printing. The Lincoln profile portrait die (BEP MISC633) traces back to BEP engraver Joseph Ourdan in 1867.

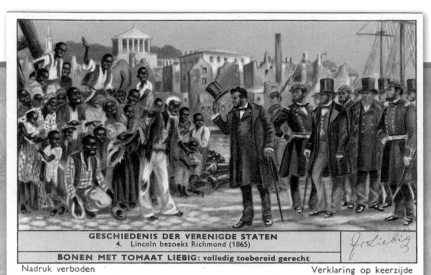

Fig. 2.114. Many of the late-19th-century lithographed trade and collectors' cards were produced in Germany, where the trade flourished. This fine example illustrates Abraham Lincoln being enthusiastically received by the freedmen and women in Richmond on April 4, 1865. It was issued by the Liebig Company in New York. Founded by Justus von Liebig in 1865, the company marketed meat extracts as health supplements.

Fig. 2.115. Isaac N. Arnold was a Lincoln colleague and politician from Illinois. In 1866 and again in 1884 he wrote influential biographies of Old Abe. Here Arnold poses in his study about the time of his second book, *The Life of Abraham Lincoln.*

Fig. 2.116. *Life* magazine (no relation to the Time-Warner periodical which commenced in 1936, when Henry Luce bought up this periodical so he could acquire its name) was a general-interest and humor magazine published 1883 to 1936. In 1887 *Life* published this interesting ad. "Who is it?" Yankee soap was a well-known product; it had been around since 1840. That the bottom portion of Lincoln's likeness alone could be so recognizable as to make this a fun activity for "bright" boys and girls and adults alike and an appealing advertising come-on shows how pervasive this image was in public consciousness by then. The likeness reproduced is not the engraving from the $100 bill but a very close copy of it.

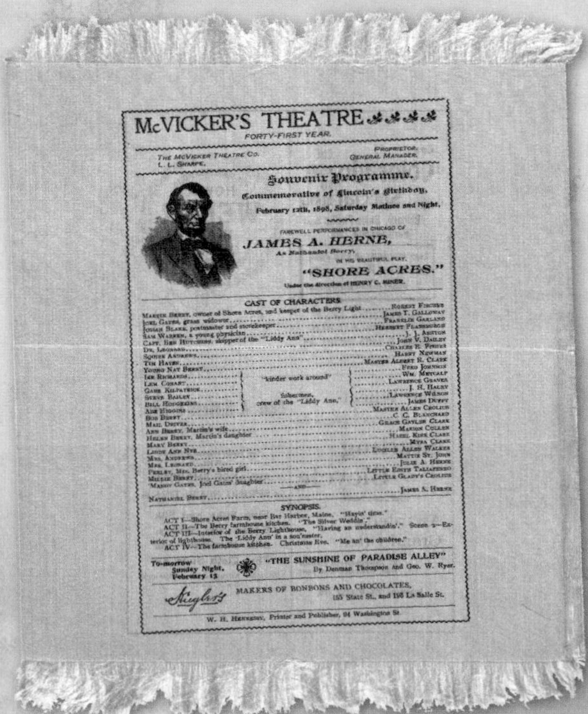

Fig. 2.117. McVicker's Theatre was a principle Chicago entertainment venue established before the Civil War. This fine silk program commemorates the February 12, 1898, staging of *Shore Acres,* honoring the anniversary of Lincoln's birth. The image is the $100 bill design.

Fig. 2.118. Incredibly, this very colorful and detailed chromolithograph that outlines Lincoln's adult achievements is unsigned. We date it to the 1890s. Its recognizable portrait is the $500 bill image.

Fig. 2.119. *Tromp l'oeil* painting was designed to fool the eye by presenting still lifes so realistically detailed that the observer would swear he could pluck the note or photo off the wall rack. The technique goes back to ancient Greece, where artists would paint "windows" in solid walls. John Haberle and John Frederick Peto were two of the principle devotees of this painting style in the United States. Haberle painted his famous *The Changes of Time* in 1888 *(a)*; and Peto his *Reminiscence of 1865* circa the 1890s *(b)*. Both are rich in Lincoln imagery.

Fig. 2.120. This silver-and-enamel Cincinnati Lincoln Club pin dates from around the 1890s.

Fig. 2.121. Homer Lee Bank Note Co. created a Lincoln portrait copied from the $100 money image, after the Berger O-92 photograph. It appeared on ornate Republican National Committee contributor receipts like this one in 1889 and 1890.

Fig. 2.122. Colorful chromolithograph tobacco labels of various brands traded on the public's affinity for Honest Abe, the Great Emancipator. Militarism and emancipation are the calling card for A. Lincoln brand *(a)*, while Compeer encompassed the whole gamut from railsplitter to emancipator for its product "made on honor" *(b)*.

Fig. 2.123. In 1870, S.S. Garrett was a deputy marshal in Shelby County, Tennessee (Memphis). In this election ticket, with its Lincoln $100-style portrait, he was running for sheriff.

Fig. 2.124. In the 1890s Moehle Lithographic Co., Brooklyn, did both of these Lincoln profile portrait labels for Abraham Lincoln cigars.

Fig. 2.125. This copper sign advertising "best quality" warranted sewing-machine needles has both Washington's and Lincoln's familiar money images.

1887 OCTOBER 22. On the same day Saint-Gaudens's Chicago standing figure of Lincoln is dedicated, *Harper's Weekly* features a two-page illustration of the statue. According to the publication: "The tall figure of the Liberator was impressive when in the clay, but the bronze, so soon as the first raw newness of the metal shall have worn off, will be much more imposing by virtue of its appropriateness to the severe treatment of the statue proper. The face itself, with its rugged features . . . forms the center and finishing-point to a figure distinguished beyond any so far seen in the United States for quiet, for introspection, and for a latent life ready to spring into action as the call of the master-mind of the greatest epoch in the history of our land." And continued: "Mr. St. Gaudens has not come at once or by one bound to this masterpiece. Always questioning his own conceptions, only too ready to destroy a model which he suspects to be inferior to his best, he has been long about the Lincoln for Chicago. . . . It is better suited, by its size and attitude as well as the proportions of the bench, to the extensive outlook it enjoys in the Chicago park."[27]

1888 SEPTEMBER. According to an extensive, illustrated article, "Presidential Campaign Medals," by Gustave Kobbé, which appears in *Scribner's Magazine,* Lincoln political medals for the campaign of 1860 number about 200 different types, including the only silver medal of the series to circulate freely "among the people." According to Kobbé, this medal is the Lincoln silver medal with "Free Territory for a Free People" (King-34). Following the Lincoln series of 1860, political medals cease to be noteworthy, in Kobbé's view. "The medals issued during subsequent campaigns are neither so varied nor so interesting in design as those struck off during the Lincoln or previous canvasses."[28]

1889. Shortly after the installation of August Saint-Gaudens's majestic standing Lincoln sculpture in Lincoln Park, Chicago, industrialist John Crerar bequeaths $100,000 to the city's South Park Commission to construct a second Lincoln memorial in the city. Once again, the city turned to Saint-Gaudens. He would spend a dozen years crafting his second masterpiece, *The Head of State.* It shows Lincoln seated on a massive throne draped with an American flag—a pose traditionally reserved for emperors and kings. The nation's CEO gazes downward introspectively, with the weighty cares of his presidency on his shoulders. The sculptor declined the president's head slightly so observers could look right into his eyes. The statue was cast in 1908, after the sculptor's death, by Roman Bronze Works in New York City. That year, it was displayed at the Metropolitan Museum of Art in New York City. It then remained in a storeroom there until it was dusted off and shipped out to the 1915 San Francisco World's Fair. After the exposition it was shipped to Chicago for the first time, but stored again for more than a decade. It would not be officially dedicated in Chicago until May 31, 1926, at Chicago's Grant Park. Architect Stanford White designed an enormous 150-foot semi-circular marble exedra (a low wall with a bench) as a backdrop for the statue, on land reclaimed from Lake Michigan.

1890. The 10-volume *Abraham Lincoln: A History,* the collaboration between Lincoln secretaries John Hay and John Nicolay, is published by The Century Co. This multi-volume biography capped the articles that had been running serially in *The Century Magazine* for more than three years. The biography included many chapters not contained in the periodical series. In addition to providing a great deal of documentary material on Lincoln, the work was also a general history of his times.

1890. Allegheny Park, Pennsylvania, public gardens feature "Lincoln's Portrait in Flowers," preserved by Philadelphia publisher C.H. Graves' sepia stereoviews, sold only by The Universal Photo Art Co.

1891. Sculptor Leonard Volk copyrights his nearly three-foot-tall statue of Abraham Lincoln displaying a copy of the Emancipation Proclamation. Bronze castings, 32.5 inches high on a 10.5-inch bronze circular base, bear his copyright claim in incised lettering along the side of the base.

1891 OCTOBER 31. The *Chicago Tribune* publishes this erroneous origin for the genesis of Alexander Gardner's incomparable "Gettysburg Lincoln" image (O-77):

THE ONLY ACCURATE AND LIFELIKE PHOTOGRAPH IN EXISTENCE. In 1864 Gen. Grant went to Washington to receive his commission as Lieutenant-General. After that ceremony was over—if ceremony it could be called between two such simple men as Grant and Lincoln—some one suggested that the occasion deserved its commemoration to the extent of a photograph of each of the principals. So they went and were photographed. A negative of each was regarded as unsatisfactory by the photographer and thrown aside. A short while ago they were discovered and printed. The pictures here represent these discarded negatives of 1864. This is probably the only true likeness of Abraham Lincoln in existence. It has all the natural defects of the actual face. The smoothing hand of the photographer, usually applied to all negatives, has never been laid upon it. It gives the man as he was, with every element of his character expressed. There is a melancholy deadness about the eyes that makes it very striking. The lower lip is surprisingly prominent. Whoever looks at it could easily appreciate that the original carried all the cares which he was known to bear, but until the eye rests upon the forehead, one's conception of Lincoln's intellectual power is not satisfied.

1891. The Abraham Lincoln Log Cabin Association copyrights a large-format photograph of the Thomas Lincoln cabin on Goosenest Prairie, near Farmington, Illinois (see figure 1.18 in *Abraham Lincoln: The Image of His Greatness*). Copies of this photograph were sold to help transport the cabin to the 1892 World's Columbian Exposition. Following the close of the fair, the cabin disappeared. It has been reconstructed on the original site as the Lincoln Log Cabin State Historic Site, with living interpreters acting in character.

1892 FEBRUARY 12. Attendees at the Lincoln banquet of the Republican Club of New York receive a T. Johnson etching of Lincoln based on an 1861 photograph supplied by Lincoln's register of the Treasury, Lucius E. Chittenden.

1892 MARCH 25. Banknote engraver Charles Burt, who created four Lincoln portraits for U.S. federal paper money and was the most influential engraver of his image during Lincoln's lifetime (and down to the present), dies.

Fig. 2.127. Photographer C.H. Graves recorded "Lincoln's Portrait in Flowers" for a hand-tinted stereoview card in 1890. The man standing behind the cut-shrub display is believed to be the unheralded creator of this Lincoln tribute.

Fig. 2.126. This splendid Abraham Lincoln profile etching by T. (Thomas) Johnson was accomplished circa 1890. Johnson did many similar pieces. The 1912 catalog that Judd Stewart did of his collection listed 17. One is inscribed "Etched for the Republican Club and distributed at its dinner February 12, 1892. From a photograph in the possession of L. E. Chittenden," Chittenden was register of the Treasury during the Lincoln administration. Johnson won a silver medal for a drawing at the Pan-American Exposition.

Fig. 2.128. Henry Bonnard Bronze Co., New York City, produced this unsigned bronze plaque circa 1890.

Fig. 2.129. This splendid Lincoln profile steel-plate security die was engraved in 1892 by Western Bank Note and Engraving Co. in Chicago. Lincoln never looked better!

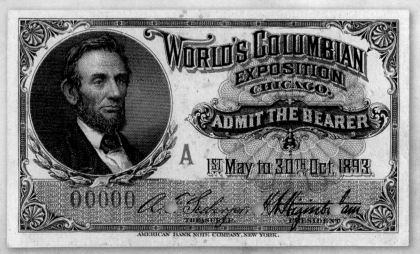

Fig. 2.130. Because the American Bank Note Co. did not capitulate to a petulant U.S. Treasury Department and surrender Charles Burt's excellent 1861 portrait die (ABNCo die 141), it could continue to use it on commercial work. For the second season of the World's Columbian Exposition in Chicago in 1893, ABNCo produced a series of fine admission tickets depicting Columbus, Washington, Franklin, a Native American, and the composer Handel as well as one showing Illinois's favorite son, Abe Lincoln. The Lincoln ticket used a cropped version of ABNCo die 141, shown on this proof that came forward through the American Bank Note Co. archives sales of recent years.

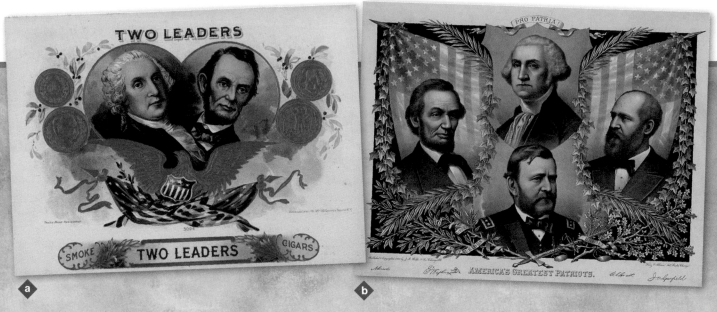

Fig. 2.131. The specifics of these two circa-1890 lithographs differ but their intentions are similar—whether American Leaf Co. is peddling its Two Leaders cigars *(a)*, or J.H. Wolfe & Co., Chicago, is inviting your business with its "America's Greatest Patriots" calendar art *(b)*. Both companies wanted the public to associate them with greatness . . . in products, service, whatever.

Fig. 2.132. Davenport, Iowa, horticulturist O.P. Nichols loved Abraham Lincoln, and he never threw away any scrap of paper with Lincoln's image on it. His paperwork, his checks, and in this case his Union Savings Bank passbook cover, passed down through Iowa dealer Doc Carberry, have proved a collecting bonanza for Lincolnphiles over the past several decades.

Fig. 2.133. Philipp Hake, of Hoboken, New Jersey, patented a process of illuminating embossed paper on April 7, 1891, under which patent this embossed-leather postcard was manufactured by Tanner Souvenir Co., New York. The process applied color to the sides and adjacent areas of the ridges, and a different color to the opposite ridge sides and adjacent areas, "producing a design shaded in two or more colors." These postcard novelties were sold from the 1890s forward, and postally used cards are especially desirable. This card is an excellent embossing in reverse of the Lincoln $500 bill portrait.

Fig. 2.134. Sojourner Truth was a free black abolitionist and women's rights activist, who traveled from Michigan to visit Abraham Lincoln at the White House on October 29, 1864. Around 1893 Albion College professor and artist Franklin C. Courter painted the scene of the woman seated, with Lincoln standing examining a Bible, with the title *Lincoln Showing Sojourner Truth the Bible Presented Him by the Colored People of Baltimore*. The painting was exhibited at the World's Columbian Exposition in 1893, but sadly was lost in a 1902 fire. Fortunately Battlecreek, Michigan, photographer Fred Perry had photographed the canvas, and another Battlecreek photographer, R.D. Bayley, popularized this image as a cabinet-card photo, which was further disseminated through copy photographs and prints. Shown is Bayley's photograph.

1892 MAY 30. Sculptor Leonard Volk's standing bronze figure of Abraham Lincoln holding his Emancipation Proclamation is dedicated at Washington Park, Rochester, New York.

1892 NOVEMBER 19. Shortly after the wide publication of the "Rice" portrait of Abraham Lincoln, Henry C. Whitney's *Life on the Circuit with Lincoln, with Sketches of Generals Grant, Sherman and McClellan, Judge Davis, Leonard Swett, and Other Contemporaries,* is copyrighted. A reproduction of the "Rice" photo serves as the frontispiece in Whitney's massive tome. He attributes this "Gettysburg Lincoln" portrait (O-77)—now known to have been taken by Alexander Gardner on November 8, 1863—thus: "The photographer was Rice, of Washington City. The sitting was had on March 9th, 1864."[29] He also reprints the erroneous *Chicago Tribune* report of March 9, 1864, regarding the occasion when the photograph was alleged to have been taken by "Rice." Ironically, this attribution appears near the back of the book immediately prior to a section in which Whitney attempts to debunk recorded "Mistakes of History" in other writers' accounts of Lincoln. This unfortunate mistake is doubly ironic, of course, because Whitney's book—by accident of history, or by design—was actually copyrighted on the 29th anniversary of Lincoln's brief but famous November 19, 1863, remarks at a battlefield cemetery in Pennsylvania, known to history as his Gettysburg Address.[30]

1892. The Lincoln Memorial Company publishes a photo of an old "Lincoln" cabin in Washington County, Kentucky; a portrait of Lincoln based on the same model (O-92) as the federal $100 note portrait; and photographic copies of Lincoln's parents'—Thomas Lincoln and Nancy Hanks—marriage license.

1892. John Rogers produces a life-size figure of Abraham Lincoln. Rogers's compact, realistic cast-plaster groups—which included,

importantly, *Council of War* (1867), a two-foot-high group approximately 15 inches at the base, showing the trio of Lincoln, Stanton, and Grant—had been very popular in the 1860s, 1870s, and 1880s. Their popularity faded as artistic tastes changed in the 1890s. His life-size 1892 statue would win a bronze medal at the Chicago World's Columbian Exposition the following year, and thereafter would be installed at Manchester, New Hampshire.

1893 AUGUST. Saratoga Springs, New York, had, from the early 1800s, a reputation as a healthy retreat. Late in the century a company at Saratoga, New York, drilled the first of 26 wells on 24 acres it owned in the town to produce carbonic acid gas and carbonated well water. A second well was added in 1894, and in March 1896 this second well was extended to the depth of 426 feet, striking a gusher. "At this depth, or a little less, mineral water was struck. . . . the pressure of gas forced the water out of the pipe to a distance of over 40 feet in the air." This well was named the Lincoln Spring, from which the company took its corporate name, Lincoln Spring Company.

"The water proved a useful and popular mineral water, which was bottled and sold on the market." More wells were drilled, varying in depth from 88 feet to 256 feet, most requiring pumping. The company bottled and sold its mineral water as Saratoga Lincoln Water, and also compressed the carbonic acid gas into liquid form, for sale. Other companies joined drilling in the area.

In 1908 the New York State Legislature feared the natural resource would be depleted. It attempted to stop production of these drilling companies by forbidding accelerating or increasing the flow of percolating waters or natural carbonic acid gas from wells bored into the rock by pumping. Enforcement of the legislation was tied up in the courts. Eventually the State moved against the property claims by enforcing eminent domain, and in 1911 established the New York State Reservation at Saratoga.[31]

Fig. 2.135. Leonard Volk is widely remembered for casting Abraham Lincoln's beardless face and hands in 1860, but much less well known for his Lincoln busts and statues. This excellent Volk likeness of Lincoln holding his Emancipation Proclamation was installed in Rochester, New York, in 1892.

Fig. 2.136. In this 1896 ad Saratoga Lincoln Water was touted as "one of the most wonderful discoveries since . . . ether and chloroform." The medicinal water was praised as a tonic for diabetes, dyspepsia, or insomina.

Fig. 2.137. Saratoga Springs, north of New York City, was reputed to be healthy, and spas and recreational venues opened there, attracting big-city types. The Saratoga Lincoln Spring Co. bottled water from wells in amber-colored bottles like this one in the 1890s.

1893. Cabinet-card photos, likely issued by Osborn H. Oldroyd himself as a promotional venture and souvenir, show the street-elevation view of the Petersen house, with a sign in front of its stairway door to its upper floors: "This house in which Abraham Lincoln died contains the Oldroyd Lincoln Memorial Collection of over 3,000 articles relating to Abraham Lincoln. Open all hours day & evening. Admission 25¢." A U.S. flag flies from the window of the room in which Lincoln expired.

1893 AUGUST 21. George E. Bissell's standing bronze statue showing Lincoln as the Great Emancipator towering over a freed slave is dedicated at Old Carlton Burial Ground, Edinburgh, Scotland.

1894. As an offshoot of their multi-volume Lincoln biographical project, The Century Co. publishes John G. Nicolay and John Hay's *The Complete Works of Abraham Lincoln.*

1894 JULY 4. Architect Levi T. Schofield's bronze relief panels commemorating the Civil War actions of Ohio soldiers and Lincoln's Emancipation are dedicated in the Memorial Room in the base of the Cuyahoga County Soldiers' and Sailors' Memorial in the Public Square, Cleveland, Ohio. The base is surmounted by a 125-foot pillar, with inscribed brass bands, and a statue of Freedom at top, surrounded by an esplanade of bronze sculptural groupings.

1895 JULY 9. Ownership of the Lincoln National Monument (Lincoln's tomb) is transferred from the Lincoln Monument Association to the State of Illinois. The Lincoln Monument Association goes out of existence.

1895. *McClure's Magazine* commences publication of Ida M. Tarbell's series of articles on Abraham Lincoln. The previous year, owner-publisher S.S. McClure, a passionate fan of the Great Emancipator, and editor J.S. Phillips had tasked the hard-driven reporter to "add to our knowledge of Abraham Lincoln by collecting and preserving the reminiscences of such of his contemporaries as were then living," Tarbell recalled. "They established in their editorial rooms what might be called a Lincoln Bureau and from there an organized search was made for reminiscences, pictures and documents."[32]

1895. In a discussion of Abraham Lincoln's kindness, Reverend Wayland Hoyt, DD, recounts the story of Lincoln pardoning the sleeping sentry who had been court-martialed and sentenced to death. The soldier, William Scott, had been sentenced, when Lincoln paid him a visit in the field. "I knew him at once by a Lincoln medal I had long worn.[33] I was scared at first, for I had never before talked with a great man: but Mr. Lincoln was so easy with me, so gentle, that I soon forgot my fright," Hoyt quotes Scott.

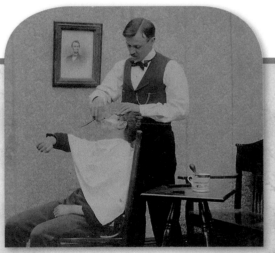

Fig. 2.138. A Gilded Age Broadway gent felt right at home getting spruced up under the watchful eye of the golden Abe from the $500 bill.

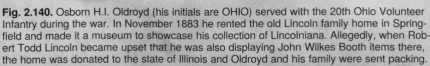

Fig. 2.139. Benjamin S. Whitehead and Chester R. Hoag formed a specialty adverting company in Newark, New Jersey. In 1896 Whitehead & Hoag patented a celluloid pinback button. This advertising button, with a lithographed image similar to the Lincoln $100 portrait, was made shortly thereafter for the American Pepsin Co., which sold chewing gum and was a heavy advertiser on such pinbacks.

Fig. 2.140. Osborn H.I. Oldroyd (his initials are OHIO) served with the 20th Ohio Volunteer Infantry during the war. In November 1883 he rented the old Lincoln family home in Springfield and made it a museum to showcase his collection of Lincolniana. Allegedly, when Robert Todd Lincoln became upset that he was also displaying John Wilkes Booth items there, the home was donated to the state of Illinois and Oldroyd and his family were sent packing.

Oldroyd landed on his feet. With government permission, he moved his family into the Petersen House, where Lincoln had died, across the street from Ford's Theatre. He turned that house into a museum, too, charged the curious a quarter to view the artifacts, and lived there with his family rent free. This circa-1893 photograph shows the house and its marquee. After years of negotiations, in 1926 the government purchased the 3,000-piece Oldroyd collection of Lincolniana for $50,000. The collection was eventually moved to Ford's Theatre, where items Oldroyd had owned are still on public display.

In conversation, Lincoln says he believes the man could not stay awake; he won't be shot the following day, but he had caused the president considerable trouble to venture down to see him.

How will you pay my bill? Lincoln asked the soldier.

Misunderstanding Lincoln's intentions, Scott suggested he could pay out of his bounty that was in the bank. "Then Mr. Lincoln put his hands on my shoulders, and looked into my face as if he was sorry, and said: 'My boy, my bill is a very large one. Your friends cannot pay it, nor your bounty, nor the farm, nor all your comrades! There is only one man in all the world who can pay it, and his name is William Scott! If from this day William Scott does his duty, so that, if I was there when he comes to die, he can look me in the face as he does now, and say, I have kept my promise, and I have done my duty as a soldier, then my debt will be paid.'"

Scott promised. The private served admirably and was killed in action.[34]

1896 January 31. S.S. McClure Co. publishes Ida M[inerva]. Tarbell's *The Early Life of Lincoln,* with 160 illustrations "and masses of new material." Tarbell, noted chiefly as a muckraking anti-monopoly journalist, "made it her business to seek out the men who had known Lincoln and were still living in the '90s, and to get from them their own homely and often not entirely consistent accounts of what Lincoln said and did in their daily companionship with him. In this way Miss Tarbell made a book of surpassing human interest, and undoubtedly preserved much valuable material that might otherwise have been lost," Lincoln historian Albert Shaw wrote.[35] *McClure's Magazine* had begun publishing Tarbell's Lincoln articles in 1895. The magazine set up a "Lincoln Bureau" to popularize Lincoln with the public. Also during this period, the magazine published many hitherto unknown or little-known images of Lincoln that were turned up by Tarbell's investigations.

1896 February 12. Jersey City Lincolnite Edwin Manners records in his diary: "A fine day; the air, cold and crisp. It is the anniversary of Lincoln's birth, and it is observed for the first time as a legal holiday, but only partially and quietly by the people, who have not fully waked up to the occasion or whose practical sense demurs at another added to our growing list of *dies non.* Our local Lincoln association, the original of its kind in America, holds its annual dinner with speeches, this evening, at Taylor's [sic] Hotel."

1896 December 18. William R. O'Donovan's bronze figure of an equestrian Lincoln is dedicated as part of the evolving design of Brooklyn's Prospect Park Plaza Soldiers' and Sailors' Memorial Arch. The arch has a companion equestrian figure of General Ulysses S. Grant (also by O'Donovan). Both riders' horses were the work of Thomas Eakins. The monument would be designated a landmark in 1973 by the New York Landmarks Preservation Commission.

Fig. 2.141. The Soldiers' and Sailors' Arch monument at the Grand Army Plaza in Brooklyn, dedicated in 1892, incorporated these bronze facing panels under the arch circa 1896, honoring Lincoln *(a)* and Grant *(b)*, commander and commanding general, on horseback. The men were sculpted by William Rudolf O'Donovan, and the horses by Thomas Eakins.

1897 MARCH 15. In a paper on political medals before the American Numismatic Society, collector Andrew C. Zabriskie says: "Abraham Lincoln has had more medals struck in his honor than any other president or presidential candidate, with the exception of Washington." And further, "The number of materials composing medals is probably more varied in the case of Lincoln than any other candidate, for I have specimens made from celluloid, india-rubber, wood, leather and even soap, which latter, however, I regret to say old Father Time is fast reducing to an unrecognizable mass."[36] Zabriskie also railed against absurd mules, such as a Lincoln die mated with a Dutch Church medal. "What should anyone imagine who comes across this medal, but that the bust of the obverse represented some good old Dutch dominie, who officiated at that church?" he asked reproachfully. The object of Zabriskie's scorn, New York die sinker George H. Lovett's Old Middle Dutch Church medal (King-28), is not even the most outrageous example

he could have cited of the multiplicity of pieces issued solely to wring additional moolah out of collectors who chase their collecting passions in folly.

1897 OCTOBER 20. A decade after the unveiling of his triumphant *Standing Lincoln* figure in Chicago's Lincoln Park, Augustus Saint-Gaudens is awarded a second commission to produce a monumental statue of Lincoln for display in the Chicago Park System. This time the sculptor's model was Amos Bixby, another man of Lincoln's height and build, from the Cornish area, according to Saint-Gaudens authority John H. Dryfhout. Saint-Gaudens's first clay model was destroyed in the sculptor's studio fire in 1904. The second model, recreated from photographs by Saint-Gaudens with extensive assistance by Henry Hering and Elsie Ward, would be completed in 1906. According to Dryfhout it was cast by Roman Bronze Foundry in New York City in that year.[37] Other sources state that it was cast posthumously in 1908.[38] It would be displayed at New York City's Metropolitan Museum of Art in 1908, very

FRANK LESLIE'S
SCENES AND PORTRAITS
OF THE
CIVIL WAR.

Fig. 2.142. The 50-cent Fractional Currency, with its portrait based on Anthony Berger's O-97/98 photograph, failed when it was overtaken by counterfeiters—surely through no fault of the engraver, Charles Burt, who provided an excellent likeness for currency use. After that failure, a so-called 1864 "life portrait" by artist Francis B. Carpenter, as replicated by Frederick Halpin's engraving, became the vehicle for popularizing this intimate Lincoln portrait. Halpin's engraving appeared on the title page of *Frank Leslie's Scenes and Portraits of the Civil War* in 1894. The work included many of the finest woodcut engravings that had appeared in the newspaper contemporaneous to the events, and was edited by Louis Shepheard Moat, with an introduction by Joseph B. Carr.

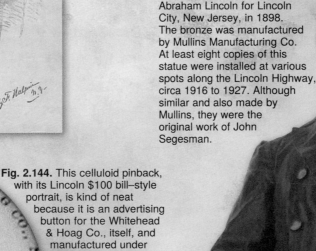

Fig. 2.143. Alonzo (Alfonso) Pelzer sculpted this figure of Abraham Lincoln for Lincoln City, New Jersey, in 1898. The bronze was manufactured by Mullins Manufacturing Co. At least eight copies of this statue were installed at various spots along the Lincoln Highway, circa 1916 to 1927. Although similar and also made by Mullins, they were the original work of John Segesman.

Fig. 2.144. This celluloid pinback, with its Lincoln $100 bill–style portrait, is kind of neat because it is an advertising button for the Whitehead & Hoag Co., itself, and manufactured under the Newark, New Jersey, firm's 1896 advertising-button patent.

likely in conjunction with its casting at Roman Bronze Works in that year. At nine feet tall, the seated Lincoln in this statue is slightly larger than the 12-foot-tall standing Lincoln in Saint-Gaudens's earlier effort, were Lincoln also to rise from his chair in Grant Park. (See entry for 1908 March 2.)

1898 MAY 30. Alonzo (Alfonso) Pelzer's seven-and-a-half-foot-tall pressed-and-hammered-copper statue of Abraham Lincoln as Emancipator is installed on a base seven feet tall, at Mountain Avenue and Lincoln Boulevard, Middlesex Borough, New Jersey. According to the Smithsonian American Art Museum Art Inventories Catalog, the work had been commissioned on January 8, 1898. The statue, formed of copper sheeting, was manufactured by W.H. Mullins Co., Salem, Ohio, for real-estate developer Silas D. Drake, according to a letter of agreement dated June 4, 1898. The purchase price was $700. "On the day the statue was dedicated, the southern part of Middlesex Borough was officially named Lincoln," according to a local historian.

Lincoln statue researcher Dave Wiegers relates that the Mullins Company formed their hammered-copper statues between positive and negative dies in pieces, which were fastened together to make the final statues. "As I understand the process," writes Wiegers, "a positive and a negative of each individual piece was made. The lower die was cast in zinc and the upper die was made of lead. The upper die was fastened to a drop hammer." The copper sheets were heated, "then placed between the dies on large presses and smashed into place. Since the hot stamping was not perfect, workers made the final perfection of the stamping (process) with hammering." Pieces were then soldered together. "When the joint was smoothed, it was almost invisible."[39]

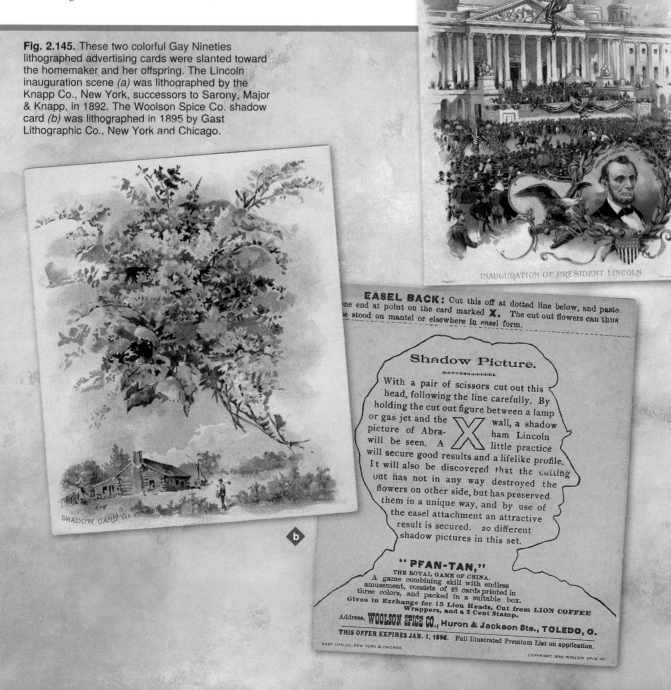

Fig. 2.145. These two colorful Gay Nineties lithographed advertising cards were slanted toward the homemaker and her offspring. The Lincoln inauguration scene *(a)* was lithographed by the Knapp Co., New York, successors to Sarony, Major & Knapp, in 1892. The Woolson Spice Co. shadow card *(b)* was lithographed in 1895 by Gast Lithographic Co., New York and Chicago.

1899 February 13. Booker T. Washington addresses the annual Lincoln observance at the Union League of Philadelphia. Washington had been scheduled to speak the previous night at the League's "Lincoln Dinner," but a violent snowstorm delayed his arrival.

1899 April 8. The Grolier Club, 29 East 32nd Street, New York City, mounts an imperial exhibition of "Engraved and Other Portraits of Lincoln" for two weeks, ending April 22, ably cataloged by Charles Henry Hart.

"This catalogue is the first attempt to make a systematic record of the engraved portraits of Abraham Lincoln, sixteenth President of the United States; and never before, as far as can be ascertained, has a special exhibition of them been undertaken," Hart wrote in the catalog's introduction. "Interest in everything pertaining to Lincoln is on the steady increase, and many valuable collections have been formed of his portraits, of the literature pertaining to him, and of personal memorials." Hart predicted presciently: "The Lincoln cult is only in its infancy. It has had but a single generation in which to grow; but as the perspective of time brings into grander

relief the noble proportions of its subject, homage and admiration for him will be bounded only by the civilized world."

The catalog and the exhibition itself (presumably) included more than 200 Lincoln images and related items owned by members of the Grolier Club, supplemented by items belonging to Major W.H. Lambert and W.C. Crane. Paintings, photographs, medals, lithographs, and engravings were on display. Significant engravings included:

No. 4, a proof on India paper, die no. 323 said to have been utilized by the U.S. Treasury to print the Lincoln 50-cent Fractional Currency portrait but actually a similar die produced by Baldwin &Gleason Co.

No. 5, a pair of Bureau [of] Engraving and Printing die proofs of an unspecified Lincoln portrait (probably the $100 bill vignette)

No. 20, by Charles Burt, an incomplete proof likely of the $500 Gold Certificate portrait vignette.

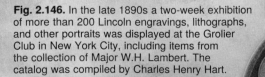

Fig. 2.146. In the late 1890s a two-week exhibition of more than 200 Lincoln engravings, lithographs, and other portraits was displayed at the Grolier Club in New York City, including items from the collection of Major W.H. Lambert. The catalog was compiled by Charles Henry Hart.

Fig. 2.147. This proof for the 1897 Lincoln Association of Jersey City banquet program employs the Baldwin & Gleason Lincoln image, ofttimes confused with the Lincoln Fractional Currency portrait.

Fig. 2.148. Cincinnati diesinker James Murdock Jr. cut the dies for this 32nd National Grand Army of the Republic Encampment medal (King-400) with its Lincoln, Washington, and McKinley portraits, a view of Cincinnati's bridge, Tyler-Davidson fountain, and an incline railroad. The reverse honors "The Three War Presidents of the U.S. of A."—a nod to the American Revolution, the Civil War, and the Spanish-American War.

Other engravings listed included the famous Lincoln works of John Chester Buttre, Thomas Doney, H.B. Hall, W.G. Jackman, T. Johnson, John D. Lovett, John C. McRae, William E. Marshall, George E. Perrine, Alexander H. Ritchie, William and Samuel Sartain, and other engravers. Highlights included the magnificent large mezzotints of John Sartain, Ritchie's engraving of Carpenter's *First Reading of the Emancipation Proclamation,* Frederick Halpin's engraving of Carpenter's life portrait, and Henry Gugler's engraving of Littlefield's painting, as well as foreign engraved Lincoln portraits from Germany, London, and Paris.

Lithographic portraits included the work of Louis Prang, J.H. Bufford, J. Magee, Kimmel & Forster, Currier & Ives, Major & Knapp, William Smith, and others.

Paintings included Francis B. Carpenter's black-and-white oil portrait from life that was a study for his Emancipation Proclamation canvas; Carpenter's black-and-white oil painting of the Lincoln family that served as a model for a Buttre engraving; Thomas Nast's black-and-white drawing of Lincoln entering Richmond, done in January 1868 and property of the Union League Club of New York; and several paintings by David Hunter Strother.

Medallic portraits included Charles Calverley's 10.75-inch circular bronze bas relief; a "bronze gilded" example of Franky Magniadas's French subscription medal, the original gold of which was presented to widow Mary Todd Lincoln; as well as a Calverley plaster medallion profile portrait that was the original model for the marble bas relief he executed for the Union League Club in 1869.

There were also bronze casts of the 1860 Volk life mask and Volk's casts of Lincoln's hands, both recast from the first replicas of the originals by Volk in New York City in 1884 and 1886, respectively, for R.W. Gilder.

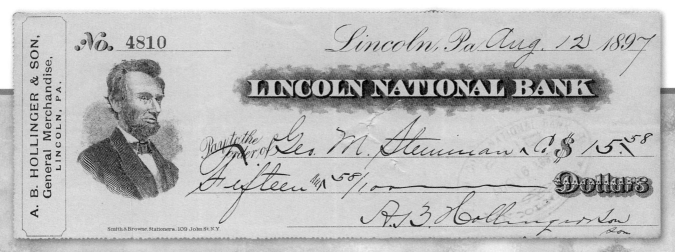

Fig. 2.149. Smith & Browne, Stationers, New York City, printed this check for the Lincoln National Bank of Lincoln, Pennsylvania. The Lincoln portrait is styled after the Brady O-87 1864 photograph. At one time the present author owned hundreds of these 19th-century checks on this account, and gave them away freely to purchasers of *Abraham Lincoln: The Image of His Greatness* as thank-yous.

Fig. 2.150. By 1899 Abraham Lincoln had been represented on U.S. federal government paper money eight times, on $10, $20, $100, $500, and 50-cent notes, by four different engraved portraits. All had been engraved by Charles Burt, whose many money images make him undoubtedly the most important engraver of Lincoln images in the 19th century. These notes circulated by the tens of millions, making Lincoln's image recognizable to every man, woman, and child in the country. Furthermore, they were widely copied in many additional media, reinforcing correct perceptions of Lincoln as patriot, statesman, honest broker, emancipator, and savior of the nation.

By century's end, however, change was in the wind. Change took many forms: the United States became an imperial nation with an overseas empire; women entered the workforce by droves, unleashed by such new inventions as the typewriter; and on the nation's folding currency a new dominant Lincoln image emerged. Hardly as insignificant as its small size might suggest, G.F.C. Smillie engraved both the small Lincoln and the companion Grant portraits for the face of the Series of 1899 $1 Silver Certificate. As can be seen on this specimen Series of 1899 $1 note (type of Friedberg-226), the principle vignette on the note's face is "The Eagle of the Capitol," the so-called Black Eagle from which collectors derive the note's nickname.

(a)

(b)

Fig. 2.151. Commencing in 1895 and continuing for several years, *McClure's Magazine* author Ida M. Tarbell uncovered much new information and unheralded photographs, which S.S. McClure published. He doubled his circulation from the reader interest these Lincoln pieces created. Shown is the February 1896 *McClure's* cover *(a)*. Many magazines followed suit, or at least paid lip service to the growing interest in Lincoln, usually in the publication's issues of February (Lincoln's birth month), April (Lincoln's death month) or November (when Lincoln gave his Gettysburg Address). Also shown is the cover of the February 1899 *Self Culture (b)*, which features a learned account by a PhD and a fine reproduction of the Berger O-91 photograph appearing on the $500 Gold Certificates.

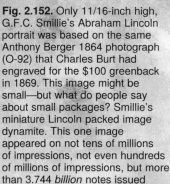

Fig. 2.152. Only 11/16-inch high, G.F.C. Smillie's Abraham Lincoln portrait was based on the same Anthony Berger 1864 photograph (O-92) that Charles Burt had engraved for the $100 greenback in 1869. This image might be small—but what do people say about small packages? Smillie's miniature Lincoln packed image dynamite. This one image appeared on not tens of millions of impressions, not even hundreds of millions of impressions, but more than 3.744 *billion* notes issued during the next 24 years. These were $1 notes that circulated everywhere, down to the lowest transactions and smallest pockets. Furthermore, when such notes got grimy, the Treasury laundered them and sent them back into the streams of commerce.

Smillie's Lincoln on the dollar and Burt's similar Lincoln on the $100 co-circulated for more than two decades, completely swamping any competing Lincoln image in the public mind. Once again, as Carl Sandburg had observed regarding Lincoln's Civil War money images, the Lincoln on the dollar bill was the Lincoln people knew, and became the Lincoln that adorned schoolroom walls, graced book covers, and launched advertising campaigns.

Fig. 2.153. I purchased this brief typed note signed by Bureau of Engraving and Printing Director Claud M. Johnson from my longtime friend, Chicago dealer Dennis Forgue, many years ago. Dennis had discovered it and brought it to the Memphis Paper Money Show especially for me to see. Although Lincoln is not shown, I regard this note as one of my most precious Lincoln items. On February 3, 1899, in the week before Lincoln's birthday, Director Johnson forwarded a proof impression (shown at left) of Smillie's Lincoln portrait to his boss, Treasury assistant secretary William B. Howell. Soon Americans across the nation would have the opportunity to see Smillie's work, too, on their $1 bills.

Fig. 2.154. On June 2, 1890, the U.S. government introduced a dark-brown four-cent definitive postage stamp (Scott 222), engraved and printed by the American Bank Note Co. This is a close copy of the O-92 pose, but actually is based on a portrait painted by John H. Littlefield, who slightly altered Lincoln's bangs to clean up his widow's cap. In 1894 the Bureau of Engraving and Printing took over printing the stamps, and triangles were engraved in the upper corners. On June 20, 1898, the United States seized the Spanish island of Guam, in the Pacific, during the Spanish-American War. Thirteen months later, on July 7, 1899, the United States introduced its own postage stamps, overprinted GUAM, to the island. Only 50 sheets of 100 (5,000 total) of the four-cent Lincoln issue (Scott A90) were overprinted for use there.

Fig. 2.155. This Lincoln bond-coupon vignette proof is puzzling. The portrait is unmistakably a closer crop of Smillie's 1899 Silver Certificate portrait. According to Dr. Franklin Noll, contract historian at the Bureau of Engraving and Printing Historical Resource Center, the vignette was used on a bond coupon.

Fig. 2.156. Silas H. Dunning was secretary of a social organization (founded in Chicago in 1884) that took Lincoln's name. William Dewitt Dunning (no doubt related) was the group's president. Both Dunnings were employed by Illinois railroads. Lincoln Council No. 68 National Union organized annual Lincoln Day celebrations on February 12 in Chicago, beginning in 1888. The 1890 affair drew a crowd of 3,000 to Central Music Hall. The society's logo appropriated the Lincoln O-92 money image.

Fig. 2.157. The recipient of this colorful red-white-and-blue badge in 1900 was the vice president of the Lincoln-McKinley Association of Veteran Voters of the United States, headquartered in St. Louis. The group prided itself on owning a flag that was waved at the time Abraham Lincoln carried the party's presidential nomination at the 1860 Republican Convention in Chicago. Once again, the Lincoln portrait is the money image based on the O-92 photo.

Fig. 2.158. If G.F.C. Smillie's Lincoln portrait on the dollar bill was the left jab of Lincoln imagery, Marcus Baldwin's 1903 engraved portrait based on the same model was a right cross when it was introduced on the five-cent definitive postage stamp (Scott 304) a little over three years later. First issued January 20, 1903, this new series of stamps replaced the Series 1894 Bureau-issue stamps. Baldwin's portrait is nearly indistinguishable from the dollar portrait, and an excellent case study in branding. Almost overnight virtually all the official Lincoln imagery flowing from government presses (except the high-value Gold Certificates) and seen by the average citizen was this one-and-the-same image.

Fig. 2.159. This small (about four inches square), irregularly shaped plaque (King-944) was sculpted by Paul W. Morris and cast by Henry Bonnard Bronze Co. Founders, New York. It was a table favor for a 1900 Lincoln Day Dinner.

Fig. 2.160. Lincoln Carriage Co., Greensburg, Indiana, manufactured "high grade" vehicles, and took for its logo a Lincoln portrait of the style of the high-grade Lincoln $500 note redeemable in gold. Interestingly, the company came by its name natively. It was founded in 1829 by L. and A. Lincoln, and owned from 1880 by Levi A. Lincoln. It manufactured sleighs, landaus, phaetons, open buggies, carriages, and democrats (note, a democrat carriage was a small, simple buggy of the cheapest kind).

1900 February. Andrew C. Zabriskie, Henry Russell Drowne, and Woodbury G. Langdon organize an exhibit of American historical medals and coins at the American Numismatic and Archaeological Society—"the history of the American continent, told in coins and medals." Zabriskie's contribution was his medals of Abraham Lincoln. The exhibition was open to the public, and in May it would be sent to Paris for display at the World's Fair.

1900 February 12. Poet Edwin Markham reads his "Lincoln, the Man of the People" at a Lincoln birthday celebration in New York City. The poem had been requested by the Republican Club of New York City, which held the dinner. Markham's poem was later published in his book *Lincoln and Other Poems,* printed in October 1901 by McClure, Phillips & Co. He also recited the poem at the dedication of the Lincoln Memorial in 1922, an event which appeared in a four-minute-long newsreel. In that year a new edition of "Lincoln, the Man of the People" appeared with 17 etchings by Bernhardt Wall. Markham recited this and his "Ode to Abraham Lincoln" at poetry readings, and signed many broadside imprints of this famous poem for those attending these events.

1900. Doubleday & McClure Co. and McClure, Phillips & Co. publish Ida M. Tarbell's four-volume *The Life of Abraham Lincoln,* drawn from original sources and containing many speeches, letters, and telegrams thitherto unpublished, and illustrated with many reproductions from original paintings, photographs, and other images.

1900 May 30. Sculptor Charles H. Niehaus's seated bronze statue of Abraham Lincoln is installed at Hackley Square, Muskegon, Michigan.

1901. M.P. Rice copyrights Alexander Gardner's August 9, 1863, photograph (Ostendorf-70) of a seated Abraham Lincoln resting his arm on a book on a table. It will be remembered that it was Rice who, earlier, copyrighted Gardner's "Gettysburg Lincoln" image, in 1891.

1901 September 26. Lincoln's mortal remains are interred for a final time in the rebuilt Lincoln Memorial in Springfield, Illinois.

1902 May 23. Sculptor William Granville Hastings's bronze statue *Lincoln and Liberty* is installed at Rockdale and Main avenues in Avondale, Cincinnati, Ohio. The monument was the gift of Union veteran and shipping magnate Charles Clinton, who gave it to the Cincinnati Public Schools. The cost of the 19-foot-high memorial was reportedly $4,000. (Another account states the statue was unveiled December 23, 1902.)

1902 September 30. A seated bronze figure of Abraham Lincoln by sculptor Charles H. Niehaus is installed in the Grand Court inside the Buffalo & Erie County Historical Society. In the 1930s it would be moved to a position at the south portico steps of the building.

1903 April 12. The Nebraska legislature creates the Lincoln Centennial Memorial Association, and approves state funds for the creation of a suitable memorial at the Nebraska State Capitol in the city of Lincoln (for which Abraham Lincoln was the namesake). In 1909 the association would commission Daniel Chester French to provide a statue. His standing bronze figure shows Lincoln in a relaxed stance, with hands clasped in front of him as if he had just finished delivering his Gettysburg Address. Architect Henry Bacon, who also later collaborated with French on the Lincoln Memorial, provided the set-ting for French's statue: a pedestal and a granite backdrop on which the text of the speech is inscribed. The memorial would be dedicated on September 2, 1912, with the principal speaker being the noted, golden-throated orator and native son, William Jennings Bryan.

1903 June 19. A bronze near-replica of sculptor George Bissell's standing statue of Lincoln for Edinburgh, Scotland (without the prostrate freed slave), is erected in Clermont, Iowa, the gift to his hometown of former Iowa governor William Larrabee, who had admired Bissell's 1893 work. Bissell's facsimile stands in Lincoln Park in Clermont.

1903 June 23. Presbyterian minister Louis Albert Banks, DD, traces the history of the Lincoln Legion abstinence society organized by Dr. Howard H. Russell's Anti-Saloon League the previous year. Banks's pamphlet, *The Lincoln Legion: The Story of Its Founder and Forerunners,* was published by The Mershon Co. According to the author, Lincoln's example as a total-abstinence lawyer and anti-liquor orator should inspire others to take up his cause. The League circulated pledge cards requesting individuals to sign by classes—the Red Pledge, limited to a time stated on the card; the White Pledge, for total lifetime abstinence; or the Blue Pledge, for children until up to age 21, renewable for life after reaching 15 years of age.

1903. To mark the 55th anniversary of the Lincoln-Douglas debates, President Theodore Roosevelt dedicates a plaque in "Debate Square," Freeport, Illinois.

1903 October 29. Sculptor Charles Mulligan's heroic-sized bronze statue of Lincoln as an orator is dedicated at Rosamond Grove Cemetery, near the town of Rosamond, Illinois. The work was the gift of Captain John and Mary Kitchell, in memory of Union soldiers and sailors and their commander-in-chief. The base is inscribed with a portion of Lincoln's Gettysburg Address. Captain Kitchell said the statue was meant to "emphasize in the loftiest and most impressive manner the sublime thoughts which [Lincoln] had uttered on that memorable occasion." A duplicate is at Oak Woods Cemetery in Chicago.

1904. The Century Co. brings out a new printing of Nicolay and Hay's 10-volume *Abraham Lincoln: A History.*

1904. John Frederick Peto paints *Lincoln and the 25 Cent Note,* a *trompe l'oeil* still life showing a wooden board with an Abraham Lincoln portrait and other objects tacked to it. In the lower-right corner a Fractional Currency note is pasted to the board. The dates of Lincoln's birth and death are scratched into the wood. Peto painted several other *trompe l'oeil* paintings with Lincoln themes: *Portrait of Lincoln* (1899), *Lincoln and the Star of David* (1904), *Reminiscence of 1865* (1897, current location unknown), and *Reminiscences of 1865* (1897, at the Minneapolis Institute of Arts). In each instance observed, Peto's model for the Lincoln portrait was a carte de visite or cabinet photo of the O-92 pose.

1904 March 6. The *New York Times* publishes an illustration and notice lamenting the destruction of the "priceless" stuffed mascot, Old Abe, of the Eighth Wisconsin Infantry Regiment, at the recent fire in the Wisconsin State Capitol. Once, after the war, P.T. Barnum had unsuccessfully offered $20,000 for the privilege of exhibiting the bird, the account read.

1904 September 7. William Granville Hastings's bronze statue of *Lincoln and Liberty* is unveiled at Bunker Hill, Illinois, at the intersection of North Washington Street and Fayette Street. It is said to be one of four in existence. Union veteran Captain Charles Clinton donated the statue to the community during a Grand Army of the Republic celebration attended by 700 people, including Illinois's wartime governor, Richard Yates.

Fig. 2.161. This circa-1900 bronze plaque appears to be signed "J. Mueller." It measures 9.75 inches in its longest dimension.

Fig. 2.162. William Granville Hastings's *Lincoln and Liberty* monument was dedicated in Bunker Hill, Illinois, on September 7, 1904. A similar group had been installed in Cincinnati two years earlier. The standing figure of Lincoln minus Liberty was erected at the Green County Court House, Jefferson, Iowa.

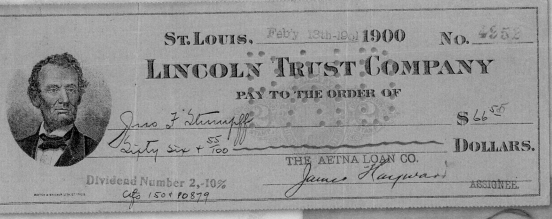

Fig. 2.163. Buxton & Skinner Lith., St. Louis, employed a likeness similar to the $500 Gold Certificate (based on the Berger O-91 photograph) on this turn-of-the-century Aetna Loan Co. dividend check drawn on the Lincoln Trust Company of St. Louis.

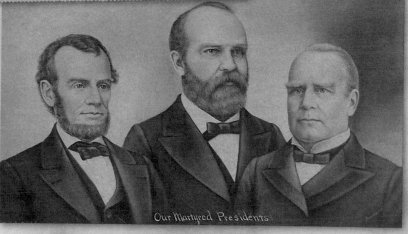

Fig. 2.164. In 1901 the dark cloud of praesicide cast its long shadow across the land once again. This cabinet-card-size photo on a jumbo mount, by "Shaw," is titled "Our Martyred Presidents." The composite includes a Lincoln image taken from a print based on the same source as the Lincoln money images on the $1 Silver Certificate and $100 Legal Tender Note.

1905 February 10. The forerunner of the Lincoln National Life Foundation, Fort Wayne, Indiana, acquires John Rogers's *The Council of War* statue depicting Lincoln, Stanton, and Grant.

1905 March 25. Sculptor Charles J. Mulligan's standing bronze figure of a youthful Lincoln as a railsplitter is installed at Garfield Park, Chicago, Illinois, according to Donald Charles Curham—however, local sources contend the statue was erected in 1911. Either way, it was donated by the city's West Park commissioners. It is located northwest of the intersection of Central Park Avenue and Washington Boulevard.

1905 June 12. Fort Wayne, Indiana, attorney Perry Randall urges the name "Lincoln" be adopted for a new insurance company. He argued that the name of Abraham Lincoln would convey to prospective customers a powerful message of integrity. Board member Randall's exact quote was: "We want a name so proud that men and women will give their lives to keep it stainless. We want a name so simple and strong that the whole world will remember it and love it. There is only one name in all the world that will fill these requirements, Abraham Lincoln."

Seven weeks later, on July 28, the new company would request from Lincoln's only living heir, his son Robert, permission to use a picture of the martyred president on its letterhead. Robert replied on August 3: "I find no objection whatever to the use of a portrait of my father upon the letterhead of such a life insurance company named after him as you describe; and I take pleasure in enclosing you, for that purpose, what I regard as a very good photograph of him." The company adopted the Marshall engraving of Lincoln as its logo.

At some later date Robert Todd Lincoln furnished managers of the company a copy of Anthony Berger's February 9, 1864, photograph of his father (O-92), which he preferred, and which was then

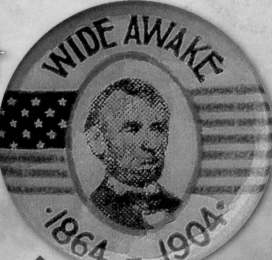

Fig. 2.165. At the turn of the century, a portrait based on the Gardner "Gettysburg Lincoln" image (O-77)—taken two weeks before Lincoln's famous battlefield-cemetery dedication address— highlights this splendid colored Ever First cigar-box inner lid for the nickel cigar. Gardner's exquisite photograph was not an important Lincoln image until it was rediscovered by M.P. Rice, who copyrighted it and released cabinet cards printed from Gardner's original 1863 glass-plate negative, in 1891. For the generation in between, it was almost unknown, but after that time it came to be an important model for book and periodical illustrations of the Great Emancipator.

Fig. 2.166. In 1904 both this splendid Lincoln pop-out half dollar (possibly a souvenir of the St. Louis World's Fair) *(a)* and this red-white-and-blue Wide Awake political pin *(b)* employed the ubiquitous Lincoln money image.

widely current in engraved form in public circulation on the $1 bill and the $100 bill. Engravings based on this photograph by G.F.C. Smillie and Charles Burt, respectively, then graced the Series of 1899 $1 Silver Certificates (Friedberg-226) and the Series of 1880 $100 United States Notes (F-181, and various additional varieties). Most 21st-century readers would know this image, however, as the portrait of Lincoln that has appeared on $5 notes of various classes for most of the preceding century, from the large-size Series of 1914 Federal Reserve Notes (F-832–891) through small-size $5 notes of various classes to the Federal Reserve Note of the Series of 1995 (F-1985).

Early on the company adopted the tagline "Its Name Indicates Its Character," attached to an image of Lincoln, generally a representation of the $5 image or (earlier) a copy of Marshall's painting and engraving. This may be seen on examples of the company's logo with both the Marshall and the Berger Lincoln portraits.

1905 June 14. *Lincoln, the Orator,* a bronze standing statue by Charles J. Mulligan, depicting Lincoln clutching papers in his left hand and raising his right arm to emphasize a rhetorical point, is erected in Oak Woods Cemetery on Chicago's South Side in the presence of the graves of many Union and Confederate deceased.

1905 August 28. Thomas Lincoln's farm is ordered sold on the courthouse steps of Hodgenville, Kentucky. Three bidders vied at the auction. One, a whiskey distiller, "planned to use the property to advertise his 'Lincoln Birthplace Whiskey,'" according to Jonathon Mann. The winning bidder, representing *Collier's Magazine,* paid $3,600. "A year of fund raising by members of The Lincoln Farm Association (including Samuel Gompers and William Jennings Bryan) was sufficient to restore the cabin to its original site," Mann added.[40] Additional fundraising was undertaken by the association, for upkeep.

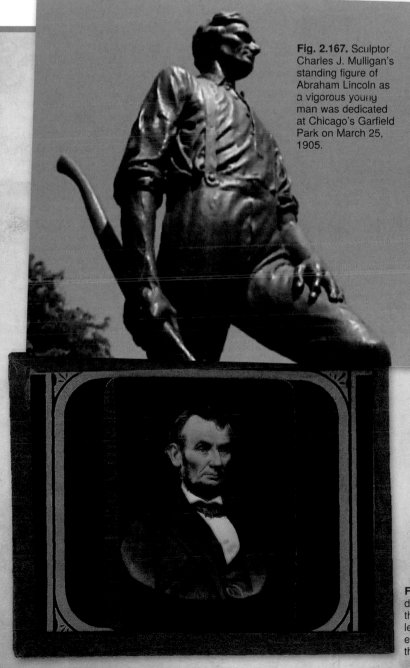

Fig. 2.167. Sculptor Charles J. Mulligan's standing figure of Abraham Lincoln as a vigorous young man was dedicated at Chicago's Garfield Park on March 25, 1905.

Commissioner's SALE!

Of the Abraham Lincoln Birthplace.

A. W. Linforth, Trustee in Bankruptcy, for R. W. Dennette, Plaintiff, against David Greer, et al, Defendants. Notice of Sale in Equity.

By virtue of a Judgment and Order of Sale of LaRue Circuit Court rendered at the May term thereof, 1905, in the above styled cause, the undersigned will on

MONDAY, August 28, 1905,

between the hours of 10 o'clock, A. M., and 3 o'clock, P. M., at the Court House door in Hodgenville, LaRue County, Ky. Being the first day of the August term of the LaRue County Court, proceed to expose to Public Sale, to the highest bidder, at public outcry, the following described property, viz:

The Lincoln Spring farm, Abraham Lincoln's birth place, situated in LaRue county, Ky., on the Hodgenville and Magnolia road, two and one-half miles South of Hodgenville, Ky., and is bounded on the north by Frank Spalding and James L. Friend's land; on the east by the lands of the Andrew Goff's heirs and ——; south by the lands belonging to the heirs of Henry Cissell; on the west by the lands of W. E. Tucker, and the boundary contains one hundred, ten and one-half acres. For a description of this boundary by metes and bounds, courses and distances, see judgment rendered in this case.

Terms: *Sale will be made on a credit of six, twelve and eighteen months, payable to A. W. Linforth, trustee in bankruptcy, for R. W. Dennette, for the use and benefit of those concerned. The purchaser will be required to give bond with approved security, for payment of the purchased money, in equal installments, to have the force and effect of a judgment, bearing legal interest from date of sale, with a lien reserved upon said property until all the purchase money is paid.*

L. B. Handley,

Special Commissioner of the LaRue Circuit Court.

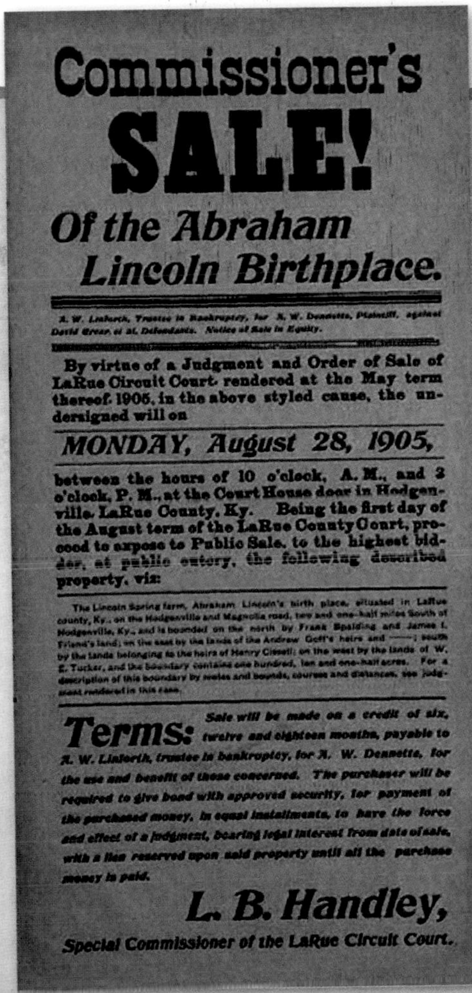

Fig. 2.168. In May 1905 the LaRue County, Kentucky, Circuit Court ordered Thomas Lincoln's Sinking Spring farm, on which Abraham Lincoln was born, to be sold in a bankruptcy sale on the steps of the courthouse in Hodgenville on August 28, 1905. Three bidders vied, and the property was purchased by a representative for a magazine magnate, who paid $3,600 for the property.

Fig. 2.169. In these days of the Internet, video games, PowerPoint displays, and satellite TV, lantern slides may not seem high tech, but these projectable images (colorized in this case) were used to illustrate lectures, school lessons, and leisure pursuits in the quiet days of the early 20th century. This slide is one of several in the author's collection that feature the predominant Lincoln money image of the time.

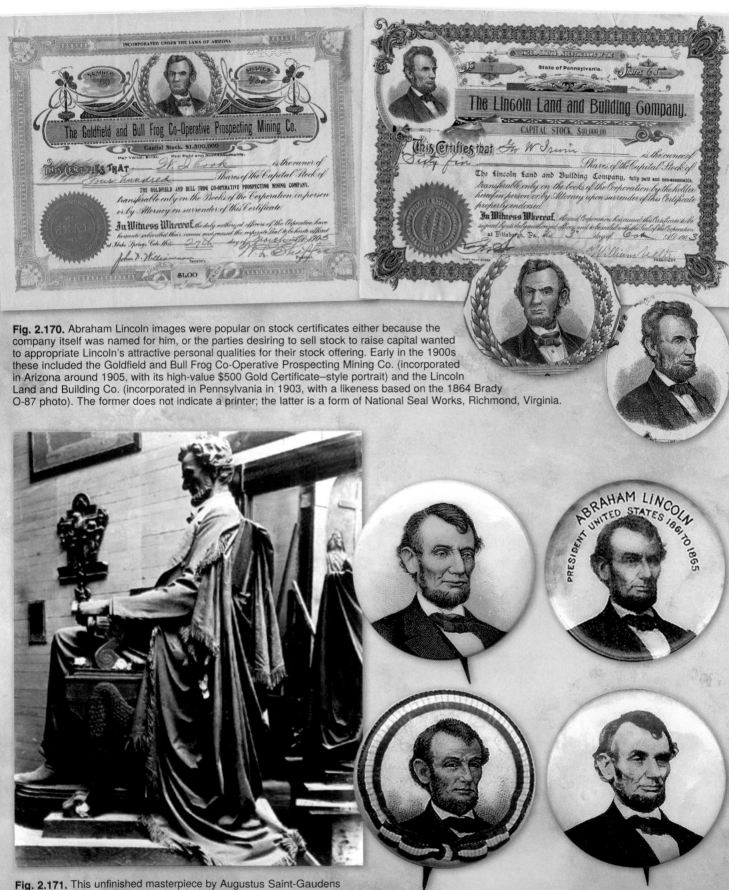

Fig. 2.170. Abraham Lincoln images were popular on stock certificates either because the company itself was named for him, or the parties desiring to sell stock to raise capital wanted to appropriate Lincoln's attractive personal qualities for their stock offering. Early in the 1900s these included the Goldfield and Bull Frog Co-Operative Prospecting Mining Co. (incorporated in Arizona around 1905, with its high-value $500 Gold Certificate–style portrait) and the Lincoln Land and Building Co. (incorporated in Pennsylvania in 1903, with a likeness based on the 1864 Brady O-87 photo). The former does not indicate a printer; the latter is a form of National Seal Works, Richmond, Virginia.

Fig. 2.171. This unfinished masterpiece by Augustus Saint-Gaudens was created between 1895 and 1904, but was lost in a fire that destroyed much of the work in his studio. The ailing sculptor was aided by photographs such as this, and by the help of assistants Henry Hering and Elsie Ward, in recreating his seated figure, which was finally cast posthumously, to great acclaim.

Fig. 2.172. All four of these pinbacks date to early in the 20th century, nominally 1905. Each displays a lithographic interpretation similar to the predominant Lincoln money image of the period. Unfortunately, all were anonymously issued.

1905 SEPTEMBER 22. The sitting president of the United States, Theodore Roosevelt, says of his predecessor in the national hot seat: "It is impossible to conceive of a man farther removed from baseness, farther removed from corruption, from mere self-seeking; but it is also impossible to conceive of a man of more sane and healthy mind." This is in the introduction to the seven-volume *The Writings of Abraham Lincoln,* published by P.F. Collier & Son. A representative of Collier's had purchased the Lincoln Spring Farm, Abraham Lincoln's birthplace, in August 1905.

1906. The Century Co. publishes John G. Nicolay's *A Short Life of Abraham Lincoln,* a single-volume biography condensed from Nicolay and Hay's *Abraham Lincoln: A History.*

1906. John G. Nicolay's daughter Helen Nicolay authors *The Boys' Life of Abraham Lincoln,* published by The Century Co., her father's publisher.

1906 JANUARY 25. Former president Grover Cleveland endorses the goals of the Lincoln Farm Association: "I am strongly in favor of the contemplated movement to make the birthplace of Abraham Lincoln a memorial which shall arouse and stimulate reverent and patriotic sentiments in the minds of the American people. It seems to me that this should be done directly by the individual effort of our people, and that the memorial for all time to come should be in their especial keeping."

1906 JANUARY 27. President Theodore Roosevelt endorses the goals of the Lincoln Farm Association: "I heartily approve of the movement to make the birthplace of Abraham Lincoln a national park, so that the building in which he was born may be preserved to illustrate the real conditions of his birth and childhood. It seems to me . . . most assuredly his birthplace should be preserved in such shape as will enable us, as a nation, to realize vividly the condition from which the second of our two great Presidents sprang to mold our destiny for good."

1906 APRIL 18. Lincoln School, located on 5th Street between Market and Mission streets in San Francisco, succumbs to the flames touched off by the Great San Francisco Earthquake. The blaze was captured by photographer W.J. Street. The fire also claimed Pietro Mezzara's Lincoln statue outside the school, the first large-scale memorial to Abraham Lincoln in this country.

1906 NOVEMBER 30. Charles Barmore, New York City, copyrights an etched copper plate with a design "after a photograph by Rice 1864." According to Charles de Kay in the *New York Times,* "Mr. Charles Barmore of Chicago and New York issues limited editions of etchings, mezzotints, or line engravings after paintings, daguerreotypes, or photographs of authors, statesmen, heroes, and eminent jurists."[41]

1907 JANUARY 2. Artist Charles R. Huntington of New York City copyrights two oil portraits of Abraham Lincoln (H91072, I20492).

1907 JANUARY 9. The Lincoln Club of Brooklyn, New York, copyrights a painting of Abraham Lincoln, 48 by 59 inches, showing Lincoln "seated on a plain mahogany chair with a red velvet or plush seat."

Fig. 2.173. New York City coin dealer Tom Elder issued a great many small Lincoln narrative medals that described events in his life, including this one (DeLorey-22) in December 1907, in anticipation of the Lincoln birth centenary. The piece was made by C.H. Hanson, Chicago.

Fig. 2.174. The 50-year anniversary of the seven Lincoln-Douglas debates came up in 1908, right on the eve of the Lincoln birth centennial. This veteran's badge was worn by a former Union soldier at the Alton, Illinois, celebration, October 15, 1908.

1907 JANUARY 24. New York City sculptor Victor David Brenner copyrights his Lincoln profile-portrait design for a medal or plaque in bronze, silver, or gold with an obverse portrait of Lincoln (I20614). He also copyrights a photo of the same.[42] This copyright claim appears on most of the large bronze rectangular plaques Brenner produced, but not on the circular medallions with a revised portrait. An adaptation of this revised portrait would subsequently appear on the U.S. cent beginning in 1909 and continuing down to the present day.

Fig. 2.175. The United States government has floated loans since its beginning to pay contingent expenses. Most investors would have cashed their interest checks, but for some reason Mr. Pierson did not cash this small check. All the better for collectors and historians, who can see that the Treasury impressed the Charles Burt money image on its pay warrants of that era.

Fig. 2.176. Victor David Brenner created a durable profile portrait of Abraham Lincoln in 1907, leading up to the Lincoln centenary. Ultimately, of course, a variation of Brenner's portrait was adapted for the smallest-denomination U.S. coin, where it would find itself in virtually every cash transaction at a time when nearly *all* retail transactions were cash transactions. Before then, however, the enterprising Brenner adapted the portrait in a variety of ways to market the image to consumers. Two are shown here: a large 6.75-inch circular version mounted on wood *(a)*, and a rectangular bronze plaque mounted on a wooden shield *(b)*.

Fig. 2.177. The purchaser of this real-estate bond would have been impressed by the likeness of Abraham Lincoln appearing on the Nebraska farm loan, which is similar to that which appeared on the $500 Gold Certificate. This W.A. and G.L. Woodward Brothers certificate was printed by the State Journal Co., Lincoln, Nebraska.

1907 JANUARY 24. The Lincoln Club of Brooklyn, New York, registers a copyright claim to a Lincoln portrait log for the group.

1907 FEBRUARY. E.P. Dutton & Co. in New York and J.M. Dent & Co. in London co-publish the *Speeches and Letters of Abraham Lincoln, 1832–1865.* This work was based with permission on John G. Nicolay and John Hay's 1894 publication *The Complete Works of Abraham Lincoln,* published by The Century Co.

1907. Howard Pyle paints a moody picture of a pensive Abraham Lincoln seated at his desk with his massive correspondence load; it will appear in *Harper's Magazine.*

1907 MARCH 5. P.P. Caproni & Brother, Boston, Massachusetts, copyright two life-size busts of Lincoln, one with a beard, and the other clean shaven.

1907 MARCH 15. Lincoln Trust Company, New York City, registers its claim to a copyright for a Lincoln portrayal.

1907 MAY 9. Sculptor Theodore Metzler of Brooklyn copyrights a bust of Abraham Lincoln on a pedestal.

1907 AUGUST 3. The Art Institute of Chicago stages a memorial exhibition of "The Works of Augustus Saint-Gaudens," to run for eight weeks. Included were 115 pieces of sculpture, photographs, and lesser works, including "casts of most of the larger works of Saint-Gaudens, and a large number of medals, plaques, coins and reliefs." The traveling exhibit would also make stops at the Corcoran Gallery in Washington, D.C., the Metropolitan Museum of Art in New York City, and the Carnegie Institute in Pittsburgh.[43]

1907 DECEMBER. Coin dealer Thomas Elder commissions the first medal in his 26-medal "Lincoln Biographical Series" (King-350, DeLorey-19). In all, through about 1939, Elder would commission 44 Lincoln medals.

1907 DECEMBER 16. *The Dial* calls special attention to the publication by Houghton, Mifflin & Co. of *Abraham Lincoln,* by Carl Schurz and Truman H. Bartlett. The exquisitely appointed work reprints Schurz's 1891 tribute to Lincoln and packages it with Bartlett's "The Portraits of Lincoln." The book "is one of the notable publications of a year marked by its wealth of good things," *The Dial* reported. The French memorial medal obverse was embossed on the book's front cover. "The portraits of Lincoln, of which a long series is reproduced, make, particularly in connection with Mr. Bartlett's essay, a fascinating study," the reviewer added.[44]

1908 FEBRUARY 12. The first annual meeting and dinner of the Lincoln Fellowship of New York City is held at Delmonico's.

1908 FEBRUARY 12. A seven-foot-tall standing bronze statue of Abraham Lincoln is dedicated inside Bancroft Public School, Omaha, Nebraska. Lincoln is depicted with his right arm behind his back and his left hand clasping his lapel.

Fig. 2.178. Prior to the Lincoln birth centennial, this brochure drummed up interest in Robert Hewitt's *The Lincoln Centennial Medal.* A bronze medal sculpted by Jules Edouard Roiné was packaged in a book, published by G.P. Putnam's Sons, with a blue buckram cover, for $5; a silver edition in a leather-bound book, limited to 100, was available for $12. A single gold specimen of the medal was struck for Lincoln collector Major William H. Lambert.

Fig. 2.179. U.S. secretary of state and orator William Jennings Bryan was defeated as a Democratic presidential candidate by Republicans three times, but he was still a favorite son of his home state and its capital, Lincoln, Nebraska, named in honor of Old Abe upon Nebraska's admission to the Union, March 1, 1867. On this attractive red-white-and-blue postcard published by I. Grollman in 1908, Lincoln's portrait again is that of the dominant Lincoln money image of that era.

1908 March 2. A memorial exhibition of the works of the late Augustus Saint-Gaudens opens at the Metropolitan Museum of Art, New York City. "Arrangements have been made for the casting of the standing Lincoln of Chicago. . . . While the later Lincoln, seated, destined also for Chicago, will be seen here, in the bronze, for the first time," pre-publicity for the exhibition reported.[45]

1908 May 8. Congress accepts Eugene Meyer Jr.'s donation to the United States of a huge marble sculpture of a beardless Abraham Lincoln's head, made by sculptor Gutzon Borglum. This was a study for the massive bearded head of Lincoln that Borglum designed at Mount Rushmore. The bust today is on display under the U.S. Capitol Rotunda.

Fig. 2.180. In 1908, the year before the Abraham Lincoln centennial observance, a portrait of Lincoln based on the O-92 Berger photo was appearing on U.S. $1 Silver Certificates (by G.F.C. Smillie), $100 U.S. Legal Tender Notes (by Charles Burt), and the five-cent U.S. postage stamp (by Marcus Baldwin; variety Scott 315 was in use by then). Additionally, Burt's 1882 Lincoln portrait based on O-91 was also appearing on $500 Gold Certificates. With the centennial fast approaching, some influential party at the U.S. Treasury thought it would be a good idea to deploy the O-92 image on a new series of $100 Gold Certificates, as well. Accordingly this die (BEP MISC 7046) was prepared. Portions of the plate are credited to a team comprised of Edward M. Hall, George U. Rose Jr., Robert Ponickau, and Edward E. Meyers. For unknown reasons, this elegant note was never issued.

Fig. 2.181. Sculptor Gutzon Borglum's impressive white marble beardless bust of Lincoln was a gift to the United States from Eugene Meyer Jr. Borglum also designed the impressive stand on which it sits. Congress accepted the gift on May 8, 1908. The sculptor also prepared a large plaster cast of the head, which is now on display at the Abraham Lincoln Presidential Library and Museum in Springfield, Illinois.

1908 June 13. The Lincoln Boulder is dedicated at Nyack, New York. Schoolchildren of Nyack contributed funds to move a large boulder from the shore of the Hudson River to a space in front of the Nyack Carnegie Library, and have a plaque with the Gettysburg Address inscribed mounted on the rock.

1908. Sculptor Gutzon Borglum prepares a large plaster head cast of a beardless Abraham Lincoln (of the marble version now in the Rotunda of the U.S. Capitol in Washington, D.C.). A bronze copy would be placed in front of Lincoln's tomb in Springfield. Other copies may be seen at the University of California and in New York City. For 35 years the plaster study greeted visitors at the entrance of the Illinois State Historical Library in the Old State Capitol. It is now on display at the Abraham Lincoln Presidential Library and Museum. Borglum also made "a slightly sadder-looking version of this face," acquired after World War I by the Detroit Institute of Arts, according to historians at the ALPLM.

1908 October. G.P. Putnam's Sons, publishers of *Putnam's Monthly & The Reader,* a magazine of literature, art, and life, and also the publisher of Robert Hewitt's *The Lincoln Centennial Medal* (a book with a medal by Roiné) touts the latter venture in the former publication. "It is a curious as well as an interesting fact that one of the most successful likenesses of Lincoln should have been made by a Frenchman. The medal by Edward Roiné, here reproduced, is destined to become famous, and it was a happy thought to select it for perpetuation in book form," the publication exhorted.[46]

1908 October 1. Sculptor Franz Zelezny's standing bronze figure of Abraham Lincoln is installed near the southeast corner of the Central High School grounds, Omaha, Nebraska. Student donations funded the sculpture, which would later be moved to Lincoln School at 11th and Center streets after Dodge Street's regrading. It would subsequently be moved to the Bancroft School.

1908 October 21. Osborn H. Oldroyd, operating a personal museum in the Petersen House in which Lincoln died in Washington, D.C., copyrights a 20-page memorial program for the "Centenary of the Birth of Abraham Lincoln, 1809–1909."

Fig. 2.182. Printed literature abounded for the upcoming Lincoln centennial. Shown are the 1908 ninth edition of Osborn H. Oldroy's *Program of Exercises* for the centenary observance *(a)*, the Methodist-Episcopal Church Freedmen's Aid Society *Lincoln Centennial Song Service (b)*, and the *Lincoln Souvenir Book (c)*, each of which employs cover portraiture that would have been intimately familiar to recipients of these pamphlets.

Fig. 2.183. This resinous cast of Roiné's obverse die for Hewitt's *Lincoln Centennial Medal* appeared in a recent auction, where it was purchased by Lincoln collector Rich Jewell, who supplied this image. The cast is translucent and is lit from behind, as shown here.

1908 OCTOBER 23. Less than four months before the celebration of the Lincoln centennial, in the short space of five days, the U.S. Copyright Office at the Library of Congress receives three different compilations of Lincoln's sayings, speeches, and letters. Works represented were from Francis D. Tandy Co., A. Wessels Co., and Brentano's, all of New York.

1908 NOVEMBER 25. McClure Newspaper Syndicate, New York City, files copyrights on a dozen Lincoln articles by Ida M. Tarbell, including "Lincoln's Three Love Stories" and "Lincoln Fails at Making Money."

1908 FALL. G.P. Putnam's Sons, New York and London, issues an aluminum medal, which they distribute to the book trade, concurrent with release of their book, *The Lincoln Centennial Medal*. The small aluminum medal (King-347) pledges that on Lincoln's birthday following, the medal dies for the large Roiné profile medal will be canceled and donated to the American Numismatic Society.

1908 DECEMBER 5. *Publishers Weekly*, the trade magazine of the Publishers' Board of Trade and American Book Trade Association, takes notice of the release of the G.P. Putnam's Sons volume *The Lincoln Centennial Medal*, containing the excellent 2-1/2–inch medal by French classicist Roiné. "The publication presents the famous Roiné medal of Lincoln," a reviewer wrote. "Among his medallic work the Lincoln medallion included in this volume has found great favor and, in the opinion of authorities, will remain the authoritative medallic presentation of the great American."

The book's text presented "the most noteworthy and characteristic utterances of Abraham Lincoln."[47] Also included in the medal volume were essays by Richard Lloyd Jones on the Lincoln Centennial, and Dr. George N. Olcott on the medalist and his medal.

The edition with silver medals, limited to 100, was signed and numbered and priced at $12; an open edition included bronze medals, at $5. A gold-medal edition was also sold, but apparently not widely advertised. A single gold specimen was struck to the order of Philadelphia Lincoln enthusiast Major William H. Lambert.[48]

1908 DECEMBER 20. During the previous month, the Metropolitan Museum of Art, New York City, received the donation of "Plaster casts of the original model of Lincoln Centennial medal by Roiné" from the Medallic Art Co., through Robert Hewitt.[49]

1908 DECEMBER 23. Douglas Volk authenticates duplicates of a cast of Lincoln's left hand, originally cast by his father, Leonard Volk, on May 20, 1860. These plaster casts would be mounted on wooden plaques in the shape of a shield. On certificates of authenticity on the backs of the plaques, the junior Volk wrote: "This cast of the hand of Lincoln was made from a replica of the one taken from life by my father, the late Leonard W. Volk, in Springfield, Ill., the Sunday following Lincoln's first nomination for the Presidency. The hand is from a copy recently remodeled and restored myself by direct comparison with the original cast." He hand-signed in pen/ink: "DOUGLAS VOLK—NEW YORK—December 23 RD 1908."

1909. *McClure's Magazine* publisher R.B. McClure issues a portfolio of photogravure reproductions of six famous photographs in his collection, including *Lincoln the President*, the famous Cooper Union portrait; Lincoln on the line of battle; an artist's conception of the Lincoln family; *Abraham Lincoln*; and "the first portrait ever made of Lincoln."

1909. The Oldroyd Lincoln Memorial Collection, located in the house where Lincoln died (at 516 Tenth Street NW, Washington, D.C.) displays for the centenary of Lincoln's birth 100 portraits, including the L. Groelrier lithograph of the 1860 portrait painted by Hicks, a photograph of Saint-Gaudens's *Standing Lincoln* sculpture in Chicago, several prints, and more than 90 original and copy photographs.

1909. Boston Sculpture Co., Melrose, Massachusetts, sells large, 31-inch-tall plaster busts of Abraham Lincoln for display in family parlors and elsewhere. (See figure 2.187.)

Fig. 2.184. In 1908 the newly established Medallic Art Co. in New York City struck this aluminum medal (King-347) touting the fact that the Lincoln Centennial medal dies would be defaced and donated to the American Numismatic Society on February 12, 1909, to assure buyers of the limited nature of the minting. According to numismatic cataloger Robert King, a thousand of these medals were struck and sent to the book trade to publicize the venture.

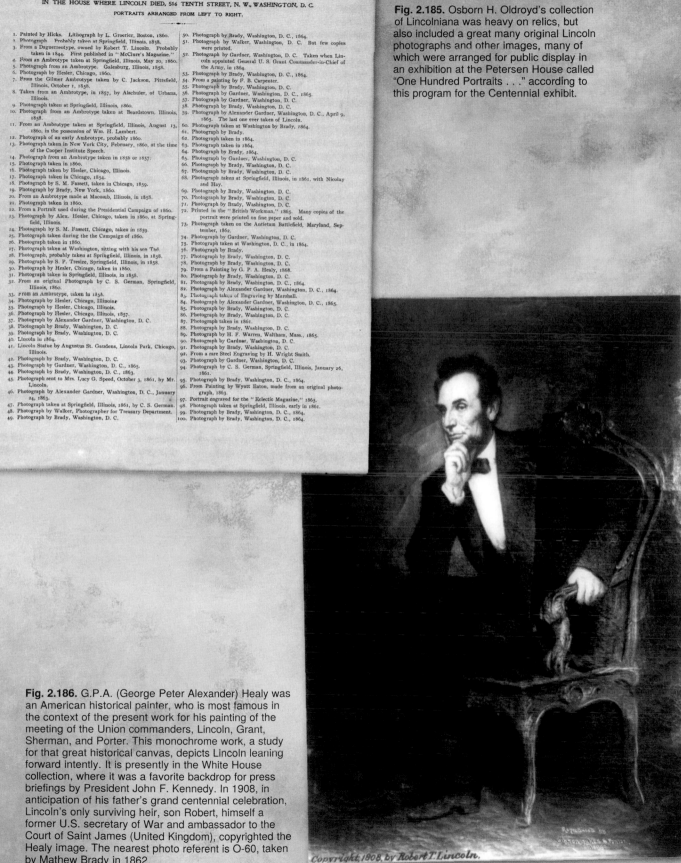

THE CENTENARY OF ABRAHAM LINCOLN'S BIRTH.

ONE HUNDRED PORTRAITS OF LINCOLN FROM THE OLDROYD LINCOLN MEMORIAL COLLECTION,

IN THE HOUSE WHERE LINCOLN DIED, 516 TENTH STREET, N. W., WASHINGTON, D. C.

PORTRAITS ARRANGED FROM LEFT TO RIGHT.

1. Painted by Hicks. Lithograph by L. Groerier, Boston, 1860.
2. Photograph. Probably taken at Springfield, Illinois, 1858.
3. From a Daguerreotype, owned by Robert T. Lincoln. Probably taken in 1844. First published in "McClure's Magazine."
4. From an Ambrotype taken at Springfield, Illinois, May 20, 1860.
5. Photograph from an Ambrotype. Galesburg, Illinois, 1858.
6. Photograph by Hesler, Chicago, 1860.
7. From the Gilmer Ambrotype taken by C. Jackson, Pittsfield, Illinois, October 1, 1858.
8. Taken from an Ambrotype, in 1857, by Aischuler, of Urbana, Illinois.
9. Photograph taken at Springfield, Illinois, 1860.
10. Photograph from an Ambrotype taken at Beardstown, Illinois, 1858.
11. From an Ambrotype taken at Springfield, Illinois, August 13, 1860, in the possession of Wm. H. Lambert.
12. Photograph of an early Ambrotype, probably 1860.
13. Photograph taken in New York City, February, 1860, at the time of the Cooper Institute Speech.
14. Photograph from an Ambrotype taken in 1856 or 1857.
15. Photograph taken in 1860.
16. Photograph taken by Hesler, Chicago, Illinois.
17. Photograph taken in Chicago, 1854.
18. Photograph by S. M. Fassett, taken in Chicago, 1859.
19. Photograph by Brady, New York, 1860.
20. From an Ambrotype made at Macomb, Illinois, in 1858.
21. Photograph taken in 1860.
22. From a Portrait used during the Presidential Campaign of 1860.
23. Photograph by Alex. Hesler, Chicago, taken in 1860, at Springfield, Illinois.
24. Photograph by S. M. Fassett, Chicago, taken in 1859.
25. Photograph taken during the the Campaign of 1860.
26. Photograph taken in 1860.
27. Photograph taken at Washington, sitting with his son Tad.
28. Photograph, probably taken at Springfield, Illinois, in 1858.
29. Photograph by S. P. Tresize, Springfield, Illinois, in 1858.
30. Photograph by Hesler, Chicago, taken in 1860.
31. Photograph taken in Springfield, Illinois, in 1858.
32. From an original Photograph by C. S. German, Springfield, Illinois, 1860.
33. From an Ambrotype, taken in 1858.
34. Photograph by Hesler, Chicago, Illinois.
35. Photograph by Hesler, Chicago, Illinois.
36. Photograph by Hesler, Chicago, Illinois, 1857.
37. Photograph by Alexander Gardner, Washington, D. C.
38. Photograph by Brady, Washington, D. C.
39. Photograph by Brady, Washington, D. C.
40. Lincoln in 1864.
41. Lincoln Statue by Augustus St. Gaudens, Lincoln Park, Chicago, Illinois.
42. Photograph by Brady, Washington, D. C.
43. Photograph by Gardner, Washington, D. C., 1865.
44. Photograph by Brady, Washington, D. C., 1863.
45. Photograph sent to Mrs. Lucy G. Speed, October 3, 1861, by Mr. Lincoln.
46. Photograph by Alexander Gardner, Washington, D. C., January 24, 1863.
47. Photograph taken at Springfield, Illinois, 1861, by C. S. German.
48. Photograph by Walker, Photographer for Treasury Department.
49. Photograph by Brady, Washington, D. C.
50. Photograph by Brady, Washington, D. C., 1864.
51. Photograph by Walker, Washington, D. C. But few copies were printed.
52. Photograph by Gardner, Washington, D. C. Taken when Lincoln appointed General U. S. Grant Commander-in-Chief of the Army, in 1864.
53. Photograph by Brady, Washington, D. C., 1864.
54. From a painting by F. B. Carpenter.
55. Photograph by Brady, Washington, D. C.
56. Photograph by Gardner, Washington, D. C., 1865.
57. Photograph by Gardner, Washington, D. C.
58. Photograph by Brady, Washington, D. C.
59. Photograph by Alexander Gardner, Washington, D. C., April 9, 1865. The last one ever taken of Lincoln.
60. Photograph taken at Washington by Brady, 1864.
61. Photograph by Brady.
62. Photograph taken in 1864.
63. Photograph taken in 1864.
64. Photograph by Brady, 1864.
65. Photograph by Gardner, Washington, D. C.
66. Photograph by Brady, Washington, D. C.
67. Photograph by Brady, Washington, D. C.
68. Photograph taken at Springfield, Illinois, in 1861, with Nicolay and Hay.
69. Photograph by Brady, Washington, D. C.
70. Photograph by Brady, Washington, D. C.
71. Photograph by Brady, Washington, D. C.
72. Printed in the "British Workman," 1865. Many copies of the portrait were printed on fine paper and sold.
73. Photograph taken on the Antietam Battlefield, Maryland, September, 1862.
74. Photograph by Gardner, Washington, D. C.
75. Photograph taken at Washington, D. C., in 1864.
76. Photograph by Brady.
77. Photograph by Brady, Washington, D. C.
78. Photograph by Brady, Washington, D. C.
79. From a Painting by G. P. A. Healy, 1868.
80. Photograph by Brady, Washington, D. C.
81. Photograph by Brady, Washington, D. C., 1864.
82. Photograph by Alexander Gardner, Washington, D. C., 1864.
83. Photograph taken of Engraving by Marshall.
84. Photograph by Alexander Gardner, Washington, D. C., 1865.
85. Photograph by Brady, Washington, D. C.
86. Photograph by Brady, Washington, D. C.
87. Photograph taken in 1861.
88. Photograph by Brady, Washington, D. C.
89. Photograph by H. F. Warren, Waltham, Mass., 1865.
90. Photograph by Gardner, Washington, D. C.
91. Photograph by Brady, Washington, D. C.
92. From a rare Steel Engraving by H. Wright Smith.
93. Photograph by Gardner, Washington, D. C.
94. Photograph by C. S. German, Springfield, Illinois, January 26, 1861.
95. Photograph by Brady, Washington, D. C., 1864.
96. From Painting by Wyatt Eaton, made from an original photograph, 1863.
97. Portrait engraved for the "Eclectic Magazine," 1865.
98. Photograph taken at Springfield, Illinois, early in 1861.
99. Photograph by Brady, Washington, D. C., 1864.
100. Photograph by Brady, Washington, D. C., 1864.

Fig. 2.185. Osborn H. Oldroyd's collection of Lincolniana was heavy on relics, but also included a great many original Lincoln photographs and other images, many of which were arranged for public display in an exhibition at the Petersen House called "One Hundred Portraits . . ." according to this program for the Centennial exhibit.

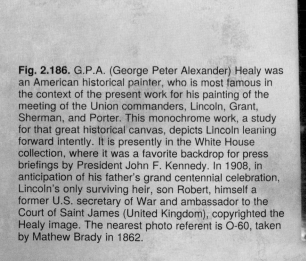

Copyright, 1908, by Robert T. Lincoln.

Fig. 2.186. G.P.A. (George Peter Alexander) Healy was an American historical painter, who is most famous in the context of the present work for his painting of the meeting of the Union commanders, Lincoln, Grant, Sherman, and Porter. This monochrome work, a study for that great historical canvas, depicts Lincoln leaning forward intently. It is presently in the White House collection, where it was a favorite backdrop for press briefings by President John F. Kennedy. In 1908, in anticipation of his father's grand centennial celebration, Lincoln's only surviving heir, son Robert, himself a former U.S. secretary of War and ambassador to the Court of Saint James (United Kingdom), copyrighted the Healy image. The nearest photo referent is O-60, taken by Mathew Brady in 1862.

Fig. 2.187. Boston Sculpture Co. marketed this 31-inch-tall plaster bust for the Lincoln centennial.

Fig. 2.188. In 1909 an artist at the American Lithographic Co., New York, created this close copy of the G.P.A. Healy and Brady O-60 pose titled *The Great American Reconciler*, for Reconciler cigars. Note the stogie in Lincoln's left hand. Overall this is arguably the most attractive of the many Lincoln tobacco chromolithographs. Note in 1909 this image was priced at $2.40 per hundred. Today a lucky owner would have to part with a thousand dollars for a single copy.

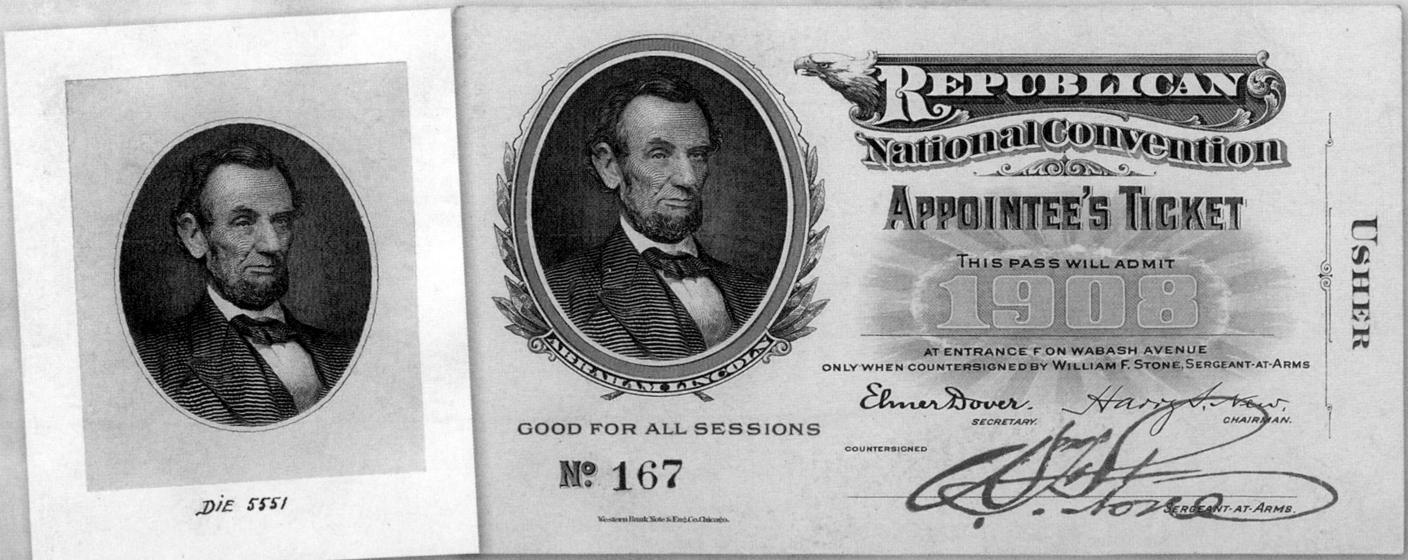

Fig. 2.189. In 1901 the American Bank Note Co., which had engraved the modified O-92 Lincoln portrait for the four-cent U.S. postage stamp of 1890 (Scott 222), acquired the Western Bank Note & Engraving Co., located in Chicago, and continued to operate the business under that name. At WBNECo an engraver for the western branch engraved this similar modified O-92 Lincoln portrait, which was used in 1908 on a Republican National Convention ticket. The slight difference between this portrait and the portrait of Lincoln on the folding currency in the delegates' pockets would have been lost on all but the most perceptive of the partisans gathered at the party's Chicago national convention.

1909 January 1. President Theodore Roosevelt pens his personal tribute to Abraham Lincoln for the upcoming centennial of his birth. Roosevelt commented on Lincoln's kindness and eloquence. "Lincoln's work and Lincoln's words should be, and I think more and more are, part of those formative influences which tend to become living forces for good citizenship among our people," the nation's then-current leader wrote in an essay published in the February issue of *The American Review of Reviews.* TR especially praised Lincoln's Gettysburg Address and Second Inaugural Address for their "wisdom, and dignity, and earnestness, and in a loftiness of thought and expression which makes them akin to the utterances of the prophets of the Old Testament."[50]

1909 January 2. President Theodore Roosevelt writes the widow of sculptor Augustus Saint-Gaudens, requesting permission to have a photograph taken of her late husband's new seated figure of Abraham Lincoln, for use as a model for a portrait engraver so a stamp could be issued for Lincoln's birthday a month later. An heroic plaster had been lent by the sculptor's widow for display in Washington, D.C., in 1908, after having been cast that year in New York City at Roman Bronze Works. According to Lincoln philatelic expert Eliot A. Landau, Saint-Gaudens's widow replied along the lines of, "Please do, I feel very honored." The photograph was taken; the engraving was made, and the carmine two-cent stamp (Scott 367–369) was released on February 12 for the centennial of Lincoln's birth.

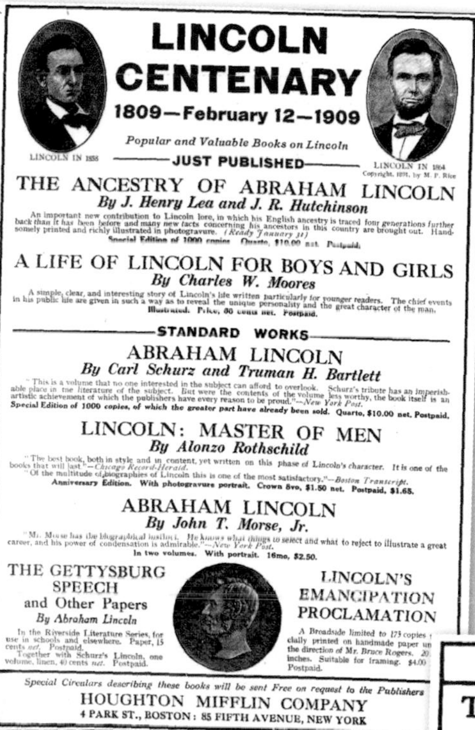

"The angle [of] Lincoln's head on [Saint-] Gaudens' working bust accounts for the somewhat introspective attitude of Lincoln's head on the 367–369 stamps," a philatelic writer observed.[51]

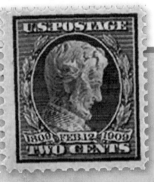

Fig. 2.190. The 1909 Abraham Lincoln centennial stamp (Scott 367–369) bears this likeness of Lincoln, engraved by Marcus W. Baldwin after the head on Augustus Saint-Gaudens's second Lincoln bronze masterpiece—his *Seated Lincoln*—because President Theodore Roosevelt importuned the sculptor's widow for the privilege after he had observed a plaster model of the recently cast statue on display in Washington, D.C.

LINCOLN CENTENARY

1809—February 12—1909

Popular and Valuable Books on Lincoln

LINCOLN IN 1858 — LINCOLN IN 1864 — Copyright, 1891, by M. P. Rice

JUST PUBLISHED

THE ANCESTRY OF ABRAHAM LINCOLN
By J. Henry Lea and J. R. Hutchinson
An important new contribution to Lincoln lore, in which his English ancestry is traced four generations further back than it has been before and many new facts concerning his ancestors in this country are brought out. Handsomely printed and richly illustrated in photogravure. *(Ready January 31)*
Special Edition of 1000 copies. Quarto, $10.00 net. Postpaid.

A LIFE OF LINCOLN FOR BOYS AND GIRLS
By Charles W. Moores
A simple, clear, and interesting story of Lincoln's life written particularly for younger readers. The chief events in his public life are given in such a way as to reveal the unique personality and the great character of the man.
Illustrated. Price, 60 cents net. Postpaid.

STANDARD WORKS

ABRAHAM LINCOLN
By Carl Schurz and Truman H. Bartlett
"This is a volume that no one interested in the subject can afford to overlook. Schurz's tribute has an imperishable place in the literature of the subject. But were the contents of the volume less worthy, the book itself is an artistic achievement of which the publishers have every reason to be proud."—*New York Post.*
Special Edition of 1000 copies, of which the greater part have already been sold. Quarto, $10.00 net. Postpaid.

LINCOLN: MASTER OF MEN
By Alonzo Rothschild
"The best book, both in style and in content, yet written on this phase of Lincoln's character. It is one of the books that will last."—*Chicago Record-Herald.*
"Of the multitude of biographies of Lincoln this is one of the most satisfactory."—*Boston Transcript.*
Anniversary Edition. With photogravure portrait. Crown 8vo, $1.50 net. Postpaid, $1.65.

ABRAHAM LINCOLN
By John T. Morse, Jr.
"Mr. Morse has the biographical instinct. He knows what things to select and what to reject to illustrate a great career, and his power of condensation is admirable."—*New York Post.*
In two volumes. With portrait. 16mo, $2.50.

THE GETTYSBURG SPEECH and Other Papers
By Abraham Lincoln
In the Riverside Literature Series, for use in schools and elsewhere. Paper, 15 cents *net.* Postpaid.
Together with Schurz's Lincoln, one volume, linen, 40 cents *net.* Postpaid.

LINCOLN'S EMANCIPATION PROCLAMATION
A Broadside limited to 175 copies
cially printed on handmade paper un
the direction of Mr. Bruce Rogers. 20
inches. Suitable for framing. $4.00
Postpaid.

Special Circulars describing these books will be sent Free on request to the Publishers

HOUGHTON MIFFLIN COMPANY
4 PARK ST., BOSTON : 85 FIFTH AVENUE, NEW YORK

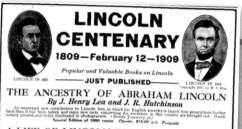

Fig. 2.191. This Houghton Mifflin Co. book ad, published running up to the Lincoln centennial, is perplexing. It clearly displays Roiné's Lincoln Centennial Medal for Robert Hewitt, a promotional item for competitor G.P. Putnam's Sons centennial book. You'll note that the Putnam volume is not offered for sale here, but the somewhat gratuitous use of the medal obverse design is prominent. The other book ad by G.P. Putnam's Sons actually *does* offer the Hewitt-Roiné-Putnam volume and medal. One cannot help but speculate that the advertising department at the *Atlantic Monthly* goofed when preparing its January 1909 issue.

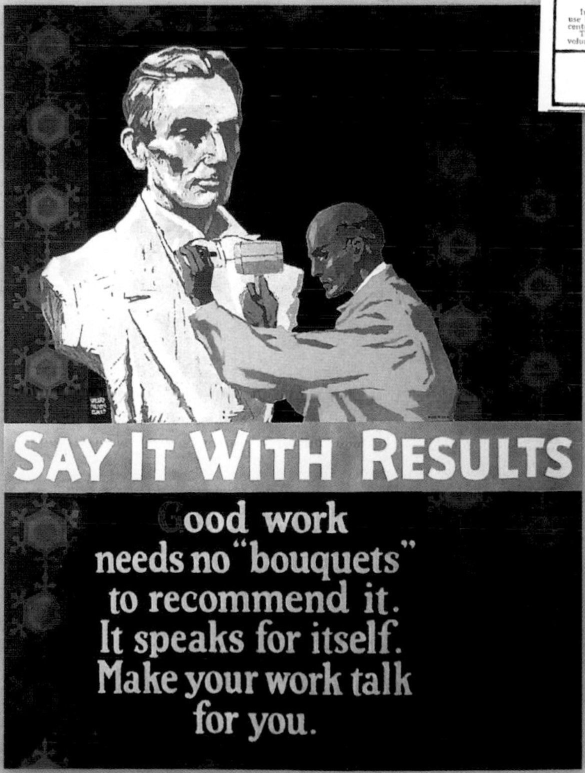

Fig. 2.192. This motivational poster, "Say It With Results," links the uniqueness of both the snowflake authored by the Creator with the uniqueness of the sculptor's masterpiece and its model, Abraham Lincoln the Individual.

The Lincoln Centenary

The Lincoln Centennial Medal

A volume presenting the famous Roiné Medal, together with the most noteworthy and characteristic utterances of Abraham Lincoln.

Bronze Edition.—*Crown 8vo, with the medal in bronze, 2½ inches in diameter, mounted artistically on boards.* $5.00 *net.*

Silver Edition.—*8vo, with the medal in silver, artistically mounted on boards. Limited to 100 signed and numbered copies.* $12.00 *net.* (*All Sold.*)

On the 12th of February, 1909, the dies of the medal are to be cancelled and then deposited in the collection of the American Numismatic Society. After that date no more copies of the medal or of the book containing the medal can be produced.

Gettysburg and Lincoln
The Battle, The Cemetery, and the National Park
By Henry S. Burrage, D.D., Brevet-Major Maine Vols.
8vo. *With 27 Illustrations.* $1.50 *net.*
This interesting volume is well illustrated and equipped with tactical maps.

Abraham Lincoln and The Downfall of American Slavery
By Noah Brooks
Author of "Henry Knox: a Soldier of the Revolution," etc.
No. 11. Heroes of the Nations.
Crown 8vo, cloth, $1.50, *Half leather,* $1.75
". . . . . The work you have prepared, presents the events which it narrates, while with sufficient fulness, with a compactness and interest that could not be surpassed."
—*Robert T. Lincoln.*

Lincolnics
Familiar Sayings of Abraham Lincoln.
Collected and Edited by Henry L. Williams
No. 145. Ariel Booklet Series.
32°. *Frontispiece in photogravure. Flexible red leather,* 75 *cents.*

New York G. P. Putnam's Sons London

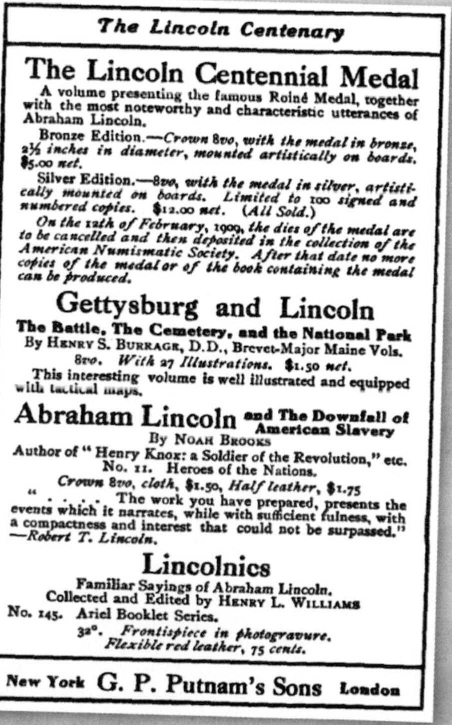

Fig. 2.193. On land the Spanish-American War was fought on foot and horseback. As this 1908 Camp Lincoln, Illinois, view shows, the mechanized cavalry was still in the future as the Illinois National Guard posed for this picture postcard, published by the *Illinois State Register*, with the American flag and a Lincoln O-92 money image.

Fig. 2.194. While a beardless image of Abraham Lincoln may have been appropriate, publisher Jules Bien & Co. went straight for the jugular when designing this colorful, embossed Lincoln boyhood-cabin view, copyrighted in 1908.

Fig. 2.195. New York coin dealer Tom Elder published 44 different Lincoln medal types (or many more, counting metal varieties), most of them by C.H. Hanson of Chicago, as is this aluminum piece (DeLorey-19), "Time Increases His Fame." Elder's reverse revisited an earlier U.S. Mint medal which proclaimed the same rippling sentiments for George Washington (Baker 91). "Time Increases His Fame" was no less appropriate this time around.

Fig. 2.196. The "official" engravings of the Berger O-92 portrait not only appeared on postage stamps, paper money, and government checks, but also on a somewhat bewildering mass of government bonds (usually of the $1,000 value). As we see here on this proof, it was also utilized on $1,000 promissory notes when the assistant U.S. treasurer or other disbursing official could not come up with the cash to make a payment.

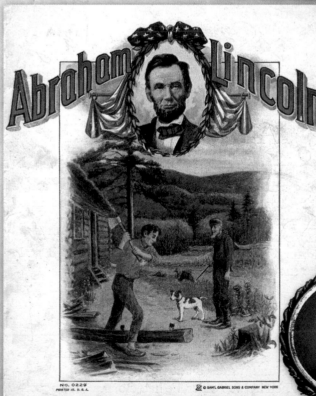

Fig. 2.197. Illustrators A.M. Turner and Harriet Kaucher created the delightful *Lincoln, the Rail-Splitter* and portrait *(a)* based on the Gettysburg Lincoln O-77 photo. Their work contributed to Calista McCabe Courtenay's children's book, *Abraham Lincoln*, published by Sam'l Gabriel Sons Co. A similarly well-done Gettysburg Lincoln appears on this mounted celluloid pinback with vestiges of its original (presumed) Lincoln-Douglas or birth-centennial anniversary ribbon *(b)*.

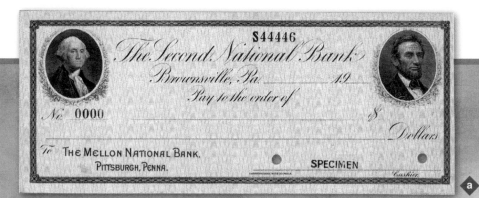

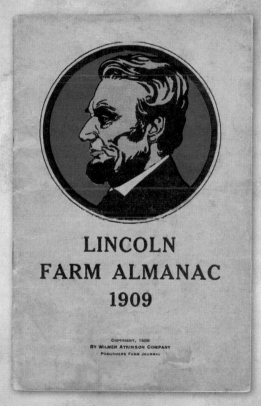

Fig. 2.198. By the early 20th century, when these two draft specimens were printed, ABNCo still had the original Lincoln paper-currency portrait die available. It was created for the company in early 1861 by engraver Charles Burt. This, it will be remembered, was the most plentiful Lincoln image of his lifetime and also the most important, as the "official" government portrait of Abe on the nation's currency, and it was modeled for postage stamps and other uses.

Although ABNCo had several other Lincoln portrait dies also available, its Philadelphia branch utilized the old-time money image with a Washington portrait on drafts of both the Second National Bank (Brownsville, Pennsylvania) and the Bank of North America (Philadelphia). The latter was the oldest bank in the United States, allowed to keep its historic name when it took a National Bank charter.

Fig. 2.199. Many millions of *Lincoln Farm Almanacs* must have been printed and distributed, judging by how common they still are today. The 1909 almanac was copyrighted in 1908 by publisher Wilmer Atkinson Co., also publisher of the *Farm Journal*, established in 1877.

Fig. 2.200. This very numismatic cigar-box inner label for A. Lincoln cigars is adorned by likenesses of gold medals awarded at Paris expositions and an absolutely splendid depiction of the then-current $500 Gold Certificate Lincoln O-91 portrait *(a)*. The American Lithographic Co. created a far less elegant label that is nevertheless very symbolic for the Los Idolos ("The Idols") brand, by combining the portraiture with the paired eagles *(b)*. Yeah, we get it—and consumers at the time did, too. Both the Washington and Lincoln images are their money images.

1909 JANUARY 7. Bureau of Engraving and Printing engraver Marcus Baldwin commences work on a Lincoln centennial two-cent postage stamp. His engraving was based on a photo of a plaster bust of August Saint-Gaudens's seated statue at Grant Park, Chicago.

1909 JANUARY 9. Horatio Sheafe Krans pens the preface to *The Lincoln Tribute Book,* published by G.P. Putnam's Sons' Knickerbocker Press. The subtitle of this book is *Together with a Lincoln Centenary Medal, from the Second Design Made for the Occasion by Roiné,* and the work includes Roiné's small facing-portrait Lincoln medal. Krans described the Lincoln medal collection of Robert W. Hewitt (who commissioned both this and the larger profile Lincoln medal that appeared in the *Lincoln Centennial Medal* volume late the previous year) as the largest in existence. Of Hewitt it was said that his "unrivaled collection of Lincoln medals has made him known to numismatists and collectors everywhere."[52] According to Krans, the second Hewitt Lincoln centennial medal book was priced modestly compared to the "costly" 1908 volume. This new work contained appreciations of Lincoln from a variety of sources.

1909 JANUARY 12. Bureau of Engraving and Printing engraver Marcus Baldwin's two-cent Lincoln Centennial postage stamp die, PO 450, is approved.

1909 JANUARY 18. Postmaster General George von L. Meyer approves the die for a two-cent Lincoln Centennial postage stamp (Scott 367).

1909 JANUARY 22. A joint resolution of Congress calls for an Abraham Lincoln centennial postage stamp to be issued on February 12. As detailed herein, however, preparation of the stamp had been in progress since early January.

1909 JANUARY 23. Poet Edwin Markham, New Brighton, New York, copyrights his poem "Lincoln, the Man of the People" (A228917). Markham would receive a second copyright on this poem in 1919, and three years later he would be selected to read it aloud at the dedication of the Lincoln Memorial in Washington, D.C.

1909 JANUARY 30. A Treasury press release states that an Abraham Lincoln portrait would probably be used on the half dollar, but that legislation might be necessary. The U.S. Treasury informs the editor of *The Numismatist:*

> President Roosevelt has given his consent to the placing of the head of Lincoln on one of the popular coins. He conferred today with Director Leach, of the mint, and details are now under advisement. Victor D. Brenner, the New York sculptor, has submitted to the director some models of Lincoln busts, and these have been shown to the president. The head of Lincoln will adorn one side of the coin and the customary coat of arms the other. It is probable that the half dollar piece will be selected as the principal coin to bear the Lincoln head, but some legislation may be necessary to make the change.

Brenner later claimed the choice of denomination was his own. "You see the life of a coin is 25 years, according to law, and the time

Fig. 2.201. Geo. D. Barnard & Co., St. Louis, utilized a profile engraving of Lincoln on this customers draft in favor of the Lincoln National Bank of Lincoln, Illinois.

Fig. 2.202. In this March 1909 ad *(a)*, Doubleday offered five Lincoln titles, including Ida M. Tarbell's two-volume biography "endorsed by the President's friends." The Lincoln History Society *(b)* was a marketing effort for Tarbell's four-volume edition of her Lincoln biography.

a

b

for the cent and the five-cent piece has expired," he wrote. "It seemed to me that the nickel already had a very practical design, and so I turned my attention to what would be most fitting for the one-cent coin."[53] According to the U.S. Mint director's annual report written late in 1909, Secretary of the Treasury Franklin MacVeagh approved Brenner's Lincoln cent design in July. But small changes had occupied the designer, including removing his last name from the bottom of the coin's reverse, replaced by his initials, "V.D.B." Coinage of the cent commenced at the Mint on June 10. According to reports, more than 20 million were struck and stockpiled before the Mint took its summer furlough on July 1. Newspaper articles fueled anticipation of the new coin's release during the spring and summer. Finally, the first examples were released to the public on August 2, to long lines of eager recipients. One of the first recipients of the new coin was designer Brenner himself, who put them up in cardboard holders, which he autographed and presented to his friends.

1909 JANUARY 31. Sculptor Bela Lyon Pratt writes that his Lincoln Centennial medal for New York City "came out better than could have been expected. They are making them of four sizes and of both bronze and silver."

1909 FEBRUARY. We owe James Grant Wilson for this delightful Lincoln numismatic anecdote. One evening late in 1864, Wilson was dining with the president when Secretary William Seward and Congressman E.B. Washburne from Galena, Illinois, were announced. Seward and Washburne were excited to show Lincoln "the large gold medal, just received from the Philadelphia Mint, which was voted by Congress to General Grant for the capture of Vicksburg" (Julian MI-29, by Anthony C. Paquet). Lincoln opened the morocco case containing the medal in an upside-down position. After a long pause, Wilson remarked, "What is the obverse of the medal, Mr. President?" Lincoln looked up, turned to Seward, and said, "I suppose by his obverse the Colonel means t' other side!" "There was no sting in this," Wilson wrote, "and the victim joined in the general laugh."

"Indeed, Lincoln was too kind-hearted," he continued, "to exercise his trenchant power of repartee. 'Wit laughs at everybody; humor laughs with everybody,'" Lincoln commented.[54]

Wilson had previously reported this recollection in 1904 in *The Cornhill Magazine.*

1909. The Lincoln History Society, New York, reprints Ida M. Tarbell's four-volume biography *The Life of Lincoln.*

1909 CIRCA. New York's fine jewelers Tiffany & Co. commission J.E. Roiné to design an Abraham Lincoln portrait medallion. The seven-inch-diameter bronze medallions were produced by Gorham Manufacturing Co. Tiffany's had its medallions mounted on half-inch-thick black-and-cream marble plaques, 8.5 by 11 inches in size, with a support mounted to the back so they would stand up on a shelf. Tiffany's sold this plaque in its store on New York's Fifth Avenue during the Lincoln centennial. Non-Tiffany Roiné bronze medallions of this size, struck by Gorham, were mounted on 9- by 11-inch wood, to be hung on walls.

Fig. 2.203. French sculptor Jules Edouard Roiné created 19 memorable Lincoln medals and plaques, according to Edgar Heyl and Robert P. King. This unlisted seven-inch bronze portrait medallion, commissioned by Tiffany & Co., New York City, and made by Gorham, was his masterpiece. Tiffany sold it mounted on an 8.5 by 11–inch marble plaque with a kickstand so it would stand up on a shelf. A less expensive edition was also sold mounted on an oak plaque that could be mounted on a wall.

1909 JANUARY. E.P. Dutton & Co. in New York and J.M. Dent & Co. in London co-publish the Illinois Lincoln Centennial Commission's project by reprinting *Speeches and Letters of Abraham Lincoln, 1832–1865.* This work was previously published in February 1907 by the same publishers, based, with permission, on John G. Nicolay and John Hay's 1894 *The Complete Works of Abraham Lincoln,* published by The Century Co. The new edition included an introduction by Richard Watson Gilder and essays by several additional contributors.

1909. A facing portrait of Abraham Lincoln in stained glass is incorporated into the center of the dome of the First Methodist Church, University Place, Lincoln, Nebraska.

1909. New membership certificates are issued for the Lincoln Farm Association, by the American Bank Note Co. The litho employed the O-92 $100 Lincoln portrait pose, replacing a Marshall-model portrait by the New York Bank Note Co. (used by the group on earlier membership certificates from about 1906).

1909 FEBRUARY. Editor Albert Shaw comments in *The American Review of Reviews,* in an article on "The Lincoln Centennial," that there "is little question that Congress will in some way provide for a Lincoln Museum at Washington, in which will be deposited all important collections of Lincoln Relics that may be hereafter acquired by the Government."[55]

1909 FEBRUARY. In the same issue of *The American Review of Reviews* referenced above, editor Albert Shaw also takes particular notice of the release of Jules Edouard Roiné's Lincoln centennial medal and the accompanying volume published by Putnam & Sons. "The copies of the medal which is described as the most beautiful representation of Lincoln's features ever made, were struck under the instructions of Mr. Robert Hewitt, the collector of Lincoln medals, who is the owner of the copyright."[56]

Fig. 2.204. In 1909 a facing portrait of Abraham Lincoln in stained glass was incorporated into the center of the dome of the First Methodist Church, University Place, Lincoln, Nebraska.

Fig. 2.205. Osborn H. Oldroyd put together the core of the Lincoln collection which the National Park Service displays today at the Ford's Theatre National Historic Site. He displayed his artifacts and commemorative pieces in Lincoln's Springfield home and in the Petersen House, in which Lincoln died. Here Oldroyd poses with a small number of his Lincoln medallions.

Fig. 2.206. The Lincoln Farm Association adopted a Lincoln logo patterned after the Marshall portrait, as appears on its letterhead *(a)* and this honorary membership certificate *(b)*. As the Lincoln centennial neared, however, the association got with the program of the times and switched to a different Abraham Lincoln portrait for its logo. Unequivocally, it selected the Lincoln O-92 money image as its new identity (see figure 3.19 in *Abraham Lincoln: The Image of His Greatness*).

1809 • ABRAHAM • LINCOLN • 1865

An immigrant to the United States from Lithuania, sculptor Victor David Brenner attempted to wring every cent he could out of his Lincoln profile design. He created many Lincoln plaques unknown to Glenn Smedley's catalog of Brenner's works. This rare bronze is one of them. Although mounted on a green marble tablet similar to the more familiarly seen large plaque, this early version does not have the 1907 copyright notice seen on those pieces running up the right edge of the field. However, it is signed in cursive "V.D. Brenner / Sc." It also has a different title block at the bottom: 1809 • ABRAHAM LINCOLN • 1865. This plaque is larger than the 8-1/4 by 10-5/8–inch plaque that is widely and erroneously claimed to have been the model for the cent. This example measures 11-1/2 by 14-3/4 inches. The marble tablet is 13 by 16-1/2 inches.

Whatever the model, Brenner's Lincoln profile would proliferate in the next century on the bronze cent, to become the idol carried in every man, woman, and child's pocket.

Chapter 3

Lincoln the Idol

1909 – 1959

The "Lincoln Half Century," commencing with the Lincoln centennial observance in 1909, turned Abraham Lincoln, the Ideal American, into Abraham Lincoln, the American Idol of the nation's civil religion. The decades saw the erection of more than two dozen important memorials to the patron saint of American exceptionalism, the progress of the self-made man. Although parochial shrines dotted the landscape throughout America, the locus of this national veneration became the axis between the Lincoln Birth Temple in Kentucky, the National Lincoln Temple in Washington, D.C., and the national pantheon on Mount Rushmore, conceived and dedicated as America's national "Shrine of Democracy."

The legend of the poor Lincoln born on the American frontier, who had raised himself up by his bootstraps to the pinnacle of the American dream, the White House, where he had saved the nation and become its martyr, to a restored Union, became a passion plays that lit up the stage and silver screen with regularity, creating successive waves of patriotic national revivals.

The Lincoln amulet, the Lincoln cent, was conceived, and its purpose hardly hidden, as the patriotic calling card of this universal Lincoln veneration. The purpose of portraying Lincoln as the first citizen to be elevated to the role of the Caesar on the nation's coinage was to make his image omnipresent in the minds, hearts, hands, and pockets of *every* American, high and low, on a minute-by-minute daily basis. On the cent Lincoln became part and parcel of virtually every commercial transaction, tying Lincoln consciousness to national commerce and individual livelihood.

It was conceived by Lincolnphile Republican U.S. president Theodore Roosevelt as a daily reminder of the nation's indebtedness to the nation's savior. Roosevelt vividly recalled as a six-year-old boy in New York witnessing the aftermath of the Lincoln assassination, its effect on his family and the public, and the events of the Lincoln veneration in New York City at the time. As a young boy, Teddy witnessed the Lincoln funeral procession up the city's Broadway from the window of his grandfather's mansion. As a grown man, Roosevelt admired his Republican forbear, the Western outdoorsman and war president who had saved the nation and freed the black race.

Fig. 3.1. This excellent Abraham Lincoln essay-contest silver portrait medal (King-493) was awarded by the *Philadelphia Public Ledger* in 1909. It was struck by J.E. Caldwell & Co., Philadelphia, a firm that lasted 170 years until it went out of business in November 2009. The King reference is incorrect; it was not "J.B. Caldwell," as stated therein.

Fig. 3.2. The *Collier's* magazine Abraham Lincoln centennial issue featured Charles R. Huntington's 1906 Lincoln portrait based on the same photographic model as the then-current $500 bill engraving.

Lincoln was not only Roosevelt's greatest hero from boyhood, but also the subject of Roosevelt's adult man-crush. In 1901, when President William McKinley became the third chief executive to be assassinated, Vice President Theodore Roosevelt stepped into his predecessors' shoes as nation's leader. As president, Roosevelt placed a portrait of Lincoln in his White House office and vowed to make all his decisions in the spirit of "what Lincoln would have done." "I think of Lincoln all the time," Roosevelt confessed. Another time, he wrote, "The more I study . . . the more I feel . . . the towering greatness of Lincoln." Roosevelt's great friend in Washington, his secretary of State, John Hay, had been one of Lincoln's personal secretaries and was—with John Nicolay—Lincoln's most eminent biographer. Hay regaled Roosevelt with intimate stories of the Civil War president, and presented Roosevelt a gold pinky ring with a lock of Lincoln's hair inside under glass. Roosevelt wore the ring to his 1905 inaugural, and said it made him ever mindful to administer the Constitution in the spirit of the Great Emancipator. On the centennial of Lincoln's birth, February 12, 1909, Roosevelt dedicated the laying of the cornerstone for the Lincoln birth memorial temple in Hodgenville, Kentucky.

The Lincoln cent was soon to become not only the most prolific but also the most pervasive symbol in American history. In the "Lincoln Half Century," 1909 to 1959, its profile became universally known as if a birthright to every American child. The cent followed Americans around the globe, becoming a symbol not just of American commerce, but also of America itself. Wherever America was known, and longed for, people the world over came to know this round ambassador of American identity. America was a country where a poor, disadvantaged boy could rise up in society to become an admired and successful man. He might even, as had Lincoln, become the president of these United States, the American Caesar himself. The promise of the penny was a powerful image and beacon not only to America's own people, but also to the poor and disadvantaged the world over, for whom the simple cent became a promise in kind, too. It was fitting that it was executed by an immigrant artisan, who had left his native Lithuania for the better prospects America offered those who labor not in vain, and who had found his own success among his adopted countrymen, to whom he gave one of the nation's most powerful symbols.

Ironically, the Lincoln brand on the cent does not engage the viewer directly. Instead the idol stares off symbolically into the future. It is not this effigy's purpose to minister, nor to console the viewer, but rather to inspire him and her. The demigod of American civil religion ministers to the God-breathed aspiration in the bosom of all mankind. Every child, so it is said in the American canon, can walk in Lincoln's footsteps no matter how humble the circumstances of birth, education, or prospects. The copper amulet is a tangible memento in the American civil religion of upward mobility. Thanks to Roosevelt and sculptor Victor David Brenner, we can hold this dream in our energetic hands as well as conceiving it in our eager hearts.

Fig. 3.3. Collectors will find a plethora of paper items relating to the Lincoln centennial. *Hints*, "The Entertainment Magazine," employed the familiar John Chester Buttre engraving on its cover *(a)*. A Sunday school booklet *(b)* used the William Edgar Marshall likeness, and the official dedication booklet for Adolph A. Weinman's statue in the Hodgenville, Kentucky, town center suitably showed his seated bronze figure *(c)*.

The first Lincoln cent was struck in May 1909. By the time the U.S. Treasury released the first examples of this eagerly awaited coin to the public in August, the pent-up demand to receive this sacramental offering created long and steady lines at distribution points. This was the first United States regular-issue coin to depict an American president. During the next 100 years, 470 billion of these small coins infiltrated every nook and cranny, crevice, and interstice in American society. A profile portrait was also adopted for use on the regular U.S. four-cent postage stamp prior to the first-class letter rate being increased in the 1950s, and another similar profile when the definitive issue was changed in 1965.

The cent profile was not just pervasive—it was popular, too. Over time the Lincoln profile became so ingrained in American consciousness that no context was necessary to create instant Pavlovian recognition responses wherever it was employed. The Lincoln profile image anointed its context with all the positive attributes associated to Lincoln in the minds of the citizenry, as the American demigod. Lincoln profiles appeared elsewhere on signs, on advertising, and anywhere a manufacturer or merchandiser desired to create this positive brand identification.

1909 FEBRUARY 8. The Historical Society of Pennsylvania celebrates the Lincoln centennial at a special meeting. Major William H. Lambert read a paper on the Gettysburg Address, and brought an extensive selection from his personal Lincoln collection to supplement the Society's own treasures in an exhibition of Lincoln autographs and relics that continued through the week.

Lambert's Lincolniana on display included a lock of the president's hair, his law-office ink stand, several canes presented to him, various books he owned, numerous holographic signed letters and notes in his hand, legal documents, and a Lincoln & Herndon fee book. Also on display: Lambert brought his example of the French memorial medal as well as silver and bronze specimens of the Victor David Brenner Lincoln medal; and bronze, silver, and (the unique) gold examples of the Lincoln Centennial medal by Roiné. Lambert also displayed two original Lincoln ambrotypes, an original Lincoln daguerreotype, a dozen contemporary card photographs, and various souvenirs, according to an account of the event.

Among items on display from the Society's collection was the letter Lincoln wrote July 13, 1863, following Ulysses Grant's victory at Vicksburg. "I do not remember that you and I ever met personally," Lincoln wrote. "I write this now as a grateful acknowledgement for the almost inestimable service you have done the country. . . ." Then Lincoln explained how he would have taken Vicksburg, and concluded, "I now wish to make the personal acknowledgment that you were right, and I was wrong. Yours very truly. A. Lincoln."[1]

1909 FEBRUARY 12. The *Philadelphia Public Ledger* awards silver medals "for merit in essay on Abraham Lincoln." The medals were produced by Philadelphia manufacturing jeweler J.E. Caldwell & Co. They have an excellent profile bust on the obverse and, on the reverse, a representation of a *Ledger* front page featuring stories about the Lincoln centennial, the president's biography, and his policies in office. (See figure 3.1.)

Fig. 3.5. The U.S. Mint struck this gold medal (King-311) for the Lincoln centennial, reprising engraver George T. Morgan's 1886 obverse portrait from the Mint's presidential-medal series (Julian PR-12) with new lettering and no beaded border, and paired it with a commemorative reverse taken from Lincoln's Second Inaugural Address.

Fig. 3.6. This privately issued medal by Sheeler-Hemsher Co., Philadelphia, was apparently unknown to King. The brass-foundry medal's obverse also employs Morgan's obverse design cast, directly from the original 1886 U.S. Mint medal obverse.

Fig. 3.4. These three Lincoln centennial pinbacks illustrate the many municipal, commercial, and essay-contest buttons issued then.

1909 FEBRUARY 12. The dies of the Lincoln centennial medal by Jules Edouard Roiné, issued by Robert Hewitt and contained in a book published by G.P. Putnam's Sons, are cancelled and deposited with the American Numismatic Society, according to an aluminum medal stuck by Medallic Art Co., New York. This was one of the first productions of the new firm, which had also struck the Lincoln centennial medal itself. It might be noted that Hewitt's book—and the medal, by extension—was dedicated to Archer M. Huntington, then president of the American Numismatic Society, who doubtless underwrote the entire venture as a private philanthropy.

1909 FEBRUARY 12. The Lincoln Centennial Association holds a banquet honoring the 100th anniversary of the birth of Abraham Lincoln at the Illinois State Armory, Springfield, Illinois.

1909 FEBRUARY 23. Cahn & Van Wagenen Music Publishing Co. copyright "Pictures on the Flag," words by L.A. Barber and music by J. Fred Baldwin. Its five-cent sheet music includes a beardless Lincoln portrait. The colorful sheet-music copyright was issued to the same parties on March 28, 1909.

Other commemorative anthems written for the Lincoln birth centennial included "Our Lincoln Ode," by W.C. Washburn and Joseph Surdo, copyrighted December 7, 1908; "The Birthday of Lincoln," by Geo. B. Jennings Co., copyrighted January 18, 1909; "Lincoln Day Program," by E.C. Bolles and D.L. Maulsby, copyrighted January 8, 1909; "Lincoln Memorial Song," by L.S. Collins and Laura Sedgwick Collins, copyrighted on February 10 and February 16, 1909; "Our Lincoln," by W.C. Washburn and Joseph Surdo, copyrighted February 4, 1909; "The Lincoln March," by Will Huff, copyrighted March 6 and March 25, 1909; "Song of the Emancipation Proclamation," by P.J. Bacon, copyrighted April 2, 1909; and "Abe Lincoln Centennial March," by Warren D. Troutman, copyrighted May 10, 1909.

1909 FEBRUARY. Robert Hewitt loans his collection of about 600 Lincoln medals to the Metropolitan Museum of Art for public display during the Lincoln centennial. "This collection . . . issued between 1860 and 1909 forms almost a complete medallic history of the martyred President, in which the slavery question, the Campaign of 1860, the Civil War, the second election in 1864, the assassination and other

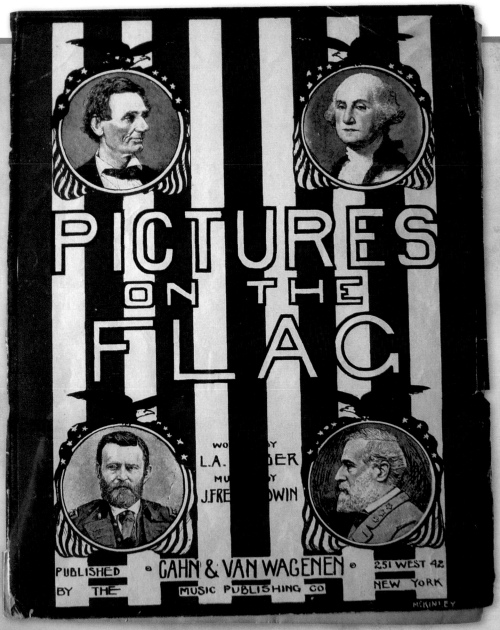

Fig. 3.7. This colorful sheet music, published by Cahn & Van Wagenen, greeted the Lincoln centennial in 1909. The pairing of warring Civil War generals U.S. Grant and Robert E. Lee with the founding father and the nation's savior shows that the healing of the rift between the North and South—which Abraham Lincoln desired—had come to pass in some measure.

events of the President's life are illustrated," according to the Museum's monthly bulletin in April, when the exhibition was still in place.[2]

1909 FEBRUARY 24. The Loup City, Nebraska, high school dedicates a 36-inch-tall bronze bust of Abraham Lincoln at the school.

1909 MARCH. *Putnam's Magazine* features a seven-page, illustrated article on Robert Hewitt's Lincoln medal collection, giving the publication another excuse to tout its two Lincoln medal books published in conjunction with Hewitt.

The article, penned by Montgomery Schuyler, traced Hewitt's "nearly half a century" inclination toward numismatics of Lincoln to the excellent advice given him years before by his neighbor, historian George Bancroft, "to specialize his collecting." "The result is a collection of medallic Lincolniana probably unequalled in number and extent," Schuyler affirmed.[3] More than 800 Lincoln medals were then presently known to collectors, according to Schuyler, "and what a recall of old times it is to look over Mr. Hewitt's collection!" he continued. The author described the French medal struck for presentation to Lincoln's widow from the proceeds of 40,000 French citizens. "One notes with pain," Schuyler wrote, "that the original is 'announced for sale.'"[4] The hardly unbiased reporter wrote effusively when describing Roiné's large profile medal for Hewitt. In contrast to most of the Lincoln medals, which have historic but little artistic interest, "This has the pretension to attain the highest grade of the medallic art of the young twentieth century," he wrote, "with

what success readers can judge for themselves. At all events, the fact that the Metropolitan Museum of Art has accepted the gift of the original design of it, indicates that in the judgment of accomplished critics the work is of high artistic quality."[5] Schuyler ended his observations with the hopes that Hewitt's lifelong interest in building the collection would safeguard "it permanently from dispersal."

1909 APRIL 20. During the previous month, the Metropolitan Museum of Art, New York City, acquires two Abraham Lincoln medals via donation by Mr. and Mrs. Frederick S. Wait, described as: "bronze medal, Abraham Lincoln, by C.E. Barber; copper medal, Abraham Lincoln, by W.H. Key."[6]

1909 MAY 26. The first Civil War campaign badge by Francis D. Millet, with a portrait bust of Abraham Lincoln on the obverse, is awarded to Major General Charles F. Humphrey.

1909 MAY 31. Sculptor Adolph A. Weinman's seated bronze figure of Abraham Lincoln is dedicated in the public square of Lincoln's birth town of Hodgenville, Kentucky.

1909 JUNE. *The Numismatist* reports: "Information from Washington indicates that the now long-anticipated Lincoln cent will not be issued before August. When examples from the supposed completed dies were submitted to President Taft, it is said that he asked for the motto 'In God We Trust' to be placed on the coin." That inscription was added, above Lincoln's head, to the obverse die.

Fig. 3.8. This close-up shows the Weinman statue's head at Hodgenville, Kentucky.

Fig. 3.9. J. Henri Ripstra was a Chicago numismatist and medalist. This is an unlisted gold example of Ripstra's small portrait plaque (King-840).

1909 June 22. Four weeks after the dedication of Adolph A. Weinman's seated bronze statue of Abraham Lincoln in the president's birthplace of Hodgenville, Kentucky, a replica of the statue is dedicated at the University of Wisconsin Madison campus, on Bascom Hill. The president of the university's board of regents singled out the statue as "a sign to all future generations of the high ideals of American citizenship." The Wisconsin statue was secured through the work of UW alumnus Richard Lloyd Jones, a generous gift of $6,500 from benefactor Thomas E. Brittingham, and another $1,500 paid by the university.

Over the years the liberal UW student body would take the Lincoln ideal less than seriously. In 1944 the campus newspaper joked that the statue did indeed reflect upon campus morals—"Lincoln stood up every time a virgin walked by"—and that quip was a byword on campus for decades thereafter. In the next decade, the Lincoln statue would be painted red for a student protest of McCarthyism. During the sixties, it was outfitted with flamboyant pink flamingos and other indignities.

1909 July 1. Milnor Dorey copyrights *Abe Lincoln: A Musical Play in Two Acts,* based on the boyhood and youth of Abraham Lincoln, with music adapted from traditional American melodies by Bryceson Treharne.

1909 July 14. Treasury Secretary Franklin MacVeagh approves the Lincoln cent design, five weeks after the first coins were struck.

1909 July 23. The Lincoln Mining Co. Stockholder's Syndicate employs the American Financial Agency Co. to represent the interests of its members.

1909. Baker & Taylor Co. publishes the multiple-volume autobiography of John Bigelow, Lincoln's appointee as consul to France. Bigelow provided extensive insights into the overt campaign, waged by Napoleon III's totalitarian French government, to suppress the public subscription among French citizens for the gold medal in Lincoln's honor, to be presented to his widow Mary. In addition to banning public congregations to support subscriptions, French officials stole subscription lists and prohibited striking of the medal in France. This delayed but did not thwart the French republicans' progress toward having the medal eventually struck in Switzerland. Novelist Victor Hugo wrote Mrs. Lincoln: "If France had the freedom enjoyed by republican America, not thousands, but millions among us would have been counted as admirers."

1909 August. Mary Shipman Andrews's inexpensive (50 cents) book for the Lincoln Centennial, *A Perfect Tribute,* published by

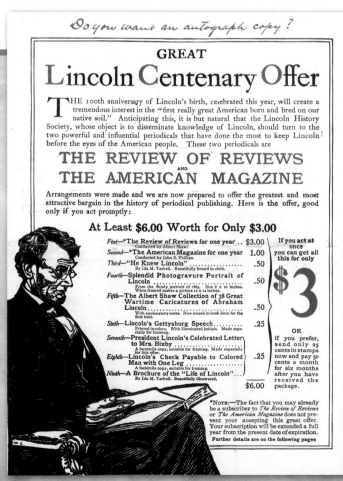

Fig. 3.10. For the centennial the Lincoln History Society partnered with two periodicals to present the "Great Lincoln Centenary Offer," subscriptions and works by Albert Shaw and Ida M. Tarbell.

Fig. 3.11. A great variety of Abraham Lincoln postcards was issued in conjunction with the Lincoln centennial. This wonderful, embossed medallion postcard made in Germany is one of the author's favorites. All the colored images are in relief.

Scribner, is a runaway bestseller in Northern bookstores, ranking at or near the top of every nonfiction sales list for the quarter. It was number 4 in New Haven; number 2 in New York City downtown; number 1 in Chicago; number 4 in Cleveland; number 3 in Denver; number 4 in Kansas City; number 1 in Milwaukee; number 3 in Minneapolis; number 2 in Pittsburgh; number 2 in Providence; number 1 in St. Paul; and number 1 in Worcester.[7]

1909 AUGUST 10. A measure of the popularity of the new Abraham Lincoln portrait cent is the public's thirst for the coin. The initial supply of the popular cents, allegedly 25 million coins, would be reported depleted only eight days after their first public release.

1909 AUGUST 15. Newspapers continue to report on the controversy over the size and prominence of the Lincoln cent designer's initials on the reverse of the coin. According to one of these accounts, Treasury Secretary MacVeagh "said that he did not know that the initials would appear in embossed form on the pennies, and that he was surprised when he saw the prominent place they had been given in the design." Accordingly, it was said, "MacVeagh announced today he had decided to have the minting of the new

Lincoln pennies stopped and that new dies will be prepared eliminating the initials of the designer, which now appear so prominently, and substituting the single initial 'B' in an obscure part of the design. The Secretary said that none of the pennies issued so far would be called in, but that the minting would be stopped because a sufficient supply was on hand." Actually, MacVeagh had ordered the prominent initials removed and the presses stopped on August 4, only two days after the coin's official release.

1909 AUGUST. The American Numismatic Association convention in Montreal passes a resolution protesting the removal of sculptor Victor David Brenner's initials from the new Lincoln cent's reverse.

1909 OCTOBER 20. During the previous month, the Metropolitan Museum of Art, New York City, received from sculptor and coin designer Victor D. Brenner a gift of two Proof 1909 cents and two bronze examples of the Panama Canal medal. The design process of the medal first suggested to President Theodore Roosevelt that he recommend the cent redesign to Brenner.[8]

Fig. 3.13. The U.S. Mint galvano for Victor David Brenner's Lincoln cent shows that the sculptor originally proposed to feature his entire last name on the coin's reverse (a). The Mint limited the presentation to his initials (b), but when Treasury bigwigs saw the first cents, they stopped the Mint presses and ordered even the initials removed. Thereafter, the sculptor handed out to friends and admirers "autographed" cents with cards, like the one shown (c).

Legality of Selling Lincoln Cents.

To the Editor of The New York Times:
Is it not an infringement of the law to permit the new Lincoln pennies to be sold for more than their full value? During the past few days I saw several boys selling these pennies three for 5 cents in the vicinity of the Sub-Treasury, New York City. The selling of the "Billiken" coins and other similar souvenirs seems equitable, but should the selling of America's genuine currency in excess of its par value be permissible any more than the passing of counterfeit currency? Will some kind reader express his views in regard to the foregoing either in the affirmative or the negative?
CHARLES E. SCHAFRANCK.
Brooklyn, Aug. 11, 1909.

Fig. 3.12. *New York Times* reader Charles E. Schafranck complained over sales of the extremely popular, newly introduced Lincoln cent at 5¢ each in the paper's August 12, 1909, issue.

Fig. 3.14. Greenduck Co., Chicago, produced many Lincoln centennial items. We believe this unsigned piece is one of them. The small 32-millimeter copper medal was distributed by The Outlet Co., Providence, Rhode Island. Three unillustrated but similar reverse dies are listed by King, so it is presently impossible to tell whether the item shown is King-340, 341, or 342.

1910. "Lincoln, A Token" (King 242, DeLorey 47), designed and issued by Thomas Elder and modeled by Jules Édouard Roiné, is struck by Henri Weil for Deitsch Brothers, New York.

1910 CIRCA. Peerless Press, Oklahoma City, Oklahoma, publishes a women's suffrage postcard, "Oklahoma Women / Want Votes For Women / Let The People Rule / Women Are People," with a quote attributed to Abraham Lincoln: "I go for all sharing the privileges of the government who assist in bearing its burdens, by no means excepting women."

1910 FEBRUARY 12. Tresal Bronzing-Plating Co., New York, produces a bronze plaque with a right-facing profile of Abraham Lincoln for the Republican Club of the City of New York celebration.

1910 MARCH. Robert Todd Lincoln expresses dismay with himself that, during the Lincoln centennial a year earlier, he did not bring forward into prominence the French gold medal in his father's honor given his mother in 1866 and then in his possession. This is according to an article in *Putnam's Magazine* authored by "J.B.G." (the publication's editor, James B. Gilder). "It is of gold . . . the thickness is about a quarter of an inch—perhaps a little more," Robert Lincoln wrote Gilder. "It is a very handsome medal, which I trust will always be properly cherished by my father's descendants."[9]

1910 MARCH 12. Among items on display at the American Numismatic Society International Medallic Exhibition of Contemporary Medals are cent designer Victor David Brenner's original plaster models for the coin's obverse and reverse, and the copper galvano die shells made from those plasters.

1910 MAY 11. The Lincoln Wigwam Table is unveiled at the Chicago Wigwam (in Chicago at Market and Lake streets) to mark the 50th anniversary of Abraham Lincoln's nomination as Republican candidate for president.

1910 MAY 30. Central High School, Manchester, New Hampshire, acquires sculptor John Rogers's *Council of War,* depicting President Abraham Lincoln, Secretary of War Edwin Stanton, and General Ulysses S. Grant.

1910 SEPTEMBER 27. A standing bronze statue of Lincoln by sculptor J. Otto Schweizer is installed at the Pennsylvania state memorial at Gettysburg battlefield, the largest at the national historic site. Names of every Pennsylvanian who fought at Gettysburg were inscribed.

1910 NOVEMBER 2. Bureau of Engraving and Printing engraver G.F.C. Smillie completes die no. 7795, a Lincoln portrait for the $100 postal-bond coupon.

Fig. 3.15. The Chicago Daughters of the American Revolution desired to mark the location of Abraham Lincoln's 1860 nomination for the Lincoln centennial, but the plaque was not completed, installed, and dedicated until 15 months later.

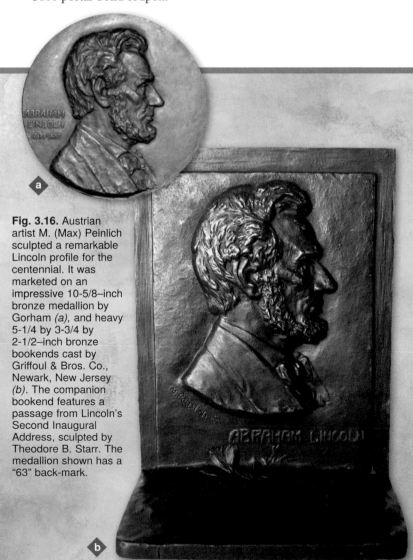

Fig. 3.16. Austrian artist M. (Max) Peinlich sculpted a remarkable Lincoln profile for the centennial. It was marketed on an impressive 10-5/8–inch bronze medallion by Gorham *(a)*, and heavy 5-1/4 by 3-3/4 by 2-1/2–inch bronze bookends cast by Griffoul & Bros. Co., Newark, New Jersey *(b)*. The companion bookend features a passage from Lincoln's Second Inaugural Address, sculpted by Theodore B. Starr. The medallion shown has a "63" back-mark.

1911. An *Encyclopedia Britannica* article by H. Lawrence Swinburne describes the original ribbon on the Union Civil War veterans' badge as having a blue stripe in the center, divided by a white line, with red stripes on its outer edges. Although this award was established to honor Union vets, in today's politically correct times modern restrikes have the medal suspended from a half-and-half blue-and-grey ribbon.

1911 MAY 30. Sculptor Gutzon Borglum's viewer-friendly statue of Lincoln seated on a bench is dedicated at the Essex County Courthouse, Newark, New Jersey. The memorial was a gift of Amos H. Van Horn, whose will set aside $25,000 for a Lincoln monument to be dedicated in memory of Lincoln Post, No. 11, Department of New Jersey, Grand Army of the Republic.

1911 JUNE 13. Sculptor and medalist James Earle Fraser writes U.S. Mint Director George E. Roberts: "I think your idea of the Lincoln head is a splendid one and I shall be very glad to make you some sketches as soon as possible and let you see them. I think they should be reduced to the actual size of the coin; otherwise we will not be really able to judge them, even in the sketch period. I will have that done here, where I can watch the process." These 1911-dated electrotrials would be produced in white metal, depicting a large bust facing left in profile, almost completely filling the proposed obverse of a design to replace the then-current Liberty Head nickel. A similar treatment of a composite Indian head, also by Fraser, would be adopted two years later for the new five-cent coin.

Fig. 3.17. Ardent Lincoln admirer Gutzon Borglum parlayed his monumentally sized beardless Lincoln head in the U.S. Capitol rotunda into a commission for a Lincoln sculpture for Newark, New Jersey. Flying in the face of tradition, which insisted on placing Lincoln on the highest of pinnacles in public statuary, Borglum's viewer-friendly Lincoln sat on a bronze bench at ground level before the Court House when unveiled there in 1911.

Fig. 3.18. Sculptor J. Otto Schweizer's standing bronze of Abraham Lincoln was installed at the Pennsylvania state memorial at Gettysburg battlefield.

Fig. 3.19. These two Lincoln National Bank checks from the 1910s, without printers' imprints, have likenesses after the Marshall portrait and the $500 bill portrait modeled on O-91.

1911 JUNE 14. A bronze Lincoln statue by sculptor Frank E. Elwell is dedicated at East Orange, New Jersey.

1911 JUNE 30. Actor Ralph Ince portrays Abraham Lincoln in the movie *The Battle Hymn of the Republic,* the first of nine silver-screen portrayals of Old Abe that he will perform through 1921.

1911 JULY 3. The last Abraham Lincoln birth-centennial medal by Jules E. Roiné is struck for the Grand Army of the Republic, by Joseph Davison's Sons, Philadelphia.

1911 AUGUST 1. The *New York Times* publishes sculptor Isidore Konti's plea that the design for the statue of the proposed Lincoln Memorial in Washington, D.C., be the result of an open competition among "independent sculptors."

"Open competition in all ages has had gratifying results. . . . Of the few artistic monuments our National Capital possesses, those of recognized artistic merits are the outcome of that system," Konti stated. "Let the American sculptors have their chance to demonstrate what they can do," he urged. "There is more talent among them than is generally known and appreciated. Perhaps the great opportunity will bring forth the genius who will master it," he added.

Konti's July 29 missive was in response to an earlier article in the *Times* suggesting that open competitions bring forth unsatisfactory results. Konti listed about a dozen contrary instances to back his argument that an as-yet-unheralded sculptor's design may be the best choice for the national monument.[10]

1911 NOVEMBER 8. Dedication ceremonies are held for Adolph A. Weinman's impressive standing bronze statue of Abraham Lincoln that J.B. Speed of Louisville presented to the Commonwealth of Kentucky in the Rotunda of the State Capitol in Frankfort. The new building had opened a year earlier. Weinman also executed the seated statue of Lincoln that is on US 31-East in the center of Lincoln's birthplace, Hodgenville, Kentucky.

1912 JANUARY 22. A bronze bust of Abraham Lincoln by Henry K. Bush-Brown is installed at the Gettysburg Soldier's National Cemetery, flanked by bronze tablets inscribed with Lincoln's oratory, against a backdrop of a low, curved white-marble wall.

1912 FEBRUARY 11. The *New York Times* feature story, "When Lincoln Was the Target of Bitter Critics," illustrates what the newspaper calls "cartoonists and professional jesters [taking] their fling at the President before he faced the problems of the White House and long afterward."

Fig. 3.21. Adolph A. Weinman, who had sculpted a seated figure of Lincoln for the Hodgenville centennial celebration, turned out this standing figure for the rotunda of the Kentucky State Capitol in Frankfort two years later. The monument was the gift of J.B. Speed of Louisville.

Fig. 3.20. J.E. Roiné's Lincoln centennial medal for the Grand Army of the Republic (King 299–301) *(a)* was struck by Jas. Davison's Sons, Philadelphia, from three distinct obverse dies. Shown is King-301, from the third obverse die, with Roiné's initials removed. Later, according to Dick Johnson, Medallic Art Co. acquired one of the dies and restruck the piece from the cancelled die. The die *(b)* that struck the medal shown still survives and was sold in a recent numismatic auction.

1912 FEBRUARY 12. The grand re-opening of the Lincoln School, originally built in 1859 as Burlington Union School, is held in Burlington, Wisconsin.

1912 MARCH. The Women's Relief Corps' Department of Massachusetts presents a bronze bust of Abraham Lincoln by Leonard Volk to the State of Massachusetts. The bust and a bronze table containing the text of Lincoln's Gettysburg Address were installed in Doric Hall, on the second floor of the Massachusetts statehouse.

1912 CIRCA. Following the destruction of the Pietro Mezzara Lincoln statue in San Francisco (due to the fires started by the Great San Francisco earthquake of 1906), a Lincoln Memorial Fund committee is started up by members of the Lincoln Grammar School Association to solicit subscriptions "to aid and assist in the erection of a memorial in San Francisco to the memory of Abraham Lincoln." Subscription diplomas were printed by Britton & Rey. A likeness of Lincoln similar to that which would shortly appear on the $5 Federal Reserve Notes and Federal Reserve Bank Notes adorns a patriotic cartouche at the head of the certificates.

Fig. 3.22. Western Bank Note Co., Chicago, printed this souvenir card of the famous Bixby Letter, sent by Abraham Lincoln in 1864 to a Massachusetts woman who had purportedly lost five sons in the Union cause. The eloquent missive was widely published at the time, although scholarship has called into question how many sons actually died for the Union. Some scholars question whether the letter was even written by Lincoln, suggesting presidential secretary John Hay as its source. The excellent engraved portrait, based on O-83, bears the 1909 copyright of Charles Barmore, New York.

Fig. 3.23. The Lincoln Protective League was organized in Springfield, Illinois, in June 1911 to promote a "strong protective tariff policy for the welfare of the American laborer, farmer and manufacturer." The league was a reaction to "the betrayal of Republican principles by a Republican administration," according to spokesman William Hale Thompson.

Fig. 3.24. Shortly after the oldest memorial sculpture to Abraham Lincoln (crafted in August 1865 by Pietro Mezzara) perished in the fire started by the great San Francisco earthquake of 1906, a group of prominent Californians started "The Lincoln Memorial Fund . . . to aid and assist in the erection" of another memorial in San Francisco to Lincoln's memory. This certificate, with a likeness similar to that on the $1 Silver Certificates and $100 Legal Tender notes of the period, was lithographed by Britton & Rey, San Francisco.

1912. Social reformer Jane Addams's autobiographical *Twenty Years at Hull-House with Autobiographical Notes,* published by Macmillan, recalls the unrest in Chicago in summer 1894, "when Chicago was filled with federal troops sent there by the President of the United States, and their presence was resented by the governor of the state. . . . I walked the wearisome way from Hull-House to Lincoln Park—for no cars were running regularly at that moment of sympathetic strikes—in order to look at and gain magnanimous counsel, if I might, from the marvelous St. Gaudens statue which had been but recently placed at the entrance of the park. . . . [N]ever did a distracted town more sorely need the healing of 'with charity towards all' than did Chicago at that moment, and the tolerance of the man who had won charity for those on both sides of 'an irrepressible conflict.'"[11]

1912 JULY. Sculptor Jules Roiné finds a second suitor for his small Lincoln centennial medal design for the City of New York—Illinois Watch Co., maker of the A. Lincoln watch.

Illinois Watch Co., Springfield, would advertise its Lincoln watch fob by Roiné for free in *The Railway Conductor* magazine from at least July to December 1912, and in the *Railroad Telegrapher* magazine from at least January to July 1913. "Write for a Lincoln Medal and a descriptive folder of these watches," the ad read.

1912 SEPTEMBER 2. Daniel Chester French's bronze statue of Abraham Lincoln is dedicated at Lincoln High School, Lincoln, Nebraska. On the same day a standing bronze statue of Lincoln by French was dedicated at the Nebraska State Capitol in Lincoln. The carved granite backdrop, by architect Henry Bacon, has Lincoln's Gettysburg Address inscribed. Silver-tongued orator William Jennings Bryan was the dedication speaker.

1912 NOVEMBER 1. Francis Ford makes his first silver-screen appearance as Abraham Lincoln, in *On Secret Service.* Ford would additionally play Lincoln in five films, most memorably in *The Heart of Lincoln,* which was released February 9, 1915.

1913 FEBRUARY 12. A Lincoln statue is dedicated in the Broken Bow, Nebraska, high-school building.

1913 APRIL 19. Alexander Groves presents a larger-than-life-size bronze statue, of Abraham Lincoln standing with his hand resting on a column and holding his second inaugural address, to Webster City High School. The statue was the work of Chicago sculptor George E. Ganiere. Groves presented the Lincoln statue in memory of his son, who attended the school, class of 1895.

Fig. 3.25. In 1912 the Illinois Watch Co., manufacturer of the A. Lincoln pocket watch, gave away small Lincoln medals and fobs in the design Bela Lyon Pratt had created for the New York City Lincoln centennial medal.

Fig. 3.26. Empire Distillery's Lincoln money-portrait brand graced its Old Empire Straight Whiskey bottle labels and the company's letterhead. This letter advised a West Virginia hotel to pick up, pay up, or shut up.

DETAIL OF THE STATUE OF LINCOLN BY DANIEL CHESTER FRENCH MADE FOR THE CITY OF LINCOLN, NEBRASKA, AND TO BE UNVEILED DURING THE PRESENT YEAR.

Fig. 3.27. A decade before he achieved immortality with his seated marble figure of Abraham Lincoln at the Lincoln Memorial, sculptor Daniel Chester French produced this reverent standing Lincoln for Lincoln, Nebraska (a). The installation, including the inscription of his Gettysburg Address on the wall behind him, was the contribution of architect Henry Bacon, who also not coincidentally designed the Lincoln Memorial. French's Lincoln was celebrated in *The Century Magazine* in March 1912 (b).

Fig. 3.28. In the early 20th century, the "Big Five" of Lincoln collectors included Joseph Benjamin Oakleaf (a) and Judd Stewart (b), whose bookplates are shown, as well as Daniel Fish, William H. Lambert, and Charles W. McClellan.

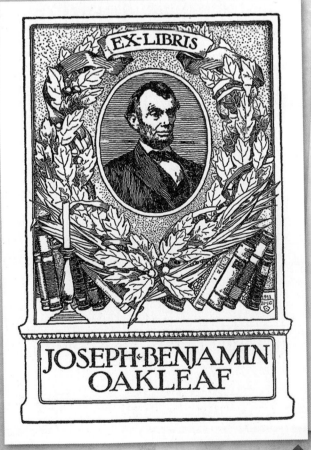

Fig. 3.29. Rudolph Bohunek's portrait of Lincoln, similar to the $500 bill image modeled on O-91, was reproduced as a chromolithograph on canvas by Illinois Watch Co., Springfield, and sent to dealers as a point-of-purchase display to boost sales of the company's A. Lincoln pocket watch.

1913 JULY 1. The Lincoln Highway Association organizes at Detroit, Michigan, with Henry Joy as its first president. Carl Fisher, the "father" of the movement, commenced an auto-tour scouting routes for the proposed transcontinental Lincoln Highway. On September 14 a provisional "Proclamation Route" would be drawn, revised on October 1. Construction of segments would commence in 1914 at Mooseheart and Malta, Illinois. The association solicited contributions, assigning "membership" certificates to donors. Automobile enthusiast President Woodrow Wilson contributed $5 and was assigned LHA certificate #1.

1913 SEPTEMBER 14. The Lincoln Highway Association, founded "to immediately promote and procure the establishment of a continuous improved highway from the Atlantic to the Pacific, open to lawful traffic of all descriptions and without toll charges," proclaims by fiat the existence of such a continuous route through the states of New York, New Jersey, Pennsylvania, Ohio, Indiana, Illinois, Iowa, Nebraska, Colorado, Wyoming, Utah, Nevada, and California.

"Whereas," its founders wrote, "It is now proper to declare the results of deliberation and inspection in the hope that the wisdom and care in selection may insure united sentiment, and with the prayer that this record will appeal to the hearts of all patriotic Americans to the end that plans and activities toward construction may go immediately forward, therefore be it Resolved, That the Lincoln Highway now is and henceforth shall be an existing memorial in tribute to the immortal Abraham Lincoln." The organizers appealed "to state authorities and all officials to properly dedicate, to re-mark and rename the said described highway with the Lincoln Highway insignia." An early traveler on the Lincoln Highway was a young army officer, Dwight D. Eisenhower, who took part in a U.S. Army cross-country convoy. The army vehicles averaged 5-3/4 miles per hour on the two-month-long jaunt, but Ike credited that trip with his vision for the interstate highway program he inaugurated as president in 1956.

1913 OCTOBER 13. A bronze statue of Abraham Lincoln by Lorado Taft's student George E. Ganiere is dedicated in Burlington, Wisconsin. The statue was the gift of local dentist Dr. Francis Meinhardt, who approved the model but died before it was cast. The original model is on display at the Burlington Historical Society Museum.

1913. The Illinois Watch Co., Springfield, uses smallish framed chromolithographs on canvas of an Abraham Lincoln portrait by Rudolph Bohunek as a sales tool to promote the company's "A. Lincoln" pocket watch. (The canvas of approximately 10 by 7 inches was in a gold frame of 14 by 11 inches.)

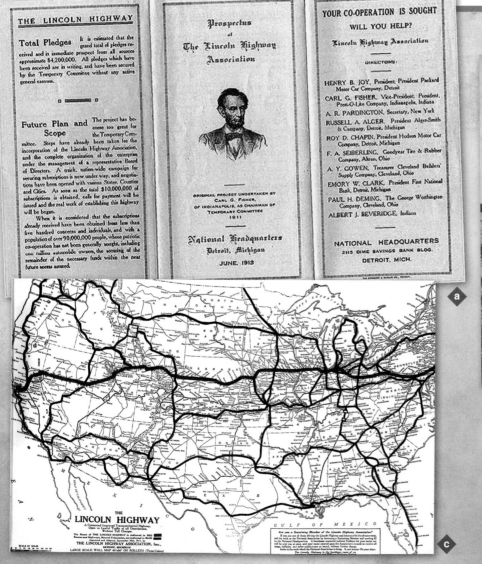

Fig. 3.30. In 1913 the Lincoln Highway Association proclaimed a transcontinental thoroughfare across plain and river and mountain from sea to shining sea, and requested local support (a). In mid-1915 a federal government expedition found this mud flat "on a deserted stretch of Lincoln Highway." (b) It would take nearly two decades for an interconnected, hard-paved road to mirror the association's 1913 aspirations and the map that the association published shortly thereafter (c).

In 1907 the company had introduced its "A. Lincoln" watch, which proved a great success, with more than 100,000 sold by 1928. In 1913, the firm hired the Bohemian artist Bohunek to paint a portrait of Lincoln, which they turned into a chromolithograph. Bohunek, born in Bohemia and trained in Prague, had worked in New Orleans from 1909 to 1911, then settled in Chicago in 1913, the year the watch company's print was first produced. He based the image on an 1864 photograph of Lincoln by Anthony Berger (O-91), which was also the model for the Lincoln portrait appearing at the time on the $500 Gold Certificate.

The framed print was sent to watch dealers around the country to be used to help promote the Lincoln watch. In the lower right is an embossing in a circle for the Illinois Watch Company and advertising "The Lincoln Watch."

1914. Poet Vachel Lindsay's "Abraham Lincoln Walks at Midnight" is published in *The Congo and Other Poems.* Writing in iambic pentameter quatrains, Lindsay described the "mourning figure" of Lincoln pacing the streets of Springfield, Illinois, on the eve of World War I. The apparition is "sleepless" because of "the bitterness, the folly, and the pain" that are abroad in our world.

1914. Judge Joseph Cunningham, reputed to be "the last living associate of Lincoln in 'riding the circuit,'" conceives of marking sites of the Eighth Circuit courthouses and roads used by Lincoln riding from county seat to county seat. The Illinois Daughters of the American Revolution took up the cause and organized the Lincoln Circuit Marking Association as a means of raising money and involving non-DAR members in the effort. Over the next seven years, during which time Coles County and other courthouses at which Lincoln practiced were added, telephone poles would be marked with the association's logo, metal plaques would be placed at county lines where Lincoln traversed from one county to another, and each county seat would be marked by a bronze plaque designed by Henry Bacon with bas relief by sculptor Georg Lober.

1914 MARCH 25. The Metropolitan Art Association, New York City, puts the Lincolniana library of the late Major William H. Lambert of Philadelphia on public display at Anderson Galleries prior to the three-day (April 1–3), five-session auction of the collection of this member of the "Big Five" (of Lincoln collectors of the early 20th century).

1914 SEPTEMBER 16. A preliminary sculpture competition at the Chicago Art Institute is conducted by the Illinois State Art Commission, seeking statues of Abraham Lincoln and Stephen A. Douglas to be erected on the State Capitol grounds in Springfield. The state legislature had voted appropriations of $50,000 and $25,000 respectively for the projects in 1913. The commission selected four Lincoln and three Douglas sculptors to be paid to enlarge their models for the final selection. The chosen models were displayed at the Art Institute for two weeks. Commissioners included sculptors Lorado Taft and Leonard Crunelle.

Fig. 3.31. Whitehead & Hoag, Newark, New Jersey, struck this 32-millimeter pocket piece (King-471) for the September 24–26, 1912, meeting marking the 50th anniversary of the convention of the Loyal Governors of the War of 1861–2 (which had expressed support for the Lincoln administration in the war's dark days).

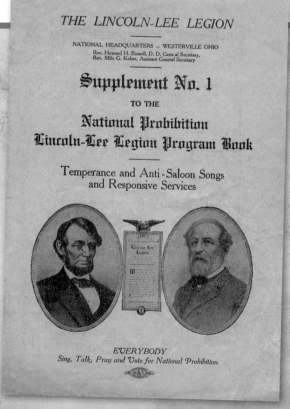

Fig. 3.32. In 1912 the name of the Lincoln League, a temperance society founded in 1903 by Reverend Howard H. Russell, DD, was changed to the Lincoln-Lee Legion to broaden its appeal among white Southerners. The group signed individuals to pledges of abstinence *(a)*, and urged "Everybody [to] sing, talk, pray and vote for National Prohibition." Once again the dollar-bill money image depicted Lincoln on the pamphlet *(b)*.

Ultimately, Andrew O'Connor's standing figure representing Lincoln's "Farewell to Springfield" speech would be selected. The 10-and-a-half-foot-tall bronze statue on a large granite base would be dedicated on October 5, 1918. British Lincoln biographer Lord Charnwood (William Arthur Smith Benson) gave the keynote address, and Illinois poet Vachel Lindsay recited his poem "When Lincoln Walks at Midnight in Springfield." The beardless head of O'Connor's statue became Mint engraver George T. Morgan's inspiration for the profile bust on the 1918 Lincoln–Illinois Centennial commemorative half dollar. Gilbert P. Riswold's statue of Lincoln's rival Douglas was dedicated the same day, the centennial of the first meeting of the Illinois General Assembly.

1914 OCTOBER 2. Secretary of the Treasury William Gibbs McAdoo approves face and back designs for Series of 1915 large-size $5 Federal Reserve Bank Notes with the Charles Burt portrait of Abraham Lincoln (BEP die MISC 1029). The face die was executed as BEP die FR4, credited by the Bureau of Engraving and Printing to Edward M. Hall, Robert Ponickau, Harry L. Chorlton, Edward E. Myers, Joachim C. Benzing, George F.C. Smillie, and Frank Lamasure. (See figure 3.38.)

1915. Henry B. Joy, president of the Packard Motor Car Company and also the Lincoln Highway Association, acquires a hammered-copper copy of Alonzo (Alfonso) Pelzer's New Jersey statue of the Great Emancipator, made by John G. Segesman. The statue would be installed in the Packard Administration Building for four years, but stored during building renovations in 1919. It would be dedicated February 3, 1919, according to the *Smithsonian American Art Museum Art Inventories Catalog.*

According to Lincoln statue chronicler Dave Wiegers, Segesman was a junior or a main sculptor for the Mullins Company from 1896 to the late 1920s, when he retired, and the Mullins Co. "got out of the sculpture business." Wiegers discovered a 1948 letter by Segesman in which he explained: "In 1915, I got orders to make a life-size model of Abraham Lincoln." Segesman said he copied Lincoln's face from a Volk life mask, to which he added a beard and eyes after studying paintings of Lincoln. "Segesman writes that all of the Lincolns strung out along the Lincoln Highway were all made from the model he sculpted in 1915. . . . Most of the Segesman Lincoln pieces went up between 1915 and 1921. . . . It is evident from looking at the Pelzer Lincoln (in New Jersey) and the Segesman Lincolns that they are similar but different. I think that the Pelzer is overall a better Lincoln," Wiegers wrote.[12] According to a 1937 letter from the Mullins Sales Department that Wiegers discovered, in 1915 statues were sold to Wooster (Ohio), Boise (Idaho), Lincoln Motor Co., and Packard Motor Co. "The Wilkinsburg Lincoln was done in 1916," he added.[13] In all, eight of the Segesman statues have been traced by researcher Dave Wiegers: Boise, ID; Brighton, MI; Detroit, MI; St. Cloud, MN; Fremont, NE; Middletown, OH; Wooster, OH; and Wilkinsburg, PA.

Fig. 3.33. On July 4, 1914, a memorial to Abraham Lincoln was dedicated in Oslo, Norway, to celebrate the 100th anniversary of Norway's constitution. The Lincoln bust by Norwegian-American sculptor Paul Fjelde was a gift from Norwegian immigrants to North Dakota. However, it was so generally little known in the United States that when U.S. sailors visited it for this publicity picture, it was captioned as having occurred in Copenhagen, Denmark!

Fig. 3.34. Lincoln money images graced both organization and commercial pinbacks in the decade before the First World War, including this red-white-and-blue Lincoln Jefferson Liberty League pin *(a)* and this golden pinback touting Ward's Tip Top Bread *(b)*.

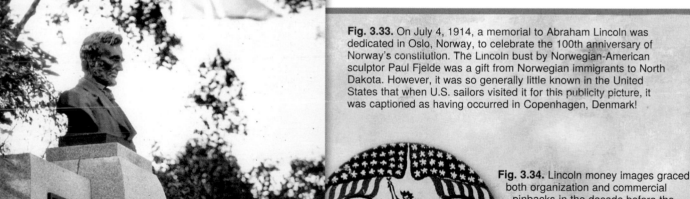

1915 FEBRUARY 12. A 10-and-a-half-foot-high sandstone pedestal to hoist a future Lincoln statue in the Idaho capital city of Boise is dedicated at the Idaho's Soldiers Home by Governor Moses Alexander. Idaho secretary of state George R. Barker called the future monument "the shrine of the nation's political saint." The statue itself, called *Lincoln the Emancipator,* would be dedicated on July 12, 1915, after arriving from the Ohio foundry of W.H. Mullins. This statue is credited to John G. Segesman, said to be a copy of Alfonso Pelzer's New Jersey tribute to the Great Emancipator.

1915 FEBRUARY 20. Abraham Lincoln proved a popular subject for this nation's world-class artists displaying their wares in the rebuilt city of San Francisco. A broad range of Lincoln items populated the Department of Fine Arts at the Panama-Pacific International Exposition, which opened in San Francisco for a nine-month run. Lincoln sculpture included works by Cyrus Dallin, George Etienne Ganiere, Daniel Chester French (lent by the State of Nebraska), Augustus Saint-Gaudens (lent by the Lincoln Monument Fund), and Adolph A. Weinman (a study for his seated figure at Hodgenville, a bust, and a photograph of his *Standing Lincoln* in the Kentucky State Capitol in Frankfort), and a photographic reproduction of Henry K. Bush-Brown's *Lincoln at Gettysburg.* Lincoln medals on display included both a medal and a plaque by Victor D. Brenner. Paintings included Francis B. Carpenter's somber monochromatic portrait of Lincoln (lent by the Union League Club of the City of New York). Prints, engravings, and etchings included Thomas Johnson's Lincoln portrait (lent by Robert Fridenberg), beardless and bearded portraits by Gustav Kruell (the latter lent by Frederick Keppel & Co., New York), and additional Lincoln works by George Meinhausen and Max Rosenthal.[14]

1915. The Lincoln Highway Association releases its first *Complete and Official Road Guide of the Lincoln Highway.* The association sponsored a Motion Picture Caravan to film the Lincoln Highway. "Seedling" miles were constructed in various states along the route.

1915 JUNE 14. A memorial is dedicated to Lincoln's Farewell Speech, February 11, 1861, at Springfield's Great Western Railroad Depot, erected by the Springfield Chapter of the Illinois Daughters of the American Revolution. There Abraham Lincoln had delivered a brief, spontaneous, and moving farewell address to a crowd of about 1,000 from the rear platform of the train that was taking him on the first leg of his journey to inauguration as this country's 16th president.

1915 JUNE 22. Sculptor Victor David Brenner copyrights an Abraham Lincoln profile plaque design. Companion bronze plaques by Gorham showing Lincoln and George Washington in profile within 25-inch-diameter circles centered on 33-inch squares would be presented by the Women's Historical Society of Pennsylvania to the City of Pittsburgh, on February 12, 1919, and February 22, 1921, respectively. They are mounted in the City-County Building.

Fig. 3.35. Cent designer Victor David Brenner created this Abraham Lincoln profile plaque for the Panama-Pacific International Exposition in 1915. Cast by Gorham, it was presented to the Alleghany County City-County Building (Pittsburgh City Hall) on February 12, 1919, by the Women's Historical Society of Pennsylvania.

1915 July 3. Sculptor Peter Bisson's granite statue of Lincoln is installed at Lincoln Park, Long Beach, California.

1915 October 1. One of seven hammered-copper copies of Alfonso Pelzer's statue of the Great Emancipator, by John G. Segesman and manufactured by W.H. Mullins, Salem, Ohio, to be placed along the Lincoln Highway, is dedicated at the College of Wooster, north of downtown Wooster, Ohio. Over the years since, the statue would be moved to three locations on campus, suffering natural and criminal depredations. It was restored by local blacksmith Stewart Simonds and returned to campus for display in 1997.

1915 October. An extensively illustrated article, "Plaques and Medallions by Victor David Brenner," is featured in *The Survey*, along with Paul U. Kellogg's "Two New Worlds and a Sculptor's Clay," also about Brenner.

According to Kellogg: "Practically everybody in the United States, practically every day in the year, carries a pocket piece which is the handiwork of the same designer. This is the Lincoln penny . . . [C]oins are itinerant teachers to eye and touch, they reach the poorest homes and most out of the way villages . . . They can leave a habit, if not a craving, for beauty, which will be less and less satisfied with what is ugly and shapeless and dull in the things of daily use. They can at strange and unexpected times touch a burdened life or fire a young one with the moral force inlaid in the seamed face of a Lincoln. Thus, by slow but all embracing experience, common standards may be raised; thus, by the strategy of building up inside human lives a craving and recognition of what is beautiful and enduring, peace may achieve something more imperishable than cathedrals; thus, out of Russia came a servant to democracy."[15]

Fig. 3.36. A great deal of mystery surrounded the seven identical Abraham Lincoln statues by John G. Segesman placed variously along the Lincoln Highway. Many were historically miscredited to artist Alfonzo Pelzer. Recently Lincoln statue researcher Dave Wiegers sorted it out, restoring Segesman's credits, which he generously supplied for the present book. Shown is the Segesman statue that originally appeared in front of the Lincoln plant in Detroit at Wyoming & Ford Road, as it looked in 1950.

Fig. 3.37. This splendid red-white-and-blue badge for a veterans' reunion in Wooster, Ohio, features the Lincoln money image.

1916 JANUARY 1. The Lincoln Safe Deposit Company, New York City, registers copyright to a logo consisting of a silhouette bust of Abraham Lincoln, showing a right profile by J.M. Gaspard. Two days later, the company would register a left-profile Lincoln silhouette, also by Gaspard. On January 11 and 12, it would register a second set of right and left profile designs.

1916 JANUARY 14. Artist George Edward Hall copyrights his front-view bust portrait of Lincoln.

1916 JANUARY 25. Sculptor Adolph Alexander Weinman copyrights his *Hodgenville Lincoln* and *Lincoln of the Capitol* statues (seated and standing, respectively) (J212364, J212365).

1916 JANUARY 27. The National Lincoln Chautauqua Association copyrights its logo. Chautauqua were summer educational camps and programs in rural communities.

1916. The American Numismatic Society Lincoln plaquette (King 302), by Jules Édouard Roiné and struck by Whitehead & Hoag, is re-issued by Medallic Art Co.[16]

1916 FEBRUARY 16. Bureau of Engraving and Printing engraver Marcus Baldwin visits the Library of Congress and National Gallery to study Abraham Lincoln portraits in preparation for engraving the large Lincoln portrait for the Bureau's "Series of the Presidents."

1916 MARCH 20. New York City sculptress Laura Gardin copyrights *Pioneer of the Lincoln Highway,* a statuette group of a man in a pioneer costume riding a horse. The copyright was in Gardin's maiden name. She had married fellow sculptor (and her mentor) James Earle Fraser on November 27, 1913, the same year that his American Bison / Indian Head nickel entered circulation.

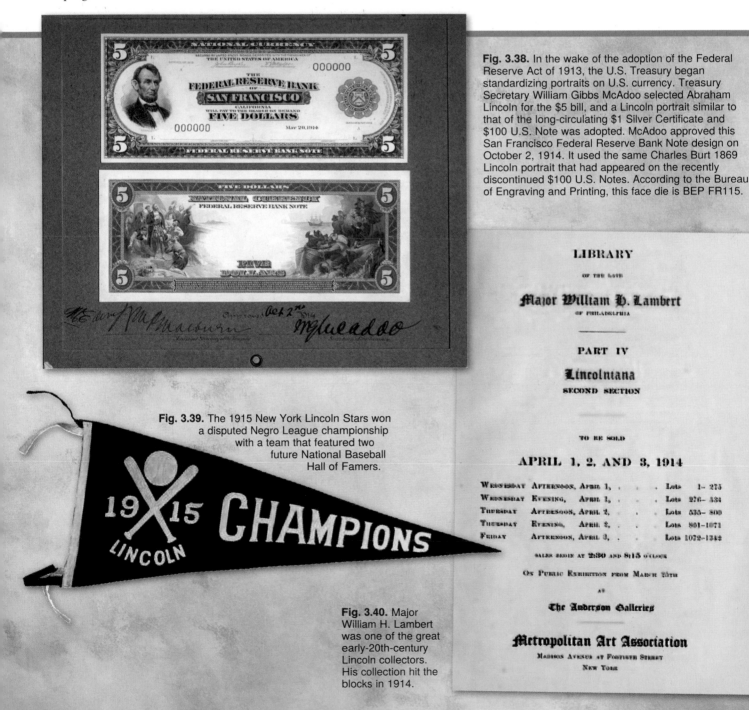

Fig. 3.38. In the wake of the adoption of the Federal Reserve Act of 1913, the U.S. Treasury began standardizing portraits on U.S. currency. Treasury Secretary William Gibbs McAdoo selected Abraham Lincoln for the $5 bill, and a Lincoln portrait similar to that of the long-circulating $1 Silver Certificate and $100 U.S. Note was adopted. McAdoo approved this San Francisco Federal Reserve Bank Note design on October 2, 1914. It used the same Charles Burt 1869 Lincoln portrait that had appeared on the recently discontinued $100 U.S. Notes. According to the Bureau of Engraving and Printing, this face die is BEP FR115.

Fig. 3.39. The 1915 New York Lincoln Stars won a disputed Negro League championship with a team that featured two future National Baseball Hall of Famers.

Fig. 3.40. Major William H. Lambert was one of the great early-20th-century Lincoln collectors. His collection hit the blocks in 1914.

Fig. 3.41. In 1916 Marcus W. Baldwin, who had created a Lincoln portrait based on O-92 for U.S. postage stamps, created this wonderful "Large Presidential Portrait" for the Bureau of Engraving and Printing based on the same model. "M.W. Baldin / Sculpt. 1916" appears at lower right, beneath the truncation.

Fig. 3.42. In 1914 the Abraham Lincoln monument in Norway joined George Bissell's *Lincoln and Liberty,* the first Lincoln memorial in Europe, which had been erected in Edinburg, Scotland, in 1893. The legend on the monument reads: "To preserve the jewel of liberty in the framework of freedom"—a philosophy that imminently would be sorely tried on the Continent by the Kaiser's war machine.

Fig. 3.43. By 1915, when the International Order of Odd Fellows convened in Springfield, the Smillie Lincoln $1 portrait based on the O-92 model had been joined by a similar $5 portrait, which borrowed Charles Burt's old $100 image, on Federal Reserve Notes and Federal Reserve Bank Notes. The Order went along with the trend on this fine pocket mirror.

1916 APRIL 1. Two Springfield, Illinois, merchants—J.D. Roper and A.W. Kessberger— copyright a pair of copies of a bust of Abraham Lincoln by Leonard Volk.

1916 JUNE 1. Andersen Art Co., Mattapan, Massachusetts, copyrights a Lincoln Memorial Tablet by Arthur Andersen. The bas-relief plaque (G52093) shows a right-profile bust of Lincoln above his Gettysburg Address.

1916 JUNE 7. Frederic Wellington Ruckstuhl, editor of *Art World*—who, with Robert Todd Lincoln, Henry Cabot Lodge, and Judd Stewart (among others) would succeed several years later in shanghaiing the gifts of George Grey Barnard's rustic Lincoln statue to European capitals in England and France—copyrights an appropriate memorial to the Nation's Savior. Ruckstuhl's monument to Lincoln consists of a man lying on a bier with two angels attending at his head.[17]

1916 JUNE 9. A fifth copy of Alfonso Pelzer's Lincoln *Emancipator* statue is placed along the Lincoln Highway in Wilkinsburg, Pennsylvania (Pittsburgh), at the intersection of the Lincoln and Penn highways. Most of the $700 cost of the hammered-copper sculpture, accomplished by John G. Segesman for W.H. Mullins Co., was underwritten by more than a thousand school-aged children. Although life-size, the hollow copper statue is said to have weighed only 80 pounds. The Mullins Company promised it would "have all the appearance of a bronze statue."

1916 JULY 10. Adelaide Lewis Lundberg copyrights three real-photo postcards of actor and Abraham Lincoln impersonator Sam D. Drane as Lincoln.

1916 JULY 21. Sculptor Daniel Chester French, who listed his address as Glendale, Massachusetts, copyrights the working model for his statue of Lincoln seated on a bench (G52345).

Fig. 3.44. The excitement following the Lincoln centennial coincided with the rise of the motion-picture industry, which cranked out film after film reiterating the Lincoln legacy to a receptive public. Two of the earliest screen Lincolns were Francis Ford, who starred in 1915's *The Heart of Lincoln,* and Joseph Henabery, in 1915's *The Birth of a Nation.* This rare view of an early nickel theater has a large poster for *The Heart of Lincoln* between the flags to the right of its doorway *(a).* Meanwhile, Henabery's Lincoln and his Cabinet gather beneath the portrait of Washington in the president's office *(b).*

Fig. 3.45. Abraham Lincoln and General U.S. Grant impersonators and Lady Liberty join two doughboys for this Liberty Bond promotional photograph, circa 1917–1918.

Fig. 3.46. A great many unsigned Lincoln plaques were produced in the teens and twenties. This oval, cast-aluminum profile plaque measures approximately 8-1/2 by 10-1/2 inches, and its reverse is fitted out for hanging on a wall.

1916 SEPTEMBER 5. The Abraham Lincoln Birthplace Memorial is accepted by President Woodrow Wilson at the site of Thomas Lincoln's farm outside Hodgenville, Kentucky.

1916 OCTOBER 25. Jules Guerrin copyrights two symbolic illustrations of Abraham Lincoln's life.

1916 NOVEMBER 2. Lincoln sculpture at the annual Chicago Institute of Art exhibition includes works by Adolph A. Weinman (including a study for the Hodgenville seated figure), Albert Jaegers, Charles Niehaus, Charles J. Mulligan, and Hermon A. MacNeil (*Lincoln the Lawyer*); a bust by George E. Ganiere; the obverse and reverse of a Lincoln medal by Victor D. Brenner; and Gail Sherman Corbett's sketch for the Lincoln Memorial.[18]

1916 NOVEMBER 17. New York sculptor Daniel Chester French registers copyright to his "design for [a] statue of Lincoln seated in chair with hands resting on arms of [the] chair" (G53081). Five and a half years later, the 19-foot-tall, 175-ton, completed white-marble masterpiece would be dedicated in the Lincoln Memorial.

1916 NOVEMBER 21. New York sculptor George Grey Barnard copyrights his "statue of Lincoln standing with hands clasped in front" (G53105; figure 3.53). Barnard unconventionally chose to depict Lincoln as "a hero of democracy and as a man of the working class," according to historian Judith A. Rice. Barnard's Lincoln transcends the imperial and imperious portrayal that had been the standard for the half century following his elevation to saintliness in the aftermath of his assassination. This, of course, is Barnard's famous rustic Lincoln statue, which outfits the railsplitter in rumpled, worn clothes and old shoes, with his arms caressing his abdomen. Its detractors called it the "Bellyache" statue, but it was installed in Cincinnati under the patronage of the Taft family.

The portrayal caused an international stink when the Tafts proposed to donate additional copies of the statue to London and Paris. Abraham Lincoln's son Robert (and others) objected to those proceedings. Robert contended (among other things) that the unflattering portrayal of his father reflected poorly on both Lincolns' images and would also sully the image of the American presidency should Barnard's unvarnished bronze be allowed to gather attention in Europe.

Besides the Tafts, Barnard's vision had other champions, including Lincoln biographer Ida Tarbell and Lincoln idolizers Teddy Roosevelt and poet Edwin Markham.

After a copy of Augustus Saint-Gaudens's more proper standing Lincoln was selected for London, a copy of Barnard's Cincinnati statue eventually was erected in Manchester, England.[19]

Fig. 3.47. Lincoln Clubs flourished across the country. Shown is a membership card *(a)* from one such group in St. Joseph (likely Missouri), with the Western Bank Note Co. Lincoln image after Littlefield, and a pin for another club *(b)* in Portland, Maine, with the Gettysburg Lincoln image.

Fig. 3.48. Ward's Tip Top Bread used a variety of Lincoln pins as promotional prizes. This pre-WWI pinback has a rather stultified impression of Honest Abe.

Fig. 3.49. Circa 1915 R.D. Berger Mfg. Co., Chicago, ripped off the U.S. Mint's Lincoln medal designs by George T. Morgan.

1917 March 4. Benjamin Chapin Studios, Ridgefield Park, New Jersey, releases the first of its *Lincoln Cycle of Photoplays,* short films recounting the life, times, and achievements of Abraham Lincoln. Chapin is best remembered for his striking physical resemblance to the president. He had been portraying Old Abe on the stage since at least 1909, during the Lincoln centennial. He mimicked "Lincoln's walk," "Lincoln's smile," "Lincoln's twinkle," according to publicity. His Lincoln cycle was filled with "real Lincoln stories . . . through reel after reel of thrilling events and humorous experiences, flashing back and forth from White House to log cabin." A full-page advertisement on the inside front cover of *Motion Picture World* magazine (March 17) would tout "History Repeats Itself." It said: "Fifty-six years ago Lincoln was inaugurated on March 4th 1861 at 3 p.m. on the East portico of the U.S. Capitol in Washington, D.C. Today Benjamin Chapin's *Lincoln Cycle of Photoplays* inaugurated first time in public, at the Belasco Theatre Washington, D.C. March 4th, 3 p.m. 1917. Then as now the public was aroused with a war spirit. The President's Answer is announced in Benjamin Chapin's *Lincoln Cycle of Photoplays* and helps history repeat itself."

The *Lincoln Cycle* eventually consisted of 13 short films, which, after debuting in the nation's capital, toured New York City and theaters across the country. (See figure 3.61.)

1917 March 31. Sculptor George Grey Barnard's bronze figure of a rustic Lincoln is installed at Lytle Park, Cincinnati, Ohio.

Fig. 3.50. Fred Smillie's Lincoln portrait based on the Anthony Berger O-92 photos circulated throughout the marketplace, reaching every transaction and every social class. Billions of notes were necessary to grease the wheels of commerce. The stereoview card shows a Bureau of Engraving and Printing inspector examining new Silver Certificates with the Lincoln portrait *(a)*. The $1 bill became so ubiquitous prior to the First World War that it was copied on this advertising note in Brno, Czechoslovakia, suitably revalued to "1000" to give it a more impressive panache *(b)*.

Fig. 3.51. The Lincoln National Life Insurance Co. branded its corporate image alternately between the O-92 Lincoln portrait and the Marshall-style image that appears on this 1918–1919 calendar.

Fig. 3.52. These two BEP engravers, Marcus Baldwin (left) and Fred Smillie (right), created *the* iconic Abraham Lincoln image of the 20th century when they successively based their Lincoln portraits on the O-92 Berger photo for the blue 1903 Lincoln five-cent stamp and the Series of 1899 $1 Silver Certificate, respectively. Like John the Baptist, their twin portraits ushered the way for the Treasury to re-adopt Charles Burt's greenback portrait, also based on O-92 from the $100 United States Note abandoned in 1912, two years later for the $5 bill. At that point the Treasury began standardizing currency portraiture with the release of the newly created Federal Reserve Notes and Federal Reserve Bank Notes. Lincoln has lived on the face of the $5 bill ever since.

Fig. 3.53. When George Grey Barnard's colossal, rustic depiction of Abraham Lincoln was erected in Cincinnati in 1917 it was abhorred by the Lincoln mafia, who insisted that it was ugly and inappropriate. The Lincoln Cult dubbed it the "bellyache" statue, in reference to the placement of Lincoln's hands. Its proponents, who included Theodore Roosevelt, praised Barnard's workingman's depiction as being down to earth and for its virility. It certainly seems admired by the three young men here.

1917 MAY 27. The second film in actor-director-producer Benjamin Chapin's four-part *Lincoln Cycle* (a Paramount series—not a serial, as each film was entire in itself), *The Son of Democracy,* explores the life of Abe's mother Nancy Hanks Lincoln, his relationship to his father Tom Lincoln, his beginnings as a country lawyer and fledgling politician, and his answer to his "country's call." The fourth in the series, *Her Country's Call,* would be released October 1, 1917. Chapin would go on to play Lincoln in nine additional short films.

1917. To a new edition of her Lincoln biography, Ida M. Tarbell appends a new introduction defending sculptor George Grey Barnard's frontier interpretation of Lincoln and chastising critics of that approach. Barnard's work had opened up a "fundamental discussion" over the proper artistic interpretation of Lincoln.[20]

1917. Cast-iron markers are erected at each state-line crossing along the transcontinental Lincoln Highway route. The Union Pacific Railroad permits construction of the Lincoln Highway in Nebraska at the edge of its right of way.

1917 JULY 31. A memorandum of agreement is signed in Detroit, Michigan, by Henry M. Leland and Wilfred C. Leland (parties of the first part) and George H. Layng, W. Rex Johnston, and William T. Nash (parties of the second part), all of Detroit, Wayne County, to form the Lincoln Motor Company with a capital stock of $1,500,000. The company was named after Abraham Lincoln because of Henry Leland's admiration of Honest Abe.

1917 SEPTEMBER 1. The Lincoln Motor Company incorporates under the laws of the State of Michigan, and commences issuing capital stock in the amount of $100 per share to the extent of $1,500,000. The shares, printed by Goes Litho Co., Chicago, were signed by Henry M. Leland, president, and William T. Nash, secretary.

The company's first contract was to build motors for aircraft during World War I. During the war the company made Liberty engines for the government. With the signing of the armistice (November 1918), the Liberty aircraft-engine market evaporated. The partners raised new capital and in 1920 repurposed their factory as a car company of the same name. The Lelands designed a

Fig. 3.54. Henry Leland *(a)* (with a Lincoln statuette) admired Honest Abe. He founded the Lincoln Motor Co. in 1917 to build excellent products. Shown are the July 31, 1917, partnership papers *(b)* and initial stock offering *(c)*. Leland originally built motors for Army air-corps planes during World War I, and then automobiles. Unfortunately, when the tax man showed up after peace had been restored, Leland lost his company to a predatory Henry Ford, who established the Lincoln luxury-car brand on a firm footing.

MEMORANDUM OF AGREEMENT entered into this 31st day of July, 1917, by and between Henry M. Leland and Wilfred C. Leland, both of Detroit, Wayne County, Michigan, hereinafter called the parties of the first part, and George H. Layng, W. Rex Johnston and William T. Nash, all of Detroit, Wayne County, Michigan, hereinafter called the parties of the second part,

WITNESSETH:

THAT WHEREAS it is the intention of first parties to organize a Michigan corporation for the purpose of conducting a machine shop and of manufacturing, assembling and dealing in motors, transmissions, parts and accessories for motor cars, motor boats, motor cycles, aeroplanes, internal combustion engines, etc. etc., and have prepared the necessary Articles of Association for such corporation, and

WHEREAS the said first parties will give to said corporation the benefit and advantage of their reputation and high standing, both in the business and manufacturing world, and are further contributing a very large percentage of the money and financial backing and responsibility necessary to the organization of said corporation and to the conduct of its business thereafter, and

WHEREAS it is the desire of first parties to associate with themselves in the said corporation the individuals named as second parties herein, for the purpose of securing the undivided personal services, time and efforts of said second parties to the success of said company and business, and to make it possible for said second parties in the event that they do so devote themselves to the success thereof, to share in the success of the said corporation, it being, however, thoroughly understood by all parties hereto that first parties desire the association new V-8 engine and produced a Model L, which debuted in fall of 1920. "Although highly regarded for its mechanics, the Model L was criticized for its lackluster coachwork," according to automotive historian Mark A. Patrick. Sales were slow, and a weakening economic climate, coupled with a multi-million-dollar tax claim by the government against the predecessor company for its share of the company's wartime profits, threw the Lincoln Motor Company into voluntary receivership in November 1921.[21]

1917. A standing bronze statue of Abraham Lincoln, with his right arm behind his back and his left hand clasping his lapel, is installed in the Auditorium Wing of the Administration Building, Nebraska State Normal School, at Kearney, Nebraska. In recent years this statue has been located in a conference room on the second floor of Founders Hall on the campus of the University of Nebraska, Kearney.[22]

1917 NOVEMBER 29. The Union League of Philadelphia—the original Union League that made Abraham Lincoln an honorary member in 1863, awarded him a gold medal, and gave him the "freedom of the Union League House" as a show of its support for his policies—dedicates its Lincoln Memorial Room to celebrate its 55th anniversary. A life-size bronze statue of Lincoln by sculptor John Otto Schweitzer was unveiled.[23] Lincoln visited the Union League in 1864.

1917 NOVEMBER 21. Sculptor Daniel Chester French's approved 1/8-scale pencil-sketch drawing of his 19-foot-high planned statue of a seated Lincoln atop a three-step riser shows it dwarfing a representative human being. Eight days later architect Henry Bacon would provide similar pencil sketches showing how the accepted figure would fit into his memorial design.

1918 JANUARY 18. Mario Scoma of Brooklyn registers copyright to a bas-relief medallion, *Upholders of Liberty and Civilization,* showing jugate profile busts of presidents Wilson, Lincoln, and Washington. Similar designs would be registered by Arthur Edwin Wilson, Chicago, on May 8, 1918; and by Charles M. Pogue, Tucson, Arizona, copyrighted on October 11, 1918.

1918 FEBRUARY 12. Merrell Gage's seated bronze Abraham Lincoln is dedicated on the grounds of the Kansas statehouse in Topeka. Lincoln is leaning slightly forward as if to engage the viewer in conversation. (See figure 3.58.)

1918 FEBRUARY 12. A bronze Lincoln statue by sculptor Alonzo Victor Lewis is erected at Lincoln High School, Tacoma, Washington.

1918. A bronze standing Lincoln statue by W. Granville Hastings is presented by Mr. and Mrs. S.B. Wilson to the city of Jefferson,

Fig. 3.55. These original February 1917 drawings from the collections of the Library of Congress show architect Henry Bacon's ideas for the Lincoln Memorial, to encompass Daniel Chester French's monumental seated figure. Originally the sculpture was slated to be 10 feet tall, but Bacon's scale drawings—showing how it would be dwarfed by the surrounding temple—led to its height being increased to 19 feet.

Fig. 3.56. New York coin dealer Tom Elder commissioned this fine 38.1-millimeter silver medal (DeLorey 52) in late 1914, struck by C.H. Hanson Co. of Chicago. The wonderful facing portrait based on the Gettysburg Lincoln photograph (O-77) belied U.S. Mint excuses over many years that full-faced portraits were inappropriate for coin designs.

Fig. 3.57. These two bronze medallions of Abraham Lincoln were made in 1914 (by sculptor Leo F. Nock) *(a)* and in 1916 (by Jno. Williams Foundry) *(b).*

Iowa. The statue on a pedestal was erected at the Greene County Courthouse in Jefferson. An identical statue was erected in Sioux City, Iowa. A similar statue by Hastings, with the addition of a kneeling woman, is located in Cincinnati.

1918 April. A silver Lincoln Indian Peace medal (Julian IP-38), owned by Menomonee Indian Sun Fish (Philip Nacootee), is published by the Wisconsin Natural History Society. "Many Lincoln medals are said to have been given to Wisconsin Indians. This is the first which has come to the writer's attention," Charles E. Brown wrote in *The Wisconsin Archaeologist*.[24]

1918 April 30. Western Reserve Historical Society Director Wallace H. Cathcart records in his annual report to membership that the society's Abraham Lincoln medal collection numbers "about 500" pieces, including 79 donated by Mr. Palmer during the year. Other Lincolniana received during the year included medals from Lincoln Accident Insurance Co. and the Illinois Watch Co., a watch fob from the Lincoln Stove Co., and medals from the essay contests of the *Cleveland Press* and the *Toledo News Bee*.[25]

1918 May 30. A sixth copy of Alfonso Pelzer's Lincoln *Emancipator* statue, by John G. Segesman, is erected on a granite base on Victory Memorial Drive, St. Cloud, Minnesota, in honor of the city's Civil War veterans. Donors to the memorial included the Elks Club and the Gustavus Adolphus Sick Benefit Society, according to the *Smithsonian American Art Museum Art Inventories Catalog*.

1918 June 30. During the year ending June 30, 1918, Robert Hewitt donated to the Smithsonian Institution his collection of Lincolniana, "the most noteworthy addition to the numismatic collections" during the year, according to the museum's annual report. Included were 1,200 items comprised of medallions, plaques, medals, medalets, coins, tokens, and badges. Among items singled out in the curator's report were the bronze cast plaque by New Orleans sculptor J. Andrieu (King-737); the Henry Bonnard bronze plaque (King-944); Roiné's Centennial medal in bronze, gilt (likely actual gold), and aluminum (King-294); the 1910 New York Republican Club plaque (King-443); the 1913 bronze medallion by A. Frechinger (King-735); silver and bronze examples of Brenner's portrait medal (King-304); silver, bronze, and lead (being the artist's proof before the dies were hardened) examples of Roiné's American Numismatic Society plaque (King-302); two original silver Indian Peace medals (Julian IP-38/39); and many other pieces.

What the present author finds most interesting in the listing, however, are the silver and bronze examples of Paquet's 1865 Northwestern Sanitary Fair medal (Julian CM-45), since this medal in silver is *not* listed in Julian's fine reference. Many trial strikes and strikes from rejected dies are also listed, as is a silver example of the French citizens' medal to Lincoln's widow by Magniadas (King-245), and silver, bronze, and aluminum examples of Hugues Bovy's wonderful medal (probably King-230) not listed in silver or aluminum.

Fig. 3.58. Sculptor Robert Merrell Gage created this inquisitive seated Lincoln figure for Topeka, Kansas, dedicated February 12, 1918.

Fig. 3.59. Whitehead & Hoag, Newark, New Jersey, manufactured this 1918 *Pittsburg* (*sic*) *Press* Lincoln Story (Essay) Contest medal (similar to King-933, issued in 1926) with a seated figure of the president.

Fig. 3.60. Greenduck Co., Chicago, struck this small Lincoln portrait medal (King-1025) in 1917 for the Louisville, Kentucky, Automobile Dealers Assn. car show.

"The Robert Hewitt collection is remarkable for the very wide range of subjects and types of numismatic material which it covers and constitutes an epitomized medallic record of the career of President Lincoln," the curator (probably Theodore T. Belote) wrote.

"Although the bulk of the material is of purely historical and numismatic interest, many pieces are of much artistic merit as well, particularly those struck in commemoration of the Lincoln Centennial in 1909," he added.[26]

Fig. 3.61. In the World War I era, stage actor Benjamin Chapin did much to popularize Lincoln through his *Lincoln Cycle of Photoplays*, eight episodic films that he wrote, produced, directed, and starred in that told the Lincoln story *(a)*. Chapin's independently released cycle was very successful, and only ceased when the auteur died of tuberculosis in 1918. Following his death, Paramount Pictures re-released the Chapin footage under the "Son of Democracy" rubric in 1918 *(b)*.

Fig. 3.62. Congress passed the funding act of April 24, 1917, to bring the country to a war footing. If the Abraham Lincoln portrait on this $5,000 Certificate of Indebtedness model in the National Numismatic Collection of the Smithsonian Institution looks familiar, it should. It was the same Lincoln portrait adopted for the $5 note following passage of the Federal Reserve Act of 1913.

Fig. 3.63. This 1917 fob or suspended ribbon medallion *(a–b)*, employing the Bela Lyon Pratt Lincoln centennial design, celebrates the 20th anniversary of Lincoln Memorial University, Harrogate, Tennessee. It was made by Whitehead & Hoag, Newark, New Jersey. A contemporary ad (1915–1917) *(c)* for another school, the International Correspondence Schools, Scranton, Pennsylvania, marshals Lincoln's self-made legacy to promote its curriculum. The school even manufactured the quote attributed to Lincoln, often seen since.

1918 July 5. Sculptor Ella Buchanan registers copyright to her statuette of Abraham Lincoln seated in a chair with an album open in his lap and Tad standing next to him, based on the famous photograph (O-93) by Anthony Berger taken on February 9, 1864.

1918 July 29. A 16-foot-tall concrete pyramid, with a bronze plaque on one of its sloping sides, is dedicated in the front lawn of the W.H. Kratz residence at Monticello, Illinois, to commemorate the meeting at that location 60 years earlier between Stephen A. Douglas and Abraham Lincoln, first agreeing to participate in a series of debates. Details of the debates were finalized that night in the parlor of the nearby home of Mr. and Mrs. Francis E. Bryant in Bement. Bryant, an Illinois legislator, was a Douglas man. The Bement cottage has been maintained as a Lincoln-Douglas memorial to the present day.[27]

1918 September 8. A copy of sculptor Paul Fjelde's Abraham Lincoln bust is dedicated on the front lawn of the Trail County Courthouse, Hillsboro, North Dakota.

1918 September 9. U.S. Mint engraver George Morgan advises Lincoln cent sculptor Victor David Brenner that no publicity surrounded the placement of Brenner's initials back on the one-cent coin. The V.D.B. initials had been removed after only a few weeks of production in 1909; in 1918 they were quietly brought back and placed under the truncation of the bust on the obverse.

1918 September 21. Sculptor William Granville Hastings's bronze statue of Abraham Lincoln, without the companion statue of Liberty, is installed at the Green County Court House, Jefferson, Iowa.

1918 October 5. Andrew O'Connor's standing bronze statue of Abraham Lincoln at the east approach of the Illinois State Capitol is dedicated. O'Connor intended to depict Lincoln as he looked when he departed Springfield on February 11, 1861, to take up the reins as the chief executive in Washington, D.C. However, O'Connor's depiction is beardless, and by the time Lincoln left Springfield he sported a brand-new beard. Nevertheless, the entire text of Lincoln's short Farewell Address to his fellow citizens is carved into the granite slab on which the statue stands. The foundry for the statue was T.F. McGann & Sons Co., and Victoria White Granite Co. was the carver for the memorial.

1918 November 26. Frank Vittor registers copyright to the bust titled *American Thinker,* depicting Abraham Lincoln resting his chin on his right hand, patterned after the famous painting by G.P.A. Healy.

Fig. 3.64. In September 1918 William Granville Hastings's Lincoln statue was erected at the Green County Court House, Jefferson, Iowa.

Fig. 3.65. In October 1918 Andrew O'Connor's beardless statue of Abraham Lincoln was erected at the east face of the Illinois State Capitol Building, Springfield. It was meant to commemorate Lincoln's farewell address to his neighbors, February 11, 1861. Unfortunately for O'Connor, Lincoln actually sported a beard by that time.

1919 January 30. Massachusetts governor Calvin Coolidge proclaims February 12 "Lincoln Day." He recommends "its observance as befits the beneficiaries of his life and the admirers of his character in places of education and worship wherever our people meet one with another."

1919 January 31. Onorio Reotolo registers copyright to a sculptured bust of Abraham Lincoln, holding a baby in his arms, entitled *Lincoln, Protector of the Negro Race.*[28]

1919 February. Author William Heyliger tells Boy Scouts reading *Boys' Life,* "There is only one United States of America. There has been only one Abraham Lincoln. Lincoln's life is the great American romance. Born to bitter poverty in the backwoods of Kentucky. . . . They buried Lincoln with such honors as have come to few men in the history of the world. They buried his body; but his soul, his great, all-embracing soul, lives on to inspire new generations. As long as the English language endures weary men and boys will read his life, and, reading his story, will take fresh courage to carry their burdens bravely and well."

1919 February 7. Boston sculptor Truman Howe Bartlett registers copyright to an Abraham Lincoln statuette. He had earlier authored *The Portraits of Lincoln,* contained in Carl Schurz's *Abraham Lincoln: A Biographical Essay* (Houghton Mifflin & Co., 1907). Bartlett collected Lincoln photos for many years and made a rather rigorous study of Lincoln's physiognomy.

1919 February 12. Attendees at the 110th anniversary dinner of Abraham Lincoln's birth, at the Carteret Club, Jersey City, New Jersey, receive William H. Richardson's pamphlet *The 'Makings' of the Lincoln Association of Jersey City.*

1919 February 13. A Lincoln statue by sculptor John G. Segesman, manufactured by W.H. Mullins in Ohio after the Alfonso Pelzer Lincoln *Emancipator* design in Lincoln, New Jersey, is dedicated in front of the Ford Motor Company at Warren and Livernois Avenue, according to Lincoln statue authority Dave Wiegers. The statue remained at the site until 1958. "After Ford ceased building Lincoln automobiles at the plant, the statue was given to the city of Detroit," Wiegers stated.[29]

Fig. 3.66. One of the oddest of Lincoln memorials was this 16-foot-tall concrete pyramid with a bronze plaque to commemorate the 50th anniversary of Abraham Lincoln and Stephen Douglas striking a bargain to engage in a series of joint public appearances, characterized in history as the "Lincoln-Douglas Debates."

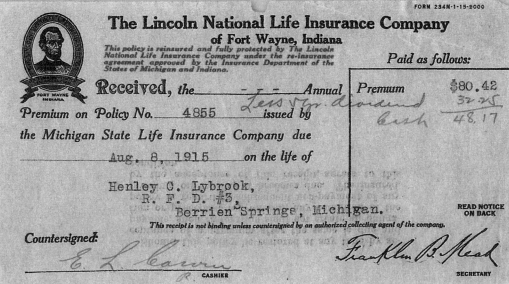

Fig. 3.67. Lincoln National Life Insurance Co. of Fort Wayne, Indiana, received Robert Todd Lincoln's permission to appropriate his father's name and identity. " Its name indicates its character" appeared on company literature like this reinsurance policy receipt (on the banner under the Lincoln portrait, based on the O-92 image). Robert was said to have supplied the original photo that the company adopted as its brand. The firm began business on September 15, 1905.

Fig. 3.68. This is not an issued $1000 Federal Reserve Note—nor even a considered design, as far as we know—however, G.F.C. "Fred" Smillie's wonderful security engraving after the Carpenter-Ritchie "First Reading of the Emancipation Proclamation" would have been a suitable reverse design for a series whose high values ($500 and above) *all* bear engravings after historical paintings in the U.S. Capitol (except the M-note, which oddly bore Marcus Baldwin's eagle design). By 1918, when the Federal Reserve Notes were released, Lincoln was already associated with $1,000 bonds. Did the Democratic administration of Woodrow Wilson put its bureaucratic foot down, saying "enough is enough"?

Fig. 3.69. The original U.S. Mint plasters show George T. Morgan's 1918 Lincoln–Illinois commemorative half-dollar designs. On the issued coin, LIBERTY is horizontal on the obverse and UNITED STATES OF AMERICA and HALF DOLLAR were moved to the reverse. Comparably, CENTENNIAL OF THE STATE OF ILLINOIS and the single date 1918 were moved to the obverse. Also, E PLURIBUS UNUM was added above the sunburst.

Fig. 3.70. A beardless, vigorous Lincoln attracted socialist artist Boardman Robinson in 1919 when he created this excellent portrait that exhibits his characteristic black-crayon-and-ink-wash technique. Robinson had resigned his position as the *New York Times'* editorial cartoonist over America's involvement in World War I. Ironically, Robinson's Lincoln portrait became iconic on World War II bond posters (such as that shown as Figure 3.103 in *Abraham Lincoln: The Image of His Greatness*). Both are signed "BR19" (for Boardman Robinson 1919), and not "B. Rig," as often cited in the works of other authors.

TRANSPORT SUNK ON VOYAGE HOME WITH WOUNDED

President Lincoln, 18,000-Ton Liner, Bound for United States, Torpedoed in War Zone.

REMAINS AFLOAT ONE HOUR

Navy Gets Meagre Report from Admiral Sims, but No News of Those on Board.

CARRIED CREW OF 700 MEN

Vessel Fully Equipped with Life-boats, and Belief Is That Loss of Life Was Not Heavy.

Special to The New York Times.

WASHINGTON, May 31.—The American troop transport President Lincoln, of 18,168 gross tons capacity, sixth in size among the vessels that have been used for our army transportation, was attacked by a German submarine at 10:40 o'clock this morning and sunk somewhere in the naval war zone.

Announcement of the loss of this important vessel, based on meagre information cabled to Secretary Daniels, from Vice Admiral William S. Sims, at London, was made by the Navy Department late this afternoon. The announcement was silent on the point as to whether there had been loss of life.

Unofficial reports indicated that the President Lincoln, which was returning from European waters to the United States, was bringing wounded men home.

The original announcement made by the Navy Department, than which the officials here professed to have no later information up to a late hour to-night, read:

"The Navy Department has received a dispatch from Vice Admiral Sims stating that the U. S. S. President Lincoln was torpedoed at 10:40 o'clock this morning and sank an hour later. The vessel was returning from Europe. No

Fig. 3.71. The SS *President Lincoln* was a military troop ship sunk by German U-boats during World War I, with much loss of life *(a)*. It had previously been a luxury ocean liner *(b)*.

LINCOLN DAY PROCLAMATION

FIVE score and ten years ago that Divine Providence which infinite repetition has made only the more a miracle sent into the world a new life, destined to save a nation. No star, no sign, foretold his coming. About his cradle all was poor and mean save only the source of all great men, the love of a wonderful woman. When she faded away in his tender years, from her deathbed in humble poverty she dowered her son with greatness. There can be no proper observance of a birthday which forgets the mother. Into his origin as into his life men long have looked and wondered. In wisdom great, but in compassion stronger, he became a leader of men by being a follower of the truth. He overcame evil with good. His presence filled the Nation. He broke the might of oppression. He restored a race to its birthright. His mortal frame has vanished, but his spirit increases with the increasing years, the richest legacy of the greatest century.

Men show by what they worship what they are. It is no accident that before the great example of American manhood our people stand with respect and reverence. And in accordance with this sentiment our laws have provided for a formal recognition of the birthday of Abraham Lincoln, for in him is revealed our ideal, the hope of our century fulfilled.

Now, therefore, by the authority of Massachusetts, the 12th day of February is set apart as

LINCOLN DAY

and its observance recommended as befits the beneficiaries of his life and the admirers of his character, in places of education and worship wherever our people meet one with another.

Given at the Executive Chamber, in Boston, this 30th day of January, in the year of Our Lord one thousand nine hundred and nineteen, and of the independence of the United States of America the one hundred and forty-third.

BY HIS EXCELLENCY THE GOVERNOR

Albert P. Langtry
SECRETARY OF THE COMMONWEALTH

Calvin Coolidge

GOD SAVE THE COMMONWEALTH OF MASSACHUSETTS

Compliments of REDFIELD-KENDRICK-ODELL Co. INC. Printers · Engravers · Map Makers *New York*

LINCOLN MOTORS

For the Baker

Down under your dough mixers, batch beaters and pan greasers you need a motor that water, steam, grease or flour cannot injure— that is the Lincoln Motor.

The insulation of the windings in the Lincoln Motor protect it against all moisture and dust. It will run under water without damage to the windings.

Lincoln Motors do the baker's work under bake shop conditions without special care or attention. They furnish the reliable and economical power for baker's machinery.

A Standard Lincoln Motor has been operated under water for nearly three years without damage to windings.

SIFTER

A Lincoln Motor operating an installation of Baker's Machinery

"Link up with Lincoln"

The Lincoln Electric Co.
Cleveland, Ohio

Buffalo   Chicago   Columbus
Detroit   Philadelphia   Pittsburgh
Toronto, Canada
Agencies in other principal cities

Fig. 3.72. In 1919 Massachusetts governor "Silent Cal" Coolidge spoke up in favor of celebrating Lincoln Day on February 12 in the commonwealth, issuing this proclamation.

Fig. 3.73. In 1916 Lincoln Electric Co. placed this ad in *Bakers Review*, stressing the "simplicity" and "honesty" of its Lincoln motor. "Link up with Lincoln" was the firm's catchphrase.

1919 FEBRUARY 13. Detroit's Henry M. Leland, founder of Lincoln Motors Co., registers copyright to two likenesses of Abraham Lincoln (J234049).

1919 FEBRUARY 18. Suitable to the occasion, members of the Pacific Coast Numismatic Society of San Francisco exhibit coins, medals, and paper money relating to Abraham Lincoln and George Washington at its monthly meeting. Member Mr. Charles B. Turrill, historian of the Lincoln Grammar School Association, delivered the principal address of the night, describing the observances in San Francisco at the death of Lincoln and the erection there of the first statue to him. A check signed by Lincoln was among items on display.

1919 MARCH 6. A. Griffoul & Bros. Co., Newark, New Jersey, copyright bookends by Julius M. Melrick, in bas relief and in the style of Gutzon Borglum's viewer-friendly, seated figure of Abraham Lincoln in Newark.

Fig. 3.74. The Lincoln Safe Deposit Company in New York City, opposite Grand Central Terminal, copyrighted several Lincoln portrait designs for logos, but settled on this somewhat uncharacteristic likeness for this 1919 label.

Fig. 3.75. After the Great War was won, the United States found itself under a deep pile of public debt, and issued a new series of Victory Liberty Loan bonds in 1919. Abraham Lincoln continued to appear on the $1,000 certificate, as this spectacular blue overprinted bond shows.

WHICH WILL SUCCEED — the one who occupies ALL his few minutes with the daily paper, or the one who, like Abraham Lincoln, is mastering a little at a time the few great books of the ages, a knowledge of which is one of the essentials of true success?

What are these few great books—biographies, histories, novels, dramas, poems, books of science and travel, philosophy and religion that so delightfully "picture the progress of civilization"?

Dr. Charles W. Eliot, from his lifetime of reading, study and teaching—forty years of it as President of Harvard University—has answered that question in the

HARVARD CLASSICS
Dr. Eliot's Five-Foot Shelf of Books

The Few Great Books That Make a Man Think Straight and Talk Well

Every well-informed man or woman should at least know something about this famous library. The free book tells about it—how Dr. Eliot has put into his Five-Foot Shelf "the essentials of a liberal education" and so arranged it that even "fifteen minutes a day" is enough.

The free book contains Dr. Eliot's own plan of reading explained by himself—and all you have to do is ask for it, because we want every Harper reader to have the advantage of the inspiration and entertainment there is in this chatty little "guide book to books."

Truly it is the most valuable little book of its kind ever written. It shows how to select a library without waste or worry, what books are worth while and what are not. Here is Dr. Eliot's best advice to you on just how and what to read.

Every Harper reader is therefore invited to have free a copy of this handsome and entertaining little book. We shall be as glad to send you a copy as you will be to have read it.

Read in the free book

those twelve vivid little essays—intimate word pictures of famous people, famous books, famous places. Perhaps you too will say: "To me the little free book opened the door of a vast new world of pleasure."

A copy free to every Harper reader; Just mail this today

P. F. Collier & Son, 416 West 13th Street, New York.
You may send me the free Harvard Classics book; no obligation.

Name _____

Address _____

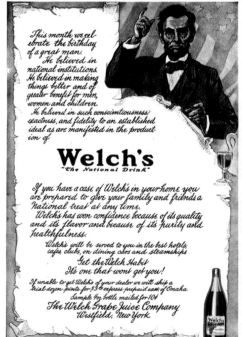

Fig. 3.76. Abraham Lincoln had little formal education, but the illustration of him curling up before the glowing hearth resonated powerfully in this 1918 ad for *Harvard Classics (a)*, published by P.F. Collier & Son, a publisher long associated with Lincoln image-building and commemoration. Most readers will have enjoyed Welch's grape juice—"The National Drink"—at one time or another, but few probably imagined that it embodied the great principles and best attributes of Lincoln himself *(b)*.

1919 MARCH 18. Sculptor George Grey Barnard writes H.S. Perris, secretary of the sponsoring group, the British-American Peace Centenary Committee, "My soul dedicated this Lincoln Bronze [the statue shipped the previous week to Manchester, England] to Democracy, to the people who by labor build life and all its contents." (See figure 3.78.)

1919 MAY 29. Artist Freeman Thorp, of Hubert, Minnesota, registers copyright to his front-view bust portrait of Abraham Lincoln (G58093).

1919 JUNE 6. A Third Liberty Loan 4-1/4% Gold Bond design with a vignette of Abraham Lincoln is approved by U.S. Treasury officials.

1919 JULY 7–SEPTEMBER 6. The U.S. Army sends a motor convoy across the Lincoln Highway from west of Washington, D.C., to San Francisco, to test the route for use by the military.

1919. Robert Todd Lincoln deposits Lincoln archival material amounting to approximately 15,000 items with the Library of Congress. Among the manuscripts were his father's drafts of the Emancipation Proclamation, his first inaugural address (which Robert misplaced for a time on the train trip east in February 1861), and a great many letters.

1919 JUNE 24. The University of Wisconsin–Madison's seated Lincoln statue, by Adolph A. Weinman, is moved 100 feet up Bascom Hill from its original location. Its new site faced the State Capitol in the newly created Lincoln Terrace, paying tribute to soldiers returning from World War I. The statue sits on a granite pedestal that is six and a half feet tall, and with its pedestal it rises a total of thirteen and a half feet.

1919 SEPTEMBER 15. A bronze duplicate of sculptor George Grey Barnard's 11-and-a-half-foot-tall, rustic bronze statue of Abraham Lincoln in Cincinnati is dedicated on Brazenose Street Square at Platt Fields, Manchester, England. The statue had been cast in fall 1917 with the expectation that it would be installed in Parliament Square

Fig. 3.77. During World War I, Liberty Loan drives filled the U.S. Treasury coffers, and created a multiplicity of debt instruments. The Lincoln money portrait was associated with the $1,000 bonds. Shown are a Third Liberty Loan bearer-bond proof *(a)*, an issued Third Liberty Loan coupon bond *(b)*, and a Fourth Liberty Loan registered bond *(c)*.

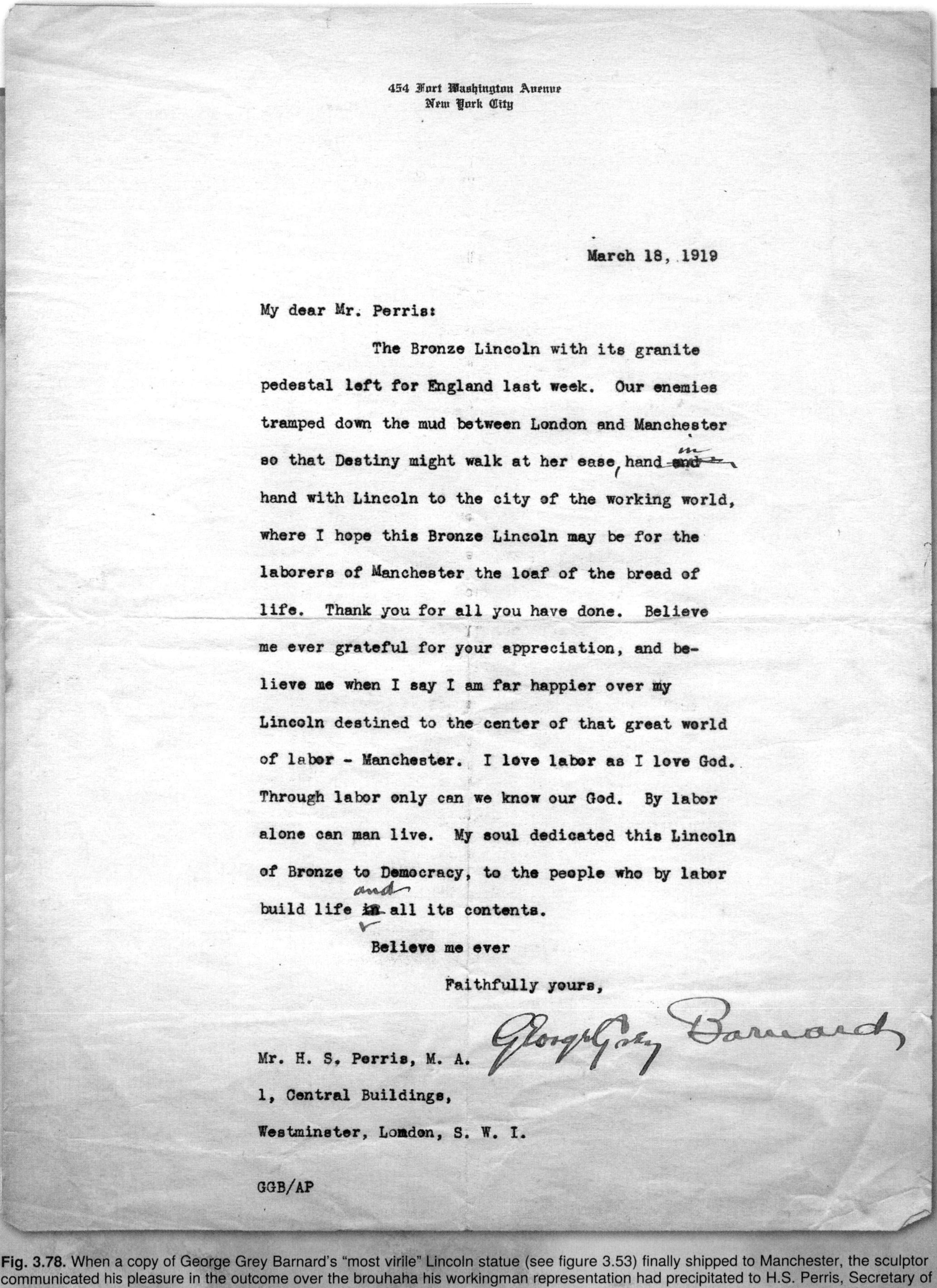

454 Fort Washington Avenue
New York City

March 18, 1919

My dear Mr. Perris:

The Bronze Lincoln with its granite
pedestal left for England last week. Our enemies
tramped down the mud between London and Manchester
so that Destiny might walk at her ease, hand in
hand with Lincoln to the city of the working world,
where I hope this Bronze Lincoln may be for the
laborers of Manchester the loaf of the bread of
life. Thank you for all you have done. Believe
me ever grateful for your appreciation, and believe me when I say I am far happier over my
Lincoln destined to the center of that great world
of labor - Manchester. I love labor as I love God.
Through labor only can we know our God. By labor
alone can man live. My soul dedicated this Lincoln
of Bronze to Democracy, to the people who by labor
build life and all its contents.

Believe me ever

Faithfully yours,

George Grey Barnard

Mr. H. S. Perris, M. A.

1, Central Buildings,

Westminster, London, S. W. I.

GGB/AP

Fig. 3.78. When a copy of George Grey Barnard's "most virile" Lincoln statue (see figure 3.53) finally shipped to Manchester, the sculptor communicated his pleasure in the outcome over the brouhaha his workingman representation had precipitated to H.S. Perris, Secretary of the British American Peace Centenary Committee, the British sponsoring group for the original installation site at Westmister, London.

in London as a symbol of Anglo-American friendship. After the Saint-Gaudens copy was chosen for that lofty honor instead, Charles Taft, the American ex-president's rich half-brother, who was making the donation, indicated he still wished the Barnard duplicate to go to England. The Manchester Art Gallery Committee advanced their city's case as the location for the monument, based on the city's long-standing commercial relations with the United States. The local newspaper, the *Manchester Guardian,* supported the quest. After Woodrow Wilson visited the city, Manchester was awarded the statue over competing cities. The reason, according to the Anglo-American Society, was the support given the North during the War Between the States by Manchester residents. Said John A. Stewart: "It is owing not a little to the way in which the English cotton spinners stood by us which enabled us to preserve the Union and bring the war to a successful conclusion. For that reason we are very grateful."

The bronze arrived in the city early in April 1919. Local officials selected the site, with the intent that the statue would later be moved to Piccadilly after renovations there. The statue was installed on a low granite base in August. At the dedication, U.S. Ambassador J.W. Davies handed over the statue. The *Manchester Guardian* applauded, reckoning while London was to get Lincoln the President, its city had received Lincoln the Man, "a statue of power and dignity." The city's other paper, the *Manchester City News,* concurred, stating the city's figure had the power "to touch the spirit of the children of future generations." It was never moved to Picca-

dilly, but remained in place at Platt Fields until the mid-1980s, when local officials decided to move it to the city center to encourage public awareness of the arts.

1919 OCTOBER 8. In a paper presented before the American Numismatic Association convention in Philadelphia, San Francisco numismatist Farran Zerbe reports that the Secret Service confiscated and destroyed blanks, stationery, and printing plates being used by Lincoln Trust Company of the Southwest having on them a portrait of Abraham Lincoln similar to that being used on federal currency, even though it had been in use for some time.

1919 OCTOBER 15. A bronze bust of Abraham Lincoln by Leonard Volk is installed at St. Andrew's Church, Hingham, England.

1919 NOVEMBER 1. Toepfert Studio, Cincinnati, registers copyright to an Abraham Lincoln statue by sculptor George Grey Barnard.

1919 NOVEMBER 3. Toepfert Studio, Cincinnati, registers copyright to a second Lincoln statue by sculptor George Grey Barnard.

1919 DECEMBER 24. Italian-American sculptor Jennaro Sorvino of New York City registers copyright to his bronze statue of Abraham Lincoln.

1919 DECEMBER 28. Fox Film Corp. debuts *The Lincoln Highwayman,* starring William Russell, about a bandit, along a mythical coastal Lincoln Highway, who preys on motorists in California.

Fig. 3.79. Another foreign commemoration of Abraham Lincoln was the post-war installation in 1919 of a nude beardless bust by Andrew O'Connor honoring the Lincoln family's ancestral parish. It was placed along with suitable inscription in a niche at St. Andrew's Church, Hingham, England.

Fig. 3.80. Promoters of the Lincoln Highway probably did not look favorably on the 1919 motion picture *Lincoln Highwayman,* about a desperado, played by William Russell, who plundered motorists on a fictional Lincoln Highway route in California.

1920 FEBRUARY 13. David Proskey, F.C.C. Boyd, Elliot Smith, and Tom Elder exhibit Lincoln medals at a meeting of the New York Numismatic Club.

1920 APRIL 5. A U.S. Senate resolution directs the Joint Committee on the Library "to engage an artist of reputation and ability to paint an oil portrait of the late Abraham Lincoln, former President of the United States, and to place the same in the Senate wing of the Capitol building, at a cost not to exceed $2,000." Several weeks later, the committee would authorize payment of $2,000 to artist Freeman Thorp for his facing portrait of Lincoln. The painting acquired by the Senate, an oil on canvas measuring approximately 29 by 24 inches, had been painted by Thorp circa 1879 from, he contended, "life sketches" in a specially created studio on the fourth floor of the Senate wing of the Capitol building. Thorp said he got close enough to sketch his hero at least twice: once when Lincoln's inaugural train had to make a stop in Geneva, Ohio, in 1861, and again at the Gettysburg battlefield in 1863. "I studied him very carefully and thoroughly from life just before his inauguration," the artist told the senators, "and later at the White House and at Gettysburg when he made his famous address, sketching him, making a descriptive delineation such as artists use, memorizing his expression and how

he looked when animated." The artist contended that these observations allowed him to create an accurate portrait of the president, and that "it would be impracticable for any future portrait painter who had not known him in life to put the real Lincoln on canvas."

Reaction to the painting was mixed. Some complained that it was too dark, but a reviewer in the Washington, D.C., *Daily Morning Chronicle* said this gave his portrait "richness of tone."

Possibly unknown to the senators, Thorp produced additional portraits of Lincoln, including a pencil drawing on cardboard, now in the collection of the Dwight D. Eisenhower Library and Museum. He also painted copies of his award-winning Lincoln portrait. One, smaller than the Senate portrait at 21 by 16.5 inches, showed up in the June 12, 2008, Heritage Galleries historical auction, where it brought only $4,780 including buyer's premium. According to research by Heritage catalogers at the time of the sale, "Painting the 'perfect' Lincoln was a lifelong mission for Thorp. . . . Our research has shown that Thorp made as many as five paintings of Lincoln from these sketches and his memories of the great man." Other Thorp Lincoln portraits have been traced at one time or another to Camp Lincoln for Boys in Minnesota, the Pequot Lakes Post Office, and Carleton College. "Thorp's daughter, Sarah Thorp Heald, donated one of the original sketches [of Lincoln]

Fig. 3.81. Artist Freeman Thorp painted this likeness after the Gettysburg Lincoln photo in 1919 and sold it to the U.S. Senate for $2,000 in 1920, under the pretext that he had observed Abraham Lincoln in life.

Fig. 3.82. This extremely high-relief bronze Art Nouveau plaque is unfortunately unsigned. The bust is mounted on a copper shell secured by screws to its period (and no doubt original) frame. The plaque is footed to facilitate its standing upright.

from life to the Crow Wing County Historical Society. The other life sketch (Gettysburg) was donated by Thorp's grandson, Joseph Heald, to Dwight Eisenhower in 1957 who placed it in the Eisenhower Museum in Abilene, Kansas." The painting in the auction was believed to have been the example formerly hanging in the Post Office building.[30] The Thorp portrait acquired by the U.S. Senate was used on the cover of the September/October 2006 issue of *Paper Money*, the award-winning official bi-monthly journal of the Society of Paper Money Collectors.

1920. W.E. Walsh of the Rotary Club, Morris, Illinois, copyrights the Rotary International's "Good Turn Token" (King 1029) with a portrait of Abraham Lincoln, an image of a Boy Scout, and the legend "No matter how much provoked, do nothing in ill temper or malice," a paraphrase from Lincoln's Cooper Union Address in which he said, regarding sectionalism: "Even though much provoked, let us do nothing through passion and ill temper." Lincoln delivered a similar line in his speech at New Haven, Connecticut, March 6, 1860.

Fig. 3.84. These 1920s pinbacks for Miller Bros. Co., Westminster, Maryland (a), and Lincoln National Life, Fort Wayne, Indiana (b), feature the Lincoln money image and the Marshall image, respectively.

Fig. 3.85. This 1920 32-millimeter "Do a Good Turn Daily" Boy Scout medal (King-1029) was sponsored by the Rotary Club of Morris, Illinois, and copyrighted by W.E. Walsh.

Fig. 3.83. Lincoln paper items of the 1920s include Massachusetts Lincolniana and coin dealer John E. Morse's calling cards imprinted on the backs of merchant scrip and old checks (in this case a century-old 1824 check) (a), an A. & J. Jewelry & Novelty Co. $10 certificate patented by Todd, Rochester, New York (b), and various checks. The Lincoln, Pennsylvania, check (c) was printed by Falconer Co., Baltimore, and the Washington, D.C., Lincoln National Bank check (d) by Young & Selden Co., Baltimore. As can be seen, each employs a different yet very common Lincoln image.

1920 JULY 1. Syracuse, New York, dealer A. Atlas Leve offers a collection of Lincoln medals for sale in *The Numismatist*.

1920 JULY 9. Long Beach, California, changes the name of its oldest park from Pacific Park to Lincoln Park. A statue of Abraham Lincoln atop a column, by sculptor Peter Bisson, had been dedicated in the park in 1915. Lincoln Park is also the home for the City Hall of Long Beach.

1920 JULY 28. A bronze duplicate of August Saint-Gaudens's standing Lincoln statue at Lincoln Park, Chicago, is dedicated in Parliament Square in London, England, resolving the bitter struggle over whether this formal statue or George Grey Barnard's more casual approach should represent our national savior in the capital of the mother country.

1920 AUGUST 23. American Numismatic Association president Waldo C. Moore exhibits broken-bank notes with portraits of Abraham Lincoln and George Washington, at the ANA convention in Chicago. Youngstown, Ohio, collector Judson Brenner displayed "a splendid collection of Lincoln medals and tokens."

1920 OCTOBER 1. Syracuse, New York, coin dealer A. Atlas Leve offers the 1865 American Numismatic and Archaeological Society's Abraham Lincoln medal for sale for $22 in "block tin." According to Leve, "only 16 struck."

Fig. 3.86. Syracuse, New York, coin dealer A. Atlas Leve was another Lincolnphile. He dealt heavily in Abraham Lincoln medals, and created a variety of covers over several years commemorating his community's fleeting association with Lincoln.

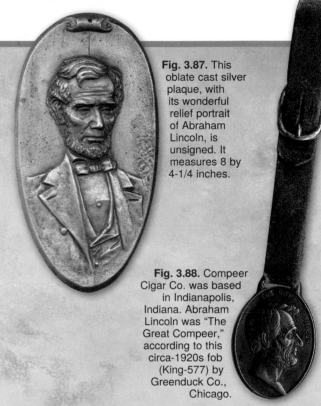

Fig. 3.87. This oblate cast silver plaque, with its wonderful relief portrait of Abraham Lincoln, is unsigned. It measures 8 by 4-1/4 inches.

Fig. 3.88. Compeer Cigar Co. was based in Indianapolis, Indiana. Abraham Lincoln was "The Great Compeer," according to this circa-1920s fob (King-577) by Greenduck Co., Chicago.

Fig. 3.89. War Savings Stamps were sold to small investors beginning in 1917, to be pasted into folders and, when full, redeemed for United States Treasury War Certificates, Defense Bonds, or War Bonds. Orange $5 stamps depicting Abraham Lincoln (Scott WS5) were introduced in December 21, 1920. The O-92–style Lincoln portrait (BEP die MISC 1139) is credited to Charles Burt in 1870 for a bond coupon. The stamp was designed by C.A. Houston. The stamp itself (BEP MISC 10323) is credited to a team headed by Fred Smillie. Joaquin C. Benzing engraved the ribbon and ornamental leaves; Edward E. Myers, the frames; and Myers and William B. Wells, the lettering and numerals. The initials S. De B. in the selvage of the pane are those of siderographer Samuel DeBinder, who laid in the plate, and who coincidentally also laid in the border plate for the 24-cent airmail stamp that was used to print the fabulous "inverted Jenny" stamps a couple of years later. These stamps are quite scarce and valuable as singles. The portion of a pane of 50 that is shown here was a Bureau of Engraving and Printing proof sheet, now in the National Numismatic Collection of the Smithsonian Institution.

Fig. 3.90. Abraham Lincoln is seen anointing Warren G. Harding and Calvin Coolidge on this 1920 campaign banner from the collection of the Library of Congress.

Fig. 3.91. Augustus Saint-Gaudens's *Standing Lincoln* in Chicago was universally acclaimed as the greatest Lincoln statue of its time. In 1919 a duplicate was installed in London, England, adjacent to Westminster Cathedral (seen in the background). The scale of the memorial is shown by the workman performing maintenance duties on it in 1955.

1921 January 1. Coin dealer A. Atlas Leve offers a "nice collection" of Lincoln medals for $50 in *The Numismatist.*

1921. The Macmillan Company publishes Ida M. Tarbell's *Boy Scouts' Life of Lincoln.* This popular juvenile title would prove durable. It would be reprinted in 1922, 1925, 1926, 1930, and 1941.

1921 February 12. Norwegian-American metal engraver Anton Erickson, of Minneapolis, celebrates Abraham Lincoln's birthday by completing on that day a unique Lincoln medal. On the obverse is a striking likeness of Lincoln, and on the other "the entire Gettysburg speech . . . including dates and the artist's name." The gold medal is the size of a cent, and "though the text cannot be read by the naked eye, it is easily deciphered when placed under a magnifying glass." Erickson had learned his art in Norway, but had immigrated to the U.S. a decade earlier.

1921 February 12. American Numismatic Association president Waldo Moore gives a Lincoln program at the Lewisburg (Ohio) Lodge, No. 571, Independent Order of Odd Fellows. Noble Grand Brother Moore gave a talk on Abraham Lincoln and displayed "a nice collection of Lincoln books, pictures, money, etc., he being the owner of many different valuable collections." At the meeting two weeks later he would treat of George Washington in a similar manner.

1921 February 23. Farran Zerbe exhibits medals of Abraham Lincoln and George Washington together with checks bearing their signatures at a meeting of the Pacific Coast Numismatic Society.

1921. Fremont, Nebraska, is the site of a copy of Alfonso Pelzer's New Jersey statue of the Great Emancipator, made by John G. Segesman. The statue was a gift from L.D. Richards. Its location was John C. Fremont Park, along the route of the Lincoln Highway. The pedestal included a bronze copy of the Gettysburg Address.

1921 April. *The Numismatist* editor Frank Duffield publishes a brief article, "Information Wanted on Die-Struck Lincoln Pieces," in which he says: "Mr. Robert P. King, Scott Building, Erie, PA, who has the distinction of being the pioneer collector of Lincoln medals and tokens, announces in our advertising pages in this month's issue that he is compiling a catalogue of die-struck Lincoln issues, and that he would like to be advised of any new or unusual issues, and also to learn the different cities issuing the large souvenir Lincoln pennies with the crude bust of Lincoln. The number of collectors of Lincoln issues has increased greatly within the last decade, and Mr. King's catalog, when issued, should be of great help to such collectors, and it is hoped they will promptly respond to Mr. King's request for information." King's ad appeared on page 180. It read: "LINCOLN MEDALS AND TOKENS. I am compiling a catalog of

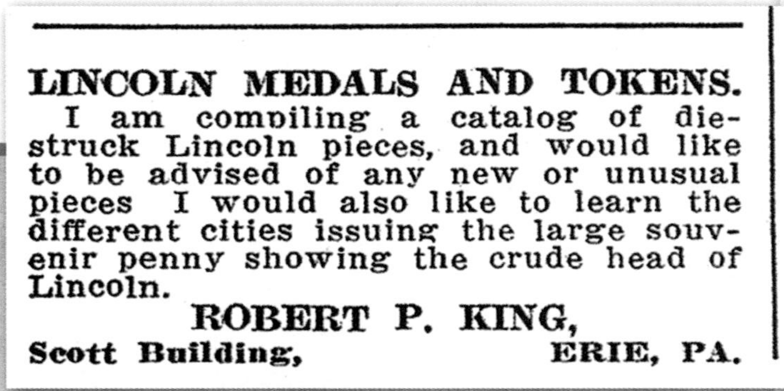

LINCOLN MEDALS AND TOKENS.

I am compiling a catalog of die-struck Lincoln pieces, and would like to be advised of any new or unusual pieces I would also like to learn the different cities issuing the large souvenir penny showing the crude head of Lincoln.

ROBERT P. KING,

Scott Building, **ERIE, PA.**

Fig. 3.92. Collector Robert P. King advertised in *The Numismatist* in 1921 for listings of "new or unusual (Lincoln) pieces" for a catalog he was compiling. The first installment would appear in that publication in 1924.

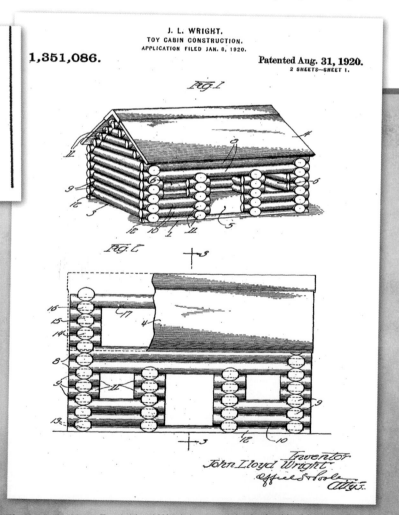

Fig. 3.93. Architect Frank Lloyd Wright's son, John L., had building-building on his mind too, when he invented and patented his "toy cabin construction" designs in 1920. His Lincoln Logs would be marketed as "America's National Toy."

die-struck Lincoln pieces, and would like to be advised of any new or unusual pieces. I would also like to learn the different cities issuing the large souvenir penny showing the crude head of Lincoln."

King's 45-word classified ad would lead directly to his publication less than three years later of an initial catalog in *The Numismatist*'s "Lincoln Number" of February 1924. King's catalog would fuel a revolution in collecting Lincolniana and, with several updates by King and later others, remain the standard cataloging for this important field. These separate listings were aggregated and reprinted to meet collector demand several times. In 1966 the Token and Medal Society (TAMS) published one such reprint printed by Edwards Brothers. Edgar Heyl followed in 1967 with an index to King's Lincolniana. Another reprint was undertaken privately by numismatic publisher Sanford Durst in June 1985. In 2008 a group of four members of the Token and Medal Society, headed by then *TAMS Journal* publisher Paul Cunningham, and including then *TAMS Journal* editor David Schenkman, Kathy Lawrence, and Fred Reed, undertook updating and revising the King list in a comprehensive way. As of this writing that work is still in progress.

1921 MAY. A. Atlas Leve offers a Lincoln medal collection for $75, including the American Numismatic and Archaeological Society medal in block tin. In July he would lower the price to $65.

1921 JUNE 22. Thomas Elder sells the magnificent collection of political medals formed by J.E. Lynch of Mineola, New York, "the finest collection of American Political Medals and Tokens up to the time of Abraham Lincoln ever offered in 410 lots, including over 250 varieties of Lincoln alone." Many of the rare pieces were pictured.

1922 FEBRUARY 4. Ford Motor Company enters the luxury-auto market by purchasing Lincoln Motor Company for $8 million so Henry Leland can pay his tax bill. Edsel Ford became president of Lincoln Motor Co. Henry Leland would try to buy the company back several months later. Ford is said to have replied, "Mr. Leland, I wouldn't sell the Lincoln plant for five hundred million dollars." In 1922 Ford asked Henry Leland's son Wilfred to leave the company, and Henry Leland resigned as well. Edsel Ford took charge, and sales doubled in a short time.

1922 FEBRUARY 9. Douglas Volk's somber Lincoln portrait, which also adorns the essay-contest medals, appears on the cover of the *Mid-Week Pictorial* weekly supplement to the *New York Times*.

1922 FEBRUARY 28. This is the date ascribed, by researcher Walter Breen, for the striking of 1922 "plain" Lincoln cents at the Denver Mint. The coins normally would have had a conspicuous "D" mintmark indicating their source, but a worn-out obverse coinage die was contaminated with grease or other debris, obliterating the mark.

1922 MAY 30. At the dedication of the Lincoln Memorial in Washington, D.C., poet Edwin Markham reads his poem, "Lincoln, Man of the People," to the one hundred thousand persons present at the ceremony and a radio audience estimated at two million more.

Fig. 3.94. When Henry Ford took over the Lincoln Motor Company in 1922, he installed his son Edsel at the company's helm. Edsel was interested in classier vehicles than his father was. In the early 1920s, he contracted with Fleetwood Metal Body Co., a top-tier automobile coachbuilder in Fleetwood, Pennsylvania. The Lincoln Fleetwood became a luxury vehicle preferred by movie stars, magnates, and socialites such as these three women, circa 1930.

Markham's work had been chosen out of 250 Lincoln poems submitted to a committee headed by Chief Justice William Howard Taft. In the third stanza, Markham wrote:

Up from log cabin to the Capitol,
One fire was on his spirit, one resolve—
To send the keen ax to the root of wrong,
Clearing a free way for the feet of God,
The eyes of conscience testing every stroke,
To make his deed the measure of a man.
He built the rail-pile as he built the State,
Pouring his splendid strength through every blow:
The grip that swung the ax in Illinois
Was on the pen that set a people free.

In later years, Markham would autograph printed copies of the poem with details of his winning the contest and accolades given the poem, signing them "Your friend, Edwin Markham." One such framed copy of the poem hung for many decades in the offices of R.M. Smythe principal John Herzog; upon sizing down after the sale of his company to Spink, he contacted the present author to inquire if he would like it. It presently hangs in this author's Lincoln Room.

Congress appropriated $2,939,720 for construction of the Lincoln Memorial, including retaining wall, approaches, and Daniel Chester French's statue of Lincoln, but excluding the lagoon and exterior roadways and walkways.[31] The pieces of French's statue, weighing 170 tons in total, had never been joined until they were put together in place.

Fig. 3.95. Stereoview cards such as this 1920s Keystone card brought the wonders of the world, the likes of the newly dedicated Lincoln Memorial, into the homes of viewers worldwide.

Fig. 3.96. Various pinbacks from the 1920s, commemorating historical events, boost the Lincoln Stove & Range Co. and other commercial and educational ventures.

Fig. 3.97. Poet Edwin Markham is seen reciting his award-winning poem "Lincoln, Man of the People" at the dedication of the Lincoln Memorial on May 30, 1922. Seated at right are Warren G. Harding and William Howard Taft.

1922 JUNE. The newly dedicated Lincoln Memorial graces the cover of *Art & Archaeology* magazine's "Lincoln Memorial Number." According to the magazine, more than 100 statues had already been lifted up to memorialize Abraham Lincoln by that time. Frank Owen Payne opines:

> Of making many books about Abraham Lincoln there is no end. . . . Monuments to Lincoln outnumber those of any other of our national heroes. . . . We fancy that it is the ambition of practically every sculptor some day to produce a statue of Lincoln. . . . [T]here has been a sufficiently large number of really good works to justify the very highest effort of any artist. . . . Abraham Lincoln furnishes a perennial theme for the artist as well as for the historian and man of letters. The triumph of democratic principles in the late war will enhance the glory of the great Emancipator wherever in future ages true Democracy shall triumph. For Lincoln was indeed the first ambassador whom the great hitherto unrepresented common people sent as plenipotentiary to the court of world affairs.[32]

Other articles in the issue include its architect Henry Bacon's description of the memorial's architecture, and muralist Jules Guerin's description of its murals.

1922 CIRCA. Sculptor Ad Meskens takes a cast of the head portion of Augustus Saint-Gaudens's *Standing Lincoln* in Lincoln Park, Chicago. Bronze 28-inch-high duplicates cast by Kunst Foundry, New York, mounted on marble, would be sold to collectors and museums. Under Lincoln's left shoulder, these duplicates bear the inscription "A. Saint Gaudens / © 1922."

1922 AUGUST 17. A limestone standing figure of Abraham Lincoln by sculptor Ira A. Correll is dedicated at Old Settlers Park, Odon, Indiana. The work was a gift of local monument carver Correll "in memory of The Pioneer Fathers and Mothers."

1922 DECEMBER 19. Postmaster General Hubert Work approves the die for a $1 Lincoln Memorial U.S. postage stamp (Scott 571).

1923 FEBRUARY. Lot Flannery's slightly-larger-than-life-size marble statue of Abraham Lincoln resting his left hand on a fasces representing the Union is restored to its original location in Washington, D.C., after having been taken down in 1919. Flannery

had won a competition to design this first memorial to the martyr in the federal District of Columbia, dedicated on the third anniversary of Lincoln's death, on April 15, 1868. He claimed to have been present at Ford's Theatre when Lincoln was assassinated.

1923 MARCH 23. The Indiana Assembly creates the Lincoln Memorial Commission, and authorizes it to purchase land and build structures as necessary, and "to prepare and execute plans for erecting a suitable memorial to the memory of Abraham Lincoln at or near his residence in the state."

1923 MAY 18. The American Institute of Architects presents its highest award, the AIA gold medal, to Lincoln Memorial architect Henry Bacon at the association's 56th annual convention in Washington, D.C. The ceremony occurred almost exactly a year after the memorial's dedication on May 30, 1922. According to an AIA historian, the medal was presented to Bacon, in an elaborate ceremony, by President Warren G. Harding on the steps of the Memorial.

> The most elaborate of all Gold Medal ceremonies was held in 1923 at the Lincoln Memorial. It honored Henry Bacon, architect of the memorial. AIA members, dressed in colorful robes, carried banners and standards. They marched down the Reflecting Pool accompanied by architecture students, who manned a series of ropes to pull Bacon, seated on a 'royal' barge, down the pool's length. Bacon sat under a golden wooden statue of a boy with a laurel wreath that represented a crown. As the barge made its way, trumpeters from the Marine Band played a 'joyous processional,' Walter's 'Prize Song' from *Der Meistersinger.* William Howard Taft, chief justice of the U.S. Supreme Court and former president of the United States, met Bacon at the bottom of the steps and presented him to President Warren G. Harding, who bestowed the Gold Medal. After the ceremony, the participants dined al fresco on the grounds of the Lincoln Memorial.[33]

Bacon would die less than a year later.

Original graphite sketches on tracing paper by Bacon at the Library of Congress reveal his "critical role in the evolution of the design, scale, and placement of the statue created by Daniel Chester French for the building's interior," a Library of Congress archivist notes. (See figure 3.99.)

Fig. 3.98. Heeren Bros. & Co., manufacturing jewelers of Pittsburgh, Pennsylvania, patented an attractive gilded and bronzed-aluminum process and produced this 32.5-millimeter medal (King-339).

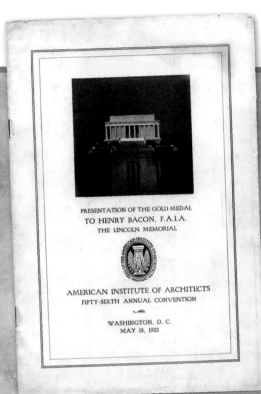

Fig. 3.99. The American Institute of Architects awarded Lincoln Memorial designer Henry Bacon the profession's highest award, the AIA gold medal, in a lavish ceremony conducted on the steps and on the lagoon of the memorial itself almost a year to the day after the memorial's dedication. Shown is a program from that ceremony.

Fig. 3.100. In the 1920s the Falconer Co. of Baltimore printed checks for Lincoln Trust Co. of Gettysburg, Pennsylvania. The $5-style money vignette based on O-92 is signed "R.H." beneath the truncation at lower left, which could indicate that it was originally done by Robert Hinshelwood for Continental Bank Note Co. prior to 1878. Various merchant imprints and the Jennie Wade Museum have been observed printed at left.

Fig. 3.102. Lincoln Birthday dinners were celebrated on land and at sea. This 1920s menu was used for one such event held on a Moore-McCormack Lines steamship.

Fig. 3.101. The approved design model for the Series of 1922 $500 Gold Certificate (Friedberg 1217, BEP die MISC 2722) continued the use of Charles Burt's "ideal" Lincoln portrait from the Series of 1882 notes. The series year was finally changed after 40 years of successive issues because of the addition of a Legal Tender clause at lower left.

Fig. 3.103. American Bank Note Co. Litho printed this 1920s Customer's Draft for Lincoln National Bank, Minneapolis, Minnesota, with the lithographic version of the company's "Men in Currency" Gettysburg Lincoln portrait.

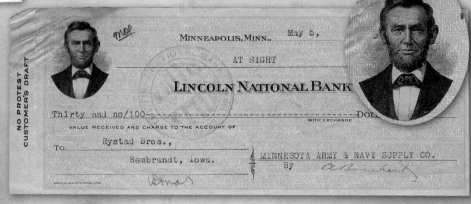

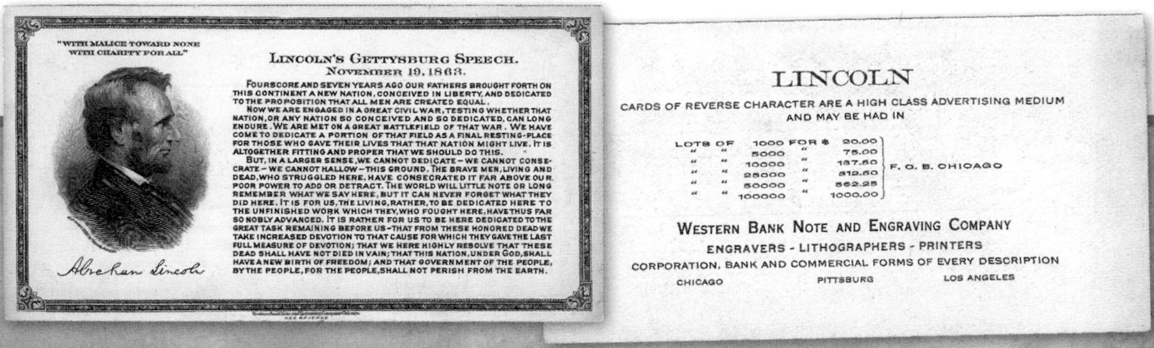

Fig. 3.104. Western Bank Note & Engraving Co., Chicago, created a fine Lincoln profile engraving based on the 1892 Thomas Johnson etching (see figure 2.126), which it used on an advertising card with the Gettysburg Address. As can be seen by the schedule on the back, it would print the card for other advertisers at rates of one or two cents per card, FOB Chicago. Note, several varieties of the card have been observed with other rates and in different sizes, and yet others with the imprint of the parent American Bank Note Co., which acquired WBNCo in 1901 and operated it as a subsidiary.

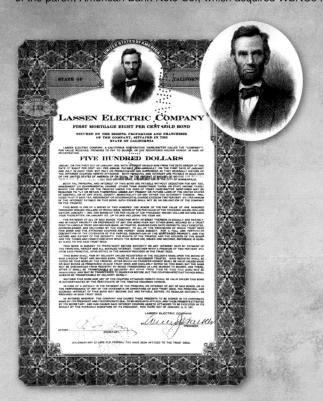

Fig. 3.105. The Gettysburg Lincoln vignette makes a powerful statement on this 1921 Lassen Electric Co. gold bond.

Fig. 3.106. Lincoln National Bank, Fort Wayne, Indiana, employed a Marshal-style portrait on this 1922 promissory note.

Fig. 3.107. The rising tide of official government portraiture after the O-92 photographic model, preferred by Robert Todd Lincoln, got an extra impetus when the Post Office released a violet three-cent stamp (Scott 555) to cover the ordinary first-class letter postage rate on February 12, 1923. On June 27, 1925, nearly 200,000 of these stamps overprinted CANAL ZONE (Scott CZ 85) were released for use there. The Lincoln portrait after the $5 model is by John Eissler.

Fig. 3.108. The owner of this circa-1920s Baby Lincoln nickel slot machine furnished the present author additional photos too. The copper medallion on the face of the machine looks like a contemporary three-inch Lincoln Lucky Penny design (see figure 3-182b) for Lincoln, Nebraska, in the author's collection.

Fig. 3.109. Abe Lincoln and eight other tall legislators represented Sangamon County in the Illinois General Assembly. All were at least six feet tall, earning the appellation "The Long Nine." The group actively sought to move the state capital from Vandalia to Springfield. In addition to Lincoln, these men were John Dawson, William F. Elkin, Ninian W. Edwards, Job Fletcher, Archer G. Herndon, Andrew McCormick, Daniel Stone, and Robert L. Wilson. This cigar-box lid is believed to date from the 1920s.

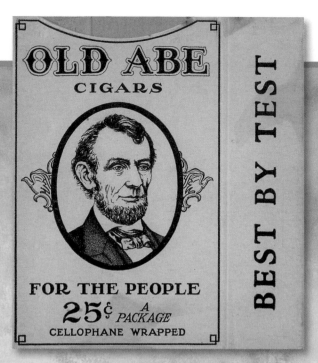

Fig. 3.110. Old Abe Cigars were cigarette-sized smokes "For the People." Memorabilia for this brand is plentiful, especially end-box labels. Not so common are cardboard packages such as this. All Old Abe memorabilia seen employs the money image that was ubiquitous in circulation by the time this circa-1920s package was filled with the small cigars.

Fig. 3.111. Gutzon Borglum had a passion for Abraham Lincoln, so much so that he named his son Lincoln. Here the sculptor poses in 1924 with a large white marble head of a beardless Lincoln that is more revealed than his similar, albeit larger, white marble study in the U.S. Capitol Rotunda. This work would eventually find its way to the Detroit Institute of Arts, a gift of local businessman Ralph Herman Booth. There it would suffer long periods in storage and the indignities of vandals while on public display.

Fig. 3.112. A world traveler in the Roaring Twenties could pick up baggage labels from Hotel Lincolns on several continents, including those in Paris, France (a), Havana, Cuba (b), and New York City (c).

Fig. 3.113. O[lga] P[opoff] Muller sculpted this pentagonal plaque (King-888) depicting Abraham Lincoln and Tad looking at the sample photograph album at the Brady Washington, D.C., studio. Muller was a decorative artist, who displayed at the Panama-Pacific Expo and the American Academy of Design. This medallium (cast iron) plaque measures approximately 7-1/4 by 4-5/8 inches. Medallium was an inexpensive metal, favored by the Decorative Arts League, that was more durable than spelter or pewter, and would take a finish such as bronze, silver, or gold. This plaque was copyrighted in 1922, and has a conjoined "MP" shopmark. Muller's design also appears on bookends, and was featured on the cover of a women's magazine of the period.

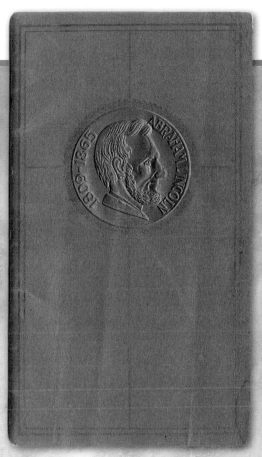

Fig. 3.114. In 1924 the Illinois Watch Co. produced this booklet touting its A. Lincoln pocket watch. Its gold-embossed cover features a medallic portrait based on the Bela Lyon Pratt medal the firm was distributing at the time as a come-on.

Fig. 3.115 This simple 1924 button *(a)* was given to those contributing to the Abraham Lincoln University Foundation Fund drive to raise money for a proposed institution of that name in Springfield, Illinois, in 1924. As the poster shows, the campaign goal was a million dollars *(b)*. This effort failed, but in the 1960s a similar campaign led to the establishment of Sangamon State University, which became the University of Illinois at Springfield in 1995.

Fig. 3.116. The effort to create the transcontinental Lincoln Highway was a patriotic red-white-and-blue affair, as the association's signage emphasized *(a)*. Here, a well-dressed family poses in front of an unidentified "L" station sign *(b)*.

1923 MAY 22. A bronze casting based on the famous head of Augustus Saint-Gaudens's *Standing Lincoln* bronze statue at Lincoln Park, Chicago, is dedicated at the Hall of Fame for Great Americans at New York University in New York City, to represent Lincoln in the Hall's pantheon. Similar 28-inch-tall bronze busts were acquired by the Brooklyn Museum's Robert B. Woodward Memorial Fund at about the same time, and by the Delaware Art Museum in 2002 as a gift from Rufus Erickson.

1923. A decade after first proposed by Carl G. Fisher to encourage building "good roads," the nation's first transcontinental highway, the Lincoln Highway, supported by auto and tire makers, sees the construction of an "Ideal Section" near Dyer, Indiana. This mile-and-a-half section was designed and built as a model for road construction along the route elsewhere. The demonstration section was funded by county and state governments and U.S. Rubber Co. It featured a "100 foot right-of-way, 40 foot paved width, 10 inch steel-reinforced concrete, underground drainage, lighted, landscaped, bridge, and pedestrian pathways," according to an historical marker erected by the Indiana Historical Bureau and other groups in 1996. Construction of the route, admittedly not all of it up to this quality, would take 15 years, from 1913 to 1928.

1923 NOVEMBER 7. Lincoln National Life Insurance Company of Fort Wayne, Indiana, dedicates its new headquarters building, with a special boardroom off the lobby, accessible to the public when not in use, with Abraham Lincoln photographs and Lincolniana on display. At the time it noted, "The effort of amassing Lincoln material is being carried on, and the Lincoln Room will be of more and more value to those who seek intimate glimpses of the man whose ideals of service were taken for the service ideals of this company." The company circulated a color postcard of the new building, with the tagline "Home Office Building—Occupied Exclusively by the Company."

1924 JANUARY 21. Associated First National Pictures releases Al and Ray Rockett's Rockett-Lincoln Film Company motion picture, *The Dramatic Life of Abraham Lincoln,* under the revised title *The Adventures of Abraham Lincoln* on some film posters. The film starred George A. Billings in the title role.

1924 FEBRUARY. Robert P. King's "Lincoln in Numismatics" appears in *The Numismatist,* the American Numismatic Association's official monthly journal. Additional articles in the issue included Allen H. Wright on Lincoln Day Menu Cards, George H. Blake on federal currency with Lincoln portraits, D.C. Wismer on obsolete currency with Lincoln portraits, F. Ray Risdon on "Why I Collect Lincolniana," and an unsigned article on Brenner's initials being restored on Lincoln cents, something first accounted for in numismatic literature in June 1922—some four years *after* they were restored without fanfare at the truncation of the bust on the obverse in 1918!

1924 FEBRUARY 12. A.L. Van den Bergen's bronze standing Lincoln is dedicated at Racine, Wisconsin. A second copy of the statue is in Clinton, Illinois, dedicated in 1931. Historians are divided over whether Lincoln grasps his Gettysburg Address or the Emancipation Proclamation in his right hand.

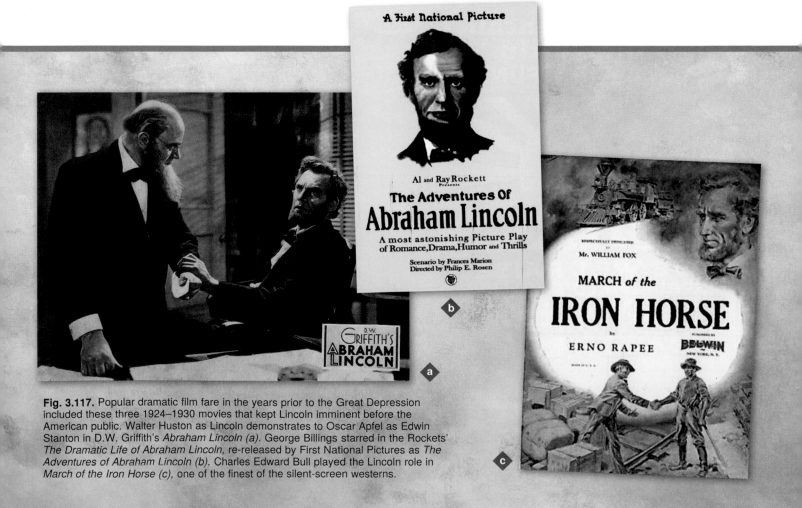

Fig. 3.117. Popular dramatic film fare in the years prior to the Great Depression included these three 1924–1930 movies that kept Lincoln imminent before the American public. Walter Huston as Lincoln demonstrates to Oscar Apfel as Edwin Stanton in D.W. Griffith's *Abraham Lincoln (a).* George Billings starred in the Rockets' *The Dramatic Life of Abraham Lincoln,* re-released by First National Pictures as *The Adventures of Abraham Lincoln (b).* Charles Edward Bull played the Lincoln role in *March of the Iron Horse (c),* one of the finest of the silent-screen westerns.

1924 March. A short list of errata to Robert P. King's "Lincoln in Numismatics" appears in *The Numismatist*. In October, the periodical would publish King's thank-you for receiving the American Numismatic Association's first-place award for an article published in the journal, presented at the organization's summer convention. King also pledged to update his list from time to time as warranted. He would indeed publish two updates, in April 1927 and August 1933.

1924 April 5. William Granville Hastings's standing Lincoln bronze statue on a base of Minnesota granite is dedicated in Grandview Park, Sioux City, Iowa, a gift of local citizens Elizabeth and John Magoun. The work was similar to a Hastings's bronze Lincoln in Jefferson, Iowa, presented to that city by Mr. and Mrs. S.B. Wilson in 1918. A third, similar, Hastings figure, with the addition of a kneeling Liberty, was installed in Cincinnati, Ohio. Another, also with the addition of Liberty, was installed at Bunker Hill, Illinois.

Fig. 3.118. Twenty years after he completed a second model, in 1926 August Saint-Gaudens's magnificent *Seated Lincoln* was officially dedicated in Chicago's Grant Park, within a magnificent 150-foot-diameter exedra designed by architect Stanford White. Unfortunately neither man was still alive to see the much-delayed, belated ceremony. Saint-Gaudens died in 1907, and White in 1906.

Fig. 3.119. The *Lincoln Library of Essential Information* was a staple of reference and community libraries in the decades before the Internet was established. The book was the brainchild of M.J. Kinsella, and provided a handy compendium of useful information. The first edition rolled off the press on February 12, 1924. This is the 1929 edition.

Fig. 3.120. The Hartford Times presented this bronze fob *(a)* (King-927) to participants in its 1923 Lincoln Story Contest. Winners (presumably) received the gilded examples listed by King. This unsigned piece was manufactured by Whitehead & Hoag, Newark, NJ, utilizing a modified Bela Lyon Pratt Lincoln bust. The Bela Lyon Pratt bust proved a durable one. Here it forms the model for Old Abe's image on a Lincoln and Lee University pendant *(b)*. The Methodist school was founded in 1925 to evidence the reformed national union.

Fig. 3.121. In 1927 New York coin dealer Tom Elder issued the second of his tiny "A Token" Lincoln medalets. According to researcher Tom DeLorey, the designer and manufacturer of this issue is unknown, but "the obverse is a crude copy" of Elder's 1910 issue modeled by Roiné, engraved by Deitsch, and struck by Medallic Art Co. The edition of 15.1-millimeter medalets included gold and aluminum pieces (shown), as well as sterling silver, German silver, copper, and gilt brass.

1924. The Lincoln Highway Association publishes its fifth edition of its *Complete and Official Road Guide of the Lincoln Highway*, the most complete (and final) edition. Over the previous decade numerous route changes had occurred as roadways were upgraded, bridges were built, and previous legs were abandoned. In 1924 Alternate Lincoln Highway routes were also established to bypass the downtowns of Philadelphia, Pittsburgh, Elkhart (Indiana), and Sacramento.

1924 July 4. Cleveland sculptor Stephen A. Rebeck's nine-foot-tall standing bronze statue of Abraham Lincoln is dedicated at Alliance, Ohio.

1924 August 7. Series of 1923 Lincoln $5 Silver Certificate "Porthole" notes are released to circulation, showing the fullest realization of Charles Burt's O-92–style portrait engraving.

1924 September 15. Sculptor Gaetano Cecere's standing bronze figure of Abraham Lincoln is dedicated at the Lincoln Memorial Bridge, Milwaukee, Wisconsin.

1924 November 11. The California Palace of Legion of Honor in San Francisco is dedicated as a memorial to veterans of the Great War (World War I). It is located at the terminus of the Lincoln Highway, which officially ended in the plaza and fountain in front of the building. The site occupies a rise in Lincoln Park in the northwest of the city overlooking the Golden Gate Bridge. This building is one of San Francisco's most beautiful art museums. Film director Alfred Hitchcock set the scene in his 1958 movie *Vertigo*, where Jimmy Stewart's character is stalking Kim Novak's character, who appears possessed by a portrait of Carlotta Valdes, at this museum.

1924 December. Coin dealer Thomas L. Elder urges numismatic and historical societies to importune Congress to pass a bill authorizing an Abraham Lincoln and/or George Washington gold dollar coin. It would be "fitting and pleasing," he said. "I venture to predict that a Lincoln gold dollar would have a great sale even among the

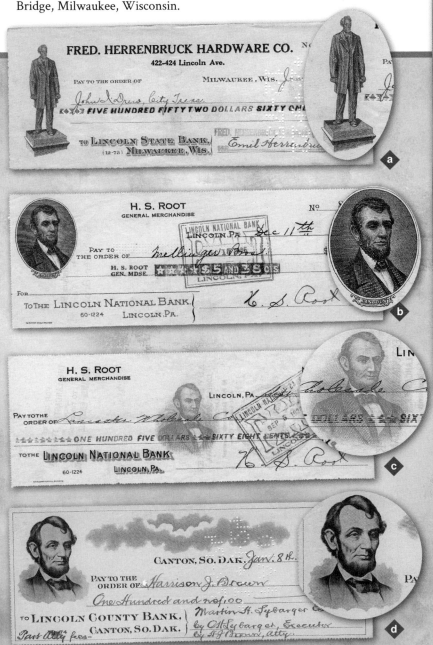

Fig. 3.122. Melodramatic, cheesy, patronizing, and even racist imagery in the 1920s and beyond permeated depictions of Abraham Lincoln and members of the black race. Even "cute" images express the widespread if subtle racism of the times. This promotional movie still is from a 1926 Hal Roach comedy depicting Farina (Allen Hoskins) saluting a Lincoln bust.

Fig. 3.123. The author has twice exhibited his unparalleled collection of Lincoln checks at the Memphis International Paper Money Show. All these checks, drafted between 1922 and 1925, show the Lincoln $5 money image based on the O-92 model, except the 1922 Lincoln State Bank of Milwaukee, Wisconsin (a), check, which displays an image of the sculptor Guetano Cecere's standing bronze figure of Lincoln that would be dedicated at the Lincoln Memorial Bridge at Milwaukee in 1924. The two Pennsylvania checks (b, c), each with a different Lincoln portrait, were printed by Falconer Co., Baltimore. The other two checks do not have printers' imprints.

laboring people, if the price were kept at about $1.50 per coin," he added.[34] Elder struck gold dollar tokens, of the Lincoln style that he recommended, in 1910, 1927, and 1939.

1925. St. Louis artist J. Wilber Gontermann's near-profile black-and-white portrait of Abraham Lincoln—patterned after the similar, familiar Douglas Volk treatments—is released as a lithograph.

1925 SEPTEMBER. Robert P. King offers for sale a 44-millimeter medal marking publication of the first installment in his "Lincoln in Numismatics" in the *Numismatist* issue of February 1924. Legends included "115th Anniversary of the Birth of Abraham Lincoln" and "To Commemorate the Publication by The Numismatist of the Robert P. King List of Coins, Medals, Tokens, Etc. of Abraham Lincoln, Feb. 1924." The medal was engraved by H.A. Gray. Mintage was 25 in silver, offered at $2.50 each; 100 in bronze, at $1; and an unspecified quantity in aluminum and lead. King would donate a bronze example and $51.56 profit from medal sales to the American Numismatic Association.[35]

1926 MARCH 8. Abraham Lincoln's only surviving son, Robert Todd Lincoln, graces the cover of *Time* magazine. The former U.S. secretary of War would die in his sleep four months later, on July 26, 1926.

1926 MAY 31. Augustus Saint-Gaudens's magnificent nine-foot-tall seated Lincoln sculpture depicting Lincoln as head of state is finally, and officially, dedicated in Chicago's Grant Park, between Michigan Avenue and Columbus Drive, within a marvelous 150-foot-wide exedra by architect Stanford White. Both Saint-Gaudens, who died in 1907, and White, who preceded him in death in 1906, were unavailable to see the fruition of their joint genius.

1926. New York Blue Ribbon Books publishes an elegant edition of *An Autobiography of Abraham Lincoln Consisting of the Personal Portions of his Letters, Speeches and Conversations,* edited by Nathaniel Wright Stephenson. The book had a photographic frontispiece of Daniel Chester French's seated Lincoln Memorial marble sculpture, and an excellent colored miniature oval portrait of Lincoln on ivory under glass "within a rectangular centerpiece comprising gilt fillets and foliate stamps." The portrait was after the then-current $500 Gold Certificate image that would have been familiar to the original purchasers of such an elegant volume. The volume was bound in crimson morocco covers, with raised bands on the spine, and gold stamped.

1926. The Abraham Lincoln Council, Boy Scouts of America, Springfield, Illinois, establishes a Lincoln Trail from New Salem to Springfield for Boy Scouts to earn Lincoln Trail medals.

1926 SUMMER. "Swim-In" organizers circulate a photograph of boys playing in the reflecting pond in front of the Lincoln Memorial, to raise awareness of the failure of Congress to appropriate money for public pools in the District of Columbia.

1926 JULY 4. A standing bronze figure of Abraham Lincoln as a lawyer, with his arms folded across his chest, by Julia Bracken Wendt, is dedicated at Lincoln Park, Los Angeles, California.

1926 OCTOBER 1. The Lincoln Club of Pittsburgh issues $20 Gold Bonds, to mature ten years later, payable "in gold coin of the United States of or equal to the present standard of weight and fineness and to pay interest thereon from the first day of April 1926, at the rate of four (4%) per cent. per annum."

1926 DECEMBER. Indiana governor Ed Jackson appoints 125 prominent Indianans to form the Indiana Lincoln Union so "that the people of [the] state in mighty unison [could] rear a national shrine honoring the Lincolns." The following year the ILU would barrage state newspapers with an advertising campaign around the theme "Fourteen States—30 Cities in the United States—have Lincoln Memorials—Indiana has none . . . What Will Indiana Do?" The committee also sent more than 200,000 campaign letters soliciting funds from Indiana citizens and institutions. Its letterhead proclaimed

Fig. 3.124. To dramatize the plight of city residents suffering through a torrid summer without congressional appropriations for Washington, D.C., municipal pools, protesters staged a "splash in" (although it was not called that at the time) during the week of the Fourth of July in 1926.

"Lincoln was a Hoosier." The ILU also published a pamphlet called *Lincoln Memorials* elsewhere and illustrated Frederick Law Olmsted Jr.'s designs for a memorial, and architect Thomas Hibben's plan for a suitable structure. "The advertisements, mailings, and pamphlets saturated the state with the memorial concept," an historian recalled.

1927 JANUARY 24. The Indiana Lincoln Memorial Commission engages landscape architect Frederick Law Olmsted Jr. to submit a plan for the proposed state memorial to its favored son. Olmsted would submit his preliminary concept on May 7, 1927.

1927 FEBRUARY 12. "Lincoln in Marble and Bronze," by William L. Stidger, is published in the *Dearborn Independent*. According to Stidger, "One who makes a careful study of the penchant there has been to interpret Lincoln in bronze and marble comes to the immediate conclusion that the sculptors of the United States have never had a subject which has inspired so many truly great pieces of lasting art as Lincoln."[36]

1927 APRIL. Robert P. King publishes the first supplement to his February 1924 listing of Lincoln exonumia, "Lincoln in Numismatics," in *The Numismatist*. By virtue of this new listing, King's original listing of 887 different tokens, medals, coins, and plaques grew to include 940 items. A second supplement by King would be published in the August 1933 issue of *The Numismatist*, extending his listings to 1,047 items.

1927 JULY 3. A standing bronze statue of Abraham Lincoln resting his hands behind him on a low wall, by Lorado Taft, is dedicated at the courthouse in Urbana, Illinois. Soon after, it would be moved to Carle Park, across from the city's high school.

1927 DECEMBER 31. Following the 1925 designation of portions of the Lincoln Highway with various federal U.S. Highway numbers (for example U.S. 1 between New York and Philadelphia; U.S. 30 from Philadelphia to Evanston, Wyoming; U.S. 530 from Evanston to Salt Lake City; and U.S. 50 in Nevada and California), the Lincoln Highway Association officially disbands "after agreeing to mark the highway one last time as a memorial to Abraham Lincoln," according to an LHA historian.

1928 FEBRUARY 12. Sculptor Haig Patigian's seated bronze statue of Lincoln is dedicated at the Civic Center (City Hall), San Francisco, California. The figure had been cast in 1926 at L. De Rome Foundry, and installed in 1927.

1928 SEPTEMBER 1. Boy Scouts nationwide erect nearly 3,000 concrete posts memorializing the Lincoln Highway. "Route changes associated with the erection of these markers were the last official alterations made to the highway by the Lincoln Highway Association," an LHA historian reported.

1928 OCTOBER 5. A standing bronze of Abraham Lincoln by sculptor George Fite Waters is unveiled in the Park Blocks of Portland,

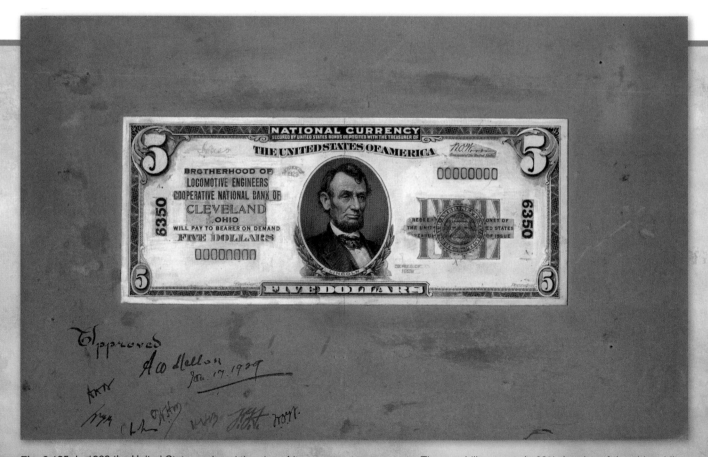

Fig. 3.125. In 1929 the United States reduced the size of its currency to save costs. The new bills were only 68% the size of the old saddle blankets. The Treasury also standardized designs on all classes of notes, with Charles Burt's Abraham Lincoln image from the $5 Federal Reserve Notes and Federal Reserve Bank Notes also carried over to United States Notes, Silver Certificates, and National Bank Notes. As can be seen, Treasury Secretary Andrew W. Mellon approved this model for national currency on January 17, 1929. Interestingly, the model has a blue seal mocked up from the small-size Silver Certificates, which had been delivered by the Bureau of Engraving and Printing to the Treasury beginning January 10. The issued National Bank Notes have a brown seal, of course.

Oregon. Lincoln stands with bowed head, capturing the anguish he went through during the war. Waters had accomplished the 10-foot-tall statue in 1926–1927 in his studio in Paris, France, and it was cast by C. Valsuani of Paris. The block surrounding is called Lincoln Square.

1929 JANUARY 17. Secretary of the Treasury Andrew E. Mellon approves the design for small-size Type 1 Series of 1929 $5 National Currency notes with the Charles Burt Lincoln portrait (BEP die 1029), according to a mockup in the National Numismatic Collection at the Smithsonian Institution.

Fig. 3.126. Sixteen years after a fund was established to replace San Francisco's Lincoln memorial (see figure 3.24), the campaign reached fruition with the dedication of Haig Patigian's seated figure of Lincoln (his model is shown) outside City Hall.

Fig. 3.127. American expatriate artists who studied in Paris are legion. Shown is young 32-year-old sculptor George Fite Waters (standing front center) in his Paris studio circa 1926–1927, with a throng of well wishers admiring his 10-foot-tall standing figure of Lincoln. Waters studied with Auguste Rodin. A bronze casting from this plaster model would be unveiled in the Park Blocks of Portland, Oregon, the following year.

1929 JANUARY 23. Illinois state senator John Robert Hamilton introduces Senate Bill No. 55, "providing for the purchase of a tract of land in Coles county, in the State of Illinois, including the Lincoln Homestead, to be used as a State Park, and making an appropriation therefor." The bill authorized not more than $25,000 for the purposes described.

1929. Medallic Art Co. acquires rights to Victor D. Brenner's 1907 Abraham Lincoln profile plaque design, and reissues bronze plaques not mounted on marble as the originals, but with a hinged, footed bronze stand attached to the back of the plaque. The plaque measures 9 by 10 inches and is still stamped with the "S. Klaber & Co. Founders N.Y." stamp and the Brenner copyright.

1929 JUNE 6. After Frank C. Ball, Muncie, Indiana, purchases approximately 22 to 30 acres (accounts vary) of the historic Thomas Lincoln farm for $32,000, which he has donated to the state, a ceremony is held for formal acceptance of the property to further the creation of a state memorial to the Lincolns' Indiana legacy.

1929 JUNE 29. Abraham Lincoln Memorial Bridge on U.S. 30, since the route is no longer known officially as the Lincoln Highway, at Blair, Nebraska, is opened across the Missouri River. It would be officially dedicated on July 26. The span would remain a toll bridge until September 29, 1962, and would be demolished in November 1991.

1929 AUGUST 27. Leonard Crunelle's bronze statue *Lincoln the Debater* commemorates the 71st anniversary of the Lincoln-Douglas debate at Freeport, Illinois. Local businessman William T. Rawleigh

donated the statue, which stands in Taylor Park in the community. This statue would become the goal for numerous Lincoln pilgrimages by Boy Scouts in the years following.

1929 SEPTEMBER 29. According to a wire-service photo published this date, "Heavy Traffic Shakes Fingers Off Statue of Abe Lincoln in Washington, D.C. Due to vibration caused by the heavy traffic in front of the District Supreme Court House in Washington, D.C., the Lincoln statue is now minus three of its fingers. The National Fine Arts Commission has recommended that to preserve the statue it should be placed inside the Court House."[37] The statue in question was the Lot Flannery statue; the missing fingers were off his extended right hand. This unfortunate turn of events came only six years after Flannery's statue of Lincoln was repositioned in front of the courthouse in the nation's capital. Underwood & Underwood published a similar photographic warning on September 26, at which time, according to that source, the problem was only two lost fingers.[38]

1929 OCTOBER 12. Local sculptor Isidore Konti's bronze statue of Lincoln is dedicated at Memorial Park, Yonkers, New York.

1929 FALL. Medalist J. Henri Ripstra engraves dies for a small commemorative plaque (51 by 39 mm) to mark the 20th anniversary of the Lincoln cent and the fifth anniversary of Victor D. Brenner's death. The plaque has a sunburst radiating on a profile, similar to that of Brenner's cent, and a freed slave. It was struck by Meyer & Wilhelm, Stuttgart, Germany. The issue was promoted by Chicago Coin Club members Dr. A.M. Rackus and Ernest Jonas. Rackus would announce the piece in the December 1929 issue of *The Numismatist*.

Fig. 3.128. In summer 1929 the Abraham Lincoln Memorial Bridge spanned the Missouri River at Blair, Nebraska, along the Lincoln Highway.

Fig. 3.129. This 1927 photograph shows progress in developing Abraham Lincoln's New Salem by recreating the village in which Lincoln lived and worked in the 1830s. The land was a gift to the local Chautauqua organization from publisher William Randolph Hearst.

1929 November. New York City's Metropolitan Museum acquires a marble head of Lincoln by George Grey Barnard.

1930 February 8. The cover of *Collier's* features a cloying illustration of a black infant nestled into the crook of Gutzon Borglum's seated sculpture of Lincoln at Newark, New Jersey. Carroll M. Sexton provided the illustration. Inside, Ida Tarbell waxed anew about Abe's ill-fated romance with Ann Rutledge.

1930 February 11. Lincoln Life Insurance Company's Lincoln Library and Museum is formally dedicated, the work of Louis A. Warren, a former minister and newspaper editor, who joined the company in 1928 to organize and expand its collection of Lincoln materials. The company's board chairman, Samuel M. Foster, welcomed guests at the ceremony: "No motive of commercialism or profit entered into our plans to assemble this wealth of Lincolniana—We seek merely to provide the means and the channel

Fig. 3.130. This circa-1930, unsigned small silver plaque celebrating Lincoln the Emancipator is credited to Chicago medalist and numismatist J. Henri Ripstra. The plaque was manufactured in Germany in .860 fine silver and bronze editions.

Fig. 3.131. In the 1920s Lot Flannery's 1868 statue of Lincoln (Washington, D.C.'s, first public memorial to the fallen hero) was replaced on a 12-foot-high pedestal rather than its original 35-foot column, in a renovation of the municipal building. However, by fall 1929 it was discovered that vibrations from local traffic had caused two fingers (and then a third) to fall off Lincoln's right hand. This photo was taken September 29, 1929.

1809 1865

LINCOLN

LINCOLN

UNDERWOOD & UNDERWOOD

through which there may continue to flow an ever increasing volume of information concerning Lincoln, especially to the youth of our land, that they may be influenced to think and to live as Lincoln did—'with malice towards none and charity for all.'" A year after he arrived, for the anniversary of Lincoln's death, Warren circulated the first issue of *Lincoln Lore,* dated April 15, 1929, as a one-page newsletter with brief articles on Lincoln that were adaptable by newspaper editors as filler material in their own publications.

1930 FEBRUARY 12. A granite bust by sculptor Andrew O'Connor is dedicated at Royal Exchange, London, England. O'Connor had created this bust in Paris in 1928. It is similar to the statue with a beardless Lincoln by O'Connor that had been installed in Springfield in 1918 east of the State Capitol, on which the 1918 Lincoln–Illinois Centennial commemorative half dollar effigy was modeled by George T. Morgan.

1930 SPRING. Sculptor Andrew O'Connor's classic statue of a seated, bearded Abraham Lincoln in robes on a stylized, plain throne is exhibited at the Spring Salon in Paris, France, where "it was judged one of the most outstanding creations at the exhibit." According to press accounts at the time, the statue had been commissioned "for the grounds of the State Capitol, Providence, R.I.," and upon completion was sent in 1931 to Gorham Manufacturing Co. in Providence to be cast. Unfortunately the local fundraising effort sputtered. When funds ran out, O'Connor was still awaiting his fee of $4,500 and Gorham was owed $5,000. The sculptor would die unpaid in 1941. Gorham would hold onto the bronze casting until 1946, when it cast around for another purchaser. The following year it would be erected at Fort Lincoln Cemetery on the site of the Civil War fort built in 1861 for the defense of Washington, D.C., just outside the District of Columbia in Prince George's County, Maryland.

Fig. 3.132. Andrew O'Connor's ill-fated seated figure of Abraham Lincoln is shown in the artist's studio in Paris, France, in 1930. This very sensitive portrayal of Lincoln in robes sitting on an unadulterated perch was sculpted by O'Connor in Paris for the State Capitol in Providence, Rhode Island, but when promoters of the venture ran out of funds, the sculptor and foundry went unpaid. The bronze remained at Gorham Foundry until 1947, when it was finally installed at Fort Lincoln Cemetery in Prince George's County, Maryland.

Fig. 3.133. Thespian Ralph Ince made his reputation portraying Lincoln in at least nine films of the teens and early twenties. This publicity photo was taken circa 1920–1921, before the Lincoln Memorial was dedicated, probably in connection with one of two Louis J. Selznick films which Ince directed and starred in as Lincoln: *The Land of Opportunity* (1920) or *The Highest Law* (1921). Seen to the left of the automobile are two children on a homemade cart.

1930. The Lincoln Bathhouse joins the Washington Bathhouse, opened a decade earlier, at the New York State Reservation at Saratoga (currently the Saratoga Spa State Park). Today, in addition to the mineral baths, the Lincoln Building houses New York's 4th Judicial District and New York's Court of Claims judges' chambers and the state park police.

1930 MAY 25. Max Bachman's beardless standing figure of Lincoln as political candidate is dedicated on Victory Memorial Drive in Minneapolis, Minnesota.

1930 JUNE 14. James Earle Fraser's nine-foot-tall bronze statue of a seated pre-presidential Abraham Lincoln seated on a rock is dedicated along the Lincoln Highway in Jersey City, New Jersey, before a crowd numbering 4,000. "I particularly wanted to make a sympathetic and human study of Lincoln," the sculptor told the *Christian Science Monitor.* "There are so many presidential Lincolns that I have hoped I might create something that would give an idea of his outdoor personality." Locals frequently refer to the melancholy portrayal as "Lincoln the Mystic."

Fig. 3.134. Circa 1930 pop-out cents, made with a Lincoln portrait die similar to the $5 paper-money image, were struck for each of the 48 states represented on the frieze of the Lincoln Memorial. The columns symbolize the 36 states (including the rebellious ones) in the Union at the time of the Lincoln administration. These encased cents with the enamel ring intact are quite scarce *(a)*. Rarer still are pop-out cents still on the original card of issue *(b)*.

Fig. 3.135. Sculptor James Earle Fraser was a lifelong admirer of Abraham Lincoln and extremely happy to snag the commission for a memorial at the Jersey City terminus of the Lincoln Highway. Fraser labored for many years over his majestic, introspective figure seated in a relaxed pose. As can be seen from the completed statue dedicated in 1931 *(a)*, and in a 1920s sketch the sculptor made while developing the concept *(b)*, Fraser abandoned his bearded presidential figure for a beardless Illinois Lincoln, in keeping with Fraser's own Midwestern roots.

1930 September 22. Sculptor Leonard Crunelle's heroic-size standing bronze figure of Abraham Lincoln as a captain during the Black Hawk War is dedicated in Dixon, Illinois, on the second day of the centenary program for the founding of Fort Dixon. The four-day event commenced September 21 with an air show and dedication of the Municipal Airport. Flyers included Jimmy Doolittle. On the day of the statue dedication, a five-mile-long parade with 100 floats illustrated the city's history.

1930 November 11. A bronze statue of Lincoln by sculptor Alonzo Victor Lewis is erected at Spokane, Washington.

1931. The last section of the Lincoln Highway is paved with a hard surface.

1931 June 10. The National Shrine of the Abraham Lincoln Fellowship is dedicated at the Hanover, Pennsylvania, home of "Mother Smith," honorary vice president no. 3 of the organization.

1931 June 12. The Lincoln Marriage Temple is opened in Piney Memorial State Park at Harrodsburg, Kentucky, on the 125th anniversary of the marriage of Abraham Lincoln's parents, Thomas Lincoln and Nancy Hanks. The shrine was built to house the cabin in which the marriage ceremony was performed.

1931 June 17. President Herbert Hoover is the featured speaker at a rededication ceremony of the refurbished Lincoln Tomb in Springfield, Illinois. A bronze replica of Gutzon Borglum's marble beardless head of Lincoln at the U.S. Capitol had been installed on a granite base outside the south entrance to the tomb. Also, small bronze copies of famous Lincoln statues had been installed in the vault. Daniel Chester French, Fred Torrey, and Leonard Crunelle were each represented by two models. Lorado Taft, Adolph Weinman, and Augustus Saint-Gaudens had one each. Additionally, Edwin Stanton's epithet, "Now he belongs to the ages," was prominently inscribed overhead inside the vault.[39]

Fig. 3.136. In a 1931 remodeling of the Lincoln Memorial in Springfield, Illinois, a bronze casting of the Gutzon Borglum head at the U.S. Capitol Rotunda was installed outside the tomb. As can be seen, millions of visitors over the years have rubbed its nose, to a shiny golden color, for good luck. The feet of the small statues within the tomb display a similar glow from visitors' love pats.

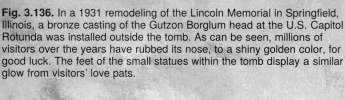

Fig. 3.137. Czech-American woodblock engraver and printer Charles Turzak distinguished himself as a black-and-white book illustrator, including in his *Abraham Lincoln: A Biography in Woodcuts*. In 1933 Turzak created this bookplate of the railsplitter himself.

1931 OCTOBER 26. Dr. Louis A. Warren calls the photograph upon which the engraving on the small-size $5 Federal Reserve Note, United States Note, National Bank Note, and Silver Certificate was based "the best known Lincoln photograph," in *Lincoln Lore,* which he edited. Warren continued: "Although Abraham Lincoln was photographed more than a hundred times, one picture of him seems to have supplanted all others in popularity. From investigations which have been made, and information now available, about the use of this photograph, it is safe to say that it has been reproduced in greater numbers that all other likenesses of the president put together."[40]

1931 NOVEMBER 11. A.L. Van Den Bergen's standing bronze statue of Abraham Lincoln is dedicated at Clinton, Illinois, near the DeWitt County courthouse. The statue is a replica of the one at Racine, Wisconsin. (See the entry for February 12, 1924.)

1932 JANUARY 19. President Herbert Hoover officially opens the Arlington Memorial Bridge that connects the ellipse around the Lincoln Memorial to the Virginia side of the Potomac River. The next day a confused Associated Press in New York City would proclaim that the "Lincoln Memorial Bridge" was open to motorists.

1932 FEBRUARY 3. At the Chicago Coin Club's 156th meeting, charter member and past president Dr. Alexander Rackus displays the "most interesting of Lincoln medals issued in Chicago"—the 1865 medal by the North Western Sanitary Fair Commission.

1932 FEBRUARY 12. Little Lovers of Lincoln Auxiliary, affiliated with the Abraham Lincoln Fellowship, is founded to "carry on and on the memory of the Saviour of our Country when the last of the honored ones who saw, heard, met or knew Lincoln have passed on to greet their leader in the spirit world."

Fig. 3.138. Nearly a decade after the Lincoln Memorial was dedicated, a bridge spanning the Potomac River, connecting the federal district with the Virginia shore, was dedicated by President Herbert Hoover on January 19, 1932. The bridge was called the Arlington Memorial Bridge because it led directly to Arlington National Cemetery, but the day following its opening, a confused Associated Press published this fine aerial photograph of some of the first traffic over the bridge, calling it the Lincoln Memorial Bridge, a certainly understandable faux pas often repeated since.

Fig. 3.139. Many states celebrated Abraham Lincoln's birthday, February 12, as a holiday. However, with or without official sanction, many more civic and religious organizations did so, often turning the celebration toward a philanthropic cause in Lincoln's name, as all of these 1930s artifacts attest.

1932 FEBRUARY 12. The Lincoln Shrine at Redlands, California, acquires a marble head of Abraham Lincoln by sculptor George Grey Barnard.

1932 FEBRUARY 12. A bronze statue by sculptor Max Kalish of a hatless Abraham Lincoln holding a paper, leaning slightly forward and giving his Gettysburg Address, is dedicated in front of the Board of Education building in Cleveland, Ohio. Kalish, a graduate of the Cleveland School of Art, had begun the statue in 1928. A collection begun among the city's schoolchildren in 1923 contributed pennies to finance a portion of the cost of the monument. The text of Lincoln's remarks was inscribed on the statue's base. The six-story Beaux-Arts building had been erected the previous year.

1932 APRIL 14. *Abraham Lincoln,* an historical drama in three acts by Walter F. Swanker, Schenectady, New York, is copyrighted.

1932 MAY 30. Sculptor Charles Keck's seated bronze Lincoln figure, showing him leaning slightly forward with his wrists resting on his knees, is dedicated at the Wabash County Court House, Wabash,

Indiana. It had been commissioned by local dry-goods merchant Alexander New. The bronze was cast by Gorham Manufacturing Co.

Although Keck portrayed a bearded presidential Lincoln sitting on a rock, his pose was heavily influenced by James Earle Fraser's quite similar, larger monumental sculpture of a beardless Lincoln, also pensively seated on a rock and leaning slightly forward with his forearms resting on his thighs. The latter work had been installed at Jersey City.

In the days between the completion of the base and the statue's dedication, townspeople packed the hollow spaces within the base with fruit jars filled with mementoes, creating a civic time capsule.

1932 SEPTEMBER 16. Sculptor Paul Manship's *Abraham Lincoln the Hoosier Youth* bronze statue is dedicated adjacent to the headquarters of Lincoln National Life Insurance Company, which commissioned it in 1928. The work shows Lincoln as he may have looked resting against an oak stump, with one hand on his dog and the other on his axe. Manship also did four relief sculptures for the statue's base to symbolize Lincoln's charity, fortitude, patriotism, and sense of justice.

Fig. 3.140. Cleveland artist Max Kalish's colossal, nearly 15-foot-tall statue of Abraham Lincoln dramatically giving his Emancipation Proclamation towers over the sculptor on a step ladder. This animated, theatrical figure was installed in Cleveland in 1932.

1932 SEPTEMBER 18. Sculptor Thomas A. Green's stone sculpture of Lincoln is erected in Lincoln Park, Springfield, Illinois.

1932 NOVEMBER. The cornerstone for the reconstruction of the Berry-Lincoln store, where the future president clerked as a youth—the first building in the restoration of Lincoln's New Salem—is laid. Eventually a representative town would be reconstructed resurrecting the frontier village of Lincoln's time.

1932 NOVEMBER 9. *New Salem Days,* a short play about Abraham Lincoln's youth written by Lucy Barton, Katonah, New York, is copyrighted.

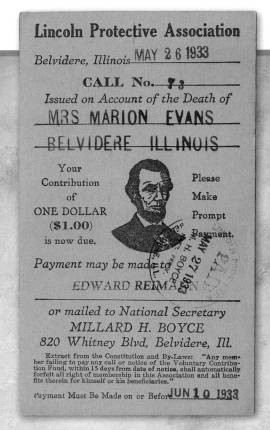

Fig. 3.141. In 1933 the Lincoln Protective Association of Belvidere, Illinois, employed a Lincoln likeness, similar to the then-current $5 portrait, on its fee-assessment cards. This mutual-benefit society had been organized in May 1905 in Allegheny, Pennsylvania, to provide life-insurance protection to its members. A similarly named company was also organized in January 1921, in Missouri.

Fig. 3.142. Charles Keck's relaxed seated figure installed in Wabash, Indiana, in 1932 owed a great deal to James Earle Fraser's similar pose. In both the figure is seated in a relaxed manner upon a rock, but Keck's Lincoln is bearded. The news photographer who snapped this image of Wabash's new monument tritely posed several of the community's black youths admiring the Great and Elevated Emancipator.

Fig. 3.143. National Cigar Company, Frankfort, Indiana's, nickel Lincoln Highway cigar was the much more prosperous 9¢ cigar when these elegant and colorful embossed sample labels were printed in the 1930s, with their continental map of the transcontinental route and feeder highways.

1933. Original plates made by photographer Alexander Hesler on June 3, 1860, are cracked in the U.S. Mail. "The Post Office paid the claim and presented the broken negatives to the Smithsonian Institution," according to Lincoln photo authority Lloyd Ostendorf.[41]

Fig. 3.144. The 1860 Alexander Hesler photograph (O-26) of Abraham Lincoln, which had been so very popular as a model for Lincoln campaign medals during his first presidential election, received a resurgence in popularity when the original glass plate cracked in the mail in 1933. After the Post Office paid off the insured party, it donated the pieces to the Smithsonian Institution. A great many prints (such as the one shown here, which shows the shards reassembled) *(a)* appeared in the press, and a variety of artists copied the likeness for uses as disparate as posters for religious literacy *(b)*, Depression scrip *(c)*, and checks dated 1930 *(d)*. The excellent likeness on the 125th-anniversary cover postmarked aboard the USS *Relief (e)* is hand drawn in pen and ink, and signed by artist "C.W."

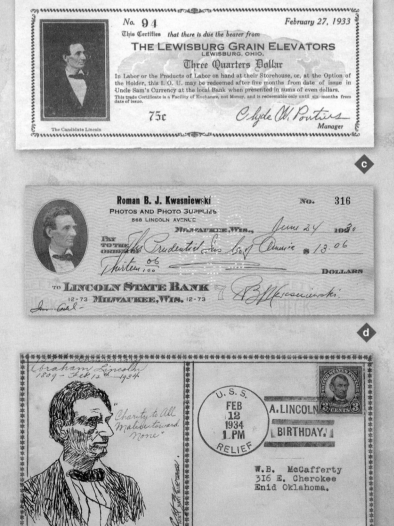

1933 FEBRUARY 27. Lewisburg Grain Elevators circulates depression scrip with images of Abraham Lincoln, in denominations of 25¢ to $5.

1933 AUGUST. A second supplement to Robert P. King's 1924 "Lincoln in Numismatics" is published in *The Numismatist,* extending his listings to 1,047 items.

1933 SEPTEMBER 3. The Lincoln Memorial Bridge, crossing the Wabash River at Vincennes, Indiana, at the spot where the Thomas Lincoln family crossed by ferry into Illinois, is dedicated.

1934 JANUARY 11. The last printing of Series of 1929 Federal Reserve Bank Notes (Kansas City $5s) is delivered to the Bureau of Engraving and Printing vault for later delivery to the bank.

THE BEAUTIFUL LINCOLN MEMORIAL BRIDGE OVER THE HISTORIC WABASH RIVER, VINCENNES, IND.

THIS BRIDGE IS ON THE SITE OF FERRY LINCOLN USED IN CROSSING WABASH IN 1830

Fig. 3.145. In 1933 the Lincoln Memorial Bridge spanned the Wabash River at the site where, according to tradition, Thomas Lincoln led his family from Indiana into Illinois.

Fig. 3.146. Sculptor Cartaino de Scarrino Paolo poses with his heroic-sized half-full-length figure of *Lincoln the Lawyer* in his studio in 1934. A bronze cast of the statue would be installed at Lincoln Memorial University, Harrogate, Tennessee, in 1949.

Fig. 3.147. Collector David W. Lange has studied and popularized the collecting of the old-time penny boards that launched thousands of change-pickers on the long coin-collecting road to becoming numismatists. Most collectors in the United States in the last hundred years started with Lincoln cents from circulation, and they needed a way to organize and store their treasures. Lange shares this 1935 Colonial Coin Holder titled "The Coin Collector, U.S. Small Cents Lincoln Head" (Lange C1cB1). The board was copyrighted by L.W. Schnelling, New York.

1934. The Lincoln National Life Insurance Company offers a free booklet penned by Louis A. Warren: "A terse, pointed biography of Abraham Lincoln by Dr. Louis A. Warren, regarded as 'the foremost living Lincoln authority' is available without cost to readers of (fill in name of magazine). An old adage of Addison's 'The real part of many a bulky volume could be put in a small pamphlet' is admirably illustrated by this brochure. A map of the Lincoln country, reproductions of the eight best known original Lincoln portraits, and the most satisfactory 'Mother and Son' portrait are features." The cover bore a Lincoln profile portrait cropped similar to that used as a model for the cent.

Fig. 3.148. U.S. currency measured 7.5 by 3.125 inches from 1861 to 1929, so the conversion over to small "Philippine" size currency, 6.14 by 2.61 inches, in 1929 was a big deal. The first small-size notes were released to circulation in July 1929, but were preceded by a media blitz to accustom the citizenry to the changeover. This included editorial cartoons and exact-size handbill advertisements of the kind printed by Western Lithograph Co., Los Angeles (a), which also familiarized recipients with the lineup of new portraiture on the new bills coming down the pike. Also shown is the approved design model (b) for the new small-size Federal Reserve Bank Note, an issued Series of 1929 Federal Reserve Bank Note for comparison (c), and the back of all the new $5 bills with an excellent engraving of the new Lincoln Memorial by Joaquin C. Benzing (d).

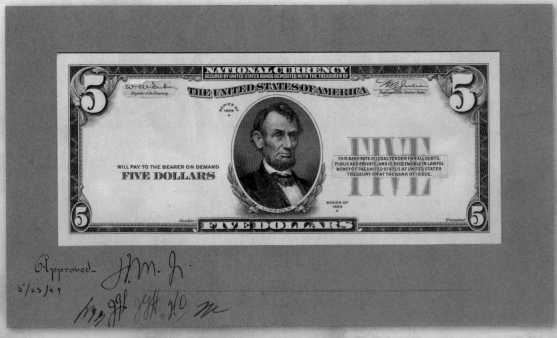

Fig. 3.149. Collectors have never had the opportunity to see this unissued Series of 1929A Federal Reserve Bank Note design, approved by U.S. Treasury Secretary Henry J. Morgenthau on May 23, 1929, in the National Numismatic Collection of the Smithsonian Institution. The reason for the considered change from Series of 1929 FRBNs was the new Legal Tender clause to be printed to the right of the Lincoln portrait. The series was never issued.

1934 MAY 23. Secretary of the Treasury Henry Morgenthau Jr. approves the design for the unissued Series of 1929A small-size $5 Federal Reserve Bank Note, with Charles Burt's portrait of Abraham Lincoln (BEP die MISC1029). "The purpose of the model was to gain authorization for the new redemption clause, which reflected the fact that the Agricultural Adjustment Act of May 12, 1933, gave National Bank Notes legal tender status," according to paper-money researcher Peter Huntoon. "There was a great flurry of discussion about the redemption clauses on notes during the 1933-4 period, and this was one outgrowth," he added.[42]

1934 MAY 26. When the "Century of Progress" Chicago World's Fair reopens for a second year, the Illinois Host Building houses "one of the most comprehensive Lincoln exhibits ever gathered." Items displayed included 72 original documents, original portraits, "an axe handle carved with his own name . . . and the 'betrothal stone,' a flat rock inscribed 'Abraham Lincoln and Ann Rutledge were betrothed here July 4, 1833.'"[43] (See figures 1.1 and 1.5.)

1934 JUNE 6. Actor Frank McGlynn Sr. portrays Abraham Lincoln in the movie *Are We Civilized?* McGlynn would appear as Lincoln in a dozen movies and short subjects, beginning in 1924 and running through World War II. His most memorable turn as the Great Emancipator would occur in *The Littlest Rebel,* starring Shirley Temple, released November 22, 1935.

1935. B&O Railroad acquires the historic Alton Railroad (formerly the Chicago & Alton Railroad) and builds—with government assistance—B&O No. 50, which is then retrofitted with a sloped front end to improve aerodynamics, and inaugurates the Abe Lincoln locomotive in service between Chicago and St. Louis operated by the subsidiary line. The route was 284 miles long, passing through Joliet, Bloomington-Normal, Springfield, and Alton. Service included a mail/baggage car, three coaches, two parlor cars, and an observation car. Two years later the Alton Railroad would add a second train, dubbed the Ann Rutledge, to provide service between St. Louis and Chicago.

1935. *The Lincoln Highway: The Story of a Crusade That Made Transportation History* is published.

1935 JULY. The Lincoln cabin bronze casting is laid in place at the Nancy Hanks Lincoln Memorial State Park. It was a symbol of the exact size of the Lincoln cabin and the original hearthstones where, as a boy, Abraham Lincoln studied by the light of the burning logs. After deciding not to purchase the replica Indiana boyhood cabin that had been displayed at the 1933 Chicago Century of Progress Exposition, and also not to replicate the Indiana Lincoln boyhood cabin, architect Thomas Hibben designed a bronze memorial that laid down the outline of the cabin based on archeological evidence, with the bottom portion of the hearth standing. In 1933 a contract was let to C.W. Hatcher of Indianapolis for $4,200. Hatcher subcontracted the work to International Art Foundries of New York City. It, in turn, subcontracted the actual metalwork to the firm of Priessman, Bauer & Co., Munich, Germany. By June 1934, a low stone wall was constructed around the site, but the bronze casting of the cabin was not ready. Plans to dedicate the cabin that summer were postponed. Meanwhile the

Fig. 3.150. Shirley Temple was the "littlest rebel," Virgie Temple, in a 1935 film of the same name. She stole the heart of both "Mr. Lincoln," played by Frank McGlynn Sr., and audiences. The film was colorized in 1994, and a promotional illustration is shown. McGlynn proved a durable Lincoln, appearing in that role in another eight films.

Fig. 3.151. In 1935 the bronze hearth and outline of Thomas Lincoln's Indiana cabin was laid in place on its archeologically determined original foundation, as a symbol of Abe Lincoln's youth, at the Nancy Hanks Lincoln Memorial State Park, raised up in honor of Lincoln's mother. This author finds the now richly patinated hearth and cabin outline the most unique, and one of the most historical and moving, of the many Lincoln memorials he has had the opportunity to visit.

"MR. LINCOLN— you won't let them shoot my daddy—will you?"

Shirley TEMPLE *as she appears in* The Littlest Rebel

U.S. dollar was devalued and squabbles among the parties resulted in a cost overrun. By May 1935, the State of Indiana gave the German firm an ultimatum: the bronze casting had to be delivered no later than June 15, 1935, or the contract would be terminated with no additional payments made. The monument was delivered in time and installed. Final cost of the bronze cabin monument was $5,797.40 in U.S. currency.

1936. Sculptor Lorado Taft completes his 8 by 9.5–foot plaster bas relief for the Lincoln-Douglas Memorial at Quincy, Illinois. A bronze casting of the panel, which illustrates the sixth Lincoln-Douglas debate (October 13, 1858) was dedicated in Washington Park, Quincy, Illinois, on October 13, 1936. It shows Lincoln standing and speaking while Judge Douglas is seated listening.

1936 February 28. Frank McGlynn Sr. plays Abe Lincoln in John Ford's motion picture *The Prisoner of Shark Island,* about the imprisonment of Dr. Samuel Mudd, who treated assassin John Wilkes Booth (played by Warner Baxter) during his flight from justice.

1936 July 25. Henry B. Joy's copy of Alfonso Pelzer's statue of the Great Emancipator by John G. Segesman for W.H. Mullins Co., which has been in storage for about 17 years after renovations at the Packard Motor Car Co. headquarters in 1919, is moved to the Boy Scout Camp Brady in Waterford, Michigan, and rededicated as an official Lincoln Pilgrimage Shrine for the Detroit Area Council of the Boy Scouts of America.

1936 August 27. Illinois governor Henry Horner dedicates the Lincoln Log Cabin State Park on the grounds of the old Thomas Lincoln Farm, which includes the a recreation of the original cabin constructed by the Civilian Conservation Corps on its original foundation.

1936 November 16. Frank McGlynn Sr. plays Abraham Lincoln once again in the beginning scenes of Cecil B. DeMille's epic motion picture *The Plainsman,* starring Gary Cooper and Jean Arthur as Billy the Kid and Calamity Jane, respectively.

1937 February. Joseph Barnet publishes "Lincoln Civil War Tokens and Cards" in the *Coin Collectors Journal,* New Series, volume 3, pp. 236–237.

1937 June 17. Three more buildings are dedicated in New Salem, Illinois, the recreated hometown of Abraham Lincoln. As part of the ceremony, 18-year-old Miss Ann Rutledge of Ottumwa, Iowa, played the part of her ancestor in a reenactment of Lincoln's courtship of Ann Rutledge at Rutledge Tavern. To that date, 16 of the original 25 buildings in the town had been recreated.

1937 September 17. The Abraham Lincoln head is dedicated at Mount Rushmore, South Dakota.

1937 October 30. The Port of New York Authority copyrights Hungarian-American sculptor Julio Kilenyi's Lincoln Tunnel medal designs (G27207).

Fig. 3.152. The history of the design and construction of the national pantheon at Mount Rushmore exhibits the bending of sculptor Gutzon Borglum's will to the realities he found "on the ground" in South Dakota's Black Hills. Originally the Lincoln head was to be to the left of Washington, according to some sources, but geologic difficulties scrapped that plan *(a)*. Then Borglum considered waist-high figures of the Washington and Lincoln, as shown in this model at the Mount Rushmore museum *(b)*. Eventually the realities of time, money, and geology determined the final product that millions have viewed in recent generations.

1937 December 25. *The New Yorker* reports on Julio Kilenyi's Lincoln Tunnel Dedication medal and the opening of the tunnel on December 22. The tunnel under the Hudson River was an impressive engineering and political achievement between the states of New York and New Jersey. Kilenyi's large, bold Lincoln portrait and Lincolnesque motto "For the further unification of the people" is an exciting design. Its reverse presents a pictorial view of the Jersey terminus and the Manhattan skyline.

1938 January. Pioneer U.S. paper-money collector Robert H. Lloyd, a friend and mentor of the present author for three decades, writes on the Lincoln Civil War scrip of C. Dautremont, Angelica, New York, in *The Numismatist.*

1938 February 11. John Carradine portrays Abraham Lincoln in *Of Human Hearts,* an intimate survey of family relationships set during the Civil War era. The movie starred Walter Huston as Reverend Ethan Wilkins (a country parson), and James Stewart as Jason Wilkins (an Army medical officer). Beulah Bondi would receive an Oscar nomination as Best Supporting Actress for her role as Mary Wilkins.

In a memorable scene, Lincoln summons surgeon Wilkins to Washington to question him about his views on amputation, his humble background, and his mother. Lincoln admonishes the soldier about his ingratitude and failure to communicate with his mother. After not hearing from him for two years, she had written to Lincoln concerned about his whereabouts and whether he was alive or dead. "Sit down at my desk. . . ." Lincoln instructs the young soldier. "Now write a letter to your mother, and tell her what an ungrateful wretch you've been and how sorry you are for it. . . . From this time forward you'll write her a letter every week. . . . If you fail, I'll have you court-martialed." Lincoln then recites a poem from *King Lear* to the memory of his own dear mother.

1938 May 4. A 13-foot-high limestone statue of Abraham Lincoln by Detroit sculptor Samuel Cashwan is dedicated at the Lincoln Consolidated School in Ypsilanti, Michigan, as a Works Progress Administration federal art project. The statue, which was unveiled by Cashwan himself, "is considered one of the best achievements of the Federal art project in Michigan," according to a press account at the time.

Fig. 3.153. In 1937 Mount Rushmore's Lincoln head *(a)* was officially dedicated (September 17) at the "Shrine of Democracy," and the Lincoln Tunnel "for a further unification of the people" was opened (December 22) between Manhattan and New Jersey. Shown is a large bronze cast of Julio Kilenyi's Lincoln Tunnel medal reverse *(b)*; the medal was given to persons of significance at the time.

1938 JUNE 14. The Illinois State Daughters of the American Revolution present the Lincoln Trail Memorial to the state, consisting of a bronze statue of Abraham Lincoln as a young man carrying a walking stick, set in place against a backdrop, limestone bas relief of a representation of the Thomas Lincoln family moving by ox cart from Indiana (where he had farmed for 14 years) into Illinois. They are led by an angel to destiny and good fortune. An inscription on the base of the memorial reads: "In the late winter of 1830 a few weeks after his 21st birthday Abraham Lincoln passed this way with his father's family entering the state of Illinois for the first time." The location, set aside as the Lincoln Trail Memorial Historic Site, marks the place where, according to tradition, the crossing of the Wabash River occurred. The monument was sculpted by Nellie Verne Walker. It lies at the west end of the Lincoln Memorial Bridge on U.S. Route 50, Lawrenceville, Illinois.

1930s. A metal desk/showcase is custom-built to house a banking ledger with entries from Abraham Lincoln's account at the Springfield Marine & Fire Insurance Company, for public display. Three bas-relief panels surrounding the skirt of the case illustrate Lincoln's sequential progress in New Salem and Springfield from (1) Pioneer and Backwoodsman to (2) Shopkeeper and Law Student to (3) Representative To The Assembly. The metal desk/showcase is currently located in the lobby of the J.P. Morgan–Chase Bank located in the original white-marble building still bearing its carved marquee proclaiming Springfield Marine Bank at 114 South Sixth Street. It faces the Old State Capitol building on the corner of Sixth and Washington streets. The bank ledger is opened to the Lincoln account, where "A. Lincoln" appears at the top, written by his banker, Robert

Irwin. After Lincoln left Springfield for Washington, Irwin made transactions as his local agent. After Lincoln's death, the account continued in the name of David Davis, administrator of the Lincoln estate until May 27, 1867. (See figure 3.167.)

1938 JULY 26. National Park Service architect Richard E. "Louie" Bishop, on leave from Washington, submits his proposal for the Indiana Nancy Hanks Lincoln–Lincoln Boyhood Memorial structures. Bishop's plan, showing two rectangular buildings joined by a semicircular cloister, would be adopted for the most part, except the memorial halls are set at angles to make a more aesthetically pleasing group.

1938 OCTOBER 15. Robert E. Sherwood's play *Abe Lincoln in Illinois* opens on Broadway at the Plymouth Theater, with Raymond Massey in the title role. Muriel Kirkland played Mary Todd, and Adele Longmire played Ann Rutledge. Playwrights Company staged Sherwood's drama. The play takes Lincoln from his childhood through his final speech in Illinois before he left for Washington, D.C. The three-act drama would run for 472 performances before ending in December 1939. The *New York Herald Tribune* called it "Not only the finest of modern stage biographies, but a lovely, eloquent, endearing tribute to all that is best in the spirit of democracy." Sherwood would receive the Pulitzer Prize in 1939 for the play. Massey reprised his role in the 1940 movie adaptation.

The work has proved perennially popular. It was adapted for television in 1945, 1950, 1951, 1957, and 1964. It was revived on stage in 1963 with Hal Holbrook, and in 1993 with Sam Waterston in the lead role. That revival won a Tony Award.

Fig. 3.154. J[oseph] C[hristian] Leyendecker created this memorable cover, resembling a bronze bust and plaque, for the February 12, 1938, front cover of the *Saturday Evening Post*. Between 1896 and 1950, Leyendecker painted more than 500 magazine covers, including 322 covers for the *Post*.

Fig. 3.155. In 1938 sculptor Nellie Verne Walker's statue of Abraham Lincoln as a young man, clutching a walking stick, was erected in front of her limestone bas relief of the Lincoln family being guided westward into Illinois by an angel.

Fig. 3.156. Robert Sherwood's stage play *Abe Lincoln in Illinois* debuted in 1938 with Raymond Massey in the title role. The following year the playwright was awarded the Pulitzer Prize for his masterpiece, which has since been adapted for film, and multiple times for television. It has also returned to Broadway, reprised on the stage by Sam Waterston and Hal Holbrook. Waterston's version won a Tony Award.

Fig. 3.157. American Eagle–Lincoln Aircraft Corp. employed a small portrait vignette after the Marshall likeness on this 1932 bond printed by W.N. Perrin & Co. Inc., New York.

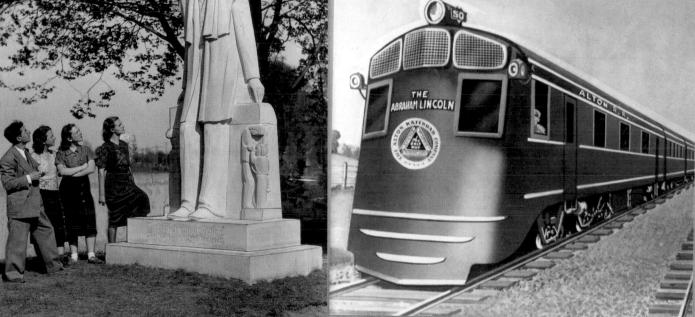

Fig. 3.158. Sculptor Samuel Cashwan created this 13-foot-tall limestone Works Progress Administration masterpiece dedicated in Ypsilanti, Michigan, in 1938. Here the sculptor and several impressionable female admirers ogle his work.

Fig. 3.159. Abraham Lincoln locomotive service between Chicago and St. Louis was offered by the Alton Rail Road, and successors from 1935, until discontinued by Amtrak in 1978. This is an artist's conception of the first Lincoln locomotive in 1935.

1938 NOVEMBER 20. The neo-Gothic Heinz Memorial Chapel at the University of Pittsburgh is dedicated as a companion structure to its famous Cathedral of Learning. Splendid stained-glass windows designed by Charles Connick, and made at his studio in Boston, total approximately 4,000 square feet in the Indiana limestone edifice. One of the window panels, representing the quality Leadership, depicts Abraham Lincoln emancipating the slaves.

Fig. 3.160. Boston artist Charles Connick designed and made this wonderful stained-glass window representing Leadership for the Heinz Memorial Chapel at the University of Pittsburgh. It was dedicated in 1938. Abraham Lincoln is shown emancipating the slaves.

Fig. 3.161. Lincoln cent and plaque designer Victor David Brenner also designed Lincoln sculptural works, including a beardless bust shown in *Abraham Lincoln: The Image of His Greatness* (see figure 2.209 in that book), and this standing dissimilar beardless figure shown circa 1917 from an article on the sculptor in B. Max Mehl's *Numismatic Monthly* in the 1930s. As far as can be determined, this standing Brenner Lincoln statue was never cast in large size for public display.

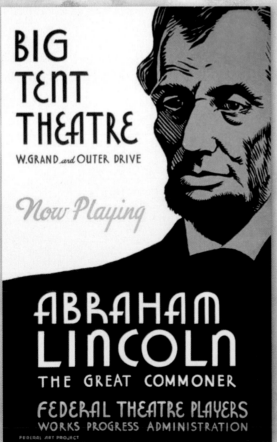

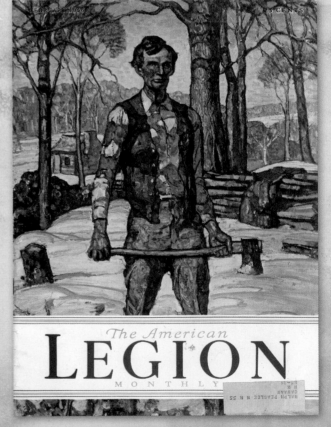

Fig. 3.162. Circa 1936 the Depression-era Works Progress Administration's Federal Art Project produced California playwright Col. F.W. Hart's socially relevant 1926 stage play *Abraham Lincoln, the Great Commoner* as part of the Illinois Federal Theatre Project. Hart presented Lincoln as a loyal friend and defender of the weak. Shown is a silkscreen poster on board in the collection of the Library of Congress. According to the Library, the unsigned head-and-shoulders portrait of Lincoln is attributed to Carken. Carken was a 1930s WPA poster illustrator whose work combined vivid visuals and playful type treatments. Unfortunately his full name is unknown.

Fig. 3.163. Legion Publishing Corp., Indianapolis, Indiana, featured Abraham Lincoln on the cover of its monthly magazine frequently. This vibrant, impressionistic watercolor by Harvey Dunn showed the Axeman Cometh in February 1936.

1939. Theodore Besterman's *A World Bibliography of Bibliographies* lists Abraham Lincoln as the fifth most written-about historical figure, behind William Shakespeare, the Italian poet Dante, the German poet Johann Wolfgang von Goethe, and the Spanish novelist Miguel de Cervantes. More ink had been used on Lincoln than on any other American, according to Besterman. Jesus was in 51st place overall, by his count. Besterman was a lecturer at the London School of Librarianship. His bibliography would be republished several times, including in 1949, 1955, and 1965.

Fig. 3.164. This 1936 convention ribbon for the Woman's Relief Corp auxiliary to the Grand Army of the Republic reproduced an illustrated portrait of Lincoln without a known photographic model.

Fig. 3.165. Another WPA Federal Art Project theatrical production was E[llsworth] P[routy] Conkle's *Prologue to Glory,* about Lincoln's early life in Illinois. This silkscreen poster for the production, staged at Maxine Elliot's Theatre, 109 West 39th Street, New York City, circa 1938, is credited to Herzog. The play was featured in the April 11, 1938, issue of *Life* magazine. Six-foot-four-inch Stephen Courtleigh played the gangly young Lincoln, and Ann Rutledge, great-grandniece of the original, played the part of Lincoln's sweetheart. Professor Conkle "disclaimed any pretense of historical accuracy" in his play, according to *Life.* The faulty depiction played into communist witch-hunting of the House Un-American Activities Committee. Republican congressman J. Parnell Thomas called the play propaganda and "Communist talk." The play also got generally lousy reviews from critics, but withal it proved very popular. After nearly a year's run on Broadway it removed to the New York World's Fair, and spun off regional productions that toured the country. It also ushered in the truly great stage drama *Abe Lincoln in Illinois*.

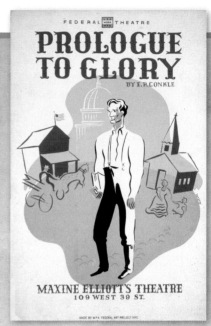

Fig. 3.166. This metal sign for Lincoln Hybrids, 30 by 12-1/2 inches in size, dramatically presents the iconic Lincoln money image as the symbol of "Honest Value." A burlap bushel seed sack for Cossack Alfalfa in the author's collection has the identical logo for Lincoln Seed & Feed Co., Sioux City, Iowa.

Fig. 3.167. Springfield Marine Fire Insurance Co., Springfield, Illinois, was Abraham Lincoln's bank before he went east for his inauguration. A bank ledger with notations from Lincoln's account has been on display in the bank's immense lobby for many years. During the 1930s a special desk/display case was constructed to house and protect the historic ledger. The case has relief panels on three sides depicting Lincoln's Illinois years.

Fig. 3.168. This program was issued for a Lincoln Day banquet by the Lincoln Club of Portland, Maine, in 1936.

Fig. 3.169. Marian Anderson's Easter Sunday concert on April 9, 1939, before an audience estimated at 75,000 at the Lincoln Memorial, is a major landmark in the civil-rights struggle in this nation. Ms. Anderson had been denied the use of Constitution Hall in Washington, D.C., by the hall's owners, the Daughters of the American Revolution.

1939 FEBRUARY 12. The City of Buffalo, New York, announces plans to erect sculptor Bryant Baker's youthful figure of Abraham Lincoln seated on a log holding a book, after receiving a $25,000 gift for that purpose. The statue would be dedicated in February 1940.

1939. Sculptor Clyde DuVernet Hunt's bronze group, *Faith, Hope and Charity* is displayed at the New York World's Fair. A standing figure of Abraham Lincoln in his familiar tall hat and a cape, representing Charity, rests his hands on a small child representing Hope and a kneeling woman representing Faith. After Hunt died in 1941, his heirs donated the statue in his memory to the town of Bennington, Vermont.

1939. At the New York World's Fair, sculptor Fred M. Torrey displays a three-foot-high plaster statue called *Abraham Lincoln Walks at Midnight,* inspired by Vachel Lindsay's poem of the same name.

1939 JUNE 9. Henry Fonda takes to the silver screen in John Ford's fictional account of lawyer Abe Lincoln in *Young Mr. Lincoln.* Lamar Trotti would be nominated for an Oscar for Best Original Story.

1939 SEPTEMBER 23. A bronze duplicate of sculptor Charles Keck's seated figure of Lincoln installed seven years earlier at Wabash, Indiana, is dedicated in Hingham, Massachusetts.

1939 NOVEMBER 5. An eight-foot-tall standing bronze figure of Abraham Lincoln, with his right arm behind his back and his left half clasping his lapel, is dedicated in the Norfolk, Nebraska, cemetery.

1940 JANUARY 20. The Indiana Lincoln Union hires National Park Service architect Richard E. "Louie" Bishop to design the state's Nancy Hanks Lincoln–Lincoln Boyhood Memorial. He would start work on the project on February 15. The Indiana Lincoln Union would approve his plans on October 7, and construction bidding would open on October 30.

Fig. 3.170. In 1939 *The Numismatic Scrapbook* editor/publisher Lee F. Hewitt issued a wooden penny flat redeemable at the Central States Numismatic Society Conference (convention), April 22–23, in Chicago.

Fig. 3.171. This style of Lincoln Brand Sunkist orange-crate labels is ubiquitous in the hobby. Virtually all seen are recent reprints.

Fig. 3.172. Sculptor Fred Torrey created a three-foot-high ceramic *Lincoln Walks at Midnight* after being inspired by Vachel Lindsay's poem of the same name. Torrey exhibited this ceramic at the New York World's Fair in 1939.

Fig. 3.173. The Lincoln Traction Co., Lincoln, Nebraska, used two varieties of this token. One was holed in the center, punching a hole in Lincoln's cheek.

Fig. 3.174. Sculptor Bryant Baker's statue of a young Abraham Lincoln was dedicated in Buffalo, New York, in February 1940.

1940 FEBRUARY. Verna Evelyn Shafter's illustration of Abraham Lincoln, George Washington, and a boy's chorus singing "America" ("My Country 'Tis of Thee") graces the cover of *The Etude Music* magazine.

1940 FEBRUARY 12. The Staten Island Chamber of Commerce listens to "the voice of old Poet [Edwin] Markham on a two-year-old recording, reciting 'Lincoln, the Man of the People,'" and eight other Markham poems about Lincoln "which Markham wrote in 1925 never before published or broadcast . . . read by Virgil Markham, the poet's fictioneer son," according to the February 19, 1940, issue of *Time* magazine.

1940 FEBRUARY 24. The cover photograph of the *Saturday Evening Post* shows Lincoln Borglum—son of sculptor Gutzon Borglum—and workmen on a scaffolding repairing Mount Rushmore.

1940 MARCH 16. The weekly half-hour *Lincoln Highway* radio show debuts on the NBC Red Network. Master of ceremonies for the episodic drama was John T. McIntire. Stars included Mary Astor, Lucille Ball, Ralph Bellamy, Joan Bennett, Rita Hayworth, Walter Huston, Raymond Massey, Ethel Merman, Maureen O'Sullivan, Vincent Price, Sophie Tucker, Burgess Meredith, and John Barrymore. The show's theme song was "God's Country and Lincoln Highway." It was broadcast live from the network flagship, WEAF in New York City, and carried "coast to coast" over 48 stations. In April 1941, the *New York Times* would report the show was being carried on 75 stations. Advertising was handled by Benton & Bowles. Its sponsor was Hecker Products Corporation, makers of Shinola Shoe Polish. After 117 programs, the show would cease airing on June 6, 1942.

Fig. 3.175. In 1939 Henry Fonda was a big hit in *Young Mr. Lincoln*, director John Ford's motion picture for 20th Century Fox.

Fig. 3.176. NBC Radio broadcast the half-hour "Lincoln Highway" program for 27 months beginning March 1940. The weekly dramas starred the biggest names from Hollywood and the New York stage. The show's sponsor was Benton & Bowles, makers of Shinola Shoe Polish.

Fig. 3.177. The little European country of San Marino recalled (on a set of three- and five-lira stamps) Abraham Lincoln's May 7, 1861, letter recognizing the principality as "one of the most honored in all history" and accepting the honorary citizenship awarded him by that state on January 22 prior to his inauguration. Shown is one of the souvenir sheets (Scott 187) for that issue of September 3, 1937. The sculpture reproduced on the stamps was by Ray[mond Granville] Barger, winner of the 1937 Prix de Rome award for sculpture. "Ray Barger Scultore" is credited in small type at the bottom of the design.

1940 June 11. The Indiana Lincoln Union approves a plan for sculpted panels to adorn an architect's design for the Indiana Nancy Hanks Lincoln–Lincoln Boyhood Memorial.

1940. The Association for Library Service to Children awards its coveted Caldecott Medal to *Abraham Lincoln* by Ingri and Edgar Parin d'Aulaire, published by Doubleday.

1940. Italian-American muralist Vincente (Vincent) Aderente, whose beautiful Lincoln portrait in the collection of the present author graced the cover of *Abraham Lincoln: The Image of His Greatness,* completes his massive (approximately 8-by-35-foot) Lincoln tribute mural at Lincoln Savings Bank, Broadway and Union, Brooklyn, New York. The central portion of the mural, which traces the transit of Abraham Lincoln's life from his rude birth cabin of 1809 to his magnificent memorial shrine dedicated in 1922, shows Lincoln turned in profile clasping his lapel and delivering his Gettysburg Address oration, which is printed on panels at the viewer's far left and far right. Also behind Lincoln to the viewer's left are a series of pre-presidential vignettes from his Kentucky cabin at far left, and people from his early life including Ann Rutledge standing in front of the platform, and friends and neighbors. In front of him to the viewer's right are the Armstrongs, his law partner John Todd Stuart, examples of Lincoln's charity, generals Robert E. Lee and U.S. Grant shaking hands, Mary Todd Lincoln and one of their sons, and several Cabinet members including Stanton, Seward, and Bates. The Lincoln Memorial is high on a symbolic hill to the far right. "The artist included a portrait of his son-in-law with his granddaughter, Glenn, seated on his shoulder," according to family information supplied to the Smithsonian Institution Research Information System by Glenn King, Aderente's granddaughter. In 1983, the bank name was changed to Federal Lincoln Savings Bank, FSB. In 2010, the bank was sold, and unfortunately the new owners removed the mural and placed it in storage at the bank, King advised this author.[44]

Fig. 3.178. Doubleday published Ingri & Edgar Parin d'Aulaire's charming Lincoln biography in 1939. The following year, the book won the Association for Library Service to Children's coveted Caldecott Medal.

a **Fig. 3.179.** Vincente Aderente, who painted the portrait used as cover art on *Abraham Lincoln: The Image of His Greatness,* also created a memorable Lincoln image in a mural he was commissioned to do for Lincoln Savings Bank, Broadway and Union, Brooklyn, New York, in 1940 *(a)*. The mural depicts Lincoln's life from boyhood cabin to sainthood at the Lincoln Memorial. The central portion shows a bearded Lincoln standing on a platform speaking to his friends and neighbors. In his past, Ann Rutledge in a pink dress admires the man he has become. A young girl in the crowd on her father's shoulders is Aderente's daughter Glenn King. A close-up of the Lincoln portrait *(b)* and another Lincoln sketch by Aderente *(c)* are also shown, courtesy of Ms. King.

Fig. 3.180. This gold bond for Lincoln Bank & Trust Co., Louisville, Kentucky, was issued in 1929 before the stock-market crash threw the country into a great depression and forced the United States off the gold standard.

1940. A seven-and-a-half-foot-tall, Art Deco standing bronze sculpture of Abraham Lincoln as a gaunt, strapping young man in shirt sleeves as a rail-fence mender using a post-hole digger, entitled *Abe Lincoln, Rail Joiner,* by American sculptor Louis Slobodkin, is dedicated at the U.S. Department of the Interior building in Washington, D.C. The design had originally been submitted in a national competition for relief-panel decoration of the Federal Building at the 1939–1940 New York World's Fair. Slobodkin, a children's book illustrator, did not win the competition, but instead was asked to enlarge his design as a free-standing statue. Accordingly, he sculpted a 15-foot-tall plaster, which was installed in the Federal Building's sculpture court. However, before the fair opened the commissioner general of the World's Fair commission ordered it to be removed from display and broken up into small pieces because

he considered it too "modern," "ridiculous," and "ugly." The sculptor pleaded his case to the press, backed by the art community, and his attorney threatened suit. Slobodkin demanded his small model back and a commission for a large bronze version, which he received in an out-of-court settlement. Accordingly his large bronze went on display at the Corcoran Gallery in October 1939, and thereafter was installed at the Interior Department, where historian Edward Steers Jr. calls it the Capitol's forgotten Lincoln tribute.

1940 JULY 4. During Germany's occupation of Norway, the first of annual anti-Nazi protests is organized in Oslo at the site of the Abraham Lincoln statue, made by Norwegian-American sculptor Paul Fjelde, which had been presented to the people of Norway by Norwegian-Americans in North Dakota and dedicated there July 4,

Fig. 3.181. *Young Lincoln,* sculptor Louis Slobodkin's 1939 vocational statue of Lincoln in shirtsleeves as a rail-joiner using a post-hole digger was deemed ugly and inappropriate for display at the New York World's Fair by exposition officials. When the sculptor threatened a lawsuit, he was given a contract for a large bronze based on his model, but the completed statue was hidden in a Washington courtyard, becoming the "unknown" Lincoln statue in the nation's capital.

Fig. 3.182. Lincoln profile portraits on medals are invariably facing the viewer's right, and cannot help but be compared to the amulet, idol design on the ubiquitous cent. These four examples are roughly contemporary to the late 1930s or the 1940s. They include a 12-1/2–inch bronze plaque attributed to Ralph J. Menconi (a), a cheap 3-inch Lincoln, Nebraska, Lucky Penny souvenir (b), a 3-inch glass paperweight etched to appear as a 1909 Lincoln cent (c), and a 3-inch plastic savings bank for the Lincoln Savings Bank of Brooklyn (d–e) (not coincidentally the bank for which Vincente Aderente had painted his Lincoln mural in 1940).

Fig. 3.183. Lucky pennies were common souvenirs, often cheaply made. Although this one for Lincoln's New Salem features a somewhat indifferent Lincoln cent profile, it has an excellent perspective relief of the first Berry-Lincoln store at the restored attraction.

1914. This is the only statue in Frogner Park not the work of Norwegian sculptor Gustav Vigeland. This silent protest at the Lincoln statue would be renewed each July 4 during the course of the wartime occupation, right under the eyes of the occupying army. Replicas of the bust are found at the Trail County Courthouse, Hillsboro, and a museum at Geneseo, Illinois. Fjelde's original plaster bust is in the collection of the Allen Memorial Library, Valley City State University (North Dakota).

1940 December 10. Ground is broken for the Indiana State Nancy Hanks Lincoln–Lincoln Boyhood Memorial buildings and cloister at Lincoln City, Indiana, by general contractor W.A. Armstrong, Terre Haute, Indiana.

1941 February 10. Norman Rockwell's painting *The Long Shadow of Lincoln* appears on the cover of the *Saturday Evening Post*.

1941 May. *Boys' Life* publishes photos of scouting pilgrimages to Abraham Lincoln statues in Jersey City, New Jersey, and Muskegon,

Michigan. The previous month the magazine had published pictures of similar pilgrimages to Lincoln statues in Freeport, Illinois, and Brooklyn, New York.

1941 May. Indiana sculptor Elmer H. "Dan" Daniels's half-scale clay models for the five heroic-scale panels adorning the state's Nancy Hanks Lincoln–Lincoln Boyhood Memorial at Lincoln City, Indiana, are approved by a committee comprised of artistic consultant sculptor Lee Lawrie, Indiana governor Henry Schricker, and members of the Indiana Lincoln Union and the Indiana Department of Conservation. These models had succeeded "definitive sketches" consisting of 16-by-27-inch clay models previously made by Daniels. After final approval, plaster casts were made of the larger models, and the Department of Conservation hired stone carvers to work from the plaster models. The ten-ton, eight-foot-tall by thirteen-and-a-half-foot-wide Indiana limestone panels were completed one year later, according to a National Parks Service history of the memorial.

Fig. 3.184. William Bradley Studios on West 43rd Street in New York City supplied properties and stage settings to New York theatrical productions and "moving picture manufacturers." The company also supplied prop money (see *Show Me the Money! The Standard Catalog of Motion Picture, Television, Stage and Advertising Prop Money*, by the current author). This green currency lookalike was the back of one of the firm's advertising notes, circa 1940, that featured a gold currency–looking impression of Washington and an eagle and shield on the face.

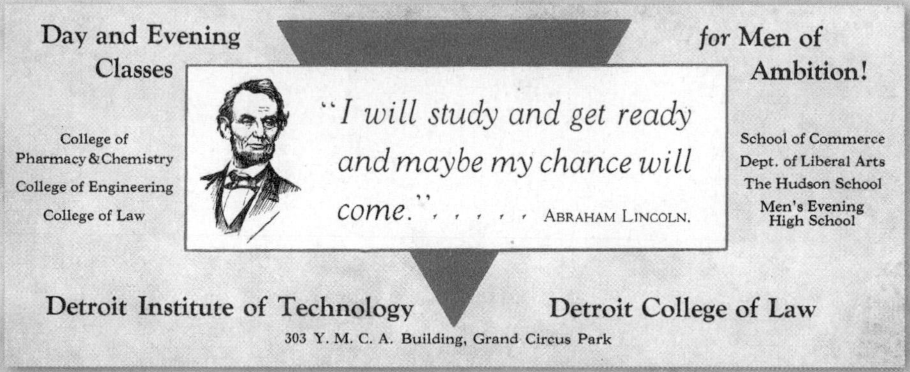

Fig. 3.185. The motivational quote on this circa-1940 Detroit Institute of Technology / Detroit College of Law ink blotter is completely bogus. It is not accepted in *The Collected Works of Abraham Lincoln*, published by the Abraham Lincoln Association, but is quoted time and again by educators, self-help gurus, religious speakers, devotional and daily-calendar manufacturers, and motivational writers. Recently, best-selling author Bill O'Reilly was taken in by it and bloviated in *The O'Reilly Factor for Kids: A Survival Guide for America's Families*.

The slogan was popularized beginning around 1915 by International Correspondence Schools, Scranton, Pennsylvania, in an extensive national advertising campaign. (See figure 3.63.) It's a good sentiment; it's just not Lincoln's. In 1915, it was easy to make up Lincoln quotes out of whole cloth since the corpus of his works was so diffuse. It's not so easy today.

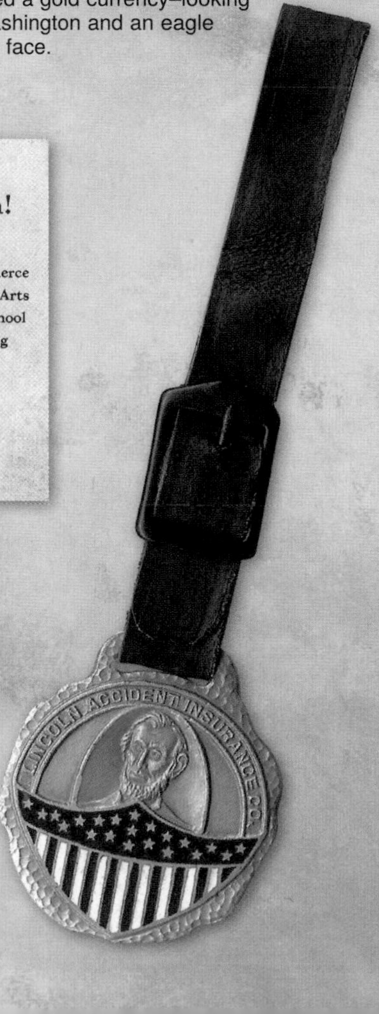

Day and Evening Classes

for Men of Ambition!

College of Pharmacy & Chemistry
College of Engineering
College of Law

"I will study and get ready and maybe my chance will come." . . . . . ABRAHAM LINCOLN.

School of Commerce
Dept. of Liberal Arts
The Hudson School
Men's Evening High School

Detroit Institute of Technology — Detroit College of Law

303 Y. M. C. A. Building, Grand Circus Park

Fig. 3.186. The present author has documented 29 insurance companies with *Lincoln* in their corporate names. Lincoln Accident Insurance was incorporated in Oklahoma on October 19, 1923, and commenced business on December 5 of that year. It sold life and health insurance, and almost immediately employed T.H. Noble & Co. and Greenduck Co., both of Chicago, to strike this wonderful medallic fob (King-557) with patriotic red-white-and-blue enameling.

1941 MAY 16. Carl Sandburg stages *The World of Carl Sandburg*, including readings from his Abraham Lincoln biography, at a dinner-theater presentation at Christ Church of Chicago. Price of a ticket was a dollar.

1941 MAY 21. The cornerstone is laid for construction of the limestone Nancy Hanks Lincoln Memorial Hall at Lincoln State Park in honor of Nancy Hanks Lincoln and Abraham Lincoln.

1941 AUGUST 4. The Indiana Department of Conservation hires Indiana sculptor Elmer H. "Dan" Daniels to sculpt the panels adorning the semi-circular Indiana Nancy Hanks Lincoln–Lincoln Boyhood Memorial at Lincoln City, Indiana. Daniels was hired for $12,000 per year for two years, but records show he ultimately received $25,000 for the project. Said Daniels: "I may get a bigger job some day, but I doubt if I will ever have a more significant one."

1942. New York City publisher Leverett S. Gleason's *Picture Digest* magazine, 114 East 32 Street, publishes a special issue. Cover designer Jo Chasin had conjoined portraits of Franklin D. Roosevelt and his shadow Abraham Lincoln. It christened Roosevelt with the tagline "FDR: The New Lincoln."

"The greatest individuals in human history have been those whose finest deeds and utterances were based on the desires and destinies of majorities of their people. . . . Abraham Lincoln was such a leader, his greatness firmly rooted in a whole nation's move toward freedom in years of critical struggle. Franklin Delano Roosevelt is such a leader, his greatness of the same national scope—in a period of even more critical importance," editor Gabriel Zakin wrote.

Articles included "How Will FDR Guide Us in Our War for Survival?", "The New Deal in Peace and in War!", and "Why is Roosevelt Great?" Other content included pictures of wartime factory conversions, details of New Deal spending programs, and public-service ads for war bonds and stamps.

1942. Composer Irving Berlin writes his paean to Honest Abe titled "Abraham." It commences "Upon a February morn / A tiny baby boy was born / Abraham, Abraham / When he grew up this tiny babe / Folks all called him Honest Abe / Abraham, Abraham / In eighteen sixty, he became / The sixteenth president / And now he's in the hall of fame / A most respected gent / That's why we celebrate / This blessed February date / Abraham, Abraham."

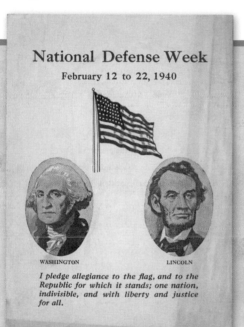

Fig. 3.187. War clouds in Europe ginned up a national patriotism expressed by pairing Abraham Lincoln and George Washington on this National Defense Week pamphlet *(a)* (note the "week" was 11 days long, encompassing both national heroes' birthdates). Similarly, current president Franklin D. Roosevelt was paired with Lincoln on the cover of a paperback digest *(b)*.

a

b

Fig. 3.188. The State of Illinois provided small cards of thanks to its World War II veterans. Two styles are known. Shown is the Columbian Bank Note Co. card with an Abraham Lincoln profile, issued when Dwight H. Green was governor (1941–1949).

Fig. 3.189. We think of Hallmark as publishing greeting cards, but as any customer at a Hallmark Shop can attest, the company has printed lots of other paper items, such as this wonderful patriotic bridge tally card from the 1940s. Scores were recorded on the back of the card and the tally could be hung up to celebrate victorious matches at a bridge or social club.

1942 JANUARY 5. Indiana Lincoln Union secretary Paul V. Brown reports purchase of a marble bust of Abraham Lincoln by Indiana sculptor Elmer H. "Dan" Daniels, sculpted in 1939, which the ILU purchased for display in the proposed Indiana Nancy Hanks Lincoln–Lincoln Boyhood Memorial building.

1942 JANUARY. Indiana sculptor "Dan" Daniels, hired by the Indiana Lincoln Union to design and model the limestone panels for the state's Nancy Hanks Lincoln–Lincoln Boyhood Memorial, complains to the press over intrusiveness exercised by the state oversight board, slowing down the artistic process (and also his paychecks). On January 8, 1942, the Indiana Lincoln Union instructs him to muzzle such outbursts.

1942 FEBRUARY 4. Lexington, Kentucky, attorney William H. Townsend discloses an undated membership document he dates to circa 1863 making Abraham Lincoln a life director of the Missionary Society of the Methodist Episcopal Church upon payment of $150.[45] Author Edgar DeWitt Jones attributes Lincoln's membership to having heard a sermon by Bishop Matthew Simpson in 1863. "At the conclusion of the services, Lincoln joined the Society, was

made a life director and subscribed one hundred and fifty dollars." A warm friendship sprang up between the two, he continued, and "the following year Lincoln was appointed on the board of the Society's Life Managers, which office he held at the time of his death." After Lincoln's death, Simpson accompanied the funeral train and delivered a eulogy at Oak Ridge Cemetery when Lincoln was interred.[46]

1942 FEBRUARY 16. The Indiana Department of Conservation purchases a $5,000 life-insurance policy from Lincoln National Life Insurance Co., Fort Wayne, Indiana, on its sculptor hired for the panels adorning the state's Nancy Hanks Lincoln–Lincoln Boyhood Memorial.

1942 JULY 21. U.S. Mint director Nellie Tayloe Ross receives suggestions from Mint staff for coinage of zinc cents and/or silver three-cent coins.

1942 AUGUST 4. Bing Crosby sings Irving Berlin's "Abraham," celebrating Lincoln's birthday, in the Paramount Pictures film *Holiday Inn.* (Berlin would win the Oscar for "White Christmas," also sung by crooner Crosby in the movie, which received two additional Oscar

Fig. 3.190. Philadelphia's E.A. Wright Bank Note Co. created an excellent Abraham Lincoln portrait vignette after the Marshall model, employed to good effect on this 1940 Republican National Convention admission ticket. The convention nominated Wendell Willkie of Indiana, but fellow Hoosier Lincoln's coattails were not long enough to carry the day against incumbent Franklin Roosevelt.

Fig. 3.191. The logo of Wyoming's Lincoln Star Coal Co. appealed to patriotism, with the recognizable Lincoln profile surrounded by stars.

Fig. 3.192. Little-noted Indiana sculptor Elmer H. "Dan" Daniels is one of the most unsung heroes of the Lincoln-idolization movement of the first half of the 20th century. With this white marble bust, Daniels took the first step toward gaining the commission of his lifetime—the large relief panels for the Lincoln boyhood memorial at the Nancy Hanks Lincoln state park.

Fig. 3.193. Lincoln cents underwent great changes during World War II, when the government changed their composition from primarily (95%) copper to zinc-plated steel, so the copper could be used in the war effort. No cents on the old-style planchets were officially struck, but some are known—apparently from planchets that got stuck in Mint hoppers during the changeover and were later jostled loose, entering the regular production line *(a)*. In 1944, the Mint converted to planchets made from salvaged cartridge and shell cases for a period of three years. No zinc-steel cents were officially struck in 1944, but again straggler planchets were indeed coined *(b)*. These off-planchet coins are highly desirable to collectors. Meanwhile, all this change was lost on the Edward B. Marks Music Corporation, which published Siegmeister's and Kreymborg's "The Lincoln Penny" song in traditional copper color in 1943 *(c)*.

Fig. 3.194. In the 1940s Mount Rushmore came into prominence not only as a national shrine, but as a tourist destination in far-off South Dakota. People who got there could put a decal on their automobile window to prove it and as a reminder of their vacation trip. Unfortunately the recipient of the decal shown here could claim only to seeing Washington, Jefferson, and Lincoln—and not Teddy Roosevelt *(a)*. Evans Plunge, Hot Springs, South Dakota, was a spring-fed, 87-degree mineral-water pool in the Black Hills that was a tourist site long before Mount Rushmore came into being, but it couldn't hurt tourist traffic, so its proprietor stuck the national memorial's image on his circa-1940s store cards *(b–c)*. Philatelists also collect "back of the book" labels such as this 1941 sticker promoting Biblical literacy as "the rock of our republic" *(d)*.

Fig. 3.195. Aaron Copland's "Lincoln Portrait" has been a great success since introduced during World War II. It has been recorded with various symphony orchestras and narrators, this being one of the first, in 1946, by the Boston Symphony and actor Melvyn Douglas.

Fig. 3.196. Etcher Bernhard Wall created the wonderful volume of his own drawings, *Following Abraham Lincoln 1809–1865*, published in 1943. Two years earlier he created this exquisite bookplate of a youthful Abe for Lincoln collector and author Steward W. McClelland, a member of the Lincoln Fellowship of Southern California.

nominations.) According to film historians, the sequence with "Abraham" is often deleted when played on television, because Marjorie Reynolds appears in blackface, which "some TV station managers view . . . as racially insensitive, even degrading."[47] That is a shame. "Abraham" is both fervent and funny, featuring lines like "The country's going to the dogs / They shouted loud and strong / Then from a cabin made of logs / The right man came along." According to the *New York Times* review the following day, Crosby's cool sold the blackface song. "Abraham" would also appear in the similarly plotted *White Christmas,* which was released October 14, 1954.

1942 DECEMBER 23. The U.S. Treasury secretary sets the weight of the wartime steel cent at 41.5 grains (later increased to 42.5 grains).

1943 FEBRUARY 27. Coining of zinc-coated steel cents at the Philadelphia Mint begins.[48]

1943 JULY 4. A bronze statue of Mr. and Mrs. Lincoln is dedicated at Racine, Wisconsin, at East Park, now Gateway Technical College. The project was a $20,000 bequest of Racine resident Miss Lena Rosewall, "who had studied the lives of the Lincolns [and] felt Mary had done much to further her husband's career." Symbolically, sculptor Frederick C. Hibbard represented the couple with Abraham seated and Mary standing at his right side. Both are dressed in formal attire. This is reputed to be the first statue group of the Lincolns. The five-ton granite group was carved from a block weighing 11 tons.

1943. The memorial halls and semi-circular cloister at Nancy Hanks Lincoln–Lincoln Boyhood Memorial are completed, to house a museum celebrating Lincoln's 14 formative years in Indiana. Plans called for the memorial's dedication as soon as it was completed,

however, it was postponed. The memorial was designed by National Park Service architect Richard E. "Louie" Bishop, and constructed with native Indiana materials, hand-cut limestone, sandstone, and woods. The central cloisters are flanked by memorial halls dedicated to Abraham Lincoln and his mother, Nancy Hanks Lincoln. On the exterior of the semi-circular buildings are five bas-relief panels sculpted by Elmer H. Daniels. The panels depict Lincoln's times in Kentucky, in Indiana, in Illinois, and in Washington, D.C., and a central panel symbolizes his enduring legacy. Nine short quotations from Lincoln's famous speeches emphasizing his commitment to democracy and liberty are carved atop the panels and intervening portals. These quotations were selected after consultation with Dr. Louis Warren of the Lincoln National Life Foundation and Paul Angle of the Illinois State Library.

The grounds of the memorial included the grave site of Lincoln's mother (Nancy Hanks Lincoln), the site of one of Thomas Lincoln's cabins, and eventually a living-history farm depicting life in Lincoln's boyhood years, and trails showing young Abe's natural world and marking milestones along his political life. A bronze marker on the site states, in part: "You are facing the wooded knoll on which sleeps Nancy Hanks Lincoln mother of the President who lived in this Hoosier environment during the formative years of his life from 1816 to 1830. Beyond, to the north, is marked the site of the humble log cabin where she led him for a little while along the path to greatness."

1943. The Library of Congress purchases about 7,000 Mathew Brady Civil War and post-war glass negatives that had originally been acquired by E. and H.T. Anthony to settle a debt owed to that photographic-supply company by Brady.

Fig. 3.197. This 1940s Vermont Marble Co. trade card displays a wonderful Lincoln marble profile.

A CARVING ON DISPLAY AT THE MARBLE EXHIBIT, VERMONT MARBLE CO., PROCTOR, VERMONT, U.S.A.

Fig. 3.198. Fort Wayne, Indiana's, Lincoln National Life Insurance Co. produced full-size (25 by 19-1/2 inches) plaster casts of Byron Pickett's 1873 memorial plaque with an applied wall hanger, for use as incentives, prizes, and gifts to dignitaries. The plaques were produced by Massolini Art Craft Co., Cleveland. The insurance company is identified on the small metal plaque beneath the bust.

1943. Sculptor Jo Davidson produces a small Abraham Lincoln bronze bust, with the same rough-free style as his bust of Franklin D. Roosevelt.

1943 DECEMBER 15. The Treasury Department files an order in the *Federal Register* changing the composition of the cent from zinc-coated steel to 95% copper and 5% zinc.

Fig. 3.199. Of all the Abraham Lincoln shrines, the boyhood memorial is the most underrated. Elmer H. "Dan" Daniels's magnificent limestone panels surrounding the visitor's center courtyard chronicle Lincoln's lifetime in Kentucky, Indiana, Illinois, and Washington, D.C. The central panel gives symbolic meaning to Secretary of War Edwin M. Stanton's deathbed epithet, "Now he belongs to the ages."

Fig. 3.200. Sculptor Jo Davidson specialized in clay modeling, and his busts were frequently cast in bronze or terra cotta. His Abraham Lincoln bust, variously dated 1943 and 1944, is one of these. It is quite similar to the sculptor's bust of Franklin D. Roosevelt, which the present author sold in his 2003 Presidential Coin & Antique Co. public-auction sale. Both display Davidson's rough modeling technique.

1944 JANUARY 24. The Indiana Department of Conservation announces that dedication of the state's Nancy Hanks Lincoln–Lincoln Boyhood Memorial would be postponed until after the end of World War II. According to a National Parks Service historian, however, "There is . . . No record that a dedication ceremony ever took place."[49] But see the entry below!

1944 FEBRUARY 12. Lincoln's stovepipe hat and umbrella on a side table, in a patriotically outfitted entryway, appear in John Carlton Atherton's *Commemorating Lincoln's Birthday* on the *Saturday Evening Post* cover. Atherton's style of "Magic Realism" is very apparent here.

1944 FEBRUARY 12. Sculptor Avard Fairbanks's bronze statue of Abraham Lincoln holding an axe is dedicated at Ewa Plantation Elementary school, Ewa Beach, Hawaii. The statue had been commissioned in June 1940, and modeled and cast in 1941, but installation was delayed by the unfolding of World War II in the Pacific Theater.

1944 MAY 20. According to the Smithsonian Institution's Research Information System Art Inventories Catalog, Elmer Harland Daniels's *Lincoln Sculptured Panels* at the Lincoln Boyhood National Memorial, Lincoln City, Indiana, are dedicated on this date. Daniels was assisted by Lee Lawrie. Carvers of the limestone panels included Albert Hoadley, Harvey Liva, and Joseph Slincard.[50]

1945. Genevieve Foster's book *Abraham Lincoln's World,* published by Scribner, is named a Newbery Honor Book in children's literature.

1945 APRIL 15. Actor Stephen Courtleigh appears on WNBT television in New York City as Abe in *Abraham Lincoln in Illinois*. Act two of the drama would be broadcast on May 20, 1945.

1945 OCTOBER 1. The Lincoln totem pole in the Hall of Flags in the Illinois Centennial Building, Springfield, is formally unveiled just prior to the annual meeting of the Illinois State Historical Society (October 5–6). Illinois State Historical Library historian Jay Monaghan had purchased the 1930s Civilian Conservation Corps copy of a 19th-century Abraham Lincoln totem pole during a summer excursion, and had parts crated and shipped back to the library, evidently with the financial backing of W.C. Hurst. The totem pole was presented to the Illinois State Museum by the Mid-Day Luncheon Club of Springfield, upon its arrival.

Fig. 3.201. Gates Rubber Company was founded by Charles Gates Sr. in Denver, Colorado, in 1911. The company prospered during World War II. When the American economy returned to a peace footing following victory, Gates printed several currency-looking handbills circulated to auto shops across the nation. "Catch a Mystery Man [and] Win a FREE $5 Bill," they state. These handbills urged mechanics to suggest new Gates fan belts to customers, because mystery shoppers employed by Gates would reward the mechanic with a $5 bill for making that suggestion. Of course, since the reward was a five-spot, Gates's ad employed Lincoln images. In addition to the $5 money portrait shown here, also observed are notes with a profile portrait, and notes with the $5 portrait flopped. All were printed by Poertner Lithographing Co., Denver, Colorado.

Fig. 3.202. United States Caramel Co., East Boston, Massachusetts, did not reach very far for the portrait shown on its 1932 American Heroes Caramel card of Lincoln, part of a set of 31 presidential cards. Of course, the company used the ubiquitous $5 bill style of portrait that would be familiar to all, including its targeted juvenile audience. Collecting and sending in all 31 cards earned the young collector "a one-pound dollar box of assorted chocolates free," and the return of his cards. Lincoln was credited as being "The Great Emancipator" in a short bio on the card back. Background color variants are known.

Fig. 3.203. Boy Scout patches frequently portray Old Abe. This Idaho scout patch has a flopped image from most Lincoln profile depictions.

1946. Counterfeiting of U.S. $5 and $100 Federal Reserve Notes and other currency is depicted in an International Criminal Police Commission (forerunner of Interpol) film, *Counterfeiting and Its Suppression*.

1946 FEBRUARY 10. Boy Scout Week in Illinois opens with 1,300 scouts hiking from the state capitol to the Lincoln Tomb, at which Eagle Scouts placed a wreath. On the 20th anniversary of this annual pilgrimage, in 1966, the route would be reversed. Patches were awarded to participants.

1946 APRIL. The odyssey of Henry B. Joy's hammered-copper copy of Alfonso Pelzer's New Jersey statue of the Great Emancipator, by John G. Segesman, continues. After being displayed at the Detroit-area Boy Scouts' Camp Brady for a decade, it was moved to the Charles Howell Scout Reservation, Brighton, Michigan, when Camp Brady was sold.

1946 JUNE 18. Republican Party delegate primary-election ballots in Wayne County, Michigan (Detroit), have an image of Abraham Lincoln superimposed on Old Glory, the Lincoln portrait being based on the old $10 greenback of the Civil War era, 90 years earlier.

1946 SEPTEMBER 8. Russian-born sculptor Boris Lovet-Lorski's eight-foot-high standing figure of Abraham Lincoln as a young lawyer is unveiled in bronze at the Macon County Building in Decatur, Illinois. The work was a gift to the city by Mr. and Mrs. Roy M. Dawson.

Fig. 3.204. These stills from the 1946 documentary *Counterfeiting and Its Suppression* are from a film produced by the International Criminal Police Commission (forerunner of Interpol).

Fig. 3.205. I personally find this 1946 Republican primary paper ballot very interesting, since it has the "throwback" Civil War–era style of Lincoln portrait made popular by Charles Burt's $10 currency engraving, after C.S. German's O-41/42 photographs, not usually seen in generations.

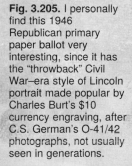

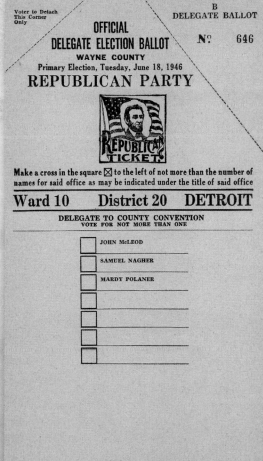

Fig. 3.206. Calendar art is collectible itself. This 1940s illustration depicts a clean-cut youth dreaming of America's past glories, a theme very receptive to a "Greatest Generation" audience ravaged by the Great Depression and a world war.

1947 February 12. G.P.A. Healy's 1868 painting *The Peacemakers* is officially hung in President Harry Truman's office on the anniversary of Abraham Lincoln's birth. The canvas depicts, life-size, a March 28, 1865, meeting of Lincoln and his commanders Admiral David Dixon Porter and generals U.S. Grant and William Tecumseh Sherman, aboard the side-wheeler *River Queen* anchored off City Point, Virginia. Healy's original masterpiece had been destroyed by fire. The example hung in the White House was a full-size copy, which had belonged to a Chicago collector for many years. It was acquired by the United States in 1947 for $10,000.

The painting would be displayed in the White House Treaty Room from the John F. Kennedy through the George W. Bush administrations. President Barack Obama would have it moved to the private President's Dining Room.

"I think the likeness of Mr. Lincoln by far the best of the many I have seen elsewhere, and those of General Grant, Admiral Porter, and myself equally good and faithful," Sherman told Isaac N. Arnold in 1872. Robert Todd Lincoln was also said to have viewed favorably its depiction of his father. In 1908, in anticipation of the coming Lincoln centennial, Robert copyrighted Healy's monochrome study of his father for the larger canvas. Several smaller copies of *The Peacemakers* by Healy are also known.

Fig. 3.207. G.P.A. Healy's 1868 painting *The Peacemakers* (measuring approximately 47 by 63 inches), depicting a council of war Abraham Lincoln held with generals Ulysses Grant and William T. Sherman and Admiral David Porter on board the steamboat *River Queen* in March 1865, came home to the White House in 1947 when it was acquired during the Truman administration. According to Robert Todd Lincoln, Healy's portrayal of his father was the "most excellent in existence." It will be remembered that in 1908, just before the Lincoln centennial observance, Robert copyrighted the Healy image of his father that was the study for this depiction.

Fig. 3.208. Once again we show poster stamps (philatelic labels) with depictions of Abraham Lincoln, both produced in 1947. The Council Against Intolerance in America was founded by James Waterman Wise in 1940, as a civil-rights and anti-defamation organization. Its goal was "combating prejudice by calling attention to American ideals, heroes, and traditions" *(a)*. It was active in the 1940s promoting African American and Jewish causes. Raymond Massey's signature role on stage and screen in *Abe Lincoln in Illinois* is patriotically recalled on his Hollywood Starstamps label *(b)*. After this stamp was issued Massey would go on to play Lincoln in three television dramas and the 1962 film *How the West Was Won*.

1947 April. Andrew O'Connor's seated figure of Abraham Lincoln is installed at Fort Lincoln Cemetery, Bladensburg, Maryland, without fanfare, after languishing at the Gorham Manufacturing Co. foundry for more than 15 years awaiting payment of the $5,000 bill for the casting of the statue.

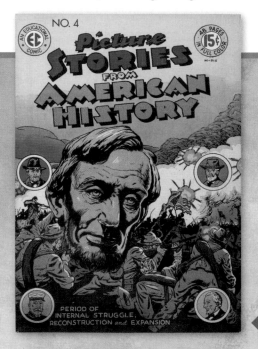

Fig. 3.209. The similarity this writer finds in these two magazine covers is their morphing of the Lincoln portrait. The illustration of the mysterious faux bust looming over the Confederate infantrymen on the April 1947 comic book *Picture Stories from American History (a)*, was drawn by Allen Simon. The June 19, 1948, cover of the *New Yorker* by Arthur Getz *(b)* similarly warps the Lincoln "Gettysburg" photo as a decorative banner being installed at Philadelphia's Municipal Auditorium in preparation for the Republican National Convention that summer. Getz was the most prolific *New Yorker* cover artist, producing a record 213 covers over a half century, 1938 to 1988.

Fig. 3.210. The designer of this attractive 1950s auto decal employed multiple photographic models for his Abraham Lincoln portrait. "The Home of Lincoln" may date this decal to prior to Illinois adopting "Land of Lincoln" as the state's slogan in 1955.

Fig. 3.211. Once again San Marino celebrated Abraham Lincoln, this time with Benjamin Franklin and George Washington, on its stamp commemorating the centenary of prepaid adhesive postage stamps in the United States. Facsimiles of the 1847 Franklin (Scott 1) and Washington (Scott 2) stamps and the 1869 Lincoln stamp (Scott 122) appear on this 15-lire stamp (Scott 269). Also issued were 3-, 35-, and 50-lire stamps.

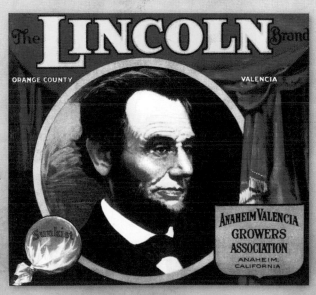

Fig. 3.212. The Independent Republic of Indonesia issued this provisional stamp in 1949, with the U.S. money portrait of Abraham Lincoln and a portrait of regime vice president Mohammad Hatta. This essay is not listed in the Scott catalog.

Fig. 3.213. This Sunkist Valencia Lincoln Brand orange-crate label for the Anaheim Valencia Growers Association sports a portrait modeled after the Brady O-87 photograph. It is believed that this is an original label that has not suffered the same reprinting as the label shown as figure 3.171 on page 182.

1947 July 19. The *Saturday Evening Post* publishes a long-lost photograph of Abraham Lincoln, known today as O-97. This numismatically historic image is believed to be the actual reference source (or a companion image) for Charles Burt's Lincoln portrait for the Bureau of Engraving and Printing, which was utilized on the Lincoln 50-cent Fractional Currency (Friedberg-1374).

The photograph was one of several recorded on glass-plate negatives by Anthony Berger at Brady's Washington, D.C., gallery on Wednesday, April 20, 1864, as photo reference material for artist Francis B. Carpenter. The cracked glass plate was discovered by Lincoln photo historian Stefan Lorant "among the unpublished diaries and sketch books of Francis B. Carpenter, painter of the famous Emancipation Proclamation picture," according to the *Post.*

This photograph was also Carpenter's reference for a portrait study of Lincoln for his *First Reading of the Emancipation Proclamation* canvas, which was thereafter engraved to resounding applause by Frederick Halpin, himself newly come from down South, where he had been employed engraving Confederate States paper money and stamps, of all things.

After publication, the *Post* offered printed duplicates of the Lincoln image, as "published for the first time anywhere in the July 19, 1947, issue of The Saturday Evening Post," to its readers.

1947 July 26. CBS Radio Network broadcasts the ceremonial "opening" of the Abraham Lincoln papers at the Library of Congress. They had been kept under seal for 21 years according to provisions of the gift from Robert Todd Lincoln, the president's only surviving direct descendant, in 1926. A distinguished body of Lincoln experts gathered for the occasion, including Carl Sandburg, James G. Randall, Paul Angle, Louis A. Warren, Roy P. Basler, Jay Monaghan, and Alfred Whital Stern.

1948 February 14. The *Collier's* front-page illustration depicts lensman Mathew Brady photographing the seated president.

1948 June 29. Senate Joint Resolution 158 is approved, "To authorize the issuance of a special series of stamps commemorative of the eighty-fifth anniversary of Lincoln's Gettysburg Address. Resolved by the Senate and House of Representatives of the United States of America in Congress assembled, That the Postmaster General is authorized and directed to prepare for issuance on November 19, 1948, a special series of 3-cent postage stamps, of such design as he shall prescribe, in commemorative of the eighty-fifth anniversary of Lincoln's Gettysburg Address." However, only a single stamp would be issued, Scott 978.

1948 October. Scrip and exonumia researcher J.J. Curto writes on the Depression scrip of Lincoln Park, Michigan, in *The Numismatist.*

1948 October 24. Fred M. Torrey's seated bronze statue of a youthful Abraham Lincoln, titled *Lincoln at Twenty-One,* is formally dedicated on Millikin University's campus, along West Main Street in Decatur, Illinois.

This magnificent photograph of Lincoln was lost for 83 years. It was discovered by Stefan Lorant, authority on Lincoln photographs, among the unpublished diaries and sketch books of Francis B. Carpenter, painter of the famous Emancipation Proclamation picture.

PUBLISHED FOR THE FIRST TIME ANYWHERE IN THE JULY 19, 1947 ISSUE OF THE SATURDAY EVENING POST

Copyright 1947. The Curtis Publishing Company

Fig. 3.214. The broken "lost" glass plate of Anthony Berger's April 20, 1864, photo (O-97) reemerged in 1947, and was published with great exuberance in the July 19, 1947, issue of the *Saturday Evening Post.* It had been discovered by Lincoln photo historian Stefan Lorant among the sketchbooks of artist Francis B. Carpenter, and was in fact the model for the "portrait from life" Carpenter painted and Halpin engraved. Curtis Publishing Company reprinted the image and an explanation on a large card stock, which it distributed at the time free for the asking.

Fig. 3.215. A large measure of Abraham Lincoln's personal papers, handed down within the family, were donated to the Library of Congress and the people of the United States by surviving son, Robert Todd Lincoln, after he had scrubbed the cache of anything he did not want preserved. Always extremely protective of his father's image and legacy, Lincoln stipulated that the papers were to remain sealed until 21 years after his own death, which occurred on July 26, 1926. The pent-up expectancy that day brought out scholars and the public in droves to view the personal letters and official messages contained in the archive. This photograph was taken on July 26, 1947, the first day the Lincoln papers were on display.

1948 December 29. The New York City Housing Authority's Abraham Lincoln Homes, comprising 14 six- and fourteen-story buildings in Manhattan, is completed. The residential development, with nearly 1,300 apartments, is located between East 132nd and East 135th streets and Fifth and Park avenues.

1949. Sculptor Cartaino de Scarrino Paolo's bronze statue *Lincoln the Lawyer* is dedicated at Lincoln Memorial University, Harrogate, Tennessee. Noted Lincoln collector and lawyer Carl W. Schaefer commissioned the work, and was the principal speaker at its dedication. The university would subsequently offer 14-1/4-inch bronze replicas for sale at $1,000 each. The career of Paolo (1882–1955) spanned six decades, and his bronzes also included Ulysses S. Grant and Robert E. Lee.

1949 February 12. Sculptor Charles Keck's bronze statue, of a seated Abraham Lincoln with his arm around a young boy standing at his right, is dedicated at the New York City Housing Authority's Abraham Lincoln Homes in Harlem, a low-rent public-housing development completed only two months earlier in northern Manhattan. Presently the development is called Abraham Lincoln Houses.

Fig. 3.216. This large bronze, called *Lincoln Statue*, by sculptor Jack Witt, guards the gate to Lincoln Memorial University, Harrogate, Tennessee. It was dedicated October 23, 1992.

Fig. 3.217. On February 12, 1949, Charles Keck's seated bronze figure of Abraham Lincoln with his sheltering arm around a young boy was dedicated at New York City's Abraham Lincoln Homes, a low-rent public housing project in Harlem. The young resident of the development seems curious about the great man depicted.

Fig. 3.218. Not all Lincoln pins are celluloid pinbacks, as these three post-WWII metal pins prove. The blue, white, and gold enamel rosette pin *(a)* was issued circa the 1950s by Lincoln Life (an Illinois life-and-health insurance company incorporated May 27, 1922); the gilt keystone-shaped pin belonged to a student at Lincoln High School *(b)*. The 1939 below the bust is the date the school opened in the newly developed African American community of Lincoln Manor in Dallas, Texas; and the state-shaped red enamel pin was also circa the 1950s by the Lincoln (Nebraska) Commercial Club *(c)*.

1949 MARCH. Gold Key publishes *Giggle Comics,* in which comic animal characters join an Abraham Lincoln bust, clad in a red-white-and-blue tie and party hat, and blow red-and-white horns to celebrate Lincoln's birthday. Lincoln's horn is propped up by a sling shot in a hotel lobby. All these proceedings bring the chagrin of the hotel redcap. The Lincoln bust had also appeared on the *Giggle Comics* covers of January 1946 (where the Great Superkatt held an umbrella over the Lincoln statue's head so he wouldn't get wet) and March 1948 (where the animals sang "Happy Birthday" to Abe).

1950 FEBRUARY 12. The Philco Television Playhouse broadcasts *Ann Rutledge,* with a vibrant Grace Kelly in the title role and Stephen Courtleigh in the role of her swain, a young Abe Lincoln.

1950 FEBRUARY 18. A golden bust of the nation's savior looms over the eerie twilight scene of a youth chopping wood at dusk outside the humble log cabin from which he came—this image on the cover of *Collier's,* "the nation's magazine." The illustrator for the cover was Walter Bomar, an accomplished graphic artist.

1950. Sawyer's Inc., Portland, Oregon, copyrights its "Abe Lincoln's New Salem" View-Master reel no. 298.

1950. Illinois governor Adlai Stevenson commissions playwright Kermit Hunter to write a play about the life and times of Abraham Lincoln in New Salem, resulting in the musical-drama *Forever This Land.* The play would be performed at Lincoln's New Salem State Park that summer season and the next. For the Lincoln bicentennial in 2009, the play was revived at the park.

Fig. 3.219. *Giggle Comics,* published by Gold Key, repeatedly teamed a Lincoln statue with comic animal characters in the late 1940s. This humorous cover appeared on the January 1946 issue.

Fig. 3.220. Illinois' Democratic governor Adlai Stevenson commissioned playwright Kermit Hunter to write a play about Lincoln's days at New Salem. *Forever This Land* was the result, and it played at New Salem State Park in summer 1950 and 1951. It was reprised for the bicentennial in 2009.

Fig. 3.221. Publisher Henry R. Luce had three great ideas: deliver timely news weekly (resulting in *Time* magazine), deliver picture stories weekly (resulting in *Life* magazine), and deliver sports features weekly (resulting in *Sports Illustrated*). From the time *Life* came on the scene in 1936, re-inventing the photo magazine, millions turned its pages weekly to see interesting sights from across the county and around the world. This straightforward "In This Temple" cover visits the lonely grandeur of the nation's secular idol. On the 137th anniversary of his birth, Lincoln's "stature continues to grow. . . . In an Elmo Roper poll released last week his popularity was greater than George Washington's, even in the South," the magazine reported inside.

Fig. 3.222. The author dates this tobacco inner label to around the 1940s, but its seller thought it was a lot earlier because of its nice gold embossing. Whatever its vintage, "Old Honesty," and "A. Lincoln," and the $5 O-92 money portrait are synonymous with quality and value.

1950 OCTOBER 20. The *Pulitzer Prize Playhouse* television-series episode "Abe Lincoln in Illinois" features Raymond Massey as Lincoln and Adele Longmire as Ann Rutledge.

1950 OCTOBER 30. The Lincoln Historical Fund Campaign, 100 North LaSalle Street, Chicago, Illinois (Governor Adlai E. Stevenson honorary chairman), solicits tax-deductible donations to purchase the Oliver R. Barrett Abraham Lincoln collection. The solicitation would prove unsuccessful, and the Barrett collection would be sold at public auction in 1952.

1950 NOVEMBER 19. On the "four score and seventh anniversary" of Lincoln's Gettysburg Address, the Library of Congress announces that Chicago Lincolniana collector Alfred Whital Stern is donating more than 7,000 Lincoln items—mostly books, monographs, and pamphlets about Lincoln, but also including such items as sheet music, prints, broadsides, and ephemera—to the Library. A specialized group consisted of original materials of Chicago sculptor Leonard Volk, including many of his studio tools, his reminiscences, and bronze castings of the life mask and hands of Lincoln.

Stern had been a Lincoln collector since the 1920s. He was a colleague of Ralph G. Newman, and a charter member of the Chicago Civil War Roundtable from 1940. His collection included copies of three speeches delivered by Lincoln during his term as a U.S. representative from Illinois; Lincoln's scrapbook documenting his debates with Stephen A. Douglas during the Illinois senatorial campaign of 1858; and materials relating to the 1860 presidential election, Lincoln's assassination, and his funeral. The collection was initially deposited in 1951, and formally presented in 1953.

Minor items in the collection included a collection of Lincoln cents, some Lincoln stamps, and first-day-of-issue covers. Librarian of Congress Luther H. Evans acknowledged the gift (in part):

"There is a profound satisfaction in your assurance that the national collection of Lincolniana shall possess the dignity, resourcefulness, meaning, and primacy to which it and the people of the United States are so eminently entitled." Stern's gift also included funds to endow its enlargement over time, and to publish a catalog of the collection's contents, which would be done in 1960, just missing the Lincoln sesquicentennial celebration. The collection now numbers more than 11,000 items.

1951 FEBRUARY. *Boys' Life* publishes current requirements for First Class scouts to receive the various Lincoln Trail medals. The Kentucky Lincoln Trail is 34 miles long, a two-day hike. Additionally, scouts must submit a 300-word book report on an approved Lincoln book, and memorize the Gettysburg Address. The Indiana Lincoln Trail is 18 miles long. Additionally, scouts must read two short histories of Lincoln furnished by the Southern Indiana Council and write a report on the hike. In Illinois, the Lincoln Trail from New Salem to Springfield is 20 miles long. Second Class scouts could qualify also. Additionally, participants must report on an approved Lincoln biography before taking the trail. The Illinois Lincoln Trail was the oldest of the three, having been established in 1926.

1951 FEBRUARY 12. Raymond Massey plays Lincoln in "Abe Lincoln in Illinois" in a *Lux Video Theatre* TV-series episode.

1951. Edwards Brothers, Ann Arbor, Michigan, publishes Donald Charles Durman's *The Statues of Abraham Lincoln,* including also the Volk and Mills life masks, the Volk casts of Lincoln's hands, and more than two dozen busts.

1951. Clara Ingram Judson's book *Abraham Lincoln, Friend of the People,* published by Follett, is named a Newbery Honor Book in children's literature.

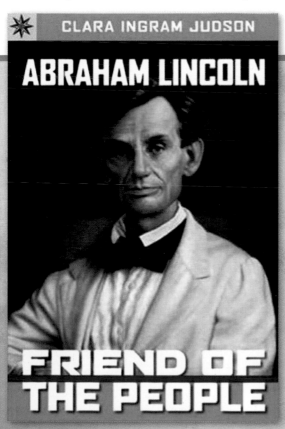

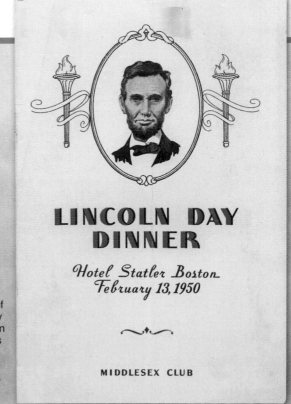

Fig. 3.223. In 1951 Clara Ingram Judson's book, *Abraham Lincoln, Friend of the People,* published by Follett, was named a Newbery Honor Book in children's literature.

Fig. 3.224. Another of the many Lincoln Day banquet and luncheon menus in the author's collection, this is for a Middlesex Club event of February 13, 1950, at Boston's swanky Hotel Statler.

1951 SEPTEMBER 26. Los Angeles–based international jewelers James and Harry Kazanjian display a 1,318-carat sapphire head of Abraham Lincoln carved from one of the five largest known sapphires. The Kazanjian Brothers valued their prized artifact at a cool quarter of a million bucks. The Lincoln carving was the first of four large sapphires fashioned by artist Norman Maness with consultation of Lincoln Borglum. Subsequently, he fashioned similar portraits of Andy Jackson, Thomas Jefferson, and Dwight D. Eisenhower, president at the time. The carver had to invent the cutting tools he used on the two-year project. In 1988 the Kazanjian Foundation would donate this patriotic quartet to the White House, where their public display caused a sensation.

1951 NOVEMBER. The Judge James W. Bollinger Lincoln Collection at the University of Iowa, Iowa City, Iowa, is dedicated.

1952 FEBRUARY 11. A Madison Avenue copywriter coins the Lincoln approbation "He was everybody, grown a little taller" in a two-page John Hancock Life Insurance Co. advertisement in *Life* magazine, with an illustration of a seated Lincoln by illustrator Frank Smith. The ad was part of a famous multi-decade (1940s, 1950s, and 1960s) campaign of personalized biographical pitches with memorable tag lines. Other prominent Americans in various fields of endeavor lauded for their accomplishments in the series included Buffalo Bill Cody ("He was there when he was needed"), George Gershwin ("He gave something rare and beautiful to us all"), Charles Evans Hughes ("He was guardian of our liberties"), Teddy Roosevelt ("His strength made all Americans strong"), George Washington ("He took a new job and the world changed"), Asher Benjamin ("He gave Freedom a House to Live in"), Francis Scott Key ("He wrote a song for the home of the brave"), Richard E. Byrd ("He made a frozen frontier tell its secrets"), Henry David Thoreau ("He heard a drummer in the forest"), Albert Einstein ("He showed us the promise of a new age"), Frederic Remington ("He gave us the Wild West for keeps"), Knute Rockne ("They called him The Man-Maker"), and of course John Hancock ("Freedom writes in a big, bold hand") himself. One-pagers from the series appeared variously.

1952 FEBRUARY 12. Parke-Bernet Galleries in New York City commences exhibiting the fabulous Oliver R. Barrett Lincoln Collection prior to its two-day sale of the collection in 842 lots on February 19 and 20. Barrett, a Chicago attorney, was the reputed greatest Lincoln collector of the first half of the 20th century. In 1949, a year prior to his death, Harcourt, Brace & Co. had published Carl Sandburg's *Lincoln Collector—The Story of the Oliver R. Barrett Lincoln Collection.*

1952 MARCH 22. Lincoln green profile-portrait penny postal cards are revalued to two cents (Scott UX40).

1952. Rutgers University Press publishes *Lincoln in Marble and Bronze,* by Dr. F. Lauriston Bullard, detailing 67 original full-figure statues and 20 replicas.

1952 JULY 20. Fourteen-year-old Abraham Lincoln enthusiast Ronald Rietveld makes a discovery in the Illinois State Historical Library, among papers donated by John Hay's daughter in 1943. Buried in the Nicolay-Hay Collection is a photograph of Lincoln in his open coffin during the time he lay in state at the New York City Hall.

According to Rietveld, who later became a California university professor, the faded brown photographic print was in a folder labeled "X:14," within a letter sent to John Nicolay in 1887 from Lewis H. Stanton, son of the secretary of War who had ordered the destruction of Jeremiah Gurney's photographs of the scene taken

Fig. 3.225. The Kazanjian brothers, James and Harry, were jewelers to the Hollywood stars in the early 1950s, when they conceived of carving four of the largest then-known sapphires into figural busts of great Americans, as a publicity stunt. The Lincoln sapphire shown, carved by Norman Maness, is 1,318 carats. In 1988 Lincoln—and companion stones in the shape of presidents Jackson, Jefferson, and Eisenhower—were donated to the White House by the Kazanjian Foundation.

Fig. 3.226. Marilyn Monroe reportedly had a "thing" for Old Abe. She posed for this publicity photo about 1951.

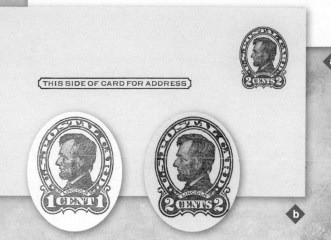

Fig. 3.227. For Lincoln's birthday advertising in 1952 a Madison Avenue copywriter coined "He was everybody, grown a little taller" to help John Hancock Life Insurance close sales. The illustration for this ad, by Frank Smith, oddly makes Lincoln look too small for his big chair, oddly out of sync with the advertising message, in this writer's view.

Fig. 3.228. On January 1, 1952, when the Post Office doubled the rate on the green penny postal card (Scott UX28) introduced in 1917, the department was possessed of a large supply of the cards still on hand after 35 years of stocking them. Initially a surcharge imprint was applied, creating a two-cent card (Scott UX40/42) *(a)*, and later a new red card (Scott UX43) *(b)* appeared at the new rate.

Fig. 3.229. Every magazine has a slant or take on the Lincoln legend. Even mystics admire Abraham Lincoln, it seems, and Lincoln cover stories sell magazines. The September 1949 issue of *Fate* discusses Lincoln's spiritualism, along with tree whisperers, fire walkers, and UFOs. The Lincoln portrait is modeled on O-118, a photo taken by Alexander Gardner on February 5, 1865. This photo image is a favorite of mystics, who claim (after the fact, of course) that the original glass plate breaking across Lincoln's brow foretold his shooting in the head two months later.

EXHIBITION FROM
TUESDAY · FEBRUARY 12

★ ★ ★ ★ ★

THE BARRETT LINCOLN COLLECTION

PUBLIC AUCTION SALE
February 19 and 20 at 1:45 and 8 p.m.

Fig. 3.230. When the State of Illinois / Illinois State Museum failed to come up with the funds to secure the Oliver Barrett Collection *en bloc,* the assemblage of original Lincoln items (several of which are pictured in this book) was put up for sale by Parke-Bernet Galleries in New York City. This sign advertised the public display of the lots and their dispersal in February 1952.

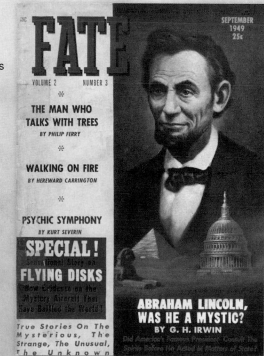

April 24, 1865. "I have found this in my father's papers and perhaps you'd like to use it," the younger Stanton had written the former presidential secretary, then at work on a massive Lincoln biography with his colleague John Hay.

1952 July 31. Regular-issue Abraham Lincoln two-cent postal cards (Scott UX43), designed by Clair A. Hutson, are introduced.

1952 August. On the 20th anniversary of Dale Carnegie's very large-circulating *Lincoln, the Unknown,* Pocket Books publishes a 25-cent paperback reissue retitled *The Unknown Lincoln,* the self-help guru's biography of Old Abe.

1952 August 11. The U.S. Post Office releases a Mount Rushmore Memorial stamp (Scott 1011) to mark the 25th anniversary of the national monument in South Dakota's Black Hills. The stamp was designed by William K. Schrage.

1952 September 15. *Life* magazine publishes Stefan Lorant's article on the newly found death picture of Abraham Lincoln, discovered by a teenager in the Nicolay-Hay papers at the Illinois State Historical Library that summer. The discoverer's name did not appear in the article, bringing Lorant much criticism from other Lincoln scholars.

1952 October 6. Illinois State Historical Librarian Harry Pratt validates discovery of the recently found death picture of Abraham Lincoln by 14-year-old Ronald Rietveld, in *Life* magazine.

1952 November 11. Methuen, Massachusetts, inventors Milton Issenberg, Daniel Issenberg, and Joseph Issenberg receive U.S. Patent no. D168155 for an ornamental Lincoln figural savings-bank bottle. The clear glass bottle was molded in the shape of a man with a beard; its black cap, in the shape of a Lincolnesque tall brimmed hat. Once the bottle was empty, the lid could be cut to make a slot for coins. Lincoln Foods, Lawrence, Massachusetts, employed the bottle to sell various milkshakes, syrups, and juices. The company used the familiar $5 note Lincoln portrait on its label.

World War II hero Milton Issenberg had returned home and joined the family business, the Lincoln Fruit and Syrup Co., in 1945. In 1954 the company would change its business style to Lincoln Foods Inc. and move into larger premises in Lawrence, Massachusetts. In 1968 the company was purchased by S.S. Pierce. In 1976 Issenberg left S.S. Pierce and founded Lincoln Food Brokers, later known as the Lincoln Food Group.

These figural bottles are plentiful today and avidly collected. Bottles with full, intact paper labels command collector premiums.

1952 November 16. Six-foot-two-inch actor Royal Dano plays Abe Lincoln in the five-part *Omnibus* television series written by James Agee. Part 2 would air November 30; Part 3, December 14; Part 4, January 11, 1953; and Part 5, February 8.

1953. A glass-plate negative at the U.S. National Archives is discovered under close inspection to show Abraham Lincoln at the Gettysburg battlefield cemetery, accompanied by his massive bodyguard Ward Hill Lamon.

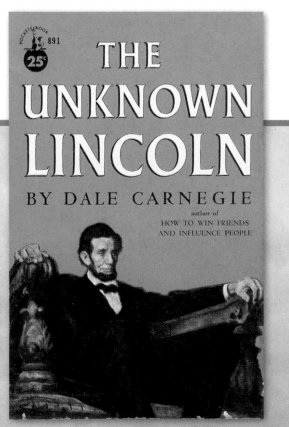

Fig. 3.231. Self-improvement guru Dale Carnegie saw Abraham Lincoln as a shining example of positive development to which his students could aspire. His 1932 biography of Lincoln (titled *Lincoln, the Unknown*) was given to graduates of his program, and many copies today are found with commemorative inscriptions inside. On the 20th anniversary a paperback 25-cent reprinting was retitled *The Unknown Lincoln.*

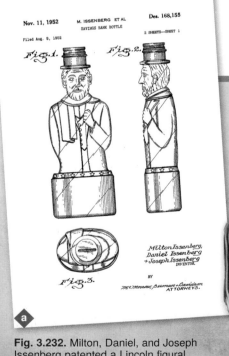

Fig. 3.232. Milton, Daniel, and Joseph Issenberg patented a Lincoln figural bottle for their Lincoln Foods company, Lawrence, Massachusetts, in 1952 (a). The clear bottles dispensed various milkshakes, syrups, and juices. They had tall black hat-shaped lids which could be cut with a slit, to reuse the friendly bottles as banks (b). Many were saved and they are plentiful on the collector market today.

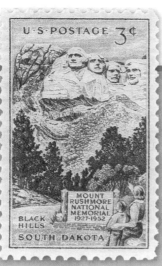

Fig. 3.233. To mark the 25th anniversary of the commencement of carving at Mount Rushmore on August 10, 1927, the Post Office issued a blue-green three-cent commemorative postage stamp (Scott 1011). The stamp design by William K. Scrage was hardly a leap, showing a woman and a child viewing the memorial. First day of issue was August 11, 1952, at Keystone, South Dakota, because August 10 was a Sunday.

Fig. 3.234. The 1952 Republican National Convention in Chicago nominated war hero Dwight D. Eisenhower. The "Land of Lincoln" convention had a Lincoln theme, including this fine profile badge.

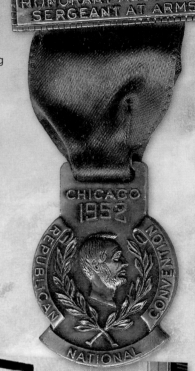

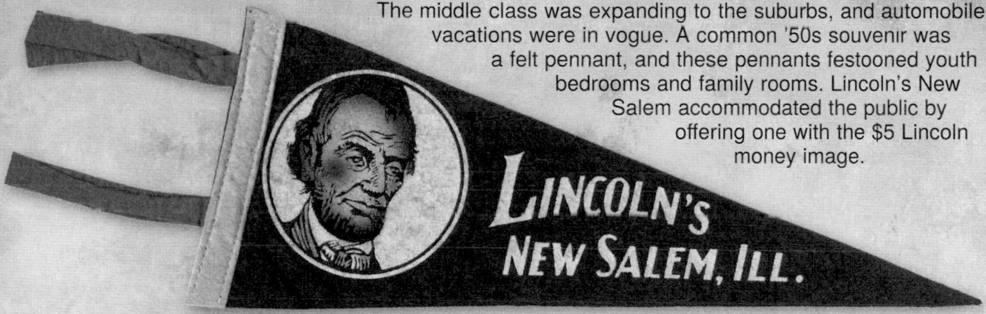

Fig. 3.235. By the 1950s, the American economy was in full swing. The middle class was expanding to the suburbs, and automobile vacations were in vogue. A common '50s souvenir was a felt pennant, and these pennants festooned youth bedrooms and family rooms. Lincoln's New Salem accommodated the public by offering one with the $5 Lincoln money image.

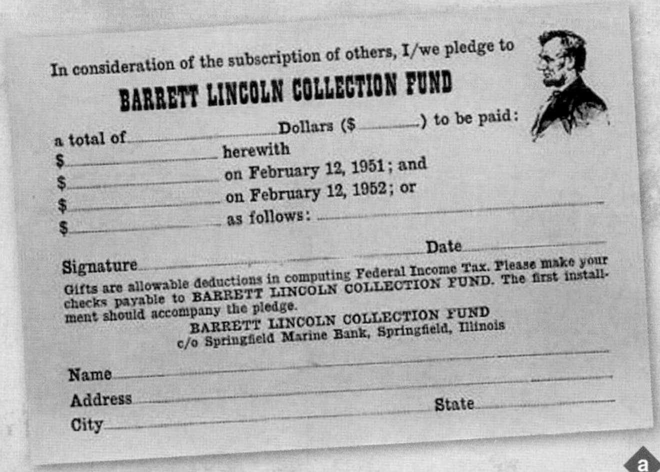

In consideration of the subscription of others, I/we pledge to

BARRETT LINCOLN COLLECTION FUND

a total of ________ Dollars ($ ________) to be paid:
$ ________ herewith
$ ________ on February 12, 1951; and
$ ________ on February 12, 1952; or
$ ________ as follows: ________

Signature ________ Date ________

Gifts are allowable deductions in computing Federal Income Tax. Please make your checks payable to BARRETT LINCOLN COLLECTION FUND. The first installment should accompany the pledge.

BARRETT LINCOLN COLLECTION FUND
c/o Springfield Marine Bank, Springfield, Illinois

Name ________
Address ________
City ________ State ________

a

b

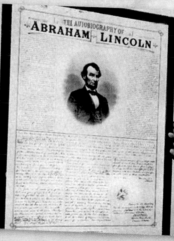

Fig. 3.236. Illinois governor Adlai Stevenson led an unsuccessful attempt to raise funds for the purchase of the Oliver Barrett Lincoln collection for the Illinois State Museum, already a depository of a significant Lincoln holding. Shown is an unfilled pledge card *(a)*, and Stevenson admiring a framed print of the Lincoln autobiography written at the behest of Jesse Fell, with its popular John Chester Buttre engraving of the O-92 image *(b)*.

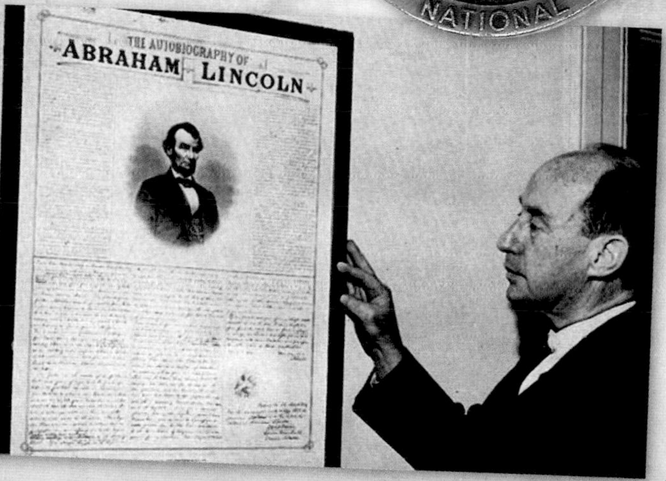

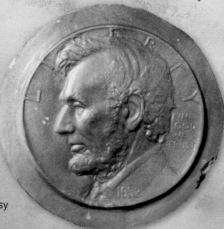

Fig. 3.237. Sculptor James Earle Fraser conceived of introducing a new Abraham Lincoln portrait on the cent for the sesquicentennial of Lincoln's birth. In 1952, he created this approximately four-inch plaster model. Fraser was at the top of his game, and this masterful design would have made a lovely cent, but he died in 1953, before he could see the project to fruition. The original plaster is shown courtesy of its owner, Jim Halperin.

1953 MARCH 10. The Illinois legislature creates the Illinois Memorial Commission. The commission chose the site for the memorial at the triangle formed by the intersections of Lincoln-Lawrence-Western on the city's north side. The commission publicized nationally for a concept. Illustrator and Lincoln photographic historian in-the-making Lloyd Ostendorf won the $1,000 prize for a "beardless and strong" depiction, the way Lincoln looked to his contemporaries in Chicago from 1849 to 1860. The Illinois House then appropriated $35,000 to the commission to undertake such a work, and Avard T. Fairbanks was commissioned to provide the statue. The culmination of the commission's activities was the erection of Fairbanks's *The Chicago Lincoln: A Chance to Portray Liberty* in the Windy City's Ravenswood neighborhood's Lincoln Square. It would be dedicated October 16, 1956.

1953. Dr. Kate Pelham Newcomb organizes a "Million Penny Parade" in Woodruff, Wisconsin, urging local schoolchildren to save their pennies so the town can build a local hospital. The media spread the story far and wide, and 1.7 million coppers rolled into town. The town got its hospital, and the fundraising stunt landed the penny visionary on the popular *This Is Your Life* television show in March of 1954. With this additional publicity, more than $100,000 in donations poured into the northern Wisconsin community. To commemorate their achievement the town erected the "world's largest penny" monument, a concrete statue weighing 17,452 pounds! The foot-thick, copper-colored "Big Penny" monument stands about nine feet high at the corner of 3rd Avenue and Hemlock Street.

1953 DECEMBER. President Dwight D. Eisenhower's Christmas card bears his portrait of Abraham Lincoln. Eisenhower, an amateur artist, did a creditable job with his Lincoln depiction.

1954 FEBRUARY 7. Abe Lincoln is formally clad in tie and top hat, with a red plaid shawl thrown over his shoulders, in Joseph Parrish's portrait gracing the *Chicago Tribune* magazine. Inside is a color-illustrated article on the restoration of Lincoln's boyhood village at Spencer County, Indiana, near Rockport.

Fig. 3.238. A very successful penny drive in Woodruff, Wisconsin, that brought the community a local hospital is commemorated by the "world's largest penny" monument, composed of nearly nine tons of concrete.

Fig. 3.239. An amateur painter, President Dwight D. Eisenhower painted a very creditable portrait of Lincoln that was used on Ike and Mamie's 1953 Christmas cards. For his models, Ike chose for the portrait the Alexander Gardner photograph (O-78) taken November 8, 1863, which is a companion photo to the more well-known Gettysburg Lincoln image. However, evidently Ike drew his inspiration for Lincoln's lower vest and gold watch chain from Anthony Berger's February 9, 1864, image (O-91), as he reproduced the more expensive-looking finer chain and guard in the portrait precisely.

A REPRODUCTION OF AN OIL PAINTING BY GENERAL EISENHOWER — 1953

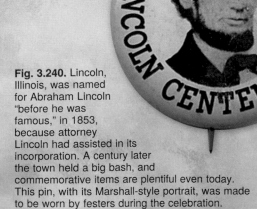

Fig. 3.240. Lincoln, Illinois, was named for Abraham Lincoln "before he was famous," in 1853, because attorney Lincoln had assisted in its incorporation. A century later the town held a big bash, and commemorative items are plentiful even today. This pin, with its Marshall-style portrait, was made to be worn by festers during the celebration.

Fig. 3.241. This high-grade, architectural brass plaque is 10-3/4 inches in diameter, and the cast bust is 1-1/4 inches in depth. It was made by the Connecticut Foundry Co., Rocky Hill, Connecticut, in 1954, according to its backmarks.

1954 FEBRUARY. Lincoln scholar and Rotary International district governor Clarendon E. Van Norman writes in *The Rotarian*: "Boy Scouts from many States . . . Come to this exciting village (New Salem), where, from a place near the entrance of Kelso Hollow Theater, they start the 20-mile trek to Springfield, marked out as the Boy Scout Lincoln Trail. Almost any Saturday or summer day, Scouts will be seen scattered along the trail, some peppy, some weary, now and then one with blistered heel—but all with hearts set on winning a Lincoln Medal for the journey. Many of these same boys may be seen returning in June to Springfield for an annual three-mile hike from the heart of the city to the Lincoln Tomb, going by the route of the Lincoln funeral procession."[51]

Fig. 3.242. By the 1950s, when both of these specimen stock certificates were printed, Western Bank Note & Engraving Co., Chicago, was being operated as the Western Division of the American Bank Note Co. Both the Lincoln National Bank, Chicago, stock (by WBNE) (a) and the Lincoln National Life Insurance Co., Fort Wayne, Indiana, stock (with the imprint of the Franklin-Lee Division of American Bank Note Co., New York) (b) have the identical profile portrait vignette.

Fig. 3.243. A Lincoln-Garfield Woman's Relief Corps ribbon from a Corvallis, Oregon, convention in 1953 reproduces the old $10 greenback portrait based on O-41/42.

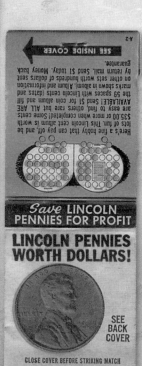

Fig. 3.244. Lincoln matchbooks are plentiful. Those pictured are of typical 1950s vintage, as far as the author can tell. These four were chosen primarily because they present as many different Lincoln images and a variety of advertisers, including an insurance company (a), an inn (b), a hotel (c), and a coin-album publisher (d).

1954 June 21. Avard Fairbanks's heroic-size, nine-foot-high bronze of Abraham Lincoln symbolically discarding his axe and taking up his law books is erected at New Salem State Historic Site. The sculptor based his Lincoln on copies of the face and hand casts by Leonard Volk. Lincoln was elected to the Illinois state legislature from the community in the 1830s.

1954 circa. Palmer Paint Sales, Detroit, Michigan, had introduced the "paint by numbers" fad to America in 1951 under the Craft Master Brand, offering "a paint set for every purse and purpose." This recreational painting venture was the brainchild of artist Dan Robbins. Kits included brushes, premixed paints, and a color-blocked canvas-board picture. Series IV had a patriotic Abraham Lincoln picture showing a bust of Abe and an American flag. Although the phenomenon was panned by many purists, the Chicago Institute of Arts said that it stimulated interest in the arts, and Dwight D. Eisenhower's appointments secretary, Thomas Edwin Stephens, mounted a gallery of finished paintings done by administration officials, in a West Wing corridor.

1954. The Library of Congress purchases approximately 10,000 Civil War and post–Civil War negatives from the daughters of Levin C. Handy, Alice H. Cox, and Mary H. Evans. Handy had been apprenticed to his famous uncle Mathew Brady, and thereafter became a famous photographer in his own right in Washington, D.C. He issued numerous prints from the Brady negatives and additional copy negatives, a number of which have come into the collection of the present author and have been used to illustrate this volume and its predecessor (see especially figure 1.59b).

1954. Lincoln University, Chester County, Pennsylvania, celebrates its centennial. A medal commemorated the event and was awarded to donors. It displays a small cent image in the front. The Lincoln profile portrait is similar to Victor David Brenner's cent effigy, surrounded by the legend "If the Son shall make you free / You shall be free indeed," and views of the school buildings. Around the periphery are the commemorative dates, a likeness of the university's main gate, and the legend "Free Persons In A Free World Through Education And Brotherhood." The school was founded in 1854 as the first school for higher education for "youth of African descent." It was renamed for Abraham Lincoln in 1866.

1954 November 19. The red-violet Lincoln four-cent first-class postage stamp (Scott 1036) is introduced.

1955 February 7. Richard Gaines plays Abe Lincoln in the *TV Readers' Digest* television-drama series episode "How Chance Made Lincoln President."

Fig. 3.245. Palmer Paint Sales' "Paint by Numbers" was the brainchild of artist Dan Robbins, and the fad swept the nation. In the fourth series of kits, circa 1954, amateur dabblers could complete this Abraham Lincoln bust and flag. Framing was optional.

Fig. 3.246. Sculptor Avard Fairbanks's nine-foot-tall statue of a strapping Lincoln symbolically tossing off his axe for mental pursuits was dedicated at New Salem State Historic Site in 1954. Here the sculptor is seen taking a measurement of the book in Lincoln's right hand, in his studio in 1953.

1955 FEBRUARY 13. Richard Boone plays Abe Lincoln in the *G.E. True Theater* episode "Love is Eternal," hosted by Ronald Reagan. Teresa Wright played Mary Todd Lincoln. The drama was based on Irving Stone's 1954 novel *Love is Eternal: A Novel of Mary Todd and Abraham Lincoln.*

1955. During this year, Lee Hewitt's *Numismatic Scrapbook* magazine publishes articles on three collectors who completed their Lincoln cent collections with coins from circulation.

1955. Harper and Brothers publishes syndicated columnist Jim Bishop's *The Day Lincoln Was Shot,* which becomes an instant bestseller and Book-of-the-Month Club selection. The reporter offered a detailed minute-by-minute dramatic account of April 14, 1865, the day President Abraham Lincoln was assassinated by thespian John Wilkes Booth. Although a dramatic retelling of events, historian Bishop went to the trouble of providing a bibliography on sources he'd consulted, and a series of photographs. The following year Raymond Massey would star opposite Jack Lemon as Booth in a live telecast adaptation of the biopic, on the *Ford Star Jubilee* dramatic series that aired February 1, 1956, and was narrated by Charles Laughton.

1955 JULY. The Abraham Lincoln School is founded in Bogota, Colombia. It was named after Lincoln because he "was thought a character of international scope, great intellectual tradition, with principles, values lived, preached with obvious achievements, persistence and perseverance to any test of honesty and integrity." Classes would commence in September 1955.

Fig. 3.247. Lincoln University, Chester, Pennsylvania, celebrated its centennial by presenting this fine medal to donors in 1954. The school had been founded in 1854 as Ashmun Institute, the first school for higher education for "youth of African descent," but was renamed for Abraham Lincoln in 1866. The Biblical quotation around the bust, "If the Son shall make you free / You shall be free indeed" is the school motto, quoted from John 8:32.

Fig. 3.248. My first coin company in the mid-1950s was Tatham Stamp & Coin, Springfield, Massachusetts, operated by Howard E. MacIntosh, with whom my dad (a stamp collector) had dealt since before he went into service in World War II. Tatham's illustrated catalogs were jam-packed with inexpensively priced material having real story appeal. The coin company issued this Lincoln store card in both bronze *(a)* and aluminum *(b)*.

Fig. 3.249. In 1955 a doubled obverse die created a Lincoln cent error that was plentiful enough to make it worth chasing, yet scarce enough to make it worthy of the pursuit. The error coin and the publicity attendant to it gave an impetus to coin collecting from circulation.

Fig. 3.250. Both of these 1950s pinbacks, for Lincoln Savings Bank *(a)* and Land of Lincoln *(b)*, have Lincoln money images.

Fig. 3.251. On April 25, 1955, Cuba released a commemorative stamp to mark the centennial of the country's first stamp. The 12-centavo stamp showed the Plaza de Fraternidad in Havana and its memorial bust there of Abraham Lincoln. Monuments to other Pan-American leaders are also found in the plaza.

1955 SEPTEMBER 25. The *New York Times* publishes T. Harry Williams's review of J.G. Randall's last volume in his four-volume Lincoln biography. "Two biographies of Lincoln written in the grand manner—multi-volumed works—have been attempted in this country, one by a great literary artist and the other by a distinguished academic scholar. First to appear was the poet Carl Sandburg's stupendous six-volume 'Abraham Lincoln: the Prairie Years' in 1936 and 'The War Years' in 1939. Almost on the heels of Sandburg's performance came 'Lincoln the President,' by J.G. Randall of the University of Illinois,

the first and only professional historian to essay a comprehensive life of Lincoln. The Lincoln of Sandburg's biography is the foremost American folk hero as viewed by a mystic impressionist who is also a prodigious investigator. The Lincoln of Randall's study is that same figure as viewed by a detached, dispassionate product of the graduate school."

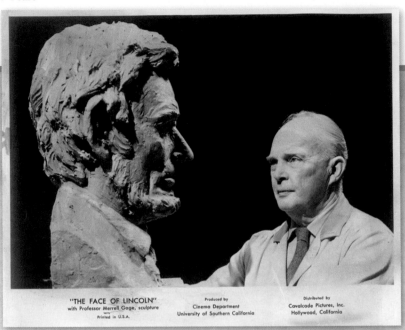

Fig. 3.252. University of Southern California sculpture professor Robert Merrell Gage's 22-minute biographical documentary *The Face of Lincoln* was made in 1955 for use in schools. The black-and-white instructional film shows Gage sculpting a large clay bust of Abraham Lincoln in real time while he recites the major events of Lincoln's life. Gage illustrates how these events altered Lincoln's appearance as he grew a beard, changed the part in his hair, and lost weight, and as his face became etched with a thousand sorrows almost too difficult to bear. The short film won an Academy Award. A half century later, the film is still worth seeing, and it is now available on the Internet at archive. org/details/face_of_lincoln.

Fig. 3.253. Another 1950s aluminum token for a Lincoln, Nebraska, Buick Auto Company has a profile of Lincoln.

Fig. 3.254. The Lincoln House restaurant gave out fine advertising matchbooks in the 1950s, with a small Lincoln likeness mirroring the $5 bill portrait.

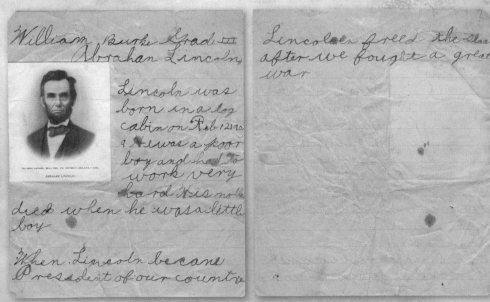
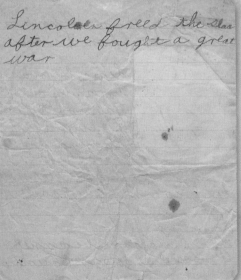

Fig. 3.255. In the mid-1950s, when this author was coming up through grade school, every schoolroom had pictures of Washington and Lincoln posted prominently, often in the front of the room. Both presidents' birthdates were school holidays, and we were taught to revere their memories. So was William Burke, Grade III, who must have been a contemporary of the present author, and who somehow found the American Bank Note "Men in Currency" Lincoln vignette patterned after O-77, the Gettysburg Lincoln photo, to illustrate his school biography.

1956. Decca Records releases a gold-label LP, *Poetry and Prose of Abraham Lincoln*, a spoken-word album (DL 8515 LP) featuring Carl Sandburg reading selections of his own writings, Orson Welles reciting the Gettysburg Address and Lincoln's Second Inaugural Address, and Walter Huston voicing Edwin Markham's "Lincoln, the Man of the People," Walt Whitman's "O Captain, My Captain," and Vachel Lindsay's "Abraham Lincoln Walks at Midnight."

1956 FEBRUARY 11. The lead item in Robert Ripley's *Believe It or Not* panel syndicated in hundreds of newspapers is titled "The Great Tragedy." It explains "5 People were in President Lincoln's box at the Ford Theatre at the moment the great emancipator was shot in 1865—And all of them were haunted by sorrow! . . . The President died the next day . . . His Assassin was slain . . . Mrs Lincoln became deranged and died in 1882 . . . Major Rathbone—present with the girl he later married—killed her in 1883 and spent the last 28 years of his life in a mental institution."

1956 FEBRUARY 11. CBS Television airs the *Ford Star Jubilee* drama "The Day Lincoln was Shot," based on Jim Bishop's best-selling book of the same title. In the climactic scene in the presidential box at Ford's Theatre, Jack Lemmon, playing Booth, sneaks behind the first couple, played by Lillian Gish and Raymond Massey, and lowers his gun point-blank at the back of the president's head.

Fig. 3.256. In the 1950s Baltimore collector Louis E. Eliasberg formed the only "complete" collection of regular-issue United States coins. That feat got him considerable publicity, and he shared his collection through public displays. Specialists since have picked incessantly at the "completeness," but his accomplishment was certainly noteworthy. Additionally, Eliasberg owned this set of 15 Lincoln medals struck in gold *(a–b)*, housed in a special frame. Illustrations of many of these medals also appear individually in the present work, courtesy of the Louis E. Eliasberg estate.

Fig. 3.257. This set of souvenir miniature photos was marketed in Springfield, Illinois, to tourists. The Lincoln home and tomb are featured on the set of 20 cards.

Fig. 3.258. This late-1950s GOP aluminum so-called dollar features bold designs on obverse and reverse. However, party fathers might wish that it had exploited a different message surrounding its conjoined portraiture of Tricky Dick, Ike, and Abe.

Fig. 3.259. Gilroy Roberts's 1954 GOP centennial-medal design was also employed in the party's 1956 national-convention badge.

1956 FEBRUARY 12. Attorney G. William Horsley recreates Lincoln's Farewell Address to Springfield during ceremonies at the historic Great Western Railroad depot, two blocks from Lincoln's Springfield, Illinois, residence. Two years later, Lincoln presenter Horsley would recreate the Lincoln-Douglas debates with Douglas presenter S. Phil Hutchinson. The depot would undergo restoration in the 1960s and pass through several administrations until being taken over in 1977 by Sangamon State University for use in training history majors. Today, although Copley Press owns the building, it is operated by the *State-Journal Register* and the Lincoln Home National Historic Site under the National Park Service.

1956 FEBRUARY 12. Dedication ceremonies are held in Detroit for a large copy of Gutzon Borglum's famous beardless bust of Abraham Lincoln emerging from a rocky base. The Detroit Institute of Arts had originally received the sculpture as a donation from local businessman Ralph Herman Booth. This prize was largely undisplayed and in storage until the 1950s, according to writer B. Nash. After being on display for slightly over a decade, the statue was the victim of 1960s hooliganism. Its nose was broken off, and it was hauled off to storage once again. Nineteen years later it reemerged, with a reattached patched-up replacement nose, and was installed near Hart Plaza on East Jefferson Avenue. In recent years, the adhe-

Fig. 3.260. Gutzon Borglum's marble Lincoln bust (see figure 3.111) was dedicated in Detroit on February 12, 1956. This is how it looked before 1960s hooligans knocked its nose off. Today the repaired statue has an unfortunate dark ring around the proboscis, caused by weathering of the adhesive used to reattach the nasal protrusion.

Fig. 3.261. In 1952 Bowman issued a set of U.S. Presidents cards with attractive artwork, including a scene recalling a youthful Abraham Lincoln wrestling Jack Armstrong, behind the iconic O-92 Lincoln money image. In 1956 Topps bought out Bowman and reissued the set from the same artwork, but in slightly smaller format. Topps reissued the set once again in 1972. This is the original Bowman card.

Fig. 3.262. "The Second Death of Abraham Lincoln" was the cover story of the June 1956 *House of Mystery* comic book. Alternate stories of Lincoln's assassination have been a staple of literature at various levels in recent decades.

Fig. 3.263. The Principality of Monaco celebrated the Fifth International Philatelic Exhibition (FIPEX) in New York City in 1956 by issuing a diamond-shaped three-franc stamp after the Hesler Lincoln photo (O-27). The biographical stamp design by Gaudan is mirrored on this first-day-of-issue card.

sive attaching the nose has turned much darker than the complexion color of the bust, causing an unsightly dark ring around Abe's nose. "I think Mr. Borglum would be greatly saddened by the sorry state of Detroit's copy of his masterpiece," Nash opined.[52]

1956 APRIL 3. The Principality of Monaco pays tribute to Abraham Lincoln with a diamond-shaped stamp issued in conjunction with the 5th International Philatelic Exhibition in New York City.

1956 OCTOBER 16. Sculptor Avard Fairbanks's *The Chicago Lincoln: A Chance to Portray Liberty* is unveiled at Ravenswood's Lincoln Square, in Chicago.

1957 JUNE 30. *BBC Sunday-Night Theatre* airs a production of "Abe Lincoln in Illinois."

1957 JULY. Acclaimed TV western director Andrew McLaglen's movie *The Abductors,* about the plot to steal Abraham Lincoln's corpse from the Springfield, Illinois, cemetery and hold it for ransom, is released. The director's father, Oscar winner Victor McLaglen, was the star. It was written by Ray Wander, loosely based on the actual events.

1957 OCTOBER 10. Fort Wayne, Indiana, Lincoln Museum director Dr. R. Gerald McMurtry presents a lecture on Abraham Lincoln medals to Fort Wayne's Old Fort Coin Club.

1958 JANUARY 1. *The Lincoln Hunters,* a sci-fi time-travel novel by Wilson Tucker, is published by Rinehart & Co., Inc.

1958. In view of the upcoming Lincoln sesquicentennial, Dell Publishing publishes the first of its "Dell Giant" color-illustrated "comic books," titled *Abraham Lincoln Life Story.* The remainder of the series would consist of juvenile fiction with subjects ranging from the Lone Ranger to Raggedy Ann and Andy, Santa Claus, Tarzan, Woody Woodpecker, and Dracula.

1958 APRIL 17. A copy of a standing statue of Abraham Lincoln by Alfonso Pelzer for Lincoln, New Jersey, with its base inscribed "Let Man Be Free," done by John G. Segesman for W.H. Mullins Co., is removed to the Skillman Branch of the Detroit Public Library. The statue had originally been erected by Lincoln Motor Company at its plant at West Warren and Livernois in Detroit, a gift of company founder Henry M. Leland.

1958 JULY 31. First-day-of-issue covers are postmarked and released at Mandan, North Dakota, because of its proximity to nearby Fort Abraham Lincoln, for the four-cent red-violet Lincoln portrait stamp. The stamp would pay the basic first-class letter rate beginning August 1, 1958. This was the first increase in first-class postage in 26 years, since 1932! Perhaps Abraham Lincoln was employed to ease the pain and to silence negative feedback.

Fig. 3.264. The 1954 Republican centennial medal design by Gilroy Roberts, conjoining profile portraits of White House residents Abraham Lincoln and Dwight D. Eisenhower, is featured on the party's 1956 *Civil Rights* brochure, issued by the Republican National Committee. This was the appeal of the party of Lincoln to African American voters after the Eisenhower administration had supported Brown v. Board of Education, which had struck down racially segregated schools in 1954. Ike won and even got 40% of black voters, but black support of the Democratic Party continued a trend from since the New Deal era.

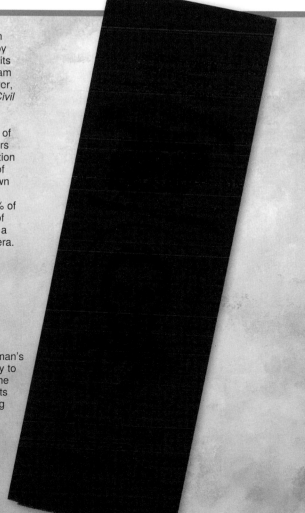

Fig. 3.265. The Woman's Relief Corps auxiliary to the Grand Army of the Republic continued its tradition of employing attractive ribbons for its annual meetings. This Springfield, Illinois, conclave ribbon sports the 1863 bearded Gettysburg Lincoln O-77–style image.

1958 OCTOBER. A 12-foot-tall, bronze statue of Abraham Lincoln by sculptor Gilbert Franklin is installed on a seven-foot-high granite pedestal in Roger Williams Park, Providence, Rhode Island. The work was financed by a memorial fund originally donated by Henry W. Harvey in 1922 in memory of his wife Georgina. By 1954 the fund had grown to $25,000, and an advisory committee of the Providence Art Club selected a location and sculptor for the project.

1958 OCTOBER 6. To commemorate the centennial of the Lincoln-Douglas debates, sculptor Avard Fairbanks's tablets with portraits of each debater respectively are installed on the east side of Old Main Street in Galesburg, Illinois.

1959 JANUARY. The Association of American Railroads' School and College Service Division releases a colorful comic book entitled *All Aboard, Mr. Lincoln!*, depicting railroad history during the Civil War. The cover illustration depicts Abraham Lincoln boarding a train.

1959 JANUARY 2. The U.S. Mint begins striking new cents with Frank Gasparro's Lincoln Memorial on the reverse. The coins would first officially be released on February 12, but examples escaped into circulation early.

Fig. 3.266. *MAD* magazine had a running Lincoln gag. This cover practically parodies the Mount Rushmore commemorative stamp (see figure 3.338), with the young mother pointing out the fifth honoree, Alfred E. Neuman, publisher William Gaines's mascot and cover boy.

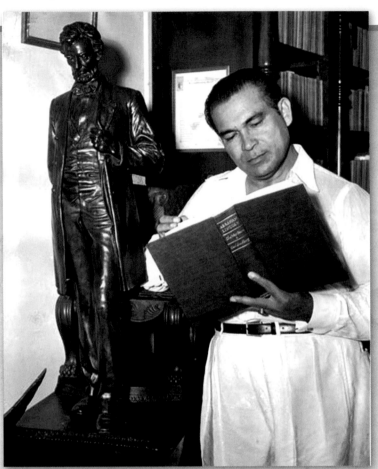

Fig. 3.267. Cuban strongman Fulgencio Batista lived in the United States for many years. In 1952, he was returned to power in a coup as an American puppet. Batista wrapped himself in Cubans' native love for Abraham Lincoln, and in many public-relations photos posed with his personal copy of Saint-Gaudens's *Standing Lincoln*. Nevertheless, his repressive rule in 1950s Havana led to his overthrow by Fidel Castro's July 26th Movement guerrilla revolution. Castro has since also skillfully attempted to manipulate Lincoln consciousness on the island.

Fig. 3.268. In 1958 Gilberton Publications' *Classics Illustrated* juvenile illustrated biography of Lincoln, dated January 1958, was translated into Greek. The original painting depicted the legendary wrestling match between Abraham Lincoln and Jack Armstrong. For the Greek edition, the publisher also shows an ancient Greek coin or medallion featuring wrestlers squaring off, which does not appear on the U.S. original. Wrestling was one of the original Olympic sports in ancient Greece.

Fig. 3.269. By the late 1950s Lincoln consciousness in America was pervasive. In those years before the 1959 sesquicentennial, Abraham Lincoln was the American secular idol. Lincoln consciousness in America is best represented by these two photos of teenage boys and girls celebrating Lincoln. The Boy Scout ceremony before the Saint-Gaudens *Standing Lincoln* in Chicago was held February 10, 1958 *(a)*. Unfortunately we don't know many specifics about the cheerleaders. However, the enthusiasm of these 1950s Lincoln High School students ringing their spirit bell *(b)* was surely duplicated at many Lincoln High Schools across the land.

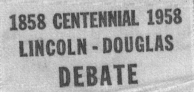

Fig. 3.270. Knox College, Galesburg, Illinois, is justly proud to have hosted the fifth Lincoln-Douglas Debate on October 7, 1858. For the centennial of that event, this ribbon was issued with a fine portrait likeness of Abraham Lincoln based on O-27 *(a)*. Although attractive and popular, O-27 can be viewed as an historically inaccurate photo since it was a post-nomination portrait taken in June 1860, nearly two years after the senatorial debate of 1858. The same anachronistic Lincoln image was modeled by sculptor Avard Fairbanks for a plaque dedicated on October 6, 1958, on Galesburg's Main Street *(b)*.

LINCOLN

The O-92 Lincoln image is *the* iconic Lincoln image. Although engraved by Charles Burt in 1869 for use on $100 Legal Tender notes and then used in 1870 on $500 Gold Certificates, the image was widely spread throughout the culture by smaller representations on $1 Silver Certificates and postage stamps beginning in the 1890s. This Burt iconic O-92 was then claimed for the $5 note after passage of the Federal Reserve Act in 1913, and spread to all classes of currency in 1929 until it became the normative Lincoln image in our culture and by extension around the world. Charles Burt's adaptation of Anthony Berger's February 9, 1864, O-92 photograph, which Robert Lincoln preferred, is the Abraham Lincoln that Americans know, the universal Lincoln icon, and the one that influenced all other media in spreading Lincoln's story and legacy.

Chapter 4

Lincoln the Icon
1959 – 2009

No U.S. presidential portrait in history has been more widely duplicated and dispersed than Anthony Berger's February 9, 1864, photograph known as O-92, except for the Washington portrait on the dollar bill and the Lincoln profile on the cent. These money portraits have inculcated the faces and features of the Father of our Country and the Nation's Savior on generations of Americans. Yankee dollars have spread these likenesses around the globe.

The O-92 likeness has been the most enduring portrait on our nation's money. It was created originally in 1869 to replace the from-life image of the yet-living Abraham Lincoln, which had been introduced on the $10 bill as a patriotic motif when the government turned to the printing press in 1861 to finance the Civil War. The new pose selected as a model for the currency image was more formal, more presidential, if you will, than the flesh-and-blood image Charles Burt had engraved eight years earlier of the newly bewhiskered president-elect. The O-92 portrait was Robert Todd Lincoln's favorite photograph of his father, although it is unknown if he was consulted in its selection for use on U.S. paper money. Burt engraved an austere likeness of the O-92 portrait that immediately appeared on new and successive series of $100 greenbacks from 1869 until circa 1913, when the feds reorganized the nation's finances with the passage of the Federal Reserve Act. By then 1,200,000 of these Lincoln C-notes had been printed and placed into circulation over a period of 45 years. During this time Burt's engraving was also adopted for Series of 1870/1875 $500 Gold Certificates, and a small engraving on the same model was employed on the Series of 1871 internal-revenue beer stamps.

The government adopted similar poses frequently on U.S. postage stamps during the succeeding decades. A likeness after a painting also based on the O-92 photograph was adopted for the four-cent postage stamps in 1890/1894. In 1903 the O-92 was once again the model for the five-cent stamp, and again in 1923 for the three-cent first-class definitive stamp. In 1920 an O-92 portrait was adopted for $5 war-savings stamps to encourage thrift and patriotism. In 1942, yet another Lincoln portrait based on O-92 appeared on a commemorative stamp issued in support of Nationalist Chinese resistance against the Chinese Communists. And still another Lincoln stamp on the O-92 model, a 25-cent airmail stamp, appeared in 1960.

While this was occurring, however, the Treasury took an even more significant

Fig. 4.1. Mint engraver Frank Gasparro worked diligently to ensure that Daniel Chester French's Lincoln statue within Henry Bacon's temple was discernible on the back of the Lincoln Memorial cent design introduced for the Lincoln sesquicentennial in 1959.

step. It adopted a similar, albeit smaller, O-92 portrait by G.F.C. "Fred" Smillie and put it on the $1 Silver Certificate. Whereas Lincoln was the dominant theme of the $100 greenbacks, this new smaller presidential portrait was paired with a similar small portrait of General U.S. Grant. Today's history portrays a sullied Grant, but his popularity with Union veterans in the decades following the Civil War was enormous, and he had been placed on U.S. currency already almost from the moment of his death in 1885. Both preservers of the Union, Lincoln and Grant, were, however, subordinated on the ubiquitous note to a symbol of national Union, the federal eagle surmounting the U.S. Capitol with its statue of Freedom atop its dome.

The adoption of this new Lincoln-Grant-Union theme for the mass-circulation dollar bill during the Republican administration of Civil War–vet president William McKinley broadcast a nationalistic and militarist message from the nation's ship of state in the wake of the U.S. victory over Spain. In its new incarnation the same Berger Lincoln portrait now became the Lincoln of the common man. From 1899 to 1923, an incredible 3,744,000,000 of these bills circulated. No longer a huge Lincoln portrait for the banker and investor, this new device reached down into all strata of society and mercantile activity. Even the street urchin could aspire to possess such a bill.

With the coming of the nation's 20th-century central bank, created by the Federal Reserve Act of 1913, also came a new currency—Federal Reserve Bank Notes, which were obligations of the respective issuing banks, and Federal Reserve Notes, which were the obligation of the system as a whole. A new series of standardized designs was adopted, and the Burt O-92 engraving was reprised for the $5 bill, the lowest denomination of these notes originally issued. For the next decade, large-size notes of both $1 and $5 denomination were co-circulated with diminishing numbers of $100 notes, all bearing this singular image of Abraham Lincoln.

Fig. 4.2. Unlike the 1909 Abraham Lincoln centennial, the 1959 sesquicentennial was a national celebration. The Library of Congress exhibition catalog *(a)* sported a beardless Lincoln image reflecting the scope of its exhibition, but the official U.S. Lincoln Sesquicentennial Commission literature *(b–d)* all featured the iconic O-92 Charles Burt Lincoln $5 bill–style portrait.

Fig. 4.3. The 1959 Lincoln Trail Boy Scout badge *(a)* and circa-1959 Washington, D.C., bronze lucky penny *(b)* have cent-like Lincoln profiles, while the small Lincoln birthplace sesquicentennial bronze medal *(c)* offers up a sculpted likeness of the $5 bill portrait.

Civil War Times

40 Cents

Vol. I, No. 1 · ...A Magazine Devoted to America's Most Exciting Period · Gettysburg, Pa., April, 1959

Lincoln and 'The Rising of a Great Wind'

From the 'Wigwam' To the White House

By BURKE DAVIS

THE VERY SMELL of war was in the air this spring of 1860, but no one seemed to care. The talk was so old. It had been in the mouth of John Calhoun, long ago, and the country had tired of it. It had been the rage somewhere back in lost memory, when old Andy Jackson had whipped South Carolina to her knees. It seemed a false echo of those times now, with Stephen Douglas, The Little Giant, roaring like an old-time Democrat.

In churches of the North protest meetings over the end of John Brown continued. The name of Harpers Ferry, a peaceful stop on the hilly banks of the Potomac, had an ominous sound. People were reading Mrs. Stowe, and companies played Uncle Tom's Cabin to huge audiences.

To the south, churches were busy, too, for in their cellars, and in armories, small companies of fashionably dressed gentlemen soldiers were at drill. In the country, plantation boys hitched horses to rails, firing pistols near the animals to train them for war.

God alone knew what the divided Democrats would do. It was scarcely better in Chicago, where the Republicans gathered for their second campaign.

ONE WHO WATCHED in Chicago was Murat Halstead, 31, of the Cincinnati Commercial, on May 15 unaware that he was watching the rise of a new American legend:

"... Chicago is attending to this Convention in magnificent style. ... The great feature is the Wigwam erected within the past month, expressly for the use of the Convention, by the Republicans of Chicago, at a cost of seven thousand dollars. It is a small edition of the New York Crystal Palace, built of boards, and will hold ten thousand. ...

"This is the morning of the first day of the Convention ... the hotelkeepers say there are more people here now than during the National Fair last year, and then it was estimated that thirty thousand strangers were in the city. ...

"... The amount of idle talking that is done is amazing. ... There are a thousand rumors afloat. ... There are now at least a thousand men packed together in the halls ... rushing each other's ribs, tramping each other's toes, and titillating each other with the gossip of the day; and the probability is, not one is possessed of a single political fact not known to the whole which is of the slightest consequence to any human being.

"The current of the universal twaddle this morning is that 'Old Abe' will be the nominee. ...

IT WAS the third day of the convention before nominations came forth.

Full of confidence on that Friday morning, about a thousand marched from their headquarters, as usual behind a magnificent band. Protracting their parade too long, some thousand men weren't able to jam into the Wigwam and were forced to wait outside with thousands of others.

Inside, nominations and seconds were made. Halstead reported:

LINCOLN'S HOME IN SPRINGFIELD—This artist's conception shows Lincoln returning from his debate with Douglas in 1858. Lincoln's beard? That, too, is the artist's conception. (Courtesy National Archives)

"The only names that produced 'tremendous applause' were those of Seward and Lincoln. Everybody felt that the fight was a higher note ... nothing was between them, and yelled accordingly.

"THE EFFECT was startling. Hundreds of persons stooped their ears in pain ... No Comanches, no panthers ever struck a higher note ... nothing was to be seen below but thousands of hats—a black, mighty swarm of hats—flying with the velocity of hornets over a mass of human heads, most of the mouths of which were open. ...

"Now the Lincoln men had to try it again, and as Mr. Delano, of Ohio, on behalf of a portion of the delegation of that state, seconded the nomination of Lincoln, the uproar was beyond description. Imagine all the hogs ever slaughtered in Cincinnati giving their death squeals together, a score of big steam whistles going, and you conceive something of the same nature ... the Lincoln boys were clearly ahead, and feeling their victory, as there was a lull in the storm, took deep breaths all around, and gave a concentrated shriek that

was positively awful, and accompanied it with stamping that made every plank and pillar in the building quiver. ...

"The New York, Michigan and Wisconsin delegations sat together, and were in this tempest very quiet. Many of their faces whitened as the Lincoln yawp swelled into a wild hosanna of victory. ..."

THE FIRST VOTE was announced, with 233 votes needed for nomination:

William H. Seward, New York, 173½. Abraham Lincoln, Illinois, 102. Edward Bates, Missouri, 48. Simon Cameron, Pennsylvania, 50½.

John McLean, Ohio, 12. Salmon P. Chase, Ohio, 49.

There were six others, with a faint scattering of votes. The second balloting began, and ended in buzzing excitement, with Lincoln gaining 79 votes; Seward, 184½; Lincoln, 181. Halstead saw history made in the third roll call:

"It was whispered about—'Lincoln's the coming man'—will be nominated this ballot.' When the roll of states and territories had been called, I had ceased to give attention to any votes but those cast for Lincoln, and had his vote added up as it was given. ... I saw under my pencil as the Lincoln column was completed, the figure 231½—one vote and a half to give him the nomination. In a moment the fact was whispered about. A hundred pencils had told the same story. The news went over the house wonderfully ... there is nothing that politicians like better than a crisis. I looked up to see who would be the man to give the decisive vote. ...

"IN ABOUT ten ticks of a watch, Cartter, of Ohio, was up. ... Every eye was on Cartter, and everybody who understands the matter at all knew what he was about to do.

"He is a large man with rather (Continued on Next Page)

Lincoln in 1860. (Courtesy National Archives)

The Author

BURKE DAVIS'S stature as writer of highly readable history grows with each of his books, the most recent of which—"To Appomattox"—is reviewed on Page 7 of this issue of Civil War Times.

A North Carolinian, Davis attended Duke University, Guilford College and graduated from the University of North Carolina. For 10 years after graduation, he worked for the Charlotte (N. C.) News as sports editor, special feature writer and associate editor. In 1947 he joined the staff of the Baltimore Sun. In 1951 he returned to North Carolina to work for the highly respected Greensboro Daily News.

Davis divides his time between special assignments for The Daily News and his books. Married and the father of two children, he lives in a colonial period house on the edge of the Guilford Courthouse battlefield.

He has written three novels, three successful Civil War biographies and "To Appomattox," the story of the last nine days of the Army of Northern Virginia. His "Jeb Stuart" won the Fletcher Pratt Award for the best book on the Civil War in 1957.

Next month's Civil War Times will carry a companion article to this one by Burke Davis. In it, Davis will relate the selection and nomination of Jefferson Davis as President of the Confederacy.

OTHER PAGES

SANDBURG'S Tribute to Lincoln .... Page 5
BALLOON Warfare, Page 9
BOOK Review Section, Pages 6, 7
STONEWALL and the Seminoles ... Back Page

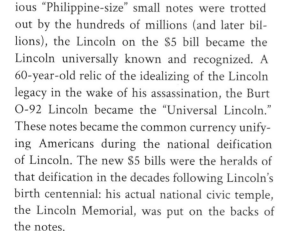

By the time the Treasury switched to a new small-size currency in the 1920s, with its standardized designs across all classes of currency—i.e., United States Notes (red seals), National Currency (brown seals), Silver Certificates (blue seals), and Federal Reserve Notes (green seals)—there was only one appropriate image of Lincoln to emblazon $5 notes of all types. Once again the Burt O-92 image, which all people everywhere were thoroughly familiar with, was employed.

Beginning in 1928 and 1929, when these various "Philippine-size" small notes were trotted out by the hundreds of millions (and later billions), the Lincoln on the $5 bill became the Lincoln universally known and recognized. A 60-year-old relic of the idealizing of the Lincoln legacy in the wake of his assassination, the Burt O-92 Lincoln became the "Universal Lincoln." These notes became the common currency unifying Americans during the national deification of Lincoln. The new $5 bills were the heralds of that deification in the decades following Lincoln's birth centennial: his actual national civic temple, the Lincoln Memorial, was put on the backs of the notes.

Fig. 4.4. The semi-monthly *Civil War Times* debuted April 1, 1959. It switched to a magazine format for its 11th issue, in April 1960. Two years later, in April 1962, the publication became *Civil War Times Illustrated*, featuring full-color covers, and reset its odometer to volume 1, issue 1, once again. In October 2002 (volume 41, issue 5), the publication reverted to its original name. Naturally, Abraham Lincoln has been featured in many issues.

Lincoln's image became omnipresent in the hands of his people, not just confined to faraway national memorials and hallowed places of national recollection. The O-92 Lincoln became the most prevalent image throughout the culture, not just on money. It was copied in schoolbooks and placed at the front of schoolrooms in all parts of the nation. When students pledged to the flag at the beginning of school each day, the Lincoln and Washington money images were enshrined there at the front of the room with Old Glory too. This image came to dominate collective consciousness.

Well before the Lincoln sesquicentennial in 1959 it had become not just universal but iconic. For most of the next 50 years this icon would become pervasive. The image represented in people's minds not only money, but all the positive virtues associated with the Lincoln icon: honesty, personal progress, value, patriotism, and the rest. The O-92 money image dominated advertising. Merchandisers of all kinds emblazoned it on projects and products, of all kinds, that they wished to be associated with Americans' love of Abraham Lincoln.

1959 FEBRUARY 12. West Berlin mayor Willy Brandt calls for the reunification of Berlin, and of Germany, at the Abraham Lincoln sesquicentennial celebrations in Lincoln's hometown of Springfield, Illinois. Said Brandt: "The German people acknowledged Lincoln's dictum that it was the duty of the people never to entrust to any hands but their own the preservation of their liberties."

1959 MARCH 24. The State of Indiana approves a building permit to construct a museum building at the state's Nancy Hanks Lincoln–Lincoln Boyhood Memorial at Lincoln City, Indiana. The State Board of Education approved a plan to collect $1 bills from the state's nearly one million schoolchildren to fund the renovation. The museum would not be built, however, because Indiana's new U.S. senator, Vance Hartke, pressured for a national memorial instead. This overtook state plans to upgrade the state memorial. Democrat Hartke complained that "the Indiana monument is not an adequate tribute to the Great Emancipator." Accordingly, on February 12, 1959, he introduced S 1024, requiring the secretary of the Interior to report to Congress the feasibility of a national monument there.

1959 APRIL 22. Indiana U.S. senator Vance Hartke's bill to determine whether the Lincoln State Park and the Nancy Hanks Lincoln

Fig. 4.5. A GOP pinback from the sesquicentennial urges a re-dedication to the ideals of the Republican Party.

JOIN IN TRIBUTE TO LINCOLN 1809 1959 and RE-DEDICATION TO THE IDEALS OF THE REPUBLICAN PARTY

Fig. 4.6. Spanish-language publications featuring Old Abe during the Lincoln sesquicentennial included *Comentario (a)* and *Biografias Selectas Presenta Lincoln (b)*. Each had a highly visible Lincoln likeness on its cover.

COMENTARIO
FEBRERO 1959 – N.º 44

EDAR
Biografias Selectas
Presenta "LINCOLN" No.51
Un episodio completo en cada número
$1.00

State Memorial were nationally significant and suitable for inclusion in the U.S. National Park System becomes law. A study subsequently undertaken by the National Park Service would determine "there were already more units in the National Park System associated with Abraham Lincoln than with any other individual," and would recommend neither for nor against the incorporation of the Indiana sites under consideration.

1959 May 12. Haiti issues four diamond-shaped stamps to commemorate the sesquicentennial of Abraham Lincoln's birth. They featured four different portraits as well as Lincoln monuments and his boyhood log cabin.

1959 July 1. San Marino honors the 150th anniversary of Abraham Lincoln's birth with an issue of portrait stamps.

Fig. 4.7. Countries on five continents celebrated the Lincoln sesquicentennial philatelically along with U.S. citizens. Shown is a first-day cover from San Marino, July 1, 1959, with four of the country's five Lincoln stamps (Scott 433–436) *(a)*; one of the three stamps from Colombia (Scott C376) *(b)*; one of the 11 Nicaraguan stamps for the sesquicentennial issued the following January 20, 1960 *(c)*; the souvenir sheet of four from Haiti (Scott C144a) *(d)*; one of the dozen stamps from Honduras with red overprint "Oficial" (Scott CO101) *(e)*; the souvenir sheet from Ghana (Scott 41a) *(f)*; and a first-day cover, December 25, 1959, of the two Taiwanese stamps (Scott 1248 and 1249) showing Lincoln and Sun Yat-sen *(g)*.

1959 July 4. *Lincoln the Friendly Neighbor*, by sculptor Avard Fairbanks, is dedicated at the Lincoln Federal Savings and Loan Association, Berwyn, Illinois. The sculptor depicted Abraham Lincoln guiding a boy and a girl to a hopeful future. Senator Paul H. Douglas spoke. On the same day a very large white-marble bust by Fairbanks was also dedicated in the bank's lobby. After the bank changed names in 1989, the statue was no longer considered appropriate, and it was given to a new Lincoln Middle School in Berwyn; the bust was sold to a private party. This statue would be rededicated at the school in 1997; a picture of it serves as an icon on the school's Facebook page.

1959. The Lincoln Highway summit memorial is erected, featuring sculptor Robert Russin's 13-foot-high bronze figure of Abraham Lincoln's head on a high granite base. The memorial was about 10 miles east of Laramie, at the highest point of the old Lincoln Highway. It took Russin nearly a year to create the enormous, hollow head, and it required ten tons of clay. Russin, a former art professor at the University of Wyoming, designed it as 30 pieces to be bolted together. The parts were cast in Mexico City. The original dedication in 1959 was at the summit of Sherman Hill, near its present location. A decade later, when Interstate US-80 was opened in southeastern Wyoming, the memorial was removed to a rest area where a visitor center was constructed.

Beneath the memorial is a plaque to Henry Joy, head of the Packard Car Company, who was the first president of the Lincoln Highway Association.

1959 December. Barely qualifying as being published for the Lincoln sesquicentennial, a supplementary listing of Lincoln exonumia is published in *The Numismatist*'s "Abraham Lincoln Number." Four specialists (Nate Eglit, George and Melvin Fuld, and Paul Ginther) increased the number of cataloged Lincoln exonumia pieces to 1,210, by supplying descriptions of another 163 additional pieces. An additional article in the issue, by Cleveland paper-money collector Nathan Gold, "Lincoln and Civil War Finance," called Old Abe "the Father of United States Paper Money." According to Gold, "It is altogether fitting and proper that Lincoln's portrait has been used on United States paper money since its inception."

1960 February 1. Avard Tennyson Fairbanks's heroic-size white marble busts *Lincoln the Youth*, *Lincoln the Pioneer*, *Lincoln the Lawyer*, and *Lincoln the President* are unveiled at Ford's Theatre. Fairbanks was joined by Senator John S. Cooper (of the Lincoln Sesquicentennial Commission) and Lincoln biographer, poet Carl Sandburg. The busts illustrate the "Four Ages of Abraham Lincoln," commissioned by Broadcast Music Inc. to accompany an award-winning series of public-service announcements broadcast nationwide for the observance of the Lincoln sesquicentennial in 1959. The busts would be given to the government of the United States by the company at a Lincoln Day dinner on February 11. *Lincoln the Lawyer* was placed in the U.S. Supreme Court Building. The other three busts were placed in the Ford Theatre Museum. A full-size copy of *Lincoln the Frontiersman* was placed in the hall of the International Copyright Bureau in Geneva, Switzerland.

Fig. 4.8. Sculptor Ralph J. Menconi sculpted an excellent set of small medals of U.S. presidents for Presidential Art Medals, Vandalia, Ohio. Both silver and bronze editions were issued. Menconi based his Lincoln portrait on the iconic $5 bill model. The firm specialized in series medals. Other series commemorated the states of the Union, signers of the Declaration of Independence, U.S. astronauts, and similar historical subjects.

A CATALOG OF THE

Alfred Whital Stern

Collection of

LINCOLNIANA

in the Library of Congress

Washington : 1960

Fig. 4.9. The *Treasure Chest* issue of February 11, 1960, employed both the Abraham Lincoln and George Washington paper-money likenesses on its cover celebrating their birth dates.

Fig. 4.10. In 1960 the Library of Congress published a catalog of the Alfred Whital Stern Lincolniana collection, which had been deposited in the Library in 1951 and formally donated two years later.

Fairbanks, an educator as well as a famed sculptor, also created monumental Lincoln sculptures, including *Lincoln the Frontiersman* (Ewa, Hawaii), the transitional *Lincoln* (Lincoln's New Salem), *The Chicago Lincoln: A Chance to Portray Liberty* (Chicago), and *Lincoln the Friendly Neighbor* (Berwyn, Illinois).

1960 FEBRUARY 21. Ford Rainey plays Abe Lincoln in the *NBC Sunday Showcase* episode of "Our American Heritage: Shadow of a Soldier," about the reminiscences of a dying Ulysses S. Grant, played by James Whitmore. Rainey would perform as Lincoln in four other shows.

1960. William Edelen popularizes misinformation about Abraham Lincoln's convictions in his book *Toward the Mystery*, published by Joslyn Morris, Publishers. According to Edelen, Lincoln said: "I have never united myself to any church because I could not give assent to the long complicated statements of Christian doctrine and dogma which characterize their articles of belief and confession of faith. When any church will require only the Great Commandment (the Jewish Shema) for belief, then I will join that church."

Edelen's book would be reprinted by the publisher in 1983. It has been picked up by non-theistic and anti-Christian groups as something of a mantra in years since. However, an exhaustive search of Lincoln's complete works has led to the conclusion that Lincoln never uttered those words attributed to him!

1960 APRIL 22. The U.S. Post Office introduces a new black-and-maroon Giori press Lincoln portrait 25-cent air-mail stamp (Scott C59), with a modern innovative design by graphic artist, type designer, and advertising art director Herb Lubalin. Pre–World War II Cooper Union graduate Lubalin pioneered inventive scaling and mixing of illustrations and phototype faces, and founded *U&lc*, an influential typographic journal (its title representing the shorthand editing mark for "uppercase and lowercase" typography). His accepted design has a stylized O-92 Lincoln portrait of the kind then current on the $5 bills, balanced by oversize type, unlike any other ever seen on a U.S. postage stamp. Lubalin's photographic models show how he played around with many type faces and sizes and renditions of the Lincoln portrait before he achieved his aesthetic—but *every* Lincoln portrait was modeled on the $5 bill image then entrenched in public consciousness.

Fig. 4.11. Innovative advertising art director Herb Lubalin experimented with various treatments of the iconic Lincoln O-92 image and typography *(a–e)* in creating the new black-and-maroon Giori press 25-cent airmail stamp *(f)* in 1960.

1960 OCTOBER 22. Moral Re-Armament releases the feature film *The Crowning Experience*, loosely based on the life of Mary McLeod Bethune, who started a school for underprivileged African American youth. The film draws inspiration from the Great Emancipator.

1960 DECEMBER 19. The Lincoln home and the Lincoln tomb in Springfield, Illinois, are designated national historic landmarks.

1961 JANUARY 11. Indiana congressman Winfield K. Denton introduces legislation, HR 2470, proposing establishment of a U.S. National Park Service unit at Lincoln City, Indiana, a proposal backed by local business interests as a boost to tourism. The bill proposed transfer of the Nancy Hanks Lincoln Memorial to the National Park Service. Despite some opposition to the plan, the state legislature would pass a joint resolution of March 6, 1961, HCR 11, supporting the proposal. On March 8, the assembly passed H 85, authorizing conveyance of 200 acres of the Nancy Hanks Lincoln Memorial to the feds, but not Lincoln State Park.

1961 MARCH 11. USS *Abraham Lincoln* (SSBN 602), a nuclear-powered, ballistic-missile–equipped submarine, is commissioned. Its keel had been laid November 1, 1958, and it had launched May 14, 1960. The sub was about 382 feet long, with a crew of 140 officers and men. It was equipped with 16 Polaris missile tubes and six torpedo tubes. Service would include a 65-day patrol during the Cuban missile crisis of October 1962.

The sub would be decommissioned at Puget Sound Naval Shipyard, Bremerton, Washington, on February 28, 1981.

1961. Sculptor Robert M. Gage's *Lincoln, the Student*, depicting a seated bronze Abraham Lincoln with a book propped open on his lap, is dedicated at Lincoln College, Lincoln, Illinois. The heroic-size bronze figure sits on a granite base outside the college's Lincoln Heritage Museum.

1961 NOVEMBER 19. A life-size bronze group called *Lincoln and Tad* is erected on the west grounds of the Iowa State Capitol in Des

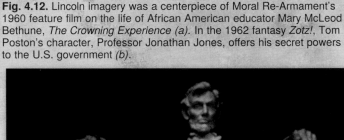

Fig. 4.12. Lincoln imagery was a centerpiece of Moral Re-Armament's 1960 feature film on the life of African American educator Mary McLeod Bethune, *The Crowning Experience (a)*. In the 1962 fantasy *Zotz!*, Tom Poston's character, Professor Jonathan Jones, offers his secret powers to the U.S. government *(b)*.

Fig. 4.13. From the height of the Cold War, this cover postmarked May 14, 1960, honors the launching of the *Abraham Lincoln* submarine, SSB(N)602, at the Portsmouth Naval Shipyard at Kittery, Maine, opposite Portsmouth, New Hampshire. The *Lincoln* cruised at 25 knots submerged, carried torpedoes, and held 16 Polaris missiles. It was active during the Cuban missile crisis of 1962.

Moines. This is sculptor Fred Torrey's and his wife Mabel's three-dimensional representation of the famous photograph of Abraham Lincoln and his young son glancing at a photographer's sample album. The installation marked the centennial of Lincoln's Gettysburg Address. Torrey did the seated Abraham figure, and Mabel the attentive, standing child. Iowa schoolchildren contributed to a penny drive to defray part of the statue's cost.

1962 FEBRUARY 10. Norman Rockwell's painting *Lincoln for the Defense* appears on the cover of the *Saturday Evening Post.*

1962 FEBRUARY 19. President John F. Kennedy signs the act authorizing the Lincoln Boyhood National Memorial, Indiana's first unit under the National Park Service. The bill passed was Congressman Winfield K. Denton's. A dedication ceremony would be held on July 10, 1962, during which Indiana governor Matthew Welsh presented a faux land deed to the U.S. secretary of the Interior. Also in attendance were Senator Vance Hartke and Congressman Denton, who had sponsored separate bills to facilitate transfer of the site into federal hands. "The program for the dedication ceremony listed poet Carl Sandburg as Honorary Chairman of the dedication committee, but there is no evidence of Sandburg's involvement in the planning, nor did he attend the ceremony," according to a National Park Service historian. On June 11, 1963, the State of Indiana actually deeded 114.5 acres to the United States of America. Secretary of the Interior Stuart Udall published a "Notice of Establishment" in the *Federal Register* of August 15, 1963, completing the formal establishment of the national memorial. On September 17, 1964, the park debuted an on-site film program, *The Establishment of Lincoln Boyhood National Memorial.* (See figure 4.16.)

Fig. 4.14. Guatemala got in late on the Lincoln sesquicentennial commemorative-stamp bonanza. In October 1960 the Central American nation issued a set of three stamps designed by Josefina v. de Polantinos. A Guatemalan stamp dealer put the five-cent, blue-violet airmail issue (Scott C248) to good use on his advertising cards mailed to collectors back in the States.

Fig. 4.15. In 1961 two seated statues of Abraham Lincoln were erected at Lincoln College, Lincoln, Illinois, and the Iowa State Capitol, Des Moines. In Robert Merrell Gage's *Lincoln, the Student* a young beardless Lincoln reads a book resting in his lap, on a plain marble perch *(a)*. In Iowa sculptor Fred Torrey shows an older, bearded Lincoln with an album propped on his lap; with the addition of Torrey's wife Mabel's companion sculpture of young Tad, we see a three-dimensional depiction of Anthony Berger's famous O-93 photograph *(b)*.

1962. Heritage Records releases the National Republican Party's *Mr. Lincoln's Party Today* LP record, with a large view of the Daniel Chester French Lincoln Memorial statue dominating its cover. On the LP, Dwight D. Eisenhower, Richard M. Nixon, Barry M. Goldwater, and Nelson A. Rockefeller issue a "declaration of Republican Belief."

1962 SEPTEMBER 5. President John F. Kennedy signs PL 87-643, eliminating tin from the Lincoln cent's composition and substituting zinc.

1962 OCTOBER 1. President John F. Kennedy, who would be inextricably linked to Abraham Lincoln by tragedy two years later, visits Lincoln's tomb in Springfield, Illinois, during the off-year congressional campaign.

1962 NOVEMBER 19. Lincoln four-cent red-violet postal cards (Scott UX48) are introduced at Springfield, Illinois.

1962 NOVEMBER 21. Currency-size advertising handbills for Paramount Pictures' Jerry Lewis comedy *It's Only Money* depict the star with a Lincolnesque beard in a Lincoln-like pose on an imitation $5 bill titled an "Enjoyment Certificate."

1960s. During the Civil War centennial and the rise of coin collecting (following publicity over the 1960 Small Date cents and the introduction of a weekly coin tabloid, *Coin World*), a great many collector mulings and restrikes are issued. In one instance, Paquet's small Lincoln profile die (previously used to make medalets listed as Julian PR-35–39) was used in conjunction with an eagle die to overstrike various gold coins, such as the 1861 gold half eagle ($5 coin) that would appear in the Stack's December 9, 2009, auction. It is speculated this item (see figure 2.31) may have been struck at this time.

Fig. 4.16. The Lincoln Boyhood National Memorial's logo celebrates the boy within the man. The Lincoln City, Indiana, park was designated a national historic landmark on December 19, 1960, and a national memorial on February 19, 1962. It was added to the National Register of Historic Places on October 15, 1966.

Fig. 4.17. Elongated, or rolled, cents are ordinary coins passed through roller dies under pressure. The process has been put to a great many commemorative and advertising uses since these small medalets were introduced at the World's Columbian Exposition in 1893. A miniature engraved Lord's Prayer, such as on this 1962 Lincoln cent, is a favorite topic.

Fig. 4.18. Democrat John F. Kennedy's presidency came just after the Lincoln sesquicentennial and simultaneous to the celebration of the Civil War centennial, during which Lincoln consciousness remained high. Kennedy self-identified with the legacy of Lincoln a century earlier by frequently speaking from a position in front of the G.P.A. Healy portrait that Robert Lincoln had admired and copyrighted in 1908. The linking of Lincoln peeking over Kennedy's shoulder was a sight to which Americans were accustomed long before Kennedy's assassination further connected the martyred presidents.

1963. A 14-foot-high bronze statue of Abe Lincoln on horseback, titled *On the Circuit*, by Anna Hyatt Huntington, is dedicated on the approach to Lincoln's New Salem. The statue was a gift to the state by the sculptor and Carlton Smith of the National Arts Foundation. The statue is located just outside New Salem State Park on Route 97. Duplicate castings were placed in Lincoln City, Oregon; Syracuse, New York; and Salzburg, Austria.

1963 FEBRUARY 20. Raymond Massey once again plays Abe Lincoln, this time in John Ford's epic *How the West Was Won.* The film won three Oscars, and was nominated for five more including Best Picture. Stars included a who's who of Hollywood A-listers: James Stewart, Debbie Reynolds, John Wayne, Carol Baker, Henry Fonda, George Peppard, Gregory Peck, Karl Malden, Eli Wallach, Carolyn Jones, and Walter Brennan.

1963 APRIL 16. The governors of Kentucky, Indiana, and Illinois convene at Kentucky Dam Village to approve plans sponsored by the American Petroleum Institute for creating a Lincoln Heritage Trail through the three states to "bring history alive for the visitor," and to promote tourism and sales of gasoline.

1963 MAY 17. The Southern Christian Leadership Conference and local ministers hold a 24-hour prayer vigil, kneeling before the Lincoln Memorial statue, to mark the ninth anniversary of the U.S. Supreme Court's decision desegregating American public schools, *Brown v. Board of Education of Topeka.* (See figure 4.23.)

1963 MAY 27. The Columbia record label releases folk singer–songwriter Bob Dylan's second studio album, *The Freewheelin' Bob Dylan*, featuring "Blowin' in the Wind," perhaps his most famous song.

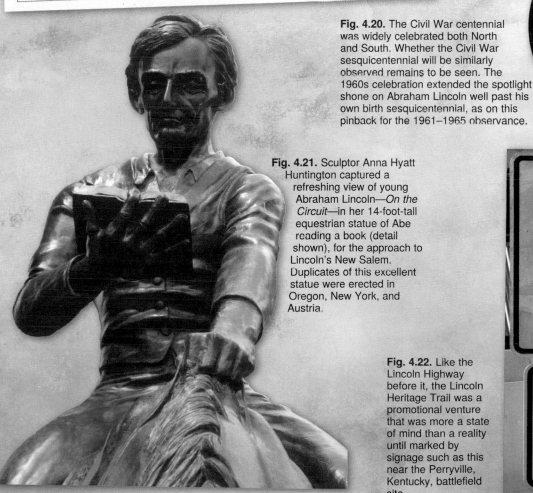

Fig. 4.19. For the 1962 motion-picture comedy *It's Only Money*, Paramount Studios distributed money-like Lincolnesque advertising handbills, called "Enjoyment Certificates," to promote the movie.

Fig. 4.20. The Civil War centennial was widely celebrated both North and South. Whether the Civil War sesquicentennial will be similarly observed remains to be seen. The 1960s celebration extended the spotlight shone on Abraham Lincoln well past his own birth sesquicentennial, as on this pinback for the 1961–1965 observance.

Fig. 4.21. Sculptor Anna Hyatt Huntington captured a refreshing view of young Abraham Lincoln—*On the Circuit*—in her 14-foot-tall equestrian statue of Abe reading a book (detail shown), for the approach to Lincoln's New Salem. Duplicates of this excellent statue were erected in Oregon, New York, and Austria.

Fig. 4.22. Like the Lincoln Highway before it, the Lincoln Heritage Trail was a promotional venture that was more a state of mind than a reality until marked by signage such as this near the Perryville, Kentucky, battlefield site.

Fig. 4.23. This is one of the most disturbing photos the present writer has ever seen. It was taken during a Civil Rights prayer vigil in 1963. Four ministers of the Gospel are kneeling within the secular temple to the Lincoln idol.

The album also includes a Side B cut, "Talkin' World War III Blues," a spontaneous anti-war "talkin' blues" number recorded April 24, 1963, at Columbia's Seventh Avenue studios in New York City. According to Dylan:

Half the people can be part right all of the time, an'
Some of the people can be all right part of the time,
But all the people can't be all right all of the time.
I think Abraham Lincoln said that.

Dylan's lines were a somewhat free paraphrase of the epigram often attributed to Abe Lincoln's September 2, 1858, speech at Clinton, Illinois: "You can fool all the people some of the time and some of the people all the time, but you cannot fool all the people all the time." This quote had been debunked by the editors of *The Collected Works of Abraham Lincoln* 10 years earlier. According to their exhaustive research: "In 1905 testimony was gathered by the *Chicago Tribune* and *Brooklyn Eagle* to prove that Lincoln used the epigram at Clinton. The testimony was conflicting and dubious in some particulars, but the epigram has remained a favorite in popular usage. Neither the report in the (Bloomington, Illinois) *Pantagraph* which provides the text of the Clinton speeches, nor any other contemporary Lincoln reference located by the present editors, makes any reference to the epigram."[1]

1963 CIRCA. Shortly after the promulgation of a Lincoln Heritage Trail marking a theoretical route connecting places important to Abraham Lincoln's life story, View-Master includes a three-reel "Lincoln Heritage Trail" set, complete with a booklet by celebrated newsman Lowell Thomas. These color 3D images, when viewed in the Sawyer firm's patented viewer, showed (to young and old alike) Lincoln's birth cabin, his home in Springfield, and other locations familiar to the Lincoln canon.

The viewing system was the brainchild of Oregonian William Gruber as a revival of the old stereoviews. It utilized Kodachrome film, which had recently been brought into widespread use. Gruber sold his idea to Harold Graves, president of Sawyer's Inc., a company that specialized in picture postcards. The system was introduced first at the 1939 New York World's Fair as an alternative to the card photograph.

1963 AUGUST 16. Pioneering African American art director Georg Olden's bold commemorative stamp marking the centennial of Lincoln's Emancipation Proclamation is released by the U.S. Post

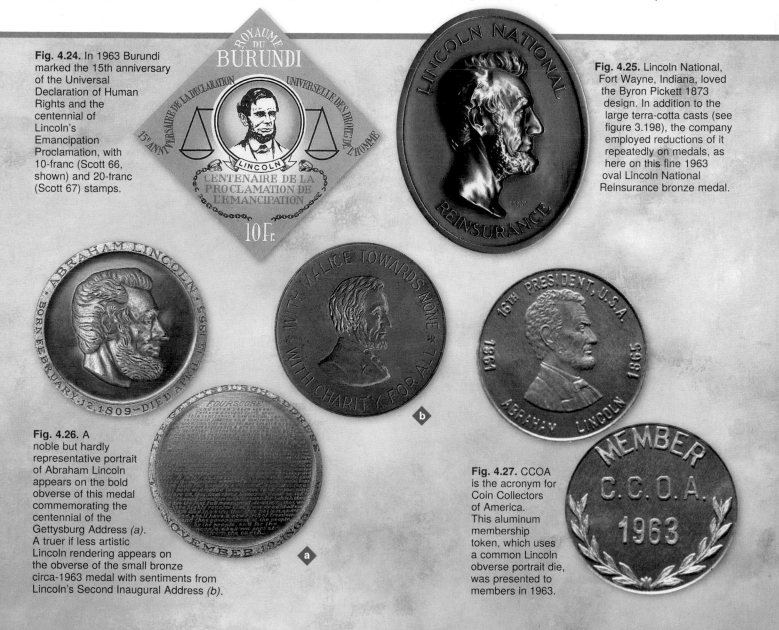

Fig. 4.24. In 1963 Burundi marked the 15th anniversary of the Universal Declaration of Human Rights and the centennial of Lincoln's Emancipation Proclamation, with 10-franc (Scott 66, shown) and 20-tranc (Scott 67) stamps.

Fig. 4.25. Lincoln National, Fort Wayne, Indiana, loved the Byron Pickett 1873 design. In addition to the large terra-cotta casts (see figure 3.198), the company employed reductions of it repeatedly on medals, as here on this fine 1963 oval Lincoln National Reinsurance bronze medal.

Fig. 4.26. A noble but hardly representative portrait of Abraham Lincoln appears on the bold obverse of this medal commemorating the centennial of the Gettysburg Address (a). A truer if less artistic Lincoln rendering appears on the obverse of the small bronze circa-1963 medal with sentiments from Lincoln's Second Inaugural Address (b).

Fig. 4.27. CCOA is the acronym for Coin Collectors of America. This aluminum membership token, which uses a common Lincoln obverse portrait die, was presented to members in 1963.

Office. Olden's design on the dark-blue, black, and red five-cent stamp features a simple but enormous broken chain link. Its introduction is featured as a landmark on *Communication Arts* magazine's "Design and Advertising Timeline" on the last half century.

Olden was the grandson of a slave, who achieved great success at the CBS television network and in commercial advertising. Reputedly, he was the first African American to design a U.S. postage stamp. At a White House ceremony in Olden's presence, President

Fig. 4.28. Sculptor David Kresz Rubins's rough-hewn, barefoot Hoosier youth was dedicated in Indianapolis in 1963, becoming a rallying point for civil-rights demonstrations thereafter.

John F. Kennedy praised the stamp as "a reminder of the extraordinary actions in the past as well as the business of the future."[2]

1963 AUGUST 28. Dr. Martin Luther King Jr. delivers his "I have a dream" speech from the steps of the Lincoln Memorial during his March on Washington for Jobs and Freedom rally. His remarks include the memorable refrain by which this event is most remembered. "I have a dream," Dr. King said in part, "that one day this nation will rise up and live out the true meaning of its creed: 'We hold these truths to be self-evident, that all men are created equal.'"

1963 SEPTEMBER 26. Sculptor David Kresz Rubin's rough-hewn bronze sculpture of Abraham Lincoln as a Hoosier youth, barefoot and clutching a book in this left hand, is dedicated at the east entrance of the State Office Building, Indianapolis. The sculpture had been copyrighted in 1962. It would become a rallying point during the civil-rights movement of the 1960s.

1964 FEBRUARY 5. The *Hallmark Hall of Fame* TV series episode "Abe Lincoln in Illinois" has Jason Robards as Lincoln.

1964 JANUARY. *Life* magazine announces the "Discovery of earliest known likeness of Abraham Lincoln," with photos by Francis Miller. The likeness shows a rather plain young man, with a wart and large ears, deep-set eyes, and a prominent nose.

1964. A bronze statue of a standing Abraham Lincoln is erected in Ciudad Juarez, Mexico, across the Rio Grande from El Paso, Texas.

1964. The Canton, New York, library displays medals, a bas relief, and several lithographs of 19th-century diesinker and medalist Salathiel Ellis, who moved to Canton in 1828 and opened up a "paintshop" on Main Street there. In the early 1840s Ellis removed to New York City, where he operated a commercial studio for more than 20 years. Ellis's commissions included designing medals for C.C. Wright, and several commissions for the U.S. Mint. The latter included the 1860 Japanese Embassy medal, and Indian Peace medals for Fillmore, Pierce, Buchanan, and Lincoln. "It was during this period when he became most renowned," a local historian observed.

Ellis and his brother James married two Willson sisters, Clarina and Melinda, of Potsdam, New York. The girls' younger cousin, Joseph Willson, became a protégé and then an associate of Salathiel Ellis's, in New York City.[3] It was Willson, of course, who engraved the reverse of the Buchanan Indian Peace medal, which was subsequently married to the Lincoln bust Ellis engraved for the Lincoln Indian Peace medal in 1862. Among its artistic representations, five children are seen playing a stick-and-ball game known as "one old cat," a contemporary of early baseball-type games.[4]

Fig. 4.31. The 1860 Lincoln-Hamlin jugate portrait medal (Dewitt/Sullivan AL 1860–31) was restruck for this attractive red-white-and-blue Lincoln inauguration centennial badge in 1961.

Fig. 4.29. From the 1940s to the 1960s, bread-label collecting was in vogue. This circa-1960s label commemorates Lincoln's Gettysburg Address.

Fig. 4.30. This 1963 Gettysburg Address Boy Scout badge has the same Abraham Lincoln profile portrait as the 1959 trail badge shown as figure 4.3a, but instead of an outsized cent on a pentagon plaque, the bust this time is appropriately on a suspension in the form of a scroll.

Fig. 4.32. After President John F. Kennedy was slain in Dallas's Dealey Plaza on November 22, 1963, the symbolic linking of the destinies of Kennedy and his presidential predecessors Lincoln, Garfield, and McKinley was made visible on this "Four Martyrs" pinback *(a)*. Other Kennedy-Lincoln mementoes included small medals such as the bronze piece pictured *(b)*, countermarked Lincoln-Kennedy cents, and similar mourning items. Both items shown have O-92 $5 bill–style Lincoln images.

Fig. 4.33. This heavy 10-1/2 by 6-1/4 by 7/8–inch Lincoln-Kennedy cast-iron plaque is believed to have been an architectural adornment. In recent years a plastic copy of the original plaque has been widely sold on the Internet. As readers can see, the author's original cast-iron piece has acquired a lovely, russet patina.

Fig. 4.34. Following the Kennedy assassination, on May 29, 1964, Honduras overprinted unsold quantities of its Lincoln birth sesquicentennial stamps with a commemorative inscription. Shown is the overprinted souvenir sheet (Scott C330a) of all six values. In the margin on the sheet the overprint also includes the Alliance for Progress emblem. Alliance for Progress was Kennedy's economic initiative to foster cooperation between North and South America.

Fig. 4.35. Togo issued a set of four stamps (Scott 454–456, C35) on October 5, 1963, to commemorate the centennial of the Emancipation Proclamation. Following John F. Kennedy's assassination, in February 1964 it overprinted the stamps with a memorial inscription (Scott 473–475, C41). As can be seen, for the souvenir sheet (Scott C41b) Togo also added a black border and a Kennedy profile, creating a very somber effect.

Fig. 4.36. Treasury Secretary C. Douglas Dillon approved this model for the Series of 1963 $5 Federal Reserve Note, bearing his and U.S. Treasurer Kathryn O'Hay Granahan's signatures.

Fig. 4.37. This tin pin with its Marshall-style Lincoln portrait was given away as a prize by the Dutch Fix en Fox weekly magazine *Historica*, circa 1959–1966. The colored shield is 19 by 19 mm. Other historical figures in the series included Rembrandt, Marie Curie, Alfred Nobel, and other international historical figures.

Fig. 4.38. Walt Disney brought Abraham Lincoln to life for the New York World's Fair in 1964, and the following year he announced plans to install the animatronic figure at his Anaheim theme park, Disneyland, as part of the park's 10th-anniversary celebration (a). Tickets (b, c) state: "So young people may have a better knowledge of the man who played such an important part in American history . . . Jiminy Cricket [and Walt Disney] invites you to be his guest to spend a few . . . 'Great Moments With Mr. Lincoln.'"

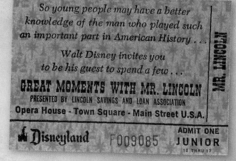

1964. A Lincoln National Life Insurance Company advertising campaign shows 1963 Lincoln cents, close up, in use in commercial transactions, with the message: "Whenever a Lincoln penny passes through your fingers, remember: You may not be able to save enough to (fill in a personal emergency, such as death, unemployment). BUT, chances are, you can afford a Lincoln Life policy which will give them protection and comfort when they need it most. Phone your Lincoln Life agent."

1965 FEBRUARY 12. President Lyndon B. Johnson places a wreath in the Lincoln Memorial at the foot of the statue there.

1965 FEBRUARY 12. Avard Fairbanks's bronze bust of *Abraham Lincoln of the Gettysburg Address* is dedicated at Lincoln Junior High School, Salt Lake City, Utah. When the school eventually closed, the bust was moved to Fairview Museum, Fairview, Utah.

1965 MARCH. Actor Robert Ryan portrays Abraham Lincoln during a re-enactment of Lincoln's second inaugural, at the U.S. Capitol.

1965. The U.S. Treasury launches its "You meet the nicest people when you buy U.S. Savings Bonds" campaign, with portraits of Abraham Lincoln and seven other individuals depicted on various denominations of bonds.

1965. Sculptor Augustus Saint-Gaudens's home and studios at Cornish, New Hampshire, become the first site administered by the National Park Service to commemorate a visual artist. To this day the park remains the only National Park unit in New Hampshire.

1965 APRIL. Magazine and commercial artist Roger Hane's bizarre, fanciful, surreal painting of Abraham Lincoln saluting at the American altar of progress and success appears on Avon Publishing's Bard Books' paperback re-release of Nathanael West's *A Cool Million* and *The Dream Life of Balso Snell*.

1965 MAY 22. "The Executioners," an episode of the Doctor Who TV series, features Robert Marsden as Abraham Lincoln.

Fig. 4.39. This 3-1/2–inch circular brass disc imprinted with the $5 bill–style portrait was sold as a souvenir at Illinois' Land of Lincoln pavilion during the 1964–1965 New York World's Fair.

Fig. 4.40. Avon's 1965 Bard imprint paperback cover for Nathanael West's two short novelettes *A Cool Million* and *The Dream Life of Balso Snell* featured Roger Hane's surreal portrayal of Abraham Lincoln saluting a memorial to American expansionism.

1965. Artist Norman Rockwell paints *Lincoln, the Railsplitter*, an 84.5 by 44.5–inch canvas depicting Abe Lincoln "transitioning from physical labor to mental pursuits." While clasping his axe, the youth's attention is directed toward a book in his other hand. Rockwell said he was inspired by Carl Sandburg's *Abraham Lincoln, the Prairie Years*. The work, which was commissioned for an advertisement by Lincoln Bank, Spokane, Washington, would be acquired by the Butler Institute of American Art, Youngstown, Ohio, in a November 2006 Christie's auction.

1965 MAY 25. Burglars plunder a currency exhibit (on loan from the Federal Reserve System) at Lincoln National Bank and Trust Co., Syracuse, New York. Among items taken were Confederate notes, gold and silver coins, and comparative pieces of genuine and counterfeit notes. Also included was a specimen set of notes from $1 to $10,000, each with all-zero serial numbers.

1965 JUNE 15. The W. Clement and Jessie Stone Foundation presents sculptor Carl Tolpo's heroic-size bronze bust of Abraham

Fig. 4.41. The centenary of Lincoln's death was visited by an outpouring of commemorative memorial stamps in distant lands. These included Ghana set of four (Scott 208–211) illustrated by a souvenir sheet (Scott 211a) *(a)*, Guatemala 7 centavos (Scott C371) of a set of five issued in 1967 *(b)*, Liberia 20 cents (Scott 424) of a set of three *(c)*, Antigua and Barbuda (Scott 760, 764) *(d)*, Upper Volta (Scott 144) *(e)*, Ras Al Khaima (Scott M24) of a set of three overprints *(f)*, Cameroun (Scott 53) *(g)*, Togo 1 franc (Scott 521) of a set of four *(h)*, India (Scott 400—not released until four years later) *(i)*, Chad (Scott C22) *(j)*, Venezuela (Scott C930) issued in 1966 *(k)*, Congo (Scott C35) *(l)*, Suriname (Scott 316) *(m)*, Cuba (Scott 952–955) *(n)*, Paraguay (Scott unlisted) *(o)*, Central African Republic (Scott C28) *(p)*, and Rwanda 30 centimes (Scott 94) of a set of six stamps *(q)*.

Lincoln to the Ford's Theatre Lincoln Museum. W. Clement Stone was co-founder of *Success Unlimited* magazine.

1965 NOVEMBER 19. The U.S. Post Office issues the first in a new "Prominent Americans" series of regular postage stamps at New York City, with a Lincoln profile against a backdrop of the wall of a log cabin. The stamp was designed by Bill Hyde of San Francisco, "based on a Mathew Brady photograph," according to the United States Post Office Department.[5] The stamp actually was based on an Anthony Berger photo (O-88) taken at Brady's Washington, D.C., gallery on February 9, 1864, similar to the pose depicted by Victor David Brenner on the U.S. cent from 1909 to present.

Fig. 4.42. The Post Office issued a very graphic, black four-cent Abraham Lincoln stamp (Scott 1282) based on the O-88/89 Anthony Berger photographic model, as part of the "Prominent Americans" series on the 102nd anniversary of the Gettysburg Address. This is the same view as seen on Victor David Brenner's cent, but by then the standard letter rate was five cents. George Washington appeared on the five-cent stamp in this series.

Fig. 4.43. During the Civil War centennial, Abraham Lincoln figured on a great many small medals. Shown is a Central States Numismatic Society reissue of J. Henri Ripstra's "tombstone" design *(a)*, struck in pure nickel in 1965. The Nevada Centennial medal struck in silver in 1964 *(b)* is an elaborate but fragile design with a Lincoln $5 bust. The 1961 Kentucky State Numismatic Society medal *(c)* honors both of the state's favorite sons, Lincoln and Jefferson Davis, and the state's prominence as the 15th state in the Union. Another O-92–style bust adorns the small bronze "Government of the People" medal *(d)* from the 1960s.

Fig. 4.44. In 1965 Topps Card Co. issued a 36-card set of Push-Pull cards. Three of the cards had Abraham Lincoln connections. On card 21, an O-92 money image of Lincoln turned into the portrait of John F. Kennedy when the holder moved the insert. On another (card 11, shown) the White House turned into Mount Rushmore. On the third, card 35, the Washington Monument became the Lincoln Memorial.

1966 FEBRUARY 13. Hal Holbrook appears on *The Ed Sullivan Show* in character as Abraham Lincoln.

1966 MARCH 3. *Jet* magazine features Jet-Ebony publisher John J. Johnson receiving the Lincoln Academy of Illinois award medal from Governor Otto Kerner. The academy was established by Kerner the previous year to pay tribute to the memory of Abraham Lincoln and honor distinguished Illinois citizens, who are thereby inducted as lau-reates of the Lincoln Academy. Others named in 1966 included football coach George Halas and architect Ludwig Mies van der Rohe.

1966 APRIL 15. A replica of Augustus Saint-Gaudens's 1887 *Standing Lincoln* statue is dedicated at Mexico City's Luis G. Urbina Park. President Lyndon B. Johnson made the presentation. The park, which has since been renamed Parque Lincoln, is in the Polanco neighborhood of Mexico City.

Fig. 4.45. More 1960s small medals with Abraham Lincoln include a tribute to Gutzon Borglum's pantheon in the Black Hills, with a quote from the sculptor on reverse *(a)*. Ralph J. Menconi's $5 bill–type bust, seen on figure 4.8, also was used on this small Presidential Art Medals uniface plaque for the American Numismatic Association's "Land of Lincoln" 1966 Chicago coin show *(b)*. The circa-1963 Lucky Penny for Gettysburg National Museum *(c)* has one of the most finely done portraits observed on such pieces.

Fig. 4.46. On April 15, 1966, the 101st anniversary of Abraham Lincoln's death, a full-size copy of Augustus Saint-Gaudens's *Standing Lincoln* statue was dedicated in Mexico City, Mexico.

1966 JUNE 2. The Visitor Center at the Lincoln Boyhood National Memorial, Lincoln City, Indiana, is opened four years after an act authorizing this national memorial was signed by President John F. Kennedy. The building, enclosing the original cloister which connected the Nancy Hanks Lincoln and Abraham Lincoln memorial halls, would be officially dedicated August 21, 1966.

1966 JULY 13. *Coin World* advises collectors holding fake multiple-struck 1964 Lincoln cents to turn them over to the U.S. Secret Service.

1966 AUGUST 21. After the National Park Service assumes control of the Nancy Hanks Lincoln Memorial, it adapts the existing structure to meet its needs by building an addition, reconfiguring the courtyard, and holding a new dedication ceremony. National Park Service Director George Hartzog Jr. spoke at the official dedication event.

1966 SEPTEMBER CIRCA. The Token and Medal Society reprints a hardback edition of Robert P. King's classic reference articles, "Lincoln in Numismatics," after securing approval from the American Numismatic Association, which owned the copyright. Although they reprinted the fruits of King's three (1924, 1927, 1933) articles, they either forgot, ignored, or considered irrelevant the 1959 "Lincoln Number" additions by TAMS members George Fuld and others.

The following year, TAMS would publish Edgar Heyl's index to King's Lincolniana, a much-needed guide to his bewildering warren of classifications and entries.

1966. A five-story fiberglass copy of the historic 19th-century Alaskan Abraham Lincoln totem pole is made from the Illinois State Museum's 1930s Civilian Conservation Corps copy of the original.

It presently sits outside the entrance to the museum in Springfield. An eight-foot-tall figure of Lincoln sits atop the pole.

1966 OCTOBER 15. The Lincoln home and the Lincoln tomb in Springfield, Illinois, are listed on the National Register of Historic Places.

1966 DECEMBER 2. Ford Rainey plays the role of Abraham Lincoln for a second time in "The Death Trap," an episode of the television series *The Time Tunnel*.

1967. Lincoln College of Professional Studies is founded in Monrovia, Liberia, West Africa, by Matthew Ogunremi, as the Lincoln Institute. It would be accredited in 1969, and currently offers associate of arts degrees in several business-related fields.

1967 FEBRUARY 12. For Abe Lincoln's 158th birthday, Fillmore Hall concert posters for the appearance of Mojo Men, Chocolate Watch Band, and Love have Abe decked out in a gray tweed suit and pink shoes, playing a pink electric guitar and wearing an oversize blue-purple-turquoise paisley stovepipe hat.

1967 APRIL 28. The Central States Numismatic Society issues a special medal set for its convention in Peoria, Illinois. The three-medal set employs J. Henri Ripstra's "tombstone" design struck in aluminum and sterling silver on diamond-shaped planchets, and a rectangular copper striking. Pieces struck in nickel have also been observed. For the show, rolled-cent enthusiast Lloyd Wagaman created a Lincoln profile design with Lincoln's dates and name surrounded by an intermittent border.

Fig. 4.47. In 1967–1969 various Middle Eastern states issued stamps honoring Abraham Lincoln's humanitarianism. The South Arabian state now known as Yemen linked John F. Kennedy with the Healy pose so admired by Kennedy and Robert Todd Lincoln (Minkus 187) *(a)*. Ras al Khaima's lovely 2 riyals (Minkus 155) *(b)* celebrated International Human Rights Year. Following the slaying of U.S. civil-rights leader Dr. Martin Luther King Jr., Manama struck off a stamp (Minkus 98) *(c)* pairing King with assassinated U.S. presidents Lincoln and Kennedy, part of a two-stamp issue. Yemen's attractive "World Racial Peace" 6-buqsha stamp (unlisted) *(d)* in 1969 was part of a two-stamp release.

1967 June circa. Edgar Heyl releases his comprehensive index to Robert King's "Lincoln in Numismatics."

1967 June. Carl W. Rinnius's 30-foot fiberglass statue of Abe Lincoln as a railsplitter is erected at the Illinois State Fair Grounds in Springfield.

1968 January 4. The U.S. Post Office introduces a new five-cent, emerald-on-white Abe Lincoln postal card (Scott UX55) at Hodgenville, Kentucky. The card was designed by Robert J. Jones.

1968 January 30. For the reopening of Ford's Theatre, *A Lincoln Evening* features a star-studded group of headliners, including

Fig. 4.48. Tall Abe gets taller. . . . In June 1967 a 30-foot fiberglass cartoon of Abraham Lincoln holding an axe, by Carl W. Rinnius, was erected at the Illinois State Fair Grounds in Springfield, Illinois.

Fig. 4.49. "PROTEST! PROTEST! PROTEST! PROTEST! Marchers at Lincoln Memorial" is how *Time* magazine described the turbulent antiwar demonstrations of the 1960s on its October 27, 1967, cover.

Fig. 4.50. Syracuse University acquired the Laura Gardin Fraser–James Earle Fraser studio collection, including the original full-size plaster model of Jimmy's 1931 Jersey City, New Jersey, seated figure of Lincoln. Before the university sold a good portion of the studio models to the National Cowboy Hall of Fame and Western Heritage Center in Oklahoma City, it had this full-size bronze casting made. It has become a center of campus activity.

Helen Hayes, Henry Fonda, Frederic March, Robert Ryan, Odetta, Harry Belafonte, Andy Williams, and Julie Harris.

1968 FEBRUARY 12. The original heroic-sized plaster that sculptor James Earle Fraser created for his seated figure of Abraham Lincoln at Jersey City, New Jersey, is debuted in its new quarters at the National Cowboy Hall of Fame and Western Heritage Center, Oklahoma City, Oklahoma. The museum acquired it from Syracuse University out of the Fraser estate (see the entry for December 13, 1968).

1968 JULY 15. Yippies (political hippies) apply for permits to camp in Lincoln Park and to rally at Soldier Field during the Democratic National Convention.

1968. A card in the *Laugh-In* card set makes funny with the ubiquitous presence of Abraham Lincoln. "Knock Knock Who's there? Abe Lincoln. Abe Lincoln Who?" Quickly the first party follows up with a pun off Lincoln's name (such as "Abe-C-D-E-F-G-H-I-J-K-L-M-N-O-P!"). *Laugh-In* was a highly rated television series at the time, featuring short funny quips and sight gags. Varieties of this quip festoon joke books.

This knock-knock joke was strikingly twisted in an episode of *M*A*S*H*, another large fan-favorite TV series. Hawkeye followed up quickly with another knock-knock and replied, "Thomas Jefferson. Was Abe Lincoln just here?" Opined humor writer Len Morse: "Hawkeye cracked himself up, but Trapper put his pillow over his head. It was a great scene of simple joy amid the horrors of war."[6]

1968 AUGUST 25. Yippies stage "Festival of Life" on Sunday in Lincoln Park Chicago, listening to MC-5 and local bands. On Monday, Black Panther Party chairman Bobby Seale spoke at a Lincoln Park rally, urging demonstrators to defend themselves from police attacks. A crowd of clergy and laymen carried a 12-foot cross, and when protesters refused to obey curfew and leave the park police cleared them out with tear gas and billy clubs.

1968 DECEMBER 13. With absolutely no fanfare at all, a truck and crane pull up in front of the Maxwell School of Syracuse University, and a nine-foot-tall, 2,700-pound replica of James Earle Fraser's 1930 seated *Mystic Lincoln* statue at Jersey City, New Jersey, is set onto a concrete pedestal in the building's courtyard, "while a few passersby stopped to gawk," according to a school spokesman. Today it is "one of the University's most photographed features and it is especially well-loved by citizens of Maxwell, who tend to think of it as their own," according to the same source.[7] Two years earlier the University had acquired the Fraser Studio collection, including the life-size plaster casting of the Lincoln statue that Fraser had completed CIRCA 1929 and from which the University's statue was

Fig. 4.51. Penn-Ohio Numismatic Association was one of the active regional coin collectors groups of the 1960s. The group's annual conventions left a rich medallic legacy including this wonderful Lincoln profile on the 1968 Penn-Ohio convention silver medal by M.R.

Fig. 4.52. The Lincoln Heritage Trail was a tri-state venture to promote tourism by mapping out the progress of Abraham Lincoln's life across the several states. This 1969-dated coin-relief medal was struck in silver (a) and bronze (b) by Medallic Art Co. in 1970. The medal reverse is signed by sculptor Trygve A. Rovelstad.

cast. A portion of these materials were subsequently sold to the National Cowboy Hall of Fame and Western Heritage Center, including the original Fraser full-size plaster. (See the entry for February 12, 1968.)

1969. Shortly after issuing its 1969 catalog, the U.S. Mint withdraws bronze restrikes of the Abraham Lincoln Indian Peace medal (Julian IP-38) from public sale. U.S. Mint brochures from 1969 and later do not list the Lincoln medal as available, according to medal expert Tony Lopez, who labels the Lincoln restrikes as "the most difficult to obtain" of the Indian Peace medal series. In *The Numismatist*, he continued, "The Mint's 1969 catalog lists the Lincoln Peace medal, so the brochure postdates it." Writing in the ANA monthly, he speculated, "The fact that the Lincoln medal apparently was the first Indian Peace medal to be discontinued by the Mint might account for its rarity."[8]

1969 MARCH 7. Lee Bergere stars as Abraham Lincoln, 23rd-century captain James T. Kirk's boyhood idol, in "The Savage Curtain," an episode of *Star Trek*.

1969 APRIL 14. On the day that the new fourth Philadelphia Mint opens at Fifth and Arch streets, the Mint also unveils its new General Motors–manufactured roller coining press by striking Lincoln cents before hundreds of onlookers.

1969 APRIL 15. India's Posts and Telegraphs Department pays honor to the centenary of Abraham Lincoln' death (four years after the fact) with a stamp issue, having a similar likeness to that on then currently circulating U.S. $5 bills.

1969 MAY. The "world's tallest Lincoln statue," a 62-foot figure of Abraham Lincoln by Minnesotan Bob Edgett, is erected at Charleston, Illinois, as a tourist attraction. Backers patterned the wire-mesh-and-fiberglass statue, supported by a steel frame, after Iron City, Michigan's, colossal figure of Paul Bunyan. The work was commissioned by the Charleston Tourism Development Corporation, and fabricated by the Gordon Specialty Co. of St. Paul, Minnesota. It would be dedicated June 1 in a new "Lincoln Memorial Park." Vandals have repeatedly—without success—attempted to topple the 18,000-pound tall fellow by felling Lincoln at the ankles; others have repeatedly splashed paint on his shoes and lower trousers.

Fig. 4.53. Twenty-third–century ship's captain James T. Kirk, played by William Shatner, meets his boyhood idol, 19th-century U.S. president Abraham Lincoln, played by Lee Bergere.

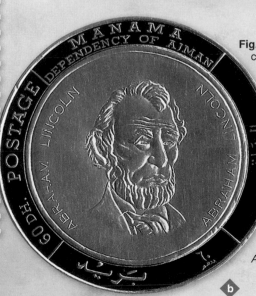

Fig. 4.54. Two more Middle Eastern states celebrated Lincoln in 1970, ever aware of the U.S. collectibles market and worldwide reverence for Old Abe. Fujeira's 2-riyals stamp (Minkus 453) *(a)* was issued May 18. Manama's large gold-foil "coin" stamp is a different breed of collectible altogether. Originally issued in November 1968 as part of a "Heroes of Humanity" series, the 60-DH Lincoln "coin" (Minkus 105 shown) *(b)*, bearing an embossing after the U.S. $5 model, was overprinted in April 1970 to mark the 25th anniversary of the United Nations, and then successively to mark *Apollo 13* and *Apollo 14* space flights.

Fig. 4.55.. . . and yet taller still. Even the 30-foot Lincoln was dwarfed in May 1969, when Bob Edgett's colossal 62-foot fiberglass statue of Lincoln pointing skyward (a) was erected at Charleston, Illinois, as a tourist attraction. Edgett is seen in his Minnesota studio with a model of the statue and the figure's head (b).

1970 June 5. Southgate, Michigan, coin collector Art Goupel's nearly four-foot-tall bust of Lincoln, comprised of 80,000 cents stuck together, goes on display at the National Bank of Detroit Money Museum. This artwork took a whole year to complete. Goupel was a collector of Lincolniana. He also took turns as a Lincoln impersonator, as for example at the 1973 Indiana State Numismatic Association convention, June 1–3, at Fort Wayne. The museum was operated by retired Admiral Oscar H. Dodson.

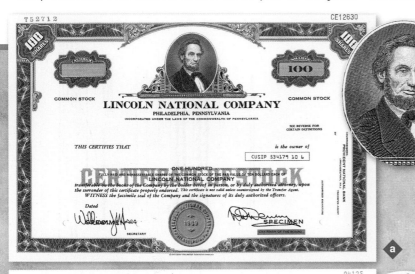

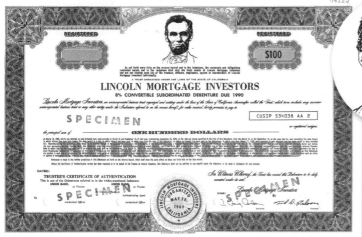

Fig. 4.56. This Lincoln National Company, Phila-delphia, stock from 1969 incorporation by Security-Columbian Bank Note Co. has a Marshall-style portrait vignette *(a)*. That same year, Lincoln Mortgage Investors stock sported an O-77–style image by Jeffries Bank Note Co. *(b)*.

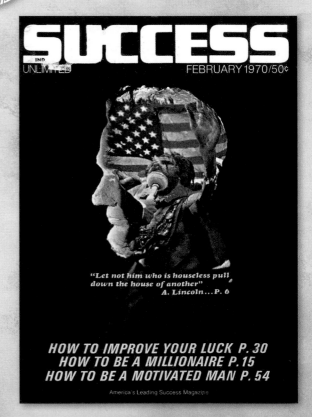

Fig. 4.57. F[red] Morton Reed (no relation to the author) was an industrial illustrator, a syndicated numismatic columnist, and a contract numismatic illustrator for *Coin World* in the 1960s and 1970s. In 1971 Reed was also the artist for the "Numistamp" series that reproduced U.S. coin designs in a realistic manner on small plaques semi-perforated like stamps. The series was evidently not a big hit, as examples are rarely encountered, but the medallic designs are excellent as this Numistamp honoring Frank Gasparro's Lincoln Memorial design shows.

Fig. 4.58. Personal-development guru and philanthropist W[illiam] Clement Stone began his *Success Unlimited* magazine in 1954. The publication's colorful February 1970 cover protested the protestors by quoting from Lincoln's March 21, 1864, letter to the New York Workingmens' Democratic Republican Association.

1970 JULY 4. Following hard on the heels of a turbulent 1960s decade of protests at the Lincoln Memorial and the National Mall, the 1970s kick off with a counter-rally. Four hundred thousand "middle Americans" turn out for a patriotic event, centered on the steps of the Lincoln Memorial and filling the National Mall. The event, called by sponsors "Honor America Day," was the brainchild of *Reader's Digest* editor-in-chief Hobart Lewis and evangelist Billy Graham. Organizers said they hoped their event would provide an "antidote for the poisons of defeatism, cynicism, and disillusionment that boil[ed] from the wells of America's unsolved problems." The festival was broadcast worldwide to 123 countries via TV and radio. Bob Hope, Dinah Shore, Jack Benny, Glen Campbell, The New Christy Minstrels, and Teresa Graves were among the performers. Dr. Graham gave the invocation.

Fig. 4.59. Michigan numismatist and Lincoln impersonator Art Goupel created this bust out of 80,000 Lincoln cents, shown on display in 1970 at the National Bank of Detroit Money Museum.

Fig. 4.60. The pushback against the protestors that had turned the National Mall and Lincoln Memorial into a counterculture venue gained impetus in 1970 when *Reader's Digest* editor-in-chief Hobart Lewis and evangelist Billy Graham staged a patriotic July 4th celebration there. Their "Honor America Day" celebration attracted an estimated 400,000, to hear Bob Hope, Jack Benny, Dinah Shore, Glen Campbell, and others perform. Dr. Graham is seen addressing the crowd.

1971. Avon Products introduces its men's aftershave products in 5-1/2-inch-tall clear-glass bottles with an image of Abraham Lincoln similar to that on the $5 bill, packaged in patriotic cardboard boxes with silver stars on a blue field, red and white alternating stripes, and the presidential seal.

1971 JUNE. For the centennial of cent designer Victor David Brenner's birth, the Chase Bank Money Museum in Rockefeller Center, New York, stages a memorial exhibit. Mint Director Eva Adams cooperates with the event. According to participant Dick Johnson, "She sent Frank Gasparro (designer of the 1959 cent reverse) [with] the original Brenner cent plaster models and the original copper galvano dieshells for both obverse and reverse made from those plaster models. Frank was most gracious. Before he let us put the items behind the wall of glass in the exhibit room he allowed each of us to have our photos taken with him, the original models, and the dieshells. Then he signed autographs all day long for the public. Unfortunately Frank had to return them to the Mint vaults after this one-day Saturday showing. The exhibit continued for several more weeks, however. Frank told us this was the first time the models and dieshells had been outside the Mint vaults since the 1910 Exhibition of the Contemporary Medal, also in New York City, at the American Numismatic Society."

1971 AUGUST 18. After the State of Illinois had donated the former home of Abraham and Mary Todd Lincoln to the United States, the home and adjacent properties were designated a national historic site, administered by the National Park Service. The site is the only one administered by the NPS in the state. Currently it is comprised of about 12 acres. In addition to the Lincoln home, which is open for free public tours, a visitor's center (with exhibits, documentary films, and today a large gift shop) caters to tourists. Additional exhibits are located in the Dean House and the Arnold House on the site.

1972. The Franklin Mint issues a 120-medal set titled "The Medallic History of the Jews of America." A 39-millimeter medal by sculptor Karen Worth has a $5 bill–type portrait of Abraham Lincoln holding a pen and a tablet with five Union soldiers in the background. Its reverse has the legend "Lincoln and the Jews: First president to take official action involving Jewish equality and anti-Jewish acts. Signed chaplaincy law," together with a bold eagle perched on a ring of stars.

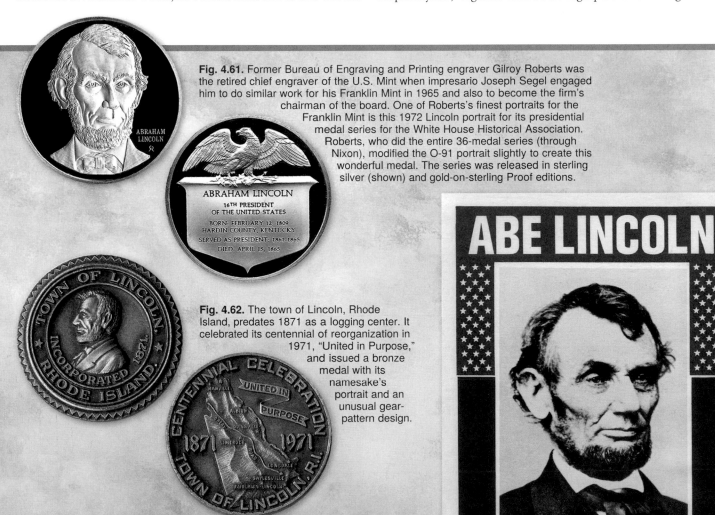

Fig. 4.61. Former Bureau of Engraving and Printing engraver Gilroy Roberts was the retired chief engraver of the U.S. Mint when impresario Joseph Segel engaged him to do similar work for his Franklin Mint in 1965 and also to become the firm's chairman of the board. One of Roberts's finest portraits for the Franklin Mint is this 1972 Lincoln portrait for its presidential medal series for the White House Historical Association. Roberts, who did the entire 36-medal series (through Nixon), modified the O-91 portrait slightly to create this wonderful medal. The series was released in sterling silver (shown) and gold-on-sterling Proof editions.

Fig. 4.62. The town of Lincoln, Rhode Island, predates 1871 as a logging center. It celebrated its centennial of reorganization in 1971, "United in Purpose," and issued a bronze medal with its namesake's portrait and an unusual gear-pattern design.

Fig. 4.63. In 1972, when Topps Card Co. reissued its series of cards honoring U.S. presidents (see figure 3.261), it also released as a premium a set of 15 "campaign posters," including this red-white-and-blue Lincoln. Most examples seen are folded from insertion in wax packs. This pristine example was purchased from the company when it sold much of its archives several years ago.

1972 AUGUST. The U.S. Secret Service takes delivery of a new presidential limousine, a 22-foot custom-built black Lincoln Continental, designed and built by Ford Motor Co. It had a roof section which opened to permit two passengers to stand during parades. The car had a wheelbase of 161 inches and was powered by a 460-cubic-inch engine.

1972 SEPTEMBER 17. The cover story published in *Chicago Tribune Magazine* is "Why Lincoln's Legacy Will Long Endure."

1972 OCTOBER 30. *The Lincoln Mask*, by V.J. Longhi, premiers at the Plymouth Theatre, starring Fred Gwynne and Eva Marie Saint. The play would flop, closing after only eight performances.

1972 DECEMBER 12. The George Schaefer play *The Last of Mrs. Lincoln*, starring Julie Harris in the title role, sees its opening night at the Anta Theatre, New York City. Written by playwright James Prideaux, the drama would earn Tony acting awards for Ms. Harris and Leora Dana, and a Drama Desk Award for Prideaux as most promising playwright. The last performance was February 4, 1973.

1973 FEBRUARY 13. Dennis Weaver stars in the NBC Lincoln birthday–themed made-for-TV movie *The Great Man's Whiskers*, retelling the familiar story about the little girl writing Lincoln and suggesting that he grow a beard. Interestingly, the Universal TV show had debuted in England May 2, 1972.

Fig. 4.64. V.J. Longhi's play *The Lincoln Mask*, starring Fred Gwynne and Eva Marie Saint, flopped on Broadway, closing after only eight performances.

Fig. 4.65. Two of the unlikeliest Lincolns performed in made-for-TV fare in the 1970s. Matt Dillon's sidekick Chester, a.k.a. Dennis Weaver, starred in *The Great Man's Whiskers (a)* on NBC television in 1974. The following year, Hal Holbrook appeared in the six-part David L. Wolper production of *Sandburg's Lincoln (b)*, also on NBC. No amount of makeup could make up for Holbrook's short frame, although he claimed to be six-feet, one-inch.

1973 NOVEMBER 7. Against the backdrop of the Lincoln assassination, and released for the 10th anniversary of the assassination of President John F. Kennedy, an indie film starring Burt Lancaster, *Executive Action*, explores the conspiracy theory that rogue intelligence agents and greedy and unscrupulous business and political groups plot, carry out, and successfully blame lone CIA operative Lee Harvey Oswald for the Kennedy slaying in Dallas.

1974 FEBRUARY 11. The Oklahoma Republican Party hosts California governor Ronald Reagan at its annual Lincoln birthday banquet, and issues a medal for the event.

1974 MAY 12. Hal Holbrook plays Lincoln in the David L. Wolper six-part TV mini-series production *Sandburg's Lincoln.* (See figure 4.65.)

1974. Sculptor Bernard Wiepper's heroic-size bronze statue, *Abraham Lincoln Walks at Midnight*, is placed near the river at the Capitol, Charleston, West Virginia. (See figure 4.71.) The 10-foot-two-inch-tall statue shows Lincoln wrapped in a robe on his nighttime vigil. The design was originally modeled by Fred M. Torrey, who was inspired by Vachel Lindsay's poem of the same name. Torrey exhibited a three-foot-tall plaster model of it at the New York World's Fair in 1939–1940. Torrey died in 1967. William Sebert Bryant purchased the plaster model from the Torrey estate. Wiepper was commissioned to model a large statue based on the Torrey design, but he contended he had also studied photographs and other busts and statues of Lincoln when he did his statue.

1974. The Lincoln Mint, Chicago, Illinois, issues a set of two dozen chronological medals illustrating the life of Abraham Lincoln (see figure 4.73), in two matched brown leatherette volumes with gold-stamped titling. One volume contained *Abraham Lincoln, an Autobiographical Narrative*, written and edited by Ralph Geoffrey Newman, with 24 original drawings by Lloyd Ostendorf. Printing was on heavy, rough paper with deckled edges in champagne-color ink.

Fig. 4.66. The 26-cent ultramarine, black, and carmine Mount Rushmore U.S. airmail stamp was released at Rapid City, South Dakota, on January 2, 1974. Designed by Robert (Gene) Shehorn, it continued the trend toward clean, modern art designs on U.S. stamps.

Fig. 4.67. In 1974 a cent shortage due to the escalating price for copper led to small-change expedients such as this one-cent note circulated June 1 by the Schwegmann Bros. Giant Supermarkets. Although such issues would have been illegal in most instances, food stores like Schwegmann's were permitted to issue coupons for making change in transactions involving food stamps, since the USDA did not supply small-denomination notes.

Congress responded to the coin-shortage crisis by enacting legislation permitting a change in the cent's metallic composition, and aluminum trial cents were struck.

Fig. 4.68. Two-term sitting California governor Ronald Reagan came to Oklahoma for Lincoln Day, February 11, 1974. This small bronze medal's somewhat stilted adaptation of the iconic $5 bill portrait is a memento of that visit.

The medal series included twenty-four 39-millimeter medals struck in two editions, one in sterling silver, and the other in 24-karat gold on sterling silver. Ostendorf's original drawing of the design for the medal preceded the chapter of the book in which it is described. Binding of the volumes was done by Ernst Hertzberg & Sons, Chicago. The edition was limited to 10,000, but nowhere near that number was actually purchased. The books were serially numbered.

Themes for the 24 medals were: (a) Kentucky Birth; (b) Indiana Years; (c) Sister Sarah; (d) Trip to New Orleans; (e) Move to Illinois; (f) Black Hawk War; (g) Postmaster & Surveyor; (h) Illinois Legislator; (i) Springfield Lawyer; (j) Marriage to Mary Todd; (k) The Lincoln Family; (l) United States Congressman; (m) The House Divided; (n) Debates with Douglas; (o) Nomination for President; (p) Presidential Election; (q) Farewell to Springfield; (r) First Inaugural; (s) Emancipation Proclamation; (t) Commander-in-Chief; (u) Gettysburg Address; (v) Second Inaugural; (w) Ford's Theatre; (x) The Memorial.

The medal reverses have short narratives describing the particular scene depicted on the obverses.

Evidence suggests that a bronze version of these medals was also struck. Unsold bronze remainders subsequently turned up in New Orleans in the 1970s as Mardi Gras carnival throws.

1974 JUNE 1. Schwegmann Bros. Giant Super Markets issue one-cent "change coupons" for use in transactions involving food stamps, since the government did not supply recipients notes of small value, but authorized local merchants to print their own small-change notes. The face design on the Schwegmann issue has a representation of a 1973 Lincoln cent obverse and the legend "Good toward any purchase or redeemable in cash."

1974 OCTOBER 11. Responding to the cent shortage of the times, Congress authorizes the Treasury secretary to diminish the amount of copper and change the ratio of zinc in the cent simply by publishing notice of intent to do so in the *Federal Register*.

1975 JANUARY 29. Custom-made Presidential U.S. Bicentennial Lincoln cent plaques debut, made by a Cleveland, Ohio, firm.

1975 FEBRUARY 26. Medallic Art Company offers 2-3/4–inch bronze restrikes of its 1909 Lincoln Centennial medal by Charles Calverley at the 1909 subscription price of $4, to introduce charter subscribers to its new newsletter, *The Art Medalist*.

1975 MARCH 19. In the pilot of *The Muppet Show*, "the end of sex and violence on television," John Lovelady voices the role of Abraham Lincoln.

1975 JUNE 27. The Lincoln Stamp Club, Lincoln, Nebraska, hosts the three-day 26th annual convention of the American Topical Association, LINPEX-TOPEX 1975, at the Radisson Cornhusker.

1975 DECEMBER 12. Arthur Hill portrays Abe Lincoln opposite Charles Durning as Stephen Douglas in NBC's *Hallmark Hall of Fame* drama "The Rivalry" (see figure 4.76). "Lincoln didn't want slavery; Douglas didn't want war," according to playwright Norman Corwin's script.

1976. Avon Products introduces its Lucky Penny Lip Gloss with two-inch-diameter plastic replicas of the rare 1909-S VDB Lincoln cent.

1976. To celebrate the U.S. Bicentennial and reap Yankee stamp collectors' dollars, the Comoros Islands issue 10-franc and 1,000-franc philatelic souvenir sheets with images of the "Gettysburg Lincoln" and the $5-note Lincoln, respectively.

Fig. 4.69. Indiana numismatist Lloyd Wagaman specialized in elongated coins and PNCs (philatelic-numismatic covers) in the 1960s and 1970s. Lloyd engraved the dies and usually signed his artwork LW, as on the truncation of this lively rolled nickel from 1973.

Fig. 4.70. During the Vietnam War era, Bell Helicopter Co. prospered greatly from the success of its "Huey" (UH-1) helicopter, which in 1972 ferried the present writer around his beat as a U.S. Army journalist in the Republic of Korea for nearly a year. This two-headed Abe medal was an advertising piece for the company and a neat, albeit well-worn, pocket piece for its owner.

Fig. 4.71. Sculptor Bernard Wiepper was engaged by William Sieberg Bryant, purchaser of the 1939 Fred Torrey plaque *Abraham Lincoln Walks at Midnight*, to translate the Vachel Lindsay–inspired Lincoln apparition into a monumental sculpture. Wiepper supplemented Torrey's design and created this 10-foot-two-inch bronze that was installed at the State Capitol, Charleston, West Virginia, in 1974.

Fig. 4.72. *Lincoln the Friendly Neighbor*, by sculptor Avard Fairbanks, was completed in 1959 and installed in front of the Lincoln Federal Savings and Loan Association, Berwyn, Illinois. It is shown here as it looked in 1973. The bank has since merged and changed its name, and the installation has since 1997 appeared in front of a local school named for Lincoln.

THE LIFE

Valuable first series from the

From Hardin County, Kentucky, to Ford's Theatre in Washington, there is no more dramatic story in American history than the life of Abraham Lincoln. For its inaugural series, the Lincoln Mint presents this superb American saga in 24 heirloom quality art medallions to be struck in .999 pure silver and solid bronze.

Historic Minting

The very minting of a complete Lincoln series is historic in scope. Seldom, if ever, has a series of art medallions been devoted to the life of a single individual. Never has a life more warranted it.

Lincoln Scholar and Historian, Ralph G. Newman's Unique Book

Such is the importance of these medals that the Lincoln Mint has commissioned the great Lincoln scholar, Ralph G. Newman, to prepare a specially numbered, limited edition book devoted to the stories behind the medals. Each medal is the subject of a complete chapter. This unique book comes to you in a beautifully bound slipcase along with two matching medallion display volumes designed to protect and display your medallions. This beautiful book is, in itself, a valuable collector's item. It is yours free with your subscription.

Ostendorf Designs

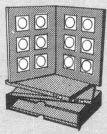

America's foremost Lincoln artist, Lloyd Ostendorf, has been commissioned to design the entire series. Each medal is a faithful reproduction of an Ostendorf original, historically accurate to the finest detail. Plates of the 24 original Ostendorf drawings are incorporated in the book.

Limited Edition. Subscription Rolls Open for Limited Time Only

Subscription rolls close March 15, 1970. Each silver medallion will be hallmarked and numbered on its edge. Your number will be assigned in the order in which your subscription is received. The earlier you order, the lower number you will get. You will retain this number throughout the entire series. No additional sets of this series will ever be struck with these dies. Upon completion of the series, the dies will be defaced and donated to Lincoln College, Lincoln, Illinois.

Larger than a Silver Dollar

The series is to be proof struck in .999 pure silver and solid bronze. The coined medallions will be full proof quality, deep bas relief, 39 millimeters

Fig. 4.73. The most ambitious Abraham Lincoln medallic tribute was the set of twenty-four 39-millimeter medals and their companion illustrated biography featuring the medal subjects by Chicago's Lincoln Mint, a division of Ero Industries. This series was released as "The Life of Lincoln" in 1974. The medals were designed by this author's mentor, Lloyd Ostendorf, and the write-ups were supplied by Lincolnphile bookstore owner Ralph Geoffrey Newman. Of course, the iconic Lincoln money image was featured prominently in the venture's profuse advertising, such as the brochure shown.

OF LINCOLN

Lincoln Mint: 24 proof-quality hallmarked medallions

in diameter. The obverse of each medallion will feature an original Ostendorf design, bordered with the name of the series and the title for that event. The reverse will bear a quotation from Lincoln's autobiographical works, describing the scene.

Distinguised Advisory Board

In addition to Ralph G. Newman and Lloyd Ostendorf, the advisory board for the Lincoln series consists of William K. Alderfer, Illinois State Historian; Dr. R. Gerald McMurtry, Director, The Lincoln National Life Foundation and Editor of "Lincoln Lore," Dr. Raymond Dooley, President of Lincoln College, Lincoln,

Illinois; and Dr. Clyde C. Walton, Director of Libraries, Northern Illinois University.

Guaranteed Cost

As a condition of your subscription, the Lincoln Mint guarantees that there will be no increase in the cost of any of your medallions regardless of fluctuations in precious metal prices, dollar devaluation or any other future event. As a work of genuine historic, artistic and intrinsic value, the Life of Lincoln series can be expected to be a continuing asset to you and your family for generations.

The Lincoln Mint

The Lincoln Mint is a division of Ero Industries, a widely diversified publicly held corporation. Backed by over half a century of coining experience, the craftsmen at the Lincoln Mint are recognized by numismatists as being among America's finest custom minters.

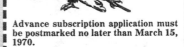

Fig. 4.74. The celebration of the U.S. Bicentennial from 1975 to 1977 (in some cases) was a marketing bonanza for other nations desirous to improve their balance of trade payments. Compared to earlier foreign stamps we begin to see a preponderance of Abraham Lincoln money images used on these later issues. Among U.S. Bicentennial–era stamps that also featured Lincoln (likely to improve their salability) were these issues from Bangladesh (Mount Rushmore, Scott 114) *(a)*; Seychelles (Scott 374) *(b)*; St. Vincent (Scott 438) *(c)*; Republic of Korea (Mount Rushmore, Scott 1036) *(d)*; the Comoros Islands (10 francs, Scott 224; 1,000 francs, Scott 232; and a 400-francs souvenir sheet with Mount Rushmore, Scott 172) *(e)*; Eynhallow, Scotland, local issue (unlisted) *(f)*; Staffa, Scotland, local issue for Washington's and Lincoln's birthdays (unlisted) *(g)*; Venezuela (Scott 1153) *(h)*; Equatorial Guinea (Mount Rushmore, Minkus 1457) *(i)*; Grenada souvenir sheet (Scott 99a) *(j)*; Guatemala (Scott C607a) *(k)*; and Chad (Scott C213), represented by a signed artist's proof *(l)*.

f

g

h

i

j

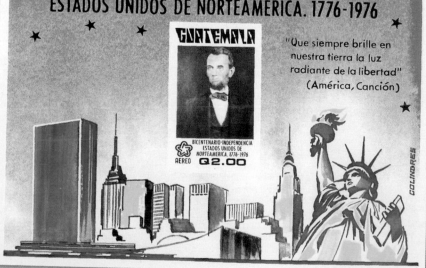

k

l

1976 FEBRUARY. A bold *Saturday Evening Post* cover by J.C. (Joseph Christian) Leyendecker shows a bronze plaque with a representation of French's Lincoln Memorial statue head flanked by an engraved legend, "With Malice Toward None" and "With Charity For All." At the bottom on a plaque is an inset of Lincoln's famous quote from his February 22, 1861, flag-raising at Philadelphia's Independence Hall: ". . . I would rather be assassinated on the spot than surrender it."

Leyendecker was one of the most prominent of American illustrators in the first half of the 20th century. Between 1896 and 1950, he painted more than 500 magazine covers, including 322 covers for the *Saturday Evening Post*. Leyendecker died in 1951. His power-ful illustration upon which the 1976 *Post* cover was based had also been utilized on the cover of February 12, 1938, but without the Lincoln quotation. The illustration has proved an enduring one. Curtis Publishing and the *Saturday Evening Post* currently sell a large framed giclée (inkjet) print of the 1938 magazine cover.

1976 MAY 3. An inventive cover illustration by illustrator Saul Steinberg, with a behatted Abe quoting "E Pluribus Unum," graces the cover of the *New Yorker* magazine.

1976 SEPTEMBER 16. Ford Rainey plays the part of Lincoln for a third time in the made-for-TV biopic *The Last of Mrs. Lincoln*, star-ring Julie Harris as Mary Todd Lincoln.

Fig. 4.76. Hallmark Hall of Fame's 1975 drama "The Rivalry" starred Arthur Hill as Abraham Lincoln and Charles Durning as Stephen A. Douglas.

Fig. 4.75. Many of the 1970s bullion pieces were melted in the great silver and gold melt of 1979–1980, when silver spiked to $50 per ounce and gold reached about $1,000 per ounce. Fortunately, this very finely detailed 1974 .999 fine one-ounce coin *(a)*, projected as an "International Silver Trade Unit," escaped the melting pot. The same fiery fate befell much of the Franklin Mint's precious-metal output of the 1960s and 1970s. Again, however, this nicely numismatic 1973 State of Illinois sterling silver medal *(b)*, with its beardless bust taken from Alexander Hesler's O-2 image, also remained for collectors to treasure.

Fig. 4.77. The *Saturday Evening Post* reprised J.C. Leyendecker's stunning 1938 *Post* cover (see figure 3.154) for its February 1976 cover. Below, on the white plaque that formerly had Lincoln's name, editors added part of Lincoln's quote from his famous flag-raising at Independence Hall in 1861 en route to Washington, D.C., and (bowing to economics of the periodical business) cover blurbs for interior contents.

Fig. 4.78. This red-white-and-blue patch was given to Scouts participating in the 1975 Lincoln Pilgrimage at Wabash, Indiana.

Fig. 4.79. Illustrator Saul Steinberg's irrepressible wit and ability to condense large concepts in spare graphical form created this memorable cover during the U.S. Bicentennial celebration period. Shown is the May 3, 1976, cover of the *New Yorker*.

1976. The National Park Service introduces a 16-minute orientation film, *Mr. Lincoln's Springfield*, at the Lincoln Home National Historic Site visitor's center.

1976 OCTOBER 14. Ford Rainey plays Lincoln for the fourth time in chapter 3 of the TV mini-series *Captains and the Kings*.

1976. A Lincoln National Life Insurance Company advertising campaign, "You probably have the name of America's tenth-largest life insurance company in your pocket," shows a large illustration of a 1976-D Lincoln cent and the company's (new) logo with a similar right-facing profile of the Great Emancipator.

1976 NOVEMBER 21. Chicago sculptor Abbott Pattison's eight-foot-tall abstract statue of Abraham Lincoln is unveiled at the south entrance of the under-construction new Lincoln Public Library in Springfield, facing the Lincoln Home National Historic Site. Sculptor Pattison said his figure, consisting of a bust of Lincoln on an abstract "body" configured of metal angles, represents "the marriage of modern Springfield and Lincoln's day. . . . It seems," he continued, "that for a modern abstract building you must straddle the resemblances to Lincoln with the lines and shape of the building. . . . The building does not call for a romantic picture of Lincoln. It was a compromise between the completely abstract and a man whom we have all admired from childhood." Traditionalists called the statue "grotesque," "an abomination," "monstrosity," and "degrading." A writer for the Illinois Humanities Council, Kim Bauer, synthesized views by calling it "a non-representational representation reflecting

the society's own confused feelings about the man who was once called 'The First American.'"9

1976 DECEMBER. Ford Rainey plays Abraham Lincoln for a fifth time, appearing in the biopic about Galen Clark, the man who created Yosemite Park. Denver Pyle starred as Clark.

1977. Lincoln National Life Insurance Company launches its "25 clues to the name of America's 10th-largest life insurance company" advertising campaign, which includes images of 25 items of Lincolniana from its Lincoln Museum collection.

1977 JULY 11. The U.S. Secret Service takes possession of a purported 1977/6 Lincoln cent overdate that had been sent to the U.S. Mint for study. On July 17, the Secret Service would pick up a fourth example of the false overdate struck from bogus dies. On July 20 two Florida men would appear at a preliminary hearing before a U.S. magistrate concerning the fraudulent coins.

1977 JULY 13. *Coin World* reports "preliminary Mint OK" of the 1977/6 Lincoln cent overdate.

1977. The Sangamon Valley room, dedicated in the new Lincoln Library, Springfield, Illinois, includes Frederick Moynihan's bronze bust of Abraham Lincoln that had hung over the front door of the city's old Carnegie Library (razed in 1974). During construction of the new building, the nearly four-score-years-old bust had been restored from the effects of bronze disease, which had discolored it and worn holes in its surface. The restoration work was undertaken

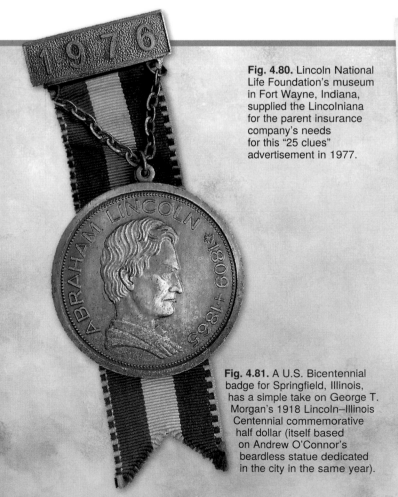

Fig. 4.80. Lincoln National Life Foundation's museum in Fort Wayne, Indiana, supplied the Lincolniana for the parent insurance company's needs for this "25 clues" advertisement in 1977.

Fig. 4.81. A U.S. Bicentennial badge for Springfield, Illinois, has a simple take on George T. Morgan's 1918 Lincoln–Illinois Centennial commemorative half dollar (itself based on Andrew O'Connor's beardless statue dedicated in the city in the same year).

Fig. 4.82. Signs of the times, in Lincoln's hometown. In November 1976, Chicago sculptor Abbott Pattison's eight-foot-tall abstract statue of Abraham Lincoln was unveiled at the south entrance of the under-construction new Lincoln Public Library, in Springfield, facing the Lincoln Home National Historic Site. As might be expected, the statue sparked controversy from traditionalists, who were aghast at the robotic metal image of the nation's savior in their midst.

by Bob Evans, then curator of art at the Illinois State Museum. The surface was restored by electrolysis, a more stable patina was applied, and the surface was waxed. "The bust is the most valuable and significant artifact saved from the old Carnegie Library," local historian Carl Volkman opined. The Sangamon Valley room includes the library's rare Lincoln and local history materials.

1977 OCTOBER. John Anderson plays the role of Abraham Lincoln in the Sunn Classics speculative fiction *The Lincoln Conspiracy*. Bradford Dillman plays assassin John Wilkes Booth.

1977 DECEMBER 16. Stephen von Zimmer is sentenced to 12 months' probation in the 1977/6 Lincoln cent overdate fraud case.

1978. Amtrak discontinues the Abraham Lincoln inter-city rail service between Chicago and St. Louis.

1978 DECEMBER 17. Springfield's 11-story Hotel Abraham Lincoln, or "the Abe," as it was known locally, falls into a heap of dust in 10 seconds after controlled explosions demolish the 53-year-old landmark. The hotel at Fifth and Capitol was just a stone's throw from the Illinois Statehouse. A large portrait of Lincoln, patterned after the "Gettysburg Lincoln" O-77 photograph, had hung over the registration desk in the lobby.

1979. Avon Products for Men introduces a figural bottle in the shape of a Lincoln bust, to sell its aftershave lotion. The bottles came in an off-white and a deep bronze color.

1979. Thieves steal the Hermon A. MacNeil bust of Abraham Lincoln on display since 1928 in Lincoln Hall, University of Illinois, Champaign, Illinois, and mount it on a tree stump at a local golf course.

Fig. 4.83. The 1977 Sunn Classic motion picture *The Lincoln Conspiracy* offered up "the worst historical abuses ever perpetuated in a Lincoln-related motion picture," according to Lincoln film connoisseur Mark Reinhart, author of *Abraham Lincoln on Screen.* John Anderson played Abe. Bradford Dillman played the show's star, John Wilkes Booth.

Fig. 4.84. Indiana numismatist Bob Julian sponsored five satirical medals in the late 1970s. The medals were designed by Warner Williams and struck by Medallic Art Co. in bronze and nickel-silver editions. Julian's 1979 Energy Crisis Medal (see, hear, speak no evil) lampooned U.S. dependence on foreign oil and the mess it had left the country in when (in the aftermath of the 1973 Arab oil embargo) per-barrel prices of crude oil spiked at over $40 during the Jimmy Carter administration. If the Abe Lincoln portrait looks familiar, it should. "Warner used the bust by Morgan on the presidential medal for the Lincoln portrait," Julian told the present writer.

Fig. 4.85. In 1977 sculptor Frederick Moynihan's traditional bronze bust of Abraham Lincoln (which had greeted visitors at the door of the Springfield, Illinois, Carnegie Library) was re-installed in the Sangamon Valley local-history room of the city's spanking-new library. The restored bust was called by a local historian "the most valuable and significant artifact saved from the old Carnegie Library."

Fig. 4.86. Collectors of Avon items know that the beauty and grooming products company employed Lincoln-themed items several times in the last few decades. This white figural bottle and a companion in deep bronze color were introduced in 1979 to market aftershave lotion to men.

BETTE MIDLER
IS

Divine Madness

Produced and Directed by MICHAEL RITCHIE
Written by JERRY BLATT, BETTE MIDLER, BRUCE VILANCH
Executive Producer HOWARD JEFFREY Director of Photography WILLIAM A. FRAKER, A.S.C.

Filmed in Panavision ® Color by Technicolor ®

A Ladd Company Release Through Warner Bros. A Warner Communications Company

Fig. 4.87. The Divine Ms. M, Bette Midler, replaced Thomas Jefferson on Mount Rushmore on this 1980 movie poster for her film *Divine Madness*.

THE PRICE OF LEADERSHIP

Fig. 4.88. The vibrant colors and aggressive masculinity of Ferdie Pacheco's *Price of Leadership*, painted originally in 1980, are reflected in the Lincoln portraiture of such modern artists as Cat Clausen. Pacheco, "The Fight Doctor," is synonymous with the ring career of Cassius Clay, a.k.a. Muhammad Ali. Art critics say Pacheco's eclectic style blurs "the boundaries between fact and fiction." We agree.

1980 JULY 17. Ex–California governor Ronald Reagan accepts the Republican presidential nomination as his party's candidate by (loosely) reminding delegates of Abraham Lincoln's claim in his first Inaugural Address: "The first Republican president once said, 'While the people retain their virtue and their vigilance, no administration by any extreme of wickedness or folly can seriously injure the government in the short space of four years.' If Mr. Lincoln could see what's happened in these last three-and-a-half years," Reagan continued, "he might hedge a little on that statement." The Great Communicator then called on the goodness of the American people: "But, with the virtues that our legacy as a free people and with the vigilance that sustains liberty, we still have time to use our renewed compact to overcome the injuries that have been done to America these past three-and-a-half years." He then laid out a straightforward, remedial plan: "First, we must overcome something the present administration has cooked up: a new and altogether indigestible economic stew, one part inflation, one part high unemployment, one part recession, one part runaway taxes, one part deficit spending and seasoned by an energy crisis. It's an economic stew that has turned the national stomach."

1981 FEBRUARY 9. Herbert Mitgang's one-man, two-act play *Mister Lincoln* kicks off season 30 of the long-running dramatic television series *Hallmark Hall of Fame*, with British Shakespearean actor Roy Dotrice in the title role. Mitgang's introspective Lincoln production had been filmed live at Ford's Theatre in Washington, D.C., the previous year, after appearing first in Edmonton and Toronto, Canada. The production would also tour locations in Australia, London, and New York City.

1981 APRIL 1. *The Lincoln Cent*, by Stephen G. Manley, is published. It would be copyrighted on April 27. The paperback book was published by Liberty Press, Muscatine, Iowa.

1981. A bronze sculpture of Abraham Lincoln is erected in Tijuana, Mexico, by Mexican sculptor Humberto Peraza y Ojeda. The statue is located in Zona Rio on the Boulevard Paseo de los Héroes. The work is said to have been a gift of the U.S. government, in appreciation of which the Mexican government reciprocated and donated a sculpture of President Benito Juarez to the United States, which was placed in San Diego's Balboa Park.

Fig. 4.89. In 1981 a statue of Abraham Lincoln by Mexican sculptor Humberto Peraza y Ojeda was erected in Tijuana as a gift of the U.S. government. A sculpture of Mexican president Benito Juarez was similarly erected in Balboa Park in San Diego.

Fig. 4.90. Herman Mitgang's one-man play *Mister Lincoln* played a national tour in 1980, including at the Morosco Theatre on West 45th Street in New York. The presentation at Ford's Theatre was broadcast as a Lincoln Birthday special, February 9, 1981, as part of the *Hallmark Hall of Fame* series. On this playbill, most of an icon $5 bill pose would have been intimately familiar to all theatergoers.

1981 JULY 22. The U.S. Treasury contracts with a Tennessee firm, Ball Corp., for copper-coated-zinc cent planchets.

1982 JANUARY 6. Issue commences for new copper-plated-zinc cents at the U.S. Mint's West Point minting facility.

1982 MAY. The Wilkinsburg, Pennsylvania, copy of Alfonso Pelzer's hammered-copper statue by John G. Segesman is stolen by vandals—all except his shoes and ankles. Police would discover the stolen Abe 10 months later, buried on a Westmoreland County farm underneath a bulldozer. The thieves were forced to pay for repair of the damage.

1982 OCTOBER 27. Issue commences for new copper-plated-zinc Lincoln cents at the Denver Mint.

1982 NOVEMBER 14. Gregory Peck takes the role of Abraham Lincoln in the six-and-a-half-hour TV mini-series *The Blue and the Grey.*

1983. The White House Preservation Fund and Dr. Maury Leibovitz donate an 18-inch-high bronze bust of Abraham Lincoln, by sculptor Jo Davidson, to the Lincoln Home National Historic Site Visitor Center. The cast had been made in 1947 by Roman Bronze Works, New York.

1983 JUNE 26. Gettysburg College professor Gabor S. Boritt institutes the first Civil War Institute at the college. Scholarly papers presented during the event, the week before the annual observance of the Battle of Gettysburg, included Dr. Mark E. Neely Jr.'s "Abraham Lincoln: the Looming Presence," and Harold Holzer's "Lincoln and the Artists."

1983 JULY 30. An Associated Press wire-service photograph of Raymond Massey announces his death: "BEST KNOWN ROLE—Actor Raymond Massey, best known for his role as Abraham Lincoln in film and on Broadway is shown as Lincoln in 'Abe Lincoln in Illinois' on Broadway in 1938. Massey died in Beverly Hills, Calif., Friday night at the age of 86. (AP Laserphoto)"

1983 SEPTEMBER 9. The American Numismatic Society's 125th-anniversary celebration is marked by a medal by sculptor Marcel Jovine, depicting a Janvier reducing-machine reduction of the 1909 Lincoln cent obverse on the plaque's reverse. Ancient and foreign coins dominated its obverse, which overall paid respect to the coiner. The Lincoln cent was chosen to symbolize the Society's role in coin and medal design since its sculptor, Victor D. Brenner, was an active member of the ANS and had the support of the Society in getting his design adopted, according to exonumia expert H. Joseph Levine. The rectangular medal was struck by Stabilimento Stefano Johnson, Milano and Roma.

1984 JANUARY. Writer Frank Jacobs and illustrator Harry North's "Famous Quotations . . . and How the People Back Then Reacted to Them" attempt to show that people nowadays are not the only generation of Americans to be "cynical, jaded, sarcastic and over-critical." The *MAD* magazine entry shows a standing Abraham Lincoln, with a portrait similar to the then-current $5 bill pose, out among a crowd saying, "A nation cannot endure half-slave and half free!" A woman in the crowd replies, "I get it! You want to abolish marriage!" A man nearby queries, "Would you settle for 40% slave . . . and 60% free?" Meanwhile, an exasperated capitalist pipes up, "Keep talking and you'll get us into a Civil War." (See figure 4.96.)

1984 FEBRUARY 12. Walter Hancock's bronze standing Abraham Lincoln sculpture is dedicated on Lincoln's birthday at the Washington National Cathedral. The sculptor portrayed Lincoln draped in a shawl with the words from his farewell remarks at Springfield inscribed on the wall behind him. In that address, Lincoln asked his fellow citizens to pray for him. An inscription on the statue reads, "Abraham Lincoln whose lonely soul God kindled is here remembered by a people their conflict healed by the truth that marches on." Lincoln's descendants contributed to supporting the costs of the statue.

1984 AUGUST 22. Jim Bishop's *The Day Lincoln Was Shot* is re-published by Gramercy.

Fig. 4.91. This £8 gold-foil local-post issue from Staffa, Scotland, with its finely embossed Lincoln $5 bill image and presidential seal (a), was issued in 1982 with a companion silver-foil stamp. Norman Rockwell's scouting painting has been borrowed several times philatelically. This 8-pence local issue for Eynhallow, Scotland (b), was used in 1978.

Fig. 4.92. The original owner of this 1980s Lincoln Club of Orange County (California) pin may have been John Wayne or Ronald Reagan, both of whom belonged to the group.

Fig. 4.93. Oscar winner Gregory Peck made a fine Lincoln in the TV mini-series *The Blue and the Gray*, which won the People's Choice Award and was nominated for four technical Emmy Awards. The series debuted in November 1982.

Fig. 4.94. Sculptor Marcel Jovine created a rectangular plaque for the 125th anniversary of the American Numismatic Society (1983). His illustration for the back of the medal illustrates the stylized process of reducing Brenner's Lincoln cent design to coinage-die size. Brenner was a Fellow of the ANS, as is the present writer.

Fig. 4.95. This French-language version of an American comic book came out in April 1983. Captain America is set upon by a malevolent spirit that has inhabited Daniel Chester French's statue in the Lincoln Memorial.

Fig. 4.96. Cartoonist Harry North surely had the iconic Lincoln $5 bill portrait in mind (and likely as a reference model, too) when he created this original art for the January 1984 issue of *MAD* magazine.

Fig. 4.97. In November 1984, the trade publication *Savings Institutions* illustrated puzzling out the profitability picture with this humorous T[erry] Sirrell Lincoln money image.

Fig. 4.96. "Bend me, shape me, any way you want me"—lyrics from a 1968 song by Cicero, Illinois, rock band The American Breed—might be Old Abe's theme song over the last century and a half. It seems anybody is free at any time to claim Lincoln's legacy for any pet initiative, product, or purpose. It's bad enough when Lincoln is misappropriated for fraudulent purposes. It is downright unconscionable, however, when the perpetrator is the United States government. When the federal government misrepresents Lincoln, no matter how worthy the goal, someone should speak up. On October 16, 1984, the Post Office issued this "A Nation of Readers" stamp (Scott 2106), one of three pro-library stamps under Postmaster General William F. Bolger, designed by Bradbury Thompson. John Y. Cole, director of the Center for the Book for the Library of Congress, was instrumental in promoting the issue of this stamp. Of course, the model for Thompson was not a book but a photo album, based on the Anthony Berger February 9, 1864, photograph, O-93. Some adult in charge should have stopped this fraud. Shown is a dual-cancel first-day cover.

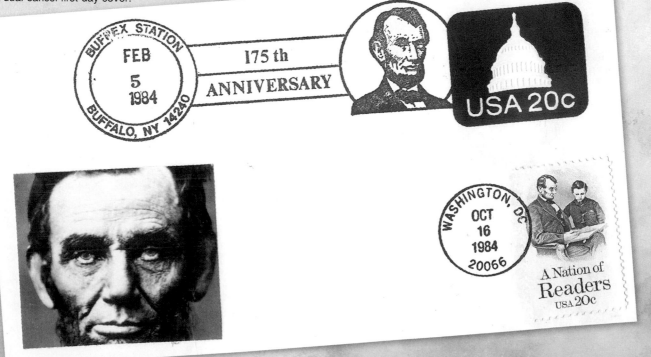

Art Buchwald
"YOU CAN FOOL ALL OF THE PEOPLE ALL THE TIME"

Fig. 4.99. Humorist Art Buchwald made a jolly old elfin Abe on the dustjacket of his 1985 best seller, *You Can Fool All of the People All the Time.*

Fig. 4.100. Collector Paul Cunningham pointed out to this writer that his Wanderung Weinsheim hiking medal was only half the image of Mount Rushmore. Lucky for this writer, he obtained the part with the Lincoln bust!

Fig. 4.101. This Series of 1985 $5 Federal Reserve Note is marked SPECIMEN, twice, in red ink. Such notes were part of a diplomatic parcel and are seldom seen individually or in the collector marketplace.

1984–85 WINTER. *Sculpture Review* publishes Theodora Morgan's article "A. Lincoln—Most Sculpted American."

1985 JUNE. Numismatic publisher Sanford J. Durst reprints Robert P. King's "Lincoln in Numismatics" as a paperback.

1985 NOVEMBER 10. Hal Holbrook takes up the role of Abraham Lincoln again, in the TV mini-series *North and South*.

1985 NOVEMBER 11. *Abraham Lincoln, the Legislator,* a colossal rose-marble statue by Avard Fairbanks, is dedicated at the U.S. Capitol, Washington, D.C. At the ceremony, Utah senator Orrin Hatch proclaimed: "When I look closely at this work of art, I see represented not only the life of our beloved president, Abraham Lincoln, but I also see imprinted in this marble the soul of its creator, the artist Dr. Avard Fairbanks." Fairbanks was 88 at the time. He would die in January 1987, two months short of age 90.

1986 MAY 14. The Henry B. Joy hammered-copper copy of Alfonso Pelzer's New Jersey statue of the Great Emancipator by John G. Segesman is rededicated at the Charles Howell Scout Reservation, Brighton, Michigan, according to the *Smithsonian American Art Museum Art Inventories Catalog.*

1986. Former U.S. Mint chief engraver Frank Gasparro creates a Statue of Liberty centennial 1886–1986 silver medal with a "Lincoln at Gettysburg" reverse. This was a very historically correct pairing, since the original impetus in 1865 that led to the erection and gifting of the Statue of Liberty to the United States by France was a memorial to Abraham Lincoln and his emancipation of the slaves.

Gasparro's Lincoln profile portrait is an excellent one, a stronger and more refined version of the low-relief profile he had created in 1982 for Chet Krause's *Numismatic News* 20th-anniversary aluminum token. This is one of the present author's favorite Lincoln small medallic portraits. The engraver shows Lincoln very animated. His depiction is remarkable for its realistic folds in the clothing. Gasparro's treatment of Lincoln's hair is reminiscent of his handling of the eagle's feathers on his proposed Liberty Head / Flying Eagle mini-dollar design in 1976. Gasparro's Statue of Liberty head is sure, also. This is one of his finest medallic designs. It will be remembered that Gasparro designed the Lincoln Memorial cent reverse that was introduced in 1959 to replace Brenner's original Wheat Ears design. This portrait gives a glimmer of what the Mint engraver could have done if he had been permitted to redesign the entire venerable copper coin on the celebration of the Lincoln sesquicentennial.

Fig. 4.102. Retired U.S. Mint engraver Frank Gasparro created a square-jawed Abraham Lincoln profile portrait for several private commissions. One version *(a)* was used in 1982 on the obverse of Chet Krause's aluminum medal marking the 30th anniversary of his weekly coin tabloid, *Numismatic News*. A similar but distinct treatment appeared on Gasparro's 1986 medal for the centennial of the Statue of Liberty *(b)*. The statue in New York Harbor was originally intended to be a tribute to Lincoln's emancipation of the slaves, but became a welcoming herald to distressed foreigners seeking a second chance.

Fig. 4.103. This 1986 Illinois commemorative automobile license plate honored the June convention of the ALPCA (Automobile License Plate Collectors Association), founded in 1954.

1986 NOVEMBER. George Grey Barnard's rustic bronze statue of Abraham Lincoln is removed from Platt Fields, Manchester, where it had been installed in 1919, to a new public space, Lincoln Square, where it is the focal point of a new development in the central city. It was remounted on a new eight-foot-tall pedestal to remove the temptation of vandalism. City fathers decided to inscribe the new taller pedestal with extracts from a letter Lincoln wrote in 1863 to the working men of Lancaster. Controversy erupted when the *Manchester Guardian* published that Lincoln's reference to "working men" in his missive had been altered in the text recorded on the pedestal to "working people" for reasons of political correctness.[10] Former Conservative lord mayor Dame Kathleen Ollerenshaw criticized the City Council: "These people are rewriting history. History is history. You cannot violate history and change, for example, what Winston Churchill said. I've never heard such bloody nonsense."[11]

1986. A USPS Mint Set of Commemorative Stamps folder cover features two bold, impressionistic portraits of Abraham Lincoln and the torch of the Statue of Liberty. A 22-cent Lincoln portrait stamp (Scott 2217g) was among a presidential series inside the folder.

1986 DECEMBER. The continuing odyssey of Henry B. Joy's hammered-copper copy of Alfonso Pelzer's New Jersey statue of the Great Emancipator by John G. Segesman resumes. After four decades at the Charles Howell Scout Reservation, Brighton, Michigan, the statue was once again moth-balled when the Boy Scout facility was sold. Two years later, Migisi Opawgan Lodge would raise $5,000 to restore the statue, which was then placed inside the Wyckoff Lodge at D-Bar-A Scout Ranch, Metamora, Michigan.

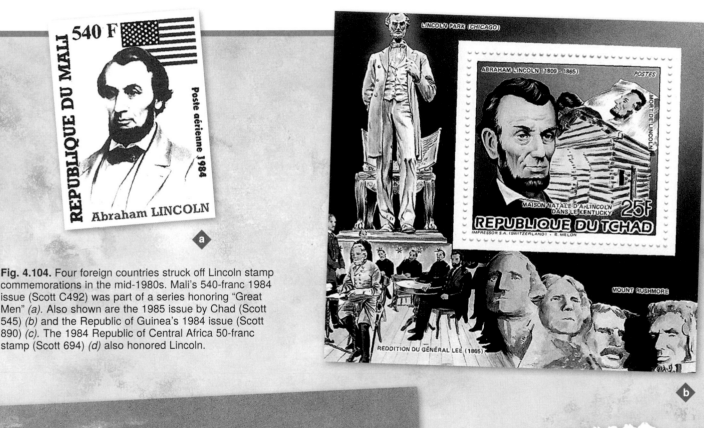

Fig. 4.104. Four foreign countries struck off Lincoln stamp commemorations in the mid-1980s. Mali's 540-franc 1984 issue (Scott C492) was part of a series honoring "Great Men" (a). Also shown are the 1985 issue by Chad (Scott 545) (b) and the Republic of Guinea's 1984 issue (Scott 890) (c). The 1984 Republic of Central Africa 50-franc stamp (Scott 694) (d) also honored Lincoln.

1986

UNITED STATES POSTAL SERVICE
MINT SET OF COMMEMORATIVE STAMPS

Fig. 4.105. "Much ado about nothing" might be the first thought of a Lincolnphile opening the U.S. Post Office 1986 Mint Set commemorative folder, after viewing the passionate cover illustration (a) with two excellent likenesses of Old Abe and the torch of the Statue of Liberty, signed by Guering. The Ameripex '86 sheet inside the folder (b) has an uninteresting 22-cent Lincoln stamp (Scott 2217) from a pen-and-ink sketch in Jerry Dadds's "woodcut style," after Brady's O-64 1864 photograph.

Presidents of
the United States: II

USA 22 — John Tyler
USA 22 — James K. Polk
USA 22 — Zachary Taylor
USA 22 — Millard Fillmore
USA 22 — Franklin Pierce
USA 22 — James Buchanan
USA 22 — Abraham Lincoln
USA 22 — Andrew Johnson
USA 22 — Ulysses S. Grant

AMERIPEX 86
International
Stamp Show
Chicago, Illinois
May 22-June 1, 1986

a

b

Abe Lincoln

Springfield 1859

Fig. 4.106. Batsman Abe Lincoln appears on this imaginative faux 1859 baseball card for the Springfield Nine, one of a series of 2 by 3-1/2–inch cards prepared by Dave Stewart in San Francisco during the 1980s. Stewart, a disabled Vietnam vet, adorned the backs of his cards with U.S. and POW/MIA flags and a legend, "Support Disabled American Veterans."

1987 FEBRUARY 15. ABC television airs the first segment of its blockbuster mini-series *Amerika*, set a decade after the Soviet Union had occupied the United States. A big-budget, 14-1/2-hour drama, it starred Kris Kristofferson, Sam Neill, Robert Urich, and Mariel Hemingway. The narrative depicted the United States under the control of a United Nations regime. American symbols like the flag had been usurped or co-opted. An Abraham Lincoln icon was still important, but so were icons of Karl Marx and Vladimir Lenin. The country's new major holiday was "Lincoln Week," which replaced the Fourth of July as a patriotic rallying point. "Indeed, the signature scene in the film was a 20-minute, dialogue-free depiction of the celebration of 'Lincoln Week' festivities . . . with both Lincoln and Lenin displayed on banners that were most likely intended to be striking and startling to television audiences of the time," according to a TV historian. Urich's character, Peter Bradford, delivered the most memorable lines from writer-director David Wrye's script in voice-over as he looked at the Lincoln Memorial: "All the kids growing up now don't have any idea of the difference between the symbol of Abraham Lincoln and what he actually stood for. You can't look at those eyes and not think of what being an American has meant. Now there's an end to it. Soon, there will be no America. We'll be history, quickly lost and distorted, like Mr. Lincoln himself. . . . I suppose there will have to be new revolutions, with new generations who will have to discover the values which our forefathers handed down to us. If those truths stop being real, maybe it's better to let them go, to let some new generation discover, as though for the first time. Maybe freedom is just one of those things you can't inherit."

1987 JUNE. A decade earlier, the Lincoln Boyhood Drama Association had been formed for the purpose of telling "the story of Abraham Lincoln's boyhood years, and at the same time, to convey the meaning of these events, both to the remainder of Lincoln's life as well as to the larger, long-term view of American history." The Association had hired playwright Billy Edd Wheeler to write a play on Lincoln's formative years. In 1985, the State of Indiana appropriated $3.35 million to construct an amphitheater at Lincoln State Park, completed in June 1987. The play *Young Abe Lincoln* would debut there that summer, "another major boon to [the park's] interpretive program," according to a National Park Service historian.

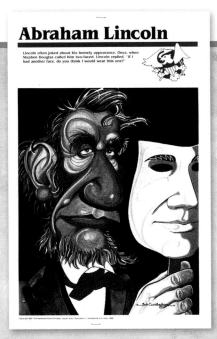

Fig. 4.107. In 1987 illustrator Bob Cunningham created a memorable advertising poster for The Perfection Form Co., Logan, Iowa. Abraham Lincoln holding a mask is quoted as saying: "If I had another face, do you think I would wear this one?"

Fig. 4.108. When my then nine-year-old son came home with his milk carton from school in 1987, he told me that he'd had to work hard to convince his teacher to let him keep the carton for his dad. I'm sure glad that his mom and I raised him right!

Fig. 4.110. Log Cabin Syrup sold its maple goodness in this commemorative tin in 1987 to celebrate a century of business. Patrick J. Towle introduced his breakfast syrup (named for his hero, Abraham Lincoln, who had lived in a log cabin) in 1887.

Fig. 4.109. Shown are three inexpensively produced Abe Lincoln and pals medals from the 1980s. The 1985 "Great Americans" medal showing Lincoln with Thomas Jefferson and George Washington *(a)* is a Mardi Gras carnival throw, tossed into admiring crowds by one of the krewes in the festival. The 1987 (60th anniversary) copper-nickel Lincoln and Mount Rushmore medal *(b)* has the familiar double-eagle reverse. The 1987 Lucky Penny *(c)* is not the kind we've seen from the 1920s forward. It does not celebrate a specific place, is only quarter-size, and has a cartoonish Lincoln profile portrait.

1987. The Bureau of Engraving and Printing experiments with microprinting, producing a Series of 1987 $5 Lincoln-portrait Federal Reserve Note with *The United States of America* repeated many times in very tiny lettering in an arc around the upper two-thirds of the Lincoln vignette. The engraved facsimile signatures on the proof are of Ortega (United States treasurer) and Baker (secretary of the Treasury), correct for the period. A 32-subject proof sheet of these hitherto unknown notes was discovered at the Smithsonian Institution in 2010 by collector-researchers Jamie Yakes and Peter Huntoon. Similar microprinting didn't appear on issued Federal Reserve Notes until the Series of 1990, on notes of $10 and higher, and on Series of 1993 for the $5s. The anti-counterfeiting measure was first used on Series of 1982 food coupons, printed by the American and U.S. Bank Note companies, Huntoon noted.

1987. Russell Friedman's *Lincoln: A Photobiography*, published by Clarion Books, wins the John Newbery Medal for children's literature. Established in 1922, the award is presented annually by the American Library Association and the Association for Library Service to Children.

1987 DECEMBER. A mile-plus-long Abraham Lincoln Memorial Bridge is opened on Interstate 39 across the Illinois River at LaSalle, Illinois. A $38 million bridge rehab project begun in February 2007 would be completed in October 2008. *Road and Bridges* magazine recognized the refurbished bridge as one of its Top 10 Bridges of 2008.

1988 FEBRUARY 15. Illustrator Lee Lorenz's *New Yorker* Valentine's Day cover shows Abe Lincoln and George Washington exchanging valentines.

Fig. 4.111. Collector Jamie Yakes discovered this unissued Series of 1987 $5 Federal Reserve Note essay in the National Numismatic Collection of the Smithsonian Institution. The note has distinctive micro-printing surrounding the vignette—a series of *The United States of America* repeated in tiny lettering. This was an anti-counterfeiting device not adopted on the $5 denomination until the Series of 1993.

Fig. 4.112. Illustration arts can create scenes impossible in history, such as Lee Lorenz's adorable *New Yorker* St. Valentine's Day cover *(a)* depicting Lincoln and Washington exchanging greeting cards, or the *Atlantic* graphic of Lincoln and Jefferson holding books to illustrate an essay by historian Doug Wilson on the two presidents' reading habits *(b)*.

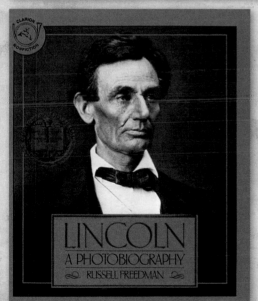

Fig. 4.113. Russell Friedman's *Lincoln: A Photobiography*, published by Clarion Books in 1987, won the 1988 John Newbery Medal for Children's Literature.

Fig. 4.114. Honest Abe Genuine Split-Rail Root Beer, Springfield, Illinois, advertised on an HO-gauge boxcar. "An honest beverage of the people, by the people and for the people!" an iconic $5-bill image states.

1988 MARCH 27. Sam Waterston plays opposite Mary Tyler Moore as the first couple, in Ernest Kinoy's adaptation of Gore Vidal's *Lincoln.*

1988 JUNE 16. Lincoln's Springfield home reopens to the public after months of remodeling. Phillip H. Wagner, of Springfield, publishes a "Special Edition" of Lincoln photographic historian Lloyd Ostendorf's fine 1961 illustrated biography, *Abraham Lincoln, The Boy and the Man,* featuring 133 of artist Ostendorf's original drawings and "101 rare Lincoln-related photos."

1988 JULY 18. Blue-and-white campaign buttons for Senator Robert F. Kennedy sport the legend "The Dream Lives On . . . Atlanta 1988" surrounding a large image of Abraham Lincoln, and smaller images of RFK, his brother JFK, and Dr. Martin Luther King Jr.

1989 FEBRUARY 17. Robert V. Barron appears as Abraham Lincoln, one of the historical figures encountered by Bill S. Preston Esq.

(Alex Winter) and Ted Logan (Keanu Reeves) in *Bill & Ted's Excellent Adventure.* When Abe accompanies the students back to San Dimas High School auditorium for their oral report, Lincoln tells the student body to "Be excellent to each other, and . . . party on dudes," bringing down the house.

1989 JULY. Lincoln Gardens, facing Chicago's *Standing Lincoln* statue by Augustus Saint-Gaudens, are donated by Credit Agricole.

1990 APRIL. After two years of display inside at Wyckoff Lodge, at Metamora, Michigan, the odyssey of Henry B. Joy's hammered-copper copy of Alfonso Pelzer's New Jersey statue of the Great Emancipator by John G. Segesman adds another chapter. It would be removed to an outdoor site at Wyckoff Lodge, and in summer 2003 placed on a newly constructed brick pedestal outside the Thomas D. Trainor Scouting Museum. "Every year, hundreds of

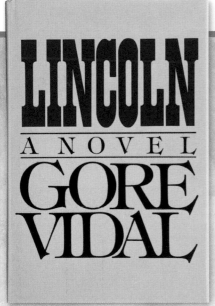

a

b

Fig. 4.115. Gore Vidal's *Lincoln (a)* was a runaway best seller in 1984 and a Book-of-the-Month Club selection. The six-foot-one-inch Sam Waterston starred in the 1988 small-screen adaptation *(b).* Director Lamont Johnson won an Emmy for his direction. Vidal depicted Lincoln, stripped of saintliness, as a cunning, shrewd, emotionally detached politician.

Fig. 4.116. Dayton, Ohio, Lincoln photo collector, historian, and illustrator Lloyd Ostendorf co-created the Lincoln photo-cataloging system (still in use) with Charles Hamilton, in their 1962 book *Lincoln in Photographs, An Album of Every Known Pose.* In the mid-1970s I was introduced to Ostendorf by Paul Agnew (his cousin and photographer), and through the next two decades Lloyd became something of a mentor to me. In his letterhead Lloyd used a small cut of O-99, Anthony Berger's 1864 photo similar to the design engraved in 1869 for U.S. Fractional Currency. Variant O-99 was derived from O-98, a pose that Lloyd discovered and then copyrighted in 1956. In 1987 Ostendorf answered one of my myriad queries on one of his O-99 Lincoln Picture Studio postcards *(a).* In 1988 Ostendorf's illustrated *Abraham Lincoln, The Boy, The Man* was reprinted in a special edition for the reopening of Lincoln's Springfield home *(b).*

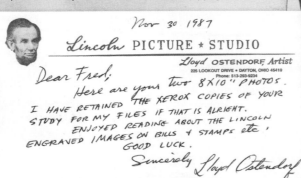

a

b

Cub Scouts and Boy Scouts make the pilgrimage to D-Bar-A Scout Ranch for a rededication ceremony to honor the life of a truly great leader, Abraham Lincoln," Scout officials said. The Lincoln Pilgrimage has been a Migisi Opawgan Lodge service project since 1959. "One thing for sure, you can always expect this event to run the second weekend of February of each year," they add.

1990 SEPTEMBER 23. Ken Burns's nine-part docudrama, *The Civil War*, commences, with Sam Waterston portraying Abraham Lincoln. The series would win two Emmy Awards.

1990 MAY 23. The Government Accounting Office, Congress's independent accounting arm, releases a statement to the U.S. House coinage subcommittee favoring continuation of the one-cent coin.

1990 NOVEMBER. Harper-Collins publishes Mario Cuomo's and Harold Holzer's *Lincoln on Democracy*. According to Holzer, the book was "inspired originally by a delegation of teachers from the Solidarity Union of Poland who had come to visit Governor Cuomo. They said to him that they really needed books now that their country was escaping from the constraints of the Iron Curtain and becoming free and independent." Cuomo suggested that they study Abraham Lincoln, but "they said that they had no Lincoln, that the Communists and the Nazis, between the two of them, had removed all of the Lincoln." So Cuomo promised he would get a book together and with Holzer wrote *Lincoln on Democracy*. The book was translated into Polish, Japanese, Hebrew, and Indonesian. "The most memorable political, diplomatic event was when Lech Walesa came from Poland to receive the first Polish language copy. That was a pretty unforgettable day. The man who had helped liberate the country and who had wanted Lincoln on the bookshelves," Holzer added.[12]

1991. Marshall Mitchell's bronze statue *Out of the Wilderness*, showing a hatless Abraham Lincoln on horseback, is installed at New Salem State Park. The Illinois Historic Preservation Agency and the Capital Development Board Art in Architecture Program commissioned this small work.

1991 NOVEMBER 19. A life-size bronze statue of Abraham Lincoln raising his stovepipe hat and gesturing as if talking to an acquaintance is installed in the Gettysburg, Pennsylvania, town square on the anniversary of Lincoln's Gettysburg Address. The installation was a gift of the Lincoln Fellowship of Pennsylvania. The statue is the work of J. Seward Johnson Jr., who calls his sculpture *The Return*. The narrative of the statue is that Lincoln is pointing toward the Wills House, where he spent the night before his famous speech, in a second-floor room, and where he put the final polish to his immortal text.

Fig. 4.117. Which is goofier: Robert V. Barron's "party on, dudes" speech in the 1989 film *Bill & Ted's Excellent Adventure (a)*, or Disney cartoon characters visiting the Lincoln Memorial on St. Vincent's 1989 two-cent stamp (Scott 1257) *(b)* or $5 stamp (Scott 1264), flying a small plane past Mount Rushmore for the World Stamp Expo '89?

Fig. 4.119. Marshall Mitchell's equestrian Lincoln statue *Out of the Wilderness* was installed at the New Salem State Park visitor center in 1991.

Fig. 4.118. As we have seen in this book and in *Abraham Lincoln: The Image of His Greatness*, politicians of all stripes have clung to the long Lincoln coattails to boost their chances or legitimize their campaigns. President George H.W. Bush's 1989 inaugural ribbon linked his presidency to Lincoln, TR, Reagan, and Ike, a not-unnatural twining for the Republican Bush-41.

1992 APRIL 4. The Akron (Ohio) Art Museum mounts a two-month-long exhibition, "An Enduring Interest: The Photographs of Alexander Gardner, One of America's First Photo-Journalists," featuring Gardner's six sessions with Abraham Lincoln at Washington, D.C., and Antietam, Maryland, which produced upward of 31 separate Lincoln images, including the magnificent portrait known to collectors and historians as the "Gettysburg Lincoln" (O-77). Gardner was Lincoln's most prolific lensman.

1992 AUGUST 27. Sculptor Lily Tolpo's bronze group *Lincoln and Douglas in Debate* is dedicated at Freeport, Illinois, close to the actual site of the event, in an area known locally as "Debate Square." The statue was dedicated on the 134th anniversary of the arguably most famous of the seven Lincoln-Douglas debates. To improve the scale of the disparately sized orators, Douglas is shown standing and gesturing and Lincoln is seated nearby on a stool with hands and legs crossed and his hat upside down on the podium next to him.

1992 SEPTEMBER. The weakened copy of Alfonso Pelzer's hammered-copper statue of the Great Emancipator by John G. Segesman in Wilkinsburg, Pennsylvania, falls off its pedestal, because repairs made to Lincoln's ankles (after the statue was stolen and recovered a decade earlier) failed. "A Wilkinsburg resident found the statue in some nearby bushes and toted it to the Wilkinsburg police on a Port Authority bus," according to Pittsburgh reporter Chris Potter.[13] For the next decade the defaced statue would reside in the Wilkinsburg Borough Building. In May 2001 it was placed on a pedestal at the former junction of the Old Lincoln Highway and the Old William Penn Highway, now Penn Avenue.

1992 OCTOBER 31. A renewed Lincoln Highway Association is organized at Ogden, Iowa, "as a non-profit organization dedicated to the interpretation and preservation of America's first transcontinental automobile road."

1993 MARCH 29. Portions of the Lincoln Highway in Green County, Iowa, near Jefferson, Grand Junction, and Scranton, are put on the National Register of Historic Places.

1993 MAY 12. With a life-size bust of Abraham Lincoln looking over his left shoulder, President Bill Clinton delivers a major economic address on the need to reduce the federal deficit at New York City's Cooper Union.

Fig. 4.120. In the early 1990s, foreign governments continued to return to the American collector trough to generate foreign exchange to feed their regimes. In the extreme, in 1991 Guyana overprinted its series of eight orchid stamps with "Fighters for Peace" and similar slogans, along with references to personalities such as Abraham Lincoln. To create additional collector varieties for the American market, Guyana officials varied ink color, and additionally imprinted some stamps "Specimen." The $7.65 stamp *(a)*, as well as the multitudinous varieties, are not listed in standard catalogs.

The following year, in 1992, Guyana issued very high-value stamps, such as a silver-foil $600 stamp with Lincoln, Churchill, Kennedy, FDR, and Martin Luther King *(b)*, for the World Thematic Stamp Expo held in Genoa, Italy, honoring the 500th anniversary of Columbus's 1492 journey. Multiple variations were also created, none of which made it into stamp catalogs. Delightful and less egregious, but still pandering, is the 1992 St. Vincent Grenadines $5 (Scott 838) *(c)* tribute to poet and Lincoln biographer Carl Sandburg, for the World Columbian Stamp Expo '92, held in Chicago.

Fig. 4.121. In 1992 Shell Oil Co. sponsored a promotion distributing small brass "coins" with likenesses and bios of U.S. presidents. The Lincoln likeness is similar to the icon portrait on the $5 bill.

Fig. 4.122. Engraver Ron Landis became famous within the numismatic community for his medallic work for The Gallery Mint, Eureka Springs, Arkansas. In 1994 Landis also produced this very creditable partial Lincoln currency-image souvenir card for the Gallery Mint Museum.

1993 July 9. Sitting on the steps of the Lincoln Memorial at sunset, Secret Service agent Frank Horrigan (Clint Eastwood) tells Abraham Lincoln, "Well, Abe, I wish I could have been there for you, pal," in the debut of the film *In the Line of Fire.*

1993 October 31. Art by Philadelphia African American artist David Bustill Bowser is featured in a comprehensive traveling display of 18th- and 19th-century African American arts and crafts opening at the Harriet Tubman Museum in Macon, Georgia. Bowser painted a contemporary Abraham Lincoln portrait in the display.

1993 December 1. Banknote Corporation of America's $20 food-coupon die proof, with a portrait based on the Gettysburg Lincoln photograph, is approved by the U.S. Department of Agriculture's Food and Nutrition Service, order 43-3198-3-0643.

1994 June 12. A revival of Robert Sherwood's *Abe Lincoln in Illinois* receives two Tony Award nominations, for Gerald Gutierrez as director and for Sam Waterston in the title role.

1995 January. A Fleer Ultra Spider-Man card set shows "Carnage U.S.A.," in which Spidey wreaks havoc on the Lincoln Memorial,

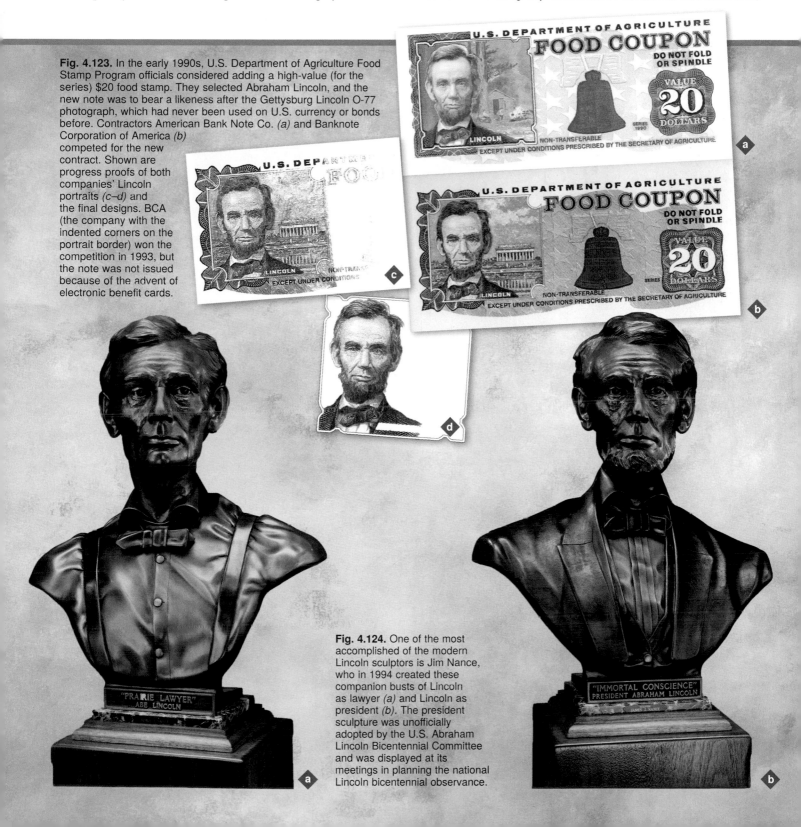

Fig. 4.123. In the early 1990s, U.S. Department of Agriculture Food Stamp Program officials considered adding a high-value (for the series) $20 food stamp. They selected Abraham Lincoln, and the new note was to bear a likeness after the Gettysburg Lincoln O-77 photograph, which had never been used on U.S. currency or bonds before. Contractors American Bank Note Co. (a) and Banknote Corporation of America (b) competed for the new contract. Shown are progress proofs of both companies' Lincoln portraits (c–d) and the final designs. BCA (the company with the indented corners on the portrait border) won the competition in 1993, but the note was not issued because of the advent of electronic benefit cards.

Fig. 4.124. One of the most accomplished of the modern Lincoln sculptors is Jim Nance, who in 1994 created these companion busts of Lincoln as lawyer (a) and Lincoln as president (b). The president sculpture was unofficially adopted by the U.S. Abraham Lincoln Bicentennial Committee and was displayed at its meetings in planning the national Lincoln bicentennial observance.

along with the Statue of Liberty, the Liberty Bell, Graceland, the Alamo, Hollywood, San Francisco, Mount Rushmore, Wrigley Field, and Coney Island. The artist for the 10-card series was Gale Heimbach.

1995 FEBRUARY. Dr. George Hoeman and Mary Myers select the C.S. German image of Abraham Lincoln for the identity for his American Civil War Home Page, providing hypertext links to the most useful electronic Civil War resources on the Web.

1995. Pennsylvania governor Tom Ridge designates a six-county, 200-mile stretch of US-30 (the old Lincoln Highway route) as the Lincoln Highway Heritage Corridor, with the intent of improving economic conditions from tourism in the region.

1995 MAY 28. Sculptor John McClarey's humorous statue, *The Last Stop*, depicting Abraham Lincoln with a small pig at his feet, is ded-icated in Taylorville, Illinois. The title refers to the town's location on the Eighth Judicial Circuit of Lincoln's time, and the subject matter recalls the wild pigs that interrupted a trial Lincoln had at Taylorville early in his legal career. The statue is located at the county historical society.

1995. A bronze bust of Abraham Lincoln mounted on an impressive, multi-tiered pedestal, by Carl and Lily Tolpo, is installed in Wauke-gan, Illinois, on the grounds of the Lake County Court House. The monument commemorates a speech Lincoln made in Waukegan.

1996 SEPTEMBER 13. Lowbrow-movement artist Van Arno debuts his latest limited-edition serigraph/silkscreen entitled *Abraham Lincoln Carried to Heaven by Raiderettes*. A naked, partially disembow-eled Lincoln is hauled skyward by two bronze, equally naked, Amazons, in Arno's depiction.

Clockwise from top left: Kris Kristofferson in "Tad," Abraham Lincoln, Abraham and Tad Lincoln, Kris Kristofferson and Bug Hall in "Tad." "Tad" is a Family Channel original movie.

Fig. 4.125. Lincoln imagery by the end of the 20th century had taken a hard turn toward ultra-imaginary, such as the 1995 Fleer Ultra Spider-Man card (Fleer 137-A) *(a)* art by Gale Heimbach (part of a 10-card mayhem set), and the ghoulish circa-1996 *Lincoln Carried to Heaven by Raiderettes* poster *(b)* by California Lowbrow artist Van Arno.

Fig. 4.126. In a 1995 Family Channel special, singer-songwriter Kris Kristofferson was cast as daddy to Bug Hall's Tad in an original movie titled simply *Tad*, depicting the Lincoln saga through the eyes of Lincoln's son. Although Kristofferson hardly looked the part, he played it earnestly and tenderly, according to Lincoln movie historian Mark Reinhart.

Fig. 4.128. In the 1970s the present author and Tom DeLorey wrote a standard catalog of error currency, so misprinted bills are near to the author's heart. This Series of 1995 Richmond district Federal Reserve Note is missing its third printing—the green overprinting that normally includes the Treasury seal and serial numbers.

The American Civil War Homepage

...but one of them would make war rather than let the nation survive, and the other would accept war rather than let it perish, and the war came.
Abraham Lincoln, 4 March 1865

Fig. 4.127. In the mid-1990s the American Civil War Homepage commenced aggregating links to Civil War resources on the Web. It employed the historically appropriate Lincoln image based on the same model as the $10 bill image current during Lincoln's lifetime on its home page in 1996 (seen here), and still does to this day under the care of Dr. George H. Hoeman of the University of Tennessee, Knoxville.

Fig. 4.129. Robert Silvers invented the Photomosaic™ technology while a student at MIT, and founded Runway Technology Inc. in 1996. Silvers's creative manipulation of myriad images to form a discernible overall pattern, such as the Gettysburg Lincoln O-77 style, was employed on the 1999 Republic of Togo 300-franc souvenir sheet (Scott unlisted), "Faces of the Millennium of Faces." Among the "1,276 Civil War photographs, the third stamp down on the right edge shows John Wilkes Booth in the upper left corner," according to Lincoln philatelic expert Angus Lincoln, of the British Lincolns. A large poster with a similar presentation by Silvers is framed in the author's Lincoln Room.

1996. The Abraham Lincoln Foundation is founded as a nonprofit organization to preserve and develop the collections of the Union League of Philadelphia, and utilize them to educate and inspire the community. The foundation makes the historical treasures of the Union League accessible to the public through tours, exhibits, symposia, and special events. The League's collections include the original Tanner manuscript recording the events of Secretary of War Edwin Stanton's interrogations of eyewitnesses to Lincoln's death (recorded that night in the Petersen House parlor), a signed copy of the Emancipation Proclamation, a vast library, and a large collection of art.

1996 OCTOBER 27. Viewers of the popular animated program *The Simpsons* catch a glimpse of an Abraham Lincoln portrait in Homer and Marge's Springfield home. Aficionados of the long-running program have cataloged more than 60 on-screen references to Lincoln in various episodes. In one, Homer goes back into time and saves Lincoln from being assassinated, then he and Abe save John F. Kennedy from a sniper's bullet.

1997 JUNE. Schiffer Publishing releases antique writer Stuart Schneider's *Collecting Lincoln, With Values*, "a Schiffer book for collectors and historians."

1997 JUNE. The City of Chicago Department of Cultural Affairs donates a seated bronze statue of a young Abraham Lincoln, by sculptor Charles Keck, to the city. The statue was placed on a three-tier riser in Senn Park at the Seven Mile House site, 5887 North Ridge Avenue. Seven Mile House, the former homestead and inn operated by the Nicholas Kransz family, was visited by candidate Lincoln in 1860. It was seven miles from downtown Chicago.

1997 JUNE 11. *The Authoritative Reference on Lincoln Cents*, by John Wexler and Kevin Flynn, is copyrighted.

1997 SEPTEMBER 28. Thieves plunder and steal a hammered-copper replica of Alfonso Pelzer's New Jersey statue of the Great Emancipator by John G. Segesman from its perch outside Detroit's Skillman Public Library.

Fig. 4.130. In the early 1990s my teenage son, Fred IV, would sometimes come up to dad's office at Beckett Publications and "hang out." Beckett was the leading publisher of sports-card and sports-personality periodicals and books at the time. Dad was vice president of publishing, and Fred IV was a collector. He would often while away the time by dashing off sketches, such as this original design employing a modern art style pioneered by Andy Warhol.

Fig. 4.131. Abraham Lincoln is associated with money, so it is easy to see why various gaming-industry manufacturers and casinos would put his image on chips for use in lieu of cold hard cash in gaming situations. These $5 Lincoln chips are from the 1990s.

1997 SEPTEMBER 30. Detroit Public Library staff retrieve their "scraped and dented" hollow bronze replica of Alfonso Pelzer's New Jersey Great Emancipator statue by John G. Segesman from a Detroit police station. The statue had been gashed and a foot was badly damaged, and it was dumped face down in front of Detroit's Clark Elementary School. It would be restored and placed inside Detroit's Burton Library to prevent further vandalism.[14]

1998 FEBRUARY 3. "Mr. Lincoln's Virtual Library," funded by a million-dollar donation by the Jones Foundation, goes online as part of the Library of Congress "American Memory" online historical collections. Lincoln impersonator Michael Krebs was on hand for the launch. Jones reminisced that as a Springfield, Illinois, paperboy he delivered newspapers to the historic Lincoln home there. "I am continuing my tradition of being a paperboy from an analog format to a digital one," he said. The virtual library allows various repositories to offer their material online in an interconnected way.

1998 MARCH. Through May, the Library of Congress displays the original draft of Abraham Lincoln's preliminary Emancipation Proclamation, its first public appearance since 1983, in its permanent, rotating "American Treasures" exhibition. This is the document Lincoln brought to a Cabinet meeting July 22, 1862, five days after the Second Confiscation Act by Congress, which gave Union forces the right to confiscate, or free, slaves held by Southerners in rebellion against the government. In recent years, according to library records, the Emancipation Proclamation was displayed to the public briefly in 1975 and 1983, and for a longer period in 1962–1963.

1998 MARCH 12. *A Quick Reference to the Top Lincoln Cent Die Varieties*, by Gary Wagnon, Karen Peterson, and Kevin Flynn, is published.

1998 APRIL 12. Turner Network Television debuts John Gray's screen adaptation of Jim Bishop's 1984 bestseller *The Day Lincoln Was Shot*, with Lance Henriksen as Abraham Lincoln and Rob Morrow as John Wilkes Booth. The program would be nominated for three Emmy Awards, for sound, cinematography, and hairstyling. Henriksen was nominated for a Golden Satellite Award for best supporting actor in a mini-series or motion picture made for television. This was the third historical novel by Bishop to be adapted for the screen. His other bios concerned the day Jesus Christ died and FDR's last year.

Fig. 4.132. The first Lincoln dollar coin was issued in 1998 by the Republic of Liberia, when its government incorporated a small image of the Daniel Chester French Lincoln Memorial statue conjoined to a profile of Ronald Reagan on a cupro-nickel coin (KM-386). Liberia also issued similar $10 and $100 coins (KM-387 and 388).

Fig. 4.133. Lance Henriksen played the title role in Turner Network Television's April 1998 made-for-cable drama *The Day Lincoln Was Shot*, a polemic film that owes little to Jim Bishop's best-selling dramatization of the same name. The film also presents a much different picture than the 1956 made-for-TV film with Raymond Massey in the title role. Imaginary scenes and motivations made the drama a potboiler, which nevertheless earned Henriksen a Golden Satellite Award nomination for best supporting actor in a made-for-TV film or mini-series.

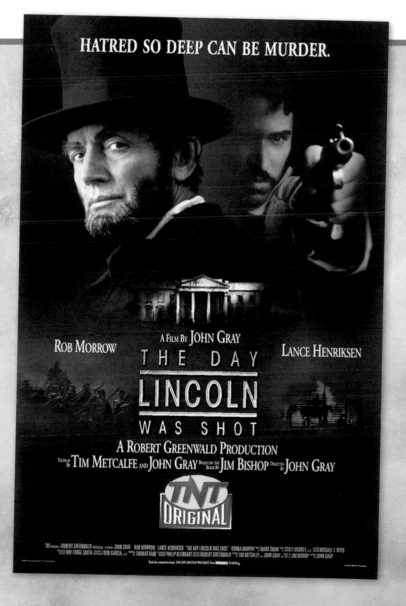

HATRED SO DEEP CAN BE MURDER.

ROB MORROW

A FILM BY JOHN GRAY

LANCE HENRIKSEN

THE DAY LINCOLN WAS SHOT

A ROBERT GREENWALD PRODUCTION

TELEPLAY BY TIM METCALFE AND JOHN GRAY BASED ON THE BOOK BY JIM BISHOP DIRECTED BY JOHN GRAY

TNT ORIGINAL

1998. Associated University Presses copyrights Frederick C. Moffatt's *Errant Bronzes: George Grey Barnard's Statues of Abraham Lincoln*, a thorough documented discussion of the controversies surrounding Barnard's rustic Lincoln likenesses. The book was published by the University of Delaware Press.

1998 June. A bronze statue of Abraham Lincoln by sculptor John McClarey is dedicated at the Russian State Library for Foreign Literature, in Moscow.

1998 November 22. John Edward Hempe, Rapid City, South Dakota, wins the International Mt. Rushmore Adult Prose Contest first-place prize—a $500 U.S. Savings Bond—for his brief essay, "Lincoln: The Reunion."

1999 February 12. The *Complete Price Guide and Cross Reference to Lincoln Cent Mint Mark Varieties*, by Brian Allen and John A. Wexler, is published.

1999 Spring. Eminent Lincoln historian Michael Burlingame's discussion of the Bixby letter leads off the Abraham Lincoln Association's launch of its newsletter, *For the People.* The newsletter was the brainchild of new ALA president Donald L. Tracy, to further make Lincoln more relevant to 21st-century Americans. Additional content in the issue included Tom Schwartz's debunking of quotations frequently attributed to Lincoln that he never uttered, a memorial to recently deceased (July 23, 1998) Lincoln promoter and Chicago book dealer Ralph Geoffrey Newman, and association news.

1999. The "Looking for Lincoln" program is instituted as a "state heritage coalition of historic sites and communities that have developed an educational and entertaining 30–45 minute Lincoln experience, either in museums, historic structures, audio driving or walking tours, etc., that create a Lincoln experience for visitors that they would judge to be educational, entertaining, and worth the time and effort to explore as a Lincoln experience," program Director Hal Smith told this author. "We hope they would agree it was worthy of their time and would be a place they would return to or recommend to others to see. We currently have about 20 historic sites and communities that have met these criteria," he added.[15]

1999 July 19. Social historian Kirk Savage's *Standing Soldiers, Kneeling Slaves*, published by Princeton University Press, traces the "slow historical stream of monumental history" by which whites stand erect and emancipated slaves bow low in America's public spaces. The prototypical example for Savage is the Thomas Ball *Emancipation Group* in Washington, D.C., which graces the book's cover. Savage recognizes the "dramatic stage for several epochal events" which have encompassed the Lincoln Memorial since its dedication in 1922. He urges, "Why not erect a monument to Reverend King within this great white temple? Not just a plaque, which has already been proposed, but a life-sized statue of King at the top of the memorial steps, where he gave his speech—a companion figure to Lincoln's, as King indeed was in that great hour of our nation's life."[16] According to the author, such a move would not diminish the Lincoln legacy but expand upon it. A commemorative inscription headed "I Have A Dream" has been inscribed in a step to commemorate Dr. King's speech there August 28, 1963. A King statue was dedicated on the National Mall in 2011.

1999 November 19. Three days after the U.S. Treasury unveils its new Lincoln-portrait $5 Federal Reserve Note design (see figure 4.138), collectorsuniverse.com publishes author Fred Reed's discussion of the implications of replacing the 85-year-old iconic Lincoln image on the bills.

Fig. 4.134. Hartford Insurance Company, Hartford, Connecticut, has long exploited the fact that both Abraham Lincoln and Robert E. Lee insured their homes (in Springfield, Illinois, and Arlington, Virginia, respectively) with the company. This 1996 ABNCo stock-certificate specimen for the Hartford Life subsidiary incorporated in Delaware employs their images with their corporate stag symbol after Sir Edwin Landseer's *Monarch of the Glen* painting.

For the People

A Newsletter of the Abraham Lincoln Association

Volume I, Number 1   Spring, 1999   Springfield, Illinois

Abraham Lincoln, John Hay, and the Bixby Letter

by Michael Burlingame

Most moviegoers are aware that Abraham Lincoln's letter of condolence to Lydia Bixby, a widow who purportedly had lost five sons in the Civil War, looms large in Stephen Spielberg's recent film, *Saving Private Ryan*. Dated November 21, 1864, the letter reads as follows: "I have been shown in the files of the War Department a statement of the Adjutant General of Massachusetts, that you are the mother of five sons who have died gloriously on the field of battle. I feel how weak and fruitless must be any words of mine which should attempt to beguile you from the grief of a loss so overwhelming. But I cannot refrain from tendering to you the consolation that may be found in the thanks of the Republic they died to save. I pray that our Heavenly Father may assuage the anguish of your bereavement, and leave you only the cherished memory of the loved and lost, and the solemn pride that must be yours, to have laid so costly a sacrifice upon the alter of Freedom. Yours, very sincerely and respectfully, A. Lincoln."

Although extravagant praise has been lavished on this document, it is surrounded by ironies. Mrs. Bixby was deemed "the best specimen of a true-hearted Union" ever seen, yet she was in fact a Confederate sympathizer who ran a whorehouse. In addition, Mrs. Bixby lied about her sons; despite her claim that five of them had been killed, she had really lost only two boys in the war.

Moreover, this beloved Lincoln letter was almost certainly composed by assistant presidential secretary John Hay. Several people, including the British diplomat John Morley, literary editor William Crary Brownell, United States Ambassador to Great Britain, Walter Hines Page, Louis A. Coolidge, a Washington correspondent for a Boston newspaper, and Spencer Eddy, Hay's personal secretary, testified that they heard Hay claim authorship or had heard that assertion made by a third party quoting Hay.

Although no direct, firsthand testimony shows that Hay claimed authorship of the Bixby letter, Hay did in 1866 tell William H. Herndon that Lincoln "signed without reading them the letters I wrote in his name."

Most Lincoln specialists have doubted that Hay composed the Bixby letter. In 1982, Mark E. Neely, Jr., declared: "There is not a scrap of reliable evidence to prove" Hay's authorship of the Bixby letter.

But there is. Hay's papers *continued on page 3*

continued on page 3

The original copy of the Bixby Letter has never been located.

Fig. 4.135. The Abraham Lincoln Association launched its newsletter *For the People* in spring 1999 with historian Michael Burlingame's critique of the Bixby Letter's authorship, and Frank Ballew's 1864 "Long Abraham Lincoln a Little Longer" post-reelection cartoon from *Harper's Weekly*.

Fig. 4.136. "Looking For Lincoln" was a 1999 Illinois initiative to involve local communities in developing educational and entertaining Lincoln venues suitable for promoting tourism. A decade later, 52 Illinois communities and sites had been marked by exhibits and story boards with the LFL logo.

Fig. 4.137. In 1999 Princeton University Press published social historian Kirk Savage's scathing assessment of 19th-century memorial statuary in the United States.

1999 NOVEMBER 19. *London Daily Mail* reviewer Peter McKay quotes gender-reassigned female author Jan Morris's jaded recollections of America's love affair with Abraham Lincoln in her lately published *Lincoln: A Foreigner's Quest*. Morris is Amerophobic, and bitterly anti-Lincoln. In his 20s (in the early 1950s), *London Times* reporter James Morris visited the United States near the zenith of Lincoln consciousness in this country. Morris recorded his impressions in the 1956 book *As I Saw the U.S.A.* What she encountered, according to her own words four decades later, had antagonized her: "the myth of Abraham Lincoln."

> The American people as a whole were almost deranged in their obsession with their 16th President, the country boy from the Middle West who, by overcoming the rebel South in the American Civil War, had ended American slavery and saved the Union. He had been assassinated at the moment of victory almost a century before, but he seemed to me, as a brash young European, all too intrusively alive. . . . [M]y own youthful prejudices against ostentatiously self-made men, cottage philosophers, role models, mimics, comic raconteurs and the University of Life, amazed and depressed me, and made me view Mr. Lincoln with a decidedly skeptic eye.

Several new editions of the work have appeared in the last decade.

2000 JANUARY 1 CIRCA. A Cheerios cereal promotion includes 10 million "first minted" Lincoln cents and 5,000 Sacagawea dollars packed in its boxes. The cents or cents/dollars were accompanied by certificates of authenticity over the facsimile signature of Mint Director Phillip N. Diehl printed on the back of the card containing the coin(s) mounted in a plastic blister pack. "This is to certify that the United States Mint at its Philadelphia, Pennsylvania facility—the largest coin manufacturing plant in the world, produced the enclosed coin(s). Your 2000-dated coin is one of the first 10,000,000 to be produced by the Mint and has been packaged by Cheerios as a special memento of the new millennium." These "Cheerios Dollars" became quite collectible and pricey five years later, when it was learned they were an early trial striking of the dollar-coin reverse. On the cereal-box coins, the features on the eagle's tail are more detailed, exhibiting veinage, and the central shaft of the center feather in the tail is raised. No such veinage appears on the rounded tail feathers of the normal coin, and the central vein is incuse. Collectors searched for terminology to describe this die difference. *Coin World*'s Bill Gibbs coined the terms "Reverse of 1999" and "Reverse of 2000" to describe the rare variety and the regular issue, respectively. Many of the prototype dollar coins were obviously spent into circulation before their significance was discovered. Independent coin-grading firms PCGS and NGC slab these Cheerios promotion coins, which draw big bucks from willing collectors. At a recent date, NGC had slabbed 390 cents and 27 of the dollar coins. No such distinctive variety has been found on the Cheerios cents. Although the scarce dollars command premiums of thousands of dollars (sets of the two coins have sold as high as $34,500 in Heritage Galleries auctions), slabbed Cheerios cents have only superficial premiums, of $20 to $40.

Fig. 4.138. The U.S. Treasury produced a poster to acquaint the public with the new U.S. Federal Reserve Note designs. The new-style, enlarged Lincoln portrait (BEP die MISC 198327-3) by Bureau of Engraving and Printing engraver Thomas Hipschen, from a design by William Fleishell, for the Series of 1999 bill is based on the same photographic model that Charles Burt engraved in 1881 for the Series of 1882 $500 Gold Certificates—Anthony Berger's 1864 O-91 image.

Fig. 4.139. In a promotion launched in January 2000, examples of the first cent and dollar coin of the new millennium were packaged in random boxes of Cheerios. This 2000 Lincoln cent was guaranteed by U.S. Mint director Philip N. Diehl to have been "one of the first 10,000,000 to be produced by the Mint." Many fewer dollars were so-packaged. The dollars, because they had an unadopted reverse die variety, have been high-valued premiums to collectors. The cents, not so much.

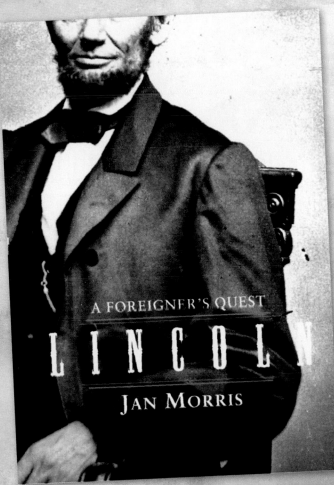

Fig. 4.140. Amerophobic British author Jan Morris found Americans "almost deranged in their obsession with their 16th president" in the 1999 book based on a visit to the States in the mid-1950s.

2000 FEBRUARY 1. Johnson Publishing Co. releases Lerone Bennett Jr.'s 652-page book *Forced Into Glory: Abraham Lincoln's White Dream.* African American scholar Bennett's insights include this comment about fooling all the people all the time (regarding Lincoln's racism):

> Lincoln is theology, not historiology. He is a faith, he is a church, he is a religion, and he has his own priests and acolytes, most of whom have a vested interest in 'the great emancipator' and who are passionately opposed to anybody telling the truth about him. Not only is Lincoln a church, he is also an industry. Hundreds, perhaps thousands, of men and women earn their living feeding the Lincoln machine, turnout out the Lincoln slogans, hairline the proclamation that never was. Over and above this, the mythological Lincoln is a defining structure in the identity system of most Americans, who are hooked on Lincoln, as on a drug, and who need periodic fixes to reaffirm their sense of reality. . . . The fascinating question here is not how people have managed to hide Lincoln, but how they have managed to hide him while writing thousands of books about him.

2000 FEBRUARY. University Press of Kansas publishes Harold Holzer's *Lincoln Seen and Heard*, which "charts his rocky road from obscure western politician to national icon," according to the publisher. The book would become the basis for a traveling road show by Holzer and various actors reading from Lincoln's works. (See also the entry for February 11, 2005.)

2000 FEBRUARY. Lincoln philatelist Eliot A. Landau's two-part article (the second segment appeared in May) in *Chronicles of the U.S. Philatelic Classics Society* conclusively demonstrates that the black 1866 Lincoln 15-cent stamp (Scott 77), based on the C.S. German photographic model (as was also the $10 greenback portrait then in wide circulation), was issued as a memorial stamp to the slain leader, who had died a year earlier. A condensed summary article offering the same argument would be published in *First Days* in 2002.

2000 FEBRUARY 21. Abraham Lincoln tops C-Span's "Presidents' Day" historians' survey of presidential leadership. Lincoln's rankings according to 87 "historians and presidential experts" surveyed were: Public Persuasion (3), Crisis Leadership (1), Economic Management (3), Moral Authority (2), International Relations (4), Administrative Skills (1), Relations with Congress (4), Vision / Setting an Agenda (1), Pursued Equal Justice for All (1), Performance Within the Context of the Times (1).

2000 JULY 7. President Bill Clinton proclaims President Lincoln's Cottage, and 2.3 acres surrounding it at the Soldier's Home, Washington, D.C., a national monument. The cottage was Lincoln's retreat from the heat and stress of Washington during the war. It would be restored and opened to the public on February 18, 2008.

Fig. 4.141. In this age of inflation, Lincoln's money image adorned this fraudulent million-dollar note in 2000. According to press reports one was tendered to a British bank, which only declined to break it because the necessary cash was not on hand at the time!

Fig. 4.142. The new larger currency portraits invited a cottage industry of "re-facing," such as this example by Fred L. Reed IV.

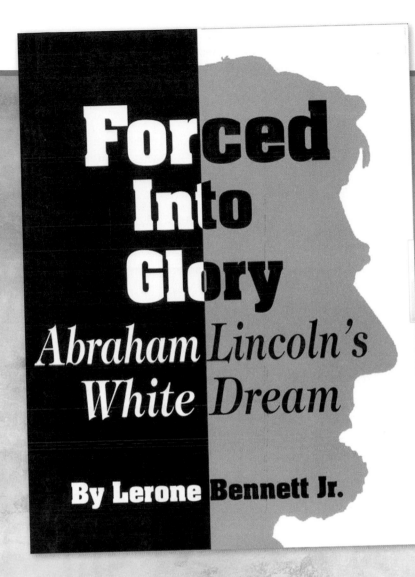

Fig. 4.143. African American scholar Lerone Bennett's *Forced Into Glory: Abraham Lincoln's White Dream* critiqued Lincoln mythology and Lincoln commerce, exclaiming that Americans are "hooked on Lincoln, as on a drug."

Fig. 4.144. This 2000 political badge employs the Lincoln money image to dramatic effect.

Fig. 4.145. This ghastly image of Abraham Lincoln appears on a playing card produced in the 1990s or early 2000s.

2001 JANUARY 9. In the "Dutch Treat" episode of the ABC *Dharma & Greg* sitcom, Ryan Stiles, playing Abraham Lincoln, declines to go to lunch with the funny couple because he already has a hat full of waffles at the ready, which he takes down and shares with Jenna Elfman's character, eliciting a great quantity of guffaws on the soundtrack. "I've got syrup in my pants," he tells Dharma, bringing forth a crescendo of laughs. A 36-second clip would be posted to YouTube on August 27, 2007, garnering 40,000 hits.

2001 FEBRUARY 8. Oxford University Press publishes The *Lincoln Enigma: The Changing Face of an American Icon*, edited by professor Gabor Boritt.

2001 FEBRUARY 10. Sculptor John McClarey's *Sitting with Lincoln* bronze, depicting a casual Lincoln sitting on a wood bench beside his stovepipe hat, reading, is dedicated in Vandalia, Illinois, south of the restored Illinois state house where Lincoln sat as a member of the state's General Assembly in the 1830s. The state house was later moved to Springfield. The statue presently resides in a small enclosure west of the Old State House.

2001 FEBRUARY 12. More than 20 different patriotic organizations present wreaths at the Lincoln Memorial in a formal ceremony sponsored by the Lincoln Birthday National Commemorative Committee.

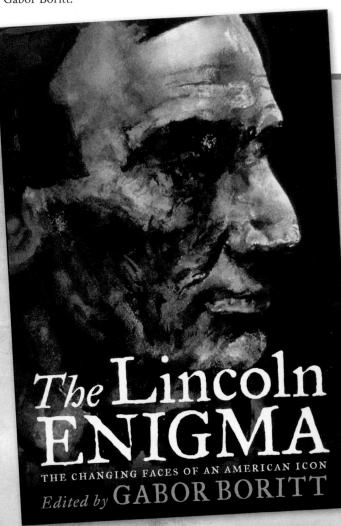

Fig. 4.146. The 2001 Oxford University Press book *The Lincoln Enigma*, edited by Lincoln scholar Gabor Boritt, explored the changing image of Lincoln in society in a series of essays. The book's subtitle is *The Changing Faces of an American Icon*.

Fig. 4.147. Taking a cue from the 19th-century *Life* magazine contest depiction of Lincoln's money image (see figure 2.116), the present author placed this ad in the January-February 2001 issue of the Society of Paper Money Collectors' award-winning magazine *Paper Money*, which he edits. The ad generated considerable comment and *results.*

Fig. 4.148. In a January 2001 episode of the sitcom *Dharma & Greg*, Americans watched Ryan Stiles as Lincoln pull waffles out of his hat, accompanied by the guffaws of a soundtrack.

Fig. 4.149. Sculptor Rick Harney's bronze figure of a relaxed Lincoln sitting on a park bench, which was unveiled on the east lawn of the McLean County Museum of History (formerly the Court House) in July 2000, continues a trend of down-to-earth humanizing in Lincoln statuary begun by Gutzon Borglum in 1911.

2001 FEBRUARY 19. University of Illinois Press publishes the seminal work on Lincoln image historiography, *The Lincoln Image: Abraham Lincoln and the Popular Print*, by coauthors Harold Holzer, Gabor S. Boritt, and Mark E. Neely Jr. Their book "documents how popular prints helped make Lincoln's a household face, deliberately crafting the image of a man of the people, someone with whom an ordinary American could identify," they write. By comparing original photographs and paintings with the prints made from them, the authors show how printmakers reworked the original images to refine or alter Lincoln's appearance in one way or another.

2001 FEBRUARY 19. The PBS series *The American Experience* kicks off a three-day, three-part presentation, "Abraham and Mary Lincoln: A House Divided," with David Morse and Holly Hunter in the title roles, and the participation of Lincoln scholars David Herbert Donald, Mark E. Neely Jr., Judge Frank J. Williams, and Doris Kearns Goodwin.

2001 MAY 7. Computer programmer William Leigh Hunt creates a portrait based on the Anthony Berger image familiar to all as the old-style $5 bill portrait, by the method of PhotoTiling. "PhotoTiled pictures are pictures that are themselves created from pictures," Hunt told this writer. Readers may have encountered such Photo-Tiled images on magazine covers or posters. For years, the present author has had a large Photomosaic™ portrait of the Gettysburg Lincoln—made up of hundreds of Civil War photographic images—by Robert Silvers hanging on a wall in his "Lincoln Room." Hunt's Lincoln was "made from 554 various pictures," he said. "The target image is a Civil War–era black-and-white photograph (the February 9, 1864, O-92 photo by Anthony Berger). Notice how a black-and-white image can be made from color pictures. In the enlarged view notice the small tile pictures come in three different sizes, giving a somewhat different look to this image," its creator said.[17]

Fig. 4.150. In 2001 Liberia issued a tiny 11-millimeter $10 gold coin (KM-unlisted) *(a)* honoring Abraham Lincoln and Jefferson Davis. The coin has a minuscule imitation of the Gardner O-77 photo. The following year Liberia issued a larger, but still small, 20-millimeter $50 gold coin *(b)*. This time the portrait resembled the iconic O-92 Lincoln money image.

Fig. 4.151. The village of Lincolnwood (formerly Tessville) in Cook County, Illinois, is proud of its namesake. It's likely that the image of Abraham Lincoln on the community's shoulder patch is modeled on a beardless Hesler photo. The village changed its name in 1936, when civic leaders were seeking a new and better image for their community.

Fig. 4.152. Charleston, Illinois, honors Abraham Lincoln and Lincoln's association with their community on their Land of Lincoln police-uniform patches.

Fig. 4.153. In 2001 computer guru William Leigh Hunt invented a program by which any group of photographs could be phototiled into a target image. Hunt's 554 personal family pictures created this O-92 representation of Lincoln. Hunt told this author he chose the O-92 image because people were familiar with it. Through an agreement with Robert Silvers, who popularized phototiled mosaics, Hunt no longer distributes his phototiling software to do pictures such as this, he told the present author.

Fig. 4.154. Early 21st-century Lincoln patches include this 2001 Detroit Boy Scout Lincoln Pilgrimage emblem *(a)* with its iconic money-image design. Another 2001 Lincoln Pilgrimage scout patch, this one from Indiana *(b)*, employs the Frank Ballew "Long Abe . . . Longer" cartoon.

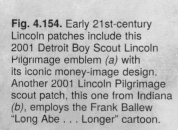

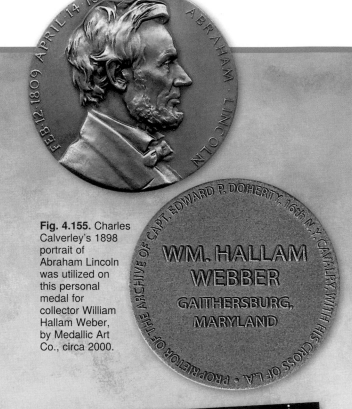

Fig. 4.155. Charles Calverley's 1898 portrait of Abraham Lincoln was utilized on this personal medal for collector William Hallam Weber, by Medallic Art Co., circa 2000.

Fig. 4.156. At the end of the 20th century several countries took opportunities to launch philatelic items on the collectors' market. Angola's 1999 "Countdown to the Millennium" *(a)* is probably the most blatantly commercial. The country issued stamps for 1940s events as disparate as the *Wizard of Oz* (it was the 1940s by the time the 1939 U.S. film got to Africa) to Pippi Longstocking, to Betty Grable to Anne Frank to the Yalta Conference, but also recognized the completion of Mount Rushmore in 1941 as a companion label on the souvenir sheet. In 2000 the Central Asian (formerly Soviet) republic of Khakasia issued a revalued stamp, honoring scouting, with Norman Rockwell's painting on it. *(b)* The same year, Rwanda printed a 300-franc stamp sheet *(c)* honoring John F. Kennedy and the U.S. space program with a gratuitous Lincoln image. Also in 2000, Turkmenistan, a West Asian former Soviet republic bordering Afghanistan and Iran, issued a series honoring U.S. presidents with the significance of Lincoln's administration highlighted by Walt Disney playing with a small scale model of his "Great Moments With Mr. Lincoln" attraction *(d)*.

2001 September. Life-size bronze figures of contestants Abraham Lincoln and Stephen A. Douglas mark the 143rd anniversary of their debate at Charleston, Illinois. The work of sculptor John McClarey, they are arranged facing one another "across a metaphorical divide" behind stone parapets (ramparts). The positioning emphasizes the disparity in their heights. According to the sculptor, both men represent the "House Divided" of their times. The statues are poised just outside the Lincoln-Douglas Debate Museum in Charleston.

Fig. 4.157. Life-size bronzes of Abraham Lincoln and Stephen A. Douglas were dedicated outside the Lincoln-Douglas Debate Museum in Charleston, Illinois, in September 2001. Sculptor John McClarey arranged the antagonists at ground level "across a metaphorical divide," putting them behind stone ramparts.

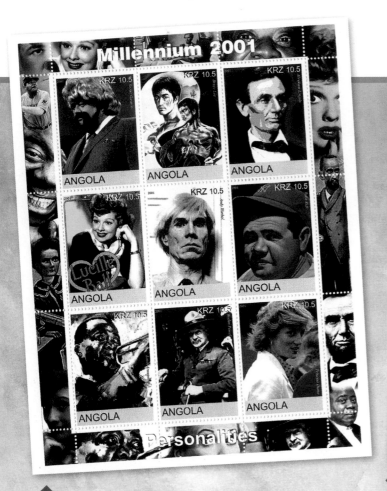

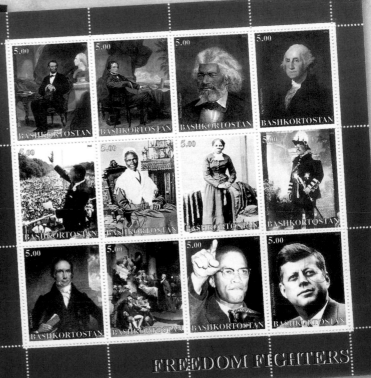

2001 October. Kent State University Press publishes Gary L. Bunker's *From Rail-Splitter to Icon: Lincoln's Image in Illustrated Periodicals, 1860–1865.* Reviewer Richard West wrote: "Bunker's book easily surpasses all of the other books devoted to Lincoln in caricature . . . because Bunker's survey of the field is comprehensive, when the others were selective, and his historical analysis is fully informed by several generations of important Lincoln scholarship."

2001 October 14. Sculptor John McClarey's bronze figure *Lincoln Draws the Line* shows Abraham Lincoln with his feet spread and pointing toward the ground to symbolically depict his stance against the spread of slavery into the territories. The life-size statue stands outside the Peoria County Courthouse in Peoria. The statue was funded by the Lincoln Statue Committee.

2001 October 20. The Kentucky Memorial at Vicksburg, Mississippi, is dedicated, featuring standing bronzes of rival presidents Abraham Lincoln and Jefferson Davis, both of whom were Kentuckians. The monument honors native Kentucky soldiers who fought at Vicksburg for both the Blue and the Grey. On May 8, 2010, a separate monument on the battlefield would be dedicated to the Kentucky Confederates who served there, under auspices of the Kentucky Division of the Sons of Confederate Veterans and the Kentucky Division of the United Daughters of the Confederacy.

2001 November 7. A subplot in an episode of the television drama *The West Wing* discusses elimination of the Lincoln cent because, as a presidential aide remarks, "They are worthless." However, a wiser head among the inner staff predicts that the proposed legislation to do away with the cent will never come up for a vote on the floor of the House of Representatives because the speaker hails from Illinois, which the aide notes "is the only state where you can put them in a toll booth. Why is that, do you suppose?"

PRESIDENT
ABRAHAM LINCOLN
(1861–1865)

LIBERIA $100

THE 16TH PRESIDENT OF UNITED STATES

e

Fig. 4.158. Turn-of-the-century millennial stamps from a half dozen foreign countries identified Abraham Lincoln as a famous individual. Angola has two different Lincoln images (O-27 and O-77) on its 2001 souvenir sheet of stamps *(a)*. Somaliland's 2001 stamp and sheet margin reproduce the C.S. German O-43 photo that shows how full Lincoln's beard had gotten only two days prior to leaving Springfield for Washington, D.C. *(b)*. Buriatia reproduces the Gardner O-77 photograph on its 2001 stamp *(c)*. Bashkortostan reproduces Alonzo Chappel's painting of Lincoln admiring Washington (see figure 1.50) on its 2001 stamp *(d)*. Liberia employed the iconic O-92 Lincoln money image on its patriotic 2001 $100 stamp *(e)*. Meanwhile Nevis celebrated the century of the teddy bear, and mischievously included a Lincoln money image *(f)*, as well as images of Napoleon, Henry VIII, and Charlie Chaplin, to sell additional souvenir sheets to a potentially broader universe of collectors.

It's A Bear's World.....
100th Anniversary of Teddy Bears

f

2001 DECEMBER 12. Augustus Saint-Gaudens's *Standing Lincoln* statue in Lincoln Park, Chicago, is designated as a Chicago Historical Landmark.

2002 JANUARY. Scholastic Press publishes Amy Cohn's and Suzy Schmidt's primary-school–aged biography *Abraham Lincoln*, with highly original art by David A. Johnson, including the Lincoln–full moon, high-hat cent profile on the book's back cover.

2002 FEBRUARY. *American Philatelist* publishes Lincoln stamp enthusiast Eliot A. Landau's "The Lincoln Story," illustrated by Lincoln campaign, mourning, and related covers from Landau's famous collection.

2002. The Wilkinsburg Historical Society underwrites repair and restoration of the city's hammered-copper copy of Alfonso Pelzer's Lincoln Emancipation statue by John G. Segesman. The hollow figure would be reinforced with an interior steel-tube skeleton, and returned to its original location beside the former historic Lincoln Highway.

2002 MAY 17. The U.S. Secret Service Office of Investigations releases findings supporting the genuineness of a purported 1959-D Lincoln cent with a Wheat Ears reverse. The Wheat Ears design had been officially retired in 1958, and all 1959 cents were supposed to have the Lincoln Memorial reverse.

2002. Economics professor Dr. Thomas DiLorenzo publishes his unflattering assessment *The Real Lincoln: A New Look at Abraham Lincoln, His Agenda, and an Unnecessary War*. DiLorenzo attacked Lincoln's racism, his centralization of power, and his economic policies.

Fig. 4.159. Several Lincoln universities exist. The Lincoln University in Jefferson, Missouri, for which this challenge coin was issued around 2000, was founded in 1866 by the 62nd and 65th Colored Infantries, according to the school seal reproduced on the "coin."

Fig. 4.160. The "World's Largest Covered Wagon," according to the *Guinness Book of World Records*, was constructed by David Bentley in 2001. It has been located several places since, as a tourist attraction. It is shown here, unfortunately defrocked of its cover, in 2009 in Lincoln, Illinois. A 12-foot-tall Abe reads a book entitled *LAW* in the front of a 40-foot-long wagon.

Fig. 4.161. Illustrator David A. Johnson's back cover art for a Lincoln biography (aimed at the juvenile market, published by Scholastic Press) playfully recreates the Lincoln cent profile image.

THE REAL LINCOLN

A New Look at Abraham Lincoln, His Agenda, and an Unnecessary War

FOREWORD BY WALTER E. WILLIAMS,
John M. Olin Distinguished Professor of Economics, George Mason University

THOMAS J. DILORENZO

Fig. 4.162. Loyola University economics and history professor Dr. Thomas DiLorenzo has been one of the chief recent critics to naysay the historical Lincoln interpretation. DiLorenzo's 2002 book *The Real Lincoln* attacks Lincoln's racism, centralization of power, and economic policies.

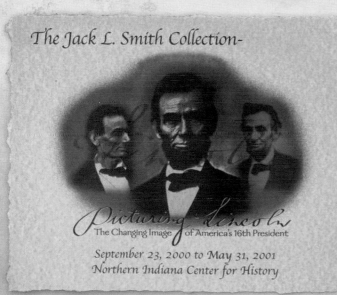

The Jack L. Smith Collection-

Picturing Lincoln
The Changing Image of America's 16th President

September 23, 2000 to May 31, 2001
Northern Indiana Center for History

Fig. 4.163. For seven months in 2000 and 2001 South Bend's Northern Indiana Center for History exhibition "Picturing Lincoln: The Changing Image of America's 16th President" featured more than 100 photographs from the Jack L. Smith Collection, as well as artifacts from Lincoln's lifetime, including the pen and inkwell used to sign the Emancipation Proclamation, and the carriage in which the Lincolns rode to Ford's Theatre on the night of the assassination.

Fig. 4.164. This Lincoln embroidered textile in the format of a $5 Silver Certificate, but with red seal and serial number (not blue), came out of England. Dealer Pam West, who found it for the present writer, had no explanation of its purpose or use. It was quite a project freehand. This writer finds it delightful!

Fig. 4.165. Collectors specializing in collecting U.S. MPC (Military Payment Currency) and related items convene once a year for a get-together in Bowling Green, Ohio, and at mini-fests around the country at large numismatic conventions. Participants are paid in MFC (Military Fest Currency), which can be collected, spent, anteed in poker games, etc. The $5 reverse shown *(a)* is Series 031, issued at Fest IV on March 1, 2003, and at other events subsequent until withdrawn on March 6, 2004. The $2 reverse shown *(b)* is Series 011, issued at Fest II on March 10, 2001, and following, withdrawn March 10, 2002, according to Joe Boling, coauthor (with Fest organizer Fred Schwan) of the classic book on World War II numismatics, *World War II Remembered*.

2002 July 24. Convicted murderer, forger Mark Hofmann, claims he made the controversial 1959-D Lincoln cent mule (declared legitimate by Treasury officials), in a letter to his sister.

2002 September 14. A dual, heroic-size bronze sculpture of Abraham Lincoln and Stephen Douglas, commemorating their first 1858 debate during the U.S. senatorial campaign, is dedicated in Ottawa, Illinois. The setting includes fountains surrounding the statues by artist Rebecca Childers Caleel, in Washington Square Park, near the site of the debate.

2002 September 23. Ira and Larry Goldberg Coins & Collectibles remove a 1959, Type of 1958 (Wheat Ears reverse), Lincoln cent from a scheduled auction sale.

2002 October 13. Sculptor Jeff Adams's innovative bronze group *Paths of Conviction, Footsteps of Fate*, which depicts Abraham Lincoln and Chief Black Hawk emerging from the same base, is dedicated beside Route 2 near Oregon, Illinois, in the Rock River Valley. "This sculpture is a reflection on the personal conviction, struggle, and fate shared by Lincoln and Black Hawk," sculptor Adams stated. Both Lincoln and the Native American chief were familiar with the area in the 1830s, when Lincoln was a captain during the Black Hawk War. Adams created the Lincoln portion using a life mask and numerous photographs as models. "My intent was to capture Lincoln's spirit, not illustrate a particular moment in history," he contended. The Black Hawk figure "sits on an incline, symbolic of the precarious position of the Native Americans during the white settlement of the prairie," he added.

2002 December 9. This is the first day of minting of Illinois state quarter dollars. The coins would be released to the Federal Reserve and the public on January 2, 2003. U.S. Mint "First Day Coin Covers" were postmarked on that date.

2003 January. Sculptor Avard T. Fairbanks's son Eugene E. Fairbanks's book, *Abraham Lincoln Sculpture Created by Avard T. Fairbanks*, is published. Extensively illustrated with family sources, the book is an excellent survey of Fairbanks's many Lincoln works.

2003 February 23. An 1885 Augustus Saint-Gaudens study of Abraham Lincoln, created in preparation for his *Standing Lincoln* monument in Chicago's Lincoln Park, is a highlight of the exhibition "Augustus Saint-Gaudens: American Sculptor of the Gilded Age," which began its national tour at the North Carolina Museum of Art, Raleigh, North Carolina.

2003 April 10. Lincoln University, Chester County, Pennsylvania, which changed its name from Ashmun School in 1866, kicks off a year-long celebration of its sesquicentennial.

Fig. 4.166. If trivializing Old Abe were not enough, early 20th-century marketers found ready currency in dressing up their imaginary characters as Abe to peddle to children and to grandparents of youngsters. Disney's 2002 movie character Stitch (a), and veteran characters Dale (b) and Goofy (c), as well as the Hanna-Barbera Smurfs (d), have donned Lincoln togs for small-scale memorabilia.

2003 OCTOBER 4. John McClarey's life-size bronze depiction of Abraham Lincoln as a surveyor is dedicated at New Salem State Historic Site, near the visitor center. Lincoln served as deputy surveyor of Sangamon County from 1833 to 1837. The statue was commissioned by the Illinois Professional Land Surveyors Association.

2004 FEBRUARY 10. The Lincoln Society of Peekskill, New York, celebrates its 100th anniversary with a gala ball and commemorative event.

2004. Topps trading card company, known for its baseball cards of the golden age of America's pastime in the 1950s and 1960s, issues an American Treasures Signature Cut Card with a valuable Abraham Lincoln autograph, card number AT-AL. The short-printed card tells its finder on the back: "CONGRATULATIONS! You have just received an authentic American Treasures Signature Cut Card of Abraham Lincoln from 2004 Topps Baseball Series 1." The card also has a 45-word biography of "one of history's greatest leaders" (Topps' words).

2004 MARCH 24. Associated Press reporter Jan Dennis reports on a movement in Lincoln, Illinois, to build a 305-foot-tall statue of Abraham Lincoln as the anchor for a theme park / tourist attraction. The projected $40 million project is the brainchild of local pastor Reverend S.M. Davis. "If we get the money, I think you'll see it go and I think you'll see it become one of the biggest tourist attractions in America," Davis is quoted saying. A statue of that height would be visible for 20 miles on the Illinois prairie. The steel-and-fiberglass structure would be patterned after Lloyd Ostendorf's painting of Lincoln christening the town of Lincoln, Illinois, with watermelon juice in 1853, according to the head of the community group seeking funds for the Long Abe. The projected height of the monument / tourist mecca, 305 feet, equals that of the Statue of Liberty and its pedestal. For further comparison, a statue of "Mother Russia" in Volgograd is 270 feet tall, while several Buddhist shrines are taller. A 500-foot-tall Maitreya Buddha statue is planned for India, and a 555-foot "Spirit of Houston" statue is on the drawing boards in Texas.

Fig. 4.167. On April 5, 2003, binding up the nation's wounds was not on the agenda for unreconstructed Sons of Confederate Volunteers and Lincolnphobes who protested the dedication of David French's life-size bronze sculpture of Abraham Lincoln and son Tad seated on a bench in Richmond, Virginia. In addition to the statue, protestors objected to the city council paying $45,000 for the plaza to show off the city's newest artwork, located on the site of the former Tredegar Ironworks. Others were more copacetic with the memorial. "Time marches on," said a civic leader. The statue was commissioned by the Richmond-based United States Historical Society.

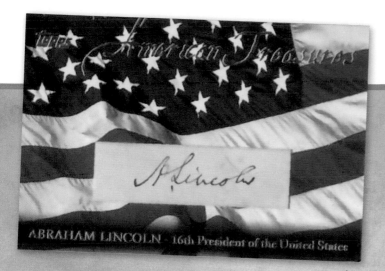

Fig. 4.169. Sculptor John McClarey's life-size bronze depicting Abraham Lincoln as a surveyor was dedicated in New Salem State Historic Site in October 2003. It was based on a pen-and-ink drawing by Lloyd Ostendorf.

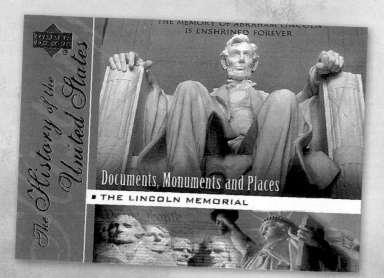

Fig. 4.168 Most of the recent limited-edition collectors' cards are pretty cheesy, but in 2004 a Topps Card Co. American Treasures card *(a)* featured a real cut signature of "A. Lincoln." Competitor Upper Deck served up Lincoln monuments in a subset devoted to memorials *(b-c)*.

Fig. 4.170. Promoters projected a 305-foot-tall Abraham Lincoln in the process of christening Lincoln, Illinois, with watermelon juice in 1853, as a theme park to attract tourism. The barrels behind the tall figure were intended to be the twin 10-story towers of a hotel. The attraction design was from an illustration by Lloyd Ostendorf.

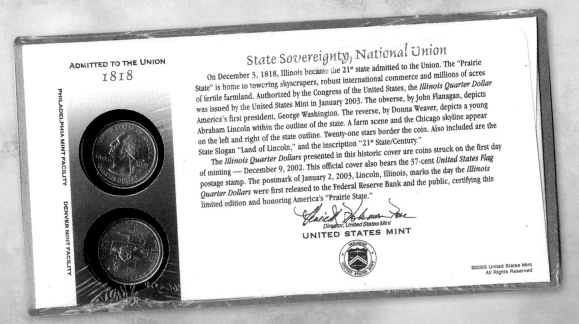

ADMITTED TO THE UNION
1818

PHILADELPHIA MINT FACILITY

DENVER MINT FACILITY

State Sovereignty, National Union

On December 3, 1818, Illinois became the 21st state admitted to the Union. The "Prairie State" is home to towering skyscrapers, robust international commerce and millions of acres of fertile farmland. Authorized by the Congress of the United States, the *Illinois Quarter Dollar* was issued by the United States Mint in January 2003. The obverse, by John Flanagan, depicts America's first president, George Washington. The reverse, by Donna Weaver, depicts a young Abraham Lincoln within the outline of the state. A farm scene and the Chicago skyline appear on the left and right of the state outline. Twenty-one stars border the coin. Also included are the State Slogan "Land of Lincoln," and the inscription "21st State/Century."

The *Illinois Quarter Dollars* presented in this historic cover are coins struck on the first day of minting — December 9, 2002. This official cover also bears the 37-cent *United States Flag* postage stamp. The postmark of January 2, 2003, Lincoln, Illinois, marks the day the *Illinois Quarter Dollars* were first released to the Federal Reserve Bank and the public, certifying this limited edition and honoring America's "Prairie State."

Director, United States Mint

UNITED STATES MINT

Fig. 4.171. The U.S. Mint issues coin covers as a product line. This Illinois state-quarter coin cover contains two quarters "struck on the first day of minting—December 9, 2002," and is postmarked on January 2, 2003, the first day of the coin's release. The commemorative reverse by Donna Weaver depicts a young Abraham Lincoln, a state map, a farm, and the Chicago skyline.

2004 MAY 11. *NCIS* (Naval Criminal Investigative Service) television-series coroner Dr. Donald "Ducky" Mallard (David McCallum) displays the bullet that killed Abraham Lincoln, and additional items from Lincoln's autopsy, to impress a female agent, on the popular CBS-Paramount crime drama.

2004 MAY 23. C-Span broadcasts Sam Waterston and Harold Holzer's presentation *Abraham Lincoln's Cooper Union Address* of February 27, 1860.

2004 JUNE 1. Houghton-Mifflin publishes Mario Cuomo's *Why Lincoln Matters Today More Than Ever.*

2004 JUNE 5. A four-part life-size bronze Lincoln family grouping by sculptor Larry Anderson is unveiled on the statehouse square by Springfield, Illinois, mayor Timothy J. Davlin. Anderson depicted Abraham holding a speech prior to arriving at the nearby statehouse, while Mary adjusts his coat. Nearby, son Willie waves to eldest son Robert a short distance away. The figures are part of Springfield's "Here I Have Lived" interpretive program, which is designed to help observers understand Lincoln in his home environment. Federal grants financed the sculptures. (See figure 4.74.)

2004 OCTOBER. Pop California artist Mark Ryden's eerie painting of Abraham Lincoln's decapitated head posed as a voyeur graces the cover of Kirsten Anderson's study *Pop Surrealism: The Rise of Underground Art*, published by Last Gasp. According to the artist, Lincoln is more icon than human to people today, and the Lincoln image has a potent impact on people because he was "King of Presidents."

Ryden described his work in 1998. "When I painted Abraham Lincoln lying on the ground giving birth from his cheek to the baby Venus delivered by Colonel Sanders I thought that was pretty original. I had at first envisioned it as Colonel Sanders giving birth to Abraham Lincoln, but upon the realization that had been done several times I cleverly added my unique twist," the artist told an interviewer for *Juxtapoz* magazine. Ryden's "lowbrow" surrealistic mixture of historical figures (such as Lincoln, Colonel Harlan "Kentucky Fried Chicken" Sanders, Michael Jackson, and Jesus Christ) with dewy-eyed blond doll figures and raw red meat in fantastical situations is popular not only with pop-culture magazines and music-album covers, but also museums like the San Francisco Museum of Modern Art, and with collectors in places like eBay. A four-minute video on YouTube shows Ryden in time-lapse fashion painting his 2010 *Pink Lincoln*, along with glimpses of several of his other Lincoln paintings, and an eclectic mix of Lincoln reference material.

2004 OCTOBER 2. Sculptor Matt Langford's figure of a standing Abraham Lincoln, holding a book and leaning on an axe, is unveiled in Covington, Kentucky, the first winner of the City of Covington's Art of Discovery Awards. Sculptor Langford says he hopes his bronze statue of young Abe Lincoln will inspire young Kentuckians to rise above their beginnings like Lincoln did by embracing the twin symbols of toil and aspiration that he took up. The statue, on a low plain base so that it is accessible to youngsters of all ages, is on the grounds of the Mary Ann Morgan Library at Fifth Street and Scott Boulevard.

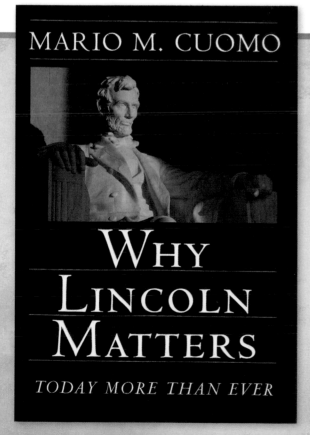

Fig. 4.172. New York's former Democratic governor Mario Cuomo wrote *Why Lincoln Matters* in 2004 to address current hot-button issues from a Lincoln perspective. This was Cuomo's second Lincoln book. In 1990, as governor, he and his aide, Lincoln scholar Harold Holzer, co-wrote *Lincoln on Democracy* to supply reference material to teachers in newly liberated Poland.

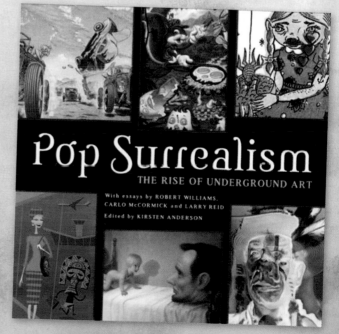

Fig. 4.173. Art critic Kirsten Anderson's 2004 study of Pop Surrealism featured artist Mark Ryden's voyeuristic image of a beheaded Lincoln on its cover.

2004 OCTOBER 10. The *Cincinnati Enquirer* reports that the recently restored statue of *Lincoln & Liberty* by William Granville Hastings, located at South Avondale Elementary School in Cincinnati, has been plagued by vandals scrawling obscene graffiti on the monument's white granite base. A 2001 restoration cost $70,000 to spruce up the then 99-year-old monument. In recent years vandals have scribbled and cut gang and other symbols into the memorial, causing the cash-strapped Cincinnati Public School system (which owns it) to scratch their heads in dismay.

2004 OCTOBER 14. The Abraham Lincoln Presidential Library opens in Springfield, Illinois. The presidential museum would open six months later, on April 19, 2005.

2004 NOVEMBER 10. The Illinois House–Joint Resolution sponsored by Representative Rich Brauer receives final approval to designate the Abraham Lincoln Parkway. On January 10, 2005, Springfield mayor Timothy J. Davlin would praise the state legislature's action as "yet another opportunity for merchants along that route to market their businesses by making a distinct connection to our 16th President. And," he would continue, "it is another way to direct people to Downtown Springfield."[18]

2005 JANUARY. NBM Comics Lit. publishes Rick Geary's black-and-white graphic novel *The Murder of Abraham Lincoln*, "a chronicle of 62 days in the life of the American Republic—March 4–May 4, 1865," as part of the publisher's Treasury of Victorian Murder.

Fig. 4.174. The purpose of city fathers in Lincoln's Springfield is to make Abraham Lincoln more human, just "one of us." Lincoln lived there, worked there, shopped there, partied there, civic leaders remind tourists. So, since June 2004, it is possible to walk up on this Lincoln family scene on the cobblestone plaza outside the Lincoln-Herndon law office. Abraham, Mary, and Willie are posed as a group *(a)*. Willie waves to eldest son Robert across the way, seen in the second picture *(b)* from Lincoln's office view of the then State Capitol Building, where Lincoln delivered his *"House Divided"* speech in 1858.

2005 January 11. *Variety*, the entertainment trade publication, reports, "Steven Spielberg is ready to embark on his long-in-the-works biopic of Abraham Lincoln." The article, bylined by Michael Fleming, was titled "Lincoln Logs in at DreamWorks." According to the report, "Spielberg has begun discussions with Liam Neeson to play the president as he steers the North to victory in the Civil War. The plan is to start production next January, sources said. . . . Spielberg has wanted to make a movie about Lincoln since 2001, when DreamWorks bought rights to a bio being written by Pulit-zer Prize–winning historian Doris Kearns Goodwin," Fleming continued. Goodwin's book was scheduled for publication in 2003 by Simon & Schuster, according to the article, under the title *The Uniter: The Genius of Abraham Lincoln*. Of course, when the book finally appeared in late 2005 its title was the more catchy *Team of Rivals: The Political Genius of Abraham Lincoln*.

2005 January 31. Zyrus Press publishes David W. Lange's *The Complete Guide to Lincoln Cents*.

Fig. 4.175. The USS *Abraham Lincoln* aircraft carrier (CVN-72) heads Carrier Strike Group Nine (the nomenclature has been changed since this patch was issued circa 2004) of currently eight surface ships, nine aircraft squadrons, and such other assets as detailed by command. Its homeport is Naval Station, Everett, Washington.

Fig. 4.176. The cover of Rick Geary's 2005 graphic novel, *The Murder of Abraham Lincoln*, features a suitably sinister view of John Wilkes Booth behind the presidential couple.

Fig. 4.177. Since the state-of-the-art Abraham Lincoln Presidential Library and Museum opened in Springfield, Illinois in 2004/2005, a vast array of merchandise has been festooned with the facility's logo, adapted from the iconic Lincoln money image. Of all the images available, administrators chose the money image because of its universal iconic character. Shown is a close-up of one of the ALPLM's items with the $5 bill logo—my very own backpack, given as a free gift to carry off all the tchotchkes I had purchased in the library's gift shop, some of which are shown in this present volume.

2005 FEBRUARY 11. "Lincoln Seen and Heard," a presentation by Lincoln scholar Harold Holzer and actor Sam Waterston, plays to rave reviews at the White House, attended by President George W. Bush, First Lady Laura Bush, legislators, current and former Cabinet members, and about a hundred other invited guests.

"Sam and Harold have had a good many reviews since they first took 'Lincoln Seen and Heard' on the road," President Bush remarked. "Perhaps the most enthusiastic review I heard came from two unimpeachable sources—Mother and Dad [laughter]—who told how much they enjoyed the performance when they saw it in Houston. Tonight we've had the special honor of listening to Lincoln's words being read in the very house where so many of them were written," he added. Bush concluded his prepared remarks on a high note: "This evening I can let you all in on a secret," he teased the audience. "Tomorrow it will be announced that Allen Guelzo, who is with us tonight, and Harold Holzer are this year's first- and second-place winners of the prestigious Lincoln Prize."[19]

The presentation included Holzer showing and describing various Lincoln photographs taken over an 18-year span, and Waterston reading from the president's writings during that time to show the correlation between Lincoln's words and his contemporary public image. "Lincoln once said he wanted to see and be seen," Holzer told the crowd. In the process, "He started out as unknown; he ended up as an icon." The hour-long performance at the White House was broadcast on C-SPAN. As noted by President Bush, the scholar and the thespian had given their presentation in numerous venues across the country, including on February 10, 2003, at the Library of Congress, a performance that was also broadcast on C-SPAN. In succeeding performances, Oscar-winning actor Richard Dreyfuss and Lincoln presenter Jim Getty also appeared with Holzer at various "Lincoln Seen and Heard" events.

2005. BRC Imagination Arts produces an animated battlefield and current-events timeline mapping of "The Civil War in Four Minutes" for the Abraham Lincoln Presidential Library & Museum, Springfield, Illinois. In addition to showing the ebb and flow of the tides of war, a counter onscreen aggregates Union and Confederate casualties through the war's end.

2005. BRC Imagination Arts produces a 17-minute layered projection and special-effects narrative, "Lincoln's Eyes," telling the story of an artist, played by Richard Doyle, who is commissioned to create a portrait of Abraham Lincoln, but who struggles to understand all the things he sees in Lincoln's eyes, including their sorrow, resolve, hope, vision, forgiveness, and more.

2005 MARCH 29. "Claudine" posts a tenement art-wall drawing of Lincoln's assassination on Yahoo's popular social file-sharing image site flickr, titled *The Fateful Day . . . September 11th 1865*. The gruesome drawing initiated several insightful comments. One, attempting to correct the dating error, was: "note: Abraham Lincoln was shot by John Wilkes Booth on the night of 11 April, 1865." A second commentator retorted: "all the info is correct, i just dont think its rite makin a picture like tht :(" A third student of history, fluent in the ways of the Internet, chimed in, verbatim: "its wierd how often september 11th comes up for tragic things, even if they are incorrect."

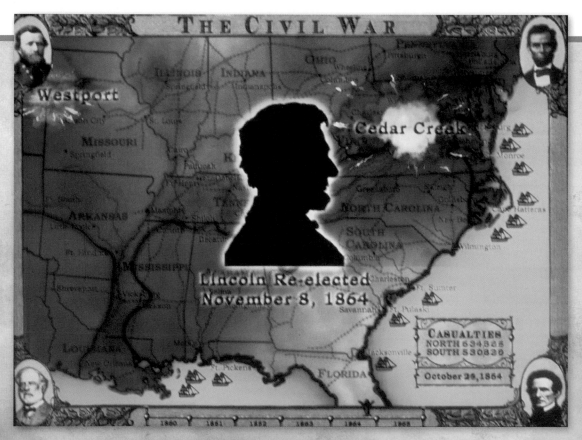

Fig. 4.178. *The Civil War in Four Minutes* was produced by BRC Imagination Arts for the Abraham Lincoln Presidential Library and Museum in 2005. An ever-evolving battle map and running count of casualties encapsulates the four-year war in as many minutes, accompanied by Jay Ungar's *Ashokan Farewell*, made famous by Ken Burns's PBS documentary *The Civil War*. If you cannot get to Springfield, the film is posted at several sites on the Internet. It is highly recommended.

Fig. 4.179. Florida paper-money dealer and prop maker Rick Reed (no relation to the author) created this ornate 5-collar prop note in 2005, employing both iconic Washington and Lincoln $1 and $5 money images and a large vignette of Ceres, goddess of agriculture.

Fig. 4.180. Grisly 2005 abandoned-building wall art relates the assassination of Abraham Lincoln and attempts to relate its impact to the September 11 Twin Towers and Pentagon attacks by Muslim extremists.

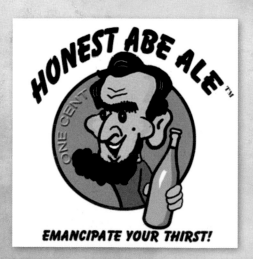

Fig. 4.181. In the 2000s a jolly Abe seems to be one kind of legacy that merchandisers are using to attract customers, whether the message is "Emancipate your thirst!" *(a)*, "Jaycee Kids," *(b)* or "Accoutrements for fun" *(c)* on packages of rubber erasers.

2005 April. Eraserhead Press publishes Chris Genoa's time-traveling comic novel *Foop!* (the sound one makes when traveling back into time—the reverse of *Poof!*, get it?), joining the Bizarro literary movement.

The protagonist and narrator, Joe, is a guide for a commercial time-traveling service whereby people can go back into time to observe famous or personal events firsthand and close-up. The Lincoln assassination is a perpetual favorite. The book opens with the narrator's observation while on guide duty:

> I've always thought that the existence of Abraham Lincoln provided conclusive visual evidence that humans are indeed descended from apes. I look at apes, and I look at men, even Cro-Magnon man, and I think, there's gott a be something in between. Where's the link? The link is Abraham Lincoln. The man looked more ape-like than some apes do when they're dressed in shorts and suspenders and wearing sunglasses. Ape Lincoln. Imagine seeing those Neanderthal cheekbones, bushy eyebrows, and way-the-hell-deep-set-back eyeballs that constantly remind you of the spooky skull underneath. I'd give him a two percent chance of being elected in the TV years. People today would lock him in a cage and throw bananas at him before they locked him in the White House. And even if he did manage to get elected I imagine people would still throw bananas at him.

At least I would. He had that same sad expression on his face that all primates have, especially Koko, that poor gorilla they taught sign language. The sad eyes and slightly protruding lower lip mirrored that mysterious inner agony that my dad once compared to the anguish a monkey at the zoo feels when it looks out into the glorious freedom beyond its cage and sees a man, its evolutionary superior and only hope for the future of life on earth, wearing a fanny pack.

Joe's mission is to shoot Lincoln for the edification of the traveling party. At first he refuses to shoot Aperham Lincoln, but relents under pressure from the boss. So Joe closes his eyes, pulls the trigger on Booth's derringer, hears a slight *tick*, and watches Lincoln's head explode. Meanwhile his boss, Burk, throws Booth over the luxury-box railing onto the stage and mouths Booth's line, "Sic Semper Tyrannis!" for the enjoyment of the time travelers.

2005 April 27. The U.S. House of Representatives passes a bill by a vote of 422–6 in favor of marking the Abraham Lincoln birth bicentennial with four commemorative cent reverses.

2005 July 4. *Time* magazine features Keya Morgan's Lincoln photograph collection. Morgan owns a large collection of Lincoln and U.S. Grant photographs.

Fig. 4.182. In 2005 the Abraham Lincoln Presidential Library and Museum opened, featuring this full-size replica of the Gutzon Borglum Lincoln marble head in the U.S. Capitol Rotunda and the bronze head at the Lincoln burial site several miles away in Springfield, Illinois.

Fig. 4.183. In 2005 the Lincoln Presidential Library received this bronze bust as a gift from sisters Vjolla and Aferdita Tafaj of Tirana, Albania. The bust is by Albanian sculptor Maksim Bushi, an instructor at the Academy of Fine Arts in Tirana. The Albanian women, who "have converted their Tirana home into the Lincoln Center of Albania," wished to show the international esteem accorded Lincoln by making their gift, they said.

2005 CIRCA. An inexpensive Napa Valley, California, wine label, Pennywise, owned by Don Sebastiani and sons, introduces a Pennywise cabernet sauvignon. Its labels sport an image of a Lincoln cent overprinted with the vintage year. Other offerings from this new label included a Pennywise petite sirah and a Pennywise merlot. A Pennywise chardonnay would be added in 2008.

2005 SEPTEMBER 15. The University of Illinois Press brings out in trade paperback *The Lincoln Image: Abraham Lincoln and the Popular Print*, by Lincoln image historians Harold Holzer, Gabor S. Boritt, and Mark E. Neely Jr. It was originally published in hardback in 2001.

2005 OCTOBER 1. Simon & Schuster publishes historian Doris Kearns Goodwin's biography *Team of Rivals: The Political Genius of Abraham Lincoln.* Pulitzer Prize winner Goodwin won the Lincoln Prize for the 912-page tome. Art director Patti Ratchford employed Alexander Hay Ritchie's engraving after Francis B. Carpenter's painting *First Reading of the Emancipation Proclamation* as the front jacket design for Goodwin's masterful study of Lincoln's skillful manipulations of his Republican rivals William H. Seward, Salmon P. Chase, Edwin M. Stanton, and Edward Bates. By "keeping his enemies closer inside his cabinet, the President deterred to a great extent his dismayed defeated rivals' disaffections and disloyalty to his person and policies, preserving the victory he had won over them at the Republican Wigwam in Chicago in May 1860," according to Goodwin's account.

2005 OCTOBER 30. Truman State University Press publishes the paperback catalog *Encounters with Lincoln: Images and Words*, by artist Thomas Trimborn. Lincoln image historian Harold Holzer recommended Trimborn's pictures, which "beautifully reflect many of the moods and character traits that made Abraham Lincoln unique, and that few artists have dared to imagine. He has captured Lincoln moving beyond the constraints of photographic models and uses his own knowledge and appreciation to fill in the blanks."

2005 DECEMBER 22. President George W. Bush signs S 1047, the Presidential $1 Coin Act of 2005, which also authorizes $50 American Buffalo bullion coinage and four reverse designs for the 2009 Lincoln cent.

2006 FEBRUARY 7. Altissimo re-releases Aaron Copland's famous *A Lincoln Portrait* with narration by former CBS news anchor Walter Cronkite and performances by the bands and choruses of the United States military services. Cronkite, in the 1960s voted the most trusted man in America, was one of scores of famous narrators for Copland's patriotic classic over the years since it was originally performed at the height of World War II, in 1942. These include Marian Anderson, Henry Fonda, Katherine Hepburn, Charlton Heston, James Earl Jones, Paul Newman, Barack Obama, Carl Sandburg, Norman Schwarzkopf, Margaret Thatcher, and Gore Vidal. (See figure 4.188.)

Fig. 4.184. A Napa, California, winery markets inexpensive cabernet sauvignon and other wines under its Pennywise cent-image label.

Fig. 4.185. No recent Abraham Lincoln book has had the impact of historian Doris Kearns Goodwin's *Team of Rivals*. The publisher changed its working title, *The Uniter*, to the more catchy label, and art director Patti Ratchford employed Alexander Hay Ritchie's engraving of Carpenter's famous painting for its dustjacket.

2006 FEBRUARY. Illinois governor Rod R. Blagojevich signs an executive order creating the Illinois Abraham Lincoln Bicentennial Commission. The governor would announce the appointment of 40 members to the commission on April 19. He also named the state's senators and congressmen ex-officio members, as well as state-government legislative and executive-branch leaders, and the mayors of Chicago and Springfield. The timing of the announcement was in conjunction with the first anniversary of the opening of the Abraham Lincoln Presidential Library and Museum in Springfield. Unlike the Reagan and Johnson presidential libraries, there are two buildings: a museum and, across the street, a library.

2006 FEBRUARY 13. Actors Liam Neeson and Holly Hunter portray Mr. and Mrs. Lincoln in *The Lincoln Family Album* at the Library of Congress. The program was narrated by Harold Holzer.

2006. Dr. Thomas DiLorenzo publishes *Lincoln Unmasked: What You're Not Supposed to Know About Dishonest Abe*, a follow-on to his controversial *The Real Lincoln*, which came out four years earlier. Lincoln was "a far worse tyrant than I portrayed him as being in that book," DiLorenzo wrote. "A thousand times worse."

2006. California Lincoln enthusiast Renee Gentry posts a title index of *Lincoln Lore* on her web site, EverythingLincoln.com, which also includes articles, podcasts, Lincolniana, a Lincoln-related bibliography, and her personal blog.

2006 MARCH 31. The American Library Association announces a list of 63 stops for the joint ALBC–National Endowment for the Humanities–Gilder-Lehrman Institute of American History traveling exhibit "Forever Free: Abraham Lincoln's Journey to Emancipation."

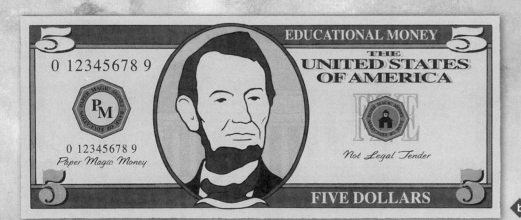

Fig. 4.186. These three imitation notes demonstrate the changeover in currency lookalikes brought on by the government's move to the new larger Lincoln portrait on the $5 note. The "Linooln" five-dollies motion-picture prop note (Reed MA10) Series 1988A *(a)*, was used in Hollywood in the 1990s. However, for reasons of economy or indifference, these notes continued in films after the changeover. In *Collateral*, for example, Tom Cruise's character uses notes like these in the 2004 DreamWorks motion picture. More in keeping with the times is the $5 Educational Money note *(b)* sold in teachers' supply stores as an educational device, and a second movie-prop note (Reed RA80b-5) *(c)* used in such films as *Mad Money* in 2008 after the currency changeover.

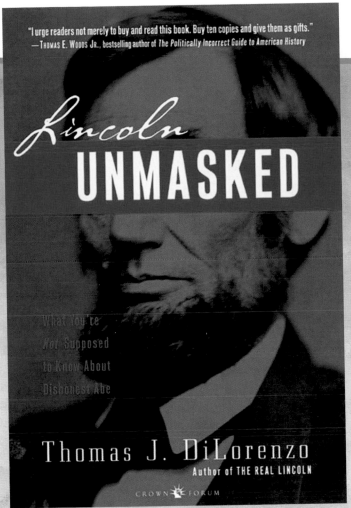

"I urge readers not merely to buy and read this book. Buy ten copies and give them as gifts."
—THOMAS E. WOODS JR., bestselling author of *The Politically Incorrect Guide to American History*

Lincoln UNMASKED

What You're Not Supposed to Know About Dishonest Abe

Thomas J. DiLorenzo
Author of THE REAL LINCOLN

CROWN FORUM

Fig. 4.187. Dr. Thomas DiLorenzo's second slap at the Lincoln piñata, his 2006 *Lincoln Unmasked*, goes further than his first book attempting to winnow the Lincoln legacy down to size by damning what the author considers Lincoln's foibles and false praises.

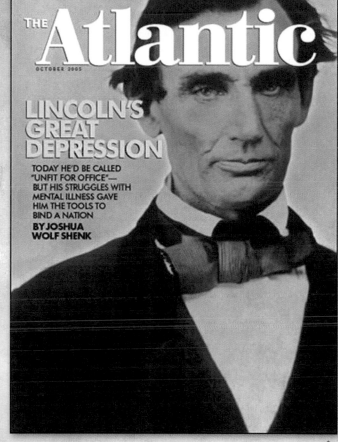

THE **Atlantic**
OCTOBER 2005

LINCOLN'S GREAT DEPRESSION

TODAY HE'D BE CALLED "UNFIT FOR OFFICE"— BUT HIS STRUGGLES WITH MENTAL ILLNESS GAVE HIM THE TOOLS TO BIND A NATION

BY JOSHUA WOLF SHENK

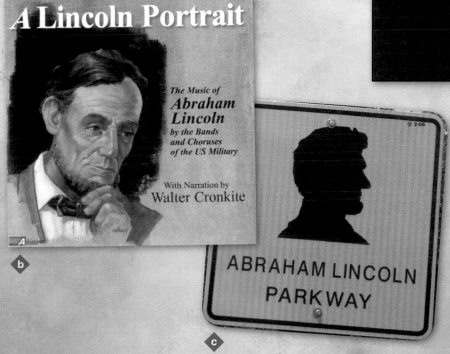

A Lincoln Portrait

The Music of **Abraham Lincoln** by the Bands and Choruses of the US Military

With Narration by Walter Cronkite

ABRAHAM LINCOLN PARKWAY

Fig. 4.188. Lincoln in the 21st century has been represented by a variety of images as art directors look for novelty for cover illustration. These 2005–2006 uses include the slightly deranged-looking 1858 Calvin Jackson O-10 portrait for the October 2005 cover story in *The Atlantic* on Lincoln's mental health *(a)*, and an introspective illustration for one of the recent re-releases of Aaron Copland's *A Lincoln Portrait* in 2005 *(b)*. Meanwhile, in February 2006 the Illinois Department of Transportation placed the readily recognizable Lincoln cent profile on new signage *(c)* for the newly redesignated Abraham Lincoln Parkway, a branded marketing concession thrown to Springfield, Illinois, merchants with the coming of the Abraham Lincoln Presidential Library and Museum.

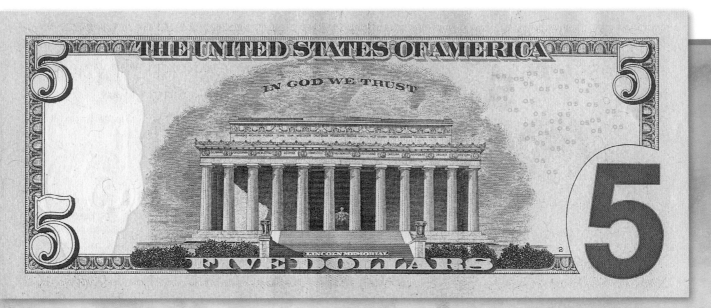

Fig. 4.189. Currency redesign, employing larger vignettes on the backs of the new notes, permitted Bureau of Engraving and Printing engraver Thomas R. Hipschen to present a recognizable Lincoln statue within the Lincoln Memorial on the backs of the new $5 Federal Reserve Notes. Shown is a Series of 2006 iteration with the addition of more colors to the formerly green back of the bill.

Fig. 4.190. Beginning in 2006, sculptor Jim Nance attempted to interest the U.S. Abraham Lincoln Bicentennial Commission in a national medal, creating excellent pre-presidential *(a)* and presidential *(b)* Lincoln portraits as examples. But when a national medal never gained traction in a Congress that was caught up in coinage commemorations for Lincoln, the lovely medal went unissued.

Fig. 4.191. The Illinois Medal of Freedom was created to honor Illinois guardsmen called up for service in America's wars since the devastation of 9/11.

2006 APRIL 18. Coin dealer and author Scott Travers purchases a bottle of Poland Spring water for $1 in change, including a valuable 1909-S VDB Lincoln cent, in Times Square, New York City, in a "National Coin Week" awareness gambit to publicize release of the fifth edition of his *Coin Collectors Survival Manual.* The ploy garners both local and national media attention.

2006 APRIL 19. A large-size (12-inch) uniface bronze foundry cast of Julio Kilenyi's Lincoln Tunnel Dedication medal reverse design for Whitehead and Hoag, Newark, New Jersey, sells for $1,375 in Stack's Coin Galleries' auction. "This imposing foundry cast was made from Kilenyi's plaster model, reduced by the Janvier lathe to produce the steel dies for striking. In includes a 16.7 mm outer flange with four tapered holes for screws to anchor it to a mahogany plaque or wall in office of public building. Such casts were presented

only to high dignitaries involved in this ambitious two-state tunnel project and are of the greatest rarity," the Stack's cataloger explained.

2006 JUNE 21. Virgin Mobile USA hosts a charity penny drive, and participants circulate "Save the Penny" petitions at New York City's Times Square. Performer Kevin Federline wore an Abraham Lincoln mask at the rally to raise awareness for the company's new one-cent text-messaging offer.

2006 JUNE 24. The Illinois adjutant general establishes the Illinois Lincoln Medal of Freedom, which may be awarded retroactively to a beginning date of September 11, 2001. The medal is awarded to military personnel mobilized in direct support of the Global War on Terror in support of Operation Iraqi Freedom, Operation Enduring Freedom, and Operation Noble Eagle. After creation of the award, the funds necessary to implement the program lagged.

Fig. 4.192. Both adults and juveniles seem to enjoy bobblehead knickknacks, and recognizable figures are stock-in-trade. Shown are three of the Lincoln bobbleheads that have created mirth in recent years.

2006 June 29. Sculptor John McClarey's evocative larger-than-life-size bronze statue titled *A Greater Task* is unveiled in the plaza across the street from the Abraham Lincoln Presidential Library and Museum.

2006 July. Sculptor Mark Lundeen's life-size bronze statue of Lincoln sitting on a bench is dedicated in Union Park, a block from the Abraham Lincoln Presidential Library and Museum in Springfield, Illinois. The artist depicted Lincoln relaxing on a bench with a copy of his Second Inaugural Address. Visitors can cuddle up to the president for a photo opportunity. The work was donated by Rick and Kim Lawrence for Siciliano Inc.

2006 July 21. The first fourth-inning Washington Nationals Presidents' Race highlights the grand reopening of the District of Columbia's RFK Stadium. The race featured costumed actors running with large foam caricature heads of presidents Abraham Lincoln, George Washington, Teddy Roosevelt, and Thomas Jefferson,

Fig. 4.193. Sculptor John McClarey produced many of the recent Abraham Lincoln sculptures, including this fine larger-than-life-size bronze, *A Great Task*, illustrating Lincoln's acceptance of the nation's call to leave Springfield and go to Washington, D.C., in 1861. The statue is located on the plaza across the street from the Abraham Lincoln Presidential Library and Museum.

"A GREATER TASK"

WHY SHOULD THERE NOT BE A PATIENT CONFIDENCE IN THE ULTIMATE JUSTICE OF THE PEOPLE? IS THERE ANY BETTER, OR EQUAL HOPE, IN THE WORLD?

ABRAHAM LINCOLN
FIRST INAUGURAL ADDRESS   MARCH 4, 1861

all of Mount Rushmore fame. The racing format has changed over time and survived removal to the Nationals' new stadium, Nationals Park. Lincoln is the usual winner of these promotions. The Racing Presidents have become local celebrities, and even sparked a "Let Teddy Win" campaign (because he never does). During the 2007 season, the ball club would give away bobblehead dolls for each of the four Racing Presidents. The Lincoln figure is 8.5 inches tall on a stand with a nameplate and the club's "W" logo, sponsored by PNC Bank. It was given away free on August 18, 2007.

2006 July 29. U.S. Senator Edward M. Kennedy narrates Aaron Copland's patriotic classic *A Lincoln Portrait* during a "Symphony by the Sea" at the Newburyport, Massachusetts, Yankee Homecoming.

2006 Summer. A contractor cleaning out an old Nelson, New Hampshire, barn prior to demolition finds seven reels of nitrate film inside, including the only known copy of a 1913 silent film about Abraham Lincoln. According to press reports, the 30-minute film *When Lincoln Paid* tells the story of the mother of a dead Union soldier who asks Lincoln to pardon a Confederate soldier whom she had turned in to authorities. It stars Francis Ford, brother of

famous director John Ford. (*When Lincoln Paid* is one of eight silents in which Ford portrayed Lincoln. No prints of the other seven Ford depictions of Lincoln are known.) The film was known from contemporary literature. It was produced by Kay-Bee Pictures and released January 31, 1913, by Mutual Film Company.

The contractor, Peter Massie, stored the film canisters in his basement for a while. Eventually he contacted a film professor at Keene State College. Professor Larry Benaquist researched the movie, and then reached out to the George Eastman House film-preservation specialists in Rochester, New York. When it was determined no other print of this film was known in archives elsewhere, Keene College applied for and received a grant from the National Film Preservation Foundation to have it restored at a Colorado laboratory. The film images were reprinted to new film stock, frame-by-frame. The process took a year to accomplish. With the help of Lincoln film historian Mark Reinhart, who owned a "crude video copy of the film that had been made from an 8-mm copy," scenes irretrievable from the nitrate copy were restored, and the entire movie was recorded to DVD. The college held a screening of the restored film on April 20, 2010.

Fig. 4.194. Contemporary sculptors increasingly see Abraham Lincoln as a man of his, and our, times. Sculptor Mark Lundeen's fine bronze likeness of Lincoln is another chance for visitors to cozy up to Father Abraham. The statue is about a block from the Abraham Lincoln Presidential Library and Museum, on the plaza across Abraham Lincoln Parkway.

On its release in 1913, *Moving Picture World* called *When Lincoln Paid* a "great war drama." According to historian Reinhart, Ford was not a particularly good Lincoln. "[H]e's kind of short and stocky," Reinhart told this writer.

"The vast majority of silent films, particularly from the early period—the first decade of the 20th century—are gone," noted Caroline Frick Page, curator of motion pictures at George Eastman House. "That's what makes these stories so incredibly special."

2006 SUMMER. Anthony W. and Tony Daniels' Great Storm Galleries, Orleans, Vermont, begins creating high-quality "cast stone"

reproductions of historical sculptures, plaques, and jewelry, focused "almost exclusively on the great American President Abraham Lincoln," Tony Daniels told the present author. Busts include works by Bissell, Volk, and Mayer. Lincoln plaques include those by Brenner and Calverley. Reproductions of life masks include both Volk and Mills. The firm also markets cut-out cents and Lincoln pins.

2006 SEPTEMBER 28. The first PCGS-graded MS-70 (denoting a perfect coin) circulation-strike Lincoln cent, a 1973 coin, brings $15,120 in a Teletrade Internet auction.

Fig. 4.195. Since 2006 Anthony W. and Tony Daniels's Great Storm Galleries, Orleans, Vermont, has sold high-quality "cast stone" reproductions of historical Lincoln sculptures and plaques. The *Let Us Have Faith* plaque is 13-1/2 by 9-1/2 inches and commemorates Lincoln's Cooper Union speech.

Fig. 4.196. Some television viewers think faux journalist–comic Stephen Colbert is a genius; others, not so much. Whether Colbert coined the term *Lincolnish* or not, he certainly popularized it on his nightly *Colbert Report*, by referring to himself by this term. The word has since been observed on t-shirts at malls. An urban dictionary on the Web defines the term in Supermanesque language as "possessing the qualities of truthiness, justice, and the Red state American way."

Fig. 4.197. As the term *Lincolnish* caught on, CafePress introduced it and an elfin Abe to a variety of products it marketed over the Internet.

2006 December 15. CAWF Fantasy Wrestling posts a seven-minute *WWE Smack Down* match video on YouTube, between martial artist turned actor Chuck Norris and railsplitter turned president Abraham Lincoln. Norris scores a KO outside the ring, leaving Lincoln flat on his back, unconscious. One hundred thousand viewers logged on to view the animated match. (See figure 4.204.)

2006 December 28. A quirky children's book that teaches a good moral, *The Boy Who Looked Like Lincoln*, is published by Puffin.

Written by Mike Reiss and illustrated by David Catrow, the book tells the story of an unfortunate tyke who resembles Abe Lincoln in appearance, right down to the wart and the beard. Kids tease him unmercifully. All he gets for birthdays is stovepipe hats. This causes eight-year-old Benjy real grief. Then he goes away to summer camp and meets other kids with even worse looks. One looks like "the back of a horse." Another, like a toaster. By the end of camp, Benjy has had an epiphany. His confidence in himself is restored, and he runs for class president.

Fig. 4.198. The Washington Nationals were an unproductive major-league baseball club through several incarnations. The new Washington Nationals were mired at or near the bottom of their National League East Division from 2005 until the miraculous 2012 season. To keep fan interest up, since July 2006 the club has staged a presidential footrace from the outfield to the infield each game. Contestants are dressed in large foam heads representing the four figures memorialized on Mount Rushmore *(a)*. As a promotion on August 18, 2007, the ball club gifted attendees with a bobblehead doll in the likeness of the Lincoln presidential race contestant *(b–c)*. At other games that season, attendees received bobbleheads for the other presidents.

Fig. 4.199. *The Simpsons* writer Mike Reiss and award-winning illustrator David Catrow created the unlikely morality tale *The Boy Who Looked Like Lincoln*, published in 2006 by Price Stern Sloan.

2007 January. The "world's largest covered wagon" (see figure 4.160), according to the *Guinness Book of World Records*, is moved to Lincoln, Illinois. It is the product of the active imagination and skilled hands of David Bentley. The wagon measures 40 feet long, 12 feet wide, and 24 feet high. Seated in the front of the wagon, a 12-foot Abe Lincoln, weighing 350 pounds, reads a book titled *LAW*. The wagon and Lincoln were completed in 2001. It had previously been located near Divemon/Pawnee, Illinois, but was moved to Lincoln because it was "rich in both Abe Lincoln and Route 66 heritage," according to Bentley and Abraham Lincoln Tourism Bureau director Geoff Ladd. The landmark was acquired for the city of Lincoln through a donation from town resident Larry J. Van Bibber. The wagon would be dedicated in March 2010, at its new site in the parking lot of Lincoln Inn, a Best Western motel, 1750 Fifth Street at the corner of Fifth Street and Route 66 in Lincoln. In June/July 2010 the wagon would be named the #1 Roadside Attraction in America, by *Reader's Digest*.

2007 January 16. Stack's, New York City, sells a 7-7/8–inch (202 mm) clear amber-colored resinous cast of Roiné's excellent bearded profile of Abraham Lincoln facing left (cf. King 305–310). A reduction of the design was used in 1908 as the obverse on a 63-millimeter copper, silver, and gold Abraham Lincoln "Liberator" medal (King 309) by the infant Medallic Art Company in New York City for inclusion in Robert Hewitt's *The Lincoln Centennial Medal* book. This medal was one of the first commissions for the new company (MACO), which owned a Janvier reducing machine. A remarkable further reduction of this design is listed as King 395, a mere 6 mm in diameter. "This medal is a reduction of No. 309," King wrote, "and is very perfect for so minute a piece." King recorded gold, silver, and copper strikings, and a unique lead striking, which he called an "artist's proof before hardening of the dies." Regarding the resinous cast, "This magnificent cast is made of a transparent amber material that glows superbly with gentle back-lighting," the Stack's cataloger wrote. (See figure 2.183.)

2007 February 10. Barack Obama announces his candidacy for president of the United States on the steps of the State House in Springfield, Illinois.

2007 February 11. David Herbert Donald and Doris Kearns Goodwin receive the Ford's Theatre Lincoln Medal at an award celebration at the White House hosted by President George W. and Mrs. Bush.

2007 March 20. A Whitest Kids U' Know three-minute-and-change skit, "What Really Happened to Abe Lincoln," appears in season 1, episode 1. Zach Cregger plays Lincoln. The skit would be posted to YouTube on June 6, 2007, and go viral, becoming an Internet sensation with nearly 4.3 million hits. After an uncensored 3:46 version without the broadcast bleeps is posted to YouTube on November 28, 2008, it records another 2.3 million views. This profane depiction of Honest Abe—who interrupts a vampire-oriented performance of *Hamlet*, irritating another member of the audience, John Wilkes Booth—becomes the one of the most-viewed depictions of Our Nation's Martyr on the Internet thus far. In what passes as humor nowadays, a morally outraged Booth climbs into the presidential box with a hammer, and, paraphrasing a pious nar-

ration of the scene, "hammers" the bullying, potty-mouthed Lincoln "in the ass to death."

2007 June. The Abraham Lincoln Presidential Library and Museum acquires the Louise Taper collection of Lincolniana. The approximately 1,500 pieces include Lincoln's well-worn stovepipe hat, his blood-stained gloves, and the handkerchief he carried the night he was assassinated. Also, the famous four-line Lincoln ditty "Abraham Lincoln is my name / and with my pen I wrote the same / I wrote in both haste and speed / and left it here for fools to read," which young scholar Lincoln wrote, in his childhood "sum book" for practicing arithmetic, as a 15-year-old. Details were not divulged, but experts estimated the collection to be valued in the $20 million neighborhood, partly financed by the presidential library's foundation and part donated by Taper.

2007 August 2. Author Gore Vidal, whose own best-selling 1984 novel *Lincoln* was made into a theatrical production and film, narrates Aaron Copland's patriotic classic *A Lincoln Portrait*, performed by the Los Angeles Philharmonic Orchestra conducted by Michael Tilson Thomas at Hollywood Bowl.

2007 September 4. "Developing the Image," part 1 of the Indiana Historical Society's three-part Lincoln Bicentennial traveling exhibition, titled "The Faces of Lincoln," opens a four-week run at the Warrick County Museum in Boonville, Indiana. This display took a look at the history of photography using some of the best and most well-known images of Abraham Lincoln. Lincoln was our first extensively photographed president, and the cataclysmic events of his presidency were also extensively photographed. Distribution of these images made Lincoln and his presidency widely known.

"Developing the Image" later would make stops of varying lengths at South Bend (Studebaker Museum, February 7, 2008), Michigan City (Public Library, March 11), Fort Wayne (History Center, April 7), Princeton (Public Library, June 2), Indianapolis (Eugene and Marilyn Glick Indiana History Center, August 6), New Castle (Henry County Historical Society and Museum, August 29), Sullivan (County Public Library, October 2), Lake Station (Historical Society and Museum, November 6), LaPorte (County Public Library, January 6, 2009), Sheridan (Public Library, January 30), Crawfordsville (Old Jail Museum, February 27), Washington (Daviess County Museum, April 16), Merrillville (Historical Society, June 4), Rush County (Historical Society (July 2), Hancock County (Cultural Center, August 20), Madison County (Historical Society, September 17), Clark-Floyd County (Tourism Convention and Visitors Bureau, November 2), Culver (Antiquarian and Historical Society, January 29, 2010), Jasper County (Historical Society, March 3), Sullivan Muncie (Cultural Center, April 2), Starke County (Public Library, May 17), the Lincoln National Memorial (June 28), Harrison College (July 26), and Lexington (Scott County Public Library, October 1).

2007 September 2. Friends of the Abraham Lincoln Historical Farm, LLC, purchase a portion of the former Thomas Lincoln farm in Coles County, which Abraham Lincoln acquired upon his father's death in 1851. The group offered penny-sized (one-14,198,352nd of an acre) lots to the public for $49.99 each, for historic preservation purposes.

2007 September 12. George Eastman House, Rochester, New York, the great repository and museum of photographic history, posts a five-and-a-half minute podcast to YouTube, entitled *The Abraham Lincoln Plate Negative,* in which Grant Romer discusses his department's conservation of the cracked glass-plate copy negative of Alexander Hesler's June 3, 1860, beardless Lincoln image known as O-26. The copy negative was one produced by George B. Ayres after he acquired Hesler's Chicago studio and its contents. After it was broken in the mail (and the mailer was paid his insurance cov-

erage), the Post Office Department donated the cracked plate to the Smithsonian Institution.

2007 September 20. The Commission of Fine Arts recommends to the Treasury designs for four 2009 circulating Lincoln cent reverses.

2007 September 20. The new Abe Lincoln $5 bill design is unveiled, digitally, online.

Fig. 4.200. In February 2007, historian and twice Pulitzer Prize winner Dr. David Herbert Donald received the Ford's Theatre Lincoln Medal from President George W. Bush at a White House ceremony. Donald's productive career spanned the 1940s, when he wrote *Lincoln's Herndon,* through the 1960s, when he coauthored with J.G. Randall the Civil War and Reconstruction history text this author used in graduate school, to his popular 1996 one-volume biography *Lincoln* (shown), to his death May 17, 2009, at age 88, having observed the Lincoln Bicentennial.

Fig. 4.201. In September 2007, the George Eastman House museum (Rochester, New York) created a short video demonstrating how experts there conserved the broken glass-plate copy negative of Alexander Hesler's O-26 Lincoln portrait.

2007 OCTOBER 2. "Creating the Image," a second portion of the Indiana Historical Society's three-part Lincoln Bicentennial traveling exhibition ("The Faces of Lincoln") opens a month-long run at the Warrick County Museum in Booneville. This display "investigates the ways that photographers, printmakers, and cartoonists tried to influence public opinion about Lincoln by altering his appearance and by placing him in make-believe situations," organizers noted.

Other stops for the display would include New Harmony (Workingmen's Institute, January 3, 2008), South Bend (Studebaker Museum, February 7), Michigan City (Barker Mansion, March 11), Bloomington (Monroe County History Center, June 4), Princeton (Public Library, June 30), Indianapolis (Eugene and Marilyn Glick Indiana History Center, August 6), Fort Wayne (History Center, September 29), New Castle (Henry County Public Library, November 17), LaPorte (County Public Library, January 6, 2009), Sheridan (Public Library, January 30), Crawfordsville (Old Jail Museum, February 27), Merrillville (Historical Society, June 4), Rush County (His-

torical Society, July 2), Hancock County (Cultural Center, August 20), Madison County (Historical Society, September 17), Clark-Floyd County (Tourism Convention and Visitors Bureau, November 2), Culver (Antiquarian and Historical Society, January 29, 2010), Jasper County (Historical Society, March 3), Sullivan Muncie (Cultural Center, April 2), Starke County (Public Library, May 17), the Lincoln National Memorial (July 30), Lexington (Scott County Public Library, August 30), and Harrison College (October 4).

2007 OCTOBER 13. A three-and-a-half-minute sketch by The Whitest Kids U' Know parodies the repartee between Abraham Lincoln and his wife Mary in the presidential box on the night of his assassination, in a YouTube video clip. Mary congratulates hubby on winning the war. Their mundane conversation is interrupted four times when John Wilkes Booth enters the box, shouts "Sic semper tyrannis," and physically assaults Lincoln in sissified ways, but is rebuffed. The last time he says he's coming back with a gun. The web site recorded 40,000 views of the video.

Fig. 4.202. The Indiana Historical Society created three roving displays for the Lincoln bicentennial that began circulating through state libraries and other public venues in 2007. "Creating the Image" was the second part of their "Faces of Lincoln" traveling exhibition. Parts 1 and 3 were "Developing the Image" and "Idealizing the Image."

Fig. 4.203. Madame Tussaud's Wax Museum, of London, New York, Washington, and similar galleries, employs realistic historical and contemporary figures as a tourist attraction, for their curiosity value. This Abraham Lincoln figure, put in a commercial airliner seat in a September 2007 publicity stunt, certainly looks real, doesn't he? Abe flew with great fanfare from La Guardia in New York City to Reagan National Airport in time to arrive at his new home at Madame Tussaud's D.C. location for an exhibit opening there on October 5.

Fig. 4.204. The story of Abraham Lincoln wrestling Jack Armstrong in New Salem continues to evoke modern fantasies. In this one, martial-arts legend Chuck Norris stomps a prostrate Lincoln in a CAWF Fantasy Wrestling *WWE Smack Down* match video. Note that Lincoln's tall black hat amazingly remained in place despite his fall to the canvas.

Fig. 4.205. A variety of factors in 2006 and 2007 piqued international philatelic interest in Abraham Lincoln, but most of it is encapsulated by the four-letter word GRED. Note the use of the Lincoln money image and other famous Lincoln portraits. Issues included the Congo's 300–Congo francs stamp and souvenir sheet which includes the Statue of Liberty, Rotary International, and kitchen sink (a); a Guinea-Bissau 500-franc stamp and souvenir sheet that ropes in Dr. Martin Luther King, Gandhi, Jimmy Carter, and the Statue of Liberty (b); a Republic of Guinea 25,000–Guinea francs Lincoln–Kennedy–Mount Rushmore stamp and souvenir sheet that includes Reagan, NASA, and the Washington Monument (c); a $2 Antigua and Barbuda stamp that was part of a humanitarian stamp series (d); the private local Easdale, Scotland, post 53-pence stamp for the 2006 World Philatelic Congress (e); S. Tomé e Prîncipe's 14,000-db Humanistas Lincoln & Rotary International stamp from a series including Gandhi, Pope John Paul II, and Albert Schweitzer (f); Liberia's $15 stamp with Norman Rockwell's Boy Scouts painting (g); and another S. Tomé e Prîncipe U.S. presidents stamp on a souvenir sheet that also manages to pay tribute to the Confederate States of America Rebel cavalry (h).

2007 October 31. Representatives Peter Roskam (R-Illinois) and Michael Castle (R-Delaware) introduce HR 4036, requiring a change in the metallic composition of the Lincoln cent.

2007 November 2. "Idealizing the Image," a third part of the Indiana Historical Society's three-part Lincoln Bicentennial traveling exhibition, titled "The Faces of Lincoln," opens a month-long run at the Warrick County Museum in Booneville. After Lincoln's assassination elevated him instantly from man to myth, his face became "a symbol of sacrifice and saintly public service," according to the Indiana Historical Society exhibition. He was revered as the "Great Emancipator" by African Americans in particular. "School-children studied him as an example of honesty, service to nation and sacrifice for right," organizers affirmed. His birthday was celebrated, and Lincoln's image "came to represent American ideals. The federal government used Lincoln's face on money, and others employed his name to make money for their commercial enterprises by trading on the virtues associated with Lincoln's name and image. Today, it is difficult to separate the man from the myth."

Other stops for the display would include South Bend (Studebaker Museum, February 7, 2008), Bloomington (Monroe County History Center, June 4), Indianapolis (Eugene and Marilyn Glick Indiana History Center, August 6), Princeton (Public Library, September 4), LaPorte (County Public Library, January 6, 2009), Sheridan (Public

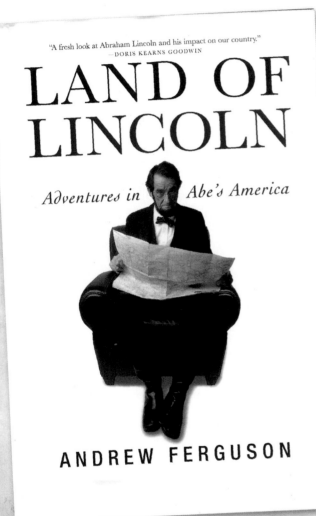

Fig. 4.206. Journalist Andrew Ferguson's 2007 *Land of Lincoln: Adventures in Abe's America* observes contemporary Lincoln currents in the United States from the Disneyfication of the Abraham Lincoln Presidential Library and Museum to the deconstructionism of the neo-Abephobes, to the generational Rorschach test that visited the erection of a Lincoln monument in the former capital of the Confederacy, Richmond, Virginia.

Fig. 4.207. Appeals to Abraham Lincoln's legacy for honesty are a powerful branding mechanism, such as in this numismatic advertisement for Heritage Auction Galleries' searchable database of more than a million numismatic auction-lot sales. Appropriately for a numismatic company, Lincoln's iconic money images were used in the ad.

Library, January 30), Crawfordsville (Old Jail Museum, February 27), Fort Wayne (History Center, April 3), Merrillville (Historical Society, June 4), Rush County (Historical Society, July 2), Hancock County (Cultural Center, August 20), Madison County (Historical Society, September 17), Clark-Floyd County (Tourism Convention and Visitors Bureau, November 2), Culver (Antiquarian and Historical Society, January 29, 2010), Jasper County (Historical Society, March 3), Sullivan Muncie (Cultural Center, April 2), Starke County (Public Library, May 17), and Lincoln National Memorial (August 30).

2007 NOVEMBER 16. The Center for Civil War Photography announces that a pair of stereo negatives taken by Alexander Gardner on November 19, 1863, in the collection of the Library of Congress, show a hidden but discernible image of Abraham Lincoln on horseback riding between two columns of soldiers on his arrival at the Gettysburg battlefield cemetery. Lincoln in the midst of the crowd was only discovered when viewed in 3D under very high magnification. In one image, Lincoln salutes the soldiers with a white-gloved hand. The following day, a "Lincoln in 3D" slideshow would be presented to the annual Lincoln Forum in Gettysburg. These images joined two other images also taken by Gardner that day, which were discovered in 1953 at the U.S. National Archives and also put forth at that time to contain views of Lincoln.

Fig. 4.208. Sculptor Jim Nance's 2007 bronze figure of Abraham Lincoln giving a speech is a traditional view of the great orator *(a)*. Meanwhile, in 2007 actor Ted Rooney playing Lincoln (advertising a sleep product in the company of a beaver) *(b)* exemplifies the "new reality" of Lincoln imagery

Fig. 4.209. The Jerry Bruckheimer–Walt Disney actioner *National Treasure: Book of Secrets* took cast, crew, and audience into a subterranean vault within Mount Rushmore as Ben Gates searched for new information about an ancestor's connection to John Wilkes Booth and the conspiracy to assassinate Lincoln.

Fig. 4.210. Bureau of Engraving and Printing engraver Thomas Hipschen's and William Fleishell's "Twinkle Eye" Lincoln portrait (BEP die MISC 198327-3) is bound to become the iconic view of the nation's 16th president during the 21st century, if it remains in place. This will happen no matter the rise of any competing image. History tells us that contemporary Lincoln money portraits become the dominant, iconic Lincoln image of their time because of two things: authority and quantity—i.e., official government sanction, and overwhelming repetitive reinforcement. This has been true since August 26, 1861, when Charles's Burt's engraving of the C.S. German pose (O-41/42) first entered the streams of commerce and consciousness on the $10 Demand Note.

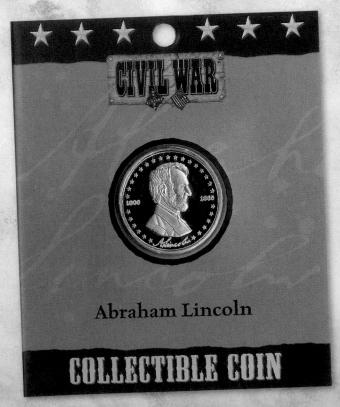

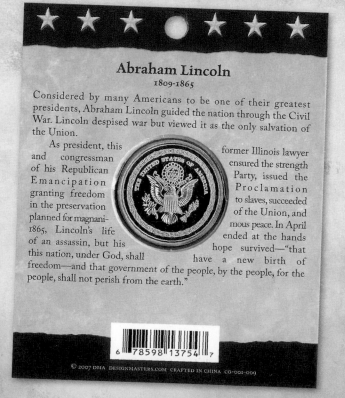

Fig. 4.211. Both my Lincoln books are printed in China, which allows a high-quality product to be produced for a lesser expense to the purchaser. I observed the growth of Asian publishing firsthand for nearly a year in the 1970s when my Authorized Army newspaper was printed in Seoul, Korea, and I understand the realities of modern publishing. But there's just something wrong when a packaged small Lincoln medal like this 2007 "Civil War . . . Collectible Coin" bears a "Crafted in China" credit line, however nice or indifferent the product and packaging are.

Fig. 4.212. Topps Card Co. employed the Gettysburg Lincoln portrait for this 2007 Turkey Red non-sports card. The T3 Turkey Red cabinet cards were premium baseball cards for Turkey Red cigarettes. The modern issue was an attempt to give historical patina to a cheap mass-produced product.

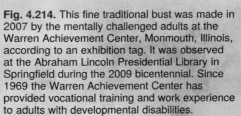

Fig. 4.213. Edward Steers Jr.'s excellent debunking of Lincoln confabulations and other errata appeared in 2007. Sales must have been helped by the attractive tall hat billboard that the publisher, University of Kentucky Press, slapped on the iconic Lincoln $5 bill portrait on the book's cover.

Fig. 4.214. This fine traditional bust was made in 2007 by the mentally challenged adults at the Warren Achievement Center, Monmouth, Illinois, according to an exhibition tag. It was observed at the Abraham Lincoln Presidential Library in Springfield during the 2009 bicentennial. Since 1969 the Warren Achievement Center has provided vocational training and work experience to adults with developmental disabilities.

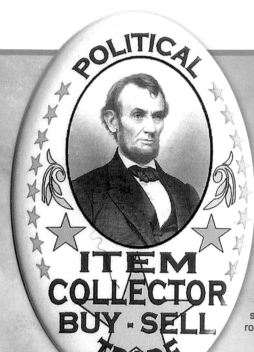

Fig. 4.215. This rather expressive button with the Lincoln money image appealed to this author, who wears it occasionally at conventions and shows to cut to the quick when searching dealers' bourse-room wares.

INDIAN HEAD CENT AND CIVIL WAR TOKEN (SET 2 OF 2)

Fig. 4.216. The Abraham Lincoln Presidential Library and Museum logo, with its iconic $5 bill Lincoln portrait and a presidential seal, was struck in medallic form for this low-relief, poorly articulated, encapsulated small souvenir bronze medal.

Fig. 4.217. Packaging for this set of replica Civil War–era small change, produced in 2007 for this author's publisher, Whitman Publishing, employs the bizarre "broomstick" haircut portrait of Lincoln (O-103) after the president got shorn prior to having Clark Mills cast a life mask of his face in plaster. These replicas are marked COPY, in accordance with the Hobby Protection Act.

Fig. 4.218. You'll just have to excuse the author on this one. But when I saw this sign on the ground propped up against a ranger's cabin in a state historic site, I couldn't help but crack up—a March 2007 anti littering campaign sign was littering the site during the Lincoln bicentennial.

Fig. 4.219. Democratic presidential candidate Barack Obama's self-identification with Abraham Lincoln spun off a host of political memorabilia, such as these two humorous 2007 campaign buttons.

Fig. 4.220. Popular fiction in print, on TV, and on the silver screen is going through a vampire craze. This cigarette case attempts to capitalize on one of the movement's excesses, portraying Abraham Lincoln as a vampire bat.

2007 DECEMBER 2. Fred Reed updates and publishes for the Bureau of Engraving and Printing Historical Resource Center a spreadsheet, "A. Lincoln on U.S. Currency," detailing the creation and use of Lincoln portrait dies at the bureau. The works are organized by photographic model, engraver, uses, dates of issue, and citations (i.e., references).

2008 JANUARY. Whitman Publishing releases Q. David Bowers's *A Guide Book of Lincoln Cents* as part of its "Official Red Book" series of numismatic references.

2008 JANUARY 30. *The Memoirs of Abraham Lincoln*, a comedy written by Peter King Beach, starring Granville Van Dusen as Lincoln, is staged at the Falcon Theatre, Burbank, California, through March 2.

2008 FEBRUARY. "A Very Brady Bank Note: One Well-Executed Photograph Helped Define America's 16th President, Influenced Scores of Portraits and Was Adapted for a Contemporary $5 Bill," by Fred Reed, appears in *The Numismatist*, the official monthly journal of the American Numismatic Association. That article would win the 2009 ANA Catherine Sheehan Literary award as the outstanding paper-money article to appear in *The Numismatist* during the previous year.

2008 FEBRUARY 1. Lincoln *"The Knob Creek Boy,"* a faux-bronze statue, is unveiled at the Hardin County, Kentucky, History Museum. According to organizers, "It gives visitors a real sense of Lincoln as they 'meet' him face-to-face and learn his story."

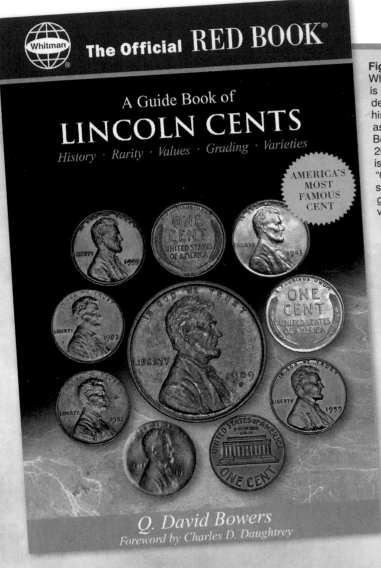

Fig. 4.221. My publisher, Whitman Publishing, LLC, is blessed to have coin dealer and numismatic historian Q. David Bowers as its numismatic director. Bowers is prodigious. His 2008 Lincoln cent book is one of the publisher's "Official Red Book" series. His foreword graces the present volume.

Fig. 4.222. The *Knob Creek Boy* statue of Lincoln was unveiled at the Hardin County Historical Museum in February 2008. The faux-bronze full-size figure represents a seven-year-old Abe seated on a keg holding a piece of sugar candy. It was made by LifeFormations Studio, Bowling Green, Ohio.

2008 FEBRUARY 7. The Indiana Abraham Lincoln Bicentennial Commission announces activities to commemorate Lincoln's 200th birthday.

2008 FEBRUARY 10. President George W. Bush presents the Ford's Theatre Lincoln Medal to retired Supreme Court justice Sandra Day O'Connor in a White House East Room ceremony.

2008 FEBRUARY 11. The Lincoln Illinois Bicentennial Commission announces a $60,000 grant to the Tinsley Project to recreate Seth Tinsley's 1850s three-story drygoods store on State House square, in which Abraham Lincoln and William Herndon rented out rooms for their law practice. The project included recreating the mercantile atmosphere that would have been a social mecca for the Lin-

colns and their friends, as well as accurately locating and restoring the actual offices in which Lincoln worked, and restoring the federal courtroom there in its original location. Two dozen other grants were also announced to support Lincoln-related sites and activities for the bicentennial, including projects to bring its observance to Illinois schools, the taping of PBS segments, traveling exhibits, and the erection of additional statuary. A $50,000 grant was awarded to the Decatur Arts Council for its program "Portraying Lincoln: Man of Many Faces Exhibit," showcasing more than 50 artists who have given expression to Lincoln's continuing influence. A small grant of $3,153 funded banners for the "Lincoln for the Next Generation" essay contest sponsored by the Illinois State Library in Springfield, challenging students to compose their own Gettysburg Address.

Fig. 4.223. The 2008 Tinsley Project is intended to redirect the visitor experience at the Lincoln-Herndon law offices in Springfield, Illinois, by recreating the mercantile nature of the building as would have been found in Lincoln's own time.

2008 FEBRUARY 12. Hodgenville, Kentucky, kicks off the Lincoln bicentennial celebration with a wreath-laying at Adolph Weinman's seated Lincoln statue in the town's Lincoln Square, followed by ceremonies at the Abraham Lincoln Birthplace National Historic Site, and a Lincoln Days luncheon at Abraham Lincoln Elementary School. At 3 p.m. the official unveiling of the Lincoln Heritage Trail took place at the Hodgenville City Center.

2008 FEBRUARY 12. The Kentucky Lincoln Heritage Trail is launched as a promotional joint venture of the Kentucky Heritage Council, Kentucky Historical Society, and Kentucky Department of Tourism, to better market the state for the upcoming Lincoln bicentennial observance. The trail is a more historically accurate circuit than the Kentucky aspect of the 1963 Lincoln Heritage Trail through Kentucky, Indiana, and Illinois, sponsored by the American Petroleum Institute.

"The Kentucky Lincoln Heritage Trail includes signature sites in Hodgenville, Louisville, Lexington, Frankfort, Elizabethtown, Nicholasville, Springfield and Richmond, as well as dozens of interpretive signs and additional historic sites across the state, all of which illuminate Lincoln's life and legacy," according to tourism officials. The Heritage Council sponsored passport promotions in 2008–2009 to encourage travel to the Lincoln-related sites in the state of Abe's birth and first years. Visitors to any of the sites or tourism offices could receive a free "passport" foldout map of the "trail," and have their passport stamped at the various sites to prove they had visited them. Participants could then enter a contest for prizes. The promotion was supported by an interactive Internet map.

During the 2009 Lincoln bicentennial year, the present author traveled the entire main trail (every site but the White Hall State Historic Site at the former home of Lincoln associate, abolitionist Cassius Marcellus Clay) and half the route a second time when he misplaced his original passport between stops. He had his passports stamped, of course, but did not enter the prize drawing. The stamped passport is a feature display of the author's Lincoln Room.

In 2010, the passport promotion was sponsored by the Kentucky Lincoln Sites Alliance, which now administers the trail. In addition to the free family-friendly passport, the promotion included an "upgraded" passport sold for $2 at select locations.

2008 FEBRUARY 12. Lincoln presenter Jim Getty and the Lexington Philharmonic perform *Lincoln's Legacy, a Musical Tribute*, at the Hardin County Performing Arts Center.

2008 FEBRUARY 12. *Abraham Lincoln—A Tribute (Ashokan Farewell)*, a four-minute video presentation of Lincoln in photographs, edited by Manuel Ortega, is posted by "Manny535" to YouTube, accompanied by the plaintive strains of Jay Ungar's *Ashokan Farewell*. In Ken Burns's documentary style, with panning and close-ups of excellent photography, having great production value, the short film is a fine survey of available Lincoln photography. It is also a fitting, traditional salute to Abe's 199th birthday.

Ashokan Farewell was composed by Ungar in 1982, and utilized extensively by Burns in his monumental 1990 made-for-TV PBS documentary *The Civil War*. The piece is a waltz in D major, written in the style of a Scots lament, usually performed by a solo violin. The video received more than a quarter million hits on YouTube.

2008 FEBRUARY 15. The University of Rochester, New York, announces it will begin putting its William Henry Seward papers online, including 72 letters written by Abraham Lincoln and 218 letters written to Lincoln.

2008 FEBRUARY 18. President Lincoln's Cottage opens at the Soldiers' Home, Washington, D.C.. The site is managed by the Armed Forces Retirement Home and the National Trust for Historic Preservation in consultation with the National Park Service.

Fig. 4.224. Kids in Lincoln's birthplace community, Hodgenville, Kentucky, attend—what else?—the Abraham Lincoln Elementary School, located almost adjacent to the Lincoln Birthplace historic site operated by the National Park Service.

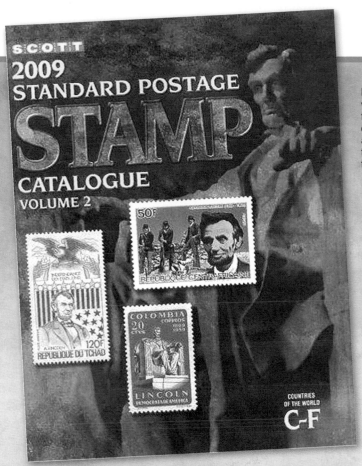

Fig. 4.232. Scott's *Standard Postage Stamp Catalogue* volumes for 2009 were released in 2008, with covers featuring foreign Abraham Lincoln stamps from the countries cataloged inside. As we've seen in this book and in *Abraham Lincoln: The Image of His Greatness*, the publisher (Amos Press Inc.) had a great many foreign Lincoln stamps from which to choose.

Fig. 4.233. Lincoln images continue to make good covers. The cover story of the May 2008 issue of *Scott Stamp Monthly (a)* was "A Stamp Tribute to Abe." The June 12, 2008, catalog for the Heritage Auction Galleries sale of political items and Americana *(b)* showed Freeman Thorp's facing portrait of Lincoln based on the O-77 Gardner photo that is similar to the one the artist sold to the U.S. Senate (figure 3.81), which he claimed had been painted from life observations.

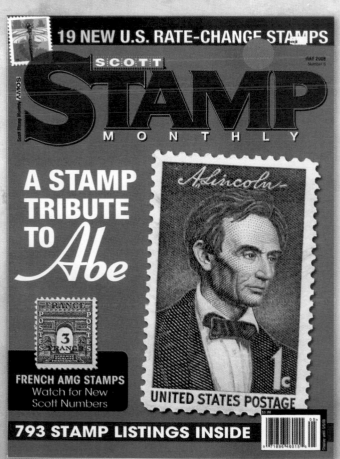

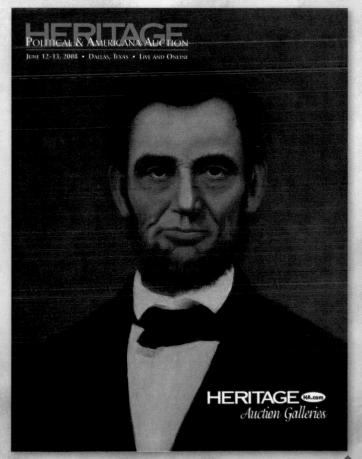

2008 MAY 6. Albino Black Sheep posts on YouTube a surreal three-and-a-half-minute video, *The Ultimate Showdown*, in which historical and fictional characters battle one another to the death. These characters run the gamut from Godzilla to Chuck Norris. Altf4 did the animated video, which includes music and lyrics by Lemon Demon. Abraham Lincoln appears in three scenes: "Abraham Lincoln popped out of his grave / And took an AK47 out from under his hat / And blew Batman away with a rat-a-tat-tat / But he ran out of bullets and he ran away / Because Optimus Prime came to save the day . . . . Abraham Lincoln came back with a machete / But suddenly something caught his leg and he tripped / Indiana Jones took him out with his whip . . . . Abraham Lincoln tried to pole vault / Onto Optimus Prime, but they [Lincoln and Jackie Chan] collided in the air / Then they both got hit by a Care Bear Stare, oooh." After a century of mayhem, Chuck Norris appears to have triumphed until a posse of villains and heroes from Gandalf to Mussolini to Superman and Hulk Hogan take him out. Ultimately a bloodstained Fred Rogers in a green sweater triumphs until he apparently commits hara-kiri. Viewers queued up to the extent of 4.3 million to catch the mayhem.

2008 MAY 10. President George W. Bush signs congressional legislation designating "The Abraham Lincoln National Heritage Area," the only National Heritage Area named for a president. The act designated the Looking for Lincoln Coalition as management entity for the heritage area, occupying 42 counties in central Illinois. Their mission is to "preserve, interpret and promote the heritage and culture of the area, in the context of Abraham Lincoln's life in Illinois." Together with partners, including the Abraham Lincoln Presidential Library and Museum, the Illinois Historic Preservation Agency, the Illinois Office of Tourism, and the National Park Service, the Looking for Lincoln initiative developed visitor-ready interpretive sites with illustrated storyboards in 52 Illinois communities. Visitors were encouraged to take rubbings

from innovative commemorative medallions mounted on the storyboards that reflect the unique story being told at the exhibit. Some communities had as few as a single LFL wayside exhibit, while Bloomington and Vandalia had 10; Decatur, 15; Quincy, 18; and Springfield 48 sites. In all, 215 exhibits were put up for the Lincoln bicentennial tourist trade. Illustrated brochures and web-site presentations were put together to guide the public walking in Lincoln's footsteps down a theoretical "Looking for Lincoln Story Trail." The brochures show Springfield's second most famous family, the Simpsons, catching up on their Lincoln lore.[21]

2008 MAY 31. A grand unveiling is held for the new Abraham Lincoln bronze sculpture in the redesigned Lincoln Square, Hodgenville, Kentucky. Lincoln is depicted at the age of seven, holding an open book, leaning against a tree trunk with his dog Honey at his side. The work had been commissioned in 2007.

2008. *Token and Medal Society Journal* publisher Paul Cunningham announces formation of a working group to correct, revise, and update Robert P. King's *Lincoln in Numismatics*. Cunningham heads a group of TAMS members working on the project, including *TAMS Journal* editor (since retired) David Schenkman, Kathy Lawrence, and Fred Reed. Publication was projected for the Lincoln bicentennial year, but completion of this large project has been delayed.

2008 JUNE. The *Journal* of the Token and Medal Society commences publishing D. Wayne Johnson's "Abraham Lincoln on Coins, Medals, and Tokens Listed by Their Artist Creators" in serial form within the magazine. Johnson's listing of all known signed Lincoln items in the categories he covers is extracted from his ongoing opus on medallic artists, *American Artists, Die-sinkers, Engravers, Medalists, Sculptors of Coins and Medals, 1652 to Date*, which he originally furnished to this author (during preparation of *Abraham Lincoln: The Image of His Greatness*), who suggested and encour-

Fig. 4.234. A very popular YouTube video, *The Ultimate Showdown*, posted by Albino Black Sheep, depicting Abraham Lincoln and various real and imaginary characters such as Jackie Chan (shown), drew more than 4.3 million viewers after it was posted in May 2008.

aged Johnson to more widely publicize his research in the *TAMS Journal* for the benefit of the entire numismatic community. Johnson's listing of hundreds of medals by more than 130 artists would be serialized in seven issues of the periodical, coinciding with the Lincoln bicentennial observance, concluding in the June 2009 issue of the bimonthly journal. The listing does not include most anonymous pieces (the majority of the Lincoln medal and token corpus to be cataloged in the TAMS-sponsored revision of King's Lincolniana catalog). "For an artist to sign his medallic creations—or for

medal researchers to learn the identity of an unsigned piece—this usually happens only for the most important items. Thus this list reflects this medallic importance of the Lincoln items to be published in this journal," journal editor David Schenkman wrote.

2008 June 9. A seven-and-a-half-minute video clip of Bill and Ted's oral report from the movie *Bill & Ted's Excellent Adventure*, including Abraham Lincoln's admonition to "Be excellent to each other, and . . . party on, dudes," nets 123,000 views on YouTube.

Fig. 4.235. On May 31, 2008, this ground-level bronze statue of a boyish Abe and his dog Honey *(a)* joined Adolph A. Weinman's seated presidential statue resting on a granite pedestal *(b)*, dedicated in 1909, in the town square of Hodgenville, Kentucky. This smallish figure was created by the Daub Firmin Hendrickson Sculpture group of Berkeley, California. No other example than the two statues of Abe Lincoln on the Hodgenville Square is necessary to demonstrate the migration of Lincoln imagery from his centennial days to the present.

2008 June 16. The sesquicentennial of Abraham Lincoln's "House Divided" speech of June 16, 1858, is commemorated at the Old State Capitol, Springfield, Illinois. *Lincoln and Douglas* author Allen Guelzo spoke, and reenactors performed historical readings from speeches by both Lincoln and Stephen A. Douglas.

2008 June 30. The Lincoln Museum, Fort Wayne, Indiana, closes.

2008 July 4. Street artist Ron English, creator of the fusion portrait *Abraham Obama*, headlines an "apolitic" art show at Gallery XIV in Boston.

2008 July. The Illinois Historic Preservation Agency spends nearly $20,000 to rehabilitate the 70-year-old Lincoln Trail Memorial in Lawrenceville, Illinois. "All eyes are focused on Lincoln sites in Kentucky, Indiana, and Illinois as we count down to the 200th anniversary of Lincoln's birth in 2009," said IHPA director Jan Grimes. "The Lincoln Trail Memorial east of Lawrenceville denotes an important part of the story and marks the beginning of Abraham Lincoln's 30 years in Illinois." General cleaning and repairs to the limestone-and-bronze memorial were undertaken, including replacing a cast bronze stick that young Abe carries,

which had been broken by vandals. The last previous restoration of the memorial had been 20 years earlier, in 1988.

2008 July 30. Whitman Publishing introduces "Mr. Lincoln," a.k.a. Lincoln presenter Dennis Boggs, to the numismatic community at the American Numismatic Association World's Fair of Money held in Baltimore. At the five-day event, "Mr. Lincoln worked for us out of the Whitman Publishing booth promoting our Baltimore Expos," Whitman Expo manager David Crenshaw noted. Boggs posed for pictures with show guests and stayed in character in conversations on the show floor. His presentation was so successful, the company would have him back for Whitman's Baltimore Coin and Collectibles Expos in November 2008 and March 2009, among others. With the advent of Whitman's new book, *Abraham Lincoln: The Image of His Greatness*, Boggs would be invited back to make appearances at Whitman's Philadelphia Expo in September 2009, Nashville Expo in May 2010, and Baltimore Expo in March 2011.

2008 August. In a four-minute *SCTV* skit, Abraham Lincoln invents a time machine, goes back into the past, and attempts several times without success to kill a young John Wilkes Booth, before dying at Booth's hand with dynamite, piano wire, and a

Fig. 4.236. Street artist Ron English created one of the most memorable of the Barack Obama images with his portrait that morphs Obama's face into Lincoln's O-77 Gardner photo features. Reproductions of this image, many in Day-Glo colors, festooned walls and other public areas. This is a "grab shot" of a window poster in Chicago in 2009.

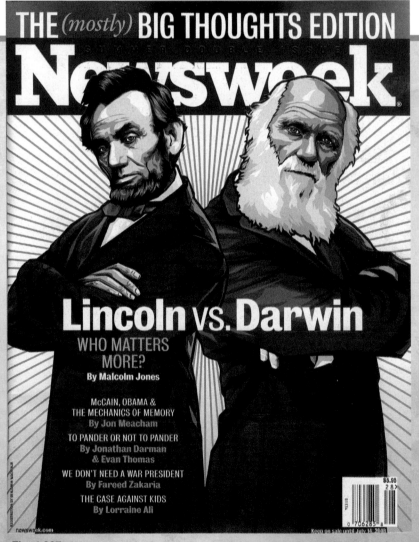

Fig. 4.237. Several periodicals, including the July 14, 2008, issue of *Newsweek*, made a big deal out of the coincidence that Abraham Lincoln and Charles Darwin were born on the same day, February 12, 1809.

blackjack in his pockets. The video makes a splash on YouTube, whose young audience finds it hilarious. One of the more sober commentators records philosophically: "This is why you should never find out who killed you in the future then . . . go back in time to try and kill them . . . it will never, EVER work."

2008 AUGUST 15. Max Powers posts on YouTube *Every Known Photograph of Abraham Lincoln*, a seven-minute slide show. Although many images are indifferently reproduced, lack chronological context, and reproduce some printed (not photographic) views, the presentation is an excellent introduction to one kind of Lincoln imagery. Remarks from some 45,000 viewers run the gamut from appreciative to picky to prickly jousts delivered by the legion of Lincoln haters and unreconstructed disunionists. A better video

along the same lines is *Abraham Lincoln—A Tribute (Ashokan Farewell)*, a four-minute animated slide show posted to YouTube on Lincoln's birthday in 2008. (See the entry for February 12, 2008.)

2008 SEPTEMBER 1. Austin, Texas, entrepreneurs Maury and Elizabeth McCoy invent and market a Lincoln Penny Portrait, consisting of an 18-by-24-inch mat with color-coded cent images on which parents and their school-aged kids can glue similarly shaded bright and tarnished Lincoln cents to create a large mosaic image of Abraham Lincoln. The portrait style chosen is the type of the Anthony Berger February 9, 1864, photograph (O-92) that was popularized on the old-style $5 bill.

McCoy's background is as a graphics designer, and his wife is an educator. The artist told this author, "I tried a few images of Abe and

Fig. 4.238. Austin, Texas, entrepreneurs Maury and Elizabeth McCoy invented the Lincoln Penny Portrait kit in 2008. After experimenting with several Lincoln portrait types, the McCoys settled on the old-style iconic $5 bill image because it was familiar to the target market and amenable to representation by variously shaded Lincoln cents.

found that this one seemed to be most easily recognized despite the lack of detail. I did try a few others to see how they looked, as well."[22]

A kit includes the poster (mat), a booklet of fun facts about Lincoln and coin collecting, assembly directions, and a 1943 steel cent, shipped in a mailing tube; buyers then provide their own cents and assemble a portrait ready for framing. A completed portrait includes 846 pennies, putting it easily within the reach of most families or school projects.

2008 September 1. Missouri delegate George Engelbach makes a seriously good Lincoln impersonation on the floor of the Republican National Convention at the Excel Center in St. Paul, Minnesota. He would be featured on TV.

2008 September 2. The three-minute GOP Convention video tribute to party elder "Abraham Lincoln" goes viral on the Internet, including more than 200,000 hits on YouTube. "He had saved the country, the country he put first, ahead of self," the narrator concluded.

2008 September. Physical improvements to US-231 from the Kentucky state line to Indiana-70 southeast of Chrisney, redesignated the Abraham Lincoln Memorial Parkway, are complete. This route extends through Spencer County in southern Indiana connecting to Interstate 64 in the north. It passes through the Lincoln boyhood–related sites of the area in and around Lincoln City, Indiana.

2008 September 6. The two-and-a-half-minute promotional video for the Detroit Electrick Six's single recording *Gay Bar* depicts multiple Lincoln-bearded and hatted actors clapping their way through gym, boudoir, and other settings, primarily in their underwear, to the catchy refrain "You're a superstar, at the gay bar. / You're a superstar, at the gay bar. / Yeah! You're a superstar, at the gay bar." The lead Lincoln lookalike is singer Dick Valentine. The song had been recorded in 2001, and was originally released June 2, 2003, off the group's debut album, *Fire*. In the original video, directed by Tom Kuntz and Mike Maguire, the references to war were considered controversial, but the Lincoln-shtick was not. Incredibly, the video grabbed 14.5 million views on YouTube!

2008 September 17. The Gilder-Lehrman Institute of American History, organizers of "Abraham Lincoln: A Man of His Time, A Man for All Times," hosts a two-day site-support orientation seminar for participants in the traveling exhibition of that name, mounted with major funding provided by the National Endowment for the Humanities.

Two exhibition sets were organized. The exhibition trail for the first set crisscrossed the country, commencing at the Civil War Institute at Gettysburg College in mid-October 2008, and then consecutively on to locations in Maryland, South Carolina, Colorado, Kentucky, Michigan, Ohio, Alabama, North Carolina, Indiana, Georgia, Florida, Illinois, Oregon, Missouri, Illinois, Pennsylvania, New Jersey, and California. Likewise, the second exhibition set logged stops in Florida, Louisiana, Illinois, California, Hawaii, California, Idaho, Pennsylvania, New York, Louisiana, Texas, Arizona, Michigan, Georgia, Iowa, Rhode Island, Ohio, Minnesota, Tennessee, and Maryland.

Local support was provided by a variety of sources. The tours would end in June 2010. Extensive promotional materials preceded the displays to tour sites. Curators for the traveling exhibition (which featured many photographs, and manuscript and printed items from the Gilder-Lehrman Collection, supplemented by additional materials from the Library of Congress and elsewhere) were University of Houston professor Steven Mintz and Oxford University professor Richard Carwardine. Extensive suggestions for educational and community involvement were also provided. Project advisors included a "who's who" of Lincoln and Civil War scholars, including Douglas Wilson, Allen Guelzo, David Blight, Thavolia Glymph, Gabor S. Boritt, Richard Carwardine, Harold Holzer, and James Oliver Horton. Another aspect of the program was sponsorship of a series of six free public lectures at the Smithsonian's National Museum of American History, discussing Lincoln's presidency and his relevancy today.

Fig. 4.239. Harold Holzer tirelessly promoted Lincoln before and during the bicentennial observance, as co-chairman of the United States Abraham Lincoln Bicentennial Commission.

2008 September 18. A werewolf-slaying Abraham Lincoln makes his debut in the counterculture Alterna graphic-novel series *Jesus Hates Zombies*, by Stephen Lindsay, with art by Steve Cobb. Lindsay began his JHZ series with the release of *Jesus Hates Zombies: Those Slack-Jaw Blues*, November 16, 2007. Thus far the murderous Lincoln has co-starred in the series in four graphic novels, the additional books being released April 29, 2009, November 25, 2009, and May 26, 2010, all authored by Lindsay and illustrated by various artists. Illustrated is volume 3, the least graphically bizarre cover.

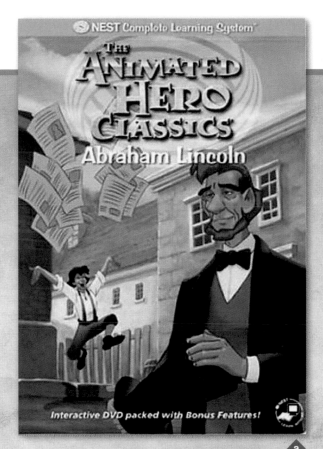

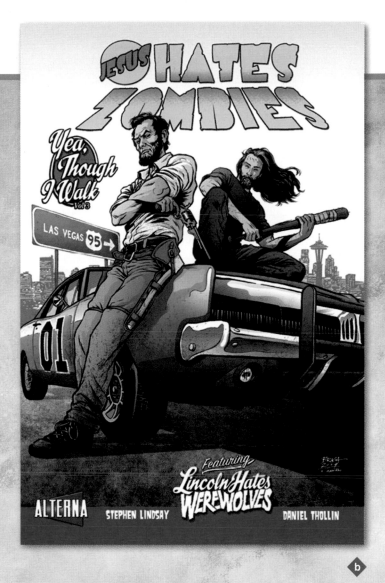

Fig. 4.240. Abraham Lincoln's roles in society today range from teacher of good values (on an *Animated Hero Classics* DVD) *(a)* to bloodthirsty, axe-wielding werewolf hunter (in the contemporary Stephen Lindsay Alterna comic-book series) *(b)*.

Fig. 4.241. In June 2008 the national weekly gallon price of conventional grades of gasoline in the United States climbed above $4 per gallon, causing a proliferation of political handbills such as the one shown, "Good For One Gallon of Gas."

2008 September 21. U.S. Mint engraver Don Everhart discusses the 2009 Lincoln cent reverses on *NBC Nightly News*.

2008 September 22. The U.S. Treasury unveils the four reverse designs chosen for the 2009 Lincoln bicentennial cents, at an outdoor event in front of the Lincoln Memorial on the National Mall. Lincoln presenter Jim Rubin was on hand for photo-ops. Rubin also attended ceremonies that day in the U.S. Capitol, unveiling the Lincoln Christmas Tree Ornament and the 2009 "We the People Calendar" sponsored by the United States Capitol Historical Society to celebrate the Lincoln bicentennial.

2008 Fall. The Illinois State Bar Association mounts an advertising campaign to burnish the image of attorneys, called "Illinois has a history of some pretty good lawyers. We're out to keep it that way," with Abraham Lincoln as their poster boy.

2008. Living History Productions updates its "President Abraham Lincoln" VHS tape in its *Animated Hero Classics* series for youngsters, by releasing an interactive video version on DVD. The series was co-produced by Nest Family Entertainment and Warner Brothers. Shows debuted in the HBO Saturday morning children's block, and then were released for home and school use supplemented by learn-

a

Fig. 4.242. Eager to get a jump on competitors in the lucrative marketplace of American collectors, these nations issued stamps under a variety of guises in 2008. Chad issued a prodigious variety of "Hope" and "Progress" souvenir sheets for Barack Obama's election against a backdrop of one of J.L.G. Ferris's paintings of Lincoln at Independence Hall in 1861 *(a)*. India commemorated the 60th anniversary of the Universal Declaration of Human Rights *(b)*. Liberia actually reprinted four of the U.S. Lincoln stamps from the past *(c)*. Guinea seemingly honored the Obama-Lincoln relationship *(d)*, but its souvenir sheets threw in Marilyn Monroe, a flag, and an orchid to appeal to buyers of those topical series, too! Gambia chose to issue a Presidential Monuments series, including the Daniel Chester French statue and Borglum's Mount Rushmore *(e, f)*.

b

c

ing materials. Their programming portrays positive values, and has earned high praise from faith-based and home-schooling organizations. These materials have also been used in more than 60,000 schools and public libraries nationwide. Many of the individual episodes have earned educational awards. The 30-minute Abraham Lincoln episode takes Lincoln from Springfield through the end of the war and his martyrdom. It was written by Brian Nissen and directed by Richard Rich. Since it is interactive, the Internet Movie Database classifies the DVD release as a "video game."

2008 OCTOBER 10. The James Earle Fraser seated Lincoln sculpture at Syracuse University adds local color in scenes from Universal Pictures' movie *The Express: The Ernie Davis Story*, debuting on screens nationwide. The movie tells the story about the Syracuse football running back who was the first black Heisman Trophy winner there, in 1961. The statue is part of the sequence when Syracuse lineman Jack Buckley gives Ernie the "white girls speech," about social segregation of black athletes and white coeds.

2008 OCTOBER 14. The *Saints Row 2* video game has a created character Abe Lincoln complete with tall black hat and beard. The tall hat was not available in the original *Saints Row* shooting game. A two-minute clip shows Flyboy513's Lincoln character getting snatched off the cruel streets and abducted by an evil general, Mr. Sunshine, but Lincoln fights his way out of a limousine in a gun battle with the general's henchmen. As Lincoln walks away, he says, "This is a bad time to be f—d up." Flyboy513's clip drew 37,000 hits.

2008 OCTOBER 23. Pseudonymously, artist MisNopalesArt posts a bearded skeletal image of Abraham Lincoln on flickr.com. The pen-and-ink sketch was titled *Abraham Lincoln Calavera ACEO*. Cal-ifornia graphic artist Jose Pulido specializes in hand-printed linocut art. Designs are "hand carved from a linoleum block and then hand printed," according to the artist, who sells his work on the Internet.

2008 OCTOBER 28. In the *Fallout 3* video game, Abe Lincoln shoots Megaton Settler in the head. The game stream also shows a post–nuclear war soldier searching through a house basement and locating a shrine to Abraham Lincoln amidst the disarray down below. Before a large, shining image of the Gettysburg Lincoln photo (O-77) are glowing lanterns, flower pots, and a bloody knife. A two-minute clip of the soldier and the shrine on YouTube garnered 570,000 hits!

Fig. 4.243. Abraham Lincoln in the culture on the eve of his bicentennial included a character in the *Saints Row 2* game (in a Flyboy 513 video) *(a)*; Jose Pulido's hand-carved linoleum block print *Abraham Lincoln Calavera ACEO (b)*; and a post–nuclear war soldier's discovery of a subterranean Lincoln shrine in the *Fallout 3* video game *(c)*.

Fig. 4.244. A large representation of George T. Morgan's 1918 Lincoln–Illinois Centennial commemorative half dollar now adorns the Arche Memorial Fountain in Chicago. The memorial, in 1916, originally marked the intersection of the east-west Lincoln Highway and north-south Dixie Highway.

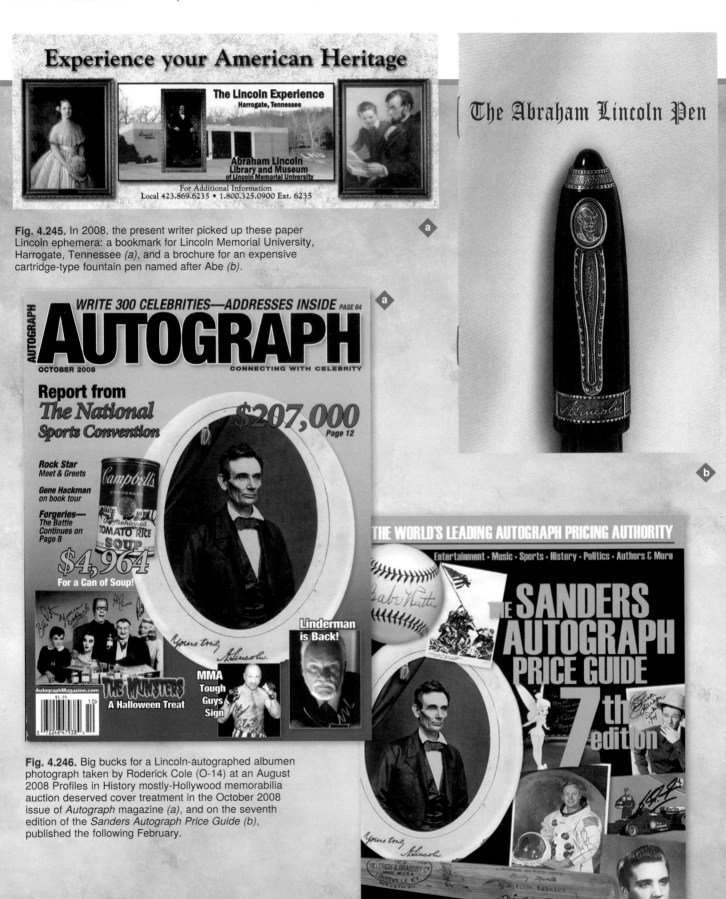

Fig. 4.245. In 2008, the present writer picked up these paper Lincoln ephemera: a bookmark for Lincoln Memorial University, Harrogate, Tennessee *(a)*, and a brochure for an expensive cartridge-type fountain pen named after Abe *(b)*.

Fig. 4.246. Big bucks for a Lincoln-autographed albumen photograph taken by Roderick Cole (O-14) at an August 2008 Profiles in History mostly-Hollywood memorabilia auction deserved cover treatment in the October 2008 issue of *Autograph* magazine *(a)*, and on the seventh edition of the *Sanders Autograph Price Guide (b)*, published the following February.

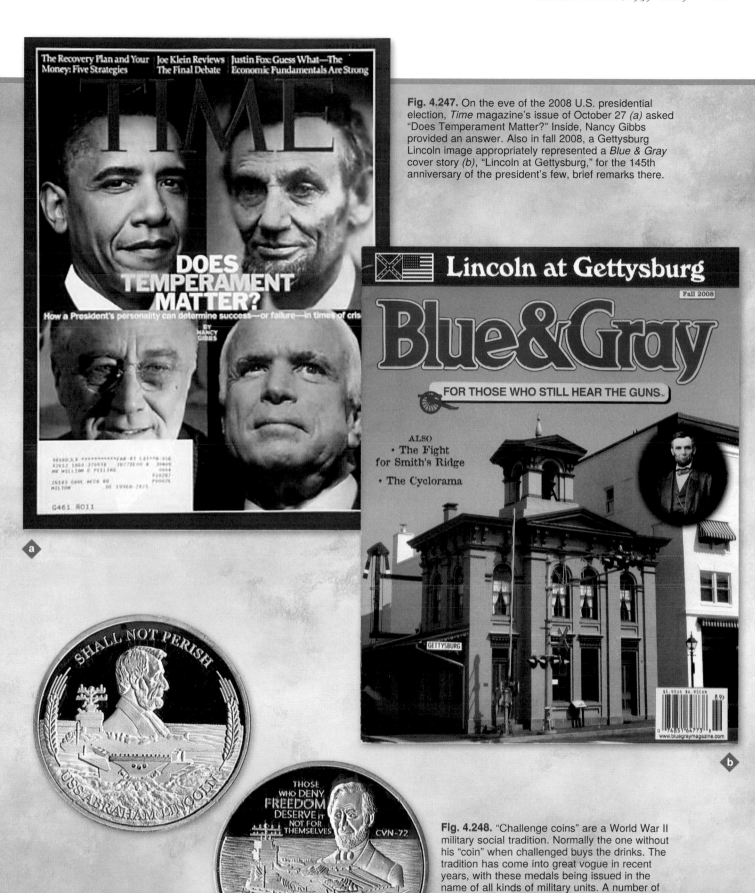

Fig. 4.247. On the eve of the 2008 U.S. presidential election, *Time* magazine's issue of October 27 *(a)* asked "Does Temperament Matter?" Inside, Nancy Gibbs provided an answer. Also in fall 2008, a Gettysburg Lincoln image appropriately represented a *Blue & Gray* cover story *(b)*, "Lincoln at Gettysburg," for the 145th anniversary of the president's few, brief remarks there.

Fig. 4.248. "Challenge coins" are a World War II military social tradition. Normally the one without his "coin" when challenged buys the drinks. The tradition has come into great vogue in recent years, with these medals being issued in the name of all kinds of military units. A number of designs are connected with the USS *Abraham Lincoln* (CVN-72) aircraft carrier. This gold-plated example is one of the better ones seen.

2008 OCTOBER 28. Cuban leader Fidel Castro rebuffs U.S. president George W. Bush's call to Cubans to "shape your own destiny" by ridding themselves of the Communist government, by linking Abraham Lincoln to Castro's fellow revolutionary, Argentine physician Ernesto "Che" Guevara. "Long Live Lincoln! Long Live Che!" Castro wrote in an editorial in the state media.

Shortly after toppling dictator Fulgencio Batista and taking power in January 1959, Castro had made an official visit to Washington, where he visited the Lincoln Memorial. He has told interviewers that he keeps a bust of Lincoln in one of his offices in Havana, according to press accounts at the time.

2008 OCTOBER 30. Gilbert Franklin's statue of Abraham Lincoln at Providence, Rhode Island, is rededicated on the 50th anniversary of its installation, after having been restored. Rhode Island chief justice Frank Williams and others officiated.

2008 OCTOBER 31. Taking a cue from the Lincoln depiction on the current $5 bills now familiar to all Americans and readers worldwide, C-Span's compendium *Abraham Lincoln: Great American Historians on Our Sixteenth President* features a large engraved likeness of Lincoln on its cover dustjacket based on the Anthony Berger February 9, 1864, photograph we know as O-91. In fact, compare a pre–Series of 2006 non-colorized $5 bill in your pocket to the cover illustration and you will see the book's publisher, PublicAffairs, utilized a tightly cropped version of Bureau of Engraving and Printing engraver Tom Hipschen's "Twinkle Eye" Lincoln security engraving from the note for their cover design—another case of art imitating life imitating art.

Fig. 4.249. Lincoln get-ups continue to be ready sellers at Halloween and for school pageants.

Fig. 4.250. An Augustus Saint-Gaudens replica in the Cuban capital of Havana continues to represent the Great Emancipator to the revolutionary people, having acquired a fine patina (and some bird poo) along the way by the eve of the Lincoln bicentennial.

2008 November 2. Lincolnphile Fred Reed submits "A New Birth of Freedom" as the theme for the upcoming 2009 American Numismatic Association–sponsored National Coin Week celebration (scheduled for April 2009, during the year of the Lincoln bicentennial). This phrase, from the conclusion to Abraham Lincoln's famous Gettysburg Address, stresses Lincoln's core belief in equality among all citizens. National Coin Week is staged annually to attract attention to the numismatic hobby.

The ANA went another direction for the April 19–25, 2009, observance. It chose the theme "Lincoln's Legacy: A Nation United," suggested by Baltimore, Maryland, collector Ryan Berman. Berman received a 50-cent Lincoln Fractional Currency note as his prize. More than 40 submissions were received, according to organizers. Other prize winners included New Jersey collectors Simon Beier and Dennis Berube for "Lincoln: A Man of Common Cents" and "Coins Communicate Lincoln's Legacy," respectively, and Californian David Sperry's "Lincoln's Legacy Makes Good Cents."

2008 November 7. The Smithsonian Institution's National Portrait Gallery opens an eight-month-long exhibition, "One Life: The Mask of Lincoln," comprising 31 memorable images of Abraham Lincoln, curated by historian David C. Ward. Included are the Lincoln plaster life masks done in 1860 by Leonard Volk and in 1865 by Clark Mills, as well as a series of portraits, lithographs, and photographs "to show the changing face that Abraham Lincoln presented to the world as he led the fight for the Union," according to Ward. Significantly, the originals of all three of the primary Lincoln money images—February 9, 1864, photographs by Anthony Berger: (O-88) modeled for the cent, (O-92) modeled for the old-style $5 notes and other bills, and (O-91) modeled for the new-style $5s—were represented by contemporary albumen silver prints, or a modern albumen print from the original 1864 wet-plate collodion negative, in the case of the cent profile.

Artists and photographers of Lincoln portraits represented included Alexander Hesler, William Judkins Thomson, John Henry Brown, Mathew Brady, George B. Ayres, George Clark, Christopher S. German, Alexander Gardner, Thomas LeMere, Adalbert Volck, Pierre Morand, Anthony Berger, Lewis E. Walker, Henry F. Warren, Lambert Hollis, engravers William Roberts and Alexander Hay Ritchie, and lithographer Leopold Grozelier. Images of Lincoln contemporaries rounding out the exhibition ran the gamut from Stephen A. Douglas and U.S. Grant to Jefferson Davis and John Wilkes Booth. The entire exhibit was also made available online. Historian Ward's keynote address based on the exhibition was also made available on the Internet as part of the Smithsonian Education Online Conference Series.

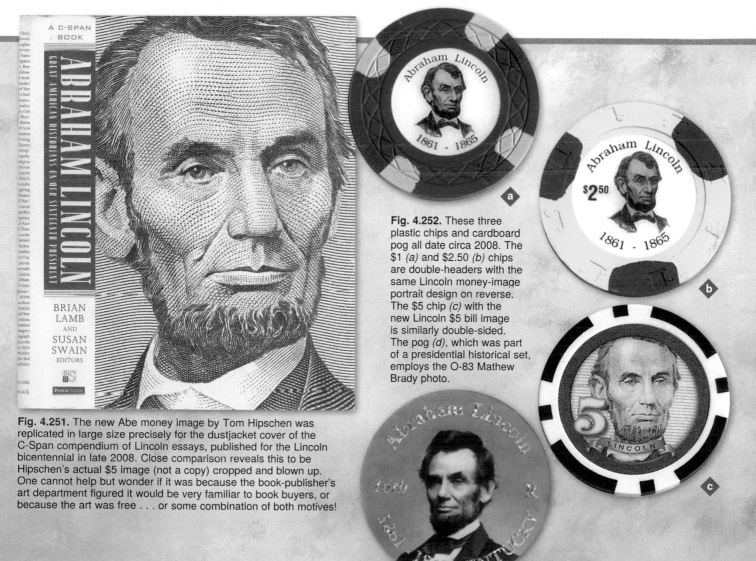

Fig. 4.251. The new Abe money image by Tom Hipschen was replicated in large size precisely for the dustjacket cover of the C-Span compendium of Lincoln essays, published for the Lincoln bicentennial in late 2008. Close comparison reveals this to be Hipschen's actual $5 image (not a copy) cropped and blown up. One cannot help but wonder if it was because the book-publisher's art department figured it would be very familiar to book buyers, or because the art was free . . . or some combination of both motives!

Fig. 4.252. These three plastic chips and cardboard pog all date circa 2008. The $1 (a) and $2.50 (b) chips are double-headers with the same Lincoln money-image portrait design on reverse. The $5 chip (c) with the new Lincoln $5 bill image is similarly double-sided. The pog (d), which was part of a presidential historical set, employs the O-83 Mathew Brady photo.

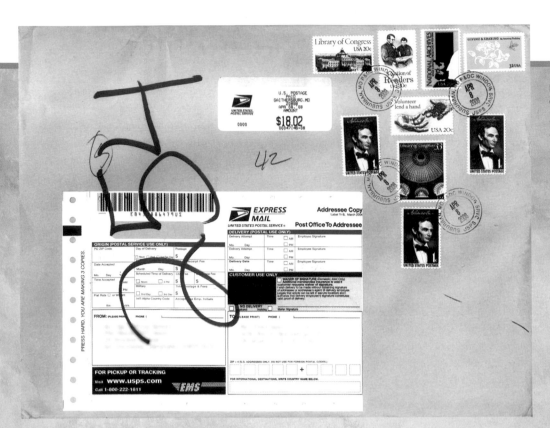

Fig. 4.253. You take your Lincoln collectibles where you can find them. Fellow Lincoln enthusiast, collector William Hallam Weber, created this fancy cover for yours truly when he employed a variety of old Lincoln postage stamps on the Express Mail envelope he sent me in April 2008.

Fig. 4.254. The Eldorado Club marketed this belt buckle, designed by Joe deBlois, in recent years.

Fig. 4.255. I know it's a patch, but the bulbous nose and prominent eyebrow on this profile of Lincoln are less than aesthetically pleasing or historically accurate. Almost any old bearded image, preferably with a tall hat, will do today.

Fig. 4.256. This copper-colored patch for the USS *Abraham Lincoln* (CVN-72) illustrates the Lincoln cent profile.

2008 November 8. The thought-provoking documentary *Abraham Lincoln: Tyrant*, a dramatically scored 4:51 video on YouTube, which relies heavily on wartime battlefield and civilian rubble photographs, receives only 15,000 views. The film's theme was that, more important even than the death and hardship inflicted on the participants and innocent civilians alike, Lincoln's invasion of the South destroyed "VOLUNTARY Union . . . Union, no longer by the consent of the governed, but by threat of violence." One needn't be firmly in the Lew Rockwell–Thomas J. DiLorenzo camp to appreciate the seriousness of the question this short film raises, and particularly to enjoy the Boston Pops Orchestra's performance of *Immolation (With Our Lives, We Give Life)*.

2008 November 8. *Washington Post* columnist David Brown writes: "It's a safe bet that Abraham Lincoln is the most recognizable American of all time. Every child in this country can name him by first grade, and so can countless millions who never set foot in the United States. His face adorns the indivisible penny (which is the best argument for retaining that beleaguered coin). He's more American than George Washington, at least when it comes to his image. A big part of the reason is photography. Lincoln was the first president whose entire political career transpired in the era when light could be magically captured and held forever."[23]

2008 November 17. On the eve of the Lincoln bicentennial observance, President George W. Bush presents National Humanities medals to Lincoln scholars Harold Holzer and Gabor S. Boritt at a White House ceremony. The National Endowment for the Humanities said Holzer was being recognized "for engaging scholarship on that crucible of our history, the American Civil War. His work has brought new understanding of the many facets of Abraham Lincoln and his era through the study of image, word, and deed." It described Boritt as a "tireless advocate for the study of Lincoln and the Civil War."

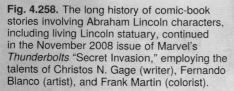

Fig. 4.257. A company called Authentic Ink sold collectors' cards in 2008 with sports and other figures commemorated. The *authentic* part was an encapsulated period Lincoln cent, such as this 1943 zinc-plated steel U.S. cent commemorating Stan Musial's 1943 Most Valuable Player performance.

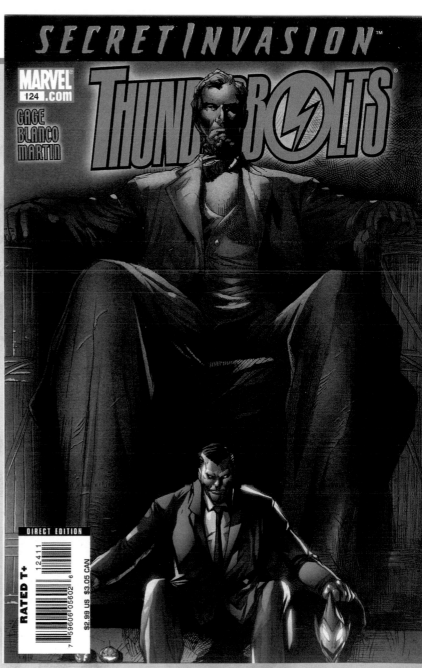

Fig. 4.258. The long history of comic-book stories involving Abraham Lincoln characters, including living Lincoln statuary, continued in the November 2008 issue of Marvel's *Thunderbolts* "Secret Invasion," employing the talents of Christos N. Gage (writer), Fernando Blanco (artist), and Frank Martin (colorist).

2008 NOVEMBER 18. First Lady Laura Bush tells students gathered at the Abraham Lincoln Birthplace National Historic Site in Hodgenville, Kentucky, "I'm delighted that boys and girls from Abraham Lincoln Elementary School are here with us today at the birthplace of America's 16th president. . . . This National Historic Site commemorates the simple log cabin where Abraham Lincoln was born. Here, we remember that the man who became our beloved president was once just a young boy—like the students here from Abraham Lincoln school. He played on the farm and he helped with difficult chores. He began his life with no special advantages—he just had a strong character and a desire to learn. Both the Lincoln Memorial in Washington and this Kentucky cabin are fitting tributes to President Lincoln. Together, these monuments tell the story of an ordinary man who answered the call to greatness and led America during a great Civil War."

2008 NOVEMBER 18. The History Channel / www.History.com and cosponsor Outback Steakhouse launch the "Give a Lincoln for Lincoln" campaign, at the Lincoln birthplace memorial, during the visit by First Lady Laura Bush, honorary chair of the National Park Foundation. "He saved our nation; let's (help) save his legacy" was the campaign's tagline. Throughout 2009 History, in association with the National Park Foundation and the National Trust for Historic Preservation, would solicit "Lincoln-head pennies and five dollar bills and more" as donations to help preserve six

sites associated with Lincoln's life and legacy. Publicity, including the campaign's logo, incorporated both current money images of Lincoln and a Lincoln cent. The goal was to raise a minimum of $200,000, or $1,000 for every year since Lincoln's birth. Sites included Abraham Lincoln Birthplace National Historical Park (Hodgenville, Kentucky), Lincoln Boyhood National Memorial (Lincoln City, Indiana), Lincoln Home National Historic Site (Springfield, Illinois), President Lincoln's Cottage at the Soldiers' Home (Washington, D.C.), Ford's Theatre National Historic Site (Washington, D.C.) and the Lincoln Memorial (Washington, D.C.). The campaign also sponsored contests for Lincoln-themed lesson plans and an art contest for students to create Lincoln coin boxes.

2008 NOVEMBER 18. The "first family of Lincoln photo collectors," heirs to the Meserve collection and legacy, authors Philip B. Kunhardt III, Peter W. Kunhardt, and Peter W. Kunhardt Jr., release their monumental study for the upcoming Lincoln bicentennial, *Looking for Lincoln: The Making of an American Icon*, published by Random House–Knopf. According to Publishers Weekly, "[T]he Kunhardts' book represents a visual and literary feast for all devotees of the sacred national idol that is Lincoln." The book was released as a companion to the PBS special also called *Looking for Lincoln,* which would premiere on February 11, 2009.

Fig. 4.259. The History Channel's "Give a Lincoln for Lincoln" campaign raised dough for preservation activities at several Lincoln national historic sites, employing both current money images to good advantage.

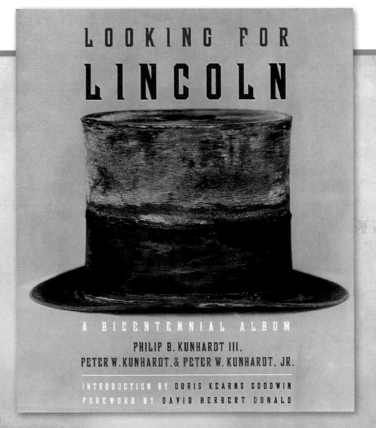

Fig. 4.260. As might be expected, the coming Abraham Lincoln bicentennial brought out a plethora of Lincoln volumes. The "first family of Lincoln portraiture," members of the Kunhardt family, contributed the excellent *Looking for Lincoln.* Publisher Knopf rolled out big guns—historians David Herbert Donald and Doris Kearns Goodwin—to provide additional commentary for the luxurious volume, printed on deckled-edge paper to resemble a hand-bound book.

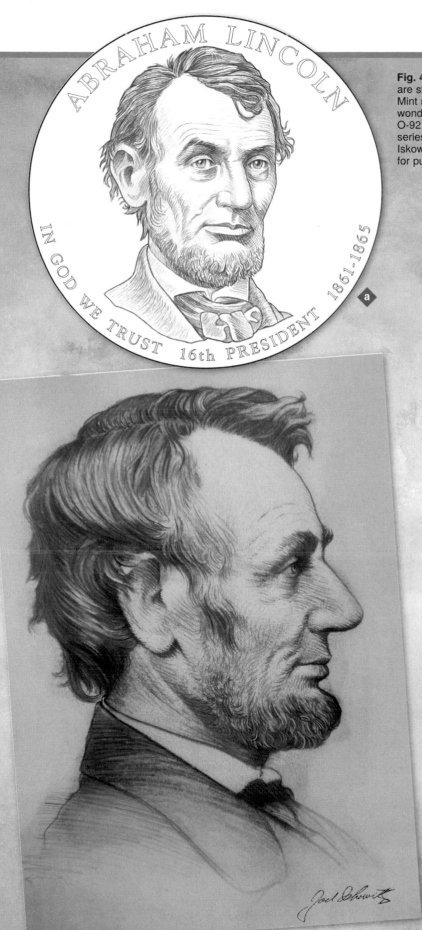

Fig. 4.261. Traditional money images of Lincoln are still popular with graphic artists today. U.S. Mint sculptor/engraver Don Everhart shared his wonderful, but unadopted, Lincoln mini-dollar O-92 design for the current U.S. presidential dollar series *(a)*. Likewise, coin and stamp designer Joel Iskowitz furnished this sensitive Lincoln O-88 *(b)* for publication in the present book.

Fig. 4.262. Meanwhile the former iconic Lincoln $5 bill image has begun to wane in use in popular culture. This Visit Springfield postcard was initially issued in the 1980s and 1990s, when this likeness was still king.

2008 November 19. U.S. Mint Deputy Director Andy Brunhart and Abraham Lincoln Bicentennial Commission co-chairman Harold Holzer unveil the design for the Abraham Lincoln bicentennial silver dollar at the 145th-anniversary ceremonies of Lincoln's Gettysburg Address. Others in attendance included Lincoln Fellowship of Pennsylvania vice president Ronald L. Hanky and historical-documentary maker Ken Burns. Availability to the public of the new coin was pegged for Lincoln's birthday, February 12, 2009.

2008 November 20. Colorado governor Bill Ritter announces formation of a "blue ribbon" panel "to study the significance of Abra-

ham Lincoln's Presidency in preparation of the 2009 bicentennial celebration." The 20-member commission's first meeting was slated for the following day. It had been authorized by Ritter's November 4 executive order.

2008 Fall. By the time of its demise, the Fort Wayne Lincoln Museum's *Lincoln Lore* had become a slickly produced but infrequently published magazine. Its "last issue" sported color reproductions of artist Wendy Allen's impressionistic *Lincoln 8* on its front cover, and another of Allen's Lincoln interpretations on the back cover. The periodical was no longer the weekly one-sheet, or

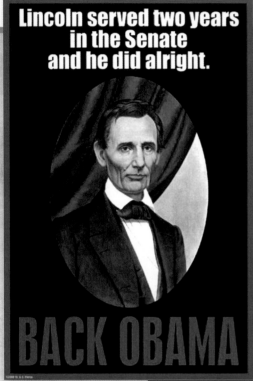

Fig. 4.263. Wilbur Pierce's pro-Obama poster during the 2008 presidential campaign claimed that lack of experience was no bar to electability. Of course, Abraham Lincoln never served in the U.S. Senate (he served one term, two years, in the House of Representatives). Obama indeed "served" there all of two years before announcing his presidential campaign in February 2007, having joined the U.S. Senate in January 2005.

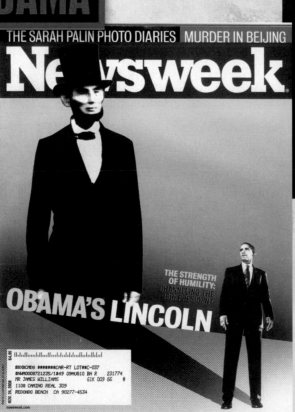

Fig. 4.264. The Eastern press was thoroughly inculcated by the Obama-Lincoln self-identification. The November 17, 2008, issue of the *New Yorker* (a), and the November 24, 2008, issue of *Newsweek* (b), artfully shared these visions with readers and newsstand gawkers.

monthly four-page, newsletter that Lincolnphiles had relied upon and cherished for more than 75 years. The swan song, under the direction of editor Sara Gabbard, was an outstanding production. The lead article was by Frank J. Williams; there were interviews with Allen Guelzo, Harold Holzer, Vernon Burton, William Lee Miller, and Harry S. Stout; and brief articles and book reviews rounded out the journal. Unfortunately, the publication had grown expensive and onerous to produce, costly to mail, and—in accord with Lincoln Financial Group's corporate change in direction—apparently superfluous to its goals. The company that had committed itself to preserving and proliferating Abraham Lincoln's lasting legacy a century earlier, and profited immensely over the years by virtue of its Lincoln brand, abandoned and orphaned its museum and publication on the very eve of the nation's Lincoln birth bicen-

tennial observance, in which by rights Lincoln National could have richly appeared stage center. Although the company left its vast Lincoln collections in strong and eager hands, alas the Lincoln mecca at Fort Wayne, and Dr. Louis A. Warren's frequent clipsheet reminder of Lincoln's virtues and importance, did not fit into the company's 21st-century vision for itself. (See the entry for December 12, 2008.)

2008 DECEMBER 1. In response to budget cuts, the State of Illinois briefly closes the Lincoln Log Cabin State Historic Site to the public.

2008 DECEMBER 1. A Civil War–era Abraham Lincoln portrait (based on his image on the then-current $10 bill) by Schoharie, New York, artist Amos Hamilton, measuring 10.5 by 14 inches on canvas, is sold by Heritage Galleries for $3,107 including buyer's premium. (See figure 1.56.)

Number 1894 / Fall 2008

Over 75 Years
Lincoln Lore®
Since 1929

Fig. 4.265. The venerable periodical *Lincoln Lore*, started by Dr. Louis A. Warren in 1929, was laid to rest in fall 2008 at the very feet of the Lincoln bicentennial observance, when Lincoln Financial Group chose to walk away from company founders' promises to preserve Lincoln's heritage as a thank-you for the cooption of the Lincoln identity, brand, and legacy. The last issue, under the direction of editor Sara Gabbard, was a bang-up one, featuring interviews and the art of Wendy Allen. The publication has since been resumed under the auspices of the Friends of the Lincoln Library.

2008 December 6. Through January 4, 2009, the White House copy of the Gettysburg Address goes on display at the Smithsonian National Museum of American History.

2008 December 8. PhD candidate Mazie Harris lectures at the Library of Congress on the change in *Vanity Fair* illustrator Henry Louis Stephens's art stemming from Lincoln's Emancipation edicts of 1862–1863. According to Harris, the Emancipation Proclamation "compelled Stephens to reconsider his previously virulently anti-abolitionist propaganda. . . . Stephens deployed color printing and caricature in an attempt to reformulate views of race relations in the North and mobilize military enlistment." (See figure 1.51.)

Fig. 4.266. Lincoln affinity was *very* relevant in the 2008 U.S. presidential campaign for politicians of all stripes, from libertarian Republican Ron Paul to Prohibition Party candidate Gene Amondson to liberal Democrat Barack Obama.

2008 December 8. The Abraham Lincoln Presidential Library & Museum, Springfield, Illinois, introduces "Bicentennial Bucks" gift certificates that can be spent at the museum. Each buck had an entry form for a prize drawing for a gala $6,000 "Night at the Museum" party, and other prizes. The bucks were *not* discount coupons: a stack of 50 $1s was $50, or $25 for 25 $1 coupons. Bucks were good for admission, food, or gift-shop items through December 31, 2010. Additionally, the Abraham Lincoln Presidential Library Foundation offered "Bundles" of the "Bucks" as a money-raising promotion. A platinum "Bicentennial Bundle" (valued at $3,400) sold for $2,000, but purchasers only received 500 Bicentennial Bucks. The rest of the value was in museum memberships and tickets. A gold bundle (valued at $1,300) netted 200 Bicentennial Bucks plus a membership and admission tickets. Silver bundles were priced at $500 (valued at $710) and paid out 150 of the bucks, plus a membership and tickets. Purchasers of bronze bundles (valued at $250) received 50 of the bucks and tickets.

2008 December 11. Preservationist and film auteur Lorre Fritchy posts on YouTube her 3:10 short film *Assassination of Lincoln: Tear-down of a Century Old Mill*, grist for her feature film (in development) *Millies*. Ms. Fritchy's film graphically depicted the destruction of the 108-year-old, six-story brick Lincoln Foods Mill in Lawrence, Massachusetts. Lincoln Foods was the originator and purveyor of the famous Lincoln bank glass figural bottles of the 1950s (see figures 3.232a and b). "As our smokestacks come down so goes our history," she contended. "The [Lincoln Foods] building should never have gotten to this point where knocking it down is the only thing we can do. . . . The only way to save Lincoln Foods at this point is on film," Ms. Fritchy said. The building was leveled to make room for a new $15 million, 32,000-square-foot U.S. Department of Homeland Security Citizenship and Immigration Services facility.

2008 December. To honor the 200th anniversary of President Abraham Lincoln's birth, February 12, 2009, the Bureau of Engraving and Printing's Historical Resource Center develops exhibits with Lincoln-related artifacts produced during the BEP's early years and from its historical collection. Three themes were explored: "Picturing President Lincoln," "Lincoln and Civil War Finance," and "Dancing the 'Legal Tender Polka': Public Reaction to Changes in

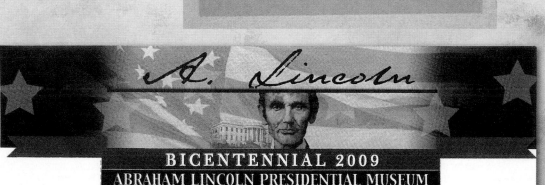

Fig. 4.267. Bicentennial Bucks was an Abraham Lincoln Presidential Library and Museum fund-raising project for the Lincoln bicentennial.

Fig. 4.268. An improvised, facing portrait of an Illinois Abe stares at visitors from a pre-bicentennial Abraham Lincoln Presidential Library and Museum senior-admission ticket.

Government Securities during the Civil War." Included in the first display were never-issued proofs of 1944 designs for $5 Federal Reserve Notes by Alvin R. Meissner and Victor S. McCloskey Jr., and for a never-issued 1944 design for a $5 Silver Certificate by an unknown BEP artist. The second exhibit included proofs of Treasury securities with Lincoln's image, while the third display featured a three-note proof sheet of Lincoln $10 Demand Note faces. Unfortunately the exhibit perpetuated the misidentification of the engraver of that first Lincoln currency image for American Bank Note Co. The engraver was Charles Burt, as reported in *Abraham Lincoln: The Image of His Greatness* and by this author elsewhere.

2008 December 12. Indiana governor Mitch Daniels announces the agreement that an Indiana consortium—including the Indiana State Museum, Allen County Public Library in Fort Wayne, the Indiana Historical Society, Indiana State Library, and Friends of the Lincoln Museum—had won the gift of the Fort Wayne Lincoln Museum collection, valued at $20 million. The donation was made by Lincoln Financial Foundation, which relocated from Fort Wayne to Philadelphia in 1999. Most of the printed documents will stay in Fort Wayne, where the ACPL plans to digitize much of the collection, but artifacts and the copies of the Emancipation Proclamation and Thirteenth Amendment will be displayed at the State Museum in Indianapolis.

"We enter Lincoln's bicentennial year with the goal of reestablishing Indiana's central place in his life. . . . Indiana pledges the most exquisite care and the widest possible public availability of these priceless pieces of our history," Daniels said.

"Lincoln is a beloved figure who has inspired generations of Americans. He spent his formative years in Indiana, and we are grateful to keep the collection here in the state," said Indiana State Museum president Barry Dressel.

A private endowment will pay expenses of the Indiana State Museum and the ACPL. Also vying for the collection had been the Smithsonian Institution / Library of Congress and the Abraham Lincoln Presidential Library and Museum.

Fig. 4.269. The U.S. Bureau of Engraving and Printing mounted three displays *(above, and the next two pages)* for the Lincoln bicentennial, featuring Lincoln paper-money, bond, and stamp portraiture. The Lincoln legacy on official government financial instruments is rich and varied, as readers of this book and of *Abraham Lincoln: The Image of His Greatness* can attest. For its exhibition, the Bureau specially printed various proofs, including a sheet of $5, $10, and $20 Demand Notes. Unfortunately, the BEP's Historical Resource Center, which supplied narrative for the displays, incorrectly identified the engraver of the Lincoln portrait on the original $10 greenbacks as Frederick Girsch (see panel "Civil War Finance" under "Two: Engraving"). This was based on since-corrected numismatic research regarding a die created by a private contractor before the Treasury engraving and printing bureau was created. In 2005, when the American Bank Note Co. archives were sold, the present author purchased the original die and ABNCo paperwork showing the engraving of the C.S. German image was done by Charles Burt for the currency. The die and roller die were illustrated in *Abraham Lincoln: The Image of His Greatness* (as figures 2.170 and 2.171), and articles on the origin of the die were published in *Paper Money, Bank Note Reporter, The Numismatist*, and even the prestigious *Lincoln Herald*. The author also informed the BEP Office of External Relations, in June 2008, that their attribution was incorrect on the Lincoln die listing the Historical Resource Center had furnished for his earlier research. Unfortunately the HRC dropped the ball when it prepared this significant and wonderfully illustrative exhibit.

The $5 Face
Francis Bicknell Carpenter
and the Emancipation Proclamation

2008 December 31. The U.S. Mint reports to Congress on the first quarter of fiscal-year 2009 that: 'The Secretary of the Treasury will mint and issue numismatic one-cent coins in 2009 with the exact metallic content as contained in the 1909 coin (95 percent copper, 5 percent tin and zinc). Numismatic coins will be those coins with a proof or uncirculated finish, and will be offered for sale in sets, i.e. proof set, uncirculated set, special one-cent coin sets. These numismatic versions will not be sold separately."[24]

2009 January 5. The numismatic trade tabloid *Coin World* introduces a weekly feature series, "The Numismatics of Lincoln," that will appear throughout his bicentennial year. Each week a different Lincoln numismatic topic would be addressed by a staff or contributing author, including the present writer, to keep alive awareness of Lincoln's grand numismatic presence in the minds of readers.

2009 January 6. Brown University's John Hay Library opens a two-month-long exhibition, "Abraham Lincoln: The Man, The Myth, The Making of a President." "Dissected endlessly by scholars, Lincoln at 200 remains an enigma, his every action open to multiple, even opposing interpretations," curator Holly Snyder wrote in the exhibition brochure. "Lincoln's complexities and his reticence in speaking about personal matters have led successive generations of authors to impute to him a wide range of qualities, beliefs and behaviors with which he had no particular association in life. This propensity to employ Lincoln's persona to promote a variety of often conflicting social, political and cultural agendas exploded after his assassination and the long period of public mourning that followed. The first crescendo of interpretation, re-interpretation and misrepresentation came in the decades just before and after the celebration of the Lincoln Centennial in 1909, and a second in our own times, with the approach of 2009," Snyder commented prophetically.

2009 January 7. The Indiana Historical Society traveling exhibit "Faces of the Civil War" opens at the Henry County Public Library in New Castle, with additional stops throughout the state through November 18, 2010.

2009 January. TD Bank rolls out a new 30-second spot in which Regis Philbin and Kelly Ripa interview Abe Lincoln, who is disappointed because the penny is so worthless that people won't even stop to pick one up off the sidewalk anymore.

2009 January 12. Jacob K. posts a found slide on Yahoo's flickr social and image-exchanging web site that creates quite a buzz. Evidently a faded Kodachrome slide degraded by exposure to sunlight over time, it shows a display of Volk's Lincoln mask and hand casts in a showcase behind glass. The image was posted backwards, but that's not what caught the attention of web-site viewers. The display is faded to a bright pink against a deep violet background, which caused several female reviewers to comment about its phallic appearance, casting a serious doubt on Lincoln's "Long Abe" nickname.

2009 January 16. An Abraham Lincoln exhibition, "A New Birth of Freedom," featuring documents from the Abraham Lincoln Presidential Library and Museum, opens at the Smithsonian's National Museum of American History. The exhibition would run through March 22.

2009 January 16. "Abraham Lincoln: An Extraordinary Life," showcasing more than 60 historical treasures associated with Lincoln's life from the collections of the Smithsonian Institution, goes

Fig. 4.270. Talk-show host Regis Philbin, holding Abraham Lincoln's hat, appears tongue-tied interviewing Old Abe for a 2009 TD Bank commercial.

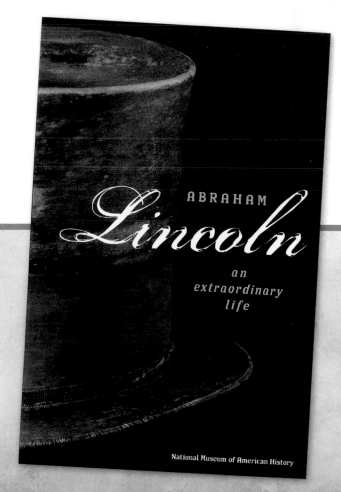

Fig. 4.271. Smithsonian Institution chair of political history, Dr. Harry R. Rubenstein, curated the museum's excellent "Abraham Lincoln: An Extraordinary Life" exhibition, featuring more than 60 treasures from the institution's collection. The illustrated companion catalog was a quick sell-out.

on display in the third-floor Rose Gallery. Included were an iron wedge Lincoln used to split wood in the early 1830s in New Salem, Illinois, the top hat he was wearing on the night he was assassinated at Ford's theatre, his patent model, and his gold pocket watch. The exhibit would remain in place through May 30, 2011. A companion, 112-page paperback color catalog by Harry R. Rubenstein, published by Smithsonian Institution Press, would debut February 1. Rubenstein is chair of the Division of Political History at the Smithsonian's National Museum of American History. The catalog represented the first time that the Smithsonian had ever published its unparalleled Lincoln collection. The exhibition, Rubenstein's symposium of the same title, and the book itself proved so popular that the book sold out and soon could only be acquired on the after-market.

2009 JANUARY 17. President-elect Barack Obama boards the Inauguration Train in Philadelphia for his trip to the inauguration in Washington, D.C.

2009 JANUARY 18. "We are One," President-elect Barack Obama's pre-inaugural celebration concert, is held at the Lincoln Memorial before a crowd estimated at 400,000 on the National Mall. Performers and speakers included Bruce Springsteen, Martin Luther King III, Marisa Tomei, James Taylor, John Mellencamp, Queen Latifah, Herbie Hancock, Sheryl Crow, Tiger Woods, Jack Black, Garth Brooks, Samuel L. Jackson, Ashley Judd, Stevie Wonder, U2, Pete Seeger, and Beyoncé. Admission was free and HBO also broadcast the event free over its normally subscription-based cable service. It was also broadcast in foreign countries.

2009 JANUARY 18. Actor Tom Hanks narrates the U.S. Armed Forces Symphony performance of Aaron Copland's patriotic classic *A Lincoln Portrait* at the "We are One" celebration at the Lincoln Memorial.

2009 JANUARY 20. Barack Obama is sworn in as president on the same Bible Abraham Lincoln used at his second inaugural.

The designer/sculptor of his official inaugural medal, Marc Mellon, said he tried to project an introspective and thoughtful Obama. "I imagined Barack Obama thinking of Lincoln and of Martin Luther King, of the historic nature of his election, and of the serious challenges he's been chosen to face."

Fig. 4.272. The Barack Obama inauguration in January 2009 created a wellspring of tabloid hype, self-consciously abetted by the January 18 Obama "We are One" pre-inaugural concert staged at the Lincoln Memorial. Shown is the January 19, 2009, front page of the *New York Post (a)*. A crowd estimated at 400,000, and a lineup of music and Hollywood A-listers, turned out for the celebration on the nation's front lawn on the National Mall in front of the Lincoln Memorial *(b)*.

2009 January 20. The Gambia issues a "Whistle Stop Tour" souvenir sheet of four stamps commemorating the inaugural journeys of Abraham Lincoln in 1861 and Barack Obama in the present day.

2009 January 21. The ApolloSpeaks blog at Newsvine.com calls attention to newly inaugurated U.S. president Barack Obama's self-conscious draping of himself in Lincoln's legacy to appropriate for himself an "image of greatness," and the "misperception that he is one of the great ones—an avatar of Lincoln, FDR or Kennedy."[25]

2009 January 23. Jim Bumgardner, alias krazydad / jbum on Yahoo's flickr social and image-sharing web site, posts a tiled

GETTYSBURG ADDRESS

View interactive mosaic @ http://www.PresidentLincoln.org

JPMorgan Chase & Co.
MacArthur
The John D. and Catherine T. MacArthur Foundation
The Chicago Community Trust AND AFFILIATES

Fig. 4.273. Jim Bumgardner created this "Four Score and Seven Poster," comprised of 572 Civil War–era images, which the Abraham Lincoln Presidential Library and Museum offered as a downloadable PDF on its web site for the Lincoln bicentennial. As of this writing it is still available, for free.

red-white-blue–tinted black-and-white image of Abraham Lincoln, based on Alexander Gardner's Gettysburg Lincoln photo (O-77), composed of 572 Civil War–era images. From a distance the target image on the poster, called *Four Score and Seven Poster*, is apparent. "I generated this mosaic for the Abraham Lincoln Presidential Library," Bumgardner wrote. "You'll find an interactive version of the mosaic here [in which the viewer can enlarge each of the small tiles] at the Abraham Lincoln Presidential library, as well as a downloadable PDF version," he continued. Bumgardner credited Chris Sparks, "who did a good deal of editorial work, and Katie Grant, who added the colors."

2009 JANUARY 31. A new National Park Service orientation film has its formal premier at the Lincoln Home National Historic Site visitor center: *Abraham Lincoln: A Journey to Greatness.* The film had debuted there earlier, in fall 2008. Starring Springfield native and

Lincoln presenter Fritz Klein in the title role, the film traces Lincoln's 24 formative years in Springfield. Arriving alone and without money, here Lincoln "would then find all the pieces of his life"—a wife and four children, a profession as a lawyer—and become the man, Abraham Lincoln. The 26-minute film was produced by Aperture Pictures at a reported cost of $200,000. It was shot over seven days in the Lincoln home, the surrounding neighborhood, the Old State Capitol, the Lincoln-Herndon Law Offices, and Lincoln's New Salem. The new docudrama replaced the 16-minute 1976 film, *Mr. Lincoln's Springfield,* which had been retired in 2002, "when it started to look dated," according to a National Park Service official. "Before Abraham Lincoln was an icon, he was a man, and before he was a president, he was a husband, a father, a young lawyer struggling to make ends meet," the film reminds the approximately 350,000 visitors to the site annually.

Fig. 4.274. President-elect Barack Obama's self-identification with Abraham Lincoln included the historic (or cheesy, depending on your understanding of historic) attempted copy of the last leg of Lincoln's train trip to his first inaugural. Obama went to Philadelphia and hopped on a special car on January 17 for a jubilant 230-mile ride into the nation's capital to kick off a four-day inaugural fest. The Gambia issued this souvenir sheet of four stamps for the 44th president's journey through Pennsylvania, Delaware, and Maryland, into D.C.

Fig. 4.275. *American History* magazine's February 2009 cover features Abraham Lincoln, but cover blurbs also plug the Thomas Jefferson–Sally Hemings affair, women's issues, and Benjamin Franklin.

2009 FEBRUARY. Abraham Lincoln's image, reputation, and legacy take front stage center in public consciousness. While it is impossible to recount the many hundreds of special events and ceremonies staged to celebrate the bicentennial of Abraham Lincoln's humble birth, those that follow indicate the scope of celebrations and importance given to this milestone anniversary by Lincoln's fellow Americans.

2009 FEBRUARY. "Darwin and Lincoln, born on the same day 200 years ago, they change the world forever; Their Genius; Their Legacies; Their Humanity," and pictures of the two bearded 19th-century gentlemen facing off dominate the cover of *Smithsonian* magazine. Inside the magazine, author Philip B. Kunhardt III writes, in part:

> From the time of his death in 1865 to the 200th anniversary of his birth, February 12, 2009, there has never been a decade in

which Abraham Lincoln's influence has not been felt. Yet it has not been a smooth, unfolding history, but a jagged narrative filled with contention and revisionism. Lincoln's legacy has shifted again and again as different groups have interpreted him. Northerners and Southerners, blacks and whites, East Coast elites and prairie Westerners, liberals and conservatives, the religious and secular, scholars and popularizers—all have recalled a sometimes startlingly different Lincoln. He has been lifted up by both sides of the Temperance Movement; invoked for and against federal intervention in the economy; heralded by anti-communists, such as Senator Joseph McCarthy, and by American communists, such as those who joined the Abraham Lincoln Brigade in the fight against the fascist Spanish government in the 1930s. Lincoln has been used to justify support for and against incursions on civil liberties, and has been proclaimed both a true and a false friend to African-Americans. . . .

Fig. 4.276. Fritz Klein appears in scenes recording Abraham Lincoln waiting at the train station prior to his departure from Springfield, Illinois, for his trip to Washington *(a)*, and drafting his first inaugural address *(b)*, in the National Park Service film *A Journey to Greatness*.

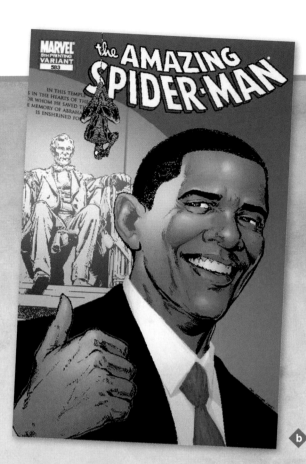

Fig. 4.277. A blitz of Lincoln-themed cover art appeared contemporaneously to the Lincoln bicentennial celebration in February 2009. Shown are the covers of the January-February 2009 *Paper Money*, official journal of the Society of Paper Money Collectors *(a)*; the January 2009 *Amazing Spider-Man* variant cover #5 *(b)*; the Winter 2009 *Smithsonian Collector's Edition (c)*; the Winter 2009 *Financial History (d)*; the February 2009 *Smithsonian (e)*; and the February 2009 *History (f)*. The Obama—Spider-Man comic (*Spider-Man* no. 583) was released January 14 and still became the top-selling comic book in January, going through five printings in all.

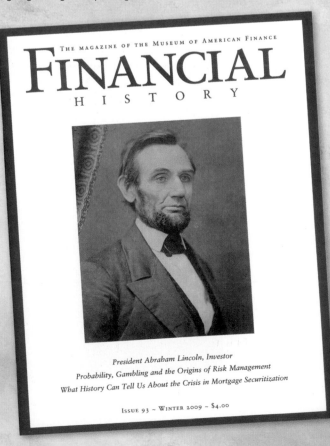

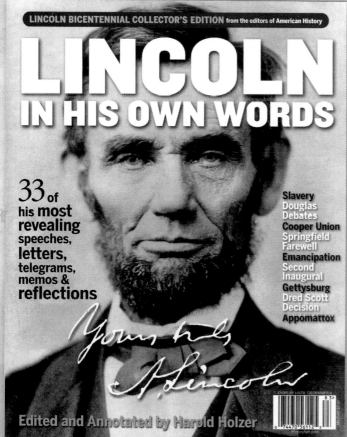

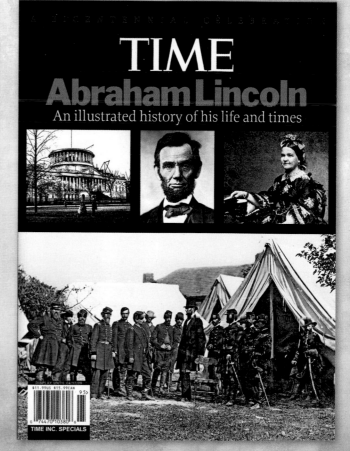

Fig. 4.278. The Gettysburg Lincoln image was unheralded, and in fact little known, until copyrighted and popularized by photographer M.P. Rice in 1891. In the years since, the universal appeal of this intimate, full-faced Lincoln portrait, which directly engages the viewer, has made it a very popular image in book and magazine illustrations. The photo is used on both of these Lincoln bicentennial collector's publications.

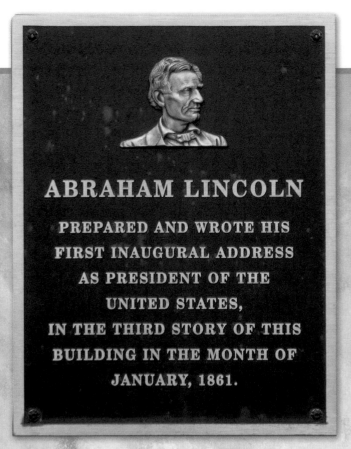

Fig. 4.279. This plaque outside the Lincoln-Herndon Law Offices in downtown Springfield, Illinois, employs the Hesler O-26 image that was so popular during the 1860 presidential campaign.

Fig. 4.280. Some enthusiasts, most notably Olympic sports fans, wear souvenir hat tacks showing their affiliations. The mania to capitalize on Abraham Lincoln for the bicentennial led to excesses such as this "Souvenir Hat Tac" [sic], purchased in one of the main national Lincoln historic-site gift shops.

Fig. 4.281. Visitors to the Abraham Lincoln Presidential Library and Museum in Springfield can pose with the Lincoln family just inside the museum's doors, in front of a White House backdrop.

2009 FEBRUARY. "Portrait of a President: Charles Burt's Engraving of Abraham Lincoln Turned the Face of a Relatively Obscure Western Lawyer into the Best-known Image of His Time," by Fred Reed, is featured in the American Numismatic Association monthly publication *The Numismatist*. This article would subsequently win the ANA's 2010 Catherine Sheehan Award as the outstanding paper-money article published in its journal in the previous year.

2009 FEBRUARY. *World Coin News* cataloger George Cuhaj's "World Coin Roundup" features new listings of Abraham Lincoln foreign-coin portraiture submitted to chief cataloger Colin Bruce by Fred Reed for inclusion in the *Standard Catalog of World Coins* in late 2008. The listings were based on research for Reed's Lincoln bicentennial book, *Abraham Lincoln: The Image of His Greatness*.

2009 FEBRUARY. *Scott Monthly Stamp Journal* publishes Lincoln philatelic expert Eliot A. Landau's article on collecting Lincoln philatelic material.

2009 FEBRUARY 1. The exhibition "From Postmaster to President: Celebrating Lincoln's 200th Birthday Through Stamps & Postal History" opens at the National Postal Museum, Smithsonian Institution. Displaying stamps and postal history, the exhibition "not only celebrates Lincoln's humble roots, but also the events from his first civil servant [sic] position as a town postmaster to his tenure as President of the United States," according to an announcement for the exhibition. Also to mark the Lincoln Bicentennial, 11 certified plate proofs for postage stamps honoring Lincoln were placed on view for 18 months in the Philatelic Gallery's pullout frames at the museum. Certified plate proofs are the last printed proof of the plate before printing of the stamps. "These plate proofs are each unique, with the approval signatures and date," a National Postal Museum spokesman said. Included were issues from 1894 to 1959 which featured Lincoln portraits.

2009 FEBRUARY 1. Ooligan Press debuts Tony Wolk's third book in his "Lincoln Out of Time" trilogy: *Lincoln's Daughter*, starring Sarah. Sarah's mother had met Abraham Lincoln in 1955 after he had been transported out of his own time. She is concerned because her stepfather, a noted Lincoln scholar, is missing. Wolk's earlier Lincoln fantasies were *Good Friday* (October 1, 2007), concerning another of Lincoln's illicit 1955 trysts, with a woman named Joan, also impregnated and haunted by the last week of Lincoln's life; and *Abraham Lincoln, A Novel Life* (February 1, 2004), which launched Lincoln on his mid-1950s sex spree in the arms of a young widow. The book jacket has a 1955 Lincoln cent in place of the "O" in Abe's surname. All three books are from the same publisher.

LINCOLN BICENTENNIAL

PORTRAIT OF A PRESIDENT

Charles Burt's engraving of Abraham Lincoln turned the face of a relatively obscure western lawyer into the best-known image of his time.

PHOTO: FRED REED

by Fred Reed ANA 3130887

I
N MARCH 1861, an itinerant engraver created the most important image of newly elected President Abraham Lincoln produced during his lifetime. This portrait was destined to shape public perception of Lincoln during his Presidency and beyond. In fact, it was the official government likeness that Abe himself carried around in his pocket in the final years of his life.

The portrait's engraver was Charles Kennedy Burt. His client was the American Bank Note Company (ABNCo), which was in dire need of a bearded likeness of Lincoln for its print work. The company's earlier, beardless image engraved by Alfred Sealey was made obsolete when Lincoln arrived in the nation's capital with a three-month growth of chin whiskers.

An expert engraver of Scottish descent, Burt delivered a wonderful portrait showing the recently hirsute chief executive as resolute and almost regal, transforming the fresh-faced prairie lawyer into the nation's commander-in-chief.

Burt's engraving was based on a likeness drawn by Luigi Delnoce from a photograph taken by Springfield, Illinois, photographer Christopher S. German on January 13, 1861. German took the photograph before Lincoln left his home in Illinois for his inauguration as the country's 16th President.

Lincoln was inaugurated as President on March 4, 1861. Burt's intaglio engraving was approved on March 30, which we know because the ABNCo Picture Engraving Proof Room Card for the die still exists. This and other documentation, ⊙

▲ Charles Burt's portrait of Abraham Lincoln appeared on federal greenbacks during the Civil War and was the image that the average American associated with the President.

Fig. 4.282. The February 2009 issue of the American Numismatic Association monthly periodical, *The Numismatist*, was one of several places the present writer corrected the previous notion of who engraved the most important Lincoln die of his lifetime (American Bank Note Co. die no. 141). This writer had published that information previously in *Paper Money* (2006), the *Lincoln Herald* (2007), and *Bank Note Reporter* (2007). The die was engraved by Charles Burt after a "Large pen & ink drawing" by artist Luigi Delnoce. Delnoce obviously based his drawing on the C.S. German O-41/42 photos. The die was approved on March 30, 1861, and was continuously in the possession of ABNCo (and later the purchaser of its archives) until sold to this writer in 2005. This was so because ABNCo wisely declined the U.S. Treasury's offer (demand) to donate their valuable property to the U.S. government to help it set up a currency bureau to compete with ABNCo for government printing contracts.

2009 FEBRUARY 1. The George Eastman House International Museum of Photography & Film exhibits the museum's conservation of a shattered glass-plate interpositive of the Alexander Hesler 1860 profile of candidate Abraham Lincoln. The museum was showcasing its two-year conservation treatment. The image, depicting a "handsome" and beardless Lincoln, was taken when he was beginning his presidential run. It is celebrated as one of the best portraits made of the 16th president. Lincoln was in agreement. "That looks better and expresses me better than any I have ever seen; if it pleases the people I am satisfied," he said.

The interpositive—an intermediate format used to generate negatives for volume production of prints—was made directly from the original wet-plate collodion negative, which captured the light from Lincoln's face during the June 3, 1860, sitting. This is the only known interpositive of this portrait. The original negative, held at the Smithsonian Institution, is shattered. This image "is the closest you will ever get to seeing Lincoln, short of putting your eyeballs on the man himself," explained Grant Romer, director of the museum's Advanced Residency Program in Photograph Conservation, who is one of the world's leading experts on 19th-century and Lincoln photography. "This is Lincoln in high definition. You can see more detail than you'll ever see in a copy print."

2009 FEBRUARY 1. Historian Michael Beschloss lists the reasons "Why Lincoln Matters" in a cover article for *USA Weekend*. Reasons for Beschloss include Lincoln's character, his embodiment of the "American Dream," his reputation with scholars and the public alike, his advancement of modern race relations, his enigmatic life details that invite inquiry, and his power with words. Most intriguing is the historian's No. 5 reason: "He remains a pop culture favorite." According to Beschloss: "Lincoln has lived on at the center of American popular culture. On TV right now, a bank commercial portrays a President Lincoln complaining that no one seems to save his pennies anymore. Even those Americans most ignorant of presidential history will encounter Lincoln cars, Lincoln Logs, companies, schools and cities named for Lincoln. A formidable engine of the Lincoln legend is the fact that in many states, especially Illinois ('Land of Lincoln'), Lincoln's birthday has been celebrated as a holiday, and schoolchildren are annually taught to understand and respect the Great Emancipator. Sadly, that holiday was supplanted in 1971 by the amorphous 'President's Day,' which places Lincoln on equal footing with leaders such as the pedestrian Millard Fillmore."

2009 FEBRUARY 4. A two-day Smithsonian Education Online Conference opens with curators and educators across the Smithsonian

Fig. 4.283. Virtually any periodical that tries can come up with a Lincoln slant if it wants to. For the bicentennial, *Bottles and Extras*, official magazine of the Federation of Historical Bottle Collectors, came up with multiple Lincoln-associated stories for its January-February 2009 issue.

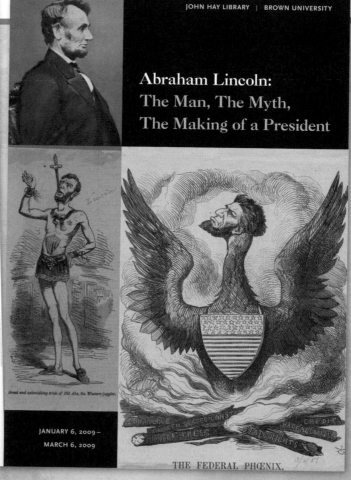

Fig. 4.284. Brown University's two-month-long Lincoln bicentennial exhibition, "Abraham Lincoln: The Man, the Myth, the Making of a President," relied upon the university's fine John Hay Library collection of Lincolniana.

"as they reveal little-known aspects of Lincoln's life and death." Speakers and their topics, based on the Smithsonian's incomparable collections related to Lincoln's life, included Pamela M. Henson ("Lincoln's Deathbed: Images of a Martyred President"), Harry Rubenstein ("Abraham Lincoln: An Extraordinary Life"), David Ward ("One Life: The Mask of Lincoln"), Tom Crouch ("Mr. Lincoln's Air Force"), Shannon Thomas Perich ("Public and Private Photography During the Civil War"), Paul Gardullo and Candra Flanagan ("The Enduring Emancipation: From President Lincoln to President Obama"), Michelle Hammond ("Sharing Lesson Ideas"), and Jeff Meade ("Stamp Stories: Philatelic Images of Abraham Lincoln and the Civil War"). All sessions were broadcast on the Internet and are still archived there, as of this writing. Meade's workshop allowed online participants to create virtual stamp collections from the National Postal Museum's collection via its Arago web site.

2009 February 6. Indiana Metal Craft produces a Lincoln bicentennial "die struck medallion," i.e., a plaque, approximately 2-3/8 by 4 inches, with a rendition of Augustus Saint-Gaudens's *Standing Lincoln* on its face, to mark the 90th anniversary of the Chicago Coin Club and the 200th anniversary of Lincoln's birth. Offered by the Chicago Coin Club, with pre-orders through April 10, 2009, were bronze, silver, and 10-karat gold medals. (See figure 5.42.)

2009 February 6. The Illinois State Museum, Springfield, Illinois, opens its 11-month-long free exhibition "From Humble Beginnings, Lincoln's Illinois 1830–1861." The exhibition would close January 10, 2010.

2009 February 7. The *New York Times* memorializes the 100th anniversary of the Lincoln cent in an article entitled "Now If Only We Could Mint Lincoln Himself."

Fig. 4.285. A commemorative license plate for Washington, D.C., sported a Lincoln bicentennial design for the 56th U.S. presidential inauguration. Since it was sold before the November 2008 election is needed to be generic.

Fig. 4.286. The Illinois State Museum, Springfield, celebrated the Lincoln bicentennial with a nearly year-long exhibition, "From Humble Beginnings: Lincoln's Illinois, 1830–1861."

Fig. 4.287. Lincoln impersonator and actor Fritz Klein starred in the new National Park Service film *A Journey to Greatness*.

2009 February 9. The "Lincoln in New York" exhibition opens at Federal Hall National Memorial in Manhattan, and runs through April 30.

2009 February 9. The four new Lincoln bicentennial U.S. postage stamps have their first day of issue, at Springfield, Illinois. These stamps featured a "scratchboard design" by Mark Summers.

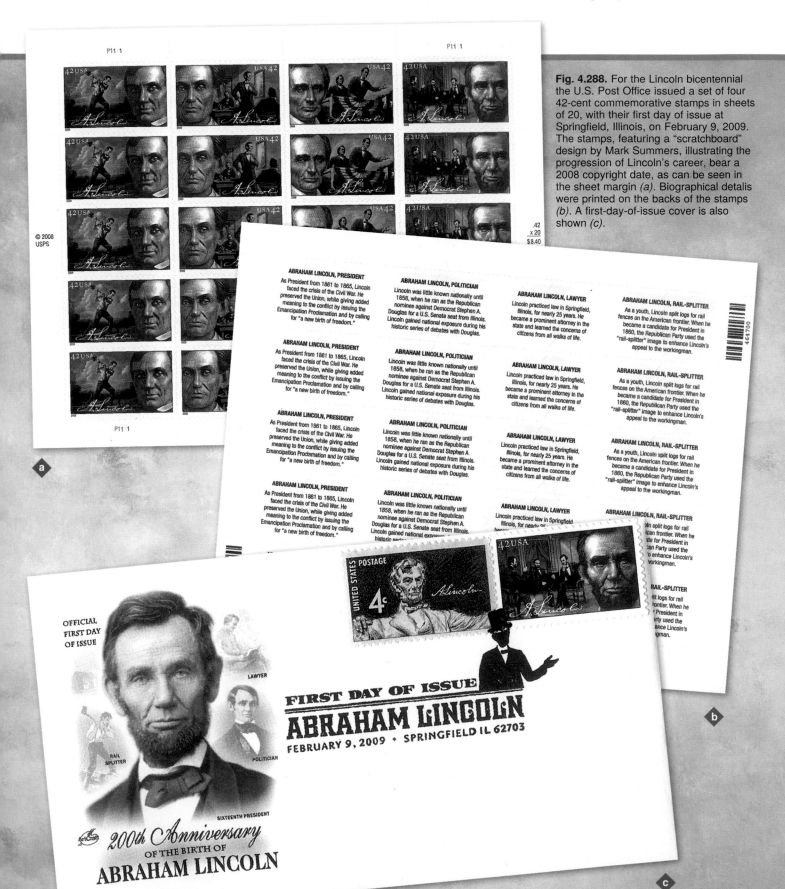

Fig. 4.288. For the Lincoln bicentennial the U.S. Post Office issued a set of four 42-cent commemorative stamps in sheets of 20, with their first day of issue at Springfield, Illinois, on February 9, 2009. The stamps, featuring a "scratchboard" design by Mark Summers, illustrating the progression of Lincoln's career, bear a 2008 copyright date, as can be seen in the sheet margin *(a)*. Biographical details were printed on the backs of the stamps *(b)*. A first-day-of-issue cover is also shown *(c)*.

Fig. 4.289. "Happy Birthday Mr. Lincoln" cards, letters, and greetings poured into various Lincoln sites from schoolchildren across the nation. Shown are greetings on display in Illinois (a) and Kentucky (b).

Fig. 4.290. The City of Springfield, Illinois, logo during its Lincoln bicentennial celebration used the familiar O-77 Lincoln image.

Fig. 4.291. On the eve of the Lincoln bicentennial the iconic "Universal Lincoln" of the 20th century still had a strong hold on scholars and collectors alike. Both the Huntington Library exhibition curator (a) and the Pennsylvania coin-show chairman (b, c) used it for advertising events beginning on February 7, 2009.

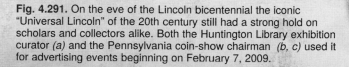

Fig. 4.292. Presidential dollar designer and engraver Don Everhart poses with his original sketch and original plaster model for his delightful golden mini-dollar coin, which employs Alexander Gardner's Gettysburg Lincoln O-77 image, as the first fully facing coin design in U.S. coinage history.

Fig. 4.293. Artist Joel Iskowitz has designed 20 U.S. coins (including the Mary Todd Lincoln First Spouse gold coin) and two congressional gold medals. He has also designed myriad foreign stamps—more than 2,000 for 40 different nations. He shared this design (a) that he produced for International Philatelic Corporation for use on worldwide stamp emissions for the Lincoln bicentennial. Iskowitz chose to depict Lincoln's domestic side in his original artwork. The artist also shows how it might have looked on a souvenir sheet for Antigua and Barbuda (b). The quotation, often given in biographies of Mary Todd Lincoln, is anecdotal, attributed to Lincoln during a reception at the White House.

a

b

Fig. 4.294. The Gilder-Lehrman traveling national exhibition "Forever Free: Abraham Lincoln's Journey to Emancipation" was featured in Lexington, Kentucky, when this writer caught up with it in late June 2009.

LINCOLN

The Bureau of Engraving and Printing credits the current Lincoln $5 bill image (BEP die MISC 198327-3) to William Fleishell III and Thomas R. Hipschen. At the time the new currency portrait was unveiled in November 1999, the BEP media-relations officer, Claudia Dickens, told me the portrait was designed by Fleishell and engraved by Hipschen. She also provided me biographies of the two engravers and additional information.

So long as this Lincoln image continues to appear on the U.S. $5 bill as the exclusive, continuous official Lincoln portrait that most people see, it will exert a tremendous power on both the public psyche and on derivative media. However, the Gettysburg Lincoln portrait, another very popular image both in the media and internationally, finally appeared on a U.S. coin (Don Everhart's recent 2010 Lincoln Presidential dollar). Were the Treasury to employ an O-77–style engraving on U.S. paper currency, too, that would no doubt become the dominant Lincoln image. If the lessons of History are to be believed, this is the future of Lincoln imagery in the present century beyond the Lincoln icon of the last century. It will mirror the American money image once again.

Chapter 5

Lincoln the Immortal

2009 and Beyond

The iconic "Universal Lincoln," the directed pose based on the O-92 model, still has a powerful sway on public consciousness. It is easy to understand why this ingrained view remains powerful in American culture. Old habits die hard. Since its appearance on U.S. paper money in 1869, it consistently appeared on notes of $100, $500, $1, and (most famously) $5 bills for a period of 131 years. Over that time it became virtually the exclusive image of Abraham Lincoln seen by most of his fellow citizens, and inextricably melded with his legacy. The iconic Lincoln on the money was the Lincoln in people's minds, hearts, and imaginations. The money image was reinforced by a series of U.S. stamps, and was replicated in popular media, in book and magazine illustrations, advertising, and other public presentations. Advertisers connected it with good value, honest and fair dealing, and other positive character traits associated with the Lincoln legend.

It is clear from history that the dominant Lincoln image going forward in the 21st century will continue to be an image modeled from Lincoln's ubiquitous, official appearance on the nation's money. If the iconic "Universal Lincoln" of last century is to be replaced in the primary view of America's 16th president in this country and around the world, that presently means either the profile portrait on the cent or the current iteration of O-91 on the $5 bill. The Lincoln profile has appeared on our nation's cent for more than a century. That image has long since achieved what marketers term "saturation." It has fully inculcated the public mind. The future of the cent, itself, has been called into question increasingly in recent years due to its cost of production and relatively small value in commerce. Replacing the Brenner profile might have made sense in 1959, or recently for the Lincoln bicentennial observance, but since it was never seriously considered at either occasion, it is doubtless the last Lincoln portrait needed for that coin.

Fig. 5.1. The Abraham Lincoln Presidential Library and Museum, Springfield, Illinois, adopted a logo that featured the modernistic facade of the museum and the old standby, iconic 20th-century Lincoln image popularized by the engraving on billions of small-size $5 bills.

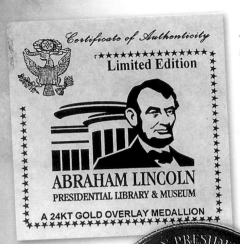

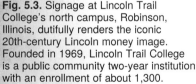

Fig. 5.2. Unfortunately the certificate of authenticity for the Abraham Lincoln Presidential Library and Museum gold-plated medal is better made than the small, low-relief, poorly articulated medal that it attests to. The medal and the ALPLM logo both employ the iconic 20th-century Lincoln money image.

Fig. 5.3. Signage at Lincoln Trail College's north campus, Robinson, Illinois, dutifully renders the iconic 20th-century Lincoln money image. Founded in 1969, Lincoln Trail College is a public community two-year institution with an enrollment of about 1,300.

The Thomas R. Hipschen–William Fleishell III O-91 "Twinkle Eye" Lincoln has been circulating since May 2000. At first the new $5s and the old-style $5s co-circulated. The half-sawbuck circulates for about two years before it is worn out and replaced, so the old O-92 bills have long since been displaced by the 10+ billion notes with the new portrait to have been issued thus far. After only a decade we already have a new generation of consumers who have entered the marketplace in the new-style Lincoln-portrait era, and scarcely have any memory of the old portrait in circulation. Advertisers, increasingly striving to capture this highly desirable, but only recently mature, market segment are already pitching the new O-91 Lincoln image at these younger consumers. Our collective memory of the old note's O-92 portrait will fade in an accelerating manner as more and more new consumers enter the marketplace without any O-92 preconceptions. The new $5 bill, with $11 billion worth in constant circulation, will increasingly become the model for Lincoln depictions in all media, as collective memory of the former "Universal Lincoln" image fades. Eventually few but numismatists and Lincoln-philes will have the same affection for it universally felt for generations.

During this time only one other non-monetary image was popular in the public marketplace. An exhaustive examination of popular-media representations of Abraham Lincoln over the last century-and-a-half-plus has revealed that since the 1890s, the intimate "Gettysburg Lincoln" O-77 portrait has been the only real competition to the Lincoln money images in public consciousness. This singular facing portrait so engages the viewer as to be charismatic in its appeal. Although it never appeared on the nation's coins or currency prior to 2010, it became a favorite with book and magazine illustrators, advertisers, and other molders of public opinion soon after it was rediscovered, copyrighted, published, and popularized by photographer M.P. Rice in 1891. It also became popular on corporate stocks, and very popular on foreign stamps.

For reasons unclear to the present writer, this fine, full-facing Lincoln portrait was never employed on the nation's money, stamps, or other official obligations until the 2009 Lincoln bicentennial. A cropped image of the portrait appeared on one of the four commemorative U.S. stamps. Significantly, it was also lately modeled in an excellent way by U.S. Mint sculptor/engraver Don Everhart for the "golden" Lincoln Presidential mini dollar coin released in 2010. Unfortunately most Americans will *never* see this coin in the foreseeable future. Most of the 97 million of these dollars will languish in Treasury and Federal Reserve vaults. History tells us that at some point in the future the burden of all these non-circulating legal-tender coins may become too much for sharp pencils at the U.S. Treasury and they will be melted down, just as unwanted non-circulating silver dollar coins have been melted in the past.

For a generation now, it has been clear that Americans will never widely use a circulating dollar coin while a circulating paper dollar is readily available. It's not just Gresham's law in action, here: nobody wants to carry a pocket full of dollar coins. We would, though, if these essentially quarter-sized mini-dollars were actually useful in commerce because the paper dollar had been abandoned. While this writer cannot foresee the public willingly abandoning Founding Father George Washington's ubiquitous paper currency . . . if it did happen, billions of U.S. Presidential dollar coins would be called into circulation, of necessity. If that happened, occasionally individuals would encounter the facing Lincoln portrait in commercial transactions. It would, subject to the vagaries of individual coin minting, be encountered on roughly one in 40 dollar coins coming to an individual, in pocket change. This could be expected to increase the visibility and popularity of this Lincoln portrait in secondary media and the public mind. But, we'll not hold our breath awaiting such an eventuality.

The use of an O-77 facing portrait on the nation's folding cash, however, would rapidly disseminate this portrait to the public purse and popular conception. The present writer has championed the use of this portrait on the nation's folding cash for more than 15 years. It is only since the publication of *Abraham Lincoln: The Image of His Greatness,* for the bicentennial, that we now know that at least twice before the recent Presidential dollar, an O-77 portrait model has been conceived for use on the nation's circulating media: in 1943, John S. Edmondson engraved a currency-sized portrait die (BEP die MISC15628), based on the Alexander Gardner O-77 photograph; and in 1993 two private banknote companies, American Bank Note Co. and Banknote Corporation of America, supplied O-77 Lincoln portraits for use on a contemplated $20 food coupon. None of these portraits would be suitable on presently configured U.S. currency, but this divine Lincoln portrait could be called upon as a model for a vibrant and new Lincoln monetary image in the future.

2009 FEBRUARY 11. The renovated Ford's Theatre is rededicated, attended by dignitaries including President Barack Obama. Renovation took 18 months and cost $25 million. Film director George Lucas and actor Sidney Poitier were awarded Ford's Theatre Lincoln medals for holding to the ideals of the 16th president.

Fig. 5.4. Iconic Lincoln money images of the old $5-bill style abounded in the Hodgenville, Kentucky, Lincoln bicentennial celebration. Lincoln National Bank's time-and-temperature signage near the Lincoln Birthplace National Historic Site was only one such instance observed by this writer in Lincoln's original hometown.

Fig. 5.7. "Lincoln walked here," proclaims a banner on a telephone pole in Marshall, Illinois, during the Lincoln bicentennial.

Fig. 5.5. This nice ribbon was offered in a display of Lincoln bicentennial memorabilia for sale. Although it clearly bears a 1993 copyright below the eagle, and of course the old-style icon Lincoln portrait, it may have been a bicentennial reissue.

Fig. 5.6. Rededication of the refurbished Ford's Theatre on February 11 was a gala affair. Honored with the Ford's Theatre Lincoln Medal were Hollywood luminaries George Lucas and Sidney Poitier. The event was also another stop on newly inaugurated president Barack Obama's Lincoln Self-identification Tour. Here the president greets a Lincoln impersonator.

2009 FEBRUARY 11. On the eve of the bicentennial of Abraham Lincoln's birth, while recently inaugurated U.S. president Barack Obama trod the same stage at Ford's Theatre over which praesicide John Wilkes Booth made his furtive getaway, *Chronicles: A Magazine of American Culture* author Justin Raimondo condemns the burlesque "cult of personality" surrounding Obama's self-identification with Abraham Lincoln and the mainstream media's culpability in perpetuating the myth. "Since we live in an age from which greatness has been banished, it's only natural for politicians, ideologues, and common demagogues to reach back into the past for models to serve as masks for their nostrums," Raimondo wrote. "Obama sees himself in our 16th president, as he admits in a 2005 essay in *Time,* and his cultists lap it up. It's pure Madison Avenue."[1]

2009 FEBRUARY 11. A gala is held at the Abraham Lincoln Presidential Library in Springfield, Illinois, for the opening of a new exhibit, "Lincoln in Illinois," displaying photographs by Ron Schramm, combined with essays by Lincoln scholars on all the Lincoln statues in Illinois. The exhibition opened to the public the following day and remained in place through September 30.

2009 FEBRUARY 11. The indie-produced short horror film *The Transient,* written and directed by Chris Lukeman, is posted to YouTube by Illini Film & Video. It stars Dave Ruthenberg in the title role as the vagrant vigilante, Blake Stubbs as his reluctant sidekick (his caseworker Steve), and well-known Abe presenter Michael Krebs as Vampire Abraham Lincoln. The film was made by University of Illinois film students in Champagne-Urbana. The Hobo Hero strives to save four score and seven virgins from Vampire Abraham Lincoln's "malicious machinations," according to the filmmakers. This witty and often clever 25-minute color film has good production values, somewhat indifferent turns at acting from its youthful cast, and an ironic take on some of Lincoln's lesser-known turns of phrase. Most viewers on the site found it quite enjoyable. The indie film was awarded the Abraham Lincoln Presidential Library Award at the Hoogland Center for the Performing Arts, Springfield, Illinois.

2009 FEBRUARY 12. *Abraham Lincoln: The Image of His Greatness,* by Fred Reed, sees its official publication date. Theretofore numismatics had been on the fringe of Lincoln-consciousness. Lincolnphiles knew about the penny, and some—grudgingly, it seemed—recognized Abe had also appeared on the $5 bill, but these depictions were regarded with little esteem. Now, with Reed's new book, numismatics was not only seen in the mainstream of Lincoln imagery, but actually assumed its rightful position as the driving engine in creating Lincoln awareness and icon imagery.

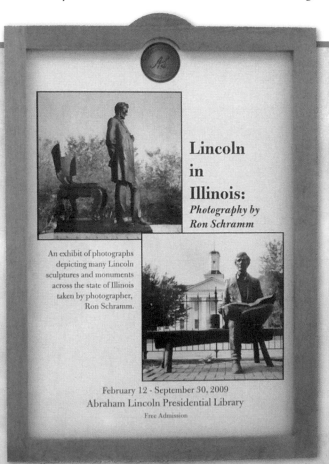

Fig. 5.8. A display of Lincoln statuary photographs (with a companion catalog by lensman Ron Schramm), "Lincoln in Illinois," opened at the ALPLM library on February 12, 2009. It ran for nearly eight months.

Fig. 5.9. Lincoln impersonator and actor Michael Krebs appeared in the short horror film *The Transient,* written and directed by Chris Lukeman, and made by University of Illinois–Champaign/Urbana film students.

Fig. 5.10. Actor Ted Rooney left his mark on Lincoln lore when he tore open his shirt to reveal a large eagle tattoo and demonstrate Lincoln's virility in a Mountain Dew commercial in March 2009.

2009 FEBRUARY 12. The first Lincoln bicentennial cent, honoring his Kentucky birth at Hodgenville, Kentucky, is officially released.

2009 FEBRUARY 12. "Art of the Stamp: Lincoln Bicentennial Exhibit" opens at the Smithsonian Institution National Postal Museum, featuring the original stamp art created by Mark Summers for the four postage stamps introduced by the U.S. Postal Service to mark the bicentennial observance. The exhibit continued until October 26, 2009.

2009 FEBRUARY 12. CNN broadcasts a six-hour block, "From Lincoln to Obama," with coverage of the day's ceremonial events. Segments highlighted displays at the Lincoln Presidential Museum, the Smithsonian Institution, and Ford's Theatre. Special emphasis in guest interviews was placed on Abraham Lincoln's conflicted feelings about abolishing slavery, the influence of Frederick Douglass in moving the reluctant president in that direction, and the importance of Barack Obama as the fulfillment of Lincoln's actions. Repeated attention was called to superficial similarities between the two men, and great emphasis was placed on the feelings of college students on Obama's election. One student mistakenly said (uncorrected) that Lincoln owned slaves. Lincoln's most important contribution—winning the Civil War—was ignored. Only Colin Powell said Lincoln's more important job was saving the Union and we should thank him for that and for, in the process, freeing the slaves.

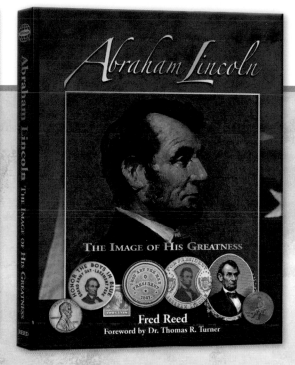

Fig. 5.12. The official publication date of the present writer's *Abraham Lincoln: The Image of His Greatness* was February 12, 2009, the 200th anniversary of Lincoln's birth. In the succeeding months, the book would win "Book of the Year" awards from the Society of Paper Money Collectors, the Professional Currency Dealers Association, and the Numismatic Literary Guild. It would also be favorably reviewed, and was one of three books featured at the Lincoln's New Salem visitor's center souvenir shop when the author visited the site unannounced in July 2009.

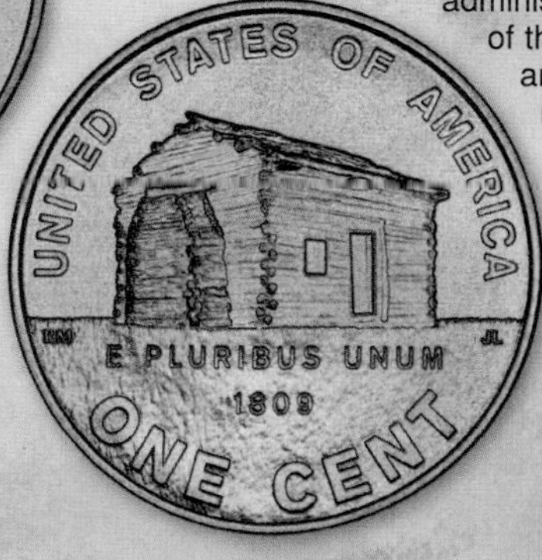

Fig. 5.11. It seemed no matter which way you turned in 2009 in some states (notably Kentucky, Indiana, and Illinois), you were headed toward another Lincoln adventure. Shown is a Lincoln Heritage Trail sign in eastern Illinois.

Fig. 5.13. The U.S. Lincoln Bicentennial Commission succeeded in getting Congress to authorize four commemorative cents for circulation throughout Lincoln's bicentennial year. The first cent, marking Lincoln's humble birth in Kentucky, was designed by Richard Masters and sculpted by Jim Licaretz. It was "officially" released in small quantities in a cash exchange on February 12 at Lincoln's Hodgenville, Kentucky, birthplace. Unfortunately the Obama administration bungled release of the commemorative cents and permitted coins by the railroad-carload to gather dust in Treasury and Federal Reserve vaults, resulting in few being seen in circulation, thus leaving many members of the public ignorant that they had been struck and "issued" at all.

Fig. 5.14. Even pipe smokers deserve a Lincoln-themed collectible, and this figural meerschaum smoking device fills the bill admirably.

2009 FEBRUARY 12. President Barack Obama speaks at the congressional tribute to Abraham Lincoln in the U.S. Capitol Rotunda, saying he feels a "special gratitude" to Lincoln and calling him "that most remarkable of men." That evening he also spoke at Springfield, Illinois, ceremonies. He appeared at the 102nd-anniversary meeting of the Abraham Lincoln Association, at the group's birthday banquet. Each person attending received a gift: *Lincoln In Illinois,* a commemorative book of photographs by Chicago photographer Ron Schramm of the statues of Lincoln in Illinois.

2009 FEBRUARY 12. The National Park Service, the Military Order of the Loyal Legion of the United States, the Lincoln Birthday National Commemorative Committee, the Abraham Lincoln Bicentennial Commission, and other groups join to honor Abraham Lincoln in the chamber of the Lincoln Memorial, Washington, D.C. In addition to the annual wreath-laying ceremony, speakers at the special event included Illinois senator Dick Durbin, ALBC co-chair Harold Holzer, ALBC commissioner Frank J. Williams, and author Nikki Giovanni.

2009 FEBRUARY 12. The Abraham Lincoln Bicentennial Commission sponsors a national teach-in on the life and legacy of Abraham Lincoln. The teach-in took place at the National Archives in Washington, D.C. Educators and students nationwide could tune in and view the event as a live webcast online. Three prominent Lincoln scholars participated in the 45-minute event: Pulitzer Prize–winning historian Doris Kearns Goodwin, Bicentennial Commission co-chair Harold Holzer, and historian Matthew Pinsker. The moderator was Dr. Libby Haight O'Connell, senior vice president for corporate outreach at A&E Television Network. Students from D.C. and northern Virginia participated as a live audience. Enrichment resources and study guides were provided for classroom use by those viewing the webcast. Reportedly more than 5,000 schools nationwide signed up in advance for the event.

2009 FEBRUARY 12. The Library of Congress opens "With Malice Toward None: The National Abraham Lincoln Bicentennial Exhibition," called "a landmark exhibit of letters, photographs, documents, and artifacts." The exhibit was curated by John Sellers. Included in the displays was the hand-written passage from Lincoln's Second Inaugural Address, with its famous "with malice toward none" closing, from which the exhibit is titled.

Also on display was the first-ever public pairing of 11-year-old Grace Bedell's letter to Lincoln suggesting that he grow a beard, and Lincoln's reply just four days later. After his election Lincoln would, of course, grow the chin whiskers and be photographed by local photographer Christopher S. German. That image would be translated into a security portrait die by Charles Burt for American Bank Note Company in March 1861, and appear on the $10 Demand Notes in 1861 and the $10 Legal Tender Notes of 1862 to 1869. This would be the image by which Lincoln would become familiar and beloved by his fellow countrymen. For, as Carl Sandburg observed in 1939, "On the $10 bill a steel engraving representing Lincoln's face became familiar to all who looked at it." The Lincoln on the money was the Lincoln everybody knew and, following his death, loved.

The Library of Congress exhibition ran through May 9, 2009, and then traveled to other institutions. It opened at the California

Fig. 5.15. Official White House photographer Pete Souza captured a jubilant President Barack Obama basking in the limelight of a Lincoln birthday celebration on February 12, 2009.

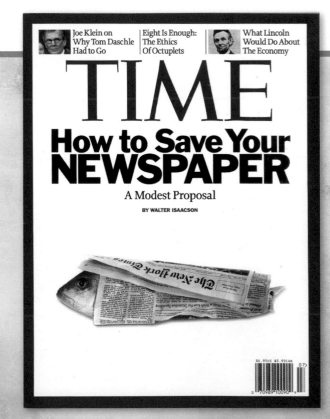

Fig. 5.16. The February 16, 2009, cover of *Time* magazine seems almost apologetic that it includes a Lincoln-slanted article inside. Instead, concept art dominates the cover of the periodical.

Museum in Sacramento on June 24 and ran there until August 22. Then it traveled to Chicago's Newberry Library (fall 2009), the Indiana State Museum in Indianapolis (winter/spring 2010), the Atlanta History Center (September 2010), and Omaha's Durham Western Heritage Museum (winter 2011).

2009 FEBRUARY 12. The National Gallery of Art, Washington, D.C., puts on public display for one year the six-foot-high plaster model (created by sculptor Daniel Chester French in 1916) which became the basis for the marble statue ensconced in the Lincoln Memorial six years later. Also in the exhibition (entitled "Designing the Lincoln Memorial: Daniel Chester French and Henry Bacon") was Bacon's original wood model of his memorial design. "Receiving the model is a coup for the gallery because the artifact hasn't traveled since 1976 from its storage space in Stockbridge, MA, where French had a country home called Chesterwood," the *Washington Post* noted. French's model was shipped in eight crates from Massachusetts. Bacon's model was on loan from the General Services Administration. The National Gallery expected more than five million visitors to view the exhibition.[2]

2009 FEBRUARY 12. Sculptor Paula B. Slater's statue *Love and Light,* a.k.a. *In Sacred Union,* is dedicated, celebrating the June 12, 1806, marriage of Abraham Lincoln's parents, Nancy Hanks and Thomas Lincoln, by Methodist pastor Rev'd Jesse Head at the home of Francis Berry in Washington County. The original "Marriage Bond and Minister's Return" were discovered by Washington County Clerk W.F. Booker in 1978.

Slater's standing figure of Lincoln stands seven miles south of the original site of the wedding, now preserved at Lincoln Homestead State Park. The Lincoln marriage cabin itself has been preserved within the Lincoln Marriage Temple at Harrodsburg, Kentucky. The figure of Lincoln is atop a pediment at the Washington County Judicial Center, across from the street from the Washington County Courthouse, Springfield, Kentucky, where those original marriage records are preserved. Completed in 1816, the Washington County Courthouse is the oldest in Kentucky still in use.

2009 FEBRUARY 12. The Chicago History Museum unveils its splendid collection of "Lincoln Treasures," including Lincoln's pocket watch, his desk, and the bed in which he died.

Fig. 5.17. All manner of schlock is festooned with Lincoln images in this consumer-is-king society—from shirts and cups *(a)* to plaques and candies *(b)*. Visitors to Lincoln shrines in his bicentennial era are faced with a difficult choice . . . pink, blue, red, or green Baby Abie sipping cups *(c)*. Sometimes the tags are the best part of the product *(d, e)*.

Fig. 5.18. On February 12, 2009, sculptor Paula B. Slater's statue *Love and Light,* a.k.a. *In Sacred Union,* was dedicated in Springfield, Kentucky, at the Washington County Judicial Center across the street from the 1816 Washington County Courthouse, the oldest in Kentucky still in use.

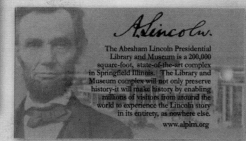

2009 FEBRUARY 12. Indiana University's Lilly Library, Bloomington, Indiana, opens the exhibition "Remembering Lincoln," putting on display 140 objects from the library's sizable Abraham Lincoln collection. The Lilly Library is the university's library for rare books and special collections. Lincoln materials have been featured prominently since it opened in 1960. The Library's Lincoln Room honors the importance of its collection, featuring the Joseph B. Oakleaf collection acquired in 1942, including 8,000 books, pamphlets, photographs, and other Lincolniana.

2009 FEBRUARY 12. The Memorial Art Gallery, University of Rochester, New York, marks the 175th anniversary of the City of Rochester with an exhibition in its Lockhart Gallery titled "Lincoln in Rochester," displaying more than 40 artworks, artifacts, and memorabilia from area collections, including those of the museum, the George Eastman House, the Rochester Historical Society, and the Seward House Museum. The display was curated by MAG director Grant Holcomb.

2009 FEBRUARY 12. The Abraham Lincoln Association of Jersey City, New Jersey, the oldest organization in the country specifically organized to preserve the memory and promote the understanding of the nation's fallen savior, holds its annual celebration of its namesake. A noon wreath-laying presentation was staged at the James Earle Fraser seated Lincoln statue at the entrance to Lincoln Park, at Kennedy Boulevard and Belmont Avenue. Dr. Jules Ladenheim gave a speech. In the evening the association hosted its 144th consecutive annual dinner tribute to Lincoln at the Casino, in the Park.

Fig. 5.19. The Kentucky Sons of Union Veterans of the Civil War issued a very attractive badge for the Lincoln bicentennial, with a Gettysburg Lincoln portrait.

Fig. 5.20. Rovere Publishing created a visually powerful and patriotic red-white-and-blue poster for the Lincoln bicentennial, with the O-77 full-facing portrait by Alexander Gardner.

Fig. 5.21. NBA journeyman Deshawn Stevenson is a man of many tattoos, including a throat tattoo rendering the Gettysburg Lincoln image in a most unusual form. Animated videos of Stevenson's Abe talking showed up, creating quite a buzz.

Fig. 5.22. Lincoln bus-bench art in Springfield, Illinois, was classlessly defaced by a juvenile with more freedom than responsibility . . . or common sense.

2009 FEBRUARY 12. David Ostro's inventive *Lincoln in Three Poses* is unveiled at Lincoln Landing, Lockport, Illinois. The bronze group depicts Abraham Lincoln bending over, dipping his hand into water, standing up, and walking resolutely away. What is inventive is that all three depictions occupy the same space emerging in three dimensions from a low wall.

2009 FEBRUARY 12. Rededication ceremonies are held at noon in Boise, Idaho, at the state Capitol building, for a life-size standing statue of the Great Emancipator cast in 1915. The statue had been removed from the Idaho State Veterans Home to the more prominent location 100 yards in front of the Statehouse. The statue was sometimes credited to Alfonso Pelzer, but officials at the time of the rededication had different ideas. They correctly credited it to John G. Segesman after a design by Pelzer, as commissioned by the city of Lincoln, New Jersey. Over the years the statue had suffered from neglect, according to local officials. Veterans organizations contributed, and a "penny drive" in local schools was held to defray costs of the restoration and relocation. The statue is revered as the oldest surviving Abraham Lincoln monument in the western United States. It is reportedly one of eight castings made between 1915 and 1926 by Mullins Manufacturing Corporation in Ohio. Lincoln was president when Idaho Territory was created, and he appointed its first territorial governor.

2009 FEBRUARY 12. Louisiana coin dealer Paul Hollis gives away the first of one million 2009 Lincoln Bicentennial cents as "a tribute to Abraham Lincoln and the introduction of the new Lincoln cent" to church groups, scouting organizations, coin clubs, elementary schools, various charities, and collectors such as yours truly.

2009 FEBRUARY 12. Eclectic Asylum Art posts a 92-second video to YouTube showing a time-lapse "Penny Art Portrait" of an artist creating a semblance of the famous O-92 old-style $5 Lincoln portrait based on Anthony Berger's February 9, 1864, photograph of the seated president. The soundtrack is Metal Patriots' recording of *The Battle Hymn of the Republic*. Cents from each of the five-score years of Lincoln cent mintage, some 1,025 in all, including the scarce 1914-D, were utilized in forming the portrait. Cents were provided by American Numismatic Association governor and coin dealer Tom Hallenbeck. More than a hundred thousand Internet surfers caught the show! In the months since, the video has also generated a long string of responses, most silly, some illiterate, and many trading misinformation of the numismatic kind. There were also posts regarding the unavailability of the 2009 Lincoln Bicentennial cents. "[I]'ve got three logs," one typed in cheerily, evidently having found three Indiana Boyhood cents showing Lincoln seated on a log, reading. "[I]f they do stop making pennies, as some have theorized, then their value should skyrocket. Save them pennies," another replied.

2009 FEBRUARY 16. On "Presidents' Day," C-Span announces that its poll of historians rated Abraham Lincoln "as the nation's best president." According to the Associated Press: "Just days after the nation honored the 200th anniversary of his birth, 65 historians ranked Abraham Lincoln as the nation's best president. . . . Lincoln was ranked in the top three in each of the 10 categories evaluated by participants. . . . The survey was conducted in December and January. Participants ranked each president on a scale of one, or 'not effective,' to 10, 'very effective,' on a list of 10 leadership qualities, including relations with Congress, public persuasion and moral authority." Lincoln scores, as reported by C-Span, were: Public Persuasion (ranked no. 2), Crisis Leadership (1), Economic Management (2), Moral Authority (2), International Relations (3), Administrative Skills (2), Relations with Congress (3), Vision / Setting an Agenda (1), Pursued Equal Justice for All (1), Performance within the Context of the Times (1).

Fig. 5.23. Benin honored Lincoln and a host of his presidential colleagues in 2009, giving both the 20th-century icon O-92 likeness *(a)* (the Buttre engraving, in fact) and the Gettysburg Lincoln O-77 image *(b)* on 660-franc full-color and monochromatic stamps.

2009 FEBRUARY 16. Marvel Comics releases a free digital comic book on President's Day, titled *Gettysburg Distress.* In it, Captain America tells Spider-Man how he traveled back in time to witness Abraham Lincoln's Gettysburg Address.

2009 FEBRUARY 20. The International Coin Club of El Paso, Texas, holds an Abraham Lincoln's Birth Bicentennial–themed three-day coin show. The first 1,000 attendees received one of the new 2009 Lincoln commemorative cents. Kids completing a Lincoln quiz were able to attend a free Kid's Auction. Attendance at the show totaled 1,350.

2009 FEBRUARY 23. "This month, in honor of the bicentennial of Lincoln's birth, the Magazines & Newspapers Center highlights *Lincoln Lore,* a bulletin published by the Lincoln Museum. The editors of this quarterly publication seek to 'interpret and preserve the history and legacy of Abraham Lincoln through research, conservation, exhibitry, and education,'" the San Francisco Public Library Herb Caen Magazines and Newspapers Center newsletter reported insightfully—but, ironically, completely oblivious to the fact that the newsletter had ceased publication months earlier.

2009 FEBRUARY 25. Disneyland announces the return of its "Great Moments with Mr. Lincoln" presentation (which had been in mothballs since 2004) "in celebration of the 200th anniversary year of Abraham Lincoln's birth." The show, featuring the world's first fully animatronic figure, was expected to resume in summer but was delayed nearly to year's end. Originally staged by Walt Disney for the State of Illinois Pavilion at the 1964 New York World's Fair, it debuted in Disneyland in the Main Street Opera House on July 18, 1965.

2009 FEBRUARY 27. *Numismatic News* editor David C. Harper laments the slow appearance of the new Lincoln Bicentennial cent in circulation. "In 31 years here," Harper wrote, "I don't remember the cents ever being later than the final half of January. . . . New Lincolns will arrive eventually," he added hopefully.

Fig. 5.24. Pennsylvania artist Wendy Allen operates the Lincoln Into Art Gallery in Gettysburg, PA. In the past 30 years she has painted more than 300 Lincoln portraits. This Lincoln #148 has the ethereality of van Gogh's *Starry Night,* to this observer's view.

Fig. 5.25. Marvel Comics, celebrating its own significant 70th anniversary, released an electronic-only Spider-Man comic book for Presidents' Day in February 2009. Captain America and Spidey triumph over a Professor Abraham von Lincolnstein in "a Marvel History-in-the-Making Classic" entitled "Gettysburg Distress." Lincolnstein steals $5 bills and "corrects" them by putting his own "twisted image" in place of old Abe. Then the web slinger and Steve Rogers (Captain America) travel back in time to witness the Gettysburg Address. The comic was posted online February 16. Cover art by Paolo Rivera depicted a rather belligerent Abe.

Fig. 5.26. Visitors to the Abraham Lincoln Home in Springfield, Illinois, received free tours and one of a series of admission tickets with various designs as an additional souvenir from the National Park Service.

2009 February 28. Lincoln scholar and retired state supreme court chief justice Frank J. Williams narrates Aaron Copland's patriotic classic *A Lincoln Portrait*, performed by the Rhode Island Philharmonic Orchestra at Veterans Auditorium, Providence, Rhode Island.

2009 March 2. An Abraham Lincoln Diet Mountain Dew commercial, with Ted Rooney as a manic wrestler Lincoln, hits the airwaves and sparks up viewers and commentary forums on YouTube. The commercial starts during one of the Lincoln-Douglas debates. It states that Lincoln's favorite sport was wrestling, and shows him stripping to reveal an eagle tattooed on his chest, while aggressively hitting people. Fans liked the ring mayhem displayed by the Lincoln character. "I just wanna shake the hand of the guy who played Lincoln, that guy is my hero," wrote one. Another remarkable commentary read: "Unfortunately, Lincoln was also a vicious mass murderer of over a half million Americans and his actions to destroy our republic led directly to the statism of TR, Wilson, America's involvement in WW I, FDR, the rise of Hitler and of Stalin and WW II. Lincoln was the Great Traitor to our republic. He is responsible (along with other later statist politicians) for much of the ruin we will suffer in coming years. Lincoln was the original American fascist." Nearly 80,000 people viewed the clip on YouTube.

2009 March 2. Former TV variety-show host Conan O'Brien presents "Lincoln as Humorist" at the newly renovated Ford's Theatre.

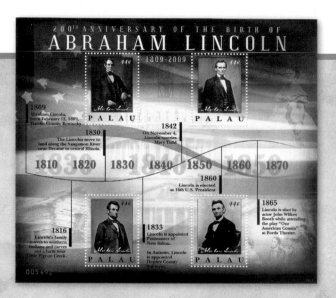

Fig. 5.27. Palau pulled out all the stops with a four-stamp set souvenir sheet that provides a mini Lincoln biography and a variety of Lincoln images. As an editor for more than 40 years, what this writer finds frustrating with the sheet, however, is how precisely certain events are dated (month-day-year), and how imprecisely others are listed (year only).

Fig. 5.28. On the newsstands during the February bicentennial celebration, due to periodicals' penchant to pre-sell post-dated issues to make them appear more timely, were these Lincoln-themed issues. Who would have expected the March 2009 issue of *Sky & Telescope* (a) or the April 2009 issue of *Wild West* to have Lincoln-related fare, especially the very memorable O-77 10-gallon cover (b)?

Fig. 5.29. This striking uniface 1-1/2-inch medal was sold during the Lincoln bicentennial, merchandised by L.W. Bristol Classics, Bristol, Tennessee.

2009 MARCH 7. The National Postal Museum hosts noted Chicago Lincoln philatelist Eliot A. Landau's "Lincoln, Slavery, and the Civil War" as the Maynard Sundman Lecture Series presentation for 2009. The 65-minute seventh annual Maynard Sundman Lecture was accompanied by a 160-page exhibition of Lincoln and ebony (African American–related) philatelic material and ancillary items from Landau's Display Class Exhibition, from which his illustrated talk was drawn. Display Class is a newly recognized exhibit class in competitive philatelic exhibiting that allows for "go withs," such as letters, photographs, documents, and artifacts to accompany covers and other philatelic material. Landau also mounted allied displays of the earliest usages of the 1909 Lincoln Centennial carmine two-cent postage stamps (Scott 367–369) to "celebrate the centennial of the centennial," and a separate display featuring "nearly all" U.S. Lincoln stamps to date. Landau was a co-designer of the Lincoln bicentennial four-stamp series. In 2003 he suggested to the Citizens Stamp Committee that the bicentennial stamps should show "not just portraits," but "should "share with us the working Lincoln." Accompanying Landau's speech was his exhibition combining philately, ephemera, and artifacts exploring Lincoln's presidency, the Civil War, and black history. A reception followed.

2009 MARCH 10. New York City Lincoln photograph collector Keya Morgan says he believes a tall figure in an 1865 carte de visite–size photograph that he purchased in February from Ulysses S. Grant VI (the Civil War general's great-great-grandson), which was discovered in a family album, is the last photograph of Abraham Lincoln from life, by photographer Henry F. Warren. It depicts a tall figure in front of the White House, and the anonymous, handwritten notation on the back "Lincoln in front of the White House." Morgan, who values his personal collection of Lincoln photographs and artifacts at $25 million, said he paid $50,000 for the card.

The story was quickly picked up by the media, including CNN the following day. According to the CNN story, because of interest in the new Lincoln image, Morgan's web site, lincolnimages.com, "received more than 5 million hits on Tuesday and crashed because of the traffic overload."[3]

The image in question shows four figures. The man at center foreground, seen nearly in profile before a low fence, is computed to be six-foot-four-inches tall, based on his location and the relative size of the other three people. The individual in question appears to be glancing back over his right shoulder in the direction of the cameraman. He is hatless and no facial details are apparent, beside what may be a beard on the right side of his face or a shadow under his jaw line.

After viewing an enlargement of the photograph, it reminds the present writer of how hobbyists expectantly searched well-worn Buffalo nickels for rare dates 50 years ago, projecting digits onto the coin surfaces by wishful thinking. Also, it should be added, the "last" photo of Lincoln known obviously post-dates this image: i.e., the casket photo that Jeremiah Gurney snapped surreptitiously while Lincoln was lying in state at the New York City Hall for public observation during his funeral train trip back to burial in Springfield (the photo that Secretary of War Edwin Stanton attempted to suppress). That image was taken six weeks after the purported date of the photograph in question.

2009 MARCH 13. The U.S. Mint commences offering rolls of the new Lincoln Bicentennial cents at nearly nine times face value ($8.95 for two rolls), plus $4.95 postage, on its web site.

2009 MARCH 13. The Bureau of Engraving and Printing offers the first in its "Lincoln Bicentennial Series" of souvenir cards, called "Humble Beginnings," at the American Numismatic Association National Money Show in Portland, Oregon.

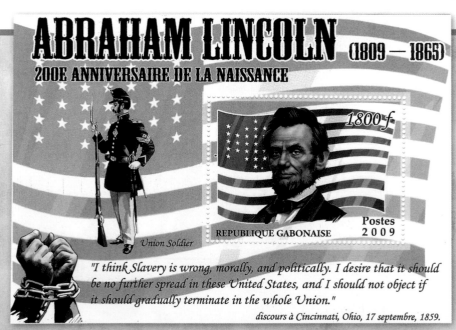

Fig. 5.30. Gabon's salute to Abe's 200th was this quite fine 1,800-franc stamp and souvenir sheet. The image is taken from O-83; the quote, Lincoln's "Black Republican" affirmation to his fellow Kentuckians from his December 17, 1859, speech across the Ohio River in Cincinnati. The flag depicted is an unusual 33-star banner, representative of 1859–1861. This is one of the present writer's favorite Lincoln bicentennial stamps, foreign or U.S.

Fig. 5.31. Union Square, the plaza across the street from the Lincoln Presidential Museum in Springfield, Illinois, sported one of a series of chronological banners. This one showed Abraham Lincoln as he appeared in 1857, when he resided in Springfield.

2009 MARCH 24. Nearing a sellout of 2009 Lincoln Bicentennial commemorative silver dollars, the U.S. Mint institutes "next-in-line" order fulfillment (processing sales in the order received, on a first-come-first-served basis) for Uncirculated examples. Three days later the Mint instituted "next-in-line" procedures for Proof examples, too.

2009 MARCH 25. Nearly 2,000 students in an Orange County, California, after-school program lay 5,491,720 Lincoln cents in a chain on a race track to eclipse the *Guinness Book of World Records* longest continuous chain of pennies, spanning 64.835 miles. The event took place at the Auto Club Speedway in Fontana. A spokesman for the childhood education program THINK (Thinking, Helping, Inspiring, Nurturing Kids Together), which sponsored the event, said that the children had collected more than 14 million pennies, the equivalent of about $146,000, or 173 miles. The penny drive commenced in February as an educational enterprise for the after-school program. Nadia Flores said the goal was to lay 8,448,800 pennies, or 100 miles, to honor the 100th anniversary of Abraham Lincoln's image being featured on the coin. Despite falling 35 miles short of its goal, the children's effort eclipsed the previous penny-laying mark of 40 miles held by a Fort Scott, Kansas, youth group. The cents were laid out in adjacent rectangular trays with printed grids linked together around the track.

2009 MARCH 26. The Bureau of Engraving and Printing offers the second in its "Lincoln Bicentennial Series" of souvenir cards, called "Family," at the Whitman Coin and Collectibles Baltimore Expo.

AMERICAN NUMISMATIC ASSOCIATION
National Money Show
Portland, Oregon - March 2009

"Lincoln Bicentennial Series"
"Humble Beginnings"

Fig. 5.32. The Bureau of Engraving and Printing intaglio print (souvenir card) program for the Lincoln bicentennial was outstanding. The cards were beautiful and they were issued efficiently early in the Lincoln bicentennial year. The first card, "Humble Beginnings," was released on March 13, 2009, at the American Numismatic Association Portland show. Engravings included Charles Burt's 1881 Lincoln portrait for the $500 Gold Certificates (BEP die MISC2722) that we have called the "Ideal" Lincoln portrait because of its size and majestic execution; a vignette of Lincoln's birthplace (BEP die MISC16064) designed by William A. Roach and engraved in 1946 by Arthur W. Dintaman; and the four-cent definitive postage stamp. Information packaged with the card calls this BEP die PO71, and credits it to Bureau engraver Lloyd B. Brook in 1894. While this may be technically correct, it is totally misleading and gives far too much credit to the bureau. The original Lincoln portrait die was engraved in 1890 by the great pictorial engraver Alfred Jones for American Bank Note Co., which had the government stamp-printing contract at the time. The stamp was designed by Tom Morris, and the letter and frame engraver was D.S. Ronaldson.

WHITMAN BALTIMORE COIN AND COLLECTIBLES CONVENTION
Baltimore, Maryland - March 2009

"Lincoln Bicentennial Series"
"Family"

Fig. 5.33. The second Bureau of Engraving and Printing card for the Lincoln bicentennial, "Family," was issued March 26 at the Whitman Coin and Collectibles Baltimore Expo. Again three Lincoln vignette dies were illustrated: the portrait of son Robert Todd Lincoln (BEP die MISC2763) was engraved by Lorenzo Hatch in 1887; Mrs. Lincoln's image, by Tom Hipschen (BEP die MISC17977) in 1972; and the Series of 1861 Lincoln 15-cent U.S. postage stamp. Once again the information card distributed with the print is somewhat disingenuous, listing the engraver and date of the die as "unknown." And once again, production of the stamp pre-dates involvement of the Treasury currency bureau, but the specifics of its issue are hardly in dispute. The stamp was issued as a memorial to Lincoln on the first anniversary of his death. National Bank Note Co. was the contractor that supplied the stamp to the government. Lincoln was engraved by Joseph Ourdan in 1866. The stamp designer was James MacDonough, and W.D. Nichols contributed the frame and probably the lettering as well.

2009 MARCH 26. Lincoln impersonator Dennis Boggs presents "an enlightening, informative, and educational look at the life of the 16th president as it might have been told by Abraham Lincoln himself," at the Whitman Coin and Collectibles Baltimore Expo. Visitors were invited to have a free souvenir photo taken with Mr. Lincoln. Whitman publisher Dennis Tucker, featured speaker at the Expo, presented "Abraham Lincoln: The Image of His Greatness" at 11 a.m. on Saturday, March 28. Tucker explored the popular depiction of Lincoln as "ideal, idol, and icon," from the book *Abraham Lincoln: The Image of His Greatness,* by Fred Reed.

2009 MARCH 26. *Numismatic News* editor David C. Harper reports a "near sellout" of Proof and Uncirculated examples of the Abraham Lincoln commemorative silver dollar. Only 2,132 coins of the 450,000 pieces being offered to collectors individually were still on hand. The remaining 50,000 Proofs of the half million coins authorized were being held for use in a special set to be offered later in the year by the U.S. Mint. Said Harper: "The Lincoln Sellout has me scratching my head—who would've thought it? The coin isn't very special—looks more like a commemorative medal."

2009 MARCH 30. "Campaign Goal: Presenting Enigmatic Figure to the Nation, 1860 Political Medals Spread Abe's Message, Image to the Masses" by Fred Reed, appears in the weekly numismatic tabloid *Coin World.*

2009 APRIL 4. "Run Where Lincoln Walked!" is the theme of the Bicentennial Lincoln Memorial Half Marathon in Springfield, Illinois. Runners started in front of the Abraham Lincoln Presidential Museum, and passed the Old State Capitol, the Lincoln-Herndon Law Office, the Lincoln Home, the current State Capitol, Washington Park, Lincoln's Tomb, and Lincoln Park.

2009 APRIL 12. A Lincoln Memorial observance pays tribute to Abraham Lincoln and the civil-rights legacy of opera star Marian Anderson. "From the moment that Marian Anderson sang to the nation from the steps of the Lincoln Memorial on Easter Sunday 1939, she anointed the memorial as a shrine to the ideals of freedom and activated the modern civil rights movement," a National Park Service spokesperson affirmed. "Seventy years later, people again gathered on Easter Sunday to pay tribute to Marian Anderson's courage and Abraham Lincoln's legacy of equality of opportunity, freedom, and democracy." A naturalization ceremony preceded the event.

2009 APRIL 13. Collectors debate the pros and cons of the "ridiculously high markup" being charged by the U.S. Mint for the new Lincoln Bicentennial cents, in *Coin World*'s Letters to the Editor forum.

2009 APRIL 15. Lot Flannery's historic standing white-marble statue of Abraham Lincoln is rededicated. The statue was originally placed in front of City Hall atop a 35-foot Tuscan pillar and dedicated April 15, 1868, on the third anniversary of Lincoln's death. In 1919, when the building, then being used as a courthouse, underwent renovation, the statue and column were dismantled and put into storage. The statue was then re-erected and unveiled on April 15, 1923, this time on a lower, 12-foot-high pedestal. In 2006 the statue was once again removed during expansion and renovation of the historic courthouse. In the interim it has been "meticulously cleaned and restored." The statue is now displayed on Indiana Avenue on the south side of the D.C. Court of Appeals, 451 Indiana Avenue NW. This new rededication was 141 years to the day it was originally installed. It thus, once again, becomes the federal district's oldest monument to Lincoln's memory.

Officials pointed out that the occasion was also important for the city generally since it was one day prior to the 147th anniversary of Lincoln's signing of "An act for the release of certain persons held to service, or labor in the District of Columbia," and for appointment of a board of commissioners to appraise slaves of loyal citizens and allow payment not exceeding an average of $300 on April 16, 1862.

The statue ceremony occurred prior to completion of the courthouse renovation.

Fig. 5.34. Lincoln presenter Dennis Boggs appeared at the March 2009 Whitman Coin and Collectibles Baltimore Expo, and several shows since. He is shown with coin dealer and Whitman Publishing author Q. David Bowers at the Whitman Philadelphia Expo in September 2009.

2009 April 17. Spink-Shreves auctions the William J. Ainsworth Collection of Abraham Lincoln's image on U.S. postage stamps, without question the finest of its kind ever formed. Winner of many philatelic exhibitions, the Ainsworth collection featured multiples of "every conceivable U.S. postal emission with Lincoln's portrait," according to a Spink spokesman. Included were postage stamps, official stamps, postal stationery, revenues, revenue stamped paper, essays, proofs, issued stamps (including singles, multiples, plate blocks, and fancy cancellations in many instances), and postal history. An exceptional hardbound sales catalog in full color was offered to prospective bidders at $30, becoming an instant reference book.

Ainsworth was a protégé of Chicago attorney and Lincoln stamp enthusiast Eliot A. Landau.

2009 April 18. The Commission of Fine Arts reviews 18 suggested reverse designs for the 2010 Lincoln cent and recommends a design with 13 stalks of wheat bound together and the legend "One Nation." However, the Mint dropped the design when collectors pointed out that the bound stalks were reminiscent of fascist and socialist coin designs. "We want an American coin design," beleaguered Mint director Edmund Moy observed.

2009 April 19. The American Numismatic Association–sponsored National Coin Week observance kicks off with the theme of "Lincoln's Legacy: A Nation United." During the week, the ANA sponsored a numismatic scavenger hunt with prizes including 1918 Lincoln–Illinois Centennial commemorative half dollars, 2009 Lincoln commemorative silver dollars, and Fractional Currency of the Civil War era.

Fig. 5.35. Preparations are seen here being made to rededicate Lot Flannery's historic white-marble statue of Abraham Lincoln in Washington, DC, during completion of the DC Court of Appeals courthouse renovation, in 2009. Rededication of the cleaned and restored statue took place on April 15—141 years to the day after the statue was first dedicated in 1868.

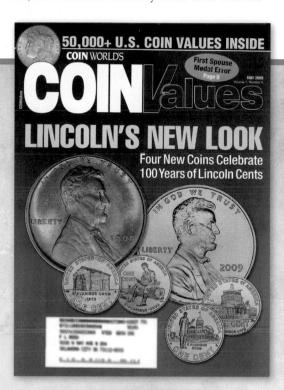

Fig. 5.36. The May 2009 issue of *Coin World's Coin Values* magazine highlighted "Lincoln's New Look" cents, but the collector tabloid *Coin World* itself was full of letters to the editor decrying the unavailability of the new coins in circulation and the high price charged by the U.S. Mint to purchase coins directly from them by the roll.

Fig. 5.37. In April 2009 the U.S. Commission of Fine Arts, established in 1910 to advise the federal government on artistic matters (including coinage), recommended this design of 13 wheat stalks bound together for the new reverse of the congressionally mandated 2010 Lincoln cent. The new design was to be symbolic of Lincoln's preservation of the Union. Collectors turned thumbs down on the design, pointing out its similarity to fascist and socialist coin designs. The U.S. Mint accommodated the outcry by adopting a shield design preferred by the Citizens Coinage Advisory Committee. "We want an American coin design," Mint director Edmund Moy observed.

2009 APRIL 22. Brian Gubicza posts *Dream Illustration–Lincoln* on flickr.com. "Goobeetsa" explains his vision as "Abe Lincoln-Bunyan was filming an infomercial in the woods." Illustrator Gibicza's vivid and colorful, childlike dream illustrations possess charm and a simple candor that is broadly appealing to his Internet followers. For example, his Lincoln-Bunyan illustration was praised for its simple geometry and perspective distortion, and called "brilliant" and "magical" by viewers.

2009 APRIL 23. The first of the Smithsonian Institution's National Museum of American History's "Abraham Lincoln Lecture Series" invites a panel to discuss "Lincoln, the Smithsonian, and Science." Moderated by Smithsonian undersecretary Richard Kurin, the panel included Marc Rothenberg, editor of the Smithsonian's Joseph Henry Papers Project; authors Thomas B. Allen and Roger MacBride Allen, who wrote *Mr. Lincoln's High Tech War: How the North Used the Telegraph, Railroads, Surveillance Balloons, Iron-Clads, High-Powered Weapons, and More to Win the Civil War;* and presidential science advisor John P. Holdren. Other programs in the series were scheduled to discuss "Lincoln, Emancipation, and Civil Rights," "Presidential Powers at a Time of War," "African Americans in the Military," and "The Public History of Lincoln."

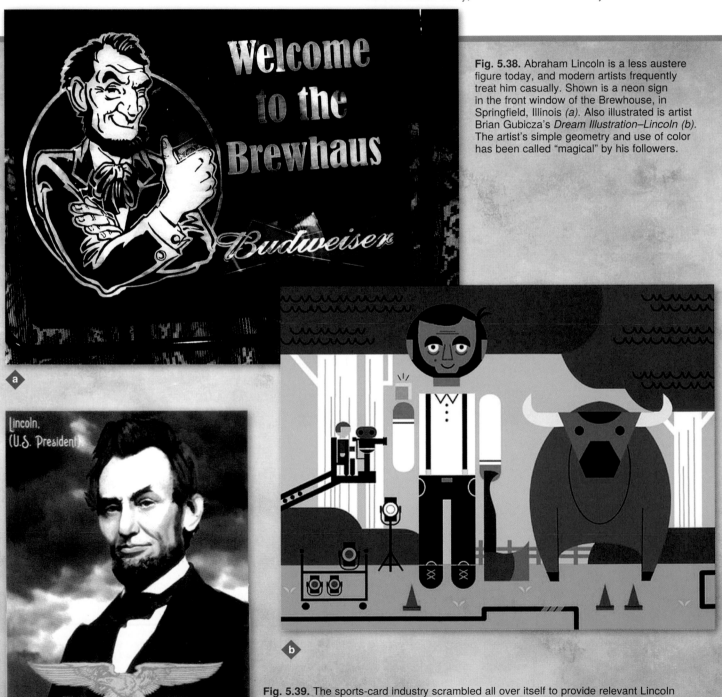

Fig. 5.38. Abraham Lincoln is a less austere figure today, and modern artists frequently treat him casually. Shown is a neon sign in the front window of the Brewhouse, in Springfield, Illinois *(a)*. Also illustrated is artist Brian Gubicza's *Dream Illustration–Lincoln (b)*. The artist's simple geometry and use of color has been called "magical" by his followers.

Fig. 5.39. The sports-card industry scrambled all over itself to provide relevant Lincoln non-sports cards for sale to collectors during the Lincoln bicentennial. Upper Deck's 2009 Goodwin Champions card "Lincoln (U.S. President)" proclaimed earnest Abe "Great Emancipator." Lincoln was card no. 16 in the set of 150, wedged in between old-time stars, slugger Dick Allen and relief pitcher Rollie Fingers. Most were sports stars, but Lyndon Johnson was card no. 36; Barack Obama, no. 44. Neither had a "Great Emancipator" nor any other mark of distinction on their card faces.

2009 APRIL 24. An official striking ceremony is held at the Nevada State Museum (formerly the Carson City Mint), for Nevada's official prooflike Abraham Lincoln bicentennial medal. Silver medals were limited to 2,009 pieces, with an unlimited copper issue. The medal was designed by Margery Hall Marshall and Karen Hopple. Medals bear the "CC" mintmark historically used on coins struck by the federal government at Carson City. The medals measure 1.5 inches in diameter. "First Day of Issue / Lincoln Commemorative Medallion" covers were also issued at Carson City, franked with Lincoln bicentennial stamps. The covers additionally state "The Silver State Honors the Bicentennial of / the birth of America's 16th President / Abraham Lincoln / 1809–2009." These covers have an impressively large circular vignette in the manner of the old-style $5 pose.

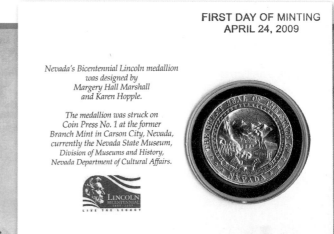

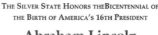

Fig. 5.40. The Nevada State Museum issued an excellent silver medal designed by Margery Hall Marshall and Karen Hopple *(a, b)*. Struck on the former Carson City Mint press at the museum, which is located in the former Mint building itself, the medal bears the historic CC mintmark on the obverse, to the left of its iconic old-style Lincoln O-92 money image. Also shown is the first-day-of-striking cover sold by the museum, also with an O-92 portrait cachet *(c)*.

Fig. 5.41. Illinois rolled out the welcome mat to Lincoln bicentennial tourists. These folks are entering from Indiana, another "land of Lincoln," as Hoosiers showed in many ways throughout the year.

2009 APRIL 25. The Chicago Coin Club annual banquet features distribution of the club's new medal depicting Augustus Saint-Gaudens's *Standing Lincoln* statue in Lincoln Park.

2009 APRIL 25. Author Fred Reed talks about his new book *Abraham Lincoln: The Image of His Greatness* at the Abraham Lincoln Book Shop, Chicago, Illinois, with host Daniel Weinberg. The interview and book signing was broadcast simultaneously and also archived on VirtualBookSigning.net. Also appearing was Canadian historian Marc Egnal, whose new book, *Clash of Extremes,* re-examined the financial struggles that led to the Civil War.

2009 APRIL 28. The Citizens Coinage Advisory Committee tables discussion of retaining the Victor David Brenner Lincoln portrait or introducing a new Lincoln portrait on 2010 and later U.S. cents. The Mint had planned to retain the Brenner portrait, and objected to further discussion of a change in portraiture on bureaucratic grounds "because it had not been listed as a topic in the meeting agenda." Discussion would be further tabled at the committee's June 29 meeting.

2009 APRIL 30. The Bureau of Engraving and Printing offers the third in its "Lincoln Bicentennial Series" of souvenir cards, called "A Nation Torn Apart," at the Central States Numismatic Society Convention in Cincinnati.

2009. Illinois artist Cathee A. "Cat" Clausen paints a vivid portrait based on the Gettysburg Lincoln image. Clausen calls her technique "pure power style," blending accurate details and passionate, instinctive brush strokes.

2009 MAY 1. Lincoln's hometown, Springfield, Illinois, holds a five-month-long "Mr. Lincoln's Bicentennial Springfield Walk" with "Here I Have Lived" historical markers distributed throughout the city.

Fig. 5.42. The Chicago Coin Club's rich tradition of medal issue continued in 2009. This plaque with a likeness after Saint-Gaudens's *Standing Lincoln* in Chicago was distributed at the club's April 25 banquet, when coincidentally this writer was also in Chicago to speak about his new Lincoln book.

Fig. 5.43. Artist Cathee A. "Cat" Clausen's visually stunning and emotionally powerful, yet realistic in style, painting recasts the familiar 19th-century Gettysburg Lincoln image and projects it into a 21st-century "beyond the American icon" manner.

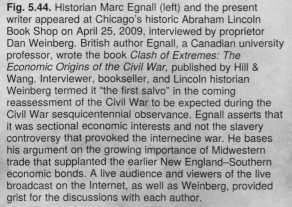

Fig. 5.44. Historian Marc Egnall (left) and the present writer appeared at Chicago's historic Abraham Lincoln Book Shop on April 25, 2009, interviewed by proprietor Dan Weinberg. British author Egnall, a Canadian university professor, wrote the book *Clash of Extremes: The Economic Origins of the Civil War*, published by Hill & Wang. Interviewer, bookseller, and Lincoln historian Weinberg termed it "the first salvo" in the coming reassessment of the Civil War to be expected during the Civil War sesquicentennial observance. Egnall asserts that it was sectional economic interests and not the slavery controversy that provoked the internecine war. He bases his argument on the growing importance of Midwestern trade that supplanted the earlier New England–Southern economic bonds. A live audience and viewers of the live broadcast on the Internet, as well as Weinberg, provided grist for the discussions with each author.

2009 MAY 4. Letter writers to Beth Deisher, editor of *Coin World,* complain about the dearth of available circulating bicentennial Lincoln cents. A Richmond, Virginia, reader complains about the U.S. Mint gouging collectors by charging $8.95 plus $4.95 postage for one each of 50-coin rolls of Philadelphia and Denver Mint cents, or 13.9¢ per coin. Meanwhile, coin dealer David Sklow reprimanded officials for the "pathetic manner used by the U.S. Mint in releasing the first 2009 Lincoln cent to the general public." Sklow also lambasted the Federal Reserve. Officials should have made release of the new cents a priority, the letter writer opined. "This four-coin program was in the planning stages for well over two years. Mint customers should not have to visit eBay and pay outrageous prices for this new cent." Sklow then recounted Mint delays in new cent orders that he has experienced. "I hope changes are made to this program prior to the release of the other three 2009 cents," he concluded. Such letters were typical of collector outrage over the bungled Lincoln Bicentennial cent program. "Where are the new Lincoln cents?" collectors asked all year long in vain, as the flood of Lincoln tributes never came.

2009 MAY 7. Historian Doris Kearns Goodwin urges graduating students at Vanderbilt University to emulate America's 16th president, during a Senior Class Day appearance. Goodwin was honored with the Nichols-Chancellor's Medal, and received a standing ovation following her speech.

2009 MAY 8. An heroic-size bronze standing Abraham Lincoln sculpture is dedicated at Hillsdale College, Ann Arbor, Michigan. Professor Allen C. Guelzo, of Gettysburg College and a two-time winner of the Lincoln Prize, gave the dedicatory address. Guelzo disparaged the cultural malaise which has toppled Lincoln off his high pedestal. "In a multicultural perspective, no triumphal, Union-saving Lincoln is allowed to emerge; multiculturalism is the celebration of ordinariness, information, and egalitarianism. Which is why most people today are interested in knowing whether Lincoln was gay rather than knowing whether he was right," the speaker said. Commenting on the statue beside him, he continued: "For a moment, the heroic has reasserted itself—not the reeking heroic of kings and emperors, but the heroic republican citizen, in broadcloth rather than in uniform . . . armed with conviction, perseverance, and ability, rather than a sword . . . standing, and always facing forward to the light."

The seven-foot-two-inch Lincoln figure was the work of sculptor Tony Frudakis, one of a series of nine historic figures commissioned by the college to celebrate contributors to the institution's "Liberty Walk." Frudakis said he based the pose, which has Lincoln's hands clasped behind his back, based on a written description of Lincoln by Francis B. Carpenter, who wrote he observed the president walking alone in the White House with his hands behind his back "carrying the weight of the world." "That resonated with me" the sculptor said.

Fig. 5.45. The third card in the Bureau of Engraving and Printing Lincoln bicentennial series, "A Nation Torn Apart," debuted at the April 30 Central States Numismatic Society show in Cincinnati. The card features the familiar iconic Lincoln portrait (in this case BEP die MISC4588), which the BEP info packet narrowly attributes to George U. Rose Jr. and Harry L. Chorlton in 1898. Again, technically correct (since messrs. Rose and Chorlton contributed the details, like the oak border and name plaque, for use on the face of a Loan of 1898 3% bond), it fails to do justice to the real artist at hand, engraver Charles Burt, who engraved the iconic Lincoln O-92 portrait parent die (BEP die no. MISC1029) in 1869 for the $100 U.S. Treasury Note. The two vignettes of soldiers are attributed to the National Bank Note Co. and Henry Gugler, left and right, respectively.

Fig. 5.46. Since Lincoln Bicentennial cents were largely unavailable, private marketers found a market for slabbed and certified "first" coins, at stiff premiums. This ANACS-certified coin was one of the first issued Formative Years coins purportedly "released" at the May 14 Indiana ceremony.

2009 MAY. Beckettmedia sells the Upper Deck 2008 SP Legendary Cuts "Hair Cut Signatures" Abraham Lincoln card (HCS-AL) on eBay for a $17,500 offer on a "Buy It Now" price of $21,400. The cut hair framed on the card was a single strand about a half inch in length, and the autograph was a full signature, "Abraham Lincoln," rather than his typical "A. Lincoln" autograph.

2009 MAY 14. The commemorative cent marking Lincoln's formative years in Indiana is officially released at the Lincoln Amphitheatre in Lincoln State Park, Lincoln City, Indiana. Children aged 18 and under received free examples of the new cent. More than 3,000 adult attendees could purchase from two to ten rolls of the new coin. All were Philadelphia-struck coins. Freedom Bank in nearly Dixie, Indiana, was in charge of the cent exchange.

2009 MAY 14. The Bureau of Engraving and Printing offers the fourth in its "Lincoln Bicentennial Series" of souvenir cards, called "Emancipation," at the Texas Numismatic Association 50th Texas State Coin and Currency Show, in Fort Worth.

2009 MAY 15. The Bureau of Engraving and Printing offers the first installment of the "Lincoln Freedom Collection—Series 2006 $5 Note Collection." It features one $5 note each of the Federal Reserve districts of Cleveland, Boston, New York, and Dallas, with the lowest serial numbers. The notes were available by district or as an entire collection through a subscription program that included all 12 Federal Reserve banks.

2009 MAY 17. Lincoln and Civil War historian David Herbert Donald dies. Donald twice won the Pulitzer Prize for biography and was a premier Lincoln scholar of the 20th century. Each year, the Abraham Lincoln Presidential Museum in Springfield, Illinois, awards the David Herbert Donald Prize for excellence in Lincoln studies.

Fig. 5.47. Once again with great fanfare but abysmal follow-through, the U.S. Mint introduced the second Lincoln Bicentennial cent (commemorating Lincoln's boyhood in Indiana) on May 14, 2009. The attractive, informally balanced railsplitter coin was designed and sculpted by Charles L. Vickers of the U.S. Mint. More than 3,000 persons attended the introduction, scarfing up two to ten rolls of Philadelphia-coined cents in an exchange, but few cents actually entered circulation.

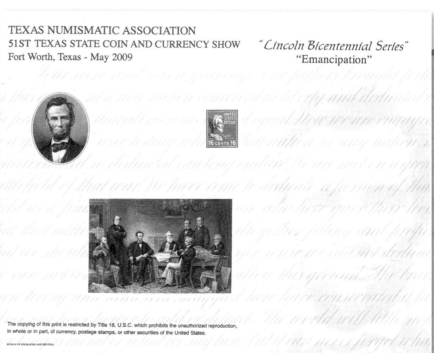

Fig. 5.48. Bureau of Engraving and Printing souvenir cards for the Lincoln bicentennial came out fast and furious during 2009, but with abysmal scholarship. Card number 4, "Emancipation," showed up on the scene May 15 at the Texas Numismatic Association convention. The issue was an unexpected treat—the first Lincoln portrait die from the BEP we'd seen with an image based on Alexander Gardner's Gettysburg Lincoln O-77 photograph. According to information supplied with the souvenir card, this portrait (BEP die MISC 15628) is ascribed to John S. Edmondson. The "Engraved portrait [was] created from photo by Gardiner" [sic] in 1943. However, in information supplied to this writer in 2008, die 15628 was attributed to another BEP engraver, Carl T. Arlt, leaving this writer to wonder who actually created the portrait he has begged the Treasury to use on U.S. currency for more than 15 years now. The other impressions include the Lincoln 16-cent stamp (BEP die PO982) credited to Carl T. Alt [sic] and James T. Vail in 1938, based on a photo of the head of Thomas Ball's Emancipation statue. The vignette at lower center is mysteriously identified as *Telegraphing in Battle* (BEP die MISC4422), engraved by Marcus Baldwin in 1897. However, as can be readily seen by even the least curious intellect, the actual vignette shown on the card is G.F.C. Smillie's engraving after Richie's engraving of Carpenter's *First Reading of the Emancipation* to the Cabinet. We showed the same vignette in *Abraham Lincoln: The Image of His Greatness* (figure 2.183 in that book). That example, which this author cataloged in 2000–2001 for Heritage Auctions along with one of the photographic models that Smillie used in 1901, was signed by Smillie and labeled "3d Pf," i.e., third proof. It was titled by Smillie, in pencil, *Signing Emancipation Proclamation.* Two years later, BEP director William Meredith would write industrialist Andrew Carnegie that G.F.C. Smillie "commands the highest salary ever paid to an engraver by the BEP or any bank note company." The Smillie Emancipation vignette and model were from the Judge Frederick Brandon Smillie–G.F.C. Smillie family archives.

2009 May 18. The Topps trading card company reveals that its new American Heritage set will contain a Lincoln card (#18) among the political heroes in the set, and also a 25-card subset (#126–150) featuring Abraham Lincoln and Barack Obama jointly. Another special was a five-card "A Hero's Journey Relics" subset with a Lincoln cut autograph, and bits of Lincoln's law-office floor and his funeral-train flag, an election cover, or portions of Lincoln's parlor curtains or wood from his home; as well as a 15-card "Hero's Journey" insert subset without relics, and a 20-card subset that incorporated actual Lincoln-related U.S. stamps. However, collectors expressed disappointment at the distressed state of the stamps used in these "special" cards.

2009 May 22. Daniel Chester French's Lincoln Memorial statue comes to life, reminds erstwhile museum security guard Larry Daley (Ben Stiller) that a house divided against itself cannot stand, and assists in subduing an insurrection led by a 3,000-year-old Egyptian pharaoh, Napoleon Bonaparte, and Al Capone, in the Twentieth Century Fox movie *Night at the Museum: Battle of the Smithsonian.*

2009 May 28. *Numismatic News* scribe Paul M. Green posthumously discusses how the hoarding of cents has altered the Lincoln cent series and the collecting of it through the years, on numismaster.com.

2009 May 28. A rare experimental 1942 aluminum Lincoln cent, Judd-2079, sells for $126,500 at Heritage Auctions' May 28, 2009, Long Beach auction. The experimental cent weighs 1.563 grams. It had been previously consigned for a March 2008 Heritage sale, but was withdrawn for further examination. It was submitted to PCGS and found to contain aluminum 98.0%, silicon 0.7%, iron 0.6%, silver 0.5%, and magnesium 0.4%.

Fig. 5.49. Topps Card Co. was the most aggressive purveyor of Lincoln bicentennial non-sports collector cards in 2009. The Topps American Heritage card with the Henry F. Warren O-112 paparazzi image shot on the White House balcony was card no. 18 in a political-heroes subset, in the format of 1952 Topps baseball cards *(a)*. The Topps "A Hero's Journey" relic card was a limited-edition insert, or "chase" card, to prop up sales to collectors trying to get a rarity *(b)*. Also shown is a regular 2009 Topps Heritage card from a set of 25 cards that attempted to capitalize on Obama-mania *(c)*, and a regular Topps 2009 "A Hero's Journey" card from the set of 15 *(d)*.

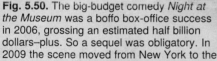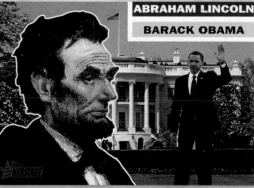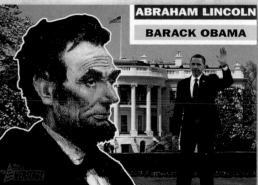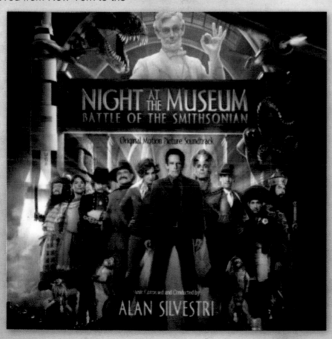

Fig. 5.50. The big-budget comedy *Night at the Museum* was a boffo box-office success in 2006, grossing an estimated half billion dollars–plus. So a sequel was obligatory. In 2009 the scene moved from New York to the nation's capital for *Night at the Museum: The Battle of the Smithsonian.* With an even bigger budget, the sequel's revenues were down in the depressed economy despite an amiable assist from Daniel Chester French's animated Lincoln Memorial statue.

2009 MAY 28. The "Hats off to Lincoln" art project, sponsored by the Springfield Rotary Club and the Springfield Area Arts Council, kicks off a display of nearly two dozen modern takes on old Abe's signature black stovepipe apparel. Springfield artist Felicia Olin created a vivid three-foot-tall (on a 57-inch base) fiberglass update of Abe's somber sombrero. She said she drew her inspiration from Vachel Lindsay's poem "Lincoln." "I just pulled out images from the poem. The poem talks about prairie fires, buffalo, and a weedy stream. So I used these images and made a picture that you follow with your eyes all the way around," Olin told a local reporter. Olin's bonnet was select for street-level viewing outside the Illinois State Museum. Artist Thom Cicchelli of Chicago, who also designed the 2003 Illinois state quarter, designed a five-foot-high birthday cake in the shape of a tall hat, titled *A Slice of History,* which was displayed in the Abraham Lincoln Presidential Library and Museum visitor center, across the street from the ALPLM proper. Other artistic entries were scattered around the city for viewing by the public.

2009 MAY 30. The Lincoln Memorial is rededicated. Four score and seven years to the day that President Warren G. Harding, Chief Justice William Howard Taft, Robert Todd Lincoln, and others attended the dedication of the Henry Bacon / Daniel Chester French temple we know as the Lincoln Memorial, Secretary of the Interior Ken Salazar led a group of speakers and performers remembering that historic event, and rededicating the memorial to Lincoln's constitutional premises that our government remains of, by, and for the People.

2009 JUNE 4. A new seated, heroic-size bronze statue of Abraham Lincoln by Ed Hamilton, and four bas-relief memorial walls, are dedicated on the Louisville, Kentucky, riverfront. The works were funded by the State of Kentucky, the Kentucky Historical Society / Kentucky Abraham Lincoln Bicentennial Commission, and private philanthropy. According to officials, "This memorial tells the story of how, as a young man, Lincoln began developing his abhorrence

Fig. 5.51. The "Hats Off to Lincoln" art project sponsored by the Springfield, Illinois, Rotary Club and the Springfield Area Arts Council invited artists to provide new visions of Lincoln's somber sombrero. The delightful results were displayed around town at various locations, as street art.

Fig. 5.53. This birthday-cake–themed *A Slice of History* display was part of the "Hats Off to Lincoln" competition in Springfield, Illinois, open to all artists. Chicago artist Thom Cicchelli, who also designed the 2003 Illinois state quarter, designed this five-foot-high birthday cake, which was displayed in the Abraham Lincoln Presidential Library and Museum visitor center at the train station, across the street from the ALPLM proper.

Fig. 5.52. In 2009, Internet creative consultant Richard Smith started a "Dollar ReDe$ign" project, offering artists a chance to propose alternatives to the drab and staid U.S. federal currency. Elias Stern suggested this approach for improving the $5 Federal Reserve Note, while retaining, but altering, the O-91 large Lincoln portrait.

of slavery while watching slaves being loaded onto riverboats on the Ohio River in Louisville." The Waterfront Park memorial features a 12-foot-high statue of Lincoln seated on a rock and looking out over the river. The rock was created by Forest Boone of Museum Rock Products. Lincoln holds a book of law, while his top hat and books labeled *Shakespeare* and *Holy Bible* lie at his feet. Four bas-reliefs (tableaux hewn from a flat surface to make a picture that stands out) illustrate four scenes that represent stories of Lincoln's life-long ties to Kentucky, the state of his birth. The four scenes illustrated are titled *Lincoln's Formative Years in Kentucky, Lincoln's Kentucky Connections, A House Divided,* and *Slavery and Emancipation.* Nationally renowned African American Louisville artist Ed Hamilton created both the Lincoln statue and the bas-reliefs. Hargreaves Associates designed the landscape and amphitheater, which face the river, providing the setting for the sculptural pieces. This spectacular site is open daily and free to the public.

Fig. 5.54. The new Waterfront Park Lincoln memorial (Louisville, Kentucky), by sculptor Ed Hamilton, dedicated June 4, 2009, is breathtaking. It features a 12-foot heroic-size bronze statue of a relaxed Lincoln looking out on the new bridge across the Ohio River within a large exedra *(a)*, and four large bronze bas-relief panels representing Lincoln's lifelong ties to his native state *(b–e)*. For my money, this was *the* outstanding celebration among the many toasts lifted toward Abe in his bicentennial year. Additionally, models for Hamilton's Lincoln statue were displayed at the city's J.B. Speed Memorial Museum during summer 2009.

Fig. 5.55. "Celebrate the Lincoln Bicentennial," this University of Louisville street banner suggests. The University's J.B. Speed Memorial Art Museum mounted a display, "Beyond the Log Cabin, Kentucky's Abraham Lincoln."

2009 June 6. "Beyond the Log Cabin: Kentucky's Abraham Lincoln," a traveling exhibit, debuts at the Kentucky Historical Society, Frankfort.

2009 June 8. "1864 Campaign Items Recall Fight Lincoln Expected to Lose; Wartime Leader Not Overly Optimistic About Chances in Presidential Election," by Fred Reed, appears in the weekly numismatic trade publication *Coin World.* This article would subsequently win the Numismatic Literary Guild award for best article on tokens and medals in a numismatic newspaper published during the preceding year.

2009 June 12. A new Lincoln monument, the Abraham Lincoln Bicentennial Plaza, honoring his Hoosier youth, is unveiled and dedicated in Lincoln State Park, Indiana. "The character and strengths he demonstrated throughout his presidency found their roots in what is now Spencer County in southern Indiana," a plaque

at the memorial reminds the viewer. "From 1816 to 1830, from ages seven to twenty one, Lincoln roamed these woods, cut down trees, and worked the fields of the family farm near Little Pigeon Creek. Here grew his love of learning, his skillful use of language and storytelling, his sense of fairness, his opposition to slavery and his ability to lead. As a lawyer and politician and ultimately as president of the United States during the Civil War, these values, strengths and abilities served Lincoln well."

The plaza was designed by architect George Morrison of Morrison Kattman Menze Inc. The outdoor display consists of a central semicircular masonry monument with stone glyphs representing Lincoln's heights as he grew up from age 7 to age 21 on his father's nearby farm. At the back of the monument is a twice-life-size bronze bust by sculptor Will Clark, on a pedestal, flanked by quotations from Lincoln's Gettysburg Address and Second Inaugural Address. The whole is surrounded by concentric circles of low bench-like

Fig. 5.56. Architect George Morrison's stone memorial chronicles Abraham Lincoln's height during his years in Indiana *(a)*. On the other side of the memorial sculptor Will Clark's bust presents a mature view of Old Abe *(b)*. This Abraham Lincoln Bicentennial Plaza at Lincoln State Park (adjacent to the Lincoln Boyhood National Memorial in Indiana) was dedicated on June 12, 2009. That evening a new play, "Lincoln," by playwright Ken Jones, debuted in the park's amphitheater *(c)*.

stones and standing columns with Lincoln quotes and narrative explanation. The memorial is comprised of native Indiana stone.

It takes its themes from Lincoln's biographical quote, "There I grew up," and from poet William Wordsworth's line, "The child is father of the man," from his 1802 poem "My Heart Leaps Up When I Behold." Later in the day of the dedication, a new play, *Lincoln*, by playwright Ken Jones, debuted in the park's amphitheatre.

Lincoln State Park is named for Lincoln's mother Nancy Hanks Lincoln. The state park includes the Little Pigeon Church, where the Lincoln family worshiped, and the grave of Lincoln's sister, Sarah. Nancy Hanks Lincoln's grave site is in the adjacent Lincoln Boyhood National Memorial, administered by the National Park Service since 1962–1963.

2009 June 13. An 1873 cover bearing the Abraham Lincoln 90-cent stamp mailed to India brings $431,000 in a New York City auction held by Siegel Auction Galleries. Known to collectors as the "Ice House Cover," the envelope is the only one collectors know of still having the stamp, which, with 22¢ other postage, paid the two-ounce foreign-letter rate. Last publicly traded in 1943, the cover was stolen in 1967 and its whereabouts were unknown until 2006. The cover had been discovered in India in 1914. The purchaser this time was collector Dr. Arthur K.M. Woo. The 90-cent Lincoln stamp of 1869 was ranked no. 5 among the 100 greatest American stamps, in the book of the same name by Janet Klug and Donald J. Sundman.

2009 June 15. "How Vast and Varied a Field . . . The Agricultural Vision of Abraham Lincoln" opens a 10-week run at the Abraham Lincoln Presidential Library and Museum, Springfield, Illinois.

2009 June 16. Congressman Joe Pitts (R-Pennsylvania) invites *Roll Call* into his office to view and photograph his collection of Abraham Lincoln sculptures.

2009 June 19. A laser-generated copy of Gutzon Borglum's twice-life-size seated Lincoln figure that has graced courthouse square in Newark, New Jersey, since 1911 is dedicated in Boise, Idaho, through the auspices of the Idaho Abraham Lincoln Bicentennial Commission. According to a local press report, a California company used a laser-scanning technique to replicate the Borglum original, the design of which is now in the public domain, in Styrofoam. Then sculptor Irene Deely made a clay maquette, which was cast by Parks Bronze Foundry in Enterprise, Oregon.

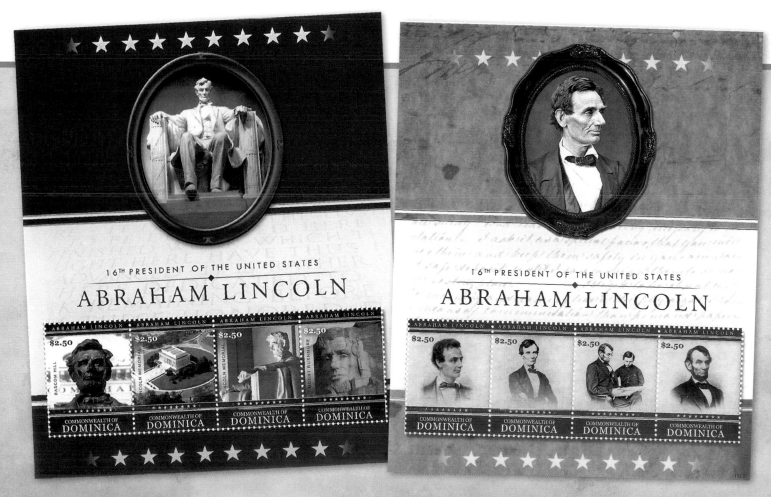

Fig. 5.57. This Commonwealth of Dominica stamp series and souvenir sheet feature Lincoln statuary and memorials. For those not familiar with Bascom Hill, it is the center of the main campus of the University of Wisconsin at Madison. Adolph Weinman sculpted the head of the statue shown, dedicated June 22, 1909. It is a duplicate of the seated figure at Hodgenville, Kentucky.

Fig. 5.58. This is a second set of Lincoln stamps issued by the Commonwealth of Dominica for the Lincoln bicentennial.

2009 June 26. Whitman Publishing's Dennis Tucker and author Fred Reed present an illustrated lecture on the new book *Abraham Lincoln: The Image of His Greatness* at the 6th Annual Society of Paper Money Collectors Authors Forum, at the Memphis International Paper Money Show. Tucker was the book's publisher.

2009 June 28. Models for Ed Hamilton's heroic-size relaxed figure of Abraham Lincoln that was placed in a special exedra at the Louisville Waterfront Park facing the Ohio River, and "Beyond the Log Cabin, Kentucky's Abraham Lincoln," go on display for 10 weeks at the J.B. Speed Memorial Museum, Louisville, Kentucky.

2009 June 29. A "Guest Commentary" (op ed), "Time to Free 2009 Lincoln Bicentennial Cents from Vaults," by Fred Reed, appears in the weekly numismatic tabloid *Coin World*. Reed supported *Coin*

World editor Beth Deisher's June 8 editorial lambasting the lackadaisical manner in which the U.S. Mint was fulfilling its congressional mandate to celebrate Lincoln's birth bicentennial. The law placed the responsibility squarely on the shoulders of Treasury Secretary Timothy Geitner, and Reed argued that Geitner had failed miserably. The writer contended that minting coins to celebrate Lincoln and then locking them up (by the millions of bags full) in Treasury and Federal Reserve vaults was no fitting commemoration, and surely not what Congress intended when it passed Public Law 109-145. Furthermore, Reed urged, "Hopefully, President Obama, a self-professed Lincoln-lover, will immediately light a fire under his underlings at Treasury and the U.S. Mint to adopt editor Deisher's sound plan to circulate these coins." The slow, small, and insignificant release of quantities of these four coins kept most of the public in the dark that they had been issued at all!

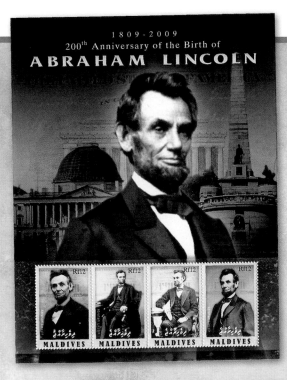

Fig. 5.39. The Maldives *(a)*, Nevis *(b)*, and the Federated States of Micronesia *(c)* all issued four-stamp Lincoln tributes in souvenir-sheet form. All these stamps are simple but well designed.

Fig. 5.60. In June 2009 Whitman publisher Dennis Tucker and this author presented an illustrated talk on *Abraham Lincoln: The Image of His Greatness* at the Sixth Annual Society of Paper Money Collectors Authors Forum. The forum annually gives authors of new books, prospective authors, and the publishing community a chance to share experiences and encouragement on the long road toward publication of a successful book.

2009 June 30. The Metropolitan Museum of Art opens a 10-week exhibition of Augustus Saint-Gaudens's coin designs and sculpture, including a bronze bust of Abraham Lincoln (based on his standing Lincoln statue in Chicago), and the bronze casts he made of Lincoln's life mask and hands, which served as models for his heroic figures. The exhibition closed October 12.

2009 July 3. Kellogg Company, Battle Creek, Michigan, displays a life-size cheese carving of Abraham Lincoln (six-foot-eight-inches, including stovepipe hat) to salute America's anniversary and the Lincoln bicentennial, and to tout its small cheese cracker. Known as the *Cheez-It Big Cheese,* the Lincoln cheese figure was carved from a 1,000-pound block of Wisconsin cheddar by Troy Landwehr. The figure was displayed to the public for three hours at 2215 Constitution Avenue NW in Washington, D.C., "in the shadow of the Lincoln Memorial." The company gave out complimentary Cheez-It crackers to onlookers, and tourists posed with the Big Cheese, himself—except for one young girl, who kicked the statue's base. Weakened by the heat, her blow sent Lincoln's head and top hat into a free fall. Carver Landwehr restored the head to its perch, but the hat "was a total loss." After the publicity stunt, a protective layer on the sculpture was peeled off and the cheese itself parceled out to various charities.

2009 July 5. "One Life: The Mask of Lincoln," an exhibition at the National Portrait Gallery, Smithsonian Institution, closes its eight-month run.

2009 July 10. *PMG Track and Price* lists 135 known $10 Demand Notes with the Charles Burt portrait of Abraham Lincoln: Friedberg-6 (New York, engraved signatures), 38 known; F-6a (New York, handwritten signatures), 5; F-7 (Philadelphia, engraved), 40; F-7a (Philadelphia, handwritten), 2; F-8 (Boston, engraved), 40; F-8a (Boston, handwritten), 2; F-9 (Cincinnati, engraved), 4; F-9a (Cincinnati, handwritten), 1; F-10 (St. Louis, engraved), 3; F-10a (St. Louis, handwritten), 0.

Fig. 5.61. Tony Landwehr created this life-size statue of Lincoln out of a half-ton block of Wisconsin cheddar cheese for display in Washington, DC, to celebrate the Fourth of July, gain publicity for sponsor Cheez-It Crackers, and benefit charity.

Fig. 5.62. Abe's hat and profile were familiar icons on street banners in Springfield, Illinois, for the city's July 4, 2009, activities.

2009 July 14. Maryland hard rockers Clutch release their ninth studio album, *Strange Cousins from the West,* with a nearly six-minute cut, *Abraham Lincoln.* Lyrics include this stanza: "Oh Abraham Lincoln carried across the street / Oh Abraham Lincoln carried across the street / The assassin, the coward shot him in the head / The assassin, the serpent struck him then he fled."

2009 July 23. Medallic Art Co., purchased by Northwest Territorial Mint, provides the original Brenner Lincoln galvano design for Signature Art Medal's "My Mind was Full of Lincoln" medal, the reverse of which was designed and sculpted by Don Everhart, according to a SAMCO spokesman.

2009 August 5. The Bureau of Engraving and Printing offers the second installment of the "Lincoln Freedom Collection—Series 2006 $5 Note Collection." It features one $5 note of each of the following Federal Reserve districts, with the lowest serial numbers: San Francisco, Philadelphia, St. Louis, and Kansas City. The notes were available by district or as an entire collection through a subscription program that included all 12 Federal Reserve banks.

2009 August 5. The co-host club for the American Numismatic Association World's Fair of Money (held in Los Angeles), the Numismatic Association of Southern California, commemorates the event by rolling elongated cents with a Lincoln profile bust imitative of Brenner's cent portrait. The design was by Oded Paz, whose initials appear to the left of the bust. They also rolled nickels, dimes, quarters, and Native American dollars with the Lincoln design and inscription.

Fig. 5.63. Signature Art Medals principles Dick Johnson and Mark Schlepphorst brought out many of the finest Lincoln bicentennial tributes. In 2009 they had Medallic Art Co. restrike the small 1907 Brenner Lincoln plaque design *(a)* with a new commemorative reverse by U.S. Mint sculptor Don Everhart *(b).* Everhart's original design shows cent designer Victor David Brenner at work on his Lincoln plaque—his "mind full of Lincoln," shown symbolically by his hovering presence. Everhart positioned Lincoln after the manner, but not as a direct copy, of the O-86 Mathew Brady image. The scale of the obverse die is indicated by the Lincoln cent positioned facing the incuse Lincoln portrait die *(c).*

Fig. 5.64. I purchased this commemorative cent folder at the Hodgenville, Kentucky, Lincoln Museum in late June 2009, more than four months after the cent was released there. It was the first Lincoln Birthplace cent I saw. None were seen in circulation in my travels in Texas, Oklahoma, Arkansas, Tennessee, or Kentucky during that time, and merchants and bankers greeted my persistent inquiries with blank stares.

Fig. 5.66. The Numismatic Association of Southern California, a host for the annual summer ANA convention now branded as the World's Fair of Money, produced commemorative elongateds for the show. They were designed by Oded Paz. Shown is a rolled cent (*a*) and a rolled nickel (*b*). Other elongated coins were also issued.

Fig. 5.65. This writer was scheduled for a book signing in August 2010 at the ANA World's Fair of Money. I'm pleased to report I was kept very busy for nearly a half hour longer than the scheduled time, meeting other Lincoln enthusiasts and signing books. I also was asked to speak at a Central States Numismatic Society educational seminar by one of the booth visitors.

2009 AUGUST 5. The Bureau of Engraving and Printing offers the fifth and last in its "Lincoln Bicentennial Series" of souvenir cards, called "Legacy," at the ANA World's Fair of Money in Los Angeles.

2009 AUGUST 6. To commemorate StampShow 2009 (the 123rd annual American Philatelic Society convention), in Pittsburgh, the APS issues free stamp pages with images of many types of U.S. regular-issue, commemorative, revenue, and miscellaneous stamps, postal cards, postal stationery, etc., with Abraham Lincoln portraits for use by hobbyists as a free download on its web site. The 16-page album supplement had spaces for each stamp type, with color images of the stamp design, as well as its Scott catalog number.

2009 AUGUST 6. *Abraham Lincoln: The Image of His Greatness* wins the Numismatic Literary Guild's "Book of the Year" award as "the work having the greatest potential impact on numismatics," at the NLG banquet in Los Angeles during the American Numismatic Association convention.

2009 AUGUST 10. "On Bonds, Honest Abe's Image Meant Legitimacy and Value; C.S. German 1861 Portrait Model for Engravings for Bonds, Currency" by Fred Reed, appears in the weekly numismatic tabloid *Coin World*.

2009 AUGUST 13. The third Lincoln Bicentennial cent, commemorating his professional life in Illinois, has its official public release in Springfield.

2009 AUGUST 13. A Topps 2004 American Treasures Signature Cut Card with an Abraham Lincoln autograph sells on eBay for $12,277.77.

2009 AUGUST 15. A life-size statue of Abraham Lincoln is unveiled on the Hillsboro Plaza, across the street from the Montgomery County (Illinois) Courthouse, to commemorate the 125th Old Settlers Days and the bicentennial of Lincoln's birth. The statue, titled *Among Friends,* is by John McClarey. It showcases Lincoln's "wide interest in entertainment and theater, an aspect of Lincoln's character not seen in other public works," according to the sculptor. The statue was cast in pieces at inBronze Studio, Gallery and Foundry, Mount Morris, Illinois. After each piece was sanded and polished, the separate pieces were welded together, the seams burnished away, and a chemical patina applied. The statue and memorial plaza was an $80,000 project underwritten by private funds. An original play, also titled *Among Friends,* by Pat Brink was performed the following week at the local Presbyterian Church.

2009 AUGUST 20. The Blue Ridge Numismatic Association celebrates its 50th annual convention with the theme "Come visit with President Lincoln!"

2009 AUGUST 24. "Pitchmen Continue to Appropriate Lincoln's Name, Portrait; Stock Certificates From Many Firms, Some Bearing His Name, Show Visage," by Fred Reed, appears in the weekly numismatic tabloid *Coin World*.

Fig. 5.66. The third of four Lincoln bicentennial cents represented Lincoln's professional life in Illinois. The successful result was a collaboration between artist Joel Iskowitz, who designed the coin's reverse, and U.S. Mint sculptor/engraver Don Everhart, who modeled the design for coining. The cent was officially "released" August 13 in Springfield, Illinois. As of this writing some 30 months later, this writer has yet to see one of these nice coins in circulation.

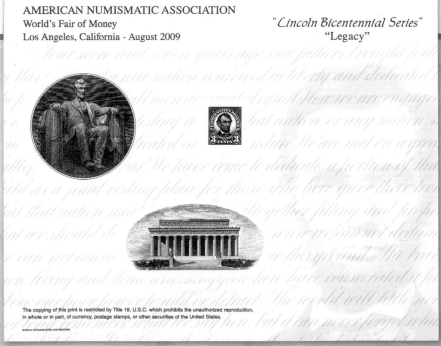

Fig. 5.67. The Bureau of Engraving and Printing concluded its successful five-souvenir-card program with the August 5, 2009, release of its "Legacy" card at the ANA World's Fair of Money in Los Angeles. The Lincoln Memorial statue engraving (BEP die MISC11363) is credited to Fredrick C. Pauling in 1926, based, of course, on the Daniel Chester French statue. The three-cent stamp (BEP die PO713) was designed by Clair Aubrey Huston. G.F.C. "Fred" Smillie had engraved the excellent O-92–style portrait in 1897–1898; it was used in 1923, by which time, ironically, he had been fired through White House political shenanigans. This stamp (Scott 555 and additional varieties) provided additional impetus toward making the O-92 portrait the "Universal Lincoln" icon of the 20th century. Joachim C. Benzing engraved the scrolls and ribbon, and Edward M. Hall the frame, numerals, and lettering, according to the information card supplied with the print. The Lincoln Memorial (BEP die MISC11539) was engraved by Joachim C. Benzing in 1927, and of course incorporated on the backs of $5 notes of all classes, Series of 1928 through Series of 1995.

2009 September 1. The Bureau of Engraving and Printing offers the third installment of the "Lincoln Freedom Collection—Series 2006 $5 Note Collection." It features one $5 note, with the lowest serial numbers, of each of the following Federal Reserve districts: Richmond, Chicago, Minneapolis, and Atlanta. The notes were available by district or as an entire collection through a subscription program that included all 12 Federal Reserve banks.

2009 September. The *Journal of American History* releases its digital history project, "Building the Digital Lincoln," providing links to a great many works of historical Lincoln significance as well as online essays, slide shows, a documentary video, and other resources for the Lincoln aficionado and scholar alike.

2009 September 15. According to the *Manchester Guardian*, filmmaker Steven Spielberg will move forward with his projected motion picture based on Doris Kearns Goodwin's bestseller *Team of Rivals*,

despite announcement that Robert Redford has a movie on convicted Lincoln assassination conspirator Mary Surratt in the works. "We are very happy that Redford will be doing this Lincoln movie," Spielberg told the trade publication *Variety,* according to *The Guardian*. "It is completely different from what our DreamWorks Lincoln movie will be, and we believe that it will add to the commercial potential of our film. Lincoln as a subject is inexhaustible," Spielberg opined.

2009 September 18. CBS posts a nearly three-minute clip from its original *Star Trek* television series showing Abraham Lincoln beaming aboard the Starship *Enterprise*. Lincoln, played by actor Lee Bergere, appeared in Season 3, episode 77. The video was evidently posted to drum up interest in the release of the *Star Trek* season 3 remastered DVD box set that would go on sale two months later, on November 18. Unfortunately the hoped-for Trekkie tsunami did not materialize. A year later the video had elicited only 2,700 views.

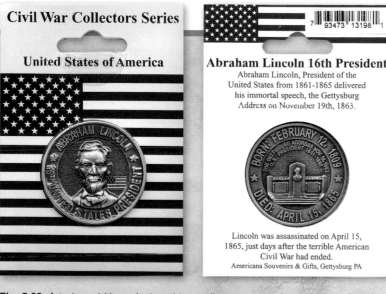

Fig. 5.68. A truly ambitious design, this small commemorative medal marketed by Americana Souvenirs and Gifts, Gettysburg, Pennsylvania, is actually slightly better-executed than it looks in these images (showing the medal inside its blister pack). It couples a Gettysburg Lincoln O-77–style bust with a small reverse representation sketching the Gettysburg Battlefield memorial with its Henry K. Bush-Brown Lincoln bust that was dedicated in 1912.

Fig. 5.69. Stack's, a New York City numismatic company, came up with interesting Lincolniana, highlighted on the Fall 2009 cover of the firm's periodic sales catalog and information vehicle, which proclaimed "Happy 200th Abraham Lincoln." Several of these pieces are also illustrated in the present work, courtesy of Stack's.

Fig. 5.70. Liberia is the most energetic of the seven foreign countries that have struck coinage in Abe's honor. Its Lincoln coins number at least 19 (and counting). For the Lincoln bicentennial, Liberia paraded out silver and silver-clad dollars *(a)* and silver-clad $5 coins with a colorized portrait of the Lincoln O-77 Gettysburg image *(b)*.

2009 September 19. "Abraham Lincoln Observer" blogger Mike Kienzler posts a "Gettysburg Lincoln" photo with Abe sporting a black eye patch over his lazy left eye to commemorate "Talk Like a Pirate Day." Appropriately, he quotes Lincoln, "Fourscore and—arrrr—seven years ago. . . ." The annual observance on September 19 was the brainchild of two Oregon men, John Baur (Ol' Chumbucket) and Mark Summers (Cap'n Slappy).

2009 September 20. A large (approximately six inches in diameter), round bronze casting of the cent profile bust, signed "V.D. Brenner" and mounted on a 10-inch-square wood plaque, sells for $960 on eBay.

2009 September 27. A bronze Lincoln bust on a pedestal is dedicated at the Abraham Lincoln Courthouse Square, Elm and Court streets, Rockford, Illinois. The sculpture was the gift of John and Suzanne Brubaker. Following a parade, a dinner was held at Veterans Memorial Hall with Lincoln interpreter Michael Krebs and Debra Ann Miller as Mary Todd Lincoln.

2009 October 1. Representative Todd R. Platts (R-Pennsylvania) and 24 cosponsors introduce HR 3712, calling for a commemorative silver dollar, $5 gold piece, and copper-nickel half dollar to mark the 150th anniversary of the Battle of Gettysburg and Lincoln's Gettysburg Address.

2009 October. The Kentucky Department of Travel receives an Excellence in Tourism Marketing second-place award for its "Saving Lincolns" television ad promoting travel deals to Lincoln-related sites in the state.

2009 October 9. The New-York Historical Society's Lincoln bicentennial exhibition "Lincoln and New York" opens at the Society's headquarters 170 Central Park West at 77th Street. A poster for the exhibition features the old-style $5 bill image and the provocative tagline, "The most beloved leader New York ever hated." The organization also staged several public programs with panels examining various aspects of Lincoln's legacy including "Lincoln's New York: The City in the 1860s" (on October 14), "Remembering David Herbert Donald: Tributes to a Great Historian" (October 21), "Lincoln's Constitution: From the Civil War Amendments to the Warren Court" (October 29), "Lincoln as Commander-in-Chief" (December 1), "Lincoln & Emancipation: An Anniversary Symposium" (January 23, 2010), and "Ex-parte Milligan: Military Commissions during the Civil War, A Supreme Court Re-enactment" (February 4).

The "Lincoln and New York" display remained in place through March 25, 2010. To kick off the exhibition, the Society also presented Tom Klingenstein's original play *Mr. Lincoln,* which dramatizes events surrounding Lincoln's epochal Cooper Union Address and the effects of meeting Lincoln then, as recounted by two witnesses many years later. The play featured Broadway actors Peter Jay Fernandez in the role of a former slave and Jane Summerhays as a New York society matron. Direction was provided by Margaret Perry. The play debuted October 9 and had 17 additional performances through mid-November.

Fig. 5.71. Two Oregon men—John Baur (Ol' Chumbucket) and Mark Summers (Cap'n Slappy)—improvised the September 19 observance of Talk Like a Pirate Day. Mike Kienzler supplied the piratical Lincoln O-77 image.

Fig. 5.72. Many readers will be very surprised to know that throughout the Civil War, New York City was a hotbed of secessionist sympathy. The New-York Historical Society's Lincoln bicentennial exhibition, "Lincoln and New York," demonstrated just that. So did the theme of its poster, *The Most Beloved Leader New York Ever Hated,* with the iconic "Universal Lincoln" image.

The Society also held a series of teacher open houses, featuring seminars on Lincoln and Lincoln's legacy, geared toward elementary, middle-school, and high-school students. These activities were supported by the National Endowment for the Humanities, the New York Council for the Humanities, PBS channel WNET, and several corporate sponsors, foundations, and individuals. The exhibition was named the best exhibit of the year by the Victorian Society, won the prestigious Barondess/Lincoln Award, and received a special commendation from the Lincoln Group of New York.

The exhibition catalog was edited by Harold Holzer. Philip Wilson Publishers released the nearly 300-page hardcover volume on October 27, 2009.

Fig. 5.73. Like John the Baptist pointing the way to Jesus of Nazareth, a carved wood figure of Lincoln heralds the location of the 62-foot-tall fiberglass giant Abe at Lincoln Springs Resort, Illinois (see figure 4.55). The tall Abe, by Bob Edgett, is surrounded at ankle level by pavilions in Abe's Garden, featuring additional carved wooden Lincoln figures. Shown are a few of these.

Fig. 5.74. A variety of outdoor murals greets visitors to Charleston, Illinois. Abraham Lincoln saying goodbye to his stepmother Sarah Bush Lincoln, painted by Glen C. Davies of Urbana, is located at 5th Street and Jackson Avenue, near the Coles County Courthouse. The exact site where the president-elect bid adieu to his beloved stepmother is seven miles south of Charleston, at the Moore Home, now a state historic site.

2009 OCTOBER 15. The U.S. Mint opens the ordering period for the Abraham Lincoln Coin and Chronicles set (a commemorative silver dollar and four commemorative cents). Orders went to a waiting list by the second day, and on October 22 the Mint officially announced a sellout.

2009 OCTOBER 16. A seated statue of a college-age Abraham Lincoln reading a textbook is dedicated at Illinois College, Jacksonville, Illinois. Although Lincoln never attended the college, he later served as its lawyer, professor Paul Spalding noted. "We have lots of connections to Lincoln, but we didn't have one thing on campus that expressed this visually," Spalding continued. "It seemed the least we could do is have a statue of Lincoln when he was in his 20s, looking toward the future," he added. The bronze by sculptors Steven Maxon and Doris Park depicts Lincoln seated on a low landscape wall, and also has a dog by his side. The statue was a gift to the school from Spalding, his wife and family, and college president Axel Steuer and

his wife and family. During the dedication ceremony, the college also bestowed an honorary degree on Lincoln posthumously.[4]

2009 NOVEMBER. The Smithsonian Institution Research Information System (SIRIS) recognizes in its database the existence and location of Vincent (Vincente) Aderente's *Portrait of Abraham Lincoln,* oil on canvas, 24 by 20 inches, which appeared on the cover of *Abraham Lincoln: The Image of His Greatness,* by the present author. The work resides in the author's collection.

2009 NOVEMBER 3. Random House's luxury Knopf imprint releases *Lincoln Life Size,* a beautiful book with images of Abraham Lincoln's face (from the collection of the heirs to the Meserve inheritance) blown up to life size. Coauthored by Philip B. Kunhardt III, Peter W. Kunhardt, and Peter W. Kunhardt Jr., the book puts the reader as close as possible to what Lincoln's contemporaries saw frozen by the lens of time.

Fig. 5.75. The U.S. Mint supplied collectors with a "Coins & Chronicles" set of Lincoln collector coins in 2009 *(a)*. It included a Proof Lincoln Bicentennial silver dollar *(b)* and four Proof cents struck in the coin's original composition of 95% copper. The Mint web site opened for orders for the set at high noon October 15, 2009, and went to a waiting list by 6 pm the following day. A certificate of authenticity over the signature of Mint Director Ed Moy certified the exacting standards used at the Mint on these numismatic issues. The impressive silver-dollar obverse was designed by Justin Kunz and engraved by Don Everhart. The reverse, with 43 words from Lincoln's Gettysburg Address, was designed and engraved by Phebe Hemphill.

Fig. 5.76. This writer sampled a goodly amount of Lincoln bicentennial schlock sold as trinkets, mementoes, and branded items of more or less utility. Quite frankly, this splendid wooden tag that was attached to one of the pieces, also sold as a laser-engraved ornament, is a better souvenir than the costly item to which it was originally attached.

Fig. 5.77. The December 2009 issue of *Illinois College Quarterly* featured a new man-about-campus, a 20ish Abe Lincoln and his faithful pooch, by sculptors Seven Maxon and Doris Park, which had been dedicated at the Jacksonville, Illinois, school in mid-October. We just know that low brick wall on which Abe sits is going to be the venue for all sorts of "Kodak moments."

2009 NOVEMBER 12. The fourth Lincoln Bicentennial cent, reflecting his presidency, is launched at Henry Shrady's U.S. Grant Memorial adjacent to the U.S. Capitol in Washington, D.C.

2009 NOVEMBER 14. A winning bidder pays $7,100 for a 2007 Razor Presidential Poker autograph cut card of Abraham Lincoln, with an encapsulated signature, "Lincoln."

2009 NOVEMBER 19. On the 146th anniversary of Abraham Lincoln's Gettysburg Address, the National Military Park's latest Lincoln statue is dedicated. Near the figure of Lincoln seated on a bench with his right hand placed on his top hat, located on Lincoln Statue Plaza, a bronze plaque mounted on a large rock gives the text of his revered comments. The statue is by Ivan Schwartz.

2009 DECEMBER 4. A youthful Abe Lincoln statue, wearing an overcoat and holding a sheaf of papers as if he had just come out of the Clark County Courthouse in Marshall, Illinois, is unveiled on the courthouse lawn. Lincoln practiced law in the courthouse. Sculptor Bill Wolfe, the high-school band, and city officials participated in the ceremony. The life-size six-foot-four-inch statue, a gift of Gerald and Jean Forsythe, is mounted on a black granite base.

Every sculptor hopes to someday be commissioned to craft a Lincoln sculpture, Wolfe said. "That's the cream of the crop, right there. . . . It's quite an honor. . . . Anytime anyone thinks about Illinois, they think about Lincoln." "We're really very pleased for the community," the donors told the local newspaper after the dedication ceremony.

Fig. 5.78. The fourth and final of the Lincoln Bicentennial cents debuted November 12 at the U.S. Grant Memorial, adjacent to the U.S. Capitol in Washington, DC. The cent was supposed to symbolize Lincoln's presidency, and the powers-that-be selected Susan Gamble's design of the unfinished U.S. Capitol dome, as engraved by Joseph F. Menna. Only a few hundred attended the rainy official ceremony, but others participated at alternate indoor coin-exchange sites. In the view of this writer, this is the least successful of the 2009 Lincoln cent designs because it fails to put Abe in the milieu. This design could as easily represent the election of Schuyler Colfax as speaker of the U.S. House of Representatives in 1862!

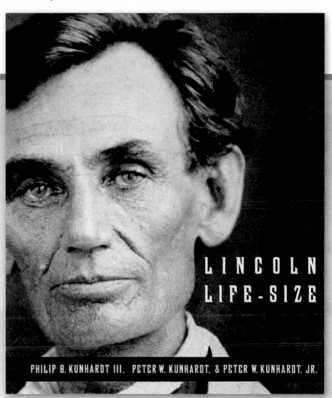

Fig. 5.79. The "first family of Lincoln photography," the Kunhardts, who are heirs to the collection and legacy assembled by pioneer Lincoln and Civil War photo collector Frederick Hill Meserve, had a second Lincoln bicentennial book published in 2009. Appearing in November, also a Knopf luxury imprint, *Lincoln Life-Size* gives readers the opportunity to stare Abraham Lincoln straight in the face, as his contemporaries saw him.

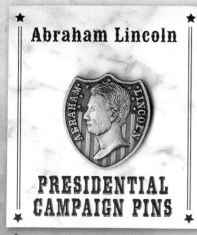

Fig. 5.80. Concessionaires stock many of the Lincoln historical sites. A series of commemorative facsimile "campaign pins" was a really nice, fairly inexpensive product. Unfortunately the spade-shaped 1860 pin *(a)* that crudely mimics Sullivan AL 1860-27 (King 22), manufactured by S.D. Childs of Chicago, is not marked COPY in accord with the Hobby Protection Act (Pub. L. 93-167) of 1973, which was passed to control imitation and replica political and numismatic items like this. The pin is marked on reverse "© 2007 DMA," and an information card on which the item was affixed identifies DMA as DesignMasters.com. The faux 1860 ferrotype copied after AL 1860-101 *(b)* with its red-white-and-blue ribbon is also not marked COPY. The cards also state each piece was a "Reproduction from Ford's Theatre National Historic Site Collection." Other pins from this series were also observed. One would hope the National Parks Service would police its vendors, but apparently not, as these were found for sale at a Lincoln National Historic Site.

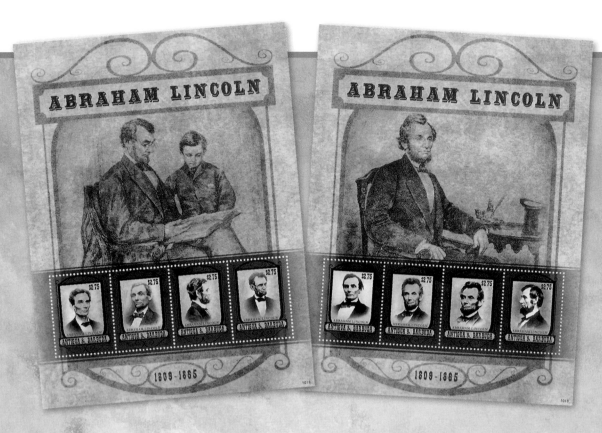

Fig. 5.81. Antigua and Barbuda issued two four-stamp Lincoln series in 2009 in souvenir-sheet form. The eight portraits shown on as many stamps are among the least traditionally popular of the Lincoln images.

Fig. 5.82. Artist Joel Iskowitz created this Lincoln at the Cooper Union original art *(a)*, and the mockup of how it would have looked as a souvenir sheet for Liberia, in 2009 *(b)*.

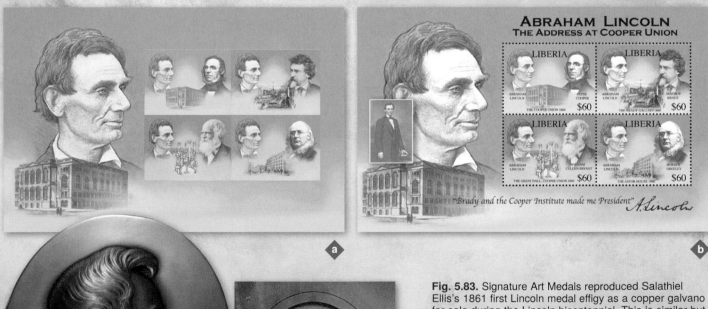

Fig. 5.83. Signature Art Medals reproduced Salathiel Ellis's 1861 first Lincoln medal effigy as a copper galvano for sale during the Lincoln bicentennial. This is similar but not the same design as used a year later on the Indian Peace medal (Julian IP-38) that Ellis did for the State Department. This first design is the item I noted in *Abraham Lincoln: The Image of His Greatness* as "1861 April 19 Minnesota sculptor Salathiel Ellis files for a patent for a medallion of President Lincoln. It is unclear if this piece was issued." While we still don't know if Ellis's first design from which this galvano was made was reproduced, I did discover a contemporary circa-1861 carte de visite of the model from which this galvano was reproduced. Unfortunately, I discovered the card too late for *The Image of His Greatness*—but then, that's what sequels are for, and here it is. This could very well be the image that Ellis used for copyright purposes. The Indian Peace medal was struck from an 1862 design for which Ellis received a design patent in August 1862.

Fig. 5.84. Additional nations climbing on the Lincoln bicentennial bandwagon in 2009 and early 2010 included St. Vincent and the Grenadines (a), Liberia (b), Sierra Leone (c), Tuvalu (d), S. Tome e Principe (e), Papua New Guinea (f), the Republic of Guinea (g), and Antigua and Barbuda (h).

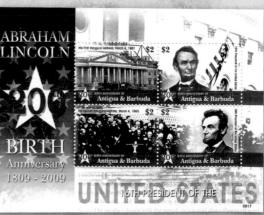

2009 DECEMBER 7. Signature Art Medals announces a new lithograph commemorating the "Inspiration of the Lincoln Cent," by artist Joel Iskowitz. It shows President Teddy Roosevelt sitting for portrait sketches by artist and cent-designer Victor David Brenner, in preparation for creation of the Panama Canal Service Medal. The imaginary illustration depicts Brenner's rectangular Lincoln plaque on a nearby table, and a beardless image of Lincoln, among natural-science artifacts in the study of the president's Sagamore Hill home.

2009 DECEMBER 14. Illinois commercial and residential developer Steve Horve wins Springfield's 12-story Abraham Lincoln Hotel and Conference Center at a foreclosure auction, for a bid of $6.5 million. The hotel billed itself as "The city's most popular event facility." The new owner of the 316-room hotel said: "I don't know how they didn't make money here." Horve noted that the hotel at 701 E. Adams Street "is a high-profile facility in the heart of a state capital."

2009 DECEMBER 18. "Great Moments with Mr. Lincoln" returns to Disneyland's Main Street Opera House after a nearly five-year absence. The show was somewhat abbreviated from its former format, but offered a "brand-new Mr. Lincoln animatronic which fea-

tures a fully electric head," according to a spokesperson for the Magic Kingdom. The new figure displays a more realistic range of facial expressions than the earlier hydraulic model. The theater lobby displays a bronze sculpture of the original Mr. Lincoln head by Blaine Gibson, patterned after the 1860 life mask by Leonard Volk. The display permits the visually impaired to "experience Lincoln's facial features," Disney officials affirm. Lincoln's voice is provided by actor Royal Dano. An outside lobby display shows a five-minute video loop of Dano's portrayal of Lincoln on the old *Omnibus* TV show. As is usual nowadays, a 4-1/2-minute YouTube video of the performance is available on the Internet for those who can't make it to California.

2009 DECEMBER 27. A Topps Heritage "American Heroes" card with a cut signature and a bit of wood from Abraham Lincoln's home sells for $7,700 on eBay, after failing to sell on a "Buy It Now" price of $19, 995. Topps also issued a similar card with a cut signature and without the wood shaving.

2010 JANUARY 6. Heritage Auctions sells an AU-58 1943 bronze Lincoln cent off-planchet error struck at the Philadelphia Mint

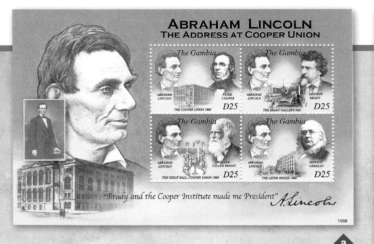

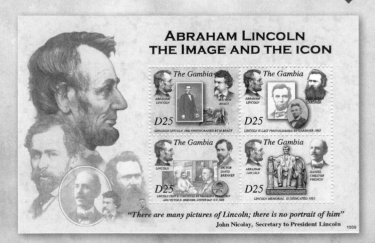

Fig. 5.85. Gambia utilized two designs by artist Joel Iskowitz for stamps and souvenir sheets utilizing his beardless Cooper Union concept *(a)* and bearded profile *(b; see figure 4.261b)*. Both sheets are mini history lessons, as the artist packs his designs with colleagues and contributors to the legacy of Abraham Lincoln's image. Also you will note that one of the stamps reproduces the artist's rich, large lithograph print that he did for Signature Art Medals, entitled *Inspiration of the Lincoln Cent (c)*. "I am very proud of my design," the artist told the present writer.

Fig. 5.86. The Abraham Lincoln Hotel and Conference Center, Springfield, Illinois, changed hands near the end of the Lincoln bicentennial year. "I don't know how they didn't make money here," the new owner said of his predecessors.

(fewer than 20 known) for $218,500 at its Florida United Numismatists auction, a 1943 cent on a Curacao 25-cent planchet for $14,950, and a 1944 cent struck on a zinc-plated steel planchet for

$25,300. Perhaps due to the buzz surrounding these sales, a second 1943 bronze cent came up for sale a month later. This VF-35 1943-S example (one of seven known to exist) brought $207,000 in Heritage's February 3 Long Beach auction.

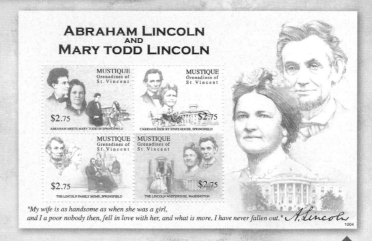

Fig. 5.87. Although announced in February, it took Walt Disney most of the rest of the Lincoln bicentennial year to gear up for its renewal of "Great Moments with Mr. Lincoln." After a nearly five-year absence, the program returned to Disneyland's Main Street Opera House a week before Christmas (a). The new head is said to reproduce more natural facial expressions, when the sound track recorded by actor Royal Dano requires them. The driver's license–like pin celebrates the return of Mr. Lincoln to Walt's palace. In late 2010, the original animatronic Abe was scheduled to go on display, too, in a new exhibit, "Walt Disney: One Man's Dream" (b).

Fig. 5.88. Artist Fred Perry shared this unpublished *Time Lincoln* artwork for this Lincoln book. Lincoln's chiseled features in this futuristic scene present a thoroughly modern take on the familiar Lincoln cent profile.

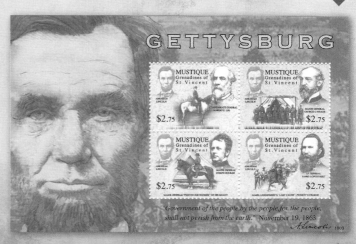

Fig. 5.89. Mustique adopted two of Joel Iskowitz's Lincoln Bicentennial designs—his domestic Abraham and Mary Todd Lincoln theme (a), and the artist's Lincoln and the generals theme (b)—for four-stamp souvenir sheets issued in 2010.

2010 JANUARY 8. Lincoln bicentennial co-chairman Harold Holzer reviews designs for Signature Art Medals' Lincoln Cooper Union plaque with designer, artist Joel Iskowitz, and company cofounder Mark Schlepphorst, at Holzer's office in the Metropolitan Museum. Holzer is senior vice president for external relations of the famed museum.

2010 JANUARY 12. The first 2010 Lincoln cents with the Shield reverse—set to debut February 11 at the Abraham Lincoln Presidential Library and Museum in Springfield, Illinois—show up in circulation a month early in Puerto Rico.

In accordance with Public Law 109-145, the U.S. Mint coined the new 2010 Lincoln cent with a redesigned reverse, by Mint Artistic Infusion Program Associate Designer Lyndall Bass, whose initials (LB) appear in small letters at the left near the bottom of the design. The reverse features a union shield with a scroll draped across it bearing the inscription E PLURIBUS UNUM ("out of many, one").

"The 13 vertical stripes of the shield represent the states joined in one compact union to support the federal government, repre-sented by the horizontal bar above. The union shield, which dates back to the 1780s, was used widely during the Civil War. In addition, the shield device is featured on frescoes throughout the halls of the U.S. Capitol Building by Constantino Brumidi, artist of the Capitol during Lincoln's presidency," a Mint spokesperson said. Bass's design was engraved by U.S. Mint sculptor-engraver Joseph F. Menna, whose initials (JFM) appear at the right near the bottom of the design.

The coin's obverse retains the original 1909 design by Victor David Brenner.

2010 JANUARY 15. Mint figures reveal the extent of the "penny malaise" engulfing the minting and circulation of the 2009 Lincoln Bicentennial cents. Mintage of the four Lincoln 2009 cents, combined, was less than half as many cents as were coined the previous year. Experts blamed this shortfall on the lagging economy and an oversupply of previously minted cents. The Mint said it struck "only" 2.35 billion cents with bicentennial reverses, compared to 5.41 billion with the predecessor Lincoln Memorial design in 2008.

Fig. 5.90. After the flap over the symbolism for the reunited Union for the 2010 new Lincoln cent reverse died down, the U.S. Mint settled on a shield design by Mint Artistic Infusion Program associate designer Lyndall Bass. The coin was engraved by Mint sculptor/engraver Joseph F. Menna. Then the Mint was faced with another snafu when cents set for public release in February at the Abraham Lincoln Presidential Library and Museum showed up a month earlier in Puerto Rico. You could buy one of these cents on eBay before you could queue up for the official exchange, and some pre-release cents were certified by postmarks and other measures.

Fig. 5.91. If we were of a mind to do so, we could fill this book with scouting patches, medals, and other memorabilia from Lincoln pilgrimages and other activities. Since that's not the purpose of this volume, we'll just show these two attractive Lincoln-themed patches celebrating the scouting centennial. Note, "LHC" on the amoeba-shaped patch stands for Lincoln Heritage Council.

2010 JANUARY. Topps, the venerable trading-card company, releases a mini-series of Chicago Cubs players cards that have digitally altered images of Abraham Lincoln looking on from the background. These variant cards include players Milton Bradley, Tyler Colvin, Ryan Dempster, and Jeff Samaradzija. The most spectacular of the five and the first one discovered by hobbyists was the Bradley card, where Lincoln's face and "Baseball Abe" appear on the outfield wall. Lincoln's other appearances were more subtle, in the shadows or out of prime focus. On Dempster's card, Abe is his shortstop. Lincoln is in the dugout on Colvin's card, and in the stands on Samaradzija's and legendary great Rogers Hornsby's cards.

The company preceded release of the cards with a news release asking "Who would Abe Lincoln's favorite team be?" Bulletin boards lit up with speculation by eager collectors. One perceptive exchange on beta.beckett.com followed this line: "Lincoln strikes me as a Chicago Cubs guy," to which another poster remarked, "Yeah . . . considering the last time they won the WS [World Series] was during his presidency." "It was all in fun," Topps director of product development Clay Luraschi said. "Since Chicago is in the 'Land of Lincoln,' we thought it would be fun to throw Abe on a couple of Cubs cards." These revelations prompted the *Abe Lincoln Observer* blogger to report, "If Abe would have lived to be 190, he would have been one frustrated Cubs fan. But then, why should he be any different than all the rest of them?" This follows a 20-year trend among card makers to insert "premium" or special "chase cards" into packs to encourage word-of-mouth and boost sales. Hobby periodicals, such as those of this author's former employer Beckett Publications, label such cards "SP" (for Short Print), indicating some degree of scarcity. Collectors greeted these new Abe variations enthusiastically. Initially their selling price on eBay approached $150—each!

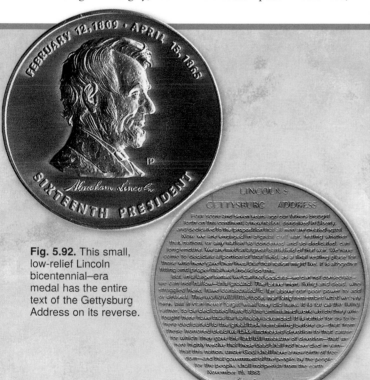

Fig. **5.92.** This small, low-relief Lincoln bicentennial–era medal has the entire text of the Gettysburg Address on its reverse.

Fig. **5.93.** A unique memorial within an historic site is the half-mile-long "Trail of Twelve Stones" at the Lincoln Boyhood National Memorial, Lincoln City, Indiana, which recounts events of Lincoln's life. Juniors could take the hike, answer a test, and qualify for prizes. As a favor the park attendant stamped a grandpa's trail guide, too—but no prize, alas.

Fig. **5.94.** Topps Card Co. didn't have enough fun peddling Abraham Lincoln cards in 2009, so it extended its sales horizon and amazed fans with several cards showing Lincoln was a fan of the Chicago Cubs. Can you spot Abe in these cards of present and vintage Cubbies?

2010 January 21. In a special ceremony, the Smithsonian Institution formally acquires Food Stamp Program coupons and related materials from the U.S. Department of Agriculture's Food and Nutrition Service. Among the items were specimens and plate proofs of a hitherto unknown Lincoln $20 food coupon, with unprecedented portraits based on the "Gettysburg Lincoln" photograph by private contractors American Banknote Company and Banknote Corporation of America. According to researcher Peter Huntoon, who examined the materials at the National Numismatic Collection in early 2010, Banknote Corporation of America "earned one distinction in December 1993, and that was to design and complete a die that won the competition for a proposed $20 bicentennial (type) coupon." The high-value $20 denomination would have been new to the series, which since 1970 had only included lower-value 50¢, $1, $2, $5, and $10 notes, as a precaution against fraudulent use of the coupons.

"Although their design was approved for use," Huntoon continued, "the $20s never went into production because electronic benefit transfer cards were coming into widespread use. Program administrators decided that implementation of the new denomination would not be cost effective." He reported this in the May/June 2011 issue of the Society of Paper Money Collectors' bimonthly journal *Paper Money*.

According to Richard Doty, the Smithsonian's senior curator of numismatics, the materials, long housed at the Agriculture Department, were headed for disposal until the previous summer, when two museum volunteers alerted curators and helped arrange for the most significant items—nearly 200 in all—to be transferred and preserved. The items include food coupons, booklets, proof sheets, early artists' designs and printer's plates. "What we did, effectively, was go over and cherrypick the collection," Doty said. "We wanted to tell a story with it." Now that story can include the approved but unissued Lincoln $20 food coupon design shown in figures 4.123a–c.

2010 January 21. Cowan's Auctions offers John Bigelow's personal copy of the French gold medal presented to Mary Todd Lincoln, with accompanying paperwork, in an American History auction. Bigelow was U.S. consul in Paris, who received the original gold medal on behalf of the U.S. government and Mrs. Lincoln in Paris and transmitted it to Secretary of State William H. Seward. The price for the bronze medal, including a leatherette case with satin lining, broken clasp, and a Parisian carte de visite of Bigelow, with some bumps to the medal, was a "steal" at only $587.50, considering its provenance.

2010 January 30. The Sundance Film Festival awards its Jury Prize in Short Filmmaking to *Drunk History: Douglass and Lincoln,* a 6:23 short film written by Derek Waters and directed by Jeremy Konner. It stars Don Cheadle and Will Ferrell in the title roles of abolitionist Frederick Douglass and emancipator Abraham Lincoln, respectively, and Zooey Deschanel as Mary Todd Lincoln. The film is narrated by an inebriated "Jen Kirkman," who—the introduction explains—has just consumed two bottles of wine and is more concerned about her weight and lack of a tan, her legs, and the location of her underpants than getting her spiel right, since after all it is a "drunk history." The film was subsequently posted on YouTube, May 25, 2010, and rang up 365,000 hits.

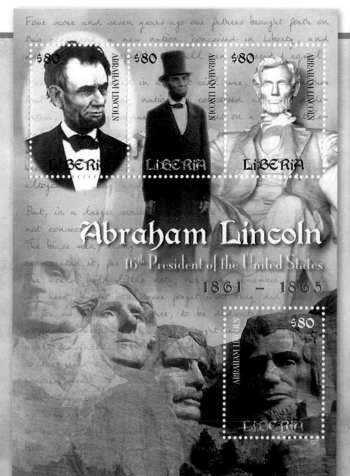

Fig. 5.95. St. Kitts's budget and/or sales aspirations were small in the Lincoln collector market. Its 2010 souvenir sheet of four Lincoln stamps offered a single common design, although French's statue makes a fine one at that.

Fig. 5.96. In 2010 Liberia issued another four-stamp souvenir sheet of Lincoln stamps.

Fig. 5.97. Comic actor Will Ferrell's turn as Old Abe took the Jury Prize in Short Filmmaking at the Sundance Film Festival in January 2010. Titled *Drunk History: Douglass and Lincoln,* the film was written by Derek Waters and directed by Jeremy Konner. Don Cheadle starred as Frederick Douglass, and Zooey Deschanel as Mary Todd Lincoln.

Fig. 5.98. Lincoln stamps were a niche for topical philatelists before the bicentennial, but even the best efforts of me and my colleague, Angus Lincoln in Great Britain, could barely keep up with the profusion of new issues that kept coming as the Civil War sesquicentennial neared. Here are some more from Sierra Leone *(a),* Grenada *(b),* the Gambia *(c),* Rwanda *(d),* St. Tome e Principe *(e),* Palau *(f),* and the Republic of Guinea *(g).*

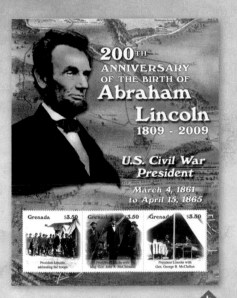

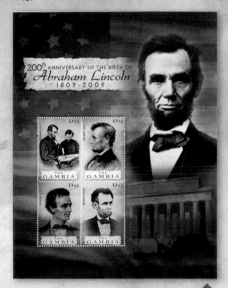

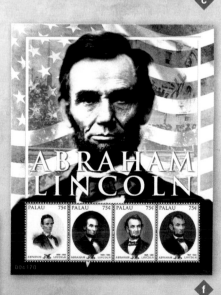

2010 FEBRUARY. "Global Tribute: Abraham Lincoln's Integrity and Dedication to Human Rights Made Him a Popular Subject on Many Countries' Commemoratives," by Fred Reed, on Lincoln-portrait foreign coins, appears in the American Numismatic Association monthly journal *The Numismatist.*

2010 FEBRUARY. Just missing the Abraham Lincoln bicentennial, the Topps card company issues Garbage Pail Kids "flashback cards" with stickers depicting a hideous juvenile caricature of Lincoln holding a "slaybill" with three bullet holes in his forehead and top hat. The art was produced by John Pound. To increase the cards' desirability with their fans, they were issued in pink-, yellow-, green-, silver- and gold-bordered parallel series, with varieties in two types (66a cards are titled "Baby Abbie" and 66b cards are titled "Lincoln Park").

According to card insiders on the Internet, these "cool" cards were among those not formerly released in the 1980s because their objectionable content was deemed too violent in the past. The Lincoln cards are prized by fanatics as unpublished "lost GPK artwork," originally created for the fifth GPK series "with images for card 66 finding itself on a test sheet before being pulled. . . . However the same image was originally conceived for the 3rd series of GPK, with the character having only one bullet hole through the top hat," according to a web site devoted to the series.[5] The fifth proof film for the original art showed up on a web site with the asking price of more than $8,000.

FEBRUARY 6, 2010. Participants in the annual Lincoln Society in Peekskill celebration learn that sculptor Richard Masloski's life-size bronze sculpture recalling Abraham Lincoln's February 19, 1861, 120-word speech at Peekskill (New York) during his train transit to his inauguration in Washington, D.C., has been cast at the Polich Foundry, and will soon be installed and dedicated at the city's new Lincoln Train Depot Museum. The museum, still under construction as of late 2011, is located at the original site of Lincoln's speech. Masloski depicts Lincoln standing holding onto a railing with his right hand, while his left hand clutches the lapel of his overcoat. The event included a Lincoln and Civil War painting exhibit by Paul R. Martin III. Receiving the group's Lincoln Legacy Award was banquet speaker, author Philip Kunhardt III.

FEBRUARY 10, 2010. U.S. Mint Director Edmund Moy holds a "penny forum" in Springfield, Illinois, on the evening before the official public release of the new Lincoln cent with the shield replacing the Lincoln Memorial on reverse. The forum "is an opportunity for coin enthusiasts to meet United States Mint Director Moy and ask questions about U.S. coinage," Mint publicity said.

FEBRUARY 10, 2010. C.A. Brown Foundry, Providence, Rhode Island, owner Steve Brown demonstrates the lost-wax casting of Signature Art Medals' Don Everhart Lincoln Cooper Union plaque to Frank Williams, a commissioner of the Lincoln Bicentennial Commission.

FEBRUARY 11, 2010. The new Lincoln "Preservation of the Union" one-cent coin is officially launched at the Abraham Lincoln Presidential Library and Museum, Springfield, Illinois.

FEBRUARY 12, 2010. Bob Lenz becomes president of the Abraham Lincoln Association.

FEBRUARY 14, 2010. A 1996 Lincoln cent overstruck on a previously struck Roosevelt dime sells for $857.98 on eBay. Fourteen bidders chased the PCGS MS-64 item from 99¢ to its closing price.

Fig. 5.99. Apparently nothing is sacred to satire . . . eventually. The card art for an unissued Garbage Pail Kids sticker card showing Abraham Lincoln shot through the head was created in the 1980s but abandoned then as too gross. But by 2010, when this sticker card was issued in a great profusion of varieties to entice collectors to chase them all, it was just the thing for six-year-olds to plaster on their lunchboxes, I guess.

Fig. 5.100. Graphic designer Jonathan Benning designed this adorable Babe Lincoln onesie, complete with beard, in July 2010. Here it is modeled exuberantly by his young niece Olivia. Her photo is used in this volume by permission of Olivia's folks, Rachel and David Benning.

FEBRUARY 2010. Fred Perry creates the first in his "Time Lincoln" series for Antarctic Press, delivering Lincoln from his assassination by John Wilkes Booth and launching him as a super hero, the supreme righter of wrongs to combat villainous dictators like Stalin and Hitler throughout history. "In his final hour, he lived a lifetime," Perry wrote. A second volume would come out in June.

Perry advised this author in August 2010 that the conclusion to the series would not be reached until Booth shows up to assassinate Lincoln in the Ford's Theatre box but finds that the president is *already* dead. "Booth did come to kill Lincoln but his shot didn't kill Lincoln; he was already dead when he fired. His pre-adventure self is pushed out of time by his post-adventure self who is in the middle of his final battle," Perry said.[6]

FEBRUARY 25, 2010. Philip B. Kunhardt III delivers the first of three lectures at the Bruce Museum, Greenwich, Connecticut, in connection with a four-month-long exhibit of approximately 70 life-size images of Abraham Lincoln's face based on original images in the Meserve-Kunhardt collection. The exhibit paralleled a book entitled *Lincoln, Life Sized*. Additional lectures included talks by Eric Foner on March 11 and Harold Holzer on April 22. The exhibition, also titled "Lincoln, Life Size," closed June 6.

FEBRUARY 25, 2010. "Great Evenings in the Great Hall, Abraham Lincoln at the Cooper Union" celebrates the 150th anniversary of "Lincoln's Right Makes Might speech that propelled Lincoln to the Presidency" at New York City's Cooper Union. The theatrical program included period music and several readers combining to perform Lincoln's famous speech in the same room and from the same lectern that launched him to the Republican nomination for president in 1860. The event was the concluding program in the Great Evenings in the Great Hall series that commenced in April 2009 as a commemoration of the Cooper Union's sesquicentennial. Narrator was noted Lincoln scholar Harold Holzer, author of *Lincoln at Cooper Union*. Speech selections were performed by former New York governor Mario Cuomo and actors Kathleen Chalfant, André DeShields, Richard Dreyfuss, and Stephen Lang. The event was free to the public and filmed for later broadcast on CSPAN's Book TV.

FEBRUARY 25, 2010. Signature Art Medals presents one of the first castings of Don Everhart's Lincoln Cooper Union plaque to officials of the educational institution, during ceremonies celebrating the anniversary of Abraham Lincoln's famous speech there. During the event, the plaque "lay on the very podium from which Lincoln delivered his address almost 150 years ago," according to company principal Mark Schlepphorst. This 7-3/8-inch plaque is *the* outstanding medallic tribute to the Lincoln bicentennial, in the present author's view. It weighs approximately three pounds. The obverse was sculpted by Everhart from the three-quarters-length "Cooper Union photograph" of Lincoln taken the day of his famous speech in 1860. The plaque's reverse, also sculpted by Everhart (from a design by Joel Iskowitz), is based on contemporary illustrations in *Leslie's Illustrated*. It shows Lincoln standing on a podium, and the large crowd on hand to hear the speech rendered in a highly detailed, personal way. Additionally, special selective patination has darkened Lincoln's coat in a realistic manner. (See figure 5.103.)

Fig. 5.101. Fred Perry's graphic-novel series *Time Lincoln* took Abe into various points in time to alter the course of history. The cover art on this novel was by Brian Denham.

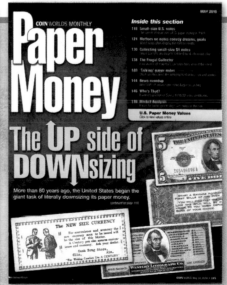
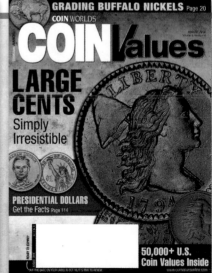

Fig. 5.102. *Paper Money Values* (a) highlighted the changeover to small-size U.S. currency in the publication's May 2010 issue. In summer 2010, its sister publication *Coin Values* (b) had a cover story on Presidential dollars, featuring the soon-to-be-released Lincoln dollar by Don Everhart.

Fig. 5.103. The Lincoln bicentennial, third aspect, Illinois cent team of Joel Iskowitz and Don Everhart combined to produce the finest medallic tribute of the Lincoln bicentennial for client Signature Art Medals. The obverse *(a)* is based on the Mathew Brady Cooper Union three-quarters-length photograph (O-17). Iskowitz's reverse design sketch *(b)* shows Lincoln on a platform speaking to a packed house, with many identifiable individuals, based on contemporary sources. Everhart sculpted both sides *(c)*. As can be seen, a special patination was applied to Lincoln's coat to make it more realistic.

2010 SPRING. Topps Card Company issues a T206 card (SR#42) for 1950s–1960s New York Yankees great centerfielder Mickey Mantle. The card also had a Lincoln four-cent black profile stamp (Scott 1282). The trouble with the pairing is that the card highlights Mantle's 1963 season stats, and the stamp's first day of issue was November 19, 1965.

2010 MARCH 2. Grand Central Publishing publishes Seth Grahame-Smith's *Abraham Lincoln: Vampire Hunter,* a horror-fantasy work seeking to capitalize on the current craze for bloodsuckers and the perennial interest in the national savior, based on the literary conceit of having derived from Abe's secret diaries. Its back-cover photo depicts a blood-stained Lincoln grasping an axe and a severed head. Grahame-Smith's book rates four stars (out of five) by reviewers on Amazon.com, an indication of the controversy it has raised, but showing evidently that more readers give it thumbs-up than thumbs-down.

A two-minute promotional video for the book by the Hachette Book Group, starring Michael Krebs as Old Abe, had drawn more than 430,000 hits on YouTube after its pre-book publication posting on February 25, 2010. According to LincolnBuff blogger Ann Tracy Mueller, "I suspect that any way we can get people enthused about Lincoln is good. And, if it takes a work like this one to reach an audience who really hadn't thought much about our sixteenth president, then that's okay." On the other hand, Richard Norton Smith, the founding director of the Abraham Lincoln Presidential Library and Museum in Springfield, Illinois, denounced the fiction of having Honest Abe portrayed as an axe-swinging slayer of the undead as "the most inane idea imaginable" and "a true bastardization of the Lincoln story."

The present author had raised a similar caution in his Abraham Lincoln Book Shop virtual book signing on the Internet, in April 2009, pointing out how off-handedly modern artists embroider the Lincoln icon nowadays. (Readers can go to virtualbooksigning. net to see exactly what I had to say nearly a year before the book's publication.)

Despite reservations in some quarters, *Vampire Hunter* landed at number 4 in its first week on the *New York Times* hardcover-fiction best-seller list. Its author was invited to make a March presentation at the Abraham Lincoln Presidential Library and Museum, and the museum offered an "exclusive" *AL: VH* t-shirt. On April 16, 2010, the vampire-book author took a turn at a solo virtual book-signing interview with Daniel Weinberg at Abraham Lincoln Book Shop in Chicago. The movie version came out June 22, 2012.

2010 MARCH 4. A Matte Proof-67+ RB 1909 V.D.B. Lincoln cent sells for more than $200,000, according to Laura Sperber of Legend Numismatics, who represented the coin's owner. Sperber noted: "Yes, the coin we had displayed and always said was not for sale got sold. While we are not releasing any specific price, we will confirm the coin set a world record above $200,000." That makes it the most valuable regular-issue Lincoln cent, she added. Representing the buyer, "the McCullagh Collection," was Brian Wagner, Milton, Washington. (See figure 5.105.)

2010 MARCH 25. Historian John J. Pitney Jr. debunks a supposed quotation that President Barack Obama attributed to Abraham Lincoln in a recent pep talk to House Democrats, just prior to consideration of the massive health-care bill, in an essay on the NPR web site. Pitney wrote: "In his remarks to Democratic lawmakers the day before they passed the health care bill, President Obama said: 'I was tooling through some of the writings of some previous presidents, and I came upon this quote by Abraham Lincoln: 'I am not bound to win, but I'm bound to be true. I'm not bound to succeed, but I'm bound to live up to what light I have.' The Lincoln quotation "was stirring. It was also bogus. There is no documentary evidence that Lincoln ever said any such thing," Pitney wrote. "It is understandable that many of these cases involve Lincoln. By quoting the Great Emancipator's words, public figures try to capture some of his magic for themselves. The temptation to touch the hem of his garment is so great that they sometimes get sloppy about fact-checking and grab for a knockoff," he scolded.[7]

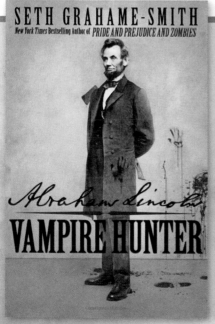

Fig. 5.104. Author Seth Grahame-Smith's *Abraham Lincoln, Vampire Hunter (a, b)* took the *New York Times* bestseller list by storm, promoting a vision of an axe-wielding murderous fellow inhabiting the soul of the man we'd believed was a compassionate Abraham Lincoln. Lincoln impersonator / actor Michael Krebs appeared in a promotional video for Grahame-Smith's novel *(c)*.

a

b

c

2010 MARCH 27. Fred Reed discusses his award-winning book *Abraham Lincoln: The Image of His Greatness* at the American Numismatic Association's National Money Show held at the Fort Worth Convention Center. Reed's well-attended 50-minute "Numismatic Theatre" PowerPoint presentation was filmed by David Lisot for CoinTelevision.com and video DVDs are available on their web site.

2010 APRIL 12. First Presbyterian Church, Springfield, Illinois, which houses the Lincoln family's church pew, dedicates installation of Thomas Trimborn's Lincoln portrait, *Lonely Leader,* during its Sunday morning service. The painting will hang permanently adjacent to the pew which the Lincoln's rented for nine years before leaving Springfield. Church records reveal Mary Todd Lincoln as a member of the church. *Lonely Leader* was previously published in Trimborn's 2005 book, *Encounters With Lincoln: Images and Words.* The artist attended the event.

2010 APRIL 14. On YouTube, a pair of animated messages entitled *Abe Speaks,* emanating from Dallas Mavericks guard Deshawn Stevenson's Abraham Lincoln throat tattoo, trash-talk opponents and urge Maverick fans to stand up and "make some noise." Stevenson, who sports multiple and varied tattoos over much of his visible upper body, got the Gettysburg Lincoln portrait tattooed below his chin whiskers while he was with the Washington Wizards. On February 13, 2010, he was traded to the Dallas Mavericks.

2010 APRIL 21. Newsweek.com publishes plastic surgeon Dr. David Hidalgo's analysis of the kinds of facelift procedures currency re-designers might have performed on our presidents if they had been cosmetic surgeons. Comparing the old $5 portrait with the two new $5 portraits (both based ironically on photographs taken only minutes apart on the same day), he writes: "President Lincoln has been treated to a full-face laser peel that has removed all blemishes and has rejuvenated his sun-damaged skin [this is the effect of a softer engraving technique with no dotted lines]. He has been treated to a haircut and an expert dye job that leaves only a few wisps of distinguished gray color. His beard has been trimmed to give him a less disheveled look. His eyebrows have been waxed to remove errant hairs. He has gotten small cheek implants that he did not need (it would have been better to fill in his hollow cheeks with fat or injectables). His naso-labial folds are a bit softer, suggesting the addition of injectable fillers. Surgically, he has been treated to a subtle rhinoplasty that retains a masculine look. The nose is straightened and the aged, drooping tip raised. He has had his lower-eyelid bags surgically removed, effectively eliminating a tired look." The doctor's comments and drawings were published in the May 3, 2010, print version of the publication as its "Back Story."

2010 APRIL 23. Thousands of Boy Scouts from across the Midwest stage the 65th annual Lincoln Pilgrimage, a three-day event at the Illinois State Fairgrounds in Springfield, the Lincoln tomb, and the Lincoln Trail Hike from New Salem, Illinois, to the Lincoln tomb, and a parade to the Old State Capitol in Springfield.

2010 MAY 7. The *Belfast Telegraph* reveals that actor Liam Neeson is "fed up waiting" for Steven Spielberg's stalled film based on the Doris Kearns Goodwin Lincoln biography to get underway. Neeson revealed he had spent five years "living with it" (the possibility of playing Abraham Lincoln on screen), had read numerous books on Lincoln, and had walked Lincoln's steps visiting locations where Abe had given famous orations. "I don't know. I think I'm past my sell-by date in my inner soul. It would depend on the script," he told the publication. "So it's either come to the plate and do it or get out of the kitchen. There are other things that I'd be quicker to pursue."[8]

Fig. 5.105. In March 2010 a Matte Proof-67+ Red and Brown 1909 V.D.B. cent reportedly changed hands for more than $200,000, as the highest-selling regular-issue Lincoln cent thus far.

Fig. 5.106. in 2010 *Newsweek* magazine asked a plastic surgeon to discover the softening of Lincoln features on the Thomas Hipschen new large-portrait $5 bills compared to the old-style iconic "Universal Lincoln" $5 bill portrait. This investigation quite simply ignored the fact that the engravings were based on two different photographic likenesses taken the same day. The silly exercise proved as ridiculous as comparing apples to oranges and speculating how one came to be red while the other was orange. For years collectors had complained that modern-issue $5 notes of the old style made Lincoln look older because the Burt portrait on earlier series were printed wet and inked more, so Lincoln's hair and beard did not look so grey. At least that was a comparison of apples.

2010 MAY. "Lincoln at Cooper Union," artist Joel Iskowitz's second lithograph for Signature Art Medals, is announced by the company. This original-concept sketch is very complex. It depicts views of the building, an illustration of Lincoln giving the speech, a carte de visite known as the Cooper Union portrait, another beardless image of Lincoln, and likenesses of Peter Cooper, Mathew Brady, and others. Iskowitz's drawing also appears on a Gambian postage-stamp souvenir sheet.

2010 MAY 29. Cheese carver Troy Landwehr unveils his 640-pound cheddar-cheese facsimile of Daniel Chester French's Lincoln Memorial seated Lincoln sculpture, on the CBS *Early Show* with host Harry Smith. The side of the throne said "Cheez-It" (Landwehr's sponsor). Landwehr told Smith it took him about 40 hours to accomplish his masterpiece. Cheddar is the carver's preferred medium—not too soft, so it doesn't melt, and not so hard that you cannot get a smooth surface to your cut. The unveiling was held the day before the anniversary of the dedication of the Lincoln Memorial in 1922.

2010 MAY 31. A unique 1959-D Lincoln cent mule error, with a Wheat Ears reverse, cleared as a genuine product of the U.S. Mint by the Secret Service, sells for $31,050 in an Ira and Larry Goldberg auction. (See *Abraham Lincoln: The Image of His Greatness,* figure 4.75.)

2010 JUNE. The *Lincoln Herald,* the long-lived journal of Lincoln scholarship published by Lincoln Memorial University, Harrogate, Tennessee, appears in print for the last time as volume 112, number 1, dated Spring 2010.

Subscribers were notified by letter that the journal was being continued as a free online publication. Editor-in-chief Dr. Thomas Turner attempted to put a smiley face on the publication's demise as a printed publication: "The good news for our readers is that due to the huge savings this will produce, the journal will be free. I readily confess that I am old enough to prefer the feel of a book in my hand and that if I had a choice I would still opt for a hard copy edition. However, times change and many journals are now publishing online, so that the *Herald* simply joins a growing trend. By slashing publishing costs, we will also be able to publish more articles in each issue; we have been limited to a very strict page count in recent years. Your editors look forward to the new format, and we pledge to work as hard as we can to maintain the high quality that you have hopefully come to expect from this journal."

Over the century-plus since the journal had commenced as the *Mountain Journal* to provide information on LMU, the publication had become the home for several generations of Lincoln scholars, providing a "Who's who" of Lincoln writers during the period, including briefly near the end the present author. News of the demise of the printed journal seemed to irritate Lincolnphiles. Internet chat rooms buzzed with rumors, including one placed in August that "The *Lincoln Herald* will start printing again. There's a new one being printed now and it's still up in the air if they ever go online. That's still great news, because that's a wonderful publication, and I'm happy to see that it's back in print." Both editor Turner and managing editor Steve Wilson confirmed to the present author that the rumor was untrue, and there were no plans to continue the revered journal in print again. (But see the entry for August 10, 2010.) Additionally, the Abraham Lincoln Library and Museum, located on the campus, deactivated the link to the *Herald* on its "Publications" page. The final issue featured a very interesting, illustrated article by Dr. Mark D. Zimmerman on the history, reproductions, and legacy of Leonard Volk's 1860 plaster life mask of Lincoln.

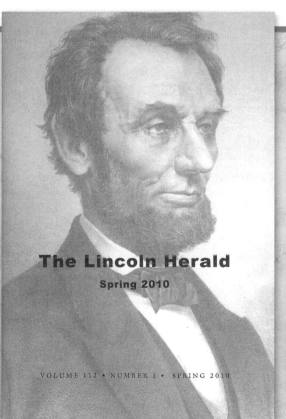

The Lincoln Herald

Spring 2010

VOLUME 112 • NUMBER 1 • SPRING 2010

Fig. 5.107. When Lincoln Memorial University announced that the Spring 2010 issue of its *Lincoln Herald* would be the last print issue of the fabled series, Lincolnphiles everywhere mourned the loss of another vehicle of Lincoln scholarship so soon after the demise of *Lincoln Lore.* After the uproar died down, LMU resumed the print publication.

Fig. 5.108. This July 2010 scout patch has a wonderful embroidered likeness of the iconic " Universal Lincoln" image.

Fig. 5.109. A 2010 Illinois Lincoln Trail Boy Scout patch was given to those completing the 20-mile New Salem to Springfield hike.

2010 June 3. A 1944-D Lincoln cent on a zinc-coated steel planchet brings $60,375 at the Heritage Auctions Long Beach sale.

2010 June 4. Grand Re-Opening Day ceremonies at the refurbished Cuyahoga County Civil War Soldiers' and Sailors' Monument in Public Square, Cleveland, include an address by Harold Holzer. The interior of the sandstone base of this magnificent monument includes a Memorial Room housing architect Levi Tucker Schofield's bronze relief panels. Rising above the base on a 125-foot column of black Quincy stone is a bronze figure of Freedom. In the monument's esplanade are four bronze groupings.

2010 June 8. The Lincoln Home National Historic Site joins Facebook as a means of improving external communication.

2010 June 15. The U.S. Mint suspends selling the three annual 2009 coin sets which include all four of the Lincoln Bicentennial cents, as well as suspending sales of two-roll sets of the Professional Life and Presidency cents.

2010 June 26. Twenty-three seconds into a 30-second GEICO commercial, "Honest" Abe Lincoln answers wife Mary's query whether her new dress makes her backside look big by hemming and hawing and then raising his right hand with thumb and forefinger spread slightly. Mary walks off in a huff. The commercial gets a quarter million hits on YouTube in 48 hours, en route to nearly 450,000 hits (and counting) as of this writing.

2010 June 30. The wooden catafalque originally built to display the mortal remains of Abraham Lincoln lying in state at the U.S. Capitol is employed for public display of the body of the late U.S. senator Robert Byrd (D–West Virginia). The catafalque has been used more than two dozen times for state observances since 1865. It is currently on display in the U.S. Capitol Visitor Center.

2010 July 1. The State of Illinois's example of the original manuscript for Lincoln's Gettysburg Address, one of five known copies in the president's hand, went back on display at the Abraham Lincoln Presidential Library and Museum. The manuscript had been in storage since 2008, allowing it to "rest," according to archivists. The state acquired the manuscript in 1944 from penny contributions by Illinois schoolchildren and a donation by Chicago department-store magnate Marshall Field III.

Fig. 5.110. Lincoln's domestic relationship was put to the test when he was asked by wife Mary whether her dress made her backside look big, and he replied reluctantly by the space between his thumb and forefinger, in a June 2010 GEICO television ad campaign.

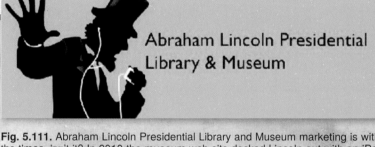

Fig. 5.111. Abraham Lincoln Presidential Library and Museum marketing is with the times, isn't it? In 2010 the museum web site decked Lincoln out with an iPod.

Fig. 5.112. One of this writer's favorite Abraham Lincoln Presidential Library and Museum souvenirs is the official museum premium chocolate bar, packaged for ALPLM by Astor Chocolate. Another favorite is the official ALPLM bottled water, furnished by Alexa Springs, Mount Ida, Arkansas.

Fig. 5.113. Many tourists collect site-specific patches. Some even wear them. This Hodgenville, Kentucky, patch was on sale during the Lincoln bicentennial era.

2010 JULY 4. U.S. ambassador Douglas W. Kmiec narrates Aaron Copland's patriotic classic *A Lincoln Portrait,* performed at Valletta, Malta, as a celebration of America's Independence Day and a tribute to our "common humanity" and "self evident truth."

2010 JULY 16. *New York Times* writer Gia Kourlas complains about the trivializing of Lincoln as a prop. "[O]f late," she wrote, "Lincoln has become a victim of commodification—featured in a GEICO ad and the subject of books like *Abraham Lincoln: Vampire Hunter.* Instead of focusing on what Lincoln stood for—or truly questioning it," such works only contribute "to the static," she concluded.[9]

2010 JULY 22. The Abraham Lincoln Presidential Library and Museum launches *From Out of the Top Hat,* a daily blog by three professional historians sharing "interesting stories and details of his [Lincoln's] life and times." Participants include James Cornelius, Thomas Schwartz, and Richard Wrightman Fox.

2010 AUGUST 1. A close-up of a current-style $5 Federal Reserve Note serves as part of the title sequence of the AMC weekly television drama series *Rubicon.*

2010 AUGUST 2. Political cartoonist Mark Fiore's 1:23 video on slateV.com exposes "Lincolngate," which parses Lincoln's Gettysburg Address irreverently to expose Lincoln's radical pro-gay marriage stance, and declaration that all persons are slaves, with voice characterizations by John Taylor.

2010 AUGUST 2. A Whitman Publishing news release reports, "*Abraham Lincoln: The Image of His Greatness* Earns Third National Literary Award."

2010 AUGUST 10. Randal, the moderator of the Lincoln-Assassination.com bulletin board, breaks the news that the *Lincoln Herald* will resume publication as a print periodical. He posted: "I talked to Mike Burkhimer tonight, and he told me *The Lincoln Herald* will start printing again. There's a new one being printed now and it's still up in the air if they ever go online. That's still great news, because that's a wonderful publication, and I'm happy to see that it's back in print."

2010 AUGUST 11. The off-Broadway musical *Abraham Lincoln's Big, Gay Dance Party* opens at the Acorn Theater, New York City, with a fictive plot, "goofy dance sequences by a stage full of Lincoln lookalikes," and an "overlong and disappointing simplistic production," according to *New York Times* reviewer Charles Isherwood. Set in Menard County, Illinois, it predictably arises from speculations over Lincoln's relationship with his friend Joshua Speed. "There's nothing naughty about my love for Joshua," the tyke portraying Abe announces, to rumblings of dismay in the audience. "It's a natural and beautiful thing. We were in love, just like your mommy and daddy, and we would have gotten married to each other if. . . ." As an adult, President Lincoln regrets that he cannot climb to the top of the Capitol Dome and scream out the name of his beloved to the Heavens. According to the theater critic, "The mystery that makes the show's title such an attention getter—the question of whether Lincoln was gay, which has exercised historians and commentators in recent years—plays no significant role in the proceedings, I'm sorry to say. With or without a kick line of dancing Lincolns, a fiery lecture on the subject from Larry Kramer, a big believer in the gay Abe, might be more entertaining than this well-meaning but overlong and disappointingly simplistic production," he added. On political as well as aesthetic reasons, some of Isherwood's readers vehemently disagreed, calling the production "relevant," "entertaining," and "engaging," while others found it "dumb" and "preachy."

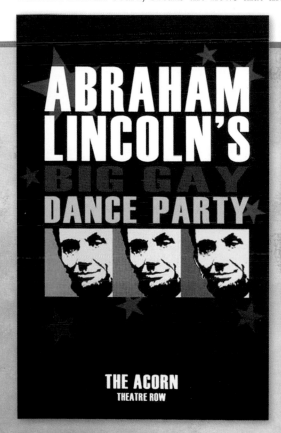

Fig. 5.114. A simple design on another of the inexpensive "Made in China" collector "coins" had two different finishes, coppery and brassy, so the vendor got two sales from some buyers looking for varieties. The designs appear to be computer-generated.

Fig. 5.115. Gay and lesbian groups are only the most recent agenda-driven segments of the Lincoln public to seek Lincoln affinity. The off-Broadway August 2010 musical *Abraham Lincoln's Big, Gay Dance Party* sought to exploit this sentiment, but got cold reviews in mainstream publications like the *New York Times.*

2010 AUGUST 12. The Token and Medal Society board of directors and cataloger Paul Cunningham agree to a plan whereby Cunningham will bring out privately the new revision to King's classic numismatic reference *Lincoln in Numismatics,* originally undertaken on behalf of TAMS by Cunningham, David Schenkman, Kathy Lawrence, and Fred Reed.

2010 AUGUST 12. The Token and Medal Society Mishler Cataloging Honorable Mention Award recognizes *Abraham Lincoln: The Image of His Greatness,* by Fred Reed.

2010 AUGUST 14. Anna Marie Wooldridge, better known by her performing name of Abbey Lincoln, dies in Manhattan. Singer-composer Wooldridge took her stage name from a symbolic conjoining of Westminster Abbey and Abraham Lincoln in the 1950s, according to her obituary. She had been born August 6, 1930.

2010 AUGUST 18. Illinois conservative candidate for governor, Adam Andrzejewski, creates Super Abe, a comic-strip superhero and righter of wrongs. In his first mission Super Abe, clad in a red-white-and-blue star-and-bar festooned costume, seizes a golden statuette labeled "Illinois Senate Seat" from the hands of Rod Blagojevich and tosses it out a nearby window to a crowd of excited onlookers, shouting "This belongs to the people of Illinois."

2010 AUGUST 20. The theme for the 51st annual Blue Ridge Numismatic Association Convention in Dalton, Georgia, is "Come visit with President Lincoln!" A Lincoln impersonator was in attendance to take pictures with conventiongoers.

2010 AUGUST 28. A massive populist "Restoring Honor" rally at the Lincoln Memorial on the 47th anniversary of Dr. Martin Luther King's "I have a dream" speech featured King's niece Alveda King, Sarah Palin, and Glenn Beck. It filled the National Mall with participants. Organizers said the purpose of the non-political rally was to call America and Americans back to our national core values. Also participating on stage were dozens of pastors, priests, and rabbis, and baseball star Albert Pujols and singer Jo Dee Masina. The rally's poster by Neal Aspinall depicts French's seated Lincoln figure from the Lincoln Memorial and the call "Join us at the steps of the Lincoln Memorial—Washington, D.C." Hundreds of thousands (NBC estimated 300,000) did just that. Proceeds from the event went to the nonprofit Special Operations Warrior Foundation, which provides college scholarships to surviving children of Army, Navy, Air Force, and Marine Corps special-operations personnel killed in combat or training, and emergency funds for families of wounded warriors so they can be bedside during their recovery.

Fig. 5.116. Conservative Illinois gubernatorial candidate Adam Andrzejewski launched the "Suber Abe" created by firebone in August 2010. Like traditional superheroes of comic-book lore, Super Abe is a genuine righter of wrongs.

Fig. 5.117. "Come visit with President Lincoln," the Blue Ridge Numismatic Association advertised for an August 2010 Dalton, Georgia, convention *(a)*. Another numismatic organization with real Lincoln roots, the Illinois Numismatic Association's logo employs a device adapted from the 1918 Lincoln–Illinois Centennial commemorative half dollar *(b)*. Both societies were celebrating their 51st anniversaries in 2010.

Fig. 5.118. Graphic artist Neal Aspinall created this very strong *Restoring Honor* poster for the massive populist rally held on the National Mall at the Lincoln Memorial on August 28, 2010. The event honored the 47th anniversary of Dr. Martin Luther King's "I Have a Dream" call for justice and equality in this country. Dr. King's niece Alveda King, Sarah Palin, Glenn Beck, baseball star Albert Pujols, and singer Jo Dee Messina headlined a program attended by a crowd of 300,000, according to NBC News.

2010 SEPTEMBER 3. The National Park Service reopens the Abraham Lincoln Birthplace National Historic Site Memorial Building following renovations to the century-old structure. The park comprises 116 acres of Thomas Lincoln's Sinking Spring farm outside Hodgenville, Kentucky. An early-19th-century Kentucky cabin inside the granite memorial building (dedicated September 4, 1916) symbolizes the one in which Lincoln was born.

2010 SEPTEMBER 5. A 2,500-pound granite statue modeled after Vinnie Ream's monumental marble sculpture of Abraham Lincoln in the U.S. Capitol is dedicated at the Galesburg, Illinois, Amtrak depot. The larger-than-life-size replica and base stand 11 feet tall, and overall weigh 11,000 pounds.

2010 SEPTEMBER 11. Robert Redford's *The Conspirator,* about the trial of Lincoln conspirator Mary Surratt, debuts at the 35th Toronto International Film Festival with Robin Wright Penn in the role of "a mother accused of aiding her son in the assassination." Gerald Bestrom played Lincoln. The movie debuted on screens nationwide April 15, 2011.

2010 SEPTEMBER 17. *Lincoln Herald* editor-in-chief Dr. Thomas Turner confirms resumption of the publication. He wrote this author in part: "It is true that the *Herald* is resuming hard copy publication. We just released the summer issue and I'm at work on the fall. I don't know whether there will ever be an electronic version. With none of the editors living in Harrogate these decisions are made by the LMU trustees and administration with very little input from the editors." Three days later, as if appointed by a higher power, my copy of the revived publication arrived in my mailbox, together with a cover letter on Abraham Lincoln Library and Museum letterhead over the signatures of Steven Wilson (*Lincoln Herald* editor and assistant director of the Abraham Lincoln Presidential Library and Museum) and Thomas D. Mackie (director of the ALLM). It read, in part: "The longest continuously published Lincoln quarterly in the country is still instituting an on-line component, but recognizing the value of the *Lincoln Herald*'s traditional service; we are continuing its hard-copy format indefinitely." An announcement is expected when the online version becomes available. Still no word as of this writing.

Fig. 5.119. Following the Lincoln bicentennial observance, the National Park Service closed the nearly century-old Memorial Building at the Abraham Lincoln Birthplace National Historic Site. The temple, housing an old Kentucky cabin reminiscent of the one in which Abe Lincoln first saw the light of day, was reopened to visitors in September 2010, following renovations.

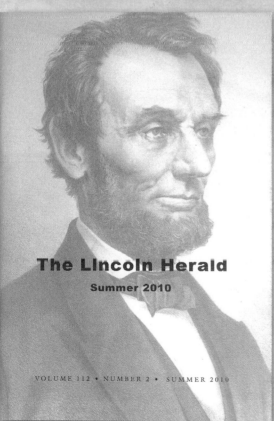

Fig. 5.120. News of the revival of the suspended print edition of Lincoln Memorial University's venerable *Lincoln Herald* lit up chat rooms, and in late September 2010 a summer issue of the magazine reached the mailboxes of formerly suspended subscribers, including this author. The return of the journal was a reason for Lincoln post-bicentennial cheer among Lincolnphiles.

Fig. 5.121 In September 2010 Robert Redford's dramatic motion picture *The Conspirator* debuted at the Toronto Film Festival with Gerland Bestrom in the role of Abraham Lincoln. The film considers the trial of Mary Surratt, played by Robin Wright Penn.

2010 September 23. *Numismatic News,* a tabloid hobby weekly, breaks the news that a 1943-D Lincoln cent made with the pre-war bronze alloy had brought $1.7 million in a private transaction between two anonymous parties. "This only-known example of a 1943 cent struck in bronze from Denver is graded MS-64 Brown by the Professional Coin Grading Service," according to the account. Purchasing and reselling the coin to an anonymous Southwestern business executive was Laura Sperber, president of Legend Numismatics. Acting as agent for the anonymous seller was Andy Skrabalak, owner of Angel Dee's Coins and Collectibles. Skrabalak says the prior owner "donated it to a charitable organization so they could sell it with all of the proceeds going to the charity."

"The 1943-D bronze cent is the most valuable cent in the world, and it took four years of aggressive negotiations with the coin's owner until he agreed to sell it," according to *Numismatic News.* The new owner is reputed to be the only collector to ever own a complete set of Philadelphia, Denver, and San Francisco 1943 bronze cents and 1944 steel cents, said Sperber. The transaction also included a 1944 Philadelphia steel cent that went for $250,000 and

a 1942 experimental cent struck in tin that was priced at $50,000, bringing the transaction total to $2 million. Sperber said the new owner of the famous 1943 and 1944 errors would display his set at the Florida United Numismatists (FUN) show in January 2011.[10]

2010 September 25. Krause Publications's Numismaster web site headlines its feature story: "Part 8: Victor Brennan [sic] and the Lincoln Cent"—such is the fading of fame.

2010 September 30. This was the deadline for the second annual Dollar ReDe$ign project competition. Entries included graphic new takes on the Lincoln image as proposals for a more mod-looking currency for this country. The annual contest, staged on the Internet by creative consultant Richard Smith, commenced in 2009. "The Dollar ReDe$ign Project hopes to bring about change for everyone. We want to re-brand the U.S. Dollar, rebuild financial confidence and revive our failing economy," Smith said. "[T]he Euro, looks so sparky in comparison it seems the only clear way to revive this global recession is to re-brand and redesign. Why not? It seems to work for everyone else," he added.

Fig. 5.122. Talk about buzz. The sale of this unique 1943 Denver Mint Lincoln cent, struck on a bronze (instead of a regular zinc-plated steel) planchet, sold for a reported $1.7 million, exciting numismatists and even the mainstream press. The coin is graded MS-64 by the Professional Coin Grading Service. Proceeds from the sale went to a charitable organization.

Fig. 5.123. After a successful kickoff in 2009, Internet creative consultant Richard Smith staged a second Dollar ReDe$ign project in fall 2010. Unrestrained by the practicalities of actually issuing a currency and securing it from vitiation by counterfeiters, the designers' Lincoln-themed notes demonstrated tremendous graphic appeal. Shown are designs produced by Reid Collier and Evan Cotter *(a)*, Mark Gartland *(b)*, Micah Perez *(c)*, and Karen McAniff *(d)*. Do you have favorites?

2010 September 30. A 20th-century gold restrike of the 1862-dated Abraham Lincoln Indian Peace medal (Julian IP-38), graded AU (About Uncirculated), brings $43,125 (including buyer's premium) in the Stack's Philadelphia Americana Sale. Ex–Louis Eliasberg Sr., the gold medal was one of 15 Lincoln gold medals that Eliasberg (who by the mid-1950s had formed the only complete collection of U.S. regular-issue coins ever assembled) owned, framed in a velvet-lined leather box. All the other medals from the boxed "set" were also offered individually, and according to a source on the auction floor during the sale, they too were purchased by the buyer of this medal, a phone bidder (#504), thus keeping the "set" together for a while longer. (See figure 3.256.)

The cataloger of this piece was fairly effusive about the 7.58-plus troy ounce gold medal: "One of the most impressive and medallically important pieces to have ever been coined from Indian Peace medal dies at the United States Mint. In the entire history of the Indian Peace medals. . . . we have never seen, nor heard of, another specimen from any of those dies coined in gold. That this piece may be the only gold example from an entire popularly collected genre of United States medals makes it not just distinctive, but of historic statue." The announcement of the sale of this medal evoked mixed reactions. Some historical-medals collectors grumbled that it wasn't original, that it was, in fact, a modern vanity piece. "I would *not* picture, much less glorify, the Eliasberg gold 76-millimeter Lincoln IPM," one told the present author. It is being "promoted as the greatest Lincoln medal ever struck . . . [but] I regard it as just bullion value as do [others, names withheld]. It's a mid-20th century 'cockamamie' (to use John J. Ford's terminology) bullion strike done at the behest of either Virgil Brand or Col. Green from modern dies. It has no historical value at all. If I had it," said the collector, who owns a great many U.S. historical medals of great significance, "I'd melt it." The cataloger speculated that the gold Lincoln Indian Peace medal was indeed struck to the order of Virgil Brand or a similar major collector, but indicated that it was early in the 20th century, suggesting that it was struck around the time of the Lincoln birth centennial.

The provenance of the complete "set" is from Judson Brenner, to "Mr. Chapman [Henry or S. H. Chapman] of Philadelphia," to T. James Clarke, to Eliasberg Sr. The "set" was purchased entire by Eliasberg in 1945 from New York City dealer Morton Stack for $5,000. The "set" was estimated to be worth $60,000 by Benjamin Stack in 1974, but only $12,000 in 1989 by Harvey Stack. In 1990, according to the auction description, dealer Q. David Bowers suggested to Louis Eliasberg Jr. "that such a set is impossible to value and that it would be advantageous to donate the set to the ANA, ANS, or Smithsonian." On sale individually, the 15 lots, the case, papers, photographs, etc., aggregated $125,177.50 (including buyer's premium). More than half of that was totaled by this medal and a gold strike of George T. Morgan's 1886 Lincoln Presidential medal (Julian PR-12), which realized $21,800 including premium. The gold IP-38 is shown as figure 1.36, and the gold PR-12 as figure 2.103a.

2010 October 14. The exhibition "Lincoln's Cabinet at the Crossroads of War—A Civil War Sesquicentennial Exhibition," based on Doris Kearns Goodwin's bestselling *Team of Rivals,* opens a 10-month run at the Abraham Lincoln Presidential Library and Museum.

2010 November 5. Disney's Hollywood Studios opens the exhibit "Walt Disney: One Man's Dream," featuring the original Disney animatronic Abraham Lincoln that appeared at the 1964–1965 New York World's Fair "Land of Lincoln" pavilion, according to Disney Parks social media director Thomas Smith.

Fig. 5.124. Additional Lincoln-themed entries in the 2010 Dollar ReDe$ign competition included these fine representatives from Micah Perez *(a)*, Jon Stefaniak *(b)*, Jose Hernandez *(c)*, and Ricardo Cerrone *(d)*. Cerrone is from Rome, Italy. Stefaniak elected to contribute a cash-card design.

2010 NOVEMBER 16. Knopf Books for Young Readers publishes Barack Obama's *Of Thee I Sing: A Letter to My Daughters,* the president's third book. In it Obama tells of 13 "heroes" from our nation's history. He says of Lincoln: "Have I told you that you are part of a family? A man named Abraham Lincoln knew that all of America should work together. He kept our nation one and promised freedom to enslaved sisters and brothers. This man of the people, simple and plain, asked more of our country—that we behave as kin." Incomprehensibly, the accompanying illustration by Loren Long shows Lincoln giving a speech in front of an American flag to an entirely white audience.

2010 NOVEMBER 18. The Abraham Lincoln Presidential dollar is released to circulation through the Federal Reserve Banks.

2010 NOVEMBER 19. The official launch ceremony is held for the Abraham Lincoln Presidential mini-dollar, designed and engraved by Don Everhart, at President Lincoln's Cottage on the grounds of the Armed Forces Retirement Home in Washington, D.C. The date coincided with the 147th anniversary of Lincoln's Gettysburg Address.

The coin's obverse features a facing portrait of Lincoln, modeled on Alexander Gardner's "Gettysburg Lincoln" photograph (O-77) taken in Washington, D.C., on November 8, 1863, just 11 days prior to Lincoln's speech at the dedication of the Pennsylvania battlefield cemetery. The president's name, dates and order of service, and the national motto "In God We Trust" also appear on the coin's obverse. For years U.S. Mint officials stubbornly contended that striking full, facing portraits on coins was impossible, despite other countries' mints successfully doing so—even in the case of Lincoln portraiture on several foreign coins based on the same photographic model that Everhart used. Now that the U.S. Mint has relented on its formerly intransigent policy, Don Everhart is to be commended for providing the American people with a truly stunning interpretation of Lincoln and a wonderful addition to our nation's coining heritage.

2010 NOVEMBER 19. DreamWorks Studio announces that two-time Oscar-winning British actor Daniel Day-Lewis will play Abe Lincoln in Steven Spielberg's stalled movie based on Doris Kearns Goodwin's bestseller, *Team of Rivals.* The screenplay was written by Pulitzer Prize winner Tony Kushner.

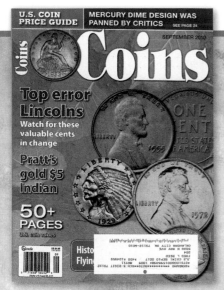

Fig. 5.125. No coin in the world is more collected than the Lincoln cent, which is a gateway drug for many lifelong collectors, including this writer. Some specialize in cent mistakes, and error Lincolns were featured in a September 2010 issue of *COINS* magazine, for which I have written a paper-money column for a number of years.

Fig. 5.126. Fans of the venerable *Lincoln Lore* were delighted to learn that the new custodians of a good portion of the former Lincoln National Life Foundation Lincoln collection resumed publication of the periodical under the joint auspices of the Allen County Public Library and the Friends of the Lincoln Collection of Indiana. Eschewing the pretentions of a slick magazine, the publication returned to its humble but strong roots offering up insight and informatino in an inexpensive newletter format.

Fig. 5.127. Signature Art Medals unveiled this unique Abraham Lincoln plaque at the ANA World's Fair of Money in Boston in August 2010. Engraved by master engraver Ron Landis, the obverse depicts Lincoln's first inauguration (*a*), and the reverse an archaic rendering of the Great Seal of the United States (*b*). R. LANDIS MMX is inscribed in tiny lettering at the bottom of the reverse.

2010 DECEMBER 2. This was the scheduled release date for the U.S. Mint's Presidential Spouse $10 commemorative coin for Mary Todd Lincoln. The obverse portrait of the .9999 fine 1/2-ounce gold coin was designed and sculpted by Phebe Hemphill. The very attractive reverse, showing Mary visiting wounded soldiers, is the design of Joel Iskowitz, as executed by Hemphill. A similar Mary Lincoln design appears on a companion U.S. Mint bronze medal, to provide an item of modest price for collectors.

2010 DECEMBER 23. This was the scheduled release date for the U.S. Mint's set comprising an Abraham Lincoln Presidential dollar and a Mary Todd Lincoln Presidential Spouse medal.

2010 DECEMBER 30. The U.S. Mint Abraham Lincoln dollar-coin cover is released on its scheduled date.

2011 FEBRUARY. Kicking off its salute to the Civil War sesquicentennial, the Abraham Lincoln Presidential Library and Museum debuts a traveling exhibit, "Abraham Lincoln: Self-Made in America." The exhibit includes seven free-standing learning stations, designed for public spaces, libraries, historical societies, and other educational and cultural institutions. Reproductions of artifacts from the Louise and Barry Taper Collection and other holdings from the ALPLM are included in the display to illustrate Lincoln's rise from humble beginnings to the pinnacle of human achievements.

2011 APRIL 2. Fred Reed speaks about his Lincoln books, research, and collection of Lincolniana at the Allen County Public Library, Fort Wayne, Indiana, as part of the Central States Numismatic Society–Old Fort Coin Club Educational Seminar. The world-class Allen County Library became the repository for much of the Lincoln National Life Foundation Lincoln Museum collections. The Library and the Friends of Lincoln collection resumed publication of *Lincoln Lore*.

2012 FEBRUARY. The Ford's Theatre Center for Education and Leadership opens across from famous Ford's Theatre and next door to the Petersen House, where Abraham Lincoln died. The facility complements the newly renovated Ford's Theatre Museum by exploring Lincoln's legacy. Construction of the $25 million facility began in July 2010, a partnership between the Ford's Theatre Society and the National Park Service. Its exhibits are nontraditional, including a three-story "tower of books," described as "a sculpture that will stack replicas of actual works atop one another to highlight how much has been written about Lincoln. Elsewhere, the center will explore how Lincoln has been portrayed or used in popular culture, with Lincoln Logs and commemorative coins among the possible attractions."[11] This definitely sounds like the kind of museum a reader fond of the present volume will enjoy!

Fig. 5.128. Do-it-yourselfer Jen Yates publicized her method of constructing penny-art tabletops on the Internet in 2010. Shown is Jen working on a desktop of her own. Her excellently designed desk features bending cents around the rounded fore-edge of the table top.

Fig. 5.130. Any Lincoln pilgrimage, and even this book, must come to an end. But Lincoln excitement won't. Lincoln imagery will continue in a vibrant and unpredictable way.

Fig. 5.129. The golden brass Abraham Lincoln Presidential mini-dollar coin released by the U.S. Mint to circulation in November 2010 was engraved by Don Everhart. Everhart's portrayal of the O-77 Gettysburg Lincoln image, with relief measuring only .0017 inches high is a masterpiece, and completely destroys the Mint's former unreasonable strictures against full-face portraiture on U.S. coinage. Everhart's initials, DE, appear on Lincoln's lapel. Everhart also designed and sculpted the common reverse for the dollar series, but it is particularly appropriate when used for the Lincoln dollar since the original impetus in France for a statue of liberty was to honor the Great Emancipator of a Race, Abraham Lincoln. The companion Mary Todd Lincoln First Spouse $10 .9999 fine half-ounce gold coin and medal, also released in November, is wonderful in its own way, too. Phebe Hemphill's design and intricate engraving on the coin's obverse depict the first lady very favorably. The coin/medal's reverse, designed by Joel Iskowitz, also was sculpted by Hemphill. In Iskowitz's scene, Mary is seen visiting wounded Union soldiers.

⋇ Notes ⋇

Chapter 1

1. "Abraham Lincoln," *Frank Leslie's Illustrated Newspaper,* October 20, 1860, 345, 347.
2. Library of Congress, American Memory, http://memory.loc.gov/mss/mal/maltext/mal015.sgm.
3. Abraham Lincoln, *Collected Works,* ed. Roy P. Basler (Brunswick, NJ: Rutgers University Press, 1953–1955), vol. 4, 183–184.
4. Lincoln, *Collected Works,* vol. 4, 334; Abraham Lincoln, Memorandum on New York Patronage, April 15, 1861, Abraham Lincoln Papers, Library of Congress, reel 15, http://memory.loc.gov/cgi-bin/query/r?ammem/mal:@field(DOCID+@lit(d0949300)).
5. Library of Congress, American Memory, http://memory.loc.gov/mss/mal/maltext/mal015.sgm.
6. Harold Holzer, *Lincoln President-Elect: Abraham Lincoln and the Great Secession Winter of 1860* (New York: Simon & Schuster, 2008), 187–188.
7. 37th Cong., 2nd sess. (July 5, 1862), 528.
8. *"Going Home to Vote": Speeches of S.P. Chase, Secretary of the Treasury, During His Visit to Ohio, With His Speeches at Indianapolis, and at the Mass Meeting in Baltimore, October, 1863* (Washington, D.C.: W.H. Moore, 1863), 25.
9. Fred H. Hackett, "The Schools of San Francisco," *The Californian,* June 1892, 294.
10. John Williams to Abraham Lincoln, in Lincoln, *Collected Works,* vol. 7, 316.
11. Abraham Lincoln to John Williams, April 25, 1864. In Lincoln, *Collected Works,* vol. 7, 316.
12. Daniel Mark Epstein, *Lincoln and Whitman: Parallel Lives in Civil War Washington* (New York: Random House, 2005), 236–237.
13. Eslanda Goode Robeson, *Paul Robeson, Negro* (New York and London: Harper & Brothers, 1930), 12.

Chapter 2

1. John Bigelow to William Seward, June 2, 1865, in *Bigelow, Retrospections of an Active Life,* vol. 3 (New York: Baker & Taylor Co., 1909), 53.
2. Ashmun Institute and Lincoln University Minutes, book 4, 977.
3. *Appleton's Annual Cyclopaedia and Register of Annual Events* (New York: D. Appleton & Co.,1867), 312.
4. "The Lincoln Medal," *American Journal of Numismatics,* May 1866, 5.
5. Osborn H. Oldroyd, *The Lincoln Memorial: Album-Immortelles* (New York: G.W. Carleton & Co., 1882), 76.
6. John Nicolay and John Hay, *Abraham Lincoln: A History,* vol. 10 (New York: The Century Co., 1890), 345.
7. Theodore W. Dimon to Mrs. Lincoln, December 26, 1866; Mrs. Lincoln to Dimon, December 27, 1866; Dimon to William H. Seward, January 7, 1867, U.S. Department of State, *Papers Relating to the Foreign Relations of the United States,* part 1 (Washington, D.C.: Government Printing Office, 1868), 217.

8. *Appleton's' Cyclopaedia,* 1867, 335.
9. U.S. Department of State, *Papers Relating to the Foreign Relations,* 216.
10. Robert P. King, *Lincoln in Numismatics* (N.p.: Token and Medal Society, 1966), 24.
11. "Abraham Lincoln by Sarah Fisher Clampitt Ames," U.S. Senate website, http://www.senate.gov/artandhistory/art/artifact/Sculpture_21_00013.htm.
12. Louis A. Warren, "Earliest Sculptors of the President," *Lincoln Lore,* no. 899 (July 1, 1946).
13. Andrew C. Zabriskie, "Lincoln Medals," *American Journal of Numismatics* (October 1872): 43.
14. Albert Shaw, "Old and New Lincoln Literature," *The American Review of Reviews,* February 1909, 249.
15. Ward H. Lamon, *Life of Abraham Lincoln* (Boston: J.R. Osgood, 1872), 339–340.
16. John Carroll Power, *An History of an Attempt to Steal the Body of Abraham Lincoln* (Springfield: H.W. Rokker, 1890), 31.
17. Greta Elena Couper, "Thomas Ball: 'In the Lap of Giants,'" http://wingedsun.com/books/articles/ball-lap.pdf.
18. Isaac N. Arnold, "Abraham Lincoln," *Proceedings of The Royal Historical Society,* June 16, 1881, 2–3.
19. John Carpenter, "Abe Lincoln Tops Many Polls, Tops a Pole," KTUU.com, November 28, 2009, www.ktuu.com/features/assignmentak/ktuu-abrahamlincolntopsmany-pol-11583507,0,5052218.story.
20. Map 1: Cornish, New Hampshire and the Surrounding Region, National Park Service website, www.nps.gov/history/nr/twhp/wwwlps/lessons/48gaudens/48locate1.htm.
21. John H. Dryfhout, *The Work of August Saint-Gaudens* (Lebanon, NH: University Press of New England, 1982), 158.
22. Isaac N. Arnold, *The Life of Lincoln,* 3rd ed. (Chicago: Jansen, McClurg & Co., 1885), 446–447.
23. William O. Stoddard to John Hay, March 25, 1885, Lincolniana at Brown, Brown University Library, http://dl.lib.brown.edu/lincoln/Lincoln_Hay/writing.html.
24. George G. Evans, *Illustrated History of the United States Mint* (Philadelphia: Author, 1885), 152–153.
25. The date of this dedication was 1887 and *not* 1897 as erroneously stated in the National Park Service brochure for the Lincoln Bicentennial observance at the Saint-Gaudens National Historic Site (http://www.nps.gov/saga/historyculture/upload/Lincoln%20project%20G.pdf).
26. Saint-Gaudens did *not* observe Lincoln beardless at this time, as stated in the National Park Service Lincoln Bicentennial brochure for the Saint-Gaudens National Historic Site.
27. "The Lincoln at Chicago," *Harper's Weekly,* October 22, 1887.
28. Gustave Kobbé, "Presidential Campaign Medals," *Scribner's Magazine,* September 1888, 341–343.

29. Henry C. Whitney, *Life on the Circuit With Lincoln, With Sketches of Generals Grant, Sherman and McClellan, Judge Davis, Leonard Swett, and Other Contemporaries* (Boston: Estes and Lauriat, 1892).
30. Whitney, *Life on the Circuit;* one of the two Library of Congress deposit copies of Whitney's work has been digitized. Near the bottom just above the publisher's imprint it has the familiar oval, purple date stamp "Library of Congress / Copyright / Nov 19 1892 / City of Washington."
31. New York (State) Legislature, Senate. "*Lincoln Spring Company v. State of New York,* Claim for the Appropriation of Land for the State Reservation for Saratoga Springs," Documents of the Senate of the State of New York, vol. 35, 1912, 81ff.
32. Ida M. Tarbell, *The Life of Abraham Lincoln* (New York: Macmillan, 1917), vol. 1, vii.
33. Probably a dog tag–type medal, sold by sutlers, which had Lincoln, McClellan, and an eagle or other patriotic device on the obverse, and a plain back on which the soldier had his name engraved.
34. Wayland Hoyt, "Some Traits and Sayings of Abraham Lincoln," *Abraham Lincoln: Tributes from his Associates* (New York: Thomas Y. Crowell & Co., 1895), 180–181.
35. Shaw, "Old and New Lincoln Literature," 249–250.
36. Andrew Zabriskie, "United States History as Illustrated by Its Political Medals," *ANS Proceedings,* 1896–1897, 41.
37. See Dryfhout 278.
38. See Grant Park National Register #92001075, 1993.
39. Dave Wiegers, personal communication to the author, October 10, 2010.
40. Jonathan Mann and Donald Ackerman, "Later Politicals, G.A.R., Commemoratives, Newspapers," *The Rail Splitter,* sale 10, lot 1087.
41. "Four Portraits of Jurists," *New York Times,* October 23, 1898.
42. Library of Congress, *Catalogue of Copyright Entries Published by Authority of the Acts of Congress of March 3, 1891, and of June 30, 1906, Part 4: Engravings, Cuts, and prints: Chromos and Lithographs; Photographs; Fine Arts* (Washington, D.C.: Government Printing Office, 1907), 220, 7975.
43. "The Augustus Saint-Gaudens Memorial Exhibition," *Bulletin of the Art Institute of Chicago,* July 1909, 12.
44. "Biography and Reminiscences," *The Dial,* December 16, 1907, 424.
45. *Bulletin of the Metropolitan Museum of Art,* February 1908, 20.
46. "The Lounger," *Putnam's Monthly & The Reader,* October 1908, 255.
47. *Publishers Weekly,* December 5, 1908, 1805.
48. Montgomery Schuyler, "A Medallic History of Lincoln," *Putnam's Magazine,* March 1909, 676–681.

49. "Complete List of Accessions November 30 to December 20, 1908," *Bulletin of the Museum of Modern Art,* January 1909, 14.

50. Theodore Roosevelt, "President Roosevelt's Tribute to Lincoln," *The American Review of Reviews,* February 1909, 171.

51. Steven J. Stratford, "Saint-Gaudens," www. us1909.com/367gaudens.html. The model for this stamp was this head on this second monumental bronze statue, and *not* Saint-Gaudens's *Standing Lincoln* figure, as averred by the National Park Service's brochure for the Lincoln Bicentennial for the Saint-Gaudens National Historic Site.

52. Horatio Sheafe Krans, preface to *The Lincoln Tribute Book: Appreciations by Statesmen, Men of Letters, and Poets at Home and Abroad, Together With a Lincoln Centenary Medal From the Second Design Made for the Occasion by (Jules Edouard) Roiné* (New York and London: G.P. Putnam's Sons, 1909), v.

53. Victor David Brenner quoted by Tom LaMarre, "Brenner's Time-Honored Lincoln," *COINS Magazine,* October 2009.

54. James Grant Wilson, "Recollections of Lincoln," *Putnam's Magazine,* February 1909, 524; for details on this medal, see *The Papers of Ulysses S. Grant,* edited by John Y. Simon, vol. 9 (Southern Illinois University Press, 1982), 504, and vol. 14, 131–132.

55. Albert Shaw, "The Lincoln Centennial," *The American Review of Reviews,* February 1909, 175.

56. Ibid., 250.

Chapter 3

1. Historical Society of Pennsylvania, "Notes and Queries," *The Pennsylvania Magazine of History and Biography* 33 (1909), 496–498.

2. *Bulletin of the Metropolitan Museum of Art,* April 1909, 69.

3. Schuyler, "A Medallic History of Lincoln," 679.

4. Ibid., 681.

5. Ibid.

6. "Complete List of Accessions, March 20 to April 20, 1909," *Bulletin of the Metropolitan Museum of Art,* May 1909, 91.

7. *The Bookman: An Illustrated Magazine of Literature and Life* 29 (March–August 1909).

8. "Complete List of Accessions August 20 to October 20, 1909," *Bulletin of the Metropolitan Museum of Art,* November 1909, 212.

9. James B. Gilder, "A French Tribute to Lincoln: The Gold Medal Presented to His Widow in 1866," *Putnam's Magazine* 7 (March 1910), 669.

10. Isidore Konti, "The Lincoln Statue: Believes It Should Be Competed for Openly by Independent Sculptors," *New York Times,* August 1, 1911, 8.

11. Jane Addams, *Twenty Years at Hull-House with Autobiographical Notes* (New York: The Macmillan Co., 1912), 32.

12. Dave Wiegers, personal communication to the author, October 8, 2010.

13. Dave Wiegers, personal communication to the author, October 10, 2010.

14. *Catalogue of the Department of Fine Arts, Panama-Pacific International Exposition* (San Francisco, CA: Wahlgreen Co., 1915).

15. Paul U. Kellogg, "Two New Worlds and a Sculptor's Clay," *The Survey* 35 (October 1915): 19–20; "Plaques and Medallions by Victor David Brenner," *The Survey* 35 (October 1915): 15–18.

16. D. Wayne Johnson, "Abraham Lincoln on Coins, Medals and TokensListed by Their Creators," part 6, *TAMS Journal* 49 (April 2009): 68.

17. Judith A. Rice, "Ida M. Tarbell: A Progressive Look at Lincoln," *Journal of the Abraham Lincoln Association* 19, no. 1 (Winter 1998). Permalink: http://hdl.handle.net/2027/spo.2629860.0019.106.

18. Art Institute of Chicago, *Catalogue of the Twenty-Ninth Annual Exhibition [of] American Oil Paintings and Sculpture, November 2 to December 7, 1916.*

19. Rice, "Ida M. Tarbell."

20. Tarbell, *Life of Abraham Lincoln,* vol. 1, xii–xiii.

21. Mark A. Patrick, *Lincoln Motor Cars: 1920–1942 Photo Archive* (Osceola, WI: Iconografix, 1996), 7.

22. "Abraham Lincoln Statue in Auditorium," Nebraska Memories, www.memories.ne.gov/cdm4/item_viewer.php?CISOROOT=/unk&CISOPTR=12&CISOBOX=1&REC=1.

23. "Lincoln Memorial Room," The Union League, http://www.unionleague.org/event-planning/lincolnmemorial.php#id=13&num=1

24. Charles E. Brown, "Additional Wisconsin Indian Medals," *The Wisconsin Archeologist* 17: 22–23.

25. Wallace H. Cathcart, *Western Reserve Historical Society Director's Report* 98 (1918): 54–55.

26. Smithsonian Institution, *Report on the Progress and Condition of the United States National Museum for the Year Ending June 30, 1918* (Washington, DC: Government Printing Office, 1919), 27, 28.

27. *Journal of the Illinois State Historical Society* 11, no. 1 (April 1918): 439–441.

28. Library of Congress, *Catalog of Copyright Entries,* G 57444, Works of Art, vols. 13–14, 400.

29. David B. Wiegers, "Detroit's Pelzer Lincoln Statue," Abe's Blog Cabin, http://abesblog-cabin.org/tag/pelzer.

30. *Abraham Lincoln* by Freeman Woodcock Thorp (American, 1844–1922), Oil on canvas, 16.5" x 21" sight size. Framed. Heritage Galleries 2008 June Political & General Americana Memorabilia Grand Format Auction #685, June 12, 2008, Lot 70095.

31. Henry Bacon, "The Lincoln Memorial Described by the Architect," *Art & Archaeology* (June 1922): 255.

32. Frank Owen Payne, "Abraham Lincoln as a Theme for Sculptural Art," *Art & Archaeology* (June 1922): 261–268.

33. "History of the American Institute of Architects," American Institute of Architects website, http://www.aia.org/about/history/AIAB028819; see also Barry Cauchon, "The Lincoln Memorial Construction & Dedication Photographs," A Little Touch of History, http://awesometalks.wordpress.com/2009/03/21/the-lincoln-memorial-construction-dedication-photographs/.

34. Thomas L. Elder, "Why Not a Washington or Lincoln Gold Dollar," *The Numismatist* (December 1924): 748–749.

35. "Lincoln Medal Issued," *The Numismatist* 38 (September 1925): 445; Robert W. Rightmire, "Lincoln's Links to the ANA," *The Numismatist* (November 2009): 65.

36. William L. Stidger, "Lincoln in Marble and Bronze," *The Dearborn Independent,* 6.

37. P&A Photos, Washington Bureau, W-211081, September 28, 1929.

38. Underwood & Underwood, "Flannery Statue of Lincoln to be Taken Down," 69235RU, September 26, 1939.

39. Illinois Department of Public Works, *Lincoln Tomb,* 1930, 13–15.

40. Dr. Louis A. Warren, *Lincoln Lore,* October 26, 1931.

41. Lloyd Ostendorf, *Lincoln in Photographs: An Album of Every Known Pose* (Dayton, OH: Morningside Press, 1985), 49.

42. Peter Huntoon, personal communication to Fred Reed, October 17, 2010.

43. A Century of Progress International Exposition, *Official Guide Book of the World's Fair of 1934* (Chicago: The Cuneo Press, 1934), 20.

44. Smithsonian Institution Research Information System, Aderente, Vincent, "Lincoln's Gettysburg Address (painting)," http://siris-artin-ventories.si.edu/ipac20/ipac.jsp?session=12859P7CW0449.10948&profile=ariall&uri=full=3100001~!413646~!50&ri=1&aspect=Browse&menu=search&source=~!siartinventories&ipp=20&spp=20&staffonly=&term=Aderente,+Vincent,+1880-1941,+painter.&index=AUTHOR&uindex=&aspect=Browse&menu=search&ri=1; Glenn King, personal communication to Fred Reed, July 25 and August 20, 2009, and January 29 and September 30, 2010.

45. Both Mr. Abraham Lincoln and Mrs. Abraham Lincoln are listed as honorary life directors of the society in *Methodist Episcopal Church, Missionary Society, Forty-Eighth Annual Report* (New York: 1867), 160.

46. Edgar DeWitt Jones, *Lincoln and the Preachers* (New York: Harper & Bros., 1948), 138–139.

47. *William J. Felchner, "Bing Crosby and Fred Astaire in Irving Berlin's Holiday Inn* (1942), www.bukisa.com/articles/248532_bing-crosby-and-fred-astaire-in-irving-berlins-holiday-inn-1942.

48. Walter Breen, *Walter Breen's Complete Encyclopedia of U.S. and Colonial Coins* (New York: Doubleday, 1988), 231; note that some sources state February 23.

49. National Parks Service, "Lincoln Boyhood National Memorial," www.nps.gov/archive/libo/adhi/adhi3.htm.

50. http://siris-artinventories.si.edu/ipac20/ipac.jsp?session= DP878F1453029.26638&profile=ariall&uri=link=3100006~211331~!3100001~!3100002&aspect=Browse&menu=search&ri=2&source=~!siartinventories&term=Daniels%2C+Elmer+Harland%2C+1905+%2C+sculptor.&index=AUTHOR.

51. Clarendon E. Van Norman, "A Rotarian in Lincoln Land," *The Rotarian* (February 1954): 14.

52. B. Nash, "Hey, Show Some Respect to Lincoln and Borglum," http://abesblogcabin.org/tag/gutzon-borglum.

Chapter 4

1. Abraham Lincoln Association, *The Collected Works of Abraham Lincoln,* ed. Roy P. Basler (Brunswick, NJ: Rutgers University Press, 1953–1955), vol. 3, 84.
2. Julie Lasky, "Medalists: Georg Olden," American Institute of Graphics Design, www.aiga. org/medalist-georgolden.
3. G. Atwood Manley, "Patient Research Discloses Story of Early Artist Salathiel Ellis," *St. Lawrence Plain Dealer,* September 13, 1961.
4. Oliver Hoover, "Baseball as Civilization: Indian Peace Medals under James Buchanan and Abraham Lincoln," *ANS Magazine,* Summer 2010, 56–70.
5. U.S. Post Office Department notice, "Post on Bulletin Board. 4-Cent Lincoln Regular Postage Stamp," U.S. Government Printing Office, 1965, OF-789-703.
6. Len Morse, "Should the 'Knock Knock Joke' Disappear?" Helium.com, http://www. helium.com/items/395175-General.
7. Dana Cooke, "A Different Lincoln," *Maxwell Perspective,* Fall 2009, http://www.maxwell. syr.edu/news.aspx?id=36507226691.
8. Tony Lopez, "Indian Peace Medals," *The Numismatist,* April 2007, 36–47.
9. Kim Bauer, "The Lincoln Legacy in Little-known Illinois Sculpture," Illinois Humanities Council, www.prairie.org/ humanities-resources/detours/lincoln-legacy-little-known-illinois-sculpture.
10. Terry Wyke, "Statue of Abraham Lincoln, Lincoln Square, Manchester," Revealing Histories, www.revealinghistories.org.uk/ the-american-civil-war-and-the-lancashire-cotton-famine/places/statue-of-abraham-lincoln-lincoln-square-manchester.html.
11. Frederick C. Moffatt, *Errant Bronzes: George Grey Barnard's Statues of Abraham Lincoln* (Mississagua, Ontario: Associated University Presses, 1968), 203.
12. Harold Holzer to Barry Cauchon, "An Awesometalk with Harold Holzer, Lincoln Scholar," http://awesometalks.wordpress.

com/an-awesometalk-with-harold-holzer-lincoln-scholar/.
13. Chris Potter, ". . .I'm pretty sure that Honest Abe didn't stop in Wilkinsburg while President. Why a statue of him there?" You Had to Ask, *Pittsburgh City Paper,* June 6, 2005, www. pittsburghcitypaper. ws/gyrobase/ Content?oid=oid%3A28988.
14. B. Nash, "Detroit's Pelzer Lincoln Statue," Abe's Blog Cabin, http://abesblogcabin.org/ tag/pelzer.
15. Hal Smith, personal communication to the author, September 21, 2010.
16. Kirk Savage, *Standing Soldiers, Kneeling Slaves* (Princeton, NJ: Princeton University Press, 1999), 212.
17. William Leigh Hunt, PhotoTiled Pictures homepage, http://web.archive.org/ web/20050217034552/home.earthlink. net/~wlhunt/index.html.
18. Timothy J. Davlin, "State of the Downtown Remarks," January 10, 2005.
19. "Weekly Compilation of Presidential Documents, Feb 21, 2005," http://www.gpo.gov/ fdsys/pkg/WCPD-2005-02-21/html/ WCPD-2005-02-21-Pg233.htm.
20. Alan Derrick, personal communication to the author, September 21, 2010.
21. "Looking for Lincoln" (Abraham Lincoln National Heritage Area brochure), www. lookingforlincoln.com/doc/LFL_VG_Web. pdf; Hal Smith, ALNHA director, personal communication to the author, September 21, 2010.
22. Maury McCoy, personal communication to the author, September 16 and 21, 2010.
23. David Brown, "Lincoln, Unexposed," *Washington Post,* November 8, 2008.
24. Edmund C. Moy, United States Mint Report to Congress on Operations from October 1 through December 31, 2008, First Quarter Fiscal Year 2008, 7, www.usmint.gov/downloads/foia/PEF09Q1.pdf.
25. ApolloSpeaks, "Barack Obama, Lincoln and the Image of Greatness," Newsvine.com, Jan-

uary 21, 2009, http://bstarz700.new.newsvine. com/_news/2009/01/21/2337173-barack-obama-lincoln-and-the-image-of-greatness.

Chapter 5

1. Justin Raimondo, "Obama as Lincoln: Mask and Mirror," *Chronicles* magazine online, http://www.chroniclesmagazine.org/ index. php/2009/02/11/obama-as-lincoln-mask-and-mirror.
2. Jacqueline Trescott, "NGA's Emancipator, In Plaster," *Washington Post,* January 16, 2009.
3. Citabria Stevens, "Photo emerges that might be last taken of Lincoln," CNN.com, http:// edition.cnn.com/2009/US/03/11/lincoln. photograph/index.html.
4. "Lincoln Now Has a Permanent Place on the Hilltop," *Illinois College Quarterly,* December 2009, 3.
5. barrenarren (Aaron J. Booten), "Garbage Pail Kids Flashback Set," http://garbage_pail_ kids.tripod.com/ US_New_Flashback_Series. htm
6. Fred Perry, personal communication to Fred Reed, August 31, 2010.
7. John J. Pitney Jr., "Honest, Mr. President: Abe Never Said It," NPR.org, www.npr.org/ templates/story/story. php?storyId=125169095.
8. "Liam Neeson 'fed up waiting' for his Lincoln film role," *Belfast Telegraph,* www.belfasttelegraph.co.uk/ entertainment/film-tv/news/ liam-neeson-lsquofed-up-waitingrsquo-for-his-lincoln-film-role-14796624. html#ixzz0yalP2blJ.
9. Gia Kourlas, "Following Lincoln Through History," *New York Times,* July 17, 2010.
10. Donn Pearlman, personal communication to Fred Reed, November 9, 2010.
11. "New Center Near Ford's Theater Aims to Expand the Lincoln Experience," *New York Times,* August 20, 2010.

☙ Select Bibliography ❧

For a more complete listing please consult www.WhitmanBooks.com/AbeBook.

Abraham Lincoln Association. *The Abraham Lincoln Quarterly,* various issues.

Abraham Lincoln Association. *Journal of the Abraham Lincoln Association,* Springfield, IL. Champaign: University of Illinois Press, various issues.

Abraham Lincoln Library and Museum, Harrogate, TN, research collections.

Abraham Lincoln Presidential Library & Museum, Springfield, IL, www.alplm.org.

Ackerman, Donald L., ed., and Jonathan H. Mann, publisher. *The Rail Splitter* 1–13 (1995–2010).

American Historical Auctions. *Historical Images and Manuscripts,* June 28, 1998.

American Numismatic Association. *The Numismatist,* various issues.

American Numismatic and Archaeological Society. *American Journal of Numismatics,* various issues.

American Numismatic Society, collections, database.

American Topical Association. *Topical Time,* various issues.

American Topical Association, ATA Americana Unit. *Americana Philatelic News,* various issues.

Anderson, Dwight G. *Abraham Lincoln: The Quest for Immortality.* New York: Alfred A. Knopf, 1982.

Bancroft, George. *Memorial Address on the Life and Character of Abraham Lincoln . . . the 12th of February, 1866.* Washington, D.C.: Government Printing Office, 1866.

Bank Note Reporter, various issues.

Bartlett, D.W. *The Life and Public Services of Hon. Abraham Lincoln . . . [and] a Biographical Sketch of Hon. Hannibal Hamlin,* Authorized edition. New York: A.B. Burdick, 1860.

Boritt, Gabor S., ed. *The Historian's Lincoln: Pseudohistory, Psychohistory, and History.* Urbana and Chicago: University of Illinois Press, 1988.

Boritt, Gabor, ed. *The Historian's Lincoln: Rebuttals, What the University Press Would Not*

Print. Gettysburg, PA: privately printed, 1988, 43 pp., erratum sheet.

Boritt, Gabor, ed. *The Lincoln Enigma.* New York: Oxford University Press, 2001.

Boritt, Gabor S., Mark E. Neely Jr., and Harold Holzer. "The European Image of Abraham Lincoln," *Winterthur Portfolio* 21 (Summer/Autumn 1986): 153–183.

Bowers, Q. David. *A Guide Book of Lincoln Cents.* Atlanta: Whitman Publishing, LLC, 2008.

———. *Obsolete Paper Money Issued by Banks in the United States, 1782–1866.* Atlanta: Whitman Publishing, 2006.

Bowers, Q. David, and David M. Sundman. *100 Greatest American Currency Notes,* Atlanta: Whitman Publishing, LLC, 2006.

Boyd, Andrew. *Memorial Lincoln Bibliography: Being an Account of Books, Eulogies, Sermons, Portraits, Engravings, Medals, etc.* Albany, NY: Andrew Boyd, Directory Publisher, 1870.

Breen, Walter. *Walter Breen's Complete Encyclopedia of U.S. and Colonial Coins.* New York: Doubleday, 1988.

Bullard, F. Lauriston. *Lincoln in Marble and Bronze.* A publication of The Abraham Lincoln Association, Springfield, Illinois. New Brunswick, NJ: Rutgers University Press, 1952.

Burdette, Roger W. *Renaissance of American Coinage, 1909–1915.* Great Falls, VA: Seneca Mill Press, 2007.

Carnegie, Dale. *Lincoln the Unknown.* New York: Pocket Books, 1932, 1952.

Carpenter, F.B. *Six Months at the White House With Abraham Lincoln: The Story of a Picture.* New York: Hurd and Houghton, 1867.

Chambliss, Carlson R. *U.S. Paper Money Guide and Handbook.* Port Clinton, OH: BNR Press, 1999.

Chandler, Robert J. "San Francisco: The Lincoln Monument That Was," *The Rail Splitter* 7, no. 1–2 (Summer/Fall 2001): 22–23.

Chicago Evening Journal, 1861–1865. Christie's, New York. Various sales catalogs, 1990–2007.

Cincinnati Daily Enquirer, 1861–1865.

Civil War Token Society. *Journal of the Civil War Token Society* (also *Copperhead Courier*), 1967–present.

Craughwell, Thomas J. *Stealing Lincoln's Body.* Cambridge, MA: Harvard University Press, 2007.

Cuhaj, George, ed. *Standard Catalog of United States Paper Money,* 25th ed. Iola, WI: Krause Publications, 2006.

Culver, Virginia and Chester L. Krause. *Guidebook of Franklin Mint Issues, 1965–1973.* Iola, WI: Krause Publications, 1974.

Cuomo, Mario M. *Why Lincoln Matters Today More Than Ever.* New York: Harcourt, Inc., 2004.

Dauer, Edward A. and Joanne C. Dauer. *American History as Seen Through Currency.* Fort Lauderdale, FL: printed privately, 2003.

DeLorey, Thomas K. *Thomas L. Elder: A Catalogue of His Tokens and Medals,* offprint from June and July 1980 articles in *The Numismatist,* card covers, 26 pages.

Dennett, Tyler, ed. *Lincoln and the Civil War in the Diaries and Letters of John Hay.* New York: Da Capo Press, Inc., 1939, 1988.

Deutsch, Kenneth L., and Joseph R. Fornieri, eds. *Lincoln's American Dream: Clashing Political Perspectives.* Washington, D.C.: Potomac Books, 2005.

DiLorenzo, Thomas J. *The Real Lincoln: A New Look at Abraham Lincoln, His Agenda, and an Unnecessary War.* Roseville, CA: Prima Publishing, 2002.

Donald, David, ed. *Inside Lincoln's Cabinet: The Civil War Diaries of Salmon P. Chase.* New York: Longmans, Green & Co., 1954.

Donald, David Herbert. *Lincoln.* New York: Touchstone Books, 1995.

Doty, Richard. *America's Money, America's Story: A Comprehensive Chronicle of American Numismatic History.* Iola, WI: Krause Publications, 1998.

Edison, Hank. "What Would Lincoln Do?" Common Dreams News Center, September 25, 2007, www.commondreams.org.

Fairbanks, Eugene F., comp. *Abraham Lincoln Sculpture Created by Avard T. Fairbanks.* Bellingham, WA: Fairbanks Art and Books, 2002.

Ferguson, Andrew. *Land of Lincoln: Adventures in Abe's America.* New York: Atlantic Monthly Press, 2007.

Fischer, Roger A. *American Political Ribbons and Ribbon Badges, 1825–1981.* Lincoln, MA: Quarterman Publications, 1985.

Fite, Gilbert C. and Jim E. Reese. *An Economic History of the United States.* Boston: Houghton Mifflin, 1959.

Frank Leslie's Illustrated Weekly, 1860–1865.

Friedberg, Arthur L., and Ira S. Friedberg. *A Guide Book of United States Paper Money.* Atlanta: Whitman Publishing, LLC, 2005.

———. *Paper Money of the United States,* 20th ed. Clifton, NJ: The Coin and Currency Institute, 2010 (and various editions).

Friedberg, Milton R. *The Encyclopedia of United States Fractional & Postal Currency.* Rockville Centre, NY: Numismatic and Antiquarian Service Corporation of America, 1978.

Fuld, George, and Melvin Fuld. *U.S. Civil War Store Cards.* N.p.: Civil War Token ociety, 1982.

———. *Patriotic Civil War Tokens,* 4th ed. Iola, WI: Krause Publications and Civil War Token Society, 1982.

Freundlich, A.L. *The Sculpture of James Earle Fraser.* N.p.: Universal Publishers, 2001.

Gilfillan, Jas. *Annual Report on the State of the Finances,* December 7, 1881.Washington, D.C.: Government Printing Office, 1881.

Goode, James M. *The Outdoor Sculpture of Washington, D.C.: A Comprehensive Historical Guide.* Washington, D.C.: Smithsonian Institution Press, 1974.

Grant, Robert W. *The Handbook of Civil War Patriotic Envelopes and Postal History,* vol. 1. Hanover, MA: printed privately, 1977.

Halliday, E.M. "Carving the American Colossus," *American Heritage* 28 (June 1977): 19–27.

Hamilton, Charles and Lloyd Ostendorf. *Lincoln in Photographs: An Album of Every Known Pose.* Dayton, OH: Morningside Press, 1985.

Harper's Weekly, 1860–1865, and various issues thereafter.

Harkness, David J. "Lincoln on Stage, Screen, and Radio," *Lincoln Herald* 7 (March 1941): 15–18.

Harris, Gordon L. *New York State Scrip and Private Issues.* N.p.: printed privately, 2001.

Hatcher, James B., ed. *Scott Specialized Catalogue of United States Stamps,* 75th ed. New York: Scott Publishing Co., 1978.

Haxby, James A. *Standard Catalog of United States Obsolete Bank Notes, 1782–1866,* 4 vols. Iola, WI: Krause Publications, 1988.

Hepburn, A. Barton. *A History of Coinage and Currency in the United States and the Perennial Contest for Sound Money.* New York: The Macmillan Co., 1903.

———. *A History of Currency in the United States.* New York: The Macmillan Company, 1924.

Herndon, William H. and Jesse William Weik. *Herndon's Lincoln: The True Story of a Great Life,* 3 vols. Springfield, IL: The Herndon's Lincoln Publishing Co., 1921.

Hessler, Gene. *The Engraver's Line: An Encyclopedia of Paper Money & Postage Stamp Art.* Port Clinton, OH: BNR Press, 1993.

———. *An Illustrated History of U.S. Loans, 1775–1898.* Port Clinton, OH: BNR Press, 1988.

———. *U.S. Essay, Proof and Specimen Notes.* Port Clinton, OH: BNR Press, 1988.

Hessler, Gene, and Carlson Chambliss. *The Comprehensive Catalog of U.S. Paper Money,* 7th ed. Port Clinton, OH: 2006.

Hewitt, Robert. *The Lincoln Centennial Medal . . .* New York: G.P. Putnam's Sons / The Knickerbocker Press, 1908.

Hill, Frederick Trevor. "The Lincoln-Douglas Debates, Fifty Years After," *The Century Magazine* 77 (November 1908): 3–19.

Hoffman, John. "Lincoln Essay Contests, Lincoln Medal, and the Commercialization of Lincoln," *Journal of the Abraham Lincoln Association* 24 (Summer 2003): 36ff.

Hogan, Jackie. Lincoln, Inc., *Selling the Sixteenth President in Contemporary America.* Lanham, MD: Rowan Littlefield, 2011.

Holzer, Harold, ed. *Abraham Lincoln Portrayed in the Collections of the Indiana Historical Society,* compiled by Emily Castle and Barbara Quigley. Indianapolis: Indiana Historical Society Press, 2006.

Holzer, Harold. *Lincoln at Cooper Union: The Speech That Made Abraham Lincoln President.* New York: Simon & Schuster Paperbacks, 2004.

———. *Washington and Lincoln Portrayed: National Icons in Popular Prints.* Jefferson, NC: McFarland & Co., Inc., 1993.

Holzer, Harold and Craig L. Symonds. *New York Times Complete Civil War, 1861–1865.* New York: Black Dog & Leventhal Publishers, Inc., 2010.

Holzer, Harold and Mark E. Neely Jr. *Mine Eyes Have Seen the Glory: The Civil War in Art.* New York: Orion Books, 1993.

Holzer, Harold, Gabor Boritt, and Mark Neely. *Changing the Lincoln Image.* Fort Wayne, IN: Louis A. Warren Lincoln Library and Museum, 1985.

———. *The Lincoln Image: Abraham Lincoln and the Popular Print.* New York: Charles Scribner's Sons, 1984.

Homren, Wayne. "Reed Promotes New Lincoln Portrait for U.S. $5 Bill," *E-Sylum,* vol. IX, November 19, 2006.

Illinois Watch Company. *The Book of A. Lincoln Watches.* Springfield, IL: Illinois Watch Co., 1924.

Jeffrey, Gary, and Kate Petty. *Graphic Nonfiction: Abraham Lincoln, the Life of America's Sixteenth President.* New York: Rosen Publishing Group, 2005.

Jones, Malcolm. "Who Was More Important: Lincoln or Darwin?" *Newsweek* 112 (July 7, 2008), pp. 30–34.

Julian, R[obert] W. *Medals of the United States Mint: The First Century, 1792–1892.* El Cajon, CA: Token and Medal Society, 1977.

Julian, R[obert] W., and Ernest E. Keusch. *Medals of the United States Assay Commission, 1860–1977.* Lake Mary, FL: Token and Medal Society, 1989.

Katz, D. Mark. *Witness to an Era: The Life and Photographs of Alexander Gardner.* New York: Viking, 1991.

King, Robert P. *Lincoln in Numismatics.* N.p.: Token and Medal Society, 1966.

Knox, John Jay. *United States Notes: A History of the Various Issues of Paper Money by the Government of the United States.* London: T. Fisher Unwin, 1885.

Krakel, Dean. *End of the Trail: The Odyssey of a Statue.* Norman: University of Oklahoma Press, 1973.

Krause, Chester L., and Clifford Mishler. *Standard Catalog of World Coins, 1901–Present.* Iola, WI: Krause Publications, 2003.

Kunhardt, Dorothy Meserve, and Philip B. Kunhardt Jr. *Mathew Brady and His World.* Alexandria, VA: Time-Life Books, 1977.

Kunhardt, Philip B. Jr., Philip B. Kunhardt III, and Peter W. Kunhardt. *Lincoln: an Illustrated Biography.* New York: Alfred A. Knopf, 1992.

——. *Lincoln Life-Size.* New York: Alfred A. Knopf, 2009.

——. *Looking for Lincoln: The Making of an American Icon.* New York: Alfred A. Knopf, 2008.

Kunkel, Mabel. *Abraham Lincoln: Unforgettable American.* Charlotte, NC: Delmar Co., 1976.

Lincoln, Abraham. *Autobiography of Abraham Lincoln.* N.p.: Americanization Department, Veterans of Foreign Wars of the United States, n.d.

——. *Abraham Lincoln Papers at the Library of Congress.* Microfilm Collection. Washington, D.C.: Library of Congress, 1947.

——. *The Collected Works of Abraham Lincoln,* 8 vols. Edited by Roy P. Basler. New Brunswick, NJ: Rutgers University Press, 1953.

——. *The Speeches of Abraham Lincoln, Including Inaugurals and Proclamations.* New York: Lincoln Centenary Association, 1908.

——. *The Works of Abraham Lincoln,* vol. 7. New York: The University Society, Inc., 1908.

Lincoln Fellowship of Wisconsin. *The Lincoln Ledger,* various issues.

Lincoln Lore, nos. 1–1900 (April 15, 1929–Summer 2012).

Luce, Henry L., ed. "The Individual in America . . . Lincoln and Modern America: The Heritage of a Free Choice in an Organized Society," *Time,* May 10, 1963, 20–25.

Luftschein, Susan. *One Hundred Years of American Medallic Art, 1845–1945.* Catalog of the John E. Marqusee Collection, Herbert F. Johnson Museum of Art, Cornell University, Ithaca, NY, 1995.

Marcovitz, Hal. *American Symbols and Their Meanings: The Lincoln Memorial.* Philadelphia: Mason Crest Publishers, 2003.

McClure, R.B. *The Abraham Lincoln Portfolio of Photogravures From the Famous McClure Collection.* New York: R.B. McClure, 1909.

McMurtry, R. Gerald. *Beardless Portraits of Abraham Lincoln.* Fort Wayne, IN: Public Library of Fort Wayne and Allen County, 1962.

——. "A Great Lincoln Collection," *Lincoln Herald* 43 (March 1941): 2–8.

——. "Lincoln Poster Stamps," *Lincoln Herald* 43 (March 1941): 9, 13.

Mead, David, and Chris Sharp. *A Little Abraham Lincoln Learns to Be Honest.* San Marcos, CA: Virtue Books, 2003.

Mearns, David C. *Lincoln Collections in the Library of Congress,* 2nd ed. Washington, D.C.: Library of Congress, 1943.

Mellon, James. *The Face of Lincoln.* New York: Bonanza Books, 1979.

Meserve, Frederick Hill, and Carl Sandburg. *The Photographs of Abraham Lincoln.* New York: Harcourt, Brace and Co., 1944.

Mihm, Stephen. *A Nation of Counterfeiters: Capitalists, Con Men, and the Making of the United States.* Cambridge, MA: Harvard University Press, 2007.

Milgram, James W. *Abraham Lincoln Illustrated Envelopes and Letter Paper, 1860–1865.* Northbrook, IL: Northbrook Publishing Co., 1984.

Miller, Francis Trevelyan. *Portrait Life of Lincoln.* Springfield, MA: The Patriot Publishing Co., 1910.

Miller, William Lee. *Lincoln's Virtues: An Ethical Biography.* New York: Alfred A. Knopf, 2002.

Moffatt, Frederick C. *Errant Bronzes: George Grey Barnard's Statues of Abraham Lincoln.* Newark: University of Delaware Press, 1998.

Monaghan, Jay. *Lincoln Bibliography, 1839–1939,* 2 vols. Collections of the Illinois State Historical Library, vols. XXXI and XXXII. Edited by Paul M. Angle, State Historian.

Moran, Michael F. *Striking Change: The Great Artistic Collaboration of Theodore Roosevelt and Augustus Saint-Gaudens.* Atlanta: Whitman Publishing, 2008.

Morris, Melvin (ed.). *Abraham Lincoln on Worldwide Stamps.* American Topical Association Handbook #135. Tucson, AZ: American Topical Association, 1998.

Neely, Mark E. Jr. *The Abraham Lincoln Encyclopedia.* New York: Da Capo Press, 1982.

Neely, Mark E. Jr. *The Last Best Hope of Earth: Abraham Lincoln and the Promise of America.* Cambridge, MA: Harvard University Press and the Huntington Library and Illinois State Historical Library, 1993.

New Orleans Bee, 1861–1865, various issues.

New York Times, 1860–1865, and various issues thereafter.

Nicolay, John, and John Hay. "Abraham Lincoln: Premier or President?" N.d., 18. pages.

Oates, Stephen B. *Abraham Lincoln: The Man Behind the Myths.* New York: Harper & Row, 1984.

Ostendorf, Lloyd. "Abraham Lincoln at Independence Hall, Philadelphia, February 22, 1861," *Saturday Evening Post,* January–February 1976.

——. *Lincoln and His Photographers.* Historical Bulletin No. 27. Madison, WI: Lincoln Fellowship of Wisconsin, 1972.

——. *Lincoln's Photographs: A Complete Album,* Dayton: Rockywood Press, 1998. 3rd edition.

——. "Signed Lincoln Photographs," *Incidents of the War,* vol. 1 (Summer 1986), 20–23.

Paper Money, various issues.

Peterson, Merrill D. *Lincoln in American Memory.* New York: Oxford University Press, 1994.

Pierand, Richard V. and Robert D. Linder. *Civil Religion & the Presidency.* Grand Rapids, MI: Academie Books, 1988.

Pratt, Harry E. *Abraham Lincoln Chronology, 1809–1865.* Springfield, IL: Illinois State Historical Library, 1957.

Pratt, Harry E. *Lincoln's Inner Circle.* Springfield, IL: Illinois State Historical Society, 1955.

Pritzker, Barry. *Mathew Brady.* New York: Crescent Books, 1992.

Randall, James G. and David Herbert Donald. *The Civil War and Reconstruction.* Lexington, MA: Heath, 1969.

Raymond, Henry J. *The Life and Public Services of Abraham Lincoln.* New York: Derby and Miller, 1865.

Reed, Fred. *Abraham Lincoln: The Image of His Greatness.* Atlanta: Whitman Publishing, 2009.

——. *Civil War Encased Stamps: The Issuers and Their Times.* Port Clinton, OH: BNR Press, 1994, 1995; revised 2nd edition in press.

Reinfeld, Fred. *The Story of Civil War Money.* New York: Sterling Publishing Co., 1959.

Reinhart, Mark S. *Abraham Lincoln on Screen: A Filmography, 1903–1998.* Jefferson, NC: McFarland & Co., 1999.

Richmond Inquirer, 1861–1865, various issues.

Rockett, Al, and Ray Rockett. *The Dramatic Life of Abraham Lincoln.* San Francisco: Souvenir Book Publishing Co., 1924,

Rose, Jon. *United States Postage Stamps of 1869.* Sidney, OH: Linn's Stamp News, 1996.

Rothert, Matt. *A Guide Book of United States Fractional Currency.* Racine, WI: Whitman Publishing, 1963.

——. "Unusual Aspects of U.S. Fractional Currency," *The Numismatist,* vol. LXXVII (August 1964), pp. 1027–1031.

Rulau, Russell. *Standard Catalog of United States Tokens, 1700–1900,* 4th ed. Iola, WI: Krause Publications, 2004.

Saad, Lydia. "Lincoln Resumes Position as Americans' Top-Rated President," February 19, 2007, www.galluppoll.com.

Sandburg, Carl. *Abraham Lincoln: The War Years,* vol. 3. New York: Harcourt, Brace & Co., 1939.

Schingoethe, Herb, and Martha Schingoethe. *College Currency: Money for Business Training.* Port Clinton, OH: BNR Press, 1993.

Schuckers, J.W. *The Life and Public Services of Salmon Portland Chase.* New York: D. Appleton and Co., 1974.

Schneider, Stuart. *Collecting Lincoln with Values.* Atglen, PA: Schiffer Publishing Ltd., 1997.

Schwartz, Barry. *Abraham Lincoln and the Forge of National Memory.* Chicago: University of Chicago Press, 2000.

——. *Abraham Lincoln in the Post-Heroic Era.* Chicago: University of Chicago Press, 2009.

——. "Iconography and Collective Memory: Lincoln's Image in the American Mind," *Sociological Quarterly,* 32, no. 3 (1991): 301–319.

——. "Lincoln at the Millennium," *Journal of the Abraham Lincoln Association,* vol. XXIV (Winter 2003), pp. 1–31.

Shaw, Albert. *Abraham Lincoln: His Path to the Presidency, a Cartoon History.* New York: The Review of Reviews Corp., 1930.

——. *Abraham Lincoln: The Year of His Election, a Cartoon History.* New York: The Review of Reviews Corp., 1930.

Shenk, Joshua Wolf. "The True Lincoln," *Time,* June 26, 2005, www.time.com.

Sherwood, Robert E. *Abe Lincoln in Illinois.* New York: The Playwrights' Co., December 25, 1939 .

Sloan, Richard, ed. *The Lincoln Log* 2–7 (October/November 1977–January, 1981).

Spaulding, Elbridge Gerry. *A Resource of War: The Credit of the Government Made Immediately Available. . . .* Buffalo, NY: Express Printing Co., 1869.

Speer, Bonnie Stahlman. *The Great Abraham Lincoln Hijack, 1876 attempt to steal the body of President Lincoln.* Norman, OK: Reliance Press, 1990.

Spink Shreves Galleries. *The William J. Ainsworth Collection: Abraham Lincoln's Image on United States Postage Stamps, April 17, 2009.* New York: Privately printed, 2009.

Stahl, Alan M., ed. *The Medal in America.* Coinage of the Americas Conference at the American Numismatic Society, New York, Sept. 26-27, 1987. New York: American Numismatic Society, 1988.

Staudenraus, P.J., ed. *Mr. Lincoln's Washington: The Civil War Dispatches of Noah Brooks,* New York: Thomas Yoselof, 1967.

Steers, Edward Jr. *Lincoln Legends: Myths, Hoaxes, and Confabulations Associated With Our Greatest President.* Lexington, KY: University Press of Kentucky, 2007.

Stevens, George. *Lincoln's Doctor's Dog and Other Famous Best Sellers.* New York: J.B. Lippincott, 1938, 1939.

Stevenson, Augusta. *Abraham Lincoln, the Great Emancipator.* New York: Macmillan Publishing Co., 1932, 1959, 1986.

Stickler, Harry D. *Trails and Shrines of Abraham Lincoln.* Chicago: Lincolniana Art and Book Association of America, 1934.

Sullivan, Edmund B. *American Political Badges and Medalets, 1789–1892.* Lawrence, MA: Quarterman Publications, 1981.

——. *Collecting Political Americana.* Hanover, MA: The Christopher Publishing House, 1991.

Sullivan, George. *Picturing Lincoln: Famous Photographs That Popularized the President.* New York: Clarion Books, 2000.

Swanson, James L. and Daniel R. Weinberg. *Lincoln's Assassins, Their Trial and Execution.* Santa Fe, NM: Arena Editions, 2001.

Swiatek, Anthony, and Walter Breen. *The Encyclopedia of United States Silver & Gold Commemorative Coins, 1892–1954.* New York: ARCO Publishing, 1981.

Taft, Horatio Nelson. *Washington During the Civil War: The Diary of Horatio Nelson Taft, 1861–1865,* 3 vols. Manuscript Division, Library of Congress, Washington, D.C., 1,240 pages.

Taft, Lorado. *The History of American Sculpture,* new edition. New York: The Macmilliam Co., 1924.

Taft, Robert. *Photography and the American Scene: A Social History 1839–1939.* New York: Dover Publications, 1938, 1964.

Tainter, J[ohn] S. "History of the Types of United States Paper Currency," *The Numismatist* 66 (August, 1953).

Taxay, Don. *An Illustrated History of U.S. Commemorative Coinage.* New York: ARCO Publishing Co., 1967.

——. *The U.S. Mint and Coinage.* New York: ARCO Publishing Co., 1966.

Taylor, Tom (Mark Lemon). *Punch, or the London Charivari,* 1861–1865.

Thomas, Benjamin P. *Abraham Lincoln.* With an introduction by Stephen W. Sears. New York: Book-of-the-Month Club, Inc., 1986.

Thomas, Christopher A. *The Lincoln Memorial and American Life.* Princeton, NJ: Princeton University Press, 2002.

Thompson, Frank. *Abraham Lincoln: Twentieth-Century Popular Portrayals.* Dallas: Taylor Publishing Co., 1999.

Tice, George. *Lincoln.* New Brunswick, NJ: Rutgers University Press, 1984.

Truesdell, Winfred Porter. *Engraved and Lithographed Portraits of Abraham Lincoln,* vol. 2., Champlain, NY: Privately printed at the Trousdale Press, 1933.

Turner, George T. *Essays and Proofs of United States Internal Revenue Stamps.* Arlington, MA: Bureau Issues Association, 1974.

Turner, Justin G., and Linda Levitt Turner. *Mary Todd Lincoln: Her Life and Letters.* New York: Alfred A. Knopf, 1987.

Waldsmith, John. *Stereo Views: An Illustrated History and Price Guide.* Radnor, PA: Wallace-Homestead Book Co., 1991.

Walsh, William S., ed. *Abraham Lincoln and the London Punch.* New York: Moffat, Yard and Co., 1909.

Ward, Geoffrey C., Ric Burns, and Ken Burns. *The Civil War: An Illustrated History.* New York: Alfred A. Knopf, 1990.

Warren, Louis A. "Unlimited Field of Lincolniana Collecting," *Hobbies,* 42 (October 1940), 1–6.

Wells, Samuel R. "Abraham Lincoln, Portrait, Character, and Biography," *American Phrenological Journal and Life Illustrated,* vol. XL (October 1864), pp. 97–98.

Westbrook, Robert A. *An Illustrated Catalogue of Early North American Advertising Notes.* New York: R.M. Smythe, 2001.

White, Charles W. "The Lincoln Cult," *Saturday Evening Post,* February 16, 1957, 36–37, 90, 92.

Wills, Garry. "Lincoln, the Power of Words in Times of War: An essay," *Life,* February 1991.

Wilson, Douglas L. *Honor's Voice: The Transformation of Abraham Lincoln.* New York: Vintage Books, 1998.

Wilson, Rufus Rockwell. *Lincoln in Caricature.* New York: Horizon Press, 1953.

——. *Lincoln in Portraiture.* New York: The Press of the Pioneers, 1935.

Wright, A.M. *The Dramatic Life of Abraham Lincoln.* New York: Grosset & Dunlap, 1925.

Yeoman, R.S. *A Guide Book of United States Coins,* 12th ed. Racine, WI: Whitman Publishing, 1958 (and other editions).

Zabriskie, Andrew C. *A Descriptive Catalogue of Political and Memorial Medals Struck in Honor of Abraham Lincoln.* New York: privately printed, 1873.

About the Author

A lifelong journalist, Fred Reed is the author, co-author or editor of more than a twenty books and has written hundreds of articles. He is owner-operator of the specialty publication company enthusiast-media.com ltd, that assists other authors to create and publish memorial works of non-fiction through his website www.fredwritesright.com. His first Lincoln book, *Abraham Lincoln: The Image of His Greatness* (Whitman, 2009) was well reviewed in both hobby and Lincoln fields, and won "Book of the Year" awards from the Professional Currency Dealers Association, Society of Paper Money Collectors, and Numismatic Literary Guild. It also received honorable mention for the Token & Medal Society's Sandra Rae Mishler Award, and was an invited Candidate for The Lincoln Group of New York's 2009 annual Award of Achievement. He recently co-authored (with noted Confederate currency authority Pierre Fricke) *History of Collecting Confederate States of America Paper Money, Vol. 1, 1865–1945.* A second volume, *1945–Present,* will complete the series.

His other works have won him numerous literary awards from the American Numismatic Association, the Society of Paper Money Collectors, the Numismatic Literary Guild, and other organizations. These include, from the SPMC, two Nathan Gold Lifetime Achievement Awards, two Literary Awards of Merit, the D.C. Wismer Award, a President's Award of Merit, and the Forrest Daniel Literary Award; from the ANA, the first-place Heath Literary Award, the Wayte and Olga Raymond Memorial Literary Award, and three consecutive Catherine Sheehan Awards; and from the NLG, "Best Specialized Book" in three categories, World Paper Money, U.S. Paper Money, and Tokens and Medals. Reed is a recipient of a National Gold Ink Award, and a gold vermeil medal from the International Philatelic Decentennial Expo PACIFICA '97. He has been editor/publisher of the Society of Paper Money Collectors' award-winning bi-monthly journal *Paper Money* for more than a decade and the Token and Medal Society's magazine *TAMS Journal* since 2010. Mr. Reed is a regular columnist for *Coin World, Bank Note Reporter,* and *Coins* magazine. His Lincoln research has been published in the *Lincoln Herald, The Numismatist,* and *Paper Money,* among other publications. His award-winning *Civil War Encased Stamps: The Issuers and Their Times* is being prepared for a revised, second edition, as well as a companion, similarly titled volume *Civil War Stamp Envelopes: The Issuers and Their Times.*

Bank Note Reporter has published many Lincoln articles by Mr. Reed, including "New $5 image likely to be iconic" (April 2011), "Illustrious past for 'Twinkle Eye,'" (March 2011), "Sweeping up $10 fakes proves a chore," (January 2009), "Feds look

Photo by Rebecca Taylor, www.myfamilylegacy.me

to second anti-photographic ink" (October 2008), "Paranoia over fakes brings call for recall," (September 2008), "Pardons of counterfeiters irked Congress" (August 2008), "Desperate Treasury approved photographic detectors" (July 2008), "Early efforts against fakers proved spotty" (April 2008), "Feds ramped up enforcement to foil fakers" (March 2008), "Bogus $10 U.S. Notes proliferated; solutions, few" (February 2008), "Auctions bring new ABNC die use to fore" (January 2008), "Federalizing didn't solve counterfeiting problems" (December 2007), "ABNC die 141 has distinguished heritage" (September 2007), "Lincoln currency portrait family tree traced" (August 2007), and "State bank note issuance grew despite problems" (April 2006).

In *Coins* magazine, Mr. Reed has published articles on Old Abe, including "'Universal' Lincoln: Burt's 1869 engraving most popular Lincoln ever" (March 2012), "Not So Fast: U.S. Treasury leans on note contractor printers" (July 2011), "Payable on Demand: Movie moguls spun Lincoln IOUs across silver screen" (January 2011), "Lincoln's Benevolence: Presidential Draft for unfortunate man famous, enigmatic" (September 2010), "Balancing Act: Anonymous writer sought relief for aching conscience" (March 2010), "Happy Birthday: Feb. 12 marks 200th anniversary of Lincoln's birth" (February 2009), "Original Greenbacks: Patent Anti-Counterfeiting Ink Proved a Bust" (September 2008), "A Noble Experiment: Dividend Checks Remain from Failed Freedman's Bank" (January 2008), "Zero in on Old Abe: Porthole Note Famous, Valuable & Aptly Named" (August 2007), "Take a wooden nickel: 'paper' collectibles include these diverse woods" (June 2007), "Your Share in America: Savings Bonds Allow Little Guy to Take Stock in America," (April 2007), "Let's Get It Right: Treasury's about face provides golden face-change opportunity" (January 2007), and "Hometown Bank Notes: Relic of Civil War, Killed Off By Great Depression" (June 2006).

His articles featured in *Coin World* on the Great Emancipator include "Not the Lincoln You Know" (February 6, 2012), "Lincoln Portrait Long Lasting" (December 19, 2011), "'Greatest' Lincoln image graces new Presidential dollar" (November 29, 2010), "Pitchmen continue to appropriate Lincoln's name and portrait" (August 24, 2009), "On bonds, Honest Abe's image meant legitimacy and value" (August 10, 2009), "Time to free 2009 Lincoln Bicentennial cents from vaults" (June 29, 2009), "1864 campaign items recall fight Lincoln expected to lose" (June 8, 2009), "Campaign Goal: presenting enigmatic figure to the nation" (March 20, 2009), "Artistic violation: James Earle Fraser researcher believes reuse of designs of Indian Head 5¢ betrays them" (October 8, 2001),

"Emancipation Proclamation: BEP should use G.F.C. Smillie's engraving" (March 26, 2001), "Emancipation Proclamation: Lincoln's edict led directly to his appearance on fractional currency" (March 19, 2001), "An icon for the ages: Cities, business schools depict president on notes" (July 24, 2000), "Abraham Lincoln: Lincoln's portraits on paper money help establish federal government image" (July 10, 2000), "Lincoln the Icon: Private banks and businesses use presidential portraits on paper money" (July 17, 2000), "New Lincoln Portrait Based on photo taken on his 55th birthday" (December 6, 1999), "Vision and Artistry: James and Laura Frasers' revitalization of U.S. coinage an international success" (January 19, 1998), "Meet the Frasers . . . Married collaborators left their mark on the nation's coinage in remarkable ways" (January 5, 1998), "Abraham Lincoln: Money shapes how Americans view the 16th President" (four-part series: February 10, 17, 24, and March 3, 1997), "Lincoln Popular Subject for Medallic Art: Commemorative Medals Frequently Use Universal Image" (March 28, 1990), "Lincoln Photos Fill Public's Need for Image: Universal Image Most Acceptable Photo of Martyred President" (March 21, 1990), "Advertising, Hollywood Use Lincoln Portrait: Legendary Honesty Wins Lincoln Place on Checks, Advertisements" (March 14, 1990), "Advertisers Quick to Use Lincoln Image: Sought to Use Portrait of 'Honest Abe' to Suggest Honesty" (March 7, 1990), "Lincoln Portrait Appears on Many Items: Early 19th Century Books Feature Illustrations Based on Portrait," (February 28, 1990), "Berger-Burt Image of Lincoln Wide-Ranging: 'Universal Lincoln' Appearances Range from Stamps to Cards" (February 21, 1990), "Lincoln: Face of Lincoln an American Institution" (February 14, 1990), and "Face Value: Lincoln Features Have Always Attracted Interest" (February 11, 1987).

Lincoln-related articles appearing in *Paper Money* include "New Nex-Gen colorized $5 FRNs are unprecedented," (July-August, 2008), "Did Abraham Lincoln's icon image on money influence his public perception-Part II?" (March-April, 2008), "Did Abraham Lincoln's icon image on money influence his public perception" (September-October 2006), and "Civil War Change Shortage Gave Rise to Curious Makeshifts" (January-February 2005).

In addition to publishing books and articles, Mr. Reed has displayed large exhibits on Lincoln at several Memphis International Paper Money Shows: *Abraham Lincoln on Non-Federal Currency*, 1999, 2007; A Checklist of Abraham Lincoln on Checks, 2002; *next-Gen, smecksGen, get with it Treasury; give us the Gettysburg Lincoln on our new $5 Federal Reserve Notes*, 2004; *Series 2004 Face Off: An A. Lincoln $5 FRN Makeover*, 2003; and *Series 1996 Face-Off: An A. Lincoln $5 FRN Makeover*, 1998. He's written about Lincoln for *E-Sylum* with "Who Is that Gent with Lincoln and Grant? Alexander II" (May 27, 2012), "Even More on Lincoln and Chase" (June 8, 2008), and "More on Salmon P. Chase and Abraham Lincoln" (May 25, 2008). He has Lincoln entries at www.wikicoins.com: "FR 93 $10 Legal Tender Note," "FR 282 Porthole note," and "FR 1800-1 Series 1929 $5 National Bank Note."

Additional articles Mr. Reed has penned on this subject include "Did Abraham Lincoln's icon image on money influence his public perception?" *The Lincoln Herald*, Winter 2007; "Did Abraham Lincoln's icon image on money influence his public perception-Part II," *The Lincoln Herald*, Summer 2012; "Emergency Money Fulfills Civil War Needs," *Civil War Token Society Journal*, Spring–Fall 1977; "'Honest Abe' Lincoln: Privately issued 19th century U.S. paper money offers many different portraits of Lincoln," *Paper Money Values*, Spring 2006; "In the 'Twinkle of an Eye': Once Popular Lincoln Photo Returns as Lincoln Icon for the 21st Century," *2000 Coin Almanac*, 1999; "New $5 Note Spiffs Up Lincoln Image," November 19, 1999, www.collectors.com; "Pliny Chase," *Journal of the Civil War Token Society*, Summer 1975; "Sculptor Fraser models proposed Lincoln cent and nickel," *Heritage Insider*, December 1999; "Shades of the Blue and Grey," *The Blue and the Grey*, October 1964–February 1965; "Shades of the Blue and Grey," *Linn's Weekly Stamp News*, April 26, 1965; "Collecting Abraham Lincoln," *Whitman Review* (January 2009), and in *The Numismatist*, "Global Tribute: Abraham Lincoln's integrity and dedication to human rights made him a popular subject on many countries' commemoratives" (February 2010), "Portrait of a President: Charles Burt's engraving of Abraham Lincoln turned the face of a relatively obscure, western lawyer into the best-known image of his time" (February 2009), "A Very Brady Bank Note: One, well-executed photograph helped define America's 16th President, influenced scores of portraits and was adapted for a contemporary $5 bill" (February 2008).

Photo Credits

All images except those listed below are from the collection of the author.

Abraham Lincoln Presidential Library & Museum: 1.55
Don Ackerman: 2.168
Larry Adams: 2.201, 3.67, 3.106
American Numismatic Association: 3.92
Architect of the Capitol: 2.32a, 2.32b, 2.49, 3.81
archive.org: 1.41, 1.53, 2.68, 2.46, 3.40
Associated Press: 4.170
C. Baker: 3.108
David Beach: 2.98, 2.122a, 2.122b, 2.131, 2.188, 2.200b, 3.54a, 3.54b, 3.54c, 3.109
Jonathan Benning: 5.100
Seth Bienstock: 3.182a
Q. David Bowers: 1.58a, 3.121a, 1.73, 2.7, 3.50a, 3.161, 5.34
S. Bruce: 4.244
Terry Bryan: 3.193c
Jim Bumgardner: 4.273
Bureau of Engraving & Printing: 4.189, 4.269a, 4.269b, 4.269c
CaféPress: 4.197
Jim Castetter: 3.39
Cathee A. "Cat" Clausen: cover, 5.43
Ed Dauer: 1.39
David DeLisle: 2.92
Tom Denly: 1.44a, 2.35b
Alan Derrick: 4.231
Lola Dupré / loladupre.com: frontispiece
Early American History Auctions: 2.56, 2.159
Paul Elman: 2.58
Don Everhart: 4.261a
Dennis Forgue: 4.19
forthegoodofillinois.org: 5.116
Galen Frysinger: 2.162, 2.167
George Eastman House: 4.201
Nathan Gibbs: 4.89
glennbeck.com: 5.118
Great Storm Galleries: 4.195
Brian Gubicza: 5.39
Hake's Americana & Collectibles: 3.34a
James Halperin: 3.237
Havana Journal Inc.: 4.250
Steve Hayden: 158c
Heritage Auctions: 1.27, 1.28, 1.30, 1.32, 1.33, 1.43, 1.56, 1.67, 1.68b, 1.69, 1.72, 2.2. 2.6, 2.10. 2.23, 2.29, 2.50, 2.59, 2.64, 2.78, 2.79, 2.89, 2.94, 2.101, 2.106, 2.125, 2.130, 2.140, 2.148, 2.157, 2.174, 2.176a, 2.176b, 2.187, p. 108, 3.13b, 313c, 3.20b, 3.29, 3.52, 3.56, 3.117, 3.121b, 3.193a, 3.193b, 3.249, 4.39

John Herzog: 3.75
Gene Hessler: 1.38
Leslie Hindman: 3.181
Wayne Homren: 3.35
Ron Horstman: 2.44
William Leigh Hunt: 4.153
Jessica Hunter, Wickliffe Public Relations: 5.61
Dr. Tony Hyman: 1.49
Jeff Harris, Indiana Historical Society: 4.202
Joel Iskowitz: 4.261b, 4.293a. 4.293b, 5.103b
Rich Jewell: 2.183
Harry Jones: 4.101
K&L Wine Merchants: 4.184
Jeremy B. Katz / JKCoinPhotography: 4.61, 4.75a, 4.75.b, 4.102b
Bob Kerstein: 3.157
Glenn King: 3.178b, 3.179a, 3.179c
Fritz Klein: 4.276a, 4.276b, 4.287
Mike Kienzler: 5.71
David W. Lange: 3.147
William Langs: 4.11a, 4.11b, 4.11c, 4.11d, 4.11f
H. Joseph Levine: 1.58b, 2.102, 4.94
Lewis Wayne Gallery: 4.96
Library of Congress: 1.15, 1.22, 159a, 1.64, 1.76, 2.3, 2.4, 2.8, 2.9, 2.12, 2.11a, 2.13, 2.30, 2.36, 2.37, 2.38, 2.40, 2.41, 2.47, 2.57, 2.62, 2.72, 2.77, 2.85, 2.90, 2.95, 2.104, 2.117, 2.134, 2.185, 2.186, 3.55, 3.72, 3.90, 3.97, 3.144b, 3.146, 3.162, 3.166, 3.230, 4.10
Lincoln Financial Foundation Collection: 4.226
lincolnandnewyork.org: 5.72
Louis Eliasberg Estate: 3.256a, 3.256b
Chris Lukeman / Kill Vampire Lincoln Productions: 5.9
marketwire.com: 5.61
Maury and Elizabeth McCoy: 4.238
Medallic Art Co.: 5.63c
Jim Nance: 4.124a, 4.124b, 4.190a, 4.190b, 4.208a
National Cowboy & Western Heritage Museum: 3.135b
National Park Service: 3.118
William S. Nawrocki: 3.13a, 3.69
New York Public Library: 1.57
Nici the 99-cent Goddess: 3.187
Mary Nowesnick: 4.97
Numismatic News: 5.37, 5.122
Orders and Medals Society of America: 4.191
Art Paradis: 2.51

Jay Parino: 2.55
Joel Patrick: 3.160
peace.maripo.com: 4.46
Don Pearlman: 5.105
Fred Perry: 5.88, 5.101
Gary Lee Price: 4.227
José Pulido: 4.243b
Fred L. Reed IV: 3.231, 4.40, 4.108, 4.130, 4.142
Richard Reed: 4.179
Rudy Riet: 4.198
David Schenkman: 2.54
Larry Schuffman: 3.77b, 3.77c
Peter Schwartz: 2.20, 2.26, 2.63
Dr. Robert Schwartz: 2.196
Neil Shafer: 4.67
Ron Sherman: 1.31
Signature Art Medals: 5.63a, 5.63b, 5.83a, 5.85a, 5.103a, 5.103c, 5.114
Richard Smith: 5.52, 5.123. 5.125
Smithsonian Institution: 1.40, 2.171, 3.38, 3.62, 3.77a, 3.89, 3.101, 3.125, 3.148b, 3.149, 4.36, 4.111, 4.123a, 4.123b, 4.123c, 4.123d
Spink Shreves Galleries: 2.15
Stack's Bowers Galleries: 1.36, 2.27, 2.31, 2.60a, 2.60b, 2.60c, 2.65, 2.67, 2.87, 2.91a, 2.91b, 2.103a, 2.150, 3.5, 3.153b
Rex Stark: 1.54
Saul Teichman: 2.42
William Tinsley: 4.110
David Tretter: 2.75
U.S. Mint: 4.1, 4.292, 5.13, 5.47, 5.66, 5.75b, 5.78, 5.90, 5.128a, 5.128b
U.S. Patent Office: 3.93; 3.232a
U.S. Treasury Department: 4.138
Gino Wang: 5.65
Washington Times: 5.21
William Hallam Webber: 4.155, 4.253
Alan Weinberg: 1.26, 1.29, 2.5, 2.120
Daniel R. Weinberg: 5.44
Dale West: 3.57a
White House Historical Association: 3.207
whitehouse.gov: 4.272b, 5.6, 5.15
Whitman image archives: 5.12
Dave Wiegers: 2.143, 4.71, 4.167
John and Nancy Wilson: 5.60
Scott Winslow: 1.17
Jen Yates: 5.127

Index